1983

THE FUTURE IS NOW

THE FUTURE IS NOW

THE FUTURE IS NOW

READINGS IN INTRODUCTORY PSYCHOLOGY

Jerome Kravitz and Walter Hillabrant

Howard University

F. E. PEACOCK PUBLISHERS, INC.
ITASCA, ILLINOIS 60143

Dedicated to
RACHEL and CHRISTIAN

Contents

vii

Introduction

Nature has provided homo sapiens with unique tools for adaptation and survival—a well developed brain and a mind which feels, perceives, thinks, wills, and reasons. Moreover, the evolution of these capabilities is far from complete. In a new evolutionary phase, the mind, previously devoted to mastery of the world, has now turned back to a self-reflective position. Through the sciences of psychology and other related disciplines, it is attempting to unravel its own mysteries.

These efforts have inspired an information explosion of such proportions that technically no one could keep abreast of all the developments in the field. We have been more than simply prolific, however, for we have indeed made much progress toward understanding ourselves. And perhaps not a moment too soon—our conquest of the external world, from the atom to the moon, has made us dangerous to ourselves, in the sense of ultimate species annihilation. To a considerable extent, our hope lies in understanding ourselves and others and in basing our personal, community, and national decisions on the best and most comprehensive knowledge of human mind and behavior we can master.

The science of psychology must always provide some vehicle for disseminating the information derived from its research findings and theoretical formulations. Usually scientists communicate among themselves through reports in scientific journals, but these are far too technical for the general public, or even the college graduate who is not continuing his education in psychology. Fortunately, the general public's need and demand for psychological information has generated a solution. The popular press—*Psychology Today, Time, Harper's, The New York Times* Magazine and many other periodicals—regularly publishes material regarding the latest advances in the field of psychology and related scientific disciplines. However, these presentations are scattered, and in pursuing them it is difficult to make out coherent themes or underlying movements. To fill this need

The Future Is Now is offered as an anthology of popular press material related to psychology. The need is great, and, literally, the future is now. This anthology is presented with the hope that it will in some way contribute to our most urgent mutual tasks—expanded self-awareness, personal growth, and species survival.

Thus *The Future Is Now* presents articles gleaned from the popular press which sample the major areas of psychology. They are grouped into eight topical headings or chapters, in line with the sectional headings found in most introductory psychology texts, so that the anthology can serve as a companion reader for introductory and contemporary psychology. The eight major headings are: (1) basic processes, (2) developmental psychology, (3) personality and individual differences, (4) social psychology, (5) problems of the individual, (6) social problems, (7) states of consciousness, and (8) therapies.

Taken together, the collection provides a broad, balanced spectrum of contemporary psychology materials selected as being personally and socially relevant to students enrolled in introductory psychology courses. It presents students with both traditional material and many of the most promising, sometimes controversial, approaches emerging from psychology and related disciplines.

Our purpose in compiling the anthology was fourfold. First, we want to acquaint the student with a broad spectrum of current psychological information, issues, and explanations.

Second, we want to provide the student and educator with the materials for instruction in the techniques and perspectives necessary for critical evaluation of popular press material related to psychology. We believe that it is this material which most students generally will have access to and which they will use as a resource as they proceed with their lives. Therefore, our educational obligation is in concert with the course instructor's to provide the student with the critical tools needed for their proper evaluation and use.

In a sense this anthology can be viewed as a type of laboratory manual. After graduation, how often will a student have access to a Skinner box or a color wheel, and how often will he or she read articles concerning psychology in the popular press? Which skill is more important to master? We think the answer is clear.

The third objective is to reaffirm for students that psychology can be relevant to their lives and interesting and fun as well. All too often college curriculums, even at the introductory levels, are geared to the training of professional psychologists, on the fallacious assumption that most students will continue their training in psychology. To the professional, the basic processes of learning, perception, and cognition; the related technologies; and the intricacies of statistics may be things of beauty, but to the student whose only academic contact with psychology will be a one-semester course, they are often boring and beside the point. While we do not recommend the deletion of the basic processes material, we do feel that there is considerable virtue in including material which is fun, interesting, and of personal and social relevance to the student. *The Future Is Now* contains that kind of material.

Our final objective is to provide readable material. Each article has been carefully screened with this criterion in mind. The result is, we believe, a text which is readable in the best sense of the term: informative, interesting, and of a high level but not pedantic.

CHAPTER I

Basic Processes

IN THE HUMAN MIND there is a vast interplay of psychological processes which are dependent for their functioning upon the most complex piece of matter in the known universe—the human brain. This chapter explores some of those processes whose ubiquitous presence qualifies them as fundamental: perception, learning, memory, and intelligence.

We are capable of knowing the world because we are able to perceive it. Psychologists and physiologists have performed a vast, still-continuing research effort in an attempt to understand how these various senses operate. Their importance can be grasped by considering the psychological consequences of the loss of any one of them. "In Search of the Mind's Eye" is concerned with the problem of visual perception and describes the connection between the eye and the brain which enables us to see. But we do more than simply see; we also remember what we perceive. "The Biology of Memory" presents some of the newest concepts which are emerging from psychologists' attempts to understand this ability.

From another perspective, we not only perceive, we also learn: to perform, how to behave in the world, to use and understand language, our way around the city, to understand. "Skinner's Utopia: Panacea or Path to Hell?" presents the principles of learning as they have been explored by B. F. Skinner, one of the most influential living psychologists in the United States. The reading also explores Skinner's speculations and recommendations, purportedly as based on his research regarding society and its future.

People are intelligent; that is, they have some degree or another of *intelligence*. How much we have is frequently of great personal and social concern. David C. McClelland's article deals with a question which is of concern to all those who have had their fates hang on a test score and which is being echoed by social critics who claim that tests are used as weapons to foster discrimination. The question is, "Do I.Q. Tests Measure Intelligence?"

The question of whether aggression and violence are basic to human psychology is debatable. Two facts are clear: Aggression and violence continue to be, as they were in the past, a dominant factor in human history, and they are of such overriding concern to some people that they consider them the fulcrum of human affairs. "Erich Fromm on Human Aggression" gives a psychoanalytic perspective to and promotes understanding of the problem, while "New Clues to the Causes of Violence" presents new findings regarding its neurophysiological basis.

Most neurophysiological studies of violence have been conducted with animals, which raises another question: What is the relationship between animal and human behavior and neurophysiology? Indeed, a new scientific specialization, sociobiology, contends that much of man's social and antisocial behavior is genetically based, as is animal behavior. "Between Man and Beast" explores this new specialization and presents many interesting and pertinent findings.

Ultimately, of course, humans depend upon the body and the brain. "Exploring the Frontiers of the Mind" presents a wealth of information concerning the latest findings in the area of brain research, while from a somewhat different perspective "The Other Hemisphere" offers fascinating recent evidence which indicates that each of the hemispheres of the human brain may be responsible for a radically different kind of psychological process. The evidence suggests that one hemisphere is in control of languages and logical processes, while the other is concerned with art, intuition, and the mystical, religious aspects of mental life.

The dependence of our mental life upon our bodies has other aspects. "New Facts on Biorhythms" presents the theory of and evidence for this new view. There is an intimate connection between the mind and the body which is as problematic as it is pervasive. The intricacies of this connection and the interactive effects of each component upon the other are explored in "The Mind–Body Link."

1. EXPLORING THE FRONTIERS OF THE MIND

The most mysterious, least-known area of man's universe does not lie in the farthest reaches of outer space. Nor is it found in the most remote Amazonian jungle or in the inky blackness of the Mariana Trench. It is located instead inside the human skull and consists of some 3½ pounds of pinkish-gray material with the consistency of oatmeal. It is, of course, the human brain.

The brain is the most important of the body's organs. The heart, after all, is merely a pump: the lungs are an oxygenation system. But the brain is the master control, the guiding force behind all of man's actions. It is the seat of all human thought and consciousness, the source of the ingenuity that made it possible for man's ancestors to survive and eventually to dominate their physically more powerful adversaries and evolve into the planet's highest form of life. Everything that man has ever been, everything he will be, is the product of his brain. It is the brain that enabled the first humanoid to use tools and that gives his genetic successors the ability to build spacecraft, explore the universe and analyze their discoveries. It is the brain that makes man man.

But it took man centuries to comprehend that there was a miraculous mechanism inside his head and begin to investigate its workings. Aristotle taught his pupils that the brain was merely a radiator or cooling system for the blood: he identified the heart as the organ of thought. Pliny the Elder was one of the first to identify the brain as "the

citadel of sense perception." But neither he nor generations of scientists who followed him had the knowledge or techniques to explore it. Investigation was also stymied by philosophical obstacles. The brain was considered the seat of the soul: its nature and its workings were considered not only unfathomable but sacrosanct.

Now man has embarked on a great voyage of discovery. In dozens of laboratories in cities round the world psychologists, biologists, physicists and chemists, recognizing that what goes on inside the brain cannot be divorced from what goes on outside, in increasing numbers are poking, prodding and analyzing the organ in an attempt to unlock its secrets. Man has split the atom, cracked the genetic code and, in a Promethean step unimaginable less than a quarter-century ago, leaped from his own terrestrial home to the moon. But he has yet to solve the mysteries of memory, learning and consciousness or managed to understand himself.

The brain is the newest and perhaps last frontier in man's exploration of himself. Crossing that frontier could have the same impact on humanity as the discovery that the earth was round. "We are like the Europeans of the 15th century," rhapsodizes one brain researcher. "We're standing on the shores of Spain or Portugal, looking out over the Atlantic. We know that there is something on the other side and that our discovery of exactly what this is will mean that things in our world will never be the same again."

The rapidly growing interest and activity

in brain research parallels an energetic, worldwide investigation of genetics that preceded James Watson and Francis Crick's 1953 discovery of the structure of the DNA molecule. Indeed, many outstanding biochemists and microbiologists who helped lay the groundwork for that monumental breakthrough have recognized that the brain now represents science's greatest challenge. Some have announced their conversion to neuroscience, the discipline that deals with the brain and nervous system. The work of the neuroscientists has already produced an exponential increase in man's understanding of the brain—and a good bit of immediately applicable knowledge as well. It has led to a host of new medical and surgical treatments for such disorders as schizophrenia, depression, Parkinson's disease and epilepsy. It has also resulted in improved and promising new techniques for relieving pain and controlling some forms of violence.

Even these accomplishments could seem insignificant once the modern Magellans attain their goal of understanding the brain's functions in thought, memory and in consciousness—the sense of identity that distinguishes man from all other known forms of life. Finding the key to these mysteries of the brain, a discovery that would suddenly explain these functions, could lead to better ways of treating the psychoses and neuroses that plague millions. It could result in identification and correction of the causes of many neurological disorders and, by revealing how the brain works, revolutionize thought, education and communication. It might even help man turn away from what some see as a headlong pursuit of self-destruction. "If man could discover why he is unique he might not destroy himself," says M.I.T. Professor Francis Schmitt, one of the leading brain researchers (p. 11). "He might respect himself more than he now does."

None of those engaged in neuroscientific research underestimate the difficulty of reaching that understanding, for the brain is an organ of enormous complexity. While a sophisticated electronic computer can store and recall some 100 billion "bits" of information, for example, the capacity of the brain seems infinite. The computer can make out a payroll, compute the trajectory of a spacecraft or figure the odds against drawing a straight flush far faster than any human. But the computer is, after all, a machine, capable of doing only what its human builders tell it to do.

The brain, on the other hand, performs a bewildering variety of far more subtle functions. It regulates man's heart and respiratory rates, controls his body temperature and tells him when to take his hands off hot stoves—all without his really being aware of that control. The brain keeps man in touch with the world around him by constantly sorting out the auditory, visual, olfactory, gustatory and tactile information his senses receive, processing it and enabling him to act upon it. It switches emotions on and off and regulates sexual drives.

Furthermore, the brain, unlike the computer, can repair itself: one area can learn to perform the functions of another in some cases of brain damage. And unlike the computer, which can be turned off at the flip of a switch, the brain remains continuously active, whether waking or sleeping. It can, like an infinitely repeated image in a hall of mirrors, think about itself as it thinks about itself thinking about itself.

The scientific effort to fathom the miracle of the brain is proceeding on many fronts, often apparently unrelated. Some of the most fascinating yet arcane work in the neurosciences is being done by zoologists like Theodore Bullock, 58, of the Scripps Institution of Oceanography in La Jolla, Calif. He is studying electric fish in order to identify interior pathways of brain commu-

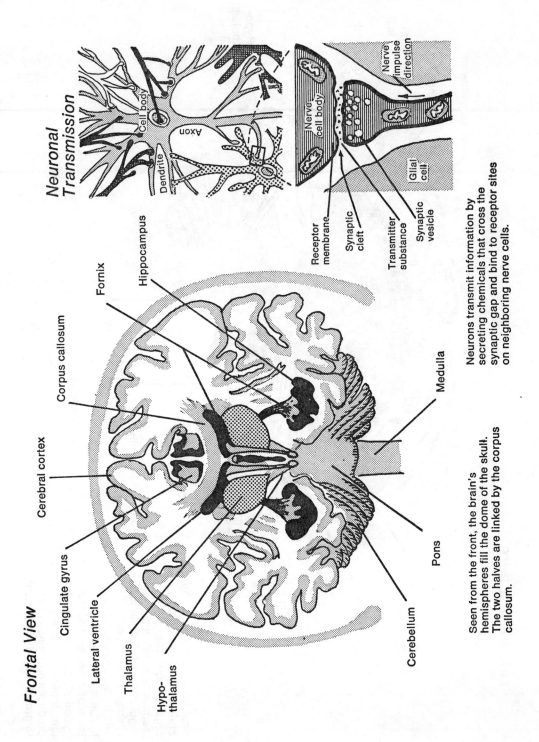

Neuronal Transmission

Cell body

Axon

Dendrite

Nerve cell body

Nerve impulse direction

Glial cell

Receptor membrane

Synaptic cleft

Transmitter substance

Synaptic vesicle

Neurons transmit information by secreting chemicals that cross the synaptic gap and bind to receptor sites on neighboring nerve cells.

Frontal View

Corpus callosum

Fornix

Hippocampus

Cerebral cortex

Cingulate gyrus

Lateral ventricle

Thalamus

Hypo-thalamus

Medulla

Pons

Cerebellum

Seen from the front, the brain's hemispheres fill the dome of the skull. The two halves are linked by the corpus callosum.

Left Hemisphere

Cingulate gyrus

Corpus callosum

Fornix

Thalamus

Pineal

Occipital lobe

Hypo-thalamus

Cerebellum.

PARIETAL LOBE

FRONTAL LOBE

TEMPORAL LOBE

Pituitary

Optic nerves

Olfactory bulb

Amygdala

Hippocampus

Pons

Medulla

Split from front to rear, the brain reveals its intricate organization. The multilobed cerebrum regulates such functions as speech, hearing and vision. The limbic system, which includes the amygdala, the hippocampus and the hypothalamus, controls the emotions; the pituitary produces hormones linked to growth and development.

THE ANATOMY OF THE BRAIN

Growing out of the spinal cord like the crown of a tree out of its trunk, the brain has several major components. The limbic system, an area that surrounds the head of the brain stem and includes such structures as the amygdala, part of the thalamus, hypothalamus and hippocampus, regulates the emotions. The pituitary, which hangs down from the brain stem like an olive from the tree, produces the hormones that influence growth and development. The cerebellum, a fist-sized structure at the rear of the brain that controls movements and coordination, enables man to touch his nose with his finger or throw touchdown passes. But it is the cerebrum that distinguishes man from other animals. Fish have little or no cerebral tissue, nor do birds. Chimpanzees, man's closest animal relatives, have larger cerebrums than most other primates, but man's is the largest.

Consisting largely of gray matter and fissured like a lunar landscape, the cerebrum dominates the human brain, filling the dome of the skull. It also makes man what he is, for it contains the areas that control thought and consciousness, the quality that enables man to remember his past, understand the present and anticipate his future.

Divided down the middle like the two halves of a walnut, the cerebral hemispheres are anatomically separate, but are cross-wired so that each controls the opposite side of the body—the left monitoring the right side, the right regulating the left. One hemisphere—the left in most people—is dominant and contains the areas that are associated with speech and hearing and involved with analytical tasks such as solving an algebra problem. The other governs spatial perception, synthesis of ideas and aesthetic appreciation of art or music. Normally these two hemispheres communicate with each other through a bundle of nerve fibers known as the *corpus callosum.* But if this connection is severed, their autonomy becomes evident. "Split brain" patients lose few of the two-handed skills already learned; they do have great difficulty learning new tasks that require both hands.

The brain is composed of two kinds of cells: neurons, or nerve cells, of which there are some 100 billion, and glia, which outnumber the neurons by a ratio of 10 to 1. Neurons, which are the functional units of the brain (glia, scientists believe, are largely "filler"), are connected to each other by means of long filaments, or dendrites, and form the body's nerve network. These cells receive sensory impulses, process the myriad bits of information pouring into the brain each moment, and transmit the brain's messages out to the various parts of the body, causing such reactions as the contracting and relaxing of muscles.

It has long been known that these messages are transmitted electrically. More recent research has shown that communication between the neurons is also chemical in nature. Neurons have bulbous endings called synapses. These secrete chemicals that cross the submicroscopic gaps between the individual cells, lock onto special sites on the dendrites of neighboring cells and cause these cells to release chemicals of their own. That action allows the passage of current from one cell to another.

The speed with which these cells can carry out their chemical transactions is, quite literally, mind-boggling. Manfred Eigen, 46, director of Germany's noted Max Planck Institute for Biophysical Chemistry in Göttingen, has found that some of the brain's chemical reactions take as little as one-millionth of a second. As many as 100,000 neurons may be involved in transmitting the information that results in as simple an action as stepping back to avoid being struck by an oncoming car. The entire process occurs in less than a second.

nication. That knowledge could lead to an understanding of how a brain communicates within itself. Other apparently tangential but vitally important research is being undertaken by Nobel-Prizewinning Immunologist Gerald Edelman, 44, of New York's Rockefeller University. Edelman notes that the immune system (TIME, March 19), which enables the body to defend itself against disease, is capable of memory. He has suggested that mechanisms similar to those that enable immunologically active cells to recognize microbes and other foreign material may also play a role in the brain's own memory system. The mechanisms could also conceivably tell cells where they fit into the "wiring diagram" of the brain while the organ is developing.

Most neuroscientists are conducting their research on cellular and sub-cellular levels, figuring that only by understanding how individual neurons work can they understand how the brain itself functions. "Studying the brain is like looking at a building called a bank and trying to figure out what it's for," says Dr. David Bodian, professor and director of the department of anatomy at Johns Hopkins University School of Medicine in Baltimore. "You can get some idea of its function by watching people go in and out. You can get an even better idea if you go inside and observe more closely."

The most advanced and exciting brain research now being conducted is directed toward discovering how the brain perceives, processes and stores information. Some scientists confine their work to only one area at a time; the brain is too complex and knowledge still too limited to do otherwise. Others, like Professor Hans-Lukas Teuber, 57, who heads M.I.T.'s department of psychology, insist on studying the three aspects together. "The way we perceive patterns, whether through sight, touch or other senses," he says "is intimately linked to the way we pattern our skilled movements, and both perception and movement inevitably involve problems of memory."

Teuber believes that such knowledge is essential for an understanding of higher brain functions, which intrigue him far more than investigations into so-called psychic phenomena. "The mystery lies where we least expect it: in sensory rather than extrasensory perception." he says. "What fascinates me is the way that you and I are able to sit opposite each other and make sounds that we receive, decode, process and then use as a basis for making more sounds. Now that is a real mystery."

Others, too, are interested in solving that mystery. Robert Galambos, 59, a professor of neurosciences at the University of California at San Diego, is attempting to track auditory impulses from the ear through the brain stem and into the cortex. He is studying several brain-wave patterns including what is called the "Aha wave," which the brain generates when it finds what it is looking for.

Hugh Christopher Longuet-Higgins of the University of Edinburgh is trying to make computer models of the way people produce sentences and understand language. Floyd Bloom, 37, chief of the laboratory of neuropharmacology at the National Institute of Mental Health in Bethesda, Md., and Walie Nauta, 57, of M.I.T., are using special staining techniques to trace the brain's neuronal pathways. "We have a long way to go," says Bloom, "but every little piece of information we gather leads us toward a better understanding of the way that the brain reacts to the outside world."

TWIN MYSTERIES

In their work all of these researchers are striving toward two major goals: explaining learning and memory. Anatomically there is no specific learning center in the brain, and there is no explanation for learning. "There is no known basis for learning; it cannot take place," says Teuber. "In fact," he adds jokingly, "as a teacher, I sometimes wonder if it does."

But learning does occur, and most researchers believe that a crucial factor in the process is protein synthesis—the creation of complex molecules. Steven Rose, 35, a professor at Britain's Open University, has found that as chicks were trained to master certain simple skills, certain brain proteins increased.

Sweden's Helger Hyden, 56, director of the Institute of Neurobiology at the University of Göteborg, has found even more convincing evidence that proteins play a role in learning. Hyden (pronounced he-*dayn*) trained rats and then killed them so that their brains could be studied. He found that certain nervous-system proteins were produced in greater amounts during the first part of learning, when the animals were striving to cope with a new problem: overtraining the animals produced no higher levels of the substances. Hyden then injected animals with antibodies against the protein, which is called S-100. The injection, which blocked the protein's activity, also caused the animals' learning rate to lessen markedly. Other findings tend to reinforce this conclusion. Protein-deficient rats learn much more slowly than well-fed animals. Also, protein-deficient children from poor families habitually trail better-fed, middle-class children in intellectual development, even when the children receive the same education.

Of equal fascination to researchers is the persistence of memory, the ability not only to store but also to recall information and experiences. In Proust's *Remembrance of Things Past*, Marcel released a flood of memories by tasting a tea-soaked *petite Madeleine*. Others have found that a memory-jogging whiff of perfume, a word, a few notes of music can conjure up similar—and often realistic—recollections of events they experienced many years earlier. A landmark discovery was made by the great Canadian neurosurgeon, Wilder Penfield, when he found that he could stimulate memories electrically. Probing a patient's brain with an electrode in order to locate the source of her epileptic seizures, Penfield was amazed when the young woman recalled an incident from her childhood in vivid detail. Penfield continued his studies and found that touching various parts of his patients' cerebral cortices with an electrode could enable them to remember songs long forgotten and experiences they thought were lost forever.

Subsequent experiments have proved that though the cortex is involved with memory, it does not act like a computer's memory bank, in which each bit of information is stored in a single electronic "cell." Memory, it has been found, is "delocalized" or spread throughout the cortex, and perhaps throughout the higher brain. Removing half the cortex may cause a proportional loss of capacity to remember, but it does not destroy specific memories.

Experiments and observations now support a three-level theory of memory. The lowest level is short-term memory, lasting no more than a few seconds; every moment of life, hundreds of sensory impressions flow into the human brain and are promptly forgotten. On the next level is medium-term memory, which lasts from a few minutes to a few hours, and enables man to remember something like a telephone number just long enough to dial it or to cram for an examination. At the highest level is long-term memory, which is sifted out of all the impressions and information entering the brain and preserved because of its importance, usefulness or vividness.

Long-term memory takes time to register

permanently on the brain. If rats are given an electric shock immediately after learning a new skill, memory of the skill is lost. If the shock is delayed for half an hour, the memory is impaired. But if 24 hours elapse between learning and shock, most of the memory remains. Human beings react in the same way.

Most researchers agree that the limbic, or feeling, brain plays a key role in long-term memory. The limbic system is concerned with affects—strong emotional experiences, for example—which people obviously remember. One part of the limbic system, the hippocampus, is indisputably vital to memory. Patients whose hippocampi have been destroyed or partially removed cannot recall new information. Dr. Robert Livingston of the University of California at San Diego postulates that the structure plays the same role in memory as the "now store" button does on a computer, determining whether a particular bit of information is to be stored or discarded.

THEORETICAL LEAP

Many researchers feel that memories are stored and recalled by a combination of macromolecules or large molecules that probably differ considerably from one individual to another. Thus they reject the notion of some science-fiction writers that memory molecules—and thereby memories—may one day be transferred from one brain to another. "The immune response is a learned reaction," says Rockefeller University's Edelman, again citing the parallel between memory and immunology. "There is no Marcel Proust for immunology. I doubt that there's one for the neurosciences!"

While focusing down on individual cells in the course of their investigations into the grand scheme of the brain, neuroscientists —like the Persian fairy tale's three princes

of Serendip—have been making fortuitous discoveries that have already resulted in improved clinical treatment of several serious illnesses. Among them:

Schizophrenia

Doctors know that two groups of drugs which include chlorpromazine and haloperidol are remarkably effective in relieving the thought disorders, hallucinations and extreme withdrawal of schizophrenia, a chronic psychosis that affects one person out of every 100. Both drugs, if administered in excess, can produce symptoms similar to those of Parkinson's disease, a neurological disorder characterized by uncontrollable tremors and lack of coordination. Parkinson's disease is caused by a lack of dopamine, a substance that transmits nerve impulses, in the brain centers that coordinate movement. Biochemical and electrophysiological studies have shown that chlorpromazine and haloperidol block the action of dopamine. Thus brain researchers suspect that schizophrenia results at least in part from an excess of dopamine.

Another clue to schizophrenia, says Dr. Seymour Kety, chief of the psychiatric research laboratories at Massachusetts General Hospital, lies in the discovery of an enzyme in the brains of both animals and man that can convert normal brain chemicals like tryptamine to dimethyltryptamine, a well-known hallucinogen. Kety and other scientists speculate that in schizophrenics such a process may be out of control.

Depression

Some severe psychiatric illnesses can now be controlled chemically. Researchers have theorized that depression may result when certain brain substances called

THE IMPRESARIO OF THE BRAIN

"To understand man, we have to understand the brain."

If man ever succeeds in reaching this goal, most neuroscientists today agree that much of the credit will belong to the author of that statement, Dr. Francis Otto Schmitt, a professor at the Massachusetts Institute of Technology. Although he is a skilled researcher in molecular biology, Schmitt is best known in his profession as a scientific impresario. He is the founder, chairman and most enthusiastic member of the M.I.T.-sponsored Neurosciences Research Program. It is from the work of this group that a comprehensive theory of brain function could well emerge.

Founded in 1962, the N.R.P. represents Schmitt's attempt to get science's "wets" (chemists) and "drys" (physicists) together to work on the mystery of the brain. The organization is a loose federation of scientists who are themselves connected with such prestigious institutions as the University of California, Germany's Max Planck Institutes and the National Institutes of Health. These researchers constitute the faculty of an "invisible university." Meeting regularly to discuss specific topics and staying in constant communication by letter and telephone, they hope to accomplish together what none could succeed in doing alone. Five of the N.R.P.'s 36 associates have won Nobel Prizes for their work in chemistry, medicine or physiology. But merely being Nobel laureates entitles them to no special consideration in what the scientific community acknowledges is a tough outfit. A couple of Nobelists were transferred to consultant status when they became too busy to participate in N.R.P.'s demanding schedule of meetings.

The dean of this unique college is as impressive as the faculty. Born in St. Louis in 1903, Schmitt studied medicine at Washington University, published two papers in *Science* before his 20th birthday and received his doctorate in physiology* before going abroad for two years of study in England and Germany. He returned to Washington U., where he remained on the faculty until moving to M.I.T. in 1941.

Schmitt pioneered the use of X-ray diffraction and polarization optics to explore the inner workings of cells, and studied molecular biology before the term was invented. Head of the team that was first in the U.S. to use an electron microscope for studying biological tissues, he is also well known for his work on collagen, the clear protein material that fills the spaces between cells. His research, which led to an understanding of how the collagen molecule is constructed, won him the coveted Lasker Award in 1956.

•

A bulky (6 ft., 200 lbs.) man with a prognathous jaw and bold forehead, Schmitt is an exceptionally articulate spokesman for his profession, promoting it in informal conversations and speeches that are remarkably free from technical jargon. "I believe the brain is knowable," he says. He is also an enthusiastic pianist and frequently entertains his friends by playing duets with his wife Barbara, a former concert pianist. Schmitt has a Teutonic dedication to hard work, moves at constant flank speed and, according to a colleague, has a tendency to "take every red traffic light as a personal affront." Asked at a recent 70th-birthday dinner if he planned to retire, Schmitt did not hesitate: "Not in the conventional sense of the word," he answered. "There are two meanings of this word, and to me, retire means to put new tires on the old chassis and get going again."

*He has since been awarded an honorary M.D. by the University of Göteborg.

monoamines are either lacking or are broken down too quickly. A new class of drugs neutralizes monoamine oxidase (MAO), the enzyme that destroys these substances. The drugs, known as MAO inhibitors, thus prolong the useful life of the monoamines in the brain. The drugs by themselves are not considered a cure for depression, but they can give relief to the victim of acute depression while psychotherapy attempts to get at the root of his problem.

Parkinson's Disease

Parkinson's disease, which afflicts over a million Americans, could once be relieved only by severing certain nerve pathways deep in the cerebrum. While the operation relieved the tremors and rigidity of the disease, patients could suffer partial paralysis and loss of speech. Now, most Parkinson's victims can be relieved by a drug known as levodihydroxyphenylalanine or L-dopa. First used successfully by George Cotzias of the Brookhaven National Laboratory, L-dopa provides a classic example of molecular chemistry at work. Normal movement depends in large part upon the action of dopamine, one of the brain's most important chemical transmitters. Parkinson's disease results from a degeneration of the cells that help produce this chemical. By boosting the level of dopamine in the brain, L-dopa helps to prevent the palsy associated with the disease.

The drug is also enabling doctors to take some tentative yet encouraging steps toward treating Huntington's chorea, a genetically-determined degenerative nerve disease that strikes its victims at about the age of 40 and kills them within 15 years. A group headed by Dr. Leslie Iverson, 36, of the British Medical Research Council's Division of Neurochemical Pharmacology, has been studying the chemical changes in brains of Huntington's victims. The team has found that victims of the disease have lower-than-normal quantities of the transmitter gamma amino butyric acid (GABA) and occasionally-elevated amounts of dopamine. They are now trying to develop drugs that will restore the balance between these chemicals.

Epilepsy

Epilepsy, which affects one person out of every 100, is caused by clusters of brain cells, or foci, that discharge electrical impulses paroxysmally. It produces violent seizures resulting in convulsions and unconsciousness, brief staring spells or episodes of uncontrollable rage. Researchers have discovered that most epileptic conditions can be controlled by a drug called Dilantin, which Dr. Frank Morrell, 47, of Chicago's Rush Medical College, believes prevents epileptic discharges from spreading to neighboring neurons.

A technique for relieving cases of epilepsy that resist treatment by drugs has been devised by Dr. Irving Cooper, 51, of St. Barnabas Hospital in New York. Cooper has found that stimulating the cerebellum electrically apparently increases its inhibitory action on the cerebrum. Cooper has implanted electronic "pacemakers" upon the cerebellums of several epileptics, as well as patients suffering from stroke-caused paralysis, cerebral palsy and from dystonia, a neuromuscular defect in which permanently flexed muscles twist and distort the limbs. The device, which stimulates the cerebellum with low-voltage jolts, has produced relief in most of the 70 cases in which it has been used. One muscular 26-year-old man suffered from daily epileptic seizures before he came to Cooper for a pacemaker. Since the machine was implanted a year ago, the man has been free of major seizures.

There are other areas in which neuroscientific research is paying dividends:

Relieving Pain

Doctors are still not sure how the brain perceives pain, but some neurosurgeons have found ways of relieving the chronic and acute discomfort associated with terminal cancer and other diseases. Dr. William Sweet, chief of neurosurgery at Massachusetts General Hospital, has found that by destroying small clusters of cells in different parts of the brain, either by freezing or by electric current, he can relieve pain without producing the degrading effects of the old-style prefrontal lobotomy, which often produced antisocial behavior and, eventually, mental deterioration. He has also found a way of dealing with *tic douloureux,* an excruciatingly painful nervous disorder involving the trigeminal nerve of the face. With his patient sedated but conscious, Sweet places electrodes in the face and destroys certain small nerve fibers that transmit pain without harming those larger fibers involved in perceiving touch.

Reducing Violence

Building on his earlier work, Sweet and others have also discovered that they can calm the violent outbursts of rage often associated with psychomotor epilepsy by destroying or partially removing the amygdala, an almond-shaped body in the limbic system of the brain. Sweet's onetime student, Dr. Vernon Mark, has performed amygdalectomies on 13 patients who exhibited violent behavior associated with a rare form of epilepsy. The operations reduced the frequency of their seizures and their aggressive outbursts. But the surgery produced no significant effects on their intelligence or ability to think.

Biofeedback Control

A handful of yoga and Zen masters have known for centuries how to control such autonomic or involuntary nervous functions as heart and respiratory rates. Rockefeller University Psychologist Neal Miller has found ways to help those with a less spiritual outlook to achieve the same kind of control. Using devices that enable patients to monitor various body functions like blood circulation and heartbeat, Miller and other researchers have trained them to raise and lower their blood pressure and hand temperatures. The phenomenon, he explains, is basically no different from other forms of learning. All learning depends on some sort of feedback to the brain—from eyes, hand or other sources—that tells the student whether he is succeeding or failing in what he is trying to do. Biofeedback-monitoring devices simply enable the patient to tell when he is consciously controlling his involuntary functions. Miller's work has been capitalized upon by charlatans and mystics who insist that biofeedback can bring a kind of instant satori to those willing to spend money for lessons and equipment. But many legitimate researchers also believe that biofeedback may prove valuable in controlling moods and dealing with certain illnesses.

While neuroscientists look forward eagerly to the day when they will understand how the brain works, some people feel that they have already gone too far. There are those who fear that new drugs and surgical techniques could be used to impose a form of "mind control" on nonconformists, tranquilize prisoners or inmates of mental hospitals, and tame those whose behavior or ideas society finds troubling. They note that psychosurgery is being widely used in Japan to calm down hyperactive children. They also observe with alarm the tendency of some school physicians to recommend drug treatment for these schoolchildren. Others, on a more philosophical level, are concerned lest the neurosciences succeed in erasing the factitious line between "mind" and "brain" and reduce man to a collection of neurons.

Neuroscientists generally appreciate their concern. "It is a measure of the distrust with which science is now viewed that people automatically think first of the evil that scientific knowledge can bring." says M.I.T.'s Teuber. "It's as if we're suffering from some sort of Manhattan Project complex."

Most neuroscientists agree that their science can be abused but doubt that it will be. Schmitt, for example, feels that fear of thought control is unreasonable. "When it comes to thought control," he says, "politicians and journalists do a better job than neuroscientists." Instead, the brain researchers stress that the benefits resulting from their research would far outweigh the dangers. An understanding of how the brain works could lead to treatments for some forms of mental retardation. A greater knowledge of what takes place during learning could result in improvement in teaching techniques. Even human intelligence might be increased as a result.

A breakthrough could also lead to the kind of social evolution that might help prevent the conflicts that now set man against man and nation against nation. "Most of our evolution has been somatic," says Schmitt. "We've changed our shape. But if we could really understand ourselves and by extension each other, we could evolve socially as well." That kind of evolution, Schmitt contends, may well be necessary for the continuation of the species. "Armies aren't the key to man's survival," he says. "Governments are not enough. Treaties are not enough. Only self-knowledge will help man to survive."

The ocean that separates man from this self-knowledge remains to be charted. Crossing it will require money, dedication, ingenuity and the development of a whole new field of science and technology. The explorers of the brain have embarked on a journey even more significant than the voyage of Columbus in 1492. Columbus discovered a new continent. The explorers of the brain may well discover a new world.

2. THE BIOLOGY OF MEMORY

Joan Arehart-Treichel

Brain investigators have attempted in recent decades to define the biological bases of memory. If such bases could be delineated, researchers might learn how to manipulate them. And manipulation of the

Reprinted with permission from SCIENCE NEWS, the weekly news magazine of science, copyright 1973 by Science Service, Inc., vol. 104, pp. 218–19.

biological processes of memory could have a profound impact on society, both positive and negative. Memory manipulation might be exploited by teachers, by physicians correcting brain diseases involving memory, by Madison Avenue in subliminal advertising, by nations engaging in psychological warfare.

"Memory research has widespread ramifications," says Robert Grenell, psychiatrist and neurobiologist at the University of Maryland Hospital. "People think memory researchers are engaged in fun and games, but it's not so."

Memory research today is largely concentrated in two areas—the chemical bases of memory and the electrophysiological bases of memory.

A leader in the field of the chemistry of memory is Georges Ungar, a pharmacologist at the Baylor College of Medicine. During the past decade, Ungar has trained animals to perform various tasks. He has then extracted chemical material from their brains and purified and isolated it. When he injects the isolated chemical material back into the brains of untrained animals, the animals act like the trained animals from which the material was taken. So it looks as if the chemical material might contain memory that can be transferred from one animal brain to another. Hence Ungar's material has come to be called "memory molecules."

The memory molecules Ungar has extracted are proteins. One, called "scotophobin," from the Greek for "fear of the dark," was taken from the brains of rats trained to fear the dark. When scotophobin was injected into untrained rats, they also feared the dark. Another molecule was taken from the brains of rats trained to ignore the sound of a loud bell. When the molecule was injected into the brains of untrained rats, they too ignored the bell. Memory molecules were also taken from goldfish trained to avoid certain colors, and to swim against adverse conditions (SN: 4/28/73, p. 268). A few months hence, Ungar intends to inject one of his memory molecules into himself and some other human volunteers.

A leader in the field of the electrophysiological bases of memory is E. Roy John of the New York Medical College. During the past 20 years, John has acquired increasing evidence that memory consists of electrical patterns that sweep through populations of nerve cells in the brain. When animals are taught certain tasks, John can see certain patterns of brain waves flicker through their brains. These waves represent a brain response to a stimulus; they are called exogenous brain waves. Soon afterward, other electrical waves ripple through the animals' brains. These waves, which appear to represent brain reaction to the stimulus, are called endogenous waves.

As an animal learns a task better and better, its endogenous brain waves become stronger and stronger. And when the animal that has learned a task is later asked to remember the task, the identical endogenous wave patterns flicker through the animal's brain. So in John's view, the endogenous waves represent traces of memory, or "engrams."

Recently John found that while memory traces are widely distributed throughout the brain, they tend to cluster in strategic areas. Traces that concern memory of a visual event are seen mostly in the visual area of the brain. Traces that concern memory of an auditory event concentrate in the auditory area of the brain.

However fascinating the chemical evidence for memory and the electrophysiological evidence for memory, they present a dilemma. Is memory chemical, or is it electrical? Might evidence from the two camps of research be reconciled?

"It's not a question of reconciliation, but of definition," Grenell insists. Learning and memory constitute a number of intricate processes. There is input of information, recognition and comparison, evaluation, short-term memory, consolidation of short-term memory, long-term memory storage, memory retrieval. Ungar, says Grenell, concerns himself with long-term memory storage. Ungar agrees. John, says Grenell, concerns himself with memory retrieval. John agrees.

So if Ungar's molecules represent long-term memory storage, and John's engrams represent memory retrieval, might memory molecules and engrams be reconciled? Ungar thinks so. "Both," he says, "are based on the assumption that new connections are established in the brain during learning."

John agrees that new connections may be established during learning, although there is no evidence for such connections. But he does not agree, on the basis of his own laboratory evidence, that memory depends on specific pathways. He does not believe that Ungar's molecules could be "produced by such pathways, or produce such pathways" in a naive brain. So John feels "there is a pretty substantial problem" in reconciling memory molecules with engrams.

On the other hand, John does not deny that Ungar's molecules do something to the brains of untrained animals. John suspects that the molecules stimulate nerve cells in the brain, as do pep pills, hormones or a number of other chemicals. As a result, an animal's behavior is altered.

J. Anthony Deutsch of the University of California at San Diego agrees. "It seems reasonable to assume," he says, "that the molecules Ungar is extracting are simply altering an animal's motivational status at the time of performance, and this is producing significant alterations in his behavior. It has nothing to do with memory as we understand it."

Yet Deutsch doesn't think electrophysiological experiments show anything about learning or memory either. On the basis of his own work, he believes that memory constitutes chemical changes as one nerve passes an electrical impulse to an adjoining nerve.

Grenell more or less agrees with Deutsch, at least as far as the recognition-comparison stages of learning and of short-term memory, are concerned. After eight years of research, Grenell has found that the nerve chemical acetylcholine facilitates the ability of a nerve to pass an electrical message to an adjoining nerve, and this facilitation is necessary for the recognition-comparison stage of learning, and for short-term memory as well. He also has results that nerve transmitters known as the catecholamines are able to inhibit nerve facilitation. He has not yet looked at the specific effects of the catecholamines on recognition-comparison and memory.

Still, Grenell does not discount that Ungar's molecules and John's engrams represent some facet of memory. "It is unlikely," he says, "that memory is purely chemical, purely electrophysiological or purely any damn thing."

Robert Thatcher, a co-worker in John's lab, also sees hope for reconciliation between chemical evidence for memory and electrophysiological evidence for memory. He speculates that Ungar's molecules, rather than storing memory, activate nerve-firing patterns in recipient brains. And the activation of these electrical patterns is the same as if the patterns had been acquired (learned). He would like to get some of Ungar's molecules, inject them into brains and see what effects the molecules have on nerve firing patterns.

It is doubtful he will be able to conduct such experiments any time soon. Too much hostility exists between chemical researchers and electrophysiological researchers. A case in point—a declaration by James Old, an investigator of the electrophysiology of memory at the California Institute of Technology: "It is an interesting state of affairs right now. It is possible to think of theories being integrated, but some [Ungar's] are not compelling. The reason they are not compelling is that it is mainly people on the crackpot fringe who have done these experiments. They really believe what they say

... The advantages of believing are so great to them, and the cost so little, they can hardly help believing. The other side, the mainstream of science, has it almost as a matter of scientific superego to quell this heresy."

"The bias is pretty rough," Grenell admits. "Biochemists have not learned physiology. Physiologists have not learned biochemistry. And neither has learned biophysics. So it gets difficult trying to put things together." The ultimate unraveling of the biology of memory, he predicts, "will come from mathematicians and physicists."

3. IN SEARCH OF THE MIND'S EYE

Rick Gore

This monkey's brain is being tapped. With a tiny tungsten electrode two Harvard scientists are intently monitoring the cryptic messages crackling along just one private line, one neural in its visual pathway. The men, David Hubel and Torsten Wiesel, immersed themselves in this world of neural chatter more than a dozen years ago. Since then they have been working with infinite patience helping to resolve one of the human brain's most provocative mysteries: how can the neuron, that commune of chemicals which by themselves are cold and inert, permit man not just to see, but to perceive? In this mechanistic age any layman can at least dimly grasp how a jolt from the brain can order a muscle to bend an elbow; but how can this same kind of nervous energy give us a perception as grand and evocative as an autumn sunset, a spring rain—or for that matter the ability to recognize something as simple as the dot over an *i*?

A man walks in a park. Perhaps the aroma of a vendor's steaming chestnuts reaches him on a sudden breeze. The cool air touches his face and makes the leaves rustle behind him, while the gravel on the pathway crunches against his feet. A soft perceptual concert is being played by innumerable agitated neurons in all the sensory seats of his brain. But the busiest groups of neurons by far are those that deliver his visual messages and make him instantly and even unconsciously aware of the world around him. They tell him he is indeed in the park he sought. A thing darts past the corner of his eye and his brain says bird, then bluejay, and noting the bluejay's constantly changing size and position tells him which way the bird is flying. A boy with a bat hits a pop fly: somehow the man knows almost instantly just about where it will land. The green of the grass is succumbing to winter brown and a stranger is sitting on one of the park's benches. He's seen him there before—how does he know this? In fact, how does the man perform all these split-second perceptual tasks with such remarkable aplomb? Day after day we are all working out data-processing miracles like these, and research now points to the fact that we do so almost entirely through the elegant, often inscrutable organization of those remarkable neurons.

Neurons first begin to handle such visual perceptions in the retina of the eye. There is a familiar (but false) analogy that compares the eyes to a camera, projecting little pictures of the outside world upside down on that rear part of the cortex that is our visual brain. Actually there is nothing like a little picture: instead each retina is sending the cortex about a million simultaneous steady streams of electrochemical data, transmitted by the more than 125 million rods and cones behind it. A far better, though still crude, analogy of how we see is found on the printed page. Seen under a magnifying glass, the printed image turns out to be nothing more than a multitude of tiny dots which the naked eye combines to form a picture. In this analogy, each dot in the picture would correspond to the "on" or "off" message of a particular retinal cell.

This mosaic of dots from the retina must then be transformed into something that has meaning. Working with their cats and monkeys, Harvard scientists Hubel and Wiesel have uncovered important clues as to how the brain begins to do this. Most important, their experiments are showing we have neurons in our brains that respond to one certain stimulus, and to nothing else. Some, for example, respond only to a line at one particular place and one precise angle. Other cells, the two men find, are more complex. They will respond to any line anywhere in their limited field of view as long as it's at the proper angle. And there are still other cells, farther back along the visual pathway, which Hubel and Wiesel call "hypercomplex." These respond to even more specific patterns, like curves or corners. Since everything we see can ultimately be reduced to a series of minute lines at angles to each other, and since most of the information we glean from our surround-

ings is concerned with edges and contours and corners, they call these basic sets of cells "the building blocks of perception."

In 1959, at about the same time that Hubel and Wiesel were making their initial discoveries at Harvard, an MIT group headed by Jerome Lettvin found what he called "bug detectors" in the retina of a frog. They consist of certain neurons that react to nothing but small dark objects that move through their receptive fields. The discovery may explain why a hungry frog will not eat dead flies set before him: because they are not moving he may not see them in terms of food. These cells are known as feature filters or pattern detectors.

Pattern detectors are no less vital to us than to the frog. We have developed a far greater repertoire of filters and use them for far more sophisticated purposes. As you read this page for example, your retina and visual cortex are analyzing progressions of black lines, angles and curves on a white background. You come across the letter E —three parallel horizontal lines each forming a right angle with the same vertical line. How we perceive that this is indeed the letter E is yet unknown. But somehow we recognize E whether it is printed small or capital, fine or large, in flashing neon or chalked on a sidewalk and half scuffed out. Thus there inevitably must be a net of neurons that can extract this pattern whenever it occurs. And thus there must be a neural model for the letter E. The leading theory today is that each signal that comes into our visual system will be compared to that model and categorized as E or non-E. We perceive by an instantaneous matching process.

No one may ever be able to trace the actual nerves that make up the neural model. In simplistic terms one might compare it to a telephone which can reach any other far away, but only if a specific set of ten numbers is dialed. In the brain, of course, even the most basic of events involves tens of thousands of neurons. The model may exist in many places in our brain, each extension having its own battery of associations. Where the neural model is and how it got there is lost in the baffling question of how memory is laid down.

Pattern recognition so dominates all perception that the brain will even fill in visual gaps. Hans-Lukas Teuber of MIT has for years studied people with head wounds that made holes in their visual cortex. He finds that patients may be completely unaware of resulting gaps in their vision because their brains somehow complete straight lines, plain-colored surfaces and all sorts of patterns across these blind spots. Such spots, or scotomas, will sometimes occur briefly during migraine attacks. Teuber recalls how his teacher, the late Karl Lashley, used to describe unusual effects of his own migraine-produced scotomas. Once when he visually "beheaded" a colleague whose face fell within the scotoma's range, Lashley's brain still kept the wallpaper pattern behind the friend's head intact. Lashley once developed a scotoma while driving along a straight Florida road; he discovered that he could make a pursuing highway patrol car "disappear" without subjectively disrupting the road or landscape.

Actually, everyone has a perfectly normal hole in his vision—the blind spot where the optic nerve leaves the retina en route to the higher centers. Yet we routinely complete the patterns across it. To find the blind spot in your right eye, first close your left eye and stare at a word on this page. Then slowly move a pencil eraser to your right. At some point—the blind spot—the eraser will briefly disappear and then return near the corner of your eye. If you have trouble finding the spot, it's just because you are used to bridging the gap with an expected pattern.

Our interpretation of these patterns depends largely on our own patterns of expectations, and our perceptions are really no more than a hypothesis. We are always "guessing" on the basis of past experience. Thus people can see different shapes in the same ambiguous object, and Hamlet could tease Polonius into admitting that a nearby cloud looked at once like a camel, a weasel and a whale. Thus a Rorschach ink blot looks to one man like a raging dragon, and to another like a playful puppy. And the two equal vertical lines below appear to be of different lengths.

We see the world as we have experienced it. At MIT, Richard Held has conducted experiments to demonstrate the importance of experience. With Alan Hein, Held raised kittens and monkeys from birth draped with cloth coverings so that they were never able to see their limbs, though they could reach about with their paws and fingers. When the coverings were removed and they could at last see their limbs, there was no coordination at all between hand and eye. For several weeks they could not reach out and locate objects they could clearly see. In another experiment, Held outfitted two men with prismatic spectacles that grossly distorted their vision. One man walked about, pushing the other in a wheelchair. The man who was active quickly adapted to his new view of the world, but his passive partner made no adjustment at all. This suggests strongly that in order to perceive an object properly we may have to establish some kind of pattern of movement in relation to it.

It is not always noticeable, but the eyes are constantly in movement. Because of the peculiar chemical requirements of the rods and cones, an image disappears if it stabilizes on the retina. So each eye has six muscles that not only focus it on the interesting object, but also keep it quivering to prevent a stabilized image. We are usually quite unconscious of our eye movements; they may be as rapid as 1/50th of a second.

There seems to be an intimate interaction between patterns of sensing and patterns of eye movement, whether it is the eyes, the rest of our bodies or the outside world that does the moving. And our brains must continually cope with all this change. A friend's face doesn't seem to shrink if he moves a few feet away—but it does, just as it would on film if you took his picture at both five and ten feet. The brain has intriguing but poorly understood mechanisms for smoothing out such transitions. If we tilt our heads to look up at a skyscraper, for example, we don't really see the skyscraper tilting back in perspective, even though what used to be its vertical lines on our retina are now sharply angled. This automatic adjustment to perspective may help explain why we are tricked by the famous Müller-Lyer arrow illusion. For decades scientists have debated why one line seems longer. A leading theory is that the angles evoke familiar, but misleading, patterns of perspective—like those an artist would use to make a line drawing seem either closer to us or farther away.

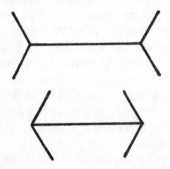

Perception is active; we constantly extract patterns from objects we see, hoping for a proper match. Stare at the little bar in the center between the cubes above if you doubt the aggressive, fluctuating nature of perception. Your mind performs all sorts of perspective gymnastics, seeking out the different patterns inherent in the cubes.

In the everyday world, patterns change frequently because we ourselves change position. To perceive this world properly our brains must take our own movements into account. Lightly tap the corner of your eye. The world seems to jump—and indeed the image on your retina is jumping. Yet if you move your eyes with your own eye muscles, there is a smooth transition. Why the difference? Because whatever center commands the eyes to move in the first place must also send a copy of its message to some crucial, but as yet unknown, way station in our sensory system. That station in turn tells the rest of our visual brain to compensate for the image change. Once again, as in the Held experiments, the act of moving our muscles ourselves seems to be essential to proper perception.

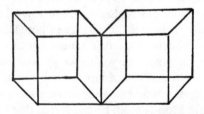

Movement of all sorts so affects our perception that many scientists are beginning to think we have a separate visual system devoted to it—centered in two little mounds, the superior colliculi, buried deeply in an old part of the brain (LIFE, Oct. 1). These mounds are evolutionary outgrowths of the optic tectum, which for lower animals, like birds and frogs, is an all-important visual center. Some superior colliculi cells respond to sound as well, and it is likely that the superior colliculi act as a kind of early warning system. A frog must move fast if it wants to catch a bug, so nature has wired in its tongue-flicking triggers close to its optic detectors. Man, too, must pay attention to rapid changes around him—after all that bluejay in the park just might have been a bee. Some superior colliculi cells have recently been found that react not to angles and lines like the Hubel and Wiesel cortical cells, but to the direction and extent of eye movements. While this warning system tells us where things are and what we should be watching, a process known as "scanning" lets us perceive the scene as a whole. When you look at the park, for example, you take in one object at a time. Only a small part of our retina, called the fovea, can focus sharply. So you scan the area with the fovea moving with unconscious speed from one point to another, from tree to bench to sidewalk. You match up object after object to patterns stored in your memory bank until you distill, in this case a park pattern. You recognize the stranger on the bench because just enough of his features—the shape of his head, the color of his hat, the cut of his clothes—fit a well-established pattern.

Your eyes jump quickly to follow any change or motion. If you try to fix them on an object, like a bush, you still find yourself breaking the bush down further, going from branch to leaf to flower, even from petal to stamen to pollen.

It is likely that each of us has characteristic scan paths. Different people will scan the same flower differently. And one person won't use the same path on flowers that he uses on trees. These scan paths, like the the the feature detectors and eye movements, must be controlled by some kind of neural network.

For years science has nibbled away at the whole area of human perception, broken it down into ever smaller units and subunits like these feature filters and scan paths and neural mounds with tongue-twisting Latin names. But perception can never be fully explained in these clinical terms. It is already obvious that we must know more about how neurons learn and remember. We must know how we focus our attention. We must understand more, too, about human motivation: why is it we often do see just what we look for? And, of course, our emotions clearly color our perceptions, adding awe to those autumn sunsets and sweetness to the spring rains. Years ago the great neurophysiologist Sir Charles Sherrington called the brain the "great raveled knot." He knew the answers lay hidden in all its tortuous pathways that feed into each other. The disentangling will be slow and arduous, but it has begun.

4. DO I. Q. TESTS MEASURE INTELLIGENCE?

David C. McClelland

Psychology has one great practical success to its credit in the twentieth century—namely the intelligence testing movement.

From *The Saturday Evening Post* (Summer 1972). Reprinted with permission. © 1972 The Saturday Evening Post Company.

Many tests have been devised which predict success in school with remarkable regularity. Literally tens of thousands of validity coefficients have been calculated, demonstrating that those who score higher on aptitude or intelligence tests usually do better in their school work. Selecting, at random, a finding which is quite typical for the United States, I recently observed in a longitudinal study to be reported by Costa (1972) that Kuhlman-Anderson I. Q. scores obtained in the sixth grade correlated 0.59 with twelfth-grade rank in class. In other words knowing how a child scores on an intelligence test when he is eleven or twelve years old enables you to predict fairly accurately how well he will be doing in school some six or seven years later. Rank in class at graduation from secondary school in turn predicts whether he can go on to the university and how good a university he will get into. As a consequence, knowing a person's intelligence-test score or scholastic-aptitude-test score has become a matter of great importance in the United States, not only to admissions officers who use it to pick people for college but also to businesses and civil service commissions who use it to decide who is "bright enough" to be a policeman, a social worker or a fireman.

Testing has therefore become big business. The Educational Testing Service which gives the Scholastic Aptitude Test used by most of the better-known colleges and universities in the United States employs around two thousand people and has a large plant spread over hundreds of acres in Princeton, New Jersey. Thousands of young people pay to take its tests annually to see if they are qualified to get into the college of their choice. The testing technology has been so sold to the American public that only in a few of the more "backward" parts of the society is it not used in the schools or businesses or civil service. And of course it is spreading fast to the rest of the world, which is beginning to discover the utility of tests for picking those who will do well in school.

To be sure, the testers themselves loudly insist that there are other important human qualities besides the ability to take scholastic aptitude tests, but as Wing and Wallach (1971) have shown, admissions officers may believe they take these other qualities into account but in fact their selection decisions can be almost perfectly predicted by aptitude-test scores alone. The desire to select more "intelligent" people for schooling or for almost any occupation proves overpowering. It quickly reduces other qualifications to insignificance.

While the intelligence-testing movement in the United States has been moving on from one triumph to the next, some questions have been raised about its theoretical underpinnings, both by scholars and by policy makers who wonder if its growing power over people's lives is justified. One difficulty with tests has long been known but little commented on, perhaps because its seriousness has not been fully appreciated. It is very simply that if academic achievement tests are taken seriously as measures of real competence, then the *quality* of education does not seem to contribute to improving competence. Back in the 1930's in the United States, a number of private schools tried to improve the quality of their education as part of what was then known as the "progressive education movement." Standardized scholastic achievement tests were used to evaluate the effects of this supposedly improved education as compared with more traditional teaching.

By and large no effects of the supposedly higher-quality education could be discovered in the test scores. The educators felt they were doing a better job but the test scores did not indicate that they were. The same finding has turned up again and again since that time. Certain colleges in the United States are widely acknowledged to be better than other colleges—in the sense that they have better faculties, more books in the library, higher endowments, better laboratory facilities, and so forth. Yet repeated studies as summarized by Jacob (1957) have failed to show any test-score differences attributable to the better education supposedly obtained in the elite colleges. If the graduates of those colleges perform better on achievement tests, it is because they scored higher on them at entrance to college, not because they received a better education subsequently.

Most recently in a very important social document on equality of educational opportunity, Coleman (1966) again showed that the *quality* of education (here in secondary school) seemed to have very little effect on the academic achievement test scores of children. In other words the children who went to poor schools with poorly trained teachers, dilapidated buildings, and crowded classrooms did no worse on the tests than children who went to excellent, well-equipped schools with low teacher-pupil ratios, once one had corrected for the initial differences in intelligence and social background of the pupils attending the two types of schools. In other words, what the test results seem to have shown over and over again is that quality of education makes no difference in improving competence.

What does make a difference are the attributes of the people getting the education —their intelligence, their social characteristics and so forth. Why then should citizens spend so much money trying to improve education? Why should educational psychologists be trying to find better ways of educating pupils? Why is money wasted on conferences to try to find ways of improving education—if in fact the data clearly show that educational variations have very little effect on academic achievement, which in turn is considered the main measure of competence for life's tasks?

One reason is that we keep suspecting that the educators may be right in continuing to think that the quality of education does make a difference. It may be the psychological testers who are wrong: their tests may simply not be adequate measures of the competence which better education produces. In fact there may even be a built-in theoretical reason why most existing tests are inadequate measures of variations in the quality of education. Most testers have worked hard to create tests which are reliable—that is, which will give the same score when the same individual is tested again. An instrument which is designed to be very reliable may not be very sensitive to changes that have actually taken place in the person through education.

But this theoretical problem has never shaken the self-confidence of the testing movement. It has continued to roll on like a juggernaut overwhelming all such doubts.

When many psychologists began to examine really seriously for the first time the assumptions on which the intelligence testing movement had been built, it took them no time at all to discover that many intelligence tests had a built-in middle-class bias. The vocabulary used in the tests was so-called "standard English," not the dialect spoken in many ghetto communities. So the children from these communities often did not even understand the instructions for the tests, let alone the words they were supposed to identify which were not part of the vocabulary in common use in their community. Correct answers to questions also often assume a standard middle-class way of life. For example, a child is asked on an intelligence test, "What would you do if you were sent to the store by your mother to buy something and you found the store didn't have it?" The "intelligent" or correct answer is supposed to be that you would go to another store to see if they had it. However, this is certainly not an intelligent answer for a ghetto child who is under strict orders from his mother to come straight home from the store because she is afraid he might be robbed or beaten if he strayed too far from familiar territory. Yet if he says he would go home he is judged by the testers to be less intelligent. It is also easy to see from these examples why there is a correlation between test performance and later performance in school because the teacher, as a representative of standard middle-class culture, will expect the same language and types of behavior as the person who made up the so-called intelligence test. The teacher will either not understand the dialect that is used in class or will give the child a lower mark for using "bad" language and the ghetto child will before long go through life stigmatized as being less intelligent and a poor student.

Looking at the problem this way forced psychologists to consider seriously another possible explanation for many of the existing correlations between intelligence test scores, doing well in school, and holding down higher-status jobs later in life. Those who control not only economic and social opportunities but also what language and values are the standards by which others will be judged, may in fact be able to use test scores to maintain their power. All one needs to assume is that more powerful families are in a much better position to help their children get higher-status jobs: they know the right people; they can send their children to the right schools; they can use their influence to get them jobs directly. So it turns out that people in higher-status jobs score higher on so-called intelligence tests.

But where is the direct evidence that the higher score on the test in fact indicated that the person was better able to do the higher-status job? As every psychologist knows, correlation does not mean causation. It doesn't follow that because professionals score higher than laborers on certain tests that it is the ability to perform those particular tests which enabled them to be professionals rather than laborers.

The reason why people have assumed that causation was involved is that the test scores were supposed to indicate how intelligent the person was, and it seems reasonable to assume that being a professional requires more of something called intelligence than being a laborer does. However, it is by no means as self-evident as it once was that these test scores measure the kind of intelligence implied by the logic of this argument. They may simply indicate that the person has the *credentials* that the power elite insists that he must have in order to hold a higher-status job. The connection between test performance and job performance may well be extrinsic rather than intrinsic. That is, being able to use the right words may have nothing to do intrinsically with whether a person is a cleverer lawyer, but those in power in a society simply decree that a person cannot be a lawyer unless he uses the correct vocabulary. In this sense the test becomes an instrument for those in power to screen out those who do not know the right words and who are therefore "unqualified" to be lawyers in the minds of those who control such things. Now such a selection procedure may be justifiable in one way or another but it does serve to make clear that the central issue is who is in power and controlling resources, not who is genetically inferior in intelligence.

American psychologists have long accepted without question Professor Terman's conclusion (1947) that his gifted children (those with higher intelligence test scores) grew up to be more successful occupationally, maritally, and socially than those of average intelligence and that they showed fewer "morally deviant" forms of psychopathology such as alcoholism or homosexuality. Yet the power analysis just carried out suggests that neither Professor Terman nor anyone else has as yet brought forward conclusive evidence that it is giftedness per se as he measured it that is responsible for these happier life outcomes. For his gifted children were also drawn very disproportionately from the ranks of the educated, the wealthy, and the powerful. This means that they had not only a better chance to acquire the characteristics measured in the test but also to be happier (since they had more money) and also to have access to higher occupations and better social standing. Maybe test scores measuring "giftedness" are simply another symptom of their generally more favorable social status.

5.   ERICH FROMM ON HUMAN AGGRESSION

Adelbert Reif

Professor Fromm, in the course of recent years, thousands of articles and books have appeared that treat the problem of human aggression under its most varied aspects—frequently, unfortunately, also in pseudoscientific fashion. Most of them show the tendency to refer to one of two diametrically opposed standpoints: either one considers aggression as an *instinct,* which in the course of evolution has been inherited from animal predecessors and, therefore, is somehow retained in unchanged form; or it is viewed, on the other hand, as *learned behavior,* as the product of cultural conditioning. In essence this literature can be divided into two groups: *pro*instinctive works, which Konrad Lorenz and his school support, and *anti*instinctive works, which criticize those theories.

The appearance of your book *The Anatomy of Human Destructiveness* has given a new direction to the discussions concerning the nature of human aggression. It is not surprising, however, that your work extends far beyond the well-known behavioristic standpoint of the anti-Lorenz

literature, "not instinct, but conditioning." You offer, among other things, the proof why human destructiveness is *not* an "inborn instinct," as Lorenz and his students think, but rather an acquired character deformation—a cultural phenomenon, not a phenomenon of nature.

Fromm: The main problem—viewed in general terms—lies in the fact that the word *aggression* is used in a nonselective and indiscriminate way; and, in fact, in the entire literature, with Freud, with Lorenz, with the behaviorists, they understand under aggression things that have nothing whatsoever to do with each other. Aggression is called the active offensive procedure of a human in the sense of the original meaning of *aggression,* derived from the Latin word *agredi,* to take a step forward. It is called aggression when someone defends himself with an act of force when his life is threatened, e.g., he shoots the threatener in order to save his own life. It is called aggression if someone enjoys torturing and controlling someone else. It is called aggression if someone has the desire to destroy humans and things. It is even called aggression, by many analysts, when the farmer plows the earth, because the earth is then somewhat "injured"; it is, so to speak, "attacked" in the act of plowing.

There is where the trick is, if I may say so. For if I designate all these acts with the same word, then I can naturally argue that what is true for defensive aggression—that is, the wish to defend oneself against an attack—is, of course, valid for the other kind of aggression, for sadism and for joy in destruction. In this way, I can simply transfer over all those actions that indicate defensive aggression to the other, the dangerous, evil aggression. That is exactly the case with Konrad Lorenz; in this is the logic of his leading proof.

That would be a quite general answer to the question concerning the total position of the instinctivists such as Konrad Lorenz and of the behaviorists such as B. F. Skinner, whose neobehaviorism is the most widely acknowledged psychological theory in American universities today. Perhaps I could add something in this connection. This total position of the behaviorists and of the instinctivists is not at all so varied as it seems. Because it is common to both schools that, to a certain degree, man as a conscious and free-acting human is completely lacking. The human being of the behaviorists is completely determined by social patterns, that is to say, by the present. The human being of the instinctivists is determined by his past, thus by the instincts that, in the course of development of man, have been built up and cultivated. Both treat humans as marionettes who move according to commands that are external to their own will and control. And here an interesting question is raised: why do the two leading schools of psychology in the 20th century propagate a model of humanity that is identical on one point, namely, that freedom, the will, the conscience, all that is specifically human, plays no role whatsoever any longer?

Q: One of the fundamental questions regarding the theories of Konrad Lorenz and his school is, certainly, can one conclude anything at all in human behavior from that of the animals? And what is more, if the creatures that are compared are not even mammals ...

Fromm: This criticism is surely completely justified and, actually, I need say nothing about it. N. Tinbergen, who is a much more careful and objective researcher than Lorenz, has already said that very clearly and has taken the position that analogies have only little value. I mean, they have actually no value at all, because what does it mean to draw a conclusion from the behavior of geese concerning Soviet-American policy, or however all these analogies appear? Also, one must not forget that, although man is in many respects an animal, it is just as important to see in how many respects he is *not* an animal. That is valid neurophysiologically, in that the human brain differs essentially from that of the primates because of the much larger and more complete neocortex. Considered psychologically, man is the only animal that is conscious of himself: of his inhibition before others, of his impotence, of the future and of death. That does not mean, however, that only man is *intelligent*—a confusion that frequently happens. The animal is also intelligent; the chimpanzee is also intelligent. I would define the concept of "intelligence" as the use of thought for the purpose of manipulating things, for the satisfaction of needs. When a chimpanzee undertakes all sorts of complicated steps in order to get hold of a banana, or solves difficult problems that involve a very complicated thought process, then he is even smarter than many men who cannot do that nearly so well. Intelligence, in this sense, is manipulating thought, thought for the purpose of manipulation; it is actually only a new organ for the accomplishment of things, an organ that is much more highly developed among the primates than with most animals. But animals *beneath* the primates also have at their disposal an amount of such manipulating intelligence. If one is to discuss it, one must say that many men, if not most, only use the manipulating intelligence of their brains and very little of that which one calls *reason* in differentiation, that is, the recognition, the consciousness of oneself, of that which one wants to know, not for the purpose of manipulating but for understanding, for forging ahead to the roots and thus to the reason for manifestations surrounding our own person.

In summing up, it can therefore be established: man not only has intelligence, man also has reason. Man is the *unique* case in nature in which life is aware of itself—completely in opposition to the animal. I believe that one can show that this factor determines all psychic reactions of man, and that all analogies just run aground on this, and this provision is completely different between man and animal in matters of brain physiology as well as in psychology.

Q: Konrad Lorenz defines aggression as a "struggle drive of animal and human directed towards companions in species" that must find manifestation. According to Lorenz, man is caught in his instincts and culture and has only a slight possibility of reducing aggression.

In opposition to this, the American anthropologist Alexander Alland writes:

Far from being tied down by biological laws, man is free to utilize fully the wide range of his biological capabilities, for as certainly as man is born with a capacity for aggression, just as certainly he is born with a capacity for empathy and sympathy, a capacity for powerlessness and a capacity for explorative behavior, which expresses itself in curiosity and in its corresponding

forms of behavior. Further, man is born with the capacity for abstract thought, with the capacity to acquire and to use language, with the capacity of being creative, with the capacity of experimenting. Whether and how these various capacities are expressed depends on the social experiences of the individual in the family and in larger social groups.

It seems to me that the confrontation of these two interpretations is of special interest in the argument with the theory of Konrad Lorenz; so I would like to ask you, Professor Fromm, to treat this fundamental problem somewhat more extensively, if you will.

Fromm: That leads to a criticism of Konrad Lorenz's entire notion about the drive of aggression. First of all, one must remember that Lorenz has the view that in the matter of aggressive drive it is a question of a self-reinforcing drive that grows until it has increased to such an extent that it has need of a release, a satisfaction. Thus, Lorenz believes that that means the aggressive drive is not a *reaction* to definite situations, but primary—as that which was seen in Freud in sexuality—a self-generating and reinforcing drive from neurophysiological causes that seeks satisfaction and, if no opportunity is presented, breaks through in "pouring out." That is a notion that one can hold with certain justification in the case of sexuality. The same is valid with hunger. Only, this notion contradicts the view and the findings of almost all neurophysiologists. On the contrary, there is a great degree of neurophysiological work that proves just the opposite, that shows that aggression is a reaction. Quite generally expressed, it is *a reaction to the threatening of vital interests of the animal or of man.* This means that aggression has developed and functions—quite in a Darwinist sense—as a protection of the survival of the individual and of the species. Aggression is not a fixed, increasing impulse, but normally—with the nature of brain processes—there exists a balance between aggressions and inhibitions, so that no active aggression exists. Aggression is first mobilized when the individual—animal or human—sees a danger that threatens his vital interests. When the danger is gone, then aggression stops once more. Thus, aggression is a *reactive defensive impulse* and not, as Lorenz thinks, a self-intensifying impulse independent of external conditions. Lorenz maintains that we have aggression not because there are, for example, various political parties—but that we have various political parties because we have need of conflict, in order to realize our aggressive drive. It is the same way with war. Man, according to Lorenz, does not become aggressive because war produces aggressiveness through reciprocal threatening—but man needs war in order to satisfy his aggressive drive. And Lorenz, following Freud in this, maintains that if man does not express his aggression, it is unhealthy and harmful to him.

The other question that you touch upon in the citation, that although man does not possess an inborn aggression drive in the nondefensive sense, conversely, brain-physiological properties such as cooperation are important in man, is corroborated by some important neurophysiologists. I have cited a whole series of neurophysiologists in *The Anatomy of Human Destructiveness,* some of whom have the view that even love and, in general, the tendency to set up goals that serve human development are built into the brain. In this there is yet another factor. When one supposes, indeed, that certain elements from earlier historical epochs and social structures are inherited, first of all, from the epochs of the hunter and gatherer, beginning with the birth of "modern" man about 50,000 years ago, then one must assume that for these hunters

and gatherers two things were essential in their whole lives: cooperation and the sharing of food. And not, as many scholars think, the desire for cruelty and for killing. The supposition that hunters are especially cruel and that they get pleasure out of it when the animals suffer, is a romantic distortion, or whatever you would call it, of the facts. A cruel hunter is a bad hunter, because his desire makes him excited. The good hunter is a hunter who behaves as a cool and unexcited beast of prey. Also, the beast of prey is not possessed by the desire to kill, but—and that is likewise proved by the physiology of the brain—the impulse to attack other animals and to kill is located elsewhere neurophysiologically than in defensive aggression.

In principle, it is correct that aggression as *defensive aggression* is built-in biologically/neurophysiologically in humans and animals and functions in the sense of preservation of the species, insofar as it is biologically fitting. This aggression, which I have designated as "benign aggression," is actually not such a great problem because it does not develop when man is not threatened; it is only a reaction to this threatenedness. Now, to be sure, it is correct that in history man has again and again been threatened, but that is a historical factor that in no way has to be. We know of numerous primitive tribes who do not threaten each other, and we can very well imagine a world and social order in which men do not threaten one another, quite in the sense of the prophets who spoke of a world order in which man has no more fear; for fear is the result of threat that leads to aggression.

It is, of course, correct that this defensive aggression occurs greater and more frequently in manifestation with man than in the case of animals, specifically for various reasons. First: the animal recognizes as a threat only that which is here and now; the animal reacts to the immediate danger. However, man, because he is man—that is, because he has a greater power of imagination—sees dangers that are not yet real at all, because he interprets and can recognize from indications that, although no danger exists for him at the moment, another tribe or another nation will attack him by surprise within a reasonable period of time. Therefore, he already reacts to the future danger, and not just to the present one.

Second: man is not the only one to have life and freedom, protection of children, etc., as vital interests—the animal has all that, too. Man has, in addition, still entirely different vital interests that have to do with being human. There are hundreds of values, institutions, persons, symbols that belong to the sphere of man, the threatening of which signifies a threat to himself. Man reacts to this threat likewise with aggression.

And then there is a third factor: man is suggestive, suggestible, capable of being influenced in a way in which an animal is not. One can "brainwash" people and tell them they are being threatened, when in actuality they are not. That is customarily done when governments are preparing for war. For example, Hitler practiced that when he arranged the surprise attack on the Gleiwitz radio station in Silesia in order to show the German people that the Poles were threatening Germany. Now that is an old trick that attacking governments have recourse to in order to mobilize aggression in the people, which only allows itself to be mobilized when every man has the feeling: "I must defend myself against an attack." If a leader should come forth today and say to the people, "We want to start a war because we want to conquer foreign countries, because we want to suppress other peoples, because we enjoy murdering," certainly, there would be no people whatsoever ready to follow him—at most, a very small minor-

ity of half-sick people. Therefore, he must mask his true intentions and suggest to the people a believable threat. Only then can he mobilize the defensive aggression.

The other question, which actually presents the big problem of which Tinbergen has spoken, is: why is man the only animal who kills members of his own species? The only animal who has joy in killing, joy in destroying, joy in torture? Among the animals, we do not find that—at least, not among the mammals. One has to, indeed—as with Lorenz—extend back to birds and fishes in order to find particular examples of sadism and joy in destruction. Actual dangerous aggression, which we meet everywhere today—for example, in the regimes of terror where the executing organs are men who often not only obey commands but are prepared for them with pleasure in killing and torture—is completely *human* and is, of course, an aggression of quite a different kind than the defensive aggression that man shares with the animals. If we want to understand the maliciousness and danger of man, then we must leave defensive aggression and biologically conditioned aggression and direct ourselves to the question: how is this malicious aggression that is typical of man conditioned, where does it come from, what are its bases? That is really the main question, too, that I have treated in *The Anatomy of Human Destructiveness.*

Q: Up to now, you have spoken of defensive aggression. What do you consider to be "malicious aggression" and what are its origins?

Fromm: There are no instincts that are not simultaneously influenced by the environment and learning factors. But here I use the concept "instinct" only quite generally because it is a popular expression with which most people can identify.

One can say that defensive aggression is a kind of instinct produced by certain sequences, stimulations and factors under the higher concept of "threatening of vital interests." As I have already explained, malicious aggression is, however, not a reaction to such threatening; that is, it is not dissected neurophysiologically as a complex of ways of reaction that are produced by means of a definite stimulus, but, and here I come to speak of the crucial point, it is a *question of character.*

Q: But what is character?

Fromm: The word *character,* as I use it here, has a meaning that stems from psychoanalysis and was used specifically by Freud for the first time—although you can read character descriptions in Balzac or Dostoevsky that outdo in abundance even Freud and, viewed theoretically, have exactly the same meaning—namely, to show character as a system of strivings that forms itself in man at a certain point of time of his life (of course, it is not entirely unchanging, although, generally, it changes little when it is once developed) and that finally determines how he acts, how he feels, how he thinks.

The discovery of the concept of character in the dynamic sense was quite an extraordinary discovery by Freud. And, remarkably, this Freudian concept of character has attracted relatively little attention. Also, his theories of the death drive and of the life or love drive have never really become popular, except with his colleagues. What was taken over from Freud was sexuality. When people speak of Freud or cite him, they speak—of course, apart from his discovery of repression, rationalization and symbol interpretation—of sexuality and above all of child sexuality as the root of all pathology, but not of his central discovery of the concept of dynamic character, which is the key to the understanding of the underlying basis of human behavior.

Perhaps a mechanism of repression or, if you will, a mechanism of resistance has contributed to this. If you ask characterologically: in fact, who are you really, what are the true motives of your action, by what are you *actually* motivated? as opposed to what you believe, or what you pretend to believe in contrast to the picture that you have of yourself or that you try to project—then one hits upon really difficult personal problems. There one unveils; there one uncovers—and no one wants to do that willingly; in the case of others, of course, but there he would have to be prepared for the others concerning themselves with him somewhat on a closer basis. And so one prefers, at the outset, not to begin with it and to dwell instead on a much more innocent theme: what went on in front of them in their parents' bedroom when they were four years old. That is naturally an enormous loss, because most of the problems of individual men, like those of society, can be understood only from the knowledge of character.

In the historical-biological sense, character develops in such a way that in a definite society individuals *want* to do what they *must* do, briefly expressed, that they are impelled by character to think in such a way, to behave in such a way, to react in such a way as is necessary under the given social conditions for the preservation of the society as a whole—and not only for the preservation of the species. For example, a man in a society of warriors must have a warlike aggressive character. He must willingly go on a campaign, he must get pleasure out of fighting and killing, etc. The same man would be quite a misfit in a society of cooperative agriculturists; there he would hardly be capable of existing because there is no place for these qualities in such a society. There he must have a character that motivates him to cooperate, to maintain friendly relations with others and to share with them.

Take the "modern" man, the man in the

cybernetic society, whom I have designated as "man of the marketplace." This man is impelled to subjugate himself to an anonymous authority, to do what the organization wants, to have little feeling. Performance is production, sufficient ambition to develop, in order to make progress, but only exactly as much as meets social requirements; for the others, on the other hand, it's enough to be satisfied with what they have. In order to bring it to a kind of formula: the alienated character is the character who conforms to the requirements of modern society. And every society produces the character that it requires.

Q: How can it be explained that in one society so many characters fit into it? How can someone develop a peaceful character in a warlike, aggressive society?

Fromm: That is an important question. It is correct to say that there are people in every society who do not fit into it. The accommodation of the members of a society is successful, of course, only on the average. When I speak here of social character as that necessary, useful character for society for the time being, that does not mean that society is successful in generating this character in all people. Because of individual or constitutional factors, there are always persons who do not conform to the social character of the society. This is partly due to negative factors; remember that there are extremely destructive people under certain social conditions who are completely incapable of sustaining any kind of human relations. That is quite certainly the case with severely ill people. On the other hand, there would be no historical development at all if there were not persons existing in every society who, exactly for the reason that they do not conform to the social character, are capable of changing and revolutionizing society.

Q: But how do these characters come about?

Fromm: That can have individual bases, resulting from quite definite family occurrences; constitutional factors can play a role, but it can also be socially motivated. Take an example: the revolutionary leaders of 1917 were, for the most part, men who came from the middle or upper class; however, they were, for individual reasons—constitutional and family factors—superior in growth over the typical character of their class and, therefore, they could become leaders who wanted to change the conditions in a way that did not conform to the traditional social character. These exceptions are enormously important historically, because they present mutations that make the social change possible if at the same time the general political and social conditions for such a change are favorable. When that is not the case, then these men probably will remain at the fringes, because no one listens to them, because no one takes notice of them; they are simply considered to be crazy and many times they even become so in their isolation. But, as I have already said, these leaders are exceptions; on the whole, the social character is produced by means of the necessity of the requirements of a society.

Q: But still now there is not just "one" society.

Fromm: That is an essential point: there is not "one" society; there are only *specific societies.* Consequently, there are also only specific human structures of energy. Viewed from the standpoint of society, all institutions—education, the school; propaganda, the newspapers; whatever— operate upon producing this social character. Or, to express it another way, society *cannot* use human energies, which are one of the original productive forces, as general energy. It must transform this energy into a *specific* energy, which is necessary for its social purposes. Where it is a question of social character, that is the transformation of general energy into specific energy, which is necessary for the society within a certain social system.

Q: What cultural-sociological significance for humanity do you derive from this conclusion?

Fromm: The significance is this: man is completely a product of social conditions. I do not speak here of "conditioning" as the behaviorists do; I am speaking of certain social systems and of the effect of such systems upon the sociologically given structure of human existence. The vital point is that man is not an empty sheet of paper upon which culture or society writes its text. Man is already born with certain necessities recumbent in his existence. To discuss these particular necessities would lead us too far astray at this point; I have written about this in various books. Only this, perhaps, as an example of what I mean: *man must have a system of orientation and of devotion.* That is, man must have a picture of the world to which he orients himself. It does not matter at all whether the picture is correct or false—even today, he does not yet have a completely correct picture (or perhaps never a completely false picture, either). But however the picture may appear, he needs it, because otherwise he cannot act. That is a basic condition for human existence that is not valid for the animal. For the animal does not have to seek out its own path, the animal is already predetermined to act in such a way that is "correct"; in this respect, it has no problems.

When I just said that man requires an object of devotion, I mean that need that man has to transcend over himself as a purely feeding and loving machine. For even if man has at his disposal all kinds of material and sexual satisfaction, he is still not happy, he is not even protected from insanity. Taking everything into consideration, we have one of the richest cultures and probably one of the most unhappy, al-

though the consciousness of being unhappy is deeply suppressed.

Q: Are you thinking of humanity in general?

Fromm: I am thinking of man in the Western industrial world, as far as he participates in the vast consumption of material things and does not belong to those whom the auto has passed by, who remain on the fringes. You see, man has more and more goods and possibilities at his disposal and in spite of that people become more and more dissatisfied. People become more destructive. Therefore, man must—and I mean this with evolution—have a goal that extends beyond himself, a devotion to something that frees him from his egocentricity. That can only happen when man appeals to something external and he conquers his egoism. That this need exists, one can, I believe, point to extensive empirical material.

Man has a need for freedom. Man can, to be sure, be brought to a point where he even loves slavery, but only one under one condition—he becomes disturbed, aggressive, stupid and fearful. For no one can enslave him and make him cheerful, happy and unaggressive. When one exceeds a certain threshold of suppression, then man avenges himself, in that he either becomes rebellious or completely destructive or of no use, or his vitality slowly dies away. History is a laboratory in which this state of affairs is demonstrated.

Permit me to say something about the sadistic character. There it depends, above all, on what one means by sadism. Freud—and it is popularly understood to be so extensively—understands sadism to be essentially a sexual phenomenon. On this point he finds support in the generally known fact that, for many people—apparently, for men more than for women, but that is again very uncertain—sexual excitement and sexual satisfaction are connected with it, when they torture another person, inflict pain on him, insult him or humble him. Now Freud has explained that sadism is a partial drive of sexuality that corresponds to an early stage of development of the libido, which then, however, has been produced independently in the case of certain people for certain reasons, and expresses either the entire content or at least an essential part of their sexual desires.

According to my view, sadism is a much more general phenomenon than that described by Freud. At the nucleus of sadism, I see the passion to control another being, that is, to completely control, to have in my power, to do with him what I will, to be, so to speak, his God, to be almighty. This situation is realized in the form of injuring someone else, to humble him physically, so that he cannot defend himself. With sadism, it must be that the other person is helpless and weak. Sadism never has a strong person as an object. One could clearly see that in the case of the Nazis; one can see that generally in sadistic psychology, that which is attractive is power over the weak. The strong one is admired, the weak one stimulates.

Naturally, there are also many other forms of complete control that are not necessarily those of physical pain or of manifest humiliation. You will find many sadistic manifestations in relationships between people that are based on the situation where one possesses complete control over the other. You see that in the case of parents, teachers, nurses, prison guards and, to a large degree, in the case of people who are in an elevated position or social situation, the kind in which one has power over others. And he who has the power uses it in order to control others. The rough forms of sadism, in that one is beaten, injured bodily or reviled, those are naturally the clearest expressions and manifestations of sadism. But they are perhaps not even the most

important at all. The most important are to be found in the relationships between people: they are the attempts of one person to gain omnipotence over others.

One can recognize a person with sadistic character quite easily: he is unfriendly, unloving, in the final analysis unsure, unproductive, he feels himself debased, and all that matters to him is to control everything and everybody, just as far as he can. Take a simple example: you see a postal official behind the counter; at 6:00 p.m. he goes off duty. It is shortly before 6:00, there are still two people standing there who have been waiting for a long time. But exactly at 6:00 p.m. he closes his counter and goes away. If you look at this person closer you will perhaps see around his thin lips a quite slight tinge of a smile of maliciousness or of enjoyment, because he has the power to compel these people to return the next day, and they have stood in line in vain. I don't bring up the question here, whether he would actually be compelled by the postal regulations to close the counter at exactly 6:00 p.m., or whether he could have worked on for two minutes longer. I am also not speaking of the question that he would probably give as an answer: well, if I stayed longer at my place of work each day, when would I then get home? This would probably explain the case rationally, if this tiny feature of satisfaction were not apparent, which is recognizable in sadists.

The behaviorists cannot see this feature, for one cannot prove it scientifically. There is no instrument with which one can grasp it. One could perhaps photograph this face, but possibly this feature would not be recognizable in the photo. But any person who is the least bit sensitive recognizes the face of a sadist.

Q: To what extent does that actually have to do with character? In what respect are character and sadism connected? You said that sadism originates from an incompetent situation and is a deep-rooted need. Wouldn't that amount to the same thing with instinct?

Fromm: Yes. I should have explained that more precisely. An instinct would not depend upon external conditions. Instinct is so strongly established that it is not lacking in some people under certain conditions and emerges in others under certain conditions. Instinct really means that a quite definite manner of reaction is built into the brain that, to be sure, is not completely independent of external circumstances, but that still functions essentially autonomously, reacts spontaneously and leads to certain motivations. Take, for example, sexuality. There one can say: that is an instinct. One does not find that with one group of people sexual desires are present and with another group of people simply are omitted. Naturally, sexual drive is stimulated by certain objects. We know, however, that if these objects are lacking, in spite of this, sexual desires and fantasies are present.

Q: Just before *The Anatomy of Human Destructiveness* appeared, you wrote in an article in *National-Zeitung:* "Probably the most important source of aggression and destructive rage is found in the *bored character.* Boredom, in this sense, is not conditioned by external circumstances, not by the lack of stimulation, for example, as in the experiments in which sensual perceptions are shut out, or as in the isolation cell of a prison. It is *a subjective factor in man himself,* an incapacity to enter into a real interest in things and people in his environment." It goes on to say: "The increase in boredom is caused by the forms and structure and the functioning of our modern industrial society."

Perhaps you could expand somewhat more upon your statement, "probably the most important source of aggression today," and also illustrate more precisely the conditions under which the destructivity develops?

Fromm: That is not simple, because there is a whole series of conditions for destructivity. One is that life loses its meaning, so that the person no longer has any hope; although he feels, to be sure, he is alive, he also feels that life is running out through his fingers like sand. He has no happiness. He never has anything that makes him feel established as a person. Insofar that he feels powerless with respect to his own existence, he has something in common with the sadist. Finally, he has a "resentment" against life, as Nietzsche calls it. He hates life because he is alive without ever having lived, for he is aware of what he is missing. He hates life because he experiences his loneliness, his isolation, and cannot attempt anything against it. He hates life because he cannot master it in any other sense, namely, in the sense of joy in living, in the sense of loving, understanding behavior, the sense of solidarity, of interest in people, in the sense of joy in the creation.

Finally, there is yet another very essential factor added to it that is probably the most important of all, and today plays a large role: I mean, the fact of boredom. You see it quite clearly in America—perhaps, too, in Germany—that what it is that the workers are complaining about is no longer primarily the more or less slight amount of their income, but boredom, which is linked to modern work. A chief problem in the disputes between labor and management is therefore the demand of the workers that this boredom be reduced. A few members of management have already begun taking steps against this problem by, for example, decentralizing the working hours again.

But where does this boredom come from? This boredom comes from the fact that man has become purely an instrument, that he develops no initiative, possesses no responsibility, that he feels himself to be only a small wheel in a machine, that he can be replaced at any time by someone else. Boredom, therefore, comes from the fact that the person is a completely alienated person —alienated from himself, from other people, from work. Boredom comes from the fact that man faces a world over which he no longer has any kind of control and in which, for this reason, too, his interest is more and more removed. That is true not only for the workers, but for the employers as well as for most people in general, with the exception of those who practice a profession that is really interesting, and that allows their own capabilities to be formed and experienced productively. That is sometimes the case with scientists, scholars, doctors and also with top managers, who, when they are located at the summit of an enterprise, can actually perform something creative, although they, too, ultimately are subjected to the law of maximalization of profit. They know that they—even though they have the most beautiful ideas—may lose their position if the profits do not increase.

Thus, in this sense, the top manager is not free any longer, either. Only when the person is interested in what he is producing —think of the fundamental meaning of "interest": to be inside something, to be in the midst of it, that is, to be possessed by something—then he is happy, he feels his own living power justified, can express it, is not isolated, feels himself united with the world and not powerless. He can love things, he can love his work and he can love people. But when he is nothing more than a minute component of a machine, if he does nothing but carry out some kind of orders—even if he is paid well for it, that does not change things at all—when he has no actual responsibility, when he can show no interest because there is just nothing interesting to do—whether he is sitting at a computer or standing at the conveyor belt is essentially all the same—then he becomes bored.

Q: What social questions result from the increasing boredom for our society?

Fromm: If we would introduce a two-hour day today instead of the seven-hour day, then I believe that our mental institutions would not suffice in the least in taking care of the victims of boredom. The bored person who cannot experience anything positive has, however, one possibility to experience intensity, and that is destruction. When he destroys life, then he experiences a sensation of dominance over life, he avenges himself on it because he was not successful in fulfilling this life with meaning. When he avenges and destroys, he proves to himself that life has not been able to cheat him.

There is extensive clinical material on this. I refer here to the numerous cases in the United States, where frequently 17- and 18-year-old people simply go out and stab a person they don't know at all and then explain, "That was the greatest moment of my life, because I saw on the pain-distorted face of this person that I surely can make an impression, that I am not completely nothing." That is a much more radical solution than sadism because it demands the negation of life itself, and through the destruction of a stranger's life one's own failure to be actually living is supposed to be compensated.

Hence, it appears to me that the destructive tendencies of today are therefore increasing so quickly because boredom is increasing, because the senselessness of life is increasing, because people are becoming more fearful, because they have no faith in the future and no hope. Also not the least, because they feel themselves cheated by all promises, by all ideologies, by all parties, by all religions. In this situation, many people see only one satisfaction, to destroy life itself, in order to avenge themselves on the deceivers and on themselves.

6. BETWEEN MAN AND BEAST—THE GENETIC–BEHAVIOR CONNECTION

V. C. deKoenigsberg

We human beings prefer to think of ourselves as a unique species. Our complicated social customs separate us from the rest of the animal kingdom. In short, we have culture. And animals are ... well ... animals.

Now, however, a small but influential group of scientists who call themselves *sociobiologists* are saying that human social customs and behavior may stem from genetics and not strictly the trimmings of culture.

Take for instance the suburban housewife-to-be who, faced with several suitors, picks one because of his potential for making good money and building and maintaining a comfortable home. She is strictly bowing to the pressures of society, a sociologist might say, not genetics.

But the sociobiologist can point to the female marsh wren. When a female marsh wren chooses a mate, says Harvard sociobiologist (and zoologist) Edward O. Wilson, she evaluates more than his physique. Male wrens have multiple mates called harems, and because of this, each female receives little help from her mate in rearing their young. So it is to the female's advantage to select a male who controls a territory of nesting sites that will protect her from predators and bad weather.

After dotting his home range with a string of half-finished roosts, explains Wilson, the male shows each one off in turn to an interested female, who selects one that

suits her best and decorates its interior with feathers and other cushy materials.

If there's a lesson to be learned from this, it's that females of most species choose mates who are good providers ... and for good survival-of-the-fittest reasons. That doesn't mean that suburban seduction rites can all be neatly explained by observing comparable behavior in wrens, but it does suggest that beneath layers of cultural conditioning, deep-seated genetic tendencies from our ancestral heritage still exert an effect on how to act. What sociobiologists like zoologist Wilson hope to accomplish is to identify these "genetic residues" by studying the behavior of animals.

To trace the origin of sociobiology, we have to go back to the 19th Century when naturalists were piecing together evolution's procession from prehistoric reptile to modern man. And as they put together skull fragments and shards of fossilized limbs, they became aware of a now-obvious fact: that skeletal architecture from species to species is very much the same. A sparrow's wing, a seal's flipper, a dog's forelimb and a man's arm are startlingly similar, indicating perhaps that all evolved from a common ancestor.

Following this evolutionary line of reasoning, Konrad Lorenz and other students of animal behavior (ethologists) searched for similarities in the *actions* of physically different creatures, such as bees and herring gulls. Here too, they found that behavior also was remarkably alike among different species, just as naturalists found similarities in skeleton design.

Reprinted with permission from *Science Digest* (July 1975), pp. 36–43. Copyright © 1975, The Hearst Corporation.

SLEUTHING GENETIC BEHAVIOR

Sociobiologists take the third step in this logic. Unlike ethologists (such as Lorenz), who study animal behavior under undisturbed field conditions, and naturalists, who probe the genetics of physical traits, the sociobiologist combines parts of both disciplines and seeks to trace the genetics of animal behavior (including humans). He studies the caste systems and modes of communication of various animal societies as well as their genetic makeup.

Sociobiologists say that natural selection, the gene-directed force that outfits living things for survival (fur for arctic dwellers, blubber for sea-going mammals) also shapes behavior. The basic idea is that animals pass on their good points to the next generation to increase their offsprings' chances of survival. By investigating the traits of animal societies, sociobiology hopes to trace this thin evolutionary thread that binds the behavior of most social animals, aiming eventually to use what it learns to illuminate human interactions.

The framework for this audacious new science is set forth in Wilson's new book, *Sociobiology: The New Synthesis* (Harvard University Press). At present, sociobiologists are seeking to explain why all animals, including humans, follow similar patterns in such areas as:

- Relations between the sexes.
- Altruism and cooperation.
- Parent-child conflicts.

Throwing himself into the first area, sexual conflict, is David Barash, a zoologist and member of the University of Washington's psychology department. Because modern man's behavior is a hopeless tangle of culturally conditioned responses and genetically inherited traits, Barash prefers to examine how animals, whose actions are not veiled by cultural masks, behave in "human" situations. And at least one type of human sexual conflict, adultery, is better understood in certain bird species.

Like most birds, mountain bluebirds are monogamous. Since a male spends plenty of time and effort caring for and protecting his offspring, he's not anxious to be cuckolded. As Dr. Barash puts it, "There's no evolutionary pay-off in raising someone else's young" (since that would amount to perpetuating a stranger's genetic legacy at the expense of one's own). So if a male bluebird suspects his mate of adultery, he might react violently.

To find out more about this, Barash placed a model male bluebird near a nesting female while her mate was out foraging for food. When the experiment was done early in the breeding season, the returning male attacked the "intruder," drove his mate from the nest, and wooed a new female with whom he raised a brood. But when Dr. Barash repeated the ruse after a female had laid her eggs, something interesting happened.

Even though the resident male attacked the model, he allowed his mate to hatch the clutch and raise their offspring. Why? Since the bluebird's brief reproductive season was already too far along to permit re-nesting, Barash reasons, the second male stayed with his seemingly errant mate for the sake of his offspring. Lesson: better to tolerate adultery and protect one's genetic "investment" in the next generation.

Extended and elaborate rites of courtship, some sociobiologists suspect, evolved among monogamous creatures to protect unsuspecting males from investing time and attention in offspring sired by others. By the courting ritual, a male has time to find out if the female he's set his cap for has already been inseminated.

Throughout the animal kingdom, Wilson points out, polygamy is the rule, monogamy the exception, and there's a sound biological reason for that. "Males invest relatively little with each mating effort," he explains in *Sociobiology,* "and it is to their advantage to tie up as many female investments as they can." Males can afford to be extravagent because they have millions of sperm to distribute, but nature demands that females be coy and cautious. At each mating a female's entire genetic portfolio is invested in a single egg, so she has to select the best of possible mates to fertilize it.

THE GENETICS OF ALTRUISM

Among social species, a key determinant of behavior appears to be another trait considered uniquely human—altruism. By feigning injury, prairie warblers lure predators away from their young. Similarly, castes of soldier termites give defenseless nymphs time to escape prey by positioning themselves directly in its path. Male mantis shrimp in combat actually exhibit what appears to be kindness toward the enemy; strikes from their hammer-shaped appendages are aimed at each other's heavily-armored tail sections where they do the least harm.

Defined in evolutionary language, "my altruism toward you," explains University of Pennsylvania sociobiologist Scott Boorman, "is any activity that makes you more likely to survive (and hence pass your genes to future generations) at the price of making me more likely to die (and so not make such a contribution myself)." But since acts of altruism seem to handicap generous individuals, why not be selfish instead?

William D. Hamilton, a British entomologist, solved that age-old riddle in 1964 when he pointed out that natural selection ultimately acts on genes, not individuals, another way of saying "blood is thicker than water." To boost his genetic contribution to posterity, Hamilton found,

an animal helps close relatives with whom he shares the most genes in common, more often than distant relatives or unrelated individuals. That way the animal makes sure that, even if he never lives to reproduce, at least some of his genes will be passed to future generations.

To test this hypothesis, Hamilton looked at the peculiar genetic attributes of the Hymenoptera, the biological order of ants, bees and wasps. Because of a reproductive quirk, females of these social species share three-quarters of their genes in common with their sisters, but only one-half with their own offspring. This being the case, one would expect hymenopteran females to contribute to the next generation by staying home and looking after their sisters instead of going out and starting families of their own. And that's exactly what they do: many female ants, bees and wasps are permanently non-reproductive "workers," who toil exclusively for the reproductive success of their sister, the queen.

Equally impressive, though less extreme, is the altruism of certain bird families, which closely resembles human nepotism. Among Florida scrub jays, for instance, "helper" sons and daughters put off laying eggs of their own to assist parents in raising younger siblings. By performing such altruistic acts as feeding nestlings and defending the low-lying nest from attack, helpers improve their own chances of survival—and of eventually starting a family of their own.

If the single breeder male in a jay family group dies or abandons his brood, studies conducted by Glen E. Woolfenden of the University of South Florida show the dominant male helper wins his place. Alternatively, as the jay population expands its territorial borders, the dominant male helper can stake out a home range, breed and raise helpers of his own.

PARENTS VS. OFFSPRING

Using altruism's strange genetic calculus as a tool, Robert Trivers, a colleague of Dr. Wilson's at Harvard's Museum of Comparative Zoology, has analyzed parent-offspring conflicts in animals, particularly those applicable to human situations. Trivers interprets the strain between the generations as the inevitable outcome of their divergent genetic interests. Parents, who are most interested in promoting their own genetic legacy, he points out, attempt to raise as many offspring to maturity as possible. In contrast, each offspring tries to monopolize its parents' attention for as long as it can. Weaning conflict, a phenomenon widespread among mammals, is one good example.

During the first weeks of a lamb's life, the ewe produces more milk than her offspring can consume. But after the fourth week, the mother supplies less milk than her growing lamb demands and the weaning process begins. Similarly, as juvenile macaques mature and learn to fend for themselves, their mothers discourage nursing with increasing firmness by plucking the infants bodily from their nipples.

In these parent-offspring conflicts, Trivers explains, children compete at a disadvantage, since they are smaller and less experienced than their elders. To compensate, they manipulate their parents through a subtle repertoire of psychological ploys. "The offspring can cry not only when it is famished," he says, "but also when it merely wants more food than the parent has elected to give. Likewise, it can begin to withhold its smile until it has gotten its way." Regression, a form of human behavior in which a person uses childish techniques to get attention, may stem from these tactics.

One important conclusion of Trivers'

analysis, however, collides head-on with more traditional views of enculturation, the socializing process by which parents teach children cultural values such as responsibility, decency, honesty and self-denial. Considering the conflict in their evolutionary strategies, Trivers says, enculturation is nothing more than a parent's devious attempts to indoctrinate children to increase their elders' lot.

That interpretation makes sense, Dr. Barash told me, because it explains why children resist such parental demands as going to bed early, studying hard, and refraining from gambling, drinking and pre-marital sex. Parents naturally encourage children to spend their time constructively (studying or mowing the lawn) rather than in frivolous pursuits (gambling), since such actions are either altruistic in themselves or prime the child for future altruism. "If the children often disagree with such parental urgings," Barash says, "this may emanate in part from their unconscious perceptions that such actions maximize the parent's fitness rather than their own."

The extent to which genetic programming influences such behavior in humans has sparked a lot of arguments between biologists and social scientists. Some sociobiologists want to relate their animal observations to comparable types of human behavior. Social scientists, however, argue that such comparisons are facile. In a creature as behaviorally complex as man, they say, how can one hope to unravel the Gordian's knot of inherited and acquired traits?

Gingerly striding the nature-nurture borderline, Dr. Barash offers a compromise position. "Human beings obviously present a special case," he says. "Certainly analysis of the human situation is greatly complicated by the tremendous interplay between genetic factors and cultural phenomena. But this is all the more reason for employing an evolutionary approach which touches all bases."

As an example of how sociobiology might illuminate human behavior, he cites such holdovers of man's primate ways as male defense of the young. Stationing himself at a dangerous crosswalk in downtown Seattle, Barash observed the behavior of parents and children about to make their way through the busy onrush of traffic.

Like their keenly alert primate counterparts, he says, human males made significantly more head sweeps than females. But among childless couples, he noted, such defensive behaviors were done the same number of times by males and females. "Our technology has substituted Chevrolets for cheetahs," he says, "but the adaptive value of appropriate behavioral tendencies may have remained unchanged."

7. THE MIND–BODY LINK

Joan Arehart-Treichel

Investigators are reporting increasingly tantalizing links between thoughts and emotions and physical disease. During the 1960s, for example, William A. Greene, a psychiatrist at the University of Rochester, studied the life history of three sets of twins. One twin out of each set had come down with leukemia. Greene found that each twin who had gotten leukemia had experienced a psychological upheaval right before. The other twins had not. So Greene concluded that psychological trauma might well be a precipitating factor in cancer, even stronger than genetic predisposition.

Clinicians also continue to be impressed by the influence of the psyche on susceptibility to physical disease. After Richard Nixon resigned as President in August 1974, a number of clots developed in his phlebitis-stricken leg. Many physicians, notably Lawrence E. Hinkle of Cornell Medical Center and Samuel Silverman of

Reprinted with permission from SCIENCE NEWS, the weekly news magazine of science, copyright 1975 by Science Service, Inc.

Harvard Medical School, are convinced that psychological stress related to the Watergate scandal may have triggered the clots.

For all the evidence linking the psyche with somatic diseases, however, there's a woeful shortage of data showing precisely how such diseases occur physiologically. As John W. Mason of the Walter Reed Army Institute of Research and a former president of the American Psychosomatic Society puts it: "There's no shortage of data relating disease to psychosocial factors. The shortage is in our knowledge of the mediating mechanisms." What's more, in view of the complex interactions between psyche and soma, it will probably be many years before scientists expose the physiological links between thoughts and emotions and physical diseases.

There are actually two kinds of evidence showing that one's thoughts and emotions have the ability to trigger somatic disease. One concerns stressful events, and their ability to trigger a welter of illnesses. The other concerns certain patterns of thoughts and emotions and their ability to trigger specific somatic diseases.

As for evidence linking stress to disease, it's plentiful and diverse. Sidney Cobb of Brown University, for example, has determined that air traffic controllers, who are under keen stress, have far greater frequency of high blood pressure, stomach ulcers and diabetes than do second-class licencees who are not under comparable stress. Cobb also studied auto workers laid off in Detroit and found that stomach ulcers were common at the time of termination. Many other laid-off workers subsequently came down with cancer, arthritis, high blood pressure, alcoholism and gout.

Probably the best known link between psychological stress and somatic disease susceptibility has been made by Thomas H. Holmes of the University of Washington and Richard H. Rahe of the Naval Health Research Center in San Diego. Holmes and Rahe have found that stressful changes in one's lifestyle over a period of time can be used to predict susceptibility to disease. They have devised a 43-item stress checklist that people can use to see whether they are likely to come down with disease in the near future. Certain stresses of life, such as death of spouse, are weighted heavier than are lesser stresses, such as Christmas or minor violations of the law.

Evidence linking particular personality types to specific disease susceptibility is also compelling. Two San Francisco cardiologists, Meyer Friedman and Ray H. Rosenman, have spent 15 years associating the aggressive, time-urgent, competitive, highly successful person (Type A) with the occurrence of heart attacks, and the counterpart, the more relaxed, easygoing person (Type B) with the lack of them. As Friedman and Rosenman write in their book, *Type A Behavior and Your Heart*, "It is the Type A man's ceaseless striving, his everlasting *struggle* with time, that we believe so very frequently leads to his early demise from coronary heart disease."

Certain personality traits have been linked with cancer. An outstanding researcher in this area is Caroline Thomas of Johns Hopkins University School of Medicine. For close to 30 years Thomas has been following Johns Hopkins medical students as they graduate, become established professionally, mature and even die. She has found, like Friedman and Rosenman, that heart attack victims tend to be high-gear persons. Suicide victims were not close to their parents in childhood and even as young people had been especially susceptible to stress. And cancer victims are low-gear persons, seldom prey to outbursts of emotions. They have feelings of isolation and unhappiness dating back to childhood (SN: 9/20/75, p. 182).

The heart attack and cancer personalities have also been confirmed by other researchers, notably Claus and Marjorie Bahnson, a husband and wife psychology team at the Eastern Pennsylvania Psychiatric Institute. As Marjorie Bahnson sees it, "The heart attack personality feels that he is under greater stress than are other people, even where this is not true. The cancer personality may be under greater stress than other people, but he will say, 'Everything is fine.'"

Provocative links have also been made between personality types and rheumatoid arthritis, asthma, stomach ulcers and some other physical diseases. For instance, four out of five rheumatoid arthritis victims are women—and many of these women have been found to share certain personality traits. They often have unfulfilled ambitions because of feelings of inadequacy harking back to childhood. Because of these frustrations, they frequently funnel their need for recognition outside the home into being exceptional housekeepers and mothers. Like cancer, rheumatoid arthritis often sets in after a particularly traumatic experience.

Certainly there is ample evidence suggesting how thoughts and emotions might actually lead to these or other somatic diseases. Largely through the work of stress pioneer Hans Selye, emotions have been found to act via the hypothalamus and pituitary gland on hormones of the adrenal glands. Other hormones, notably the hormones released by the pituitary, are also responsive to psychological stress. Edward J. Sachar of Albert Einstein College of Medicine reported in the July HOSPITAL PRACTICE. The hypothalamus is also known to link up with the autonomic nervous system. So it's quite possible that thoughts and emotions initiate disease via these nerve and hormonal pathways.

The psyche is also being linked to the immune system, the body's major barrier to disease. Selye has found that psychological stress can damage the thymus, a major gland of the immune system. Marvin Stein of the Mount Sinai School of Medicine in New York City has linked the hypothalamus to the immune system (SN: 2/1/75, p. 68). The Bahnsons, in a pilot clinical study, have found a strong correlation between depression and lowered immune competence.

What's more, physiological correlations have been made between the psyche and specific somatic diseases. According to Neal Miller, a psychologist at Rockefeller University and a pioneer in the study of the autonomic nervous system, "There is considerable clinical evidence that people under stress conditions, like combat, have stomach lesions. This is backed up by experimental evidence that . . . subjecting animals to stress will cause stomach lesions." Vernon Riley of the Northwest Research Foundation in Seattle has found that anxious mice came down with cancer; mice protected from anxiety did not (SN: 9/20/75, p. 182).

Nonetheless, tough questions still need to be answered. How might the same stress levels lead to disease in one person but not in another? How might persons with similar personalities end up with different diseases? Surely other factors than personality must also enter the picture, such as age, weight, sex, genetic predisposition, adverse environmental factors. And what is really more critical in the development of disease: the number of turbulent thoughts and emotions, or their content? In other words, are negative thoughts, emotions, and events more likely to lead to disease than positive ones?

In the absence of firm evidence, investigators disagree. In fact, in his book *Stress Without Distress,* Selye gives conflicting answers. In one place he writes, "We have seen that it is immaterial whether a stressor is pleasant or unpleasant; its stressor effect depends merely on the intensity of the demand made upon the adaptive capacity of the body." Yet in another place he writes, "Mental tensions, frustrations, insecurity and aimlessness are among the most damaging stressors, and psychosomatic studies have shown how often they cause migraine headaches, peptic ulcers, heart attacks, hypertension . . ."

The problem in proving that the psyche can cause somatic diseases is essentially this: Scientists have only a primitive notion of how thoughts and emotions are formed in the brain, and although the actions of the body are better known, their interactions with the brain and with each other have been only superficially explored.

Manson puts the matter crisply: "In our attempts to go beyond the age-old clinical observations that there is a relationship between psychological factors and disease and to get into the bodily mechanisms, we are still only scratching the surface. True, we have more sophisticated techniques than ever before, but the problem is enormously complicated and requires revolutionary innovations in research strategy. You can't take one or two hormones and study them and come up with an answer. You have to study the many interdependent hormones, perhaps eventually 15 or 20, at once. And that kind of industrial research approach is alien to the academic atmosphere. For example, I find it difficult to maintain reasonably authoritative knowledge of two or three hormones, yet I'm trying to measure ten. What is really needed are four or five additional co-workers who can each take over part of the labor, each being an authority on several hormones. Then we could cover everything at a high level of professional expertise. In other words, one major obstacle in this field is the need for new organizational approaches to developing cooperative research on a much larger scale.

"If asked where the forefront of science is at the moment," he continues, "most people would reply, at the molecular level. Certainly the analytical approach remains an important frontier. But you have the enormous question that is unique to biology compared to the physical sciences: How does it all work together? How is it all coordinated? It is the integrative approach that we're going to have to develop if we want to really understand how thoughts and emotions can lead to disease."

8. THE OTHER HEMISPHERE

Robert J. Trotter

Of all the frontiers science has yet to conquer, of all the mysteries it has yet to unravel, one of the most exciting and possibly the most important is the still uncharted human brain. Rising to meet this challenge are thousands of researchers in a number of diverse fields, each coming at the brain from a slightly different angle. Neuroscientists, brain anatomists, electrophysiologists, biochemists and other specialists in the physical sciences are all probing the brain in attempts to understand what it is and how it works. But investigations of the brain itself do not give the whole picture. Mapping the brain from an entirely different but equally valid perspective are the behavioral scientists who hope to get a better understanding of the human brain by examining not what it is but what it produces—human behavior.

Along these lines, an investigation was conducted last summer among the Inuit or Eskimo people of Baffin Island in northeastern Canada. The project, directed by anthropologist Solomon H. Katz of the University Museum of the University of Pennsylvania, dealt specifically with one of the most fascinating and fastest growing areas of brain research, cerebral asymmetry or hemispheric dominance. The researchers (including another anthropologist, a psychologist and a psychiatrist) studied the environment, lifestyle, socialization processes, art objects, eye movements and hand use of the Inuits and found what appear to be important correlations between all of these

Reprinted with permission from SCIENCE NEWS, the weekly news magazine of science, copyright 1976 by Science Service, Inc., vol. 109, pp. 218–221.

and the activity of the brain's right hemisphere.

To the naked eye, the halves of the human brain look almost like mirror images of each other, but for more than 100 years it has been known that the right and left hemispheres function differently. In 1861, Pierre Paul Broca, physical anthropologist and a founder of modern brain surgery, localized the center of articulate speech in an area of the left frontal cortex now known as Broca's area. In 1874, Carl Wernicke discovered a sensory speech center in the left hemisphere. It is concerned with the comprehension of language and is now known as Wernicke's area. Lesions in these two portions of the left hemisphere were found to cause various types of aphasia, the loss or impairment of the ability to use words as symbols or ideas.

Speech is only one ability that the hemispheres do not have in common. People who have suffered neural damage to one or the other hemisphere show a number of behavioral differences that have helped researchers delineate functional areas of the brain. An accident involving the left hemisphere can impair speech or produce aphasia. Damage exclusively to the right hemisphere does not usually disrupt linguistic abilities but can lower performance in spatial tasks, simple musical abilities, recognition of familiar objects and faces and bodily self awareness.

Since these discoveries were made, and especially in the past 20 years, the whole field of research into the differing functions of the hemispheres has blossomed. It was in 1953 that Roger W. Sperry began his far-reaching "split-brain" research. Working with Ronald E. Meyers at the California Institute of Technology, Sperry performed split-brain operations on cats. The corpus callosum, the bundle of nerve fibers that connects the hemispheres, was surgically severed, and the sensory inputs from the eyes were rearranged so that each eye fed information to only one hemisphere (instead of to both as is normally the case). After recovery from surgery, the animals were taught to solve various visual problems with one eye (and hemisphere) or the other. With the left eye blindfolded, the cat learned with its right eye and hemisphere only. When retested with the blindfold switched to the other eye, the cat showed no signs of having learned. After the corpus callosum was severed, the left hemisphere did not know what the right was learning and vice versa.

These split-brain experiments showed that the hemispheres of the brain can function independently when surgically separated. Once this was demonstrated, it became possible to use the split-brain technique to investigate various aspects of cerebral organization. But cats don't talk, and true cerebral asymmetry is not thought to exist in animals (though recent evidence suggests the possibility of hemispheric specialization in some monkeys and songbirds). It was not until the split-brain procedure was used on humans that it became possible to be more exact in descriptions of the differing functions of the right and left hemispheres of the human brain.

In the intact brain, constant communication must be maintained between the hemispheres because each side controls only one half of the body, the opposite half. If the left hemisphere decides to take a walk, this decision must be signaled not only to the right side of the body but to the right hemisphere —which in turn activates the left side of the body and produces coordinated walking. The connection between the hemispheres is made through the corpus callosum, but this arrangement does not always work to the brain's advantage. An epileptic seizure originating in one hemisphere, for instance, is communicated to the opposite side of the

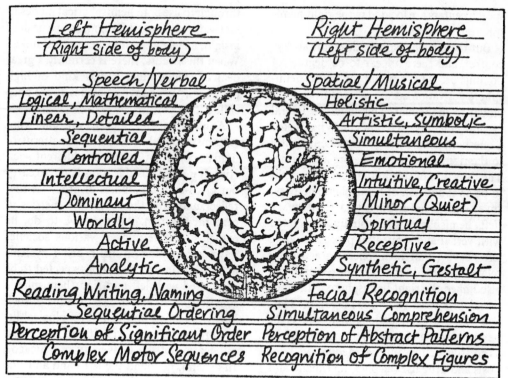

Left Hemisphere (Right side of body)	*Right Hemisphere* (Left side of body)
Speech/Verbal	Spatial/Musical
Logical, Mathematical	Holistic
Linear, Detailed	Artistic, Symbolic
Sequential	Simultaneous
Controlled	Emotional
Intellectual	Intuitive, Creative
Dominant	Minor (Quiet)
Worldly	Spiritual
Active	Receptive
Analytic	Synthetic, Gestalt
Reading, Writing, Naming	Facial Recognition
Sequential Ordering	Simultaneous Comprehension
Perception of Significant Order	Perception of Abstract Patterns
Complex Motor Sequences	Recognition of Complex Figures

Clinical and experimental evidence along with anthropological data are outlining the separate functions of the hemispheres.

brain (and then back and forth and back and forth), making the seizure much more severe. In some of the worst of these cases, the split-brain operation has been used to contain the epileptic activity to only one hemisphere.

It is these split-brain patients who have added greatly to our growing knowledge of the specific functions of the hemispheres. Sperry and others have reported that the left hemisphere is involved in logical, analytical, linear and sequential (especially time-bound) thought processes and specifically mathematical and linguistic abilities. The right hemisphere is involved in spatial relations, musical (tonal qualities), artistic, simultaneous (not constrained by time) and holistic thought processes.

Brain damage and surgical techniques have been important in mapping the brain,

but there are more subtle approaches. Handedness and eye movements have been found to be fairly reliable signs of hemispheric activation. Since the brain seems to have two "minds" that can operate independently and differently, it has been assumed that one hemisphere must be dominant. Depending on the activity involved, one hemisphere or the other must take the lead and maintain control in order to ensure coordination. Because most people are right handed (left brained), and because the speech centers are almost always located in the left hemisphere, that hemisphere has usually been considered "dominant" while the right hemisphere has been called "minor" or "quiet." (Approximately 10 percent of all people are left handed. About half of these are thought to be truly biologically left handed. That is, their speech centers are located in the right hemisphere.)

But the left hemisphere does not always control, and there appear to be degrees of dominance. The amount of right hemisphere activation seems to vary from individual to individual. This is where lateral eye movement (LEM) comes in. When asked a question, people will often glance slightly to the right or to the left before answering. The direction of this initial gaze is thought to be an indication of hemispheric activity. Investigators have found that right LEM'S (left hemisphere) are usually associated with verbal and sequential processes while left LEM'S (right hemisphere) are usually related to spatial tasks. Recent research has also linked the right hemisphere with emotional processes (SN: 10/18/75, p. 244), and there are indications that the right hemisphere may be involved in such things as creativity and intuition. Meditation, hypnosis and drug use (alcohol, marijuana and cocaine) have also been mentioned in association with right hemisphere activity. It has been suggested, for instance, that some types of drug use may be related to attempts to temporarily free the right hemisphere from the left's dominance in order to produce states of consciousness associated with the right hemisphere. "Spaced out" is a term that applies. And in typical right hemisphere fashion, it offers an integrated impression rather than an analytical description of a state of mind.

It seems likely, says Katz, "that, depending on the activity, normally the brain selectively uses one or the other hemisphere more or less during the performance of various motor activities. In a sense, while we are carrying out one activity, we may be selectively screening out another—perhaps as a child who when spoken to in the midst of daydreaming hears the words but does not know what has been said. Perhaps only in unusual circumstances do we break

through to use both hemispherical modes in focused, coordinated fashion, as in a flash of insight, as when Archimedes said 'Eureka!' When this occurs, there is certainly a great deal of exhilaration, a new kind of high point—an 'epiphany,' as James Joyce once called it."

Another line of evidence (still somewhat circumstantial) has to do with patterns of human cognition as seen in different societies. It may be possible, says Katz, to carry out cross-cultural studies of practices that reflect upon the theme of asymmetries in cerebral function. All we have to do, he explains, is determine if various societies have information in their belief systems about the kinds of behavior expected to be associated with left and right hemispheric functions. Katz has drawn up a list of such behaviors based on the anthropological literature (see ZYGON, vol. 10, no. 1, 1975, a publication of the University of Chicago). In general, he found the left hand and side of the body (right hemisphere) to be associated with the symbolic, ritualistic, mystical, mythical, omnipotent, transcendental, supernatural, evil, profane, foreign and alien. The right hand is typically associated with social order, politics, organization, social system, morality, goodness, sacred, explicitly verbal, mathematical and ordered.

Katz admits that such a list of behaviors related to one hemisphere or the other is only intuitive at present but suggests that anthropological studies will at least produce hypotheses for testing by neuropsychologists. And with that as background, he and his colleagues set out to study cerebral asymmetry among the Inuits in Frobisher Bay and Lake Harbor. (The research was supported by William and Jane Hitchcock of New York.)

If variations in cognitive style emphasizing one kind of thinking over another are possible, says Katz, one of the most likely groups manifesting orientation to right hemispheric functions would be the Inuit Eskimos. They are known for their unusual gestalt (integrated) abilities, such as drawing accurate maps of their territories. They seem to have a sort of symbiotic feeling of oneness with their environment and have traditionally depended on their well-documented ability to find their way out of the most incredible circumstances. Such abilities would probably be highly adaptive in an environment like the Arctic, which demands a high degree of visuospatial ability for survival. In short, says Katz, it would appear that these right hemisphere functions would be more highly developed in Eskimos than in modern urban populations.

The Eskimo language also reflects a high degree of spatial, right hemispheric orientation. Linguistic studies rate it as being the most synthetic of languages. American English is at the other end of the same scale and is rated as the most analytic (left hemisphere).

The Inuit people are also known for their soapstone and whalebone sculptures, wood cuts, lithographs and tapestries. This artwork has been described as "voluptuous, symbiotic and timeless in character." Figures on tapestries and in lithographs are often seen floating helter-skelter without apparent linear or three-dimensional analytic orientation. This art (especially the sculpture) not only provides additional evidence for the Inuit's spatial abilities but also affords researchers a unique opportunity to observe people carrying out work that demands tremendous spatial skills. "Hence," says Katz, "by observing and recording [videotaping] how the stone carvers use their hands and eyes in carrying out their work, we can determine if the special spatial and synthetic abilities resident in the right hemisphere are playing an important role in the creativity expressed in their carvings."

While the researchers have not finished analyzing all of their records, several clear findings have emerged that are highly suggestive of a specific role for the right hemisphere. Among the Inuit carvers (all of whom were right handed), the left hand cradles the work, moves it into new positions and feels its progress while the right hand precisely carves the details and holds the various carving tools. Even when a tool could be placed down, the left hand carried out the repositioning of the stone in space. Also, as predicted, there was a striking preponderance of holding the stone in the left visual field (right hemisphere).

These observations suggest hemispheric symmetry or at least a high degree of cooperation between the hemispheres. Katz finds an "almost perfect relationship between the right hand doing the detailed, analytical kinds of activities and the left hand doing all the spatial and touch activities." The Inuit artists produce some phenomenal representations, he says, with the left hand doing some remarkable things.

Specific conclusions from these observations are hard to reach at present, but there are some interesting implications. The Inuit environment, language and certain social behaviors (such as their emphasis on teaching by demonstration rather than by verbal instruction) all seemingly combine to foster right hemisphere activity which shows up in the Inuit life style and artwork. This suggests that modes of thinking (or hemisphere use) can be taught. It is possible that different cultures channel people into a greater or lesser reliance on one or the other hemisphere. This may eventually be confirmed as the workings of the brain are further elucidated, but even then will it have any practical import?

Several researchers have addressed this question, and as scientists so often do, they seem to be searching for symmetry:

Robert Hertz, in 1909, in a classic sociological article on the preeminence of the right hand: "If the constraint of a mystical ideal has for centuries been able to make man into a unilateral being, physiologically mutilated, a liberated and farsighted society will strive to develop the energies dormant in our right cerebral hemisphere and to assure by an appropriate training a more harmonious development of the organism."

• Jerome S. Bruner, experimental psychologist at Oxford University: "Since childhood, I have been enchanted by the fact and the symbolism of the right hand and the left—the one the doer, the other the dreamer. The right is order and lawfulness, *le droit.* Its beauties are those of geometry and taut implications. Reaching for knowledge with the right hand is science. Yet to say only that much of science is to overlook one of its excitements, for the great hypotheses are gifts carried in the left."

• Roger W. Sperry, in the National Science Foundation's March/April 1976 MOSAIC (an excellent overview of the current state of brain research): "Our educational system and modern society generally (with its very heavy emphasis on communi-

cation and on early training in the three Rs) discriminates against one whole half of the brain . . . In our present school system, the attention given to the minor hemisphere of the brain is minimal compared with the training lavished on the left or major hemisphere."

• Solomon H. Katz, speaking of right hemispheric thought processes: "Certainly, the absolutely abundant anthropological evidence that supports their manifestations from the intuitive perspective indicates that our implicit knowledge of these phenomena may be as old as humanity itself. But what is different and truly exciting this time is that we can now begin to use the knowledge as a regular part of our *scientific* understanding of the human mind in order to extend further our means of adapting to the world we live in . . . At last, our newly developing science of humanity can potentially set us free to recognize that there is more to humanity than all of our linear thinking can give us and to realize that human life viewed predominantly from left hemispheric functions is almost as flat as viewing the world through one eye."

9. NEW FACTS ON BIORHYTHMS

Ed Nelson

Like many 11-year-olds, my daughter had developed a great passion for horses. There was a pleasant riding stable near home so one June morning back in 1971 the family decided to go riding.

Reprinted with permission from *Science Digest* (May 1976), pp. 71–75. Copyright © 1976, The Hearst Corporation.

We were mounted and ready to go when my horse reared violently and fell backwards square on top of me. The saddle horn went right into my abdomen. I didn't die, but among other things I lost about 12 inches of intestine.

I can say now, with the clarity of 20/20 hindsight, I shoulda stood in bed. Proponents of biorhythm will say, "You could have had the *foresight* to know you shoulda stood in bed!"

Biorhythms supposedly could have given me that foresight. Beginning at the moment of birth, biorhythm theory states, all human lives move in predictable undulations involving three separate cycles: a physical cycle of 23 days, an emotional (or sensitivity) cycle of 28 days and an intellectual cycle of 33 days. In each cycle, half the days (the first half) are plus (good days) and half are minus (bad days). The days when the cycles switch from plus to minus or from minus to plus are called critical days. It's on these critical days when bad things can happen to you.

Critical days in the physical cycle supposedly can be the most devastating—a horse can fall on you. Emotional critical days are less catastrophic—you might start ranting and raving, cursing the horse. Critical days in the intellectual cycle are not considered to be as important, by themselves, as critical days in the other two cycles. When critical days in all three cycles coincide, it's going to be a *super*-bad day . . . says the theory. (See box, page 51.)

Science Digest took a look at biorhythms and how they affect a person's life back in August of 1973 and concluded that there might be something to it. The warning to the reader who had a critical day coming up was: "Don't panic, but be careful."

Now a fresh look is needed. Where is biorhythm theory today? More to the point, what's its track record?

Take my case. I've charted my biorhythms for 1971. What I've come to call The Day of the Horse was clearly a noncritical day. As far as being forewarned against the accident, I'd have gotten as much warning from an astrology chart.

Most of us, though, find something satisfying in regular patterns, whatever the circumstances. In a strange city, it's easier to get around on straight streets that intersect at perpendiculars. Regular, predictable working hours are easier to cope with, too. So, regular biorhythmic cycles are likewise appealing. But they're subject to many questions. Just how could they forecast troubles ahead? How can they predict our behavior?

Critical days include our weakest and most vulnerable moments, say biorhythmicists. On critical days in the physical cycle, for example, we're particularly susceptible to accidents. But certainly no responsible researcher holds that biorhythms actually can cause accidents. Those in the field insist they aren't involved in fatalism, just susceptibility.

Efforts to test the biorhythmic theory today focus heavily on accident studies. The goal: to see whether there are *significantly* more accidents on the so-called critical days than chance could account for.

Several researchers say there are. Among them is Jacob M. Sanhein, project manager at the Naval Weapons Support Center in Crane, Indiana. At the congress of the National Safety Council last fall, Sanhein presented a paper describing his study. He says that more than 40 percent of the accidents studied took place during the 20.4 percent of the time composed of victims' accident-prone days. In other words, there were twice as many accidents in those days as you would statistically expect.

But biorhythm claims still are questioned. *Science Digest* discussed them with Dr. Jerry Driessen, National Safety Council research director.

"There's no question that our various cycles are important," Dr. Driessen says, and he concedes that behavioral cycles may well be among them. "But," he adds, "the big question is, why should they begin precisely at birth?" After all, the fetus is to nearly the same extent as alive as a newborn. And what about planned birth dates—Caesarian

CHART YOUR OWN BIORHYTHMS

Biorhythm theory has staunch advocates and equally staunch detractors, as our author's research indicates. We suggest that interested readers chart their own biorhythms to see for themselves whether these "life curves" correspond to their physical, emotional and intellectual performances. First, though, let's briefly review the principles of biorhythm theory:

Actually, there are three separate biorhythms: a 23-day physical cycle, a 28-day sensitivity (or emotional) cycle and a 33-day intellectual cycle. The theory states that in each of these cycles, half the days are plus and half are minus. In the 23-day physical cycle, the first 11½ days are plus days and are therefore suitable for intensive athletic training. The second 11½ days, according to the theory, will be a time when you tire easily. The first 14 days of the 28-day sensitivity cycle theoretically are characterized by cheerfulness; the second 14 days by moodiness. The first 16½ days of the intellectual cycle are smart days; the second 16½ are dumb days. More important, though, are "critical days."

The theory states that all three cycles began on your day of birth and all began with plus days. When charted on a graph, the first half of each cycle would arc above a zero line and then would dip below that line for the second half of minus days, then hit the zero line again to continue the rhythm.

The day the cycle switches from plus to minus or minus to plus (when the curve crosses the zero line) is the much-heralded "critical day"—when accidents happen, tests are failed and empires are lost.

In the late 1930s, Hans Schwing, a behavioral scientist at the Swiss Institute of Technology, related these zero days to accidents and deaths by studying 1400 accident case histories obtained from Zurich insurance companies. Of those injured, six out of ten were at zero points on either their physical or sensitivity cycle or at zero points in both cycles simultaneously on the days of their accidents.

And of those actually killed in accidents, 65 percent died on zero or double zero days. Such days, say theorists, also claimed Custer at Little Big Horn and defeated Napolean at Waterloo.

The critical day in the intellectual cycle is not considered to be as important as critical days in the other two cycles as far as accidents are concerned. If it coincides with a critical day of another cycle, however, it has a contributory effect.

Physical or sensitivity zero days occur on an average of one day out of six, and double zero days happen about six times a year. Triple zero days occur only about once a year.

Now, back to charting *your* biorhythms. The easiest way to do it is to employ one of the many outfits that will chart these cycles for you. One service, offered by IBM, supplies you a 33-page report of about 12,000 words and a biorhythm chart for each month of the year. Called the IBM 370-145, it can be obtained through Edmund Scientific, 380 Edscorp Building, Barrington, N.J. 08007 for $15.95.

Of course, an alternative to using one of the commercial charting services is to chart your own biorhythms. All you need is a calendar, some graph paper and a little math work.

To find out how your three cycles stand for any month, add up the total number of days in your life from the day of birth to the first day of whatever month is being charted (in this case, May). Divide the total by the number of days in each cycle—23, 28 and 33 (a separate division for each). The *remainders* will show the position of each rhythm for the first day of the month.

To illustrate, let's take a fictional person whose birth date is March 8, 1936, and chart his biorhythms for May 1976:

40 Years of 365 days	14,600 days
Extra days for leap years	10
Days from March 8, 1936, up to and including May 1, 1976	54
	14,664 days

(continued)

Now we take this total of 14,664 days and divide by 23, 28 and 33:

14,664 ÷ 23 = 627 completed cycles and a *remainder of 13 days.*

14,664 ÷ 28 = 523 completed cycles and a *remainder of 20 days.*

14,664 ÷ 33 = 444 completed cycles and a *remainder of 12 days.*

This means our fictional person will begin May at the 13th, 20th and 12th days of his physical, sensitivity and intellectual cycles, respectively. The beginning of any cycle is when its plus days begin. Drawing in the curves results in the chart below (the chart is projected backwards to show how cycles began in April).

Once drawn, these charts are fairly easy to interpret. For instance, our mythical person below should enjoy a good day on the 17th when both his physical and sensitivity curves are at their peak. But during the 24-hour period of May 23 all cycles cross the zero line—a triple-zero critical day!

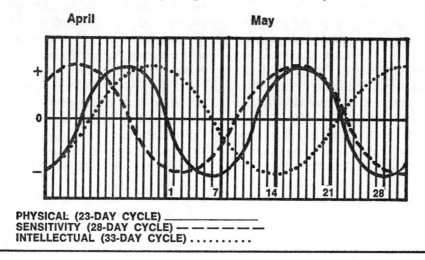

April   **May**

PHYSICAL (23-DAY CYCLE) _____
SENSITIVITY (28-DAY CYCLE) — — — — — —
INTELLECTUAL (33-DAY CYCLE) . . . .

births? Will a baby's life be significantly different if he's born a day or two or three earlier or later than he would have been naturally?

Other cycles, also apparently vital, seem to have no intimate connection with the timing of birth. There are cycles of hormone levels and cholesterol levels. A former president of the Society of Endocrinology even collected, several times a day for 16 years, specimens of his own urine. The resulting data revealed a daily cycle, a weekly cycle, a 17- to 21-day cycle, a 30-day cycle, even a yearly cycle. In such a complex of rhythms, the contention that three basic, unvarying, lifelong behavioral cycles are triggered with an infant's first breath demands explanation.

The Navy's Sanhein required birth and accident dates for a case to be included in his study. Another criterion was that the accident be primarily chargeable to the individual whose biorhythms were under study.

This selectivity follows the instruction of George S. Thommen, probably the American most influential in promoting biorhythm. His *Is this Your Day?* (Crown, 1961; also available in Avon paperback) serves as the movement's English-language bible. At a session of the 1974 National Safety Congress, he urged others to start more biorhythm projects, setting one limitation: "Select only self-caused accidents and not accidents caused by others or by circumstances."

But experienced safety professionals know accidents have many interrelated causes—that virtually *all* are, to some degree, "caused by others or by circumstances." Arbitrarily excluding some cases risks distorting the results with subjective influences. Most social scientists sternly reject such procedures.

V. Douglas Kelley, a young computer analyst at the NSC's national headquarters, flies in the face of Thommen's proposal. He will exclude none of the accidents in the biorhythm investigation he's planning. Kelley freely concedes that any biorhythmic effect could be diluted if in 1000 accidents studied, 400 were unattributable in any way to victim error. But, he says, so what? If biorhythms work, critical-day clumping—accidents happening on victims' critical days—would still show up.

There's another flaw in Sanhein's work. As do other biorhythm investigators, he passes up many statistical tests. Such tests can indicate how likely or unlikely it is that a certain percentage of *random* accidents would occur on critical days. The larger the sample, the more confidence we have in the accumulated statistical results.

In Canada, the Workmen's Compensation Board of British Columbia has a large sample. The Board studied its records of lost-time occupational accidents during the first four months of 1971—more than 13,000 cases. Keith Mason, the Board's research statistician, makes no bones about his conclusion: "The results indicate that accidents are no more likely to occur during so-called critical periods than at any other time."

When an official of the U.S. Tactical Air Command took a look at biorhythm, the theory's proponents were quick to interpret it as a sign their favorite subject was gaining still more acceptance. Actually, the Tactical Air Command's review was less than enthusiastic. In March 1972, the editor of *TAC Attack* reported on 59 TAC aviation accidents. Thirteen took place on pilots' critical days. If they had happened strictly in proportion to the amount of critical time, 12 would have occurred on these days. Less than a resounding triumph for biorhythm.

Even so, the *TAC Attack* story stirred up such interest that four flight-safety experts collaborated on another article in 1975. After many tests on 8625 pilot-involved air mishaps from Army aviation records and Navy, National Transportation Safety Board and Federal Aviation Agency cases, the results flatly ruled out biorhythms as a causal factor in aircraft accidents.

Private businesses often use biorhythm to signal when individual employees will have accident-prone days. Urging extra care for those days might improve corporate safety records, which may then be pointed to as an indication that the biorhythm theory works. But the pitch for extra caution might well have an effect even if biorhythm was a lot of bunk.

B. L. Newcomb, a New Jersey engineer, tested this possibility directly. Newcomb, in the plant engineering department of his company's factory, ran a biorhythm experiment that Thommen apparently cited as bringing a 25-percent cut in accidents.

While the plant was struggling with a rising accident rate, Newcomb had certain foremen warn their men of days they'd be more accident-prone, according to their biorhythm charts. He tested the influence of personal warnings alone by using the same approach with other crews, but gave those foremen *false* accident-prone dates. A third group was monitored, but got no special treatment.

"It's my best recollection," Newcomb told *Science Digest,* "that none of the groups had a reduction in the number of accidents. But the first test group's increase stopped. Safety talks held for the false-information group also helped, but not much. That group's rate still increased, but more slowly. The third group's rate [no safety talks] continued merrily up."

Even the young are in on biorhythm research. Stimulated by her science teacher, Suzanne Keddie, a Stockton, California, high school student, classified 150 automobile accidents and calculated each driver's biorhythms for the accident day. She concluded there was "no significant correlation" between the accidents and biorhythmic cycles, even though she accepted Thommen's injunction and considered only accidents in which a driver's error was responsible.

Despite the inexactness of biorhythmic study as a science, there is no indication that interest in it is fading. Which is fine, because scoffing at any new thesis is foolish and reckless. But thus far, many find biorhythm claims hard to buy.

I was born in 1925. Yet 50 years later I'm to believe that my physical, emotional and intellectual cycles still march rigidly forward on a schedule set way back then? In this next month, for instance, May 28 and 31 have been set to be among my critical days. I'm not holding my breath.

10. SKINNER'S UTOPIA: PANACEA, OR PATH TO HELL?

"I've had only one idea in my life—a true idée fixe. To put it as bluntly as possible—the idea of having my own way. 'Control,' expresses it. The control of human behavior. In my early experimental days it was a frenzied, selfish desire to dominate. I remember the rage I used to feel when a prediction went awry. I could have shouted at the subjects of my experiments, 'Behave, damn you! Behave as you ought!'"
B. F. Skinner's *Walden Two,* 1948

The speaker is T. E. Frazier, a character in *Walden Two* and the fictional founder of the utopian community described in that novel. He is also an alter ego of the author, Burrhus Frederic Skinner, who is both a psychology professor and an institution at Harvard.

Skinner is the most influential of living American psychologists, and the most controversial contemporary figure in the science of human behavior, adored as a messiah and abhorred as a menace. As leader of the "behavioristic" psychologists, who liken man to a machine, Skinner is vigorously opposed both by humanists and by Freudian psychoanalysts. Next week that opposition is bound to flare anew with the publication of Skinner's latest book, *Beyond Freedom and Dignity* (Knopf; $6.95). Its message is one that is familiar to followers of Skinner, but startling to the uninitiated: we can no longer afford freedom, and so it must be replaced with control over man, his conduct and his culture. This thesis, proposed not by a writer of science fiction but by a man of science, raises the specter of a *1984* Orwellian society that might really come to pass. It accounts, also, for the alarm and anger that Skinner's current popularity arouses in his opponents.

Like the utopians who preceded him, Skinner hopes for a society in which men of good will can work, love and live in security and in harmony. For mankind he wants enough to eat, a clean environment, and safety from nuclear cataclysm. He longs for a worldwide culture based on the principles of his famous didactic novel, *Walden Two.* Those principles include: communal ownership of land and buildings, egalitarian relationships between men and women, devotion to art, music and literature, liberal rewards for constructive behavior, freedom from jealousy, gossip, and—astonishingly —from the ideal of freedom. *Beyond Freedom and Dignity,* in fact, is really a nonfiction version of *Walden Two.*

DISASTROUS RESULTS

Skinner acknowledges that the concept of freedom played a vital role in man's successful efforts to overthrow the tyrants who oppressed him, bolstering his courage and spurring him to nearly superhuman effort. But the same ideal, Skinner maintains, now threatens 20th century man's continued existence. "My book," says Skinner, "is an effort to demonstrate how things go bad when you make a fetish out of individual freedom and dignity. If you insist that individual rights are the *summum bonum,* then the whole structure of society falls down." In fact, Skinner believes that Western culture may die and be replaced, perhaps, with the more disciplined culture of the Soviet Union or of China. If that happens, Western man will have lost the only form of immortality he can hope for—the survival of his way of life.

Skinner's reasoning is that freedom and free will are no more than illusions; like it

or not, man is already controlled by external influences. Some are haphazard; some are arranged by careless or evil men whose goals are selfish instead of humanitarian. The problem, then, is to design a culture that can, theoretically, survive; to decide how men must behave to ensure its survival in reality; and to plan environmental influences that will guarantee the desired behavior. Thus, in the Skinnerian world, man will refrain from polluting, from overpopulating, from rioting, and from making war, not because he knows that the results will be disastrous, but because he has been conditioned to want what serves group interests.

Is such a world really possible? Skinner believes that it is; he is certain that human behavior can be predicted and shaped exactly as if it were a chemical reaction. The way to do it, he thinks, is through "behavioral technology," a developing science of control that aims to change the environment rather than people, that seeks to alter actions rather than feelings, and that shifts the customary psychological emphasis on the world inside men to the world outside them. Central to Skinner's approach is a method of conditioning that has been used with uniform success on laboratory animals: giving rewards to mold the subject to the experimenter's will. According to Skinner and his followers, the same technique can be made to work equally well with human beings.

Underlying the method is the Skinnerian conviction that behavior is determined not from within but from without. "Unable to understand how and why the person we see behaves as he does, we attribute his behavior to a person inside," Skinner explains. Mistakenly, we believe that man "initiates, originates and creates, and in doing so he remains, as he was for the Greeks, divine. We say that he is autonomous." But Skinner insists that autonomy is a myth, and that belief in an "inner man" is a superstition that originated, like belief in God, in man's inability to understand his world. With the rise of behavioral science, understanding has grown, and man no longer needs such fictions as "something going on inside the individual, states of mind, feelings, purposes, expectancies and all of that." The fact is, Skinner insists, that actions are determined by the environment; behavior "is shaped and maintained by its consequences."

AVOIDING PUNISHMENT

To Skinner, this means that there is nothing wrong, emotionally or morally, with people who behave badly. For example, youths who drop out of school or refuse to get jobs behave as they do not because they are neurotic or because they feel alienated, but "because of defective social environments in homes, schools, factories and elsewhere." As Skinner sees it, environments are defective when they fail to make desirable behavior pay off and when they resort to punishment as a means of stopping undesirable behavior.

In short, it is punishment or reward that determines whether a particular kind of behavior becomes habitual. But Skinner believes that punishment is generally an ineffective means of control. "A person who has been punished," he writes in his new book, "is not less inclined to behave in a given way; at best, he learns how to avoid punishment. Our task is not to encourage moral struggle or to build or demonstrate inner virtues. It is to make life less punishing, and in doing so to release for more reinforcing activities the time and energy consumed in the avoidance to punishment." The way to release that time and energy is "to build a world in which people are naturally good," in which they are rewarded for wanting what is good for their culture.

But arranging effective rewards, complicated enough in the laboratory, is even more complex in the real world. Why not solve society's problems by using the much simpler physical and biological technologies we already have? Because, Skinner says, that will not work. "Better contraceptives will control population only if people use them. A nuclear holocaust can be prevented only if the conditions under which nations make war can be changed. The environment will continue to deteriorate until pollution practices are abandoned. We need to make vast changes in human behavior."

SOAP MOUTHWASH

A matter that might interest President Nixon is Skinner's belief that new ways must be found to persuade people that work is worthwhile. "Behavior used to be reinforced by great deprivation; if people weren't hungry, they wouldn't work. Now we are committed to feeding people whether they work or not. Nor is money as great a reinforcer as it once was. People no longer work for punitive reasons, yet our culture offers no new satisfactions." Moreover, "we can't control inflation if everything we might do is a threat to somebody's freedom. Yet in a long run, we are all going to suffer much more than if we were slightly restricted."

Skinner came rather slowly to his conviction that such changes can be made; his early interests, in fact, were far from psychology. Born in Susquehanna, Pa., in 1904, he was the elder son of Grace Burrhus, an amateur musician who sang at weddings and funerals, and William Skinner, a lawyer who was "a sucker for book salesmen." In his "Sketch for an Autobiography," Skinner describes his early life as "warm and stable." He lived in the same house until he went to college. He was never physically punished by his father and only once by his mother—when she washed out his mouth with soap for using a "bad word." Nevertheless, young Skinner was "taught to fear God, the police and what people will think," and his Grandmother Skinner "made sure that I understood the concept of hell by showing me the glowing bed of coals in the parlor stove." To deter him from a life of crime, Skinner's father conducted him through a county jail and on a summer vacation took him to a lecture with colored slides that depicted life in Sing Sing.

From his childhood years, Skinner was mechanically inclined. He built roller-skate scooters, steerable wagons, rafts, water pistols from lengths of bamboo, and "from a discarded water boiler a steam cannon with which I could shoot plugs of potato and carrot over the houses of our neighbors." He also devised a flotation system to separate green from ripe elderberries, which he used to sell from door to door. Although his attempts to build a glider and a perpetual motion machine ended in failure, his innovative tinkering was to pay off handsomely in the laboratory in later years.

In high school, Skinner earned money by lettering advertising show cards, played in a jazz band, and with three other boys organized an orchestra that performed two nights a week in a local movie theater. A good student, he demonstrated a flair for writing, and when he got to Hamilton College (Clinton, N.Y.) in 1922, decided to major in English.

In college, by his own admission, young Fred never fitted into student life, but became a rebel whose lack of self-understanding now amazes him. He wrote an editorial attacking Phi Beta Kappa, helped cover the walls at Class Day exercises with "bitter caricatures of the faculty," and made such a shambles of commencement ceremonies that he was warned by the college president that he would not get his degree unless he quieted down.

But at the same time he had what classmates recall as a brilliant mind, and he made full use of it. For one thing, he wrote short stories, and in his senior year sent three of them to Robert Frost, who praised them warmly.

That encouragement convinced Fred Skinner that he should become a writer. The decision, he says, was "disastrous." Recalling those "dark years," living first at home with his family and then in New York's Greenwich Village, he admits that he frittered away his time, read aimlessly, wrote very little—"and thought about seeing a psychiatrist." In his own words, he "failed as a writer" because he "had nothing important to say."

But that failure allowed Skinner to swing his attention back to one of the pet interests of his youth: animal behavior. As a boy, he had had toads and chipmunks. He also had a vivid memory of watching a troupe of trained pigeons at a county fair play at putting out a fire. Besides, he had read and been excited by some Bertrand Russell articles in the old *Dial* magazine about Johns Hopkins Psychologist John B. Watson, father of behaviorism. It was with Watson, in 1913, that psychology really emerged from its origins in philosophy to become a full-fledged scientific discipline.

Early Christian thinkers pondering the mystery of man believed that it was the "soul" that set human beings apart from animals. To them, the essence of man was his God-given spirit, immaterial, impalpable, otherworldly, something quite outside the natural world. But with the decline of religion and the rise of materialism, 17th and 18th century philosophers like Thomas Hobbes and Julien de La Mettrie increasingly viewed the soul as an aspect of the body, man as an animal, both men and animals as machines.

It was this kind of thinking that influenced Watson. Drawing, too, on the work of Pavlov, he repudiated the subjective concepts of mind and emotion and described human behavior as a succession of physical reflex responses to stimuli coming from the environment. It was the environment alone, he felt, that determined what man is : "Give me a dozen healthy infants," he wrote in 1925, "and I'll guarantee to take any one at random and train him to become any type of specialist I might select —doctor, lawyer, even beggarman and thief, regardless of his talents, penchants, tendencies, abilities." The goal of this Watsonian behaviorism was the prediction and control of behavior—which suited Skinner to perfection.

BACH FUGUES

And so, in 1928, Skinner entered Harvard with a new goal: a doctorate in psychology. His regime was spartan: "I saw no movies or plays, had scarcely any dates, and read nothing but psychology and physiology. The second year I bought a piano; but there was discipline even so: I played Bach fugues or nothing."

In these years—and subsequently—Skinner disciplined not just himself but also rats. The rats, and later pigeons, became the center of laboratory experiments in which he controlled behavior by setting up "contingencies of reinforcement"—circumstances under which a particular bit of desired behavior is "reinforced" or rewarded to make sure it will be repeated. The behavior Skinner demanded of his pigeons was bizarre—for pigeons. He made them walk figure eights, for example, by reinforcing them with food at crucial moments. The process as explained by Skinner: "I watch a hungry pigeon carefully. When he makes a slight clockwise turn, he's instantly rewarded for it. After he eats, he

immediately tries it again. Then I wait for more of a turn and reinforce again. Within two or three minutes, I can get any pigeon to make a full circle. Next I reinforce only when he moves in the other direction. Then I wait until he does both, and reinforce him again and again until it becomes a kind of drill. Within 10 to 15 minutes, the pigeon will be doing a perfect figure eight."

By a similar process, Skinner has taught pigeons to dance with each other, and even to play Ping Pong. During World War II, he conceived the idea of using pigeons in guided-missile control; three birds were conditioned to peck continuously for four or five minutes at the image of a target on a screen. Then they were placed in harness in the nose of a missile, facing a screen on which the target would appear when the missile was in flight. By pecking at the image moving on the screen, the pigeons would send corrective signals that moved the missile's fins and kept it on target. The missile called the Pelican was never used in warfare; the pigeon-aided equipment was so complex and bulky that the missile could carry little high explosive. Furthermore, Skinner mourns, "our problem was no one would take us seriously."

All of these conditioning feats were accomplished with the now-famous Skinner box. It is a soundproof enclosure with a food dispenser that a rat can operate by pressing a lever, and a pigeon by pecking a key. The dispenser does not work unless the animal has first performed according to a specially designed "schedule of reinforcement."

Explains Skinner: "One of the most powerful schedules, the variable-ratio schedule, is characteristic of all gambling systems. The gambler cannot be sure the next play will win, but a certain mean ratio of plays to wins is maintained. This is the way a dishonest gambler hooks his victim. At first the victim is permitted to win fairly often.

TWIN OAKS: ON TO WALDEN TWO

At first glance, it looks like a movie set for *Walden Two*. There is a shop building called Harmony, a farmhouse called Llano, and a dormitory called Oneida. Bulletin boards list upcoming cultural events, and young people lounge on hammocks, reading and engaging in serious discussions. The smell of farm-fresh cooking is everywhere. The resemblance to Walden Two is more than superficial. Twin Oaks, a 123-acre farm commune nestled in the foothills of Virginia's Piedmont, is a remarkable attempt to create a utopian community governed by Skinner's laws of social engineering.

•

Work is allocated by an intricate system of labor credits so that none of the 35 members have unequal burdens. Titles and honorifics have been done away with so that, in the words of the community's code, "all are entitled to the same privileges, advantages and respect." Private property is forbidden, except for such things as books and clothing, and even with that loophole, most members draw their clothing, right down to their underwear, from a massive community closet. No one is allowed to boast of individual accomplishments, to gossip ("negative speech") or to be intolerant of another's beliefs.

Behavioral engineering goes on every minute of the day. A member who gets angry, who makes demands or who gives ultimatums is simply not "reinforced," to use the behavioral term. He is ignored. What is considered appropriate behavior —cooperating, showing affection, turning the other cheek and working diligently— is, on the other hand, applauded, or "reinforced," by the group. Members are singled out for compliments if they do a job well; signs are put up telling who cleaned a room for example. Smokers who wanted to break the cigarette habit formed a group to help one another. Cigarettes were put in progressively more inconvenient spots, and each member of the group received congratulations for every day he spent without tobacco.

The use of tobacco and alcohol is, in fact, discouraged at Twin Oaks, and all drugs, including marijuana, are banned. So is television, which is considered a cultural poison. "We decided that we just weren't strong enough to stand up to television," says Kat Griebe, one of Twin Oaks' charter founders and, at 40, one of the oldest members. "Its powerful message is that of middle-class American values, which we reject—a high level of consumption, streamlined cosmetic standards of beauty, male dominance, the use of violence as a problem solver, and the underlying assumption that life should be a constant state of titillation and excitement. Life just isn't like that."

Especially, life at Twin Oaks. The favorite sports are "cooperation volleyball" and skinny-dipping in the South Anna River—false modesty is another of the sins that are not reinforced—and there is plenty of folk singing and dancing. In a departure from Skinner's rather puritanical Walden Two, sex is considered, as one member put it, a "pleasant pastime, like anything else." Adds Kat: "We don't have a very high opinion of marriage—it often becomes possessive. We do have a high regard for what Skinner calls 'abiding affection.'"

•

As yet there are no children at Twin Oaks. There is not enough "surplus labor" to care for infants, and there is no space for a separate Skinnerian nursery. Besides that, the reasoning goes, it is better not to bring children into the equation until all the adults have developed "appropriate" behavior; otherwise, bad habits would simply be reproduced in the young.

All of the utopian ventures of the early and mid-19th century—from Indiana's New Harmony on the Wabash River to Massachusetts' famed Brook Farm— eventually foundered, and Twin Oaks, too, has its problems. The major one appears to be financial. "Skinner never wrote about a poor community," laments Gabe Sinclair. "He wrote about a rich

(continued)

one." After starting with only $35,000, Twin Oaks, four years later, still finds survival a struggle. The farm brings more emotional than monetary rewards; members would find it cheaper to work at other jobs and buy their food at the market. The community's chief source of income is the sale of hammocks stitched together in Harmony, but it is not enough to make ends meet; several members are forced to take outside jobs in Richmond and Charlottesville—a direct contradiction to Walden Two's basic premise that all time should be spent in a totally controlled environment.

Beyond economics, there are serious psychological problems at Twin Oaks, and few members have stayed very long. Turnover last year was close to 70%. The ones who leave first, in fact, are often the most competent members, who still expect special recognition for their talents. "Competent people are hard to get along with," says Richard Stutsman, one of Twin Oaks' trained psychologists. "They tend to make demands, not requests. We cannot afford to reinforce ultimatum behavior, although we recognize our need for their competence. So often we have given in to them on little things, and then when a big demand arises we have to deny them." When they leave, the community not only loses their skills but also sacrifices a potential rise in its standard of living.

While it is still considerably poorer than Walden Two, Twin Oaks has gone farther toward the goal of behavioral control than might have seemed reasonably possible. It is too soon, however, to call the commune much more than a fascinating experiment.

Eventually he continues to play when he is not winning at all. With this technique, it is possible to create a pathological gambler out of a simple bird like a pigeon."

VENTURE IN SELF-THERAPY

For a while, that beguiling possibility and others suggested by Skinner left the academic world pretty cold, as did his first book, *The Behavior of Organisms,* published in 1938. "People didn't reinforce me, but my rats did," Skinner says regretfully, remembering how rewarded he felt every time his command to "Behave, damn you!" was obeyed.

He was rewarded in a different way—his first general public recognition—when in 1945 the *Ladies' Home Journal* printed a piece about another kind of Skinner box, the so-called air crib (*see box, page 62*). By the time the *Journal* article was printed, Skinner had finished writing his second book, though he did not find a publisher for

it until 1948. The work was *Walden Two,* completed in seven weeks of impassioned creativity. Writing it, says Skinner, was "pretty obviously a venture in self-therapy in which I was struggling to reconcile two aspects of my own behavior, represented by Burris and Frazier." Even today, both characters represent Skinner himself. Burris is a professor with traditional ideas, acquired in childhood, about freedom, dignity and democracy. Frazier is the antidemocratic creator of a controlled society whose views about human behavior correspond to Skinner's laboratory findings.

Visiting Frazier's planned community, Burris is both attracted and repelled—attracted by the seeming contentment of its inhabitants, repelled by their voluntary submission to the maneuverings, however well-intentioned, of its Planners and Managers. In the end, his skepticism overcome, he decides to join the community and with "euphoric abandon" wires his college head: "My dear President Mittelbach, you may take your stupid university ..."

PIGEONS AREN'T PEOPLE

Unlike Burris, the numerous and articulate anti-Skinnerians remain skeptical, if not downright hostile toward him and his followers. Yet they feel that his long, patient campaign against freedom must be studied and understood. Their criticism is directed not at Skinner the scientific technician (the soundness of his laboratory work is seldom questioned) but at Skinner the philosopher and political thinker; his proposal for a controlled society, they say, is both unworkable and evil.

Giving as an example the failure of the North Koreans to brainwash many of their G.I. war prisoners, Stanford Psychologist Albert Bandura asserts that control of human behavior on the scale advocated by Skinner is impossible. Psychologist Ernest Hilgard, also of Stanford, thinks control of mass behavior is theoretically possible but realistically improbable, because there are too many bright people who would never go along.

Skinner himself admits that "pigeons aren't people," but points out that his ideas have already been put to practice use in schools, mental hospitals, penal institutions and business firms. Skinner-inspired teaching machines have begun to produce what amounts to an educational revolution. It was after a visit to his daughter's fourth-grade arithmetic class that he invented the first device for programmed instruction in 1954. Having seen "minds being destroyed," he concluded that youngsters should learn math, spelling and other subjects in the same way that pigeons learn Ping Pong. Accordingly, machines now in use in scores of cities across the country present pupils with a succession of easy learning steps. At each one, a correct answer to a question brings instant reinforcement, not with a grain of corn that rewarded the pigeon, but with a printed statement—supposedly just as satisfying—that the answer is right.

JUVENILE OFFENDERS

Some critics, loyal Skinnerians among them, argue that this teaching process bores all but the dullest students, and that there is little solid evidence as to how well programmed instruction sticks. But Skinner insists that his devices teach faster than other methods and free teachers to give personal attention to students who are trying to master complex subjects.

In some mental hospitals, reinforcement therapy inspired by Skinner is helping apathetic or rebellious patients to behave more like healthy human beings. The staffers of one institution, for instance, were troubled by patients who insisted on trailing into the dining room long after the dinner bell sounded. Attendants tried closing the doors 20 minutes after the bell rang, refusing admittance to those who showed up any later. Gradually, the interval between bell and door closing was shortened to only five minutes, and most patients were arriving promptly. "You shift from one kind of reinforcement—annoying the guards and getting attention—to another, eating when you're hungry." says Skinner. To charges that this kind of conditioning is sadism, he replies that "the patients are going in quickly because they want to." That is strange logic: he seems to ignore the fact that the patients are compelled to "want to" unless they care to go hungry.

In yet another practical example of Skinnerism in operation, a point system for good behavior was set up for juvenile offenders—armed robbers, rapists and murderers—in the Robert F. Kennedy Youth Center in West Virginia. Though no requirements were imposed on the delinquents, they earned points if they voluntarily picked up books, or went to lectures and managed to learn something from them. With the points, they could then buy such rewards as better food, a private room, or time in front of the TV set.

"All their lives," says Skinner, "these boys have been told that they couldn't learn and that they were useless. But under conditions that reinforced them every time they progressed, their morale improved enormously. Moreover, the return rate to the school dropped from 85% to 25% after the method was instituted."

The same kind of positive reinforcement was tried a few years ago by Emery Air Freight of Wilton, Conn. To reduce the breakage that resulted when goods were packed in the wrong boxes for shipping, supervisors began complimenting packers when the correct boxes were chosen. Taking new pride in their work, the employees made virtually no mistakes, breakage ceased, and the company saved $600,000 in a year.

Mothers who practice Skinnerism—knowingly or by instinct—have an easier time with their youngsters when they reward good behavior instead of punishing bad. Explains Skinner: "If a mother goes to her baby only when he yells, she reinforces fussing. But when she goes to him while he's happy and perhaps saying 'Mama' softly, the baby will always speak to her that way."

UNCOMPROMISING VIEW

Though such apparent successes persuade Skinnerians that reinforcement is eminently practical, critics find the technique philosophically distasteful and morally wrong.

Many of their objections center around the ancient, crucial argument over free will *v.* determinism: is man in charge of himself and his destiny, or is he not? Skinner argues that belief in free will comes only from

man's need to be given credit for his "good" behavior and achievements. "Consider a woman who has a baby. It cost her a lot of pain and trouble to have it. But she didn't design that baby; it was all settled at the moment of conception what the baby was going to be like. The same thing is true when a man writes books, invents things, manages a business. He didn't initiate anything. It's all the effect of past history on him. That's the truth, and we have to get used to it." Theologians, humanists and conventional psychologists, including Freudians, cannot accept this uncompromising view. "The chief source of man's dignity," Reinhold Niebuhr wrote, "is man's essential freedom and capacity for self-determination." Carl Rogers has asserted that "over and above the circumstances which control all of us, there exists an inner experience of choice which is very important. This is the kind of thing Skinner has never been willing to recognize."

Skinner's detractors attack the whole concept of behaviorism, which Novelist Arthur Koestler, who has high amateur standing in psychology and other sciences, maintains is nothing but pseudoscience, "a monumental triviality that has sent psychology into a modern version of the Dark Ages." In ignoring consciousness, mind, imagination and purpose, Koestler says, Behaviorist Skinner and his admirers have abandoned what is most important. Similarly, Historian Peter Gay speaks of "the innate naiveté, intellectual bankruptcy and half-deliberate cruelty of behaviorism."

The gravest menace from Skinner is his authoritarianism in the view of his critics. They reject the notion that man can no longer afford freedom and believe in fact that he cannot afford the opposite. Says Harvard Social Psychologist Herbert C. Kelman: "For those of us who hold the enhancement of man's freedom of choice as a fundamental value, any manipulation of

A SKINNERIAN INNOVATION: BABY IN A BOX

In 1945, when Deborah Skinner was eleven months old, she had a rather dubious distinction: she was the most talked-about infant in America—the famous "baby in a box." The box, or "air crib" as her father called it, was his own invention, a glassed-in, insulated, air-controlled crib that he thought would revolutionize child rearing and, in line with his behaviorist theories, produce happier, healthier children.

One of the major practical problems in raising a young baby, Skinner reasoned, is the simple one of keeping it warm. The infant is usually covered by half a dozen layers of cloth—shirt, nightdress, sheet and blankets—that not only constrict movement and cause rashes, but sometimes even pose the danger of strangulation. Then there is the mother's labor in dressing and undressing the child, plus the considerable expense of buying and laundering all those clothes and blankets.

•

To eliminate those troubles, Skinner designed Deborah's crib with temperature and humidity controls so that she could be warm and naked at the same time. Besides the hoped-for results—Deborah never suffered from a rash, for instance—the crib provided an unexpected fringe benefit: the Skinners discovered that the baby was so sensitive to even the slightest change in temperature that she could be made happy simply by moving the thermostat a notch or two. "We wonder how a comfortable temperature is ever reached with clothing and blankets," Skinner wrote in a 1945 issue of *Ladies' Home Journal.* "During the past six months Deborah has not cried at all except for a moment or two when injured or sharply distressed—for example, when inoculated."

The air in the box was passed through filters, keeping Deborah free from germs and so clean that it was necessary to give her only one bath a week. There was the usual diaper change, but little other laundering; a single, 10-yd.-long sheet was stored on a spool at one end

of the compartment and rolled through into a hamper on the other end as it was soiled; it had to be laundered just once a week. The box was partially soundproofed, and a shade could be drawn over the plate-glass window.

Skinner was sensitive to criticism that Deborah was isolated. In his articles and lectures, he took pains to stress that she could watch everything that was taking place in the room about her, and that she was frequently taken out for cuddling and play. To many people, however, the air box sounded and looked like an atrocious human goldfish bowl.

The continuing controversy about the box may have partially offset the good effects Skinner hoped for when he designed it. Says Deborah, who is now an art student in London: "It was spread around that because of the box I had become psychotic, had to be institutionalized, and had even attempted suicide. My father was very concerned about these rumors, as was I. He thinks they may have affected me. After college, I had a typical half-year of depression, the sort of identity crisis that everybody I've ever known has gone through. At this point my father brought up the idea that I don't have enough faith in myself, and that the rumors may have had something to do with this."

•

In fact, Deborah, a slightly shy and earnest but nonpsychotic young woman of 27, seems to have survived the rumors rather well. Her 2½ years in the box, she thinks, did her only good. "It wasn't really a psychological experiment," she says, "but what you might call a happiness-through-health experiment. I think I was a very happy baby. Most of the criticisms of the box are by people who don't understand what it was."

Though something like 1,000 of the air cribs are in use today, Skinner's idea has not caught on with very many parents and has yet to revolutionize child rearing.

the behavior of others constitutes a violation of their essential humanity, regardless of the 'goodness' of the cause that this manipulation is designed to serve." To Kelman, the "ethical ambiguity" of behavioral manipulation is the same whether the limitation on choice comes "through punishment or reward or even through so perfect an arrangement of society that people do not care to choose."

Existential Psychoanalyst Rollo May believes that Skinner is a totalitarian without fully knowing it. "I have never found any place in Skinner's system for the rebel," he says. "Yet the capacity to rebel is of the essence in a constructive society." Richard Rubenstein, professor of religion at Florida State University, wonders what might happen to would-be rebels in a Skinnerian society: "Suppose some future controller told dissenting groups to 'behave, damn you!' What would prevent the controller from employing his own final solution?"

Skinner is skeptical about democracy. Observing that society is already using such ineffective means of behavioral control as persuasion and conventional education, he insists that men of good will must adopt more effective techniques, using them for "good" purposes to keep despots from using them for "bad" ones. In his planned society, he says, control would be balanced by countercontrol, probably by "making the controller a member of the group he controls." This would help to ensure that punishment would never be inflicted, Skinner maintains, adding that it was the use of "aversive control" (punishment) that doomed Hitler: "The Nazi system had its own destruction built right into it. When you control that way, people are out to get you."

The ultimate logical dilemma in Skinner's thinking is this: What are the sources of the standards of good and evil in his ideal society? Indeed, who decides even what

constitutes pleasure or pain, reward, or punishment, when man and his environment can be limitlessly manipulated? Skinner himself believes in Judeo-Christian ethics combined with the scientific tradition. But he fails to answer how it is possible to accept those ethics without also accepting something like the "inner person" with an autonomous conscience.

Skinner has never responded fully to any of his critics despite their number and stature. Often he has failed to understand them. Sometimes he has even branded them as neurotic or even psychotic. Occasionally he has seemed to imply that he himself is beyond criticism. "When I met him, he was convinced he was a genius," Yvonne Skinner remembers. And in *Walden Two,* Skinner's alter ego Frazier, assuming the posture of Christ on the cross, says that there is "a curious similarity" between himself and God—adding, however, that "perhaps I must yield to God in point of seniority."

In another *Walden Two* passage, Skinner sketches a more realistic self-portrait. With some bitterness his alter ego Frazier addresses Burris: "You think I'm conceited, aggressive, tactless, selfish. You're convinced that I'm completely insensitive to my effect upon others, except when the effect is calculated. You can't see in me any personal warmth. You're sure that I'm one who couldn't possibly be a genuine member of any community . . . Shall we say that as a person I'm a complete failure and have done with it?"

This awareness that he is unfit for communal life may be one reason that Skinner has never tried to start a real Walden Two, never sent a Dear-President-Mittelbach telegram to the president of Harvard. In addition, he likes his own kind of life too well to give it up even for an ideal in which he believes so intensely, and even if he felt otherwise, his wife is opposed to the idea.

Says Yvonne Skinner, a former University of Chicago English major who studied with Thornton Wilder and is herself a gifted writer: "We had tremendous arguments about *Walden Two.* I wouldn't like it: I just like change and privacy."

REFUSING INVITATIONS

Fred and Yvonne Skinner live in an attractive, modern Cambridge house complete with swimming pool, a stereo system, a grand piano, a clavichord and, in the basement study, a small organ. In a sense Skinner's own life-style is highly controlled and conditioned. His study contains a special clock that "runs when I'm really thinking. I keep a cumulative record of serious time at my desk. The clock starts when I turn on the desk light, and whenever it passes twelve hours, I plot a point on a curve. I can see what my average rate of writing has been at my period. When other activities take up my time the slope falls off. That helps me to refuse invitations."

Skinner rises at 5 a.m., writes for three hours, then walks to his Harvard office, sometimes memorizing poetry (Shakespeare or Baudelaire) on the way. There he charts the sales of *Walden Two* on a graph over his desk: the total should reach the million mark sometime in 1972. In the course of the day, he gives an occasional lecture and records his ideas in notebooks that he has always at hand. "He thinks of himself as an event in the history of man,

and he wants to be damned sure the record is straight," a colleague observes.

Skinner nonetheless allows himself some relaxation. He drinks vodka and tonic in the late afternoon, sees an occasional movie, reads Georges Simenon detective novels once in a while, and enjoys the company of friends, his two children and his grandchildren. It sounds fulfilling, but a poignant passage from a personal journal several years ago suggests an underlying sadness: "Sun streams into our living room. My hi-fi is midway through the first act of *Tristan and Isolde.* A very pleasant environment. A man would be a fool not to enjoy himself in it. In a moment I will work on a manuscript which may help mankind. So my life is not only pleasant, it is earned and deserved. Yet, yet, I am unhappy."

That sort of unhappiness wells from deep personal sources. Yet it is also related to his more universal concerns. Skinner worries about the fact that, as *Walden Two's* Frazier put it, "our civilization is running away like a frightened horse. As she runs, her speed and her panic increase together. As for your politicians, your professors, your writers—let them wave their arms and shout as wildly as they will."

That may be an accurate description of society's dilemma, but Skinner's solution seems equally frightening. To Theologian Rubenstein, *Beyond Freedom and Dignity* is an important but "terrifying" book. Skinner's "utopian projection" he says, "is less likely to be a blueprint for the Golden Age than for the theory and practice of hell."

11. NEW CLUES TO THE CAUSES OF VIOLENCE

Gene Bylinsky

Assassinations, vicious muggings, and the high and rising U.S. murder rate have pushed the subject of violence to the forefront among American concerns. At times, the nation appears to be oddly fascinated by the phenomenon. Consider, for example, the recent proliferation of grisly movies, some of which seem to glorify violence as a cult. We have been hearing an abundance of theories about the causes of violence, which variously attribute it to the war in Vietnam, to permissiveness, to drug addiction, to racial frustrations, and even to the legacy of the wild frontier.

Now science is venturing into this area of speculation and dispute. A broad interdisciplinary effort is getting under way to explore the biological nature and origins of violence. Biologists, biochemists, neurophysiologists, geneticists, and other natural scientists are probing with increasingly precise tools and techniques in a field where supposition and speculation have long prevailed. Their work is beginning to provide new clues to the complex ways in which the brain shapes violent behavior. It is also shedding new light on how environmental influences, by affecting the brain, can trigger violence. In time, these insights and discoveries could lead to practical action that may inhibit violent acts—perhaps, for example, a change in the way children are brought up, or treatment with "anti-violence" drugs. Such preventive steps might

Reprinted from *Fortune* (January 1973) by permission of publisher, pp. 73–78.
Research associate: Bro Uttal.

in the long run be more effective in controlling violent crime than either "law and order" or social reform.

By tradition, students of aggression and violence have been divided into two separate camps that hardly ever communicated with each other. On one side stood the ethologists, students of animal behavior in the wild, many of whom held that man is biologically fated to violence. At the other extreme were social scientists, who knew, or cared, little about biology. They argued that violent crime is strictly a social phenomenon, best dealt with by eliminating slums, urban crowding, and racial discrimination, and by alleviating poverty and improving the prison system.

AN IMPRINT ON THE BRAIN

The most recent research suggests that the biological and environmental causes of violence are so closely intertwined as to require a less fragmented search for remedies. The research is showing, among other things, that the environment itself can leave a physical imprint on a developing brain. The wrong kind of upbringing can make a young animal, and probably a child too, more inclined to violent behavior as an adolescent or an adult. The hopeful augury of this research is that such behavior can be prevented if steps are taken to assure that young brains develop properly.

Until a few years ago, scientists knew comparatively little about the intricate inner mechanisms of the brain that initiate and control violence. These mechanisms lie deep in an inaccessible area called the limbic system, wrapped around the brain stem, as shown in the drawing on page 68. In the limbic system, the hypothalamus stands out as the single most important control center. Regulating many of man's primitive drives, its networks of nerve cells, or neurons, direct not only aggressive and violent behavior but also the states of sleep and wakefulness, as well as sexual and feeding behavior. The front part of the hypothalamus contains networks of nerve cells that promote calmness and tranquillity. The back part regulates aggression and rage.

RESTRAINING THE HYPOTHALAMUS

Nearby lies the almond-shaped amygdala, which restrains the impulses from the hypothalamus. Another close-by structure, the septum, seems to inhibit messages from both the hypothalamus and the amygdala. The cerebellum, the large structure at the back of the brain, filters sensory impulses. The hippocampus, a short-term memory bank in front of the cerebellum, is importantly involved in ways that brain researchers do not yet adequately understand.

All these structures are functionally as well as anatomically interrelated. Electrical signals, arising in response to sensory or internal cues (e.g., sight or thought), speed along nerve pathways to activate or block the function of other nerve cells. Chemicals such as noradrenaline and dopamine, which are normally present in the brain and are known as neurotransmitters, apparently ferry these electrical signals across the tiny gaps between nerve cells, called synapses, to such control centers as the hypothalamus. At the same time, the neurons are constantly bathed in waves of background electrical activity. In still unknown ways, this background "music" apparently conveys information, too.

So complex are the organization and function of the human brain that some of its estimated 10 billion nerve cells may have as many as 100,000 connections to adjoining cells. When an aggressive act escalates into a violent one, apparently more and more of these neurons are recruited to create bigger pathways for the flow of pulses. Thus violence, as some scientists define it, is aggression gone awry.

THE CASE OF THE ENRAGED CAT

Fortunately for the advance of knowledge about human aggression, the limbic systems of animals have recently been found to bear an amazing functional resemblance to that of man. So laboratory experiments with animals (notably monkeys, cats, and mice) underpin the still limited investigations of aggression systems in the human brain.

Using fine electrodes inserted into animal brains, researchers have induced a fascinating range of aggressive behavior. Cats that normally do not attack rats, for instance, will stalk and kill a rat when stimulated in a certain area of the hypothalamus. On the other hand, a cat stimulated in another nearby region of the hypothalamus may ignore an available rat and attack the experimenter instead. Destruction of the nucleus of the amygdala will turn a friendly cat into a raging beast that claws and bites without provocation, because the signals from the hypothalamus are no longer dampened by the amygdala.

Similarly, a tumor in the hypothalamus or the amygdala can turn a peaceful person into a violent one. Such tumors occur infrequently. Corrective brain surgery remains highly controversial, however, mainly because surgeons lack precise knowledge of the aggression systems and know little about the risk of unwanted side effects from such operations. A surgical lesion—a scar-producing cut, freeze, or burn intended to destroy tissue—can increase or decrease hostile behavior, depending on its location.

Similar gaps in medical information inhibit manipulation of aggressive behavior with drugs that structurally mimic the neurotransmitter chemicals. Recent experiments by Peter Bradley, a British neuropharmacologist, show that a brain cell can be affected in different ways by the same neurotransmitter, depending on the state of the cell, the amount of neurotransmitter, and how often the chemical is administered. It also appears that during an aggressive act a general arousal of the physiological system occurs—the same type of arousal that can be produced by such peaceful activities as jogging or even a concentrated mental effort.

DYNAMITE IN THE GENES?

The complex anatomical and biochemical systems of the brain get their "orders" from the genes that determine behavior. Recent studies suggest that males have more brain cells that specialize in aggression than do females. This means that boys are more likely than girls to inherit aggressive tendencies. Very little is yet known, though, about the relationship between specific genetic defects and violence, how many such defects exist, and how frequently they might be inherited. Among the handful of anomalies discovered so far that some scientists have connected with violent behavior is the famous extra Y chromosome, which luckily appears to be inherited by fewer than two men in a thousand. (X and Y are sex chromosomes, with a normal male having an X and a Y, and a normal woman two X's.)

The Y chromosome leaped from the quiet of the laboratory four years ago and landed with a splash in newspaper headlines and courtrooms. The XYY males, usually tall, were said to have a natural propensity for violent crime. Some lawyers tried to gain reduced sentences or acquittal for their clients on the basis of their real or imagined extra Y chromosome. In France, at least, one attorney succeeded.

Some imaginative work now in progress at the University of Connecticut suggests that the Y chromosome story isn't all that simple. Researchers in the department of biobehavioral sciences, led by Benson E. Ginsburg, a noted geneticist, have designed animal breeding techniques that allow them to "tease out," as Ginsburg puts it, the contributions of individual genes and chromosomes to behavior. Their findings strongly hint that an XYY male's tendency to aggressiveness depends on whether he inherited his extra Y chromosome from a peaceful or aggressive father. The Y chromosome may act on the brain through the male sex hormones. Ginsburg and other scientists are trying to find out how this process works.

Elevating genetic probing to a new level of precision, Ginsburg and his colleagues have also shown that a Y chromosome from an aggressive father can combine with another genetic anomaly to make an animal twice as aggressive as it would be with just one genetic defect. They worked with an inbred strain of mice known as DBA 1. These mice are genetically susceptible to epileptic-type seizures that can be initiated by a high-frequency sound from a buzzer, or a bell, or even a jangling set of keys. The sound activates an enzyme system, controlled by a gene as all enzymes are, and located in the hippocampus. In a mouse, the network of neurons involved makes up

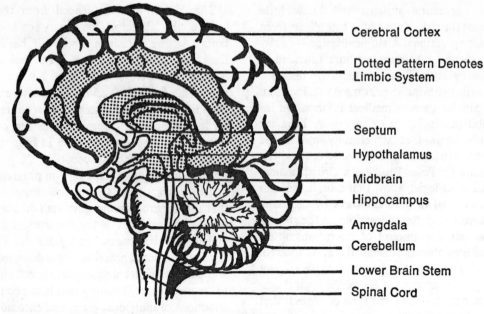

Cerebral Cortex

Dotted Pattern Denotes
Limbic System

Septum

Hypothalamus

Midbrain

Hippocampus

Amygdala

Cerebellum

Lower Brain Stem

Spinal Cord

The brain's decisions about violence are made mainly by some of the structures depicted here. The centers that initiate aggressive acts, such as the hypothalamus, lie deep in the primitive part of the brain called the limbic system. Man's more intellectual cortex exercises a restraining influence over the lower brain regions. The brain, scientists speculate, reaches decisions much as a democratic society does. Individual neurons sort out conflicting impulses and decide whether to fire an electrical pulse or not. The sum of such decisions tells a person, for instance, whether to lash out at an enemy or to remain calm.

an area the size of a pinpoint. The enzyme activated by sound, nucleoside triphosphatase, generates epileptic-like brain waves that can be recorded.

STORMY WEATHER IN THE HIPPOCAMPUS

The DBA mice, particularly males, are abnormally aggressive, apparently because of the defect in their hippocampus. In such mice, complex chemical reactions are superimposed on abnormal electrical activity in their hippocampal neurons. "You whip up an electrical storm in that region of the brain," says Ginsburg, describing his work with a touch of poetic license. Chemicals in the brain intensify the storm, he says, "as if you poured gasoline on a fire—and it went whoosh!"

The same type of storm, and in the same spot, rages in the brains of certain humans.

They are either pathologically aggressive or have been made aggressive by hippocampal stimulation. This suggests, of course, that Ginsburg and his colleagues have found a genetic anomaly underlying aggression in both mice and men. In recent years, surgeons in some hospitals have been stimulating different parts of the brains of cancer patients in an effort to find an area that might block unbearable pain. In a number of instances, where doctors have stimulated the hippocampus by administering a very mild electrical shock through an electrode, patients showed the type of rage that Ginsburg and his associates found in those DBA mice. One mild-mannered patient in his fifties suddenly brandished his bedpan as a weapon against the nurses and whoever else happened to be around. He later felt quite embarrassed and contrite.

The discovery of the consequences of these anomalies and of other types of brain damage shatters the assumption made by criminologists and sociologists that the vast majority of cases of violent behavior involve people with completely normal brains. Studies of criminals who have repeatedly committed violent offenses show that they have a higher incidence of brain damage than the general population. Moreover, recent research is uncovering subtle forms of brain damage, unrecognized until now. No one knows for sure how many people in the U.S. suffer from brain damage, but some doctors place the number at 10 million to 20 million. Not all of them are violent, of course, but in addition there are many thousands who suffer from delusions or other forms of mental disturbance that make them dangerous. David Hamburg, head of the psychiatry department at Stanford University Medical School, estimates that the nation harbors some 200,000 potential presidential assassins. "Many manage their delusions on the fantasy level,"

says Hamburg. "Others engage in other forms of violent behavior."

What many people with brain abnormalities may have in common are pathways in the brain that failed to develop properly in infancy because of faulty upbringing, just as visual nerve pathways fail to develop properly in animals deprived of light. The fault, especially during the first two years of life when the brain is growing the fastest, lies in lack of physical affection, which an infant needs as much as nourishment. Earlier researchers had usually blamed emotional, social, or learning deficiencies for behavioral disturbances in infants raised in a foundling home. But James Prescott, a young neuropsychologist at the U.S. National Institute of Child Health and Human Development, suggests that there is a more fundamental biological reason. He maintains that normal pathways in the brain do not fully develop in children deprived of such expressions of affection as touching, cuddling, and being carried about. Instead, he says, this "somatosensory deprivation" leaves them with damaged central nervous systems.

A CHICKEN-WIRE MOTHER

In a dramatic series of experiments, Harry F. Harlow, a University of Wisconsin psychologist, has demonstrated what happens when baby rhesus monkeys are deprived of their mothers. Harlow placed an infant monkey in a cage with two inanimate mother substitutes. One, covered with terry cloth and equipped with bicycle-reflector eyes, was designed to feel and look somewhat like a real rhesus mother but had no apparatus for feeding the infant. The other "mother," made of unadorned chicken wire, was unattractive to touch but contained a baby's bottle from which the infant could drink milk. Harlow found that the infant rhesus clearly preferred to spend all of its time with the nonfeeding surrogate. Even when feeding from the chicken-wire "mother," the infant would cling to his terry-cloth favorite. Harlow concluded that in infant-mother love, holding and cuddling are even more important than feeding. He also found that female monkeys who grew up with mother surrogates failed to develop maternal affection: they all seemed indifferent to their own children. Like parents who abuse their children, these monkey mothers frequently attacked, and sometimes even killed, their infants. Other researchers have recently traced three generations of human parents who batter and abuse their children. The only common characteristic of such parents, regardless of social or economic class, was that they themselves had suffered from lack of mothering and affection. Harlow wryly concluded a recent paper:

> Hell hath no fury like a woman spurned.
> With love not given, love is not returned.
> The loveless female, human or macaque,
> In place of love will substitute attack.

Can such deprived, aggressive monkeys be restored to normalcy? Experiments in Harlow's laboratory indicate that rehabilitation is possible if it is done early enough. Young monkey mothers reared in isolation sometimes regain most of their normal maternal behavior when locked in a cage with their own babies. The infant clings to the mother so persistently, despite her efforts to push it away, that eventually the baby monkey begins to serve as a therapist. Similarly, some young male monkeys reared in isolation become less aggressive when forced to play with monkeys their own age or younger.

Research into the brains of monkeys raised in isolation is just beginning, but indirect evidence already hints that such treatment induces brain damage. In humans, brain waves with abnormal, jagged "spikes" are often a telltale sign of damage. Robert G. Heath and Bernard Saltzberg, researchers at Tulane University, have recorded such spikes in the brain waves of monkeys reared by Harlow. The spikes reflect abnormal electrical activity, particularly in the cerebellum.

WHY DING FEARED DONG

Further evidence of the cerebellum's role in violence comes from the work of A. J. Berman, a neurosurgeon at Mount Sinai Medical School and the Jewish Hospital in Brooklyn. He has successfully modified autistic and aggressive behavior in isolation-reared monkeys by removing presumably abnormal sections of cerebellum that deal with the reception of sensory signals. In one experiment, Berman performed similar surgery on two monkeys called Ding and Dong, who had fought viciously and continuously. The operation turned Ding into a submissive animal, while Dong remained as aggressive as ever. Berman attributes the difference to the location of the surgery. Some tissue was removed from the midline section of Ding's cerebellum while the excision on Dong was microscopically closer to the side of that brain structure.

Berman suggests that his findings may one day be relevant to treating humans. "Walk into the back wards of any mental institution," he says, "and you'll find children whose behavior is identical with that of Harlow's monkeys."

All these and many other experiments have led a number of scientists to conclude that people who behave overaggressively may have an abnormality in the mechanism by which they perceive pleasure. In animals reared in isolation, as in pathologically violent people, the impulses resulting from the stimulation of movement and skin sensations may not be reaching their normal destinations in the brain. The feeling of pleasure may thus be experienced only partially or not at all.

This may explain, among other things, why both institutionalized children and monkeys brought up in isolation generally rock back and forth for hours on end and respond violently if touched. Adults with damaged pleasure systems similarly may be trying to derive pleasure from the rough physical contact involved in violent acts; they may, in effect, be seeking an additional stimulus. Researchers have also found that electrical stimulation of pleasure centers in the brain eliminates feelings of rage, because the brain seems to contain rival nerve systems that suppress opposing emotions chemically and electrically.

THE SCIENTIST PLAYS VICTIM

Aggressive behavior doesn't necessarily have to arise as a result of damaged networks of nerve cells; it can be easily learned, too. Albert Bandura, a pioneering psychologist at Stanford University, demonstrated almost a decade ago how effectively aggression can be taught through the power of example. He used as "victims" large, inflated plastic figures known as Bobo dolls. Small children watched both real-life and filmed attacks on the dolls, then were given an opportunity to act aggressively themselves.

In study after study, researchers discovered that boys, especially, easily learn and retain aggressive behavior. They readily act out what they have learned not only on Bobo dolls but on other children and even adults. In one typical and recent experiment, conducted by psychologist Robert M. Liebert and his associates at New York State University at Stony Brook, kindergarten children watched a short film. Later they spontaneously attacked a scientist who had appeared in the film dressed up as a hard-luck clown and had been beaten up by another researcher. Many studies show that televised violence affects children in similar ways.

Violent behavior can be set off by many other environmental conditions. For instance, Leonard Berkowitz, a University of Wisconsin psychologist, showed that the mere presence of firearms can stimulate aggressive action. He tested groups of students who were provoked and insulted by one of his colleagues. Later, the groups had a chance to administer electric shocks to their tormentor. Students in a room where a gun was casually displayed gave the investigator about 25 percent more shocks than those in a room containing no weapons. The findings suggest to Berkowitz and others that easy access to lethal weapons—about 65 percent of homicides in the U.S. are committed with guns—not only facilitates the commission of crimes but creates an atmosphere in which violence is more likely to occur.

As in the laboratory, violence in real life often begets more violence. Marvin E. Wolfgang, a noted criminologist at the University of Pennsylvania, has coined the term "subculture of violence" to describe the cluster of values, attitudes, and life styles prominent among the poor living in the slums. Violence in that setting is so common as a problem-solving mechanism, says Wolfgang, that there is no shortage of real-life models for the young to imitate.

Many other factors—frequent absence of fathers, low income, unstable employment, poor living conditions—also bend the behavior of underprivileged youths toward violence, according to Wolfgang. Under all these pressures, plus in some cases a lack of physical affection at home, adolescent blacks have the highest homicide rate of any group in the U.S.

To complicate matters, they, like other adolescents, undergo a hormonal upheaval.

Boys in particular become more aggressive as the amount of sex hormones in their bodies increases. Electron microscopy at Oxford University has recently begun to reveal structural differences between males and females in such control centers of aggression as the hypothalamus, for which sex hormones have a particular affinity.

ARE MEN STRONGER THAN MICE?

The still mysterious workings of hormones on the brain constitute only a small part of the enormous gap between what scientists have discovered and what remains to be learned about the physiology and biochemistry of violence. For example, says Benson Ginsburg, the University of Connecticut geneticist, scientists should find out whether men, through conscious control and training, can override the physiological changes involved in aggression much more effectively than, say, mice can. Another unknown is whether genetic instructions are so strong in some people as to completely mold their behavior. Answers to such questions could open the way to far more specific therapies. More effective antiviolence drugs, for instance, could be developed if we could delineate the particular enzymatic mechanisms in the brain that affect aggression.

Treatment with existing drugs, many scientists feel, is something like using a shotgun where a rifle is needed. Even so, some investigators propose that methadone-type clinics be set up to dispense drugs available now to persons prone to violence. Lithium might be useful because it appears to speed the release of serotonin, a brain chemical that seems to inhibit aggression. Michael H. Sheard, a Yale neuropharmacologist, has had some success in modifying the behavior of violent prisoners with lithium.

Other novel approaches may emerge from studies that are under way. For exam-

ple, development of a vastly improved brain-wave recording machine, now in progress at Tulane, would enable doctors to detect signals of trouble from deep in the brain without surgically implanting recording electrodes there. It may also become possible to treat damaged deep-nerve networks ultrasonically, thereby avoiding surgery.

It is clear that much more specific therapies than those in use today are needed for people who have brain damage. Vernon H. Mark and Frank R. Ervin observe in their recent book, *Violence and the Brain:* "Hoping to rehabilitate such a violent individual through psychotherapy or education, or to improve his character by sending him to jail or by giving him love and understanding—all these methods are irrelevant and will not work. It is the malfunction itself that must be dealt with, and only if this fact is recognized is there any chance of changing his behavior."

NO TROUBLE IN TAHITI

To prevent brain damage that may lead to violence, some new tactics could be tried now. "Changing child-rearing practices is probably the most important single thing we can do as a society," says Prescott. "We have to make sure that the children we have are wanted children." Prescott and others also suggest that it might be a good idea to evaluate and treat children as early as age five if they show a tendency to brutalize other children or animals or have episodes of uncontrolled rage. Such youngsters, scientists say, are good candidates for violent behavior later.

Anthropologists have gained some intriguing clues about child rearing by studying peaceful societies. Prescott surveyed data from forty-nine primitive cultures and found in thirty-six of them an amazingly strong correlation between physical affection toward infants and lack of violence. In societies where infants were treated cruelly, violence prevailed. Robert Levy, an anthropologist at the University of California at San Diego who has studied tranquil Tahiti, found that parents on the island seldom punish children by hitting them. Thus the children have no aggressive models to emulate.

Another deterrent to violence may be the habit of arguing it out. Societies that have developed highly elaborate ways of verbalizing violence are quite peaceful. In Tahiti and other Polynesian islands, people engage in "talking out acute anger, rather than taking physical action," says Levy. Similarly, Italians sometimes sound violent, but according to scientists who have studied Italy, there is far less incidence of violent offenses there than in the U.S.

This nation leads the advanced industrialized counties of the world in homicide and other violent crimes. Assaults in the U.S. occur nearly twice as often per capita as in England and Wales, and robberies are ten times as common. In 1971, the latest full year for which figures are available, 17,630 people in the U.S. were murdered. In England and Wales, West Germany, France, and Italy, which have a combined population about 3 percent larger than ours, there were only 1,948 murders—a rate almost ten times lower than that in the U.S.

By contrast with the U.S., these other industrial countries have more homogeneous populations, exert greater control over firearms, and operate with somewhat more rigid social structures. These differences may explain some, though not necessarily all, of the disparities in the rates of violence. In any case, it is clear that our methods of dealing with the problem have not proved particularly effective. Scientific investigation at last is beginning to provide surprising insights into why this is so. In time, the new research may lead to a much broader understanding of violent behavior, and, eventually, to effective means of discouraging it.

CHAPTER II

Developmental Psychology

DEVELOPMENTAL PSYCHOLOGY traditionally has focused on the particularly dramatic changes which occur as a person passes through infancy, childhood, and adolescence. Two of the articles in this chapter deal with these important developmental stages. "Giant in the Nursery: Jean Piaget," reports the epochal work and theory of this noted Swiss child psychologist. The article traces the development in humans of intelligence and rational thought, which, for Piaget, have their origin in the earliest days of life. "The Problems of Youth" presents an educator's view of how the problems of today's youth relate to their problems in the past and explores promising approaches to amelioration and solution of these difficulties.

The other readings in this section present various aspects of an enlarged view of human development which does not accept the artificial boundaries of infancy as the beginning and adolescence as the end. "Changing the Face of Birth" reports a new obstetric birth procedure and presents its rationale. The purpose of the new procedure is to make the infant's entrance into the world pleasurable and secure, rather than traumatic and painful.

"Adult Life Cycles" traces the various age-related crises and developmental problems encountered during the course of life and explores the relationship of the many things that change, grow, develop, and wane over time. "How to Cope with Male Menopause" explores the recently recognized problem of male menopause and presents some remedial approaches to it.

The last reading in this chapter, "The Thanatologist," represents a new area of specialization within psychology, one concerned with the psychology of death. This article presents the view that all concerned can and should be psychologically prepared for death. The techniques, problems, and implications of such an endeavor are explored and discussed.

Thus this chapter presents material concerning the major stages and problems encountered throughout life from birth to death. As you read it, you can evaluate your own development in light of the changes you have already experienced and those that lie ahead.

12. CHANGING THE FACE OF BIRTH

Robert J. Trotter

Imagine stepping out of a cool, dark movie theater into a hot, glaring, sunny afternoon.

Imagine being wakened from a quiet, restful sleep by the blaring noise of a brass band.

If your reflexes and senses are normal, these drastic changes are not only going to be shocking, they might be extremely painful.

Now, imagine what it would be like to experience all of these violent sensory changes if you were a naked, newborn infant. The result could be extremely traumatic. Such shock is what greets most infants at the moment of birth—according to French obstetrician Frederick Leboyer. Blinding lights, noise, cold air, harsh fabrics, being snapped into an erect position and being held aloft by one foot, being slapped on the rear end and forced to scream—these are part of what Leboyer calls the violence of birth as it takes place in the efficient, antiseptic delivery rooms of the Western world.

But there might be a better way to be born. In *Birth Without Violence* (Alfred A. Knopf, 1975), Leboyer describes, in somewhat melodramatic terms, the pain infants suffer being born in most modern delivery rooms. "What more proof do we need?" he asks. "That tragic expression, those tight-shut eyes, those twitching eyebrows . . . that howling mouth, that squirming head trying

desperately to find refuge . . . those hands stretching out to us, imploring, begging, then retreating to shield the face—that gesture of dread. Those furiously kicking feet, those arms that suddenly pull downward to protect the stomach, The flesh is one great shudder . . . Every inch of the body is crying out: 'Don't touch me!' And at the same time pleading: 'Don't leave me! Help me!' Has there ever been a more heartrending appeal?"

In answer to this appeal, Leboyer offers a method of making birth less painful and traumatic for the infant. It is a slow, quiet birth in which everything is done to protect the child from shock. The infant's sensitive eyes, for instance, are spared the glare of delivery room lamps and floodlights. "Of course," admits Leboyer, "some light is necessary to watch over the mother, so that she will not be injured when the child's head emerges." But then, he says, extinguish all lights, except a small nightlight. "And this is all to the good, since newborn infants are almost always ugly. . . . It is better that the mother discover her child by touching it."

Unnecessary noise is also eliminated. Leboyer calls for complete silence in the delivery room, instead of the loud calls, such as "push, push" that might upset the mother and could possibly be painful to the infant.

Once the child's head and arms appear, the birth can be eased along by a finger under each armpit. Supported so, the baby is gently settled on its mother's abdomen. There, for several minutes, the child is allowed to adjust slowly to its new environment while it continues to receive warmth and comfort from its mother.

The Leboyer method also eliminates the traditional slap on the rear. The infant's spinal column, while in the womb, has never been completely straight, but holding the child up by a foot snaps the spine into an erect position. This, says Leboyer, is as unnecessarily shocking and painful as the slap on the rear.

But without the slap, how does the child begin to breathe? Anoxia, or lack of oxygen, can result in irreparable brain damage and is one of the most serious dangers a child faces during the birth process. The Leboyer method attempts to avoid this danger by allowing the infant to remain on its mother's abdomen with the umbilical cord intact. In this way, the infant continues to be supplied oxygenated blood via the umbilical cord. Gradually, after several minutes, the child's lungs and respiratory system will begin to function properly, and the umbilical cord will stop pulsing. Then, says Leboyer, after perhaps five minutes, the cord can be cut. The child has continually been fed oxygen and has not been slapped.

Next, instead of placing the child on a cold scale, it is immersed in water that has been warmed to near body temperature. Here the child is gently rinsed and will eventually open its eyes and begin to move its limbs freely. The result of such a nonviolent birth, concludes Leboyer, is not a screaming, kicking, terrified infant but a relaxed and even smiling child.

Leboyer's book, compelling because of its humane approach to birth, has been a best seller in France for two years and is now being published in England, Germany, Sweden, Brazil, Italy and Holland. For the past several months, it has been selling well in the United States.

Just because the book is popular, however, does not mean that there will be immediate and drastic changes in delivery room techniques around the world. Studies have suggested a possible link between birth trauma (especially anoxia) and schizophrenia, but Leboyer offers no solid evidence that the more than 1,000 infants he has delivered by this method are any better off than children born the normal delivery room way. And it can be argued that the possible risks to mother and child in a semidarkened delivery room are more serious than any benefits that might result from the absence of bright lights.

Although Leboyer does not present specific evidence to prove the value of his method there is a growing body of evidence that might eventually bring about some changes in the way newborns are greeted. Marshall H. Klaus, for instance, is interested in the way hospital-care practices affect mothers. And his data substantiate his claim that "present hospital practices with human mothers and fathers in this country require drastic alteration." Klaus, of the department of pediatrics at the school of medicine of Case Western Reserve University in Cleveland, described his research at the recent meeting in Vermont on the prevention of psychopathology (SN: 8/9/75, p. 90).

Part of Klaus's claim is based on behavioral studies of a number of animal species as well as on studies of human maternal behavior. These observations suggest that what happens in the period immediately following delivery may be critical to later maternal behavior. Goats, sheep and cattle, for instance, show disturbances of mothering behavior if they have been separated from their young for the first hour or so after delivery. After such a separation, the mothers may fail to care for their young and may even butt their offspring away. If the mother and infant are separated for an hour on the fifth day, the mother quickly returns to the maternal behavior characteristic of her species when the pair is reunited.

Mice and rats show a lack of skill in caring for their young if mother and pup have been separated during the first few hours following delivery. Harry Harlow's studies of rhesus monkeys show that mothers who are not allowed to touch their infants, but are allowed to see them through a window, soon lose interest in those infants.

Specific patterns of behavior seem to be sensitive to factors other than separation. Pregnant rats lick their genital areas during labor and just before birth. This behavior carries over to the pups after birth. If the behavior pattern is changed, the result can be abnormal mothering. In one experiment, high collars were placed on the necks of pregnant rats to prevent self-licking. The collars were removed shortly before birth, but the rats did not lick their infants clean in the normal fashion. Instead, the mothers ate some of the pups. The mothers even refused to suckle those pups that weren't eaten.

For a period after delivery, weeks or even months, most animal species show characteristic maternal behavior patterns such as licking, nesting and grooming. Observations of humans suggest that such behavior patterns are also found in human mothers. In many societies, for instance, there is some regularized method of dealing with newborns. Anthropological studies show that in many cultures, the mother and infant are secluded during the first three to seven days after birth while the navel heals. In Israeli kibbutzim, separation does not usually occur until after the fifth day. In Russia, mothers are not separated from their infants during the first weeks of life. Klaus and his colleagues point out that "routine complete separation of mother and infant in the first days after delivery exists only in the high-risk and premature nurseries of the Western world." And even

after normal births, some degree of separation of mother and child is the standard procedure.

It is this disruption of what appears to be a normal human behavior pattern that is the subject of Klaus's research. Evidence of the danger of immediate separation of mother and child comes from studies of premature infants who were taken away from their mothers for special treatment. At the turn of the century, Pierre Budin, a specialist in infant care, noted that, "Unfortunately ... a certain number of mothers abandon the babies whose needs they have not had to meet, and in whom they have lost all interest. The life of the little one has been saved, it is true, but at the cost of the mother."

Another example comes from the work of Martin Cooney, who, in 1896, displayed a "child hatchery" that was used to isolate and protect premature infants. Cooney traveled as an exhibitor to fairs in England and the United States where he exhibited premature infants in their "hatcheries." Significantly, Cooney sometimes had difficulty getting parents to take their children back.

Because the human infant is wholly dependent on its mother or caretaker for all physical and emotional needs, the strength of the attachment bond between the two is important in determining whether a child will survive and develop optimally. The battered child syndrome, for instance, is one of the most dramatic examples of disturbed mothering. In one study of battered children, the incidence of prematurity or serious illness (problems such as Rh disease or diabetes may require immediate separation of mother and child) was 39 percent. Although many factors contribute to the battered child syndrome (such as the mother's own rearing), Klaus suggests that early separation may be a significant factor.

If the separation of mother and child immediately after birth, for medical reasons, can have such dramatic effects on the mother-child affection bond and on future behavior, then it is possible that any separation might have subtle, but still important, effects on the mother-child relationship.

In 1970, after reviewing the information on the separation of mothers and infants, Klaus and John H. Kennell concluded that "it would not be unreasonable to change many of our existing rules and regulations. However, no widespread change should take place until there is strong evidence that what we are doing is damaging, and that a change would be desirable." Since then, Klaus and his colleagues have been collecting that evidence.

They are studying the mothers of fullterm, rather than premature, infants. They are testing the hypothesis that there is a period shortly after birth that is uniquely important for the mother-to-infant attachment in humans. For the study, 28 women were selected and placed in two groups. The 14 mothers in the control group had traditional contact with their infants: a glimpse of the baby shortly after birth, brief contact and identification at 6 to 12 hours and then visits for 20 to 30 minutes every four hours for bottle feeding. In addition to this contact, the other 14 mothers, those in the extended-contact group, were given their nude babies for one hour within the first three hours of birth and also five extra hours of contact each afternoon on the first three days after delivery—a total of 16 hours of extra contact.

To determine if the additional contact altered later behavior behavior, the mothers were asked to return to the hospital one month after delivery for three separate observations. They were interviewed, observed while the child was being examined and filmed while feeding their infants. The extended-care mothers scored higher on questions related to caretaking and seemed to interact more with their infants. They were also more likely to soothe the child if it cried during the physical examination. Films showed that while feeding, the extended-contact mothers spent more time fondling and making eye-to-eye contact with their infants. The eye contact is thought to be especially important, and some researchers have even suggested that eye-to-eye contact between mother and child might be an innate releaser of maternal caretaking behavior.

The researchers concluded that the differences between the two groups in eye contact and tactile stimulation that probably occurred during the first month, in more than 200 feedings, and in numerous other encounters, may have definite effects on the infant. Studies show, for instance, that increased maternal attentiveness facilitates exploratory behavior as well as the early development of cognitive behavior in infants.

The differences between the two groups of mothers were obvious, but still, the researchers said, "It is premature to make any recommendations regarding which regimen is preferable. Caution is recommended before any drastic changes are made in hospital policies. . . . " But since that study was completed, the mothers have been seen again, at one year and at two years. The results of these observations are what has convinced Klaus that changes in hospital practices must be made.

One year after giving birth, the mothers in the two groups continued to be significantly different in their answers to interview questions and in their answers to interview questions and in their behavior during a physical examination of the child. The extended-contact mothers continued to display more fondling behavior and "en face" or eye-to-eye contact behavior. Of the mothers who had returned to work or school, the extended-contact women were more preoccupied with their babies than were the control mothers. "We were surprised at the consistency of the differences over a span of 11 months," said the researchers, who concluded that it was time for "a thorough review and evaluation of our present perinatal practices." And these changes might have to extend to fathers, notes Klaus. A study done in Sweden suggests that fathers who had extended contact with their infants during the first five days after birth were more likely to spend more time interacting with their children.

During the two-year follow-up, mother-child verbal interaction was observed and recorded. After an initial interview, each mother was left alone with her child for a "free play" period in a room containing toys. The situation was taped and analyzed, and several measures of verbal behavior were made: rate, length and variety of utterances, grammatical structure, form class and type or function of sentences.

The differences between the group were again apparent. When talking with their children, the mothers in the extended-contact group had a verbal output distinctly greater in variety and elaboration. Their utterances were somewhat longer and contained more function words (i.e., prepositions and conjunctions that are characteristic of more mature speech).

The extended-contact mothers used more appropriate forms for imparting information, for eliciting a response from the child and for elaboration on simple concepts. They addressed twice as many questions to their children and initiated more teaching behavior. The mothers in the control group used more content words, the type of concise speech one might use in giving basic information. They also used more imperatives, suggesting the use of more controlling behavior.

From these results, it appears that the extended-contact mothers have a greater awareness of the growing needs of their children to assess and interpret their widening external environment. Such sensitivity and increased attention could have a significant bearing on the child's behavior as well as on its future cognitive and linguistic development. Thus, say the researchers, permission for a mother to spend a few additional hours with her newborn infant immediately following delivery may change the linguistic environment she provides for her child in its first years of life, and this, in turn, may affect the child's learning and language far into the future.

Maternal behavior is known to be determined by a multitude of factors—the mother's genetic and cultural background, her relations with her husband and family, the planning and course of her pregnancy and her own mothering as an infant. Considering the number of determinants involved, it is surprising that just 16 hours during the first three days of life can have an effect that lasts for at least two, and perhaps many, years. And, as the researchers note, this extra contact is perhaps one of the most easily manipulated of the determinants of maternal behavior. Since an infant's mental and emotional development is dependent on its mother's behavior and care, it does not seem unreasonable, as Klaus says, that present hospital practice with regard to mothers and their newborns may have to undergo drastic alterations.

13. GIANT IN THE NURSERY—JEAN PIAGET

David Elkind

In February, 1967, Jean Piaget, the Swiss psychologist, arrived at Clark University in Worcester, Mass., to deliver the Heinz Werner Memorial Lectures. The lectures were to be given in the evening, and before the first one a small dinner party was arranged in honor of Piaget and was attended by colleagues, former students and friends. I was invited because of my long advocacy of Piaget's work and because I had spent a year (1964–65) at his Institute for Educational Science in Geneva. Piaget had changed very little since I had last seen him, but he did appear tired and mildly apprehensive.

Although Piaget has lectured all over the world, this particular occasion had special significance. Almost 60 years before, in 1909, another famous European, Sigmund Freud, also lectured at Clark University. Piaget was certainly aware of the historical parallel. He was, moreover, going to speak to a huge American audience in French and, despite the offices of his remarkable translator, Eleanor Duckworth, he must have had some reservations about how it would go.

Piaget's apprehension was apparent during the dinner. For one who is usually a lively and charming dinner companion, he was surprisingly quiet and unresponsive. About half way through the meal there was a small disturbance. The room in which the dinner was held was at a garden level and two boys suddenly appeared at the windows

and began tapping at them. The inclination of most of us, I think, was to shoo them away. Before we had a chance to do that, however, Piaget had turned to face the children. He smiled up at the lads, hunched his shoulders and gave them a slight wave with his hand. They hunched their shoulders and smiled in return, gave a slight wave and disappeared. After a moment, Piaget turned back to the table and began telling stories and entering into animated conversation.

Although I am sure his lecture would have been a success in any case and that the standing ovation he received would have occurred without the little incident, I nonetheless like to think that the encounter with the boys did much to restore his vigor and good humor.

It is Piaget's genius for empathy with children, together with true intellectual genius, that has made him the outstanding child psychologist in the world today and one destined to stand beside Freud with respect to his contributions to psychology, education and related disciplines. Just as Freud's discoveries of unconscious motivation, infantile sexuality and the stages of psychosexual growth changed our ways of thinking about human personality, so Piaget's discoveries of children's implicit philosophies, the construction of reality by the infant and the stages of mental development have altered our ways of thinking about human intelligence.

The man behind these discoveries is an arresting figure. He is tall and somewhat portly, and his stooped walk, bulky suits and crown of long white hair give him the appearance of a thrice-magnified Einstein. (When he was at the Institute for Advanced Study at Princeton in 1953, a friend of his wife rushed to a window one day and exclaimed, "Look, Einstein!" Madam Piaget looked and replied, "No, just my Piaget.") Piaget's personal trademarks are his meerschaum pipes (now burned deep amber), his navy blue beret and his bicycle.

Meeting Piaget is a memorable experience. Although Piaget has an abundance of Old-World charm and graciousness, he seems to emanate an aura of intellectual presence not unlike the aura of personality presence conveyed by a great actor. While as a psychologist I am unable to explain how this sense of presence is communicated, I am nevertheless convinced that everyone who meets Piaget experiences it. While talking to me, for example, he was able to divine in my remarks and questions a significance and depth of which I was entirely unaware and certainly hadn't intended. Evidently one characteristic of genius is to search for relevance in the apparently commonplace and frivolous.

Piaget's is a superbly disciplined life. He arises early each morning, sometimes as early as 4 A.M., and writes four or more publishable pages on square sheets of white paper in an even, small hand. Later in the morning he may teach classes and attend meetings. His afternoons include long walks during which he thinks about the problems he is currently confronting. He says, "I always like to think on a problem before reading about it." In the evenings, he reads and retires early. Even on his international trips, Piaget keeps to this schedule.

Each summer, as soon as classes are over, Piaget gathers up the research findings that have been collected by his assistants during the year and departs for the Alps, where he takes up solitary residence in a room in an abandoned farmhouse. The whereabouts of this retreat is as closely guarded as the names of depositors in numbered Swiss bank accounts; only Piaget's family, his longtime colleague Bärbel Inhelder and a trusted secretary know where he is. During the summer Piaget takes walks, meditates, writes *and* writes. Then, when the leaves begin to turn, he descends from the mountains with the several books and articles he has written on his "vacation."

Although Piaget, now in his 72nd year, has been carrying his works down from the mountains for almost 50 summers (he has published more than 30 books and hundreds of articles), it is only within the past decade that his writings have come to be fully appreciated in America. This was due, in part, to the fact that until fairly recently only a few of his books had been translated into English. In addition, American psychology and education were simply not ready for Piaget until the fifties. Now the ideas that Piaget has been advocating for more than 30 years are regarded as exceedingly innovative and even as avant-garde.

His work falls into three more or less distinct periods within each of which he covered an enormous amount of psychological territory and developed a multitude of insights. (Like most creative men, Piaget is hard put to it to say when a particular idea came to him. If he ever came suddenly upon an idea which sent him shouting through the halls, he has never admitted to it.)

During the first period (roughly 1922–29), Piaget explored the extent and depth of children's spontaneous ideas about the physical world and about their own mental processes. He happened upon this line of inquiry while working in Alfred Binet's laboratory school in Paris where he arrived, still seeking a direction for his talents, a year after receiving his doctorate in biological science at the University of Lausanne. It was in the course of some routine intelligence testing that Piaget became interested in what lay behind children's correct, and particularly their incorrect, answers. To clarify the origins of these answers he began to interview the children in the open-ended manner he had learned while serving a brief internship at Bleuler's psychiatric clinic in Zurich. This semiclinical interview procedure, aimed at revealing the processes by which a child arrives at a particular reply to a test question, has become a trademark of Piagetian research investigation.

What Piaget found with this method of inquiry was that children not only reasoned differently from adults but also that they had quite different world-views, literally different philosophies. This led Piaget to attend to those childish remarks and questions which most adults find amusing or nonsensical. Just as Freud used seemingly accidental slips of the tongue and pen as evidence for unconscious motivations, so Piaget has employed the "cute" sayings of children to demonstrate the existence of ideas quite foreign to the adult mind.

Piaget had read in the recollections of a deaf mute (recorded by William James) that as a child he had regarded the sun and moon as gods and believed they followed him about. Piaget sought to verify this recollection by interviewing children on the subject, and he found that many youngsters do believe that the sun and moon follow them when they are out for a walk. Similar remarks Piaget either overheard or was told about led to a large number of investigations which revealed, among many similar findings, that young children believe that anything which moves is alive, that the names of objects reside in the objects themselves and that dreams come in through the window at night.

Such beliefs, Piaget pointed out in an early article entitled "Children's Philosophies," are not unrelated to but rather derive from an implicit animism and artificialism with many parallels to primi-

tive and Greek philosophies. In the child's view, objects like stones and clouds are imbued with motives, intentions and feelings, while mental events such as dreams and thoughts are endowed with corporality and force. Children also believe that everything has a purpose and that everything in the world is made by and for man. (My 4-year-old son asked me why we have snow and answered his own question by saying, "It is for children to play in.")

The child's animism and artificialism help to explain his famous and often unanswerable "why" questions. It is because children believe that everything has a purpose that they ask, "Why is grass green?" and "Why do the stars shine?" The parent who attempts to answer such questions with a physical explanation has missed the point.

In addition to disclosing the existence of children's philosophies during this first period, Piaget also found the clue to the egocentrism of childhood. In observing young children at play at the *Maison des Petits,* the modified Montessori school associated with the Institute of Educational Science in Geneva, Piaget noted a peculiar lack of social orientation which was also present in their conversation and in their approaches to certain intellectual tasks. A child would make up a new word ("stocks" for socks and stockings) and just assume that everyone knew what he was talking about as if this were the conventional name for the objects he had in mind. Likewise, Piaget noted that when two nursery school children were at play they often spoke *at* rather than *to* one another and were frequently chattering on about two quite different and unrelated topics. Piaget observed, moreover, that when he stood a child of 5 years opposite him, the child who could tell his own right and left nevertheless insisted that Piaget's right and left hands were directly opposite his own.

In Piaget's view, all of these behaviors can be explained by the young child's inability to put himself in another person's position and to take that person's point of view. Unlike the egocentric adult, who can take another person's point of view but does not, the egocentric child does not take another person's viewpoint because he cannot. This conception of childish egocentrism has produced a fundamental alteration in our evaluation of the preschool child's behavior. We now appreciate that it is intellectual immaturity and not moral perversity which makes, for example, a young child continue to pester his mother after she has told him she has a headache and wishes to be left alone. The preschool child is simply unable to put himself in his mother's position and see things from her point of view.

The second period of Piaget's investigations began when, in 1929, he sought to trace the origins of the child's spontaneous mental growth to the behavior of infants; in this case, his own three children, Jacqueline, Lucienne and Laurent. Piaget kept very detailed records of their behavior and of their performance on a series of ingenious tasks which he invented and presented to them. The books resulting from these investigations, "The Origins of Intelligence in Children," "Play, Dreams and Imitation in Children" and "The Construction of Reality in the Child" are now generally regarded as classics in the field and have been one of the major forces behind the scurry of research activity in the area of infant behavior now current both in America and abroad. The publication of these books in the middle and late nineteen-thirties marked the end of the second phase of Piaget's work.

Some of the most telling observations Piaget made during this period had to do with what he called the *conservation of the object* (using the word conservation to con-vey the idea of permanence). To the older child and to the adult, the existence of objects and persons who are not immediately present is taken as self-evident. The child at school knows that while he is working at his desk his mother is simultaneously at home and his father is at work. This is not the case for the young infant playing in his crib, for whom out of sight is literally out of mind. Piaget observed that when an infant 4 or 5 months old is playing with a toy which subsequently rolls out of sight (behind another toy) but is still within reach, the infant ceases to look for it. The infant behaves as if the toy had not only disappeared but as if it had gone entirely out of existence.

This helps to explain the pleasure infants take in the game of peek-a-boo. If the infant believed that the object existed when it was not seen, he would not be surprised and delighted at its re-emergence and there would be no point to the game. It is only during the second year of life, when children begin to represent objects mentally, that they seek after toys that have disappeared from view. Only then do they attribute an independent existence to objects which are not present to their senses.

The third and major phase of Piaget's endeavors began about 1940 and continues until the present day. During this period Piaget has studied the development in children and adolescents of those mental abilities which gradually enable the child to construct a world-view which is in conformance with reality as seen by adults. He has, at the same time, been concerned with how children acquire the adult versions of various concepts such as number, quantity and speed. Piaget and his colleagues have amassed, in the last 28 years, an astounding amount of information about the thinking of children and adolescents which is only now beginning to be used by psychologists and educators.

Two discoveries made during this last period are of particular importance both because they were so unexpected and because of their relevance for education. It is perhaps fair to say that education tends to focus upon the static aspects of reality rather than upon its dynamic transformations. The child is taught how and what things are but not the conditions under which they change or remain the same. And yet the child is constantly confronted with change and alteration. His view of the world alters as he grows in height and perceptual acuity. And the world changes. Seasons come and go, trees gain and lose their foliage, snow falls and melts. People change, too. They may change over brief time periods in mood and over long periods in weight and hair coloration or fullness. The child receives a static education while living amidst a world in transition.

Piaget's investigations since 1940 have focused upon how the child copes with change, how he comes to distinguish between the permanent and the transient and between appearance and reality. An incident that probably played a part in initiating this line of investigation occurred during Piaget's short-lived flirtation with the automobile. (When his children were young Piaget learned to drive and bought a car, but he gave it up for his beloved bicycle after a couple of years.) He took his son for a drive and Laurent asked the name of the mountain they were passing. The mountain was the Salève, the crocodile-shaped mass that dominates the city of Geneva. Laurent was in fact familiar with the mountain and its name because he could see it from his garden, although from a different perspective. Laurent's question brought home to Piaget the fact that a child has difficulty in dealing with the results of transformations whether they are brought about by an alteration in the object itself or by the child's movement with respect to the object.

The methods Piaget used to study how the child comes to deal with transformations are ingenuously simple and can be used by any interested parent or teacher. These methods all have to do with testing the child's abilities to discover that a quantity remains the same across a change in its appearance. In other words, that the quantity is conserved.

To give just one illustration from among hundreds, a child is shown two identical drinking glasses filled equally full with orangeade and he is asked to say whether there is the "same to drink" in the two glasses. After the child says that this is the case, the orangeade from one glass is poured into another which is taller and thinner so that the orangeade now reaches a higher level. Then the child is asked to say whether there is the same amount to drink in the two differently shaped glasses. Before the age of 6 or 7, most children say that the tall, narrow glass has more orangeade. The young child cannot deal with the transformation and bases his judgment on the static features of the orangeade, namely the levels.

How does the older child arrive at the notion that the amounts of orangeade in the two differently shaped glasses is the same? The answer, according to Piaget, is that he discovers the equality with the aid of reason. If the child judges only on the basis of appearances he cannot solve the problem. When he compares the two glasses with respect to width he must conclude that the wide glass has more while if he compares them with respect to the level of the orangeade he must conclude that the tall glass has more. There is then no way on the basis of appearance that he can solve the problem. If, on the other hand, the child reasons that there was the same in the two glasses before and that nothing was added or taken away during the pouring, he concludes that both glasses still have the same drink although this does not appear to be true.

On the basis of this and many similar findings, Piaget argues that much of our knowledge about reality comes to us not from without like the wail of a siren but rather from within by the force of our own logic.

It is hard to overemphasize the importance of this fact, because it is so often forgotten, particularly in education. For those who are not philosophically inclined, it appears that our knowledge of things comes about rather directly as if our mind simply copied the forms, colors and textures of things. From this point of view the mind acts as a sort of mirror which is limited to reflecting the reality which is presented to it. As Piaget's research has demonstrated, however, the mind operates not as a passive mirror but rather an an active artist.

The portrait painter does not merely copy what he sees, he interprets his subject. Before even commencing the portrait, the artist learns a great deal about the individual subject and does not limit himself to studying the face alone. Into the portrait goes not only what the artist sees but also what he knows about his subject. A good portrait is larger than life because it carries much more information than could ever be conveyed by a mirror image.

In forming his spontaneous conception of the world, therefore, the child does more than reflect what is presented to his senses. His image of reality is in fact a portrait or reconstruction of the world and not a simple copy of it. It is only by reasoning about the information which the child receives from the external world that he is able to overcome the transient nature of sense experience and arrive at that awareness of permanence within apparent change that is the mark of adult thought. The importance of reason in the child's spontaneous construction of his world is thus one of the major discoveries of Piaget's third period.

The second major discovery of this time has to do with the nature of the elementary school child's reasoning ability. Long before there was anything like a discipline of child psychology, the age of 6 to 7 was recognized as *the age of reason.* It was also assumed, however, that once the child attained the age of reason, there were no longer any substantial differences between his reasoning abilities and those of adolescents and adults. What Piaget discovered is that this is in fact not the case. While the elementary school child is indeed able to reason, his reasoning ability is limited in a very important respect—he can reason about things but not about verbal propositions.

If a child of 8 or 9 is shown a series of three blocks, ABC, which differ in size, then he can tell by looking at them, and without comparing them directly, that if A is greater than B and B greater than C, then A is greater than C. When the same child is given his problem, "Helen is taller than Mary and Mary is taller than Jane, who is the tallest of the three?" the result is quite different. He cannot solve it despite the fact that it repeats in words the problem with the blocks. Adolescents and adults, however, encounter no difficulty with this problem because they can reason about verbal propositions as well as about things.

This discovery that children think differently from adults even after attaining the age of reason has educational implications which are only now beginning to be applied. Robert Karplus, the physicist who heads the Science Curriculum Improvement Study at Berkeley, has pointed out that most teachers use verbal propositions in teaching elementary school children. At least some of their instruction is thus destined to go over the heads of their pupils. Karplus and his coworkers are now attempting to train teachers to instruct children at a verbal level which is appropriate to their level of mental ability.

An example of the effects of the failure to take into account the difference between the reasoning abilities of children and adults comes from the New Math experiment. In building materials for the New Math, it was hoped that the construction of a new language would facilitate instruction of set concepts. The new language has been less than successful and the originators of the New Math are currently attempting to devise a physical model to convey the New Math concepts. It is likely that the new language created to teach the set concepts failed because it was geared to the logic of adults rather than to the reasoning of children. Attention to the research on children's thinking carried out during Piaget's third period might have helped to avoid some of the difficulties of the "New Math" program.

In the course of these many years of research into children's thinking, Piaget has elaborated a general theory of intellectual development which, in its scope and comprehensiveness, rivals Freud's theory of personality development. Piaget proposes that intelligence—adaptive thinking and action—develops in a sequence of stages that is related to age. Each stage sees the elaboration of new mental abilities which set the limits and determine the character of what can be learned during that period. (Piaget finds incomprehensible Harvard psychologist Jerome Bruner's famous hypothesis to the effect that "any subject can be taught effectively in some intellectually honest form to any child at any stage of development.") Although Piaget believes that the order in which the stages appear holds true for all children, he also believes that the ages at which the stages evolve will depend upon the native endowment of the child and upon the quality of the physical and social environment in which he is reared. In a very real sense, then, Piaget's is both a nature *and* a nurture theory.

The first stage in the development of in-telligence (usually 0–2 years) Piaget calls the sensory-motor period, and it is concerned with the evolution of those abilities necessary to construct and reconstruct objects. To illustrate, Piaget observed that when he held a cigarette case in front of his daughter Jaqueline (who was 8 months old at the time) and then dropped it, she did not follow the trajectory of the case but continued looking at his hand. Even at 8 months (Lucienne and Laurent succeeded in following the object at about 5 months but had been exposed to more experiments than Jacqueline) she was not able to reconstruct the path of the object which she had seen dropped in front of her.

Toward the end of this period, however, Jacqueline was even able to reconstruct the position of objects which had undergone hidden displacement. When she was 19 months old Piaget placed a coin in his hand and then placed his hand under a coverlet where he dropped the coin before removing his hand. Jacqueline first looked in his hand and then immediately lifted the coverlet and found the coin. This reconstruction was accomplished with the aid of an elementary form of reasoning. The coin was in the hand, the hand was under the coverlet, the coin was not in the hand so the coin is under the coverlet. Such reasoning, it must be said, is accomplished without the aid of language and by means of mental images.

The second stage (usually 2–7 years), which Piaget calls the preoperational stage, bears witness to the elaboration of the symbolic function, those abilities which have to do with representing things. The presence of these new abilities is shown by the gradual acquisition of language, the first indications of dreams and night terrors, the advent of symbolic play (two sticks at right angles are an airplane) and the first attempts at drawing and graphic representation.

At the beginning of this stage the child tends to identify words and symbols with the objects they are intended to represent. He is upset if someone tramps on a stone which he has designated as a turtle. And he believes that names are as much a part of objects as their color and form. (The child at this point is like the old gentleman who, when asked why noodles are called noodles, replied that "they are white like noodles, soft like noodles and taste like noodles so we call them noodles.")

By the end of this period the child can clearly distinguish between words and symbols and what they represent. He now recognizes that names are arbitrary designations. The child's discovery of the arbitrariness of names is often manifested in the "name calling" so prevalent during the early school years.

At the next stage (usually 7–11 years) the child acquires what Piaget calls concrete operations, internalized actions that permit the child to do "in his head" what before he would have had to accomplish through real actions. Concrete operations enable the child to think about things. To illustrate, in one study Piaget presented 5-, 6-, and 7-year-old children with six sticks in a row and asked them to take the same number of sticks from a pile on the table. The young children solved the problem by placing their sticks beneath the sample and matching the sticks one by one. The older children merely picked up the six sticks and held them in their hands. The older children had counted the sticks mentally and hence felt no need to actually match them with the sticks in the row. It should be said that even the youngest children were able to count to six, so that this was not a factor in their performance.

Concrete operations also enable children to deal with the relations among classes of things. In another study Piaget presented 5-, 6- and 7-year-old children with a box containing 20 white and seven brown wooden beads. Each child was first asked if there were more white or more brown beads and all were able to say that there were more white than brown beads. Then Piaget asked, "Are there more white or more wooden beads?" The young children could not fathom the question and replied that "there are more white than brown beads." For such children classes are not regarded as abstractions but are thought of as concrete places. (I once asked a pre-operational child if he could be a Protestant and an American at the same time, to which he replied, "No," and then as an afterthought, "only if you move.")

When a child thought of a bead in the white "place" he could not think of it as being in the wooden "place" since objects cannot be in two places at once. He could only compare the white with the brown "places." The older children, who had attained concrete operations, encountered no difficulty with the task and readily replied that "there are more wooden than white beads because all of the beads are wooden and only some are white." By the end of the concrete operational period, children are remarkably adept at doing thought problems and at combining and dividing class concepts.

During the last stage (usually 12–15 years) there gradually emerge what Piaget calls formal operations and which, in effect, permit adolescents to think about their thoughts, to construct ideals and to reason realistically about the future. Formal operations also enable young people to reason about contrary-to-fact propositions. If, for example, a child is asked to assume that coal is white he is likely to reply, "But coal is black," whereas the adolescent can accept the contrary-to-fact assumption and reason from it.

Formal operational thought also makes possible the understanding of metaphor. It is for this reason that political and other satirical cartoons are not understood until adolescence. The child's inability to understand metaphor helps to explain why books such as "Alice in Wonderland" and "Gulliver's Travels" are enjoyed at different levels during childhood than in adolescence and adulthood, when their social significance can be understood.

No new mental systems emerge after the formal operations, which are the common coin of adult thought. After adolescence, mental growth takes the form—it is hoped —of a gradual increase in wisdom.

This capsule summary of Piaget's theory of intellectual development would not be complete without some words about Piaget's position with respect to language and thought. Piaget regards thought and language as different but closely related systems. Language, to a much greater extent than thought, is determined by particular forms of environmental stimulation. Inner-city Negro children, who tend to be retarded in language development, are much less retarded with respect to the ages at which they attain concrete operations. Indeed, not only inner-city children but children in bush Africa, Hong Kong and Appalachia all attain concrete operations at about the same age as middle-class children in Geneva and Boston.

Likewise, attempts to teach children concrete operations have been almost uniformly unsuccessful. This does not mean that these operations are independent of the environment but only that their development takes time and can be nourished by a much wider variety of environmental nutriments than is true for the growth of language, which is dependent upon much more specific forms of stimulation.

Language is, then, deceptive with respect to the thought. Teachers of middle-class children are often misled, by the verbal facility of these youngsters, into believing that they understand more than they actually comprehend. (My 5-year-old asked me what my true identity was and as I tried to recover my composure he explained that Clark Kent was Superman's true identity.) At the other end, the teachers of inner-city children are often fooled by the language handicaps of these children into thinking that they have much lower mental ability than they actually possess. It is appropriate, therefore, that preschool programs for the disadvantaged should focus upon training these children in language and perception rather than upon trying to teach them concrete operations.

The impact which the foregoing Piagetian discoveries and conceptions is having upon education and child psychology has come as something of a shock to a good many educators and [to] psychological research in America, which relies heavily upon statistics, electronics and computers, Piaget's studies of children's thinking seem hardly a step beyond the prescientific baby biographies kept by such men as Charles Darwin and Bronson Alcott. Indeed, in many of Piaget's research papers he supports his conclusions simply with illustrative examples of how children at different age levels respond to his tasks.

Many of Piaget's critics have focused upon his apparently casual methodology and have argued that while Piaget has arrived at some original ideas about children's thinking, his research lacks scientific rigor. It is likely that few, if any, of Piaget's research reports would have been accepted for publication in American psychological journals.

Other critics have taken somewhat the opposite tack. Jerome Bruner, who has done so much to bring Piaget to the attention of American social scientists, acknowledges the fruitfulness of Piaget's methods, modifications of which he has employed in his own investigations. But he argues against Piaget's theoretical interpretations. Bruner believes that Piaget has "missed the heart" of the problem of change and permanence or conservation in children's thinking. In the case of the orangeade poured into a different-sized container, Bruner argues that it is not reason, or mental operations, but some "internalized verbal formula that shields him [the child] from the overpowering appearance of the visual displays." Bruner seems to believe that the syntactical rules of language rather than logic can account for the child's discovery that a quantity remains unchanged despite alterations in its appearance.

Piaget is willing to answer his critics but only when he feels that the criticism is responsible and informed. With respect to his methods, their casualness is only apparent. Before they set out collecting data, his students are given a year of training in the art of interviewing children. They learn to ask questions without suggesting the answers and to test, by counter-suggestion, the strength of the child's conviction. Many of Piaget's studies have now been repeated with more rigorous procedures by other investigators all over the world and the results have been remarkably consistent with Piaget's findings. Attempts are currently under way to build a new intelligence scale on the basis of the Piaget tests, many of which are already in widespread use as evaluative procedures in education.

When it comes to criticisms of his theoretical views, Piaget is remarkably open and does not claim to be infallible. He frequently invites scholars who are in genuine disagreement with him to come to Geneva for a year so that the differences can be discussed and studied in depth. He has no desire to form a cult and says, in fact, "To the extent that there are Piagetians, to that extent have I failed." Piaget's lack of dogmatism is illustrated in his response to Bruner:

"Bruner does say that I 'missed the heart' of the conservation problem, a problem I have been working on for the last 30 years. He is right, of course, but that does not mean that he himself has understood it in a much shorter time.... Adults, just like children, need time to reach the right ideas ... This is the great mystery of development, which is irreducible to an accumulation of isolated learning acquisitions. Even psychology cannot be learned or constructed in a short time." (Despite his disclaimer, Piaget has offered a comprehensive theory of how the child arrives at conservation and this theory has received much research support.)

Piaget would probably agree with those who are critical about premature applications of his work to education. He finds particularly disturbing the efforts by some American educators to accelerate children intellectually. When he was giving his other 1967 lectures, in New York, he remarked:

"If we accept the fact that there are stages of development, another question arises which I call 'the American question,' and I am asked it every time I come here. If there are stages that children reach at given norms of ages can we accelerate the stages? Do we have to go through each one of these stages, or can't we speed it up a bit? Well, surely, the answer is yes ... but how far can we speed them up? ... I have a hypothesis which I am so far incapable of proving: probably the organization of operations has an optimal time ... For example, we know that it takes 9 to 12 months before babies develop the notion that an object is still there even when a screen is placed in front of it. Now kittens go through the same sub-stages but they do it in three months— so they're six months ahead of the babies. Is this an advantage or isn't it?

"We can certainly see our answer in one sense. The kitten is not going to go much further. The child has taken longer, but he is capable of going further so it seems to me that the nine months were not for nothing ... It is probably possible to accelerate, but maximal acceleration is not desirable. There seems to be an optimal time. What this optimal time is will surely depend upon each individual and on the subject matter. We still need a great deal of research to know what the optimal time would be."

Piaget's stance against using his findings as a justification for accelerating children intellectually recalls a remark made by Freud when he was asked whatever became of those bright, aggressive shoeshine boys one encounters in city streets. Freud's reply was, "They become cobblers." In Piaget's terms they get to a certain point earlier but they don't go as far. And the New York educator Eliot Shapiro has pointed out that one of the Negro child's problems is that he is forced to grow up and take responsibility too soon and doesn't have time to be a child.

Despite some premature and erroneous applications of his thinking to education, Piaget has had an over-all effect much more positive than negative. His findings about children's understanding of scientific and mathematical concepts are being used as guidelines for new curricula in these subjects. And his tests are being more and more widely used to evaluate educational outcomes. Perhaps the most significant and widespread positive effect that Piaget has had upon education is in the changed attitudes on the part of teachers who have been exposed to his thinking. After becoming acquainted with Piaget's work, teachers can never again see children in quite the same way as they had before. Once teachers begin to look at children from the Piagetian perspective they can also appreciate his views with regard to the aims of education.

"The principal goal of education," he once said, "is to create men who are capable of doing new things, not simply of repeating what other generations have done—men who are creative, inventive and discoverers. The second goal of education is to form minds which can be critical, can verify, and not accept everything they are offered. The great danger today is of slogans, collective opinions, ready-made trends of thought. We have to be able to resist individually, to criticize, to distinguish between what is proven and what is not. So we need pupils who are active, who learn early to find out by themselves, partly by their own spontaneous activity and partly through materials we set up for them; who learn early to tell what is verifiable and what is simply the first idea to come to them."

At the beginning of his eighth decade, Jean Piaget is as busy as ever. A new book of his on memory will be published soon and another on the mental functions in the preschool child is in preparation. The International Center for Genetic Epistemology, which Piaget founded in 1955—with a grant from the Rockefeller Foundation, continues to draw scholars from around the world who wish to explore with Piaget the origin of scientific concepts. As Professor of Experimental Psychology at the University of Geneva, Piaget also continues to teach courses and conduct seminars.

And his students still continue to collect the data which at the end of the school year Piaget will take with him up to the mountains. The methods employed by his students today are not markedly different from those which were used by their predecessors decades ago. While there are occasional statistics, there are still no electronics or computers. In an age of moon shots and automation, the remarkable discoveries of Jean Piaget are evidence that in the realm of scientific achievement, technological sophistication is still no substitute for creative genius.

14. AN INTERVIEW WITH JAMES S. COLEMAN ON THE PROBLEMS OF YOUTH

Harold G. Shane

In the following interview, James S. Coleman, well-known to educators for the 1966 report, *Equality of Educational Opportunity* (familiarly known as the *Coleman Report*), discusses youth and their problems. More recently, Dr. Coleman, who is professor of sociology at the University of Chicago, has served as the Chairman of the Panel on Youth for the President's Science Advisory Committee. The influential report of this Committee, *Youth: Transition to Adulthood,* was published by the University of Chicago Press in 1974. It already has had an important impact upon the thinking of persons at the secondary level and in higher education.

Q. Dr. Coleman, the 1938 publication of the American Council on Education, *Youth Tell Their Story,* which was prepared by Howard M. Bell, listed the following 10 needs or problems, identified by a study of 13,500 Maryland youth, aged 16 through 24: (1) the need to equalize educational opportunities, (2) the problem of finding employment, (3) the need for greater economic security, (4) more relevant guidance, (5) better job training, (6) changes in secondary education so that schooling would better fit the needs of youth, (7) the matter of appropriate uses of leisure time, (8) better personal and social hygiene, (9) youth's indifference to civic responsibilities, and (10) the need for more community planning for youth.

Reprinted from *Today's Education: NEA Journal,* by permission of publisher and author, pp. 74–80.

After the 37 years that have intervened, do you believe that many of these problems continue to beset our 14- to 24-year-olds?

A. Yes, it seems striking to me that there are so many similarities between the kinds of problems that youth experienced in the 1930's and the difficulties they are experiencing now.

However, the problem of equalizing educational opportunities exists now in a way that wasn't yet conceived of in the 1930's. This is because discussions of equalization of opportunities at that time ignored young Blacks. Many of them were still hidden on farms in the South. They are no longer hidden, and the problem of equalizing educational opportunities between Blacks and Whites compounds the problem of equalizing educational opportunities between socioeconomic groups. Another item among the 10 that continues to confront young people regardless of whether they have low or high educational opportunity is this problem of the organization of secondary education mentioned in the 1938 study. It is still with us.

Bell's study made the implicit projection that before long virtually all students would be in school until age 18. Consequently, there had to be some conception of how we would provide a common education for all youth through senior high school. What this education should be remains an unsolved problem.

Q. Why do you think these problems persist despite the attempted social reforms of the past 40 years?

A. I believe one of the reasons is that

society has less need for young people than it ever had before. The lack of a productive, responsible role for youth—other than that of student—diminishes opportunity for young people. Also, in some ways, adults have collectively used the schools to conceal a kind of indifference on their part toward solving the serious kinds of problems of growing up that youth have—problems which are not solved by having schools merely concern themselves with reading, writing, and arithmetic.

Q. Would you say that the present apparent disintegration of the family unit—as opposed to the close family ties of the past—has been basically the result of a changed economic relationship? I refer to the present largely urban world in which parents no longer depend on children for help.

A. Yes. In the past, the family was an economically productive unit, and the child was an integral part of it. Not long ago, I bought a farm, which was not very productive but does have some cows on it. My 18-year-old son has become much more important to that farm than I am. As a consequence, he has a completely different conception of himself than if he hadn't had this kind of experience.

Q. Would you identify some of the most important fears, concerns, and problems of American youth today?

A. These differ considerably from one person to another depending on each individual's economic situation. A peculiar problem that began to appear in the 1960's, I think, is the problem of the young in affluent families. I refer to youth whose fathers, having solved the problem of economic security, have left their children with the question of "Exactly how should I make my mark?" Many middle-class young people in such circumstances experience a kind of alienation from society and demand a different pattern than that of previous generations who went to the university, got the best job they could, and worked for success in a material sense. Rejection of this standard pattern has manifested itself in alternative schools, in experimental schools, and in counterculture activities.

Q. What about the children of the poor or of the lower-middle-class families, groups which include a large portion of black youth?

A. Their problems, like those of most youth in the 1930's, involve economic matters: getting a good job or at least getting a better job than their parents had. Some of these problems probably are easier to solve than the dilemmas of affluence, because, unlike alienated youth, poor and lower-middle-class youth know where to go and how to go about succeeding, even if they often encounter difficulties.

Q. A few moments ago, you used the term *alienation*. In recent years, a great deal has been written about the alienation of youth, Dr. Coleman. What changes, if any, do you sense in the tendency of youth today to reject the world of the 1970's? Is there now a greater rejection by youth or an increasing acceptance of things-as-they-are than was the case in the 1960's?

A. There's more acceptance of our contemporary society now than four or five years ago; and the reason for that, I believe, has to do with diminished economic security. In the early 1960's, the opportunities in the world, like its resources, seemed limitless, and mundane problems of making a living appeared trivial. Young people could afford to concentrate their energies on the ills of the world.

However, as economic problems arose and began to worsen for young college graduates and for those enrolled in graduate education, their attention became much more riveted on their personal difficulties and uncertain economic future. In other words, the very limiting of their horizons tends to shift young people's attention away from social inequalities and world problems —which are especially frustrating, since they're not problems a young person (or any individual) can solve anyway—to their own problems, which they can take action to solve.

Q. Would you say that youth today are more mature and responsible than youth prior to the time our colleges erupted with protests, demonstrations, and demands for academic reforms?

A. I don't think youth are any more responsible now than in the past. One major deficiency in educational institutions as they currently exist is that they do little to inculcate responsibility. During the past several generations as the family and the neighborhood tried to transfer many of their functions to the educational system, the schools, unfortunately, either didn't or couldn't take them up.

Young people will become more responsible only when they are given more opportunities to exercise responsibility, and not before. As I just said, they now behave differently because they are more concerned with their own socioeconomic problems than with difficult-to-solve world problems or with the problems of other persons.

We can help youth to become more mature and more responsible, but to do so we have to change in one way or another the kind of educational institutions in which they spend their time.

Q. Let me explore the changing behavior of youth a bit more. In the perspective of the past decade, do you feel that our young people are becoming more conservative?

A. Yes, they are decidedly more conservative than they were in the 1960's, but it's hard to be precise about the reasons. I've already mentioned the shift to focusing on one's own problems rather than on world problems. Then another thing which

has tended to generate more conservatism and that probably will continue to do so for some time is the fact that young people are no longer an increasing fraction of the population, nor will they continue to increase in absolute numbers. In the 1960's, the growth in numbers of youth was enormous because of the baby boom that began in 1946. But now the baby boom has ended, and the number of young people will first remain constant and then go down slightly over the next 10 or 15 years.

Q. I assume that this would help to explain the lessening of radical and very liberal trends on the U.S. campus in the last two or three years.

A. Yes, I think so.

Q. I've read in several publications that young people are reaching puberty at least one year earlier than they did in the 1930's. Dr. Coleman, does this trend suggest that there is a growing gap between the physical maturity and the socioemotional maturity of youth?

A. Well, early puberty creates a gap between physical maturity and economic independence. Two trends are going in opposite directions. Seventy-five or 100 years ago, economic independence and physical maturity more or less coincided. The present gap is essentially the gap between childhood and adult life which we once called adolescence and which we now call youth.

Q. In her 1973 publication, *Dialogues with Youth,* my wife, Catherine, reported that a number of secondary students whom she interviewed felt that counseling and guidance services often were inept, lacking in relevance, and out of phase with the actual interests and motivations of teenagers. Do your experiences suggest that our schools, with the best of intentions, sometimes may be counseling students for the world of 1955 or '65 rather than the world of 1985?

A. My own experience and impressions are that high school counseling and guidance services are almost solely directed toward two activities: psychological counseling for a small fraction of students and guidance for the college-bound. Neither of these is appropriate for a large number of young people.

Unfortunately, many counselors have never had extensive experience outside the walls of the educational institutions of our society and therefore don't know how to provide guidance about the world of work. They can't be very helpful, for example, to young people who want no more formal education.

I would argue that it can be extremely valuable for a large number of young people to have a year of maturing work and service experience between high school and college. One reason they so rarely have such opportunities is because not enough counselors in high school are prepared to guide them in this area.

Q. Your comment prompts me to ask another question. What do you consider to be some alternatives to traditional content in secondary and in postsecondary education that might better serve youth?

A. To answer that question, one has to look closely at the role of schools in society. Traditionally, the school as an institution has been designed to provide the kinds of things which are not provided in naturally existing social institutions or structures, such as the home or the neighborhood. The school, as we know it today, came into being in response to the need to teach skills and competencies that many homes could not provide.

Q. Have changing times created a need for different competencies?

A. Yes. For example, since many homes or neighborhoods no longer provide the kinds of situations that develop responsibility, schools ought to give youth the chance to exercise real responsibility. As adults, they will need to have a well-developed capacity to act responsibly when other persons are dependent upon them. They will also need to be able to work cooperatively and interdependently with others. Schools, however, are generally not designed in any way for systematic development of responsibility or for interdependent work, except perhaps for certain extracurricular activities.

Consequently, we must reexamine the whole question of what the function of an educational institution in modern society should be. At the start, we need to ask ourselves, "What is it that other institutions in modern society leave undone?" Finding answers to these questions will eventually help us to decide what alternative kinds of content are needed in high school and college.

Q. Now let me ask, in what ways might the organizational structure of secondary schools, colleges, and universities be modified so as better to meet the needs of youth?

A. I'm glad you phrased the question the way you did. We must learn to look at the *whole* period of education from secondary school through college and raise the question, "What organizational structure would be most useful for young people?"

The organizational structure that currently exists is not the best for a large number of young people—particularly not for middle-class young people. I refer to the organizational structure in which young people devote full time to education through the end of college and, in some cases, up through graduate education.

Q. What do you find undesirable about that?

A. I think young people often get "school weary" and drop out because they have been cast in one role, the student role, for too long a time. They are forever being trained to act but never given the opportunity to act.

I believe that it would be a wise course for us to provide institutionalized remedies for this problem. There have been some movements in the direction of organizational change already, in the sense that some high schools allow seniors to spend part or all of their senior year at a regular job. Seniors, regardless of whether they're going to go on to the university or not, thus have some experience in various kinds of action- or service-learning settings.

An organizational change that I mentioned earlier would be extremely wise. This is to have a year of leave from education between high school and college or between the eleventh grade and twelfth grade or between the first and second year in college. The exact time isn't as important as the idea of interrupting the sequence of education with some other kind of activity—interrupting it in such a way that a person has experience in a role other than that of student.

Q. A number of social commentators, such as Alvin Toffler, have urged that our children and youth engage in socially useful work, which is often called "action" or "service" learning. Will you give your interpretation of *service learning,* Dr. Coleman, as you used it a moment ago and indicate the extent to which you believe it might provide alternatives to traditional secondary education?

A. *Action* or *service learning* as these terms are now used is very similar to some of the recommendations that our panel made with regard to the reorganization of secondary and postsecondary education. Our recommendations included both the possibility of some kind of responsible productive work throughout the period of high school and the period of college, and the possibility of a fulltime period of responsible work during an intervening year between high school and college.

We know that projects like the Peace Corps, the Civilian Conservation Corps of the 1930's, and the current Youth Conservation Corps were and are successful. We need both more viable federal programs and more federally sponsored opportunities of this kind. At present only about 20,000 young persons can take part each year in service or action learning programs, such as VISTA and the Peace Corps. This compares with an annual population of 18-year-olds that numbers about 4 million.

Q. This leads directly to another related question. For the past several years, a number of educators have been questioning the merit of uniform compulsory school attendance beyond age 15. Some even feel that schooling might, in rare instances, be interrupted at age 13 or 14. If steps are taken to avoid exploitation of the young and a revival of child labor, what is your position with regard to an earlier school-leaving age than is now customary?

A. I think compulsory education in general is a bad thing. In fact, I believe that *anything* compulsory is bad. However, if a policy change were made to do away with compulsory education or to lower the school-leaving age to 14 or 15, it would weaken equality of educational opportunity.

Q. I'm sure the readers of *Today's Education* would like you to explain in more detail why this might be so.

A. Let me be explicit. It would have no effect on the middle-class young people who are now feeling the strains of too much school. But changing present school attendance laws would have a primary effect on lower-class young people, who already tend to drop out of high school.

I think it would be valuable to have more flexible attendance policies, but those flexible policies cannot be laissez-faire policies which merely change the age of compulsory attendance. If there is a change in which there is some alternation of school and work, then other necessary changes would need to be made to insure equality of educational opportunity. By *equality of educational opportunity* in this case, I mean that we need specific procedures for encouraging youth to return to school after they have left. This would require not only improved guidance services but institutionalized structures and program changes to facilitate leaving and returning.

Q.   There have been a number of youth studies made between your present one and Howard Bell's 1938 report. Are there studies which have explored the attitudes of adults toward youth rather than youth's attitudes toward military service, the economy, and other things in their world? And have there been any inquiries into teachers' attitudes toward children and youth?

A.   I can't cite any such studies offhand. I think, incidentally, that studies of this sort might be extremely valuable. An essential part of the current problem is simply that adults have mutually agreed to relegate young people to schools. By doing this, adults assume that they then are free to turn their attention to other things.

We must very seriously question whether the adult community can afford to be as inattentive to and as uninterested in young people as it has been.

Q.   Before we terminate our discussion, Dr. Coleman, I'd like to look toward the future by looking backward a bit. How would you amend or modify for the 1970's or for the early 1980's your widely discussed report treating equality of educational opportunity, a report you prepared in the 1960's? Have there been developments or changes of an encouraging or discouraging nature with regard to education equity?

A.   To discuss all the ways I would now modify my study would take much too long. But let me say, in the context of our present discussion, that one of the sources of inequality of educational opportunity at the secondary school level lies in some of the things we have been discussing. It lies in the narrow focusing of education on cognitive skills rather than on all of the capabilities young people will need to have to become adults.

Institutionalized education in America just doesn't give enough attention to those dimensions of learning in which our youth can find the most satisfaction, motivation, and "real world" success. I don't mean that schools should not address themselves to academic matters. Rather, I am saying that because of the very nature of our schools' narrow cognitive focus, disadvantaged young persons are made even more disadvantaged. The kind of modification that I would like to see in secondary and postsecondary education is one that would not reduce or replace academic learning, but would augment it with experiences and activities that use a wider range of abilities and aim toward a broader sense of maturity.

15.   ADULT LIFE CYCLES

Paul T. Libassi

He wants to settle down and even gives it a try—seducing his brother's bride-to-be in a final, single-minded attempt to stabilize his life. But he just can't hack it. Emotional involvement seems beyond him. Love and commitment have no place among his lame feelings of anguish and ennui.

So Robert Dupea is running. From a culture-crammed country estate on a private island in Puget Sound to a cramped California bungalow. From a promising career as a concert pianist to whatever dead-end job seems handiest at the time. Scenery shifts, but nothing changes. Dupea is always quitting things, because, as he says, they'll get bad if he stays.

It takes a moment, but when we meet Dupea on a sun-baked oil field in Bob Rafelson's fine 1970 film, *Five Easy Pieces,* we recognize him. He is that familiar American man—unattached, disassociated, spiritually disenfranchised. The transient, unsettled lifestyle of his 20s is catching up with him. At 32, he feels suffocated by the chaos his "world" is in, and with reason. "If he can't reach a significant start toward settling down by about age 34," says Dr. Daniel Levinson, "his chances of forming a reasonably satisfying life structure are quite small."

Robert Dupea is one of Dr. Levinson's "case histories." A social psychologist affiliated with the Connecticut Mental Health Center and Yale University, Levinson and his team of researchers have "examined" Dupea and the characters of other films, novels and plays, including the movie *Getting Straight,* Eugene O'Neill's *The Iceman Cometh,* Edward Albee's *Who's Afraid of Virginia Wolff,* and John Barth's *Chimera.* Along with the 40 biographies of "real life" individuals, they have used their findings to spell out the stages of normal adult development—something curiously missing from modern textbooks on psychology, as if, somehow, at age 21, development grinds to a halt.

Freud and Piaget scoured the terrain of childhood for clues to why we do the things we do. Others have mapped nuances of growth and development during adolescence. But until psychologist Eric Erikson came along, adulthood was practically regarded as a featureless psychological landscape. Indeed, says UCLA psychiatrist Roger Gould, "Adulthood is still seen as a period of marking time and is not seen as a progression of stages much like the phases of rapid and slow growth of childhood and adolescence."

Along with Dr. Levinson and Harvard psychiatrist George Vaillant, Gould set to work recently to chart the topography of adult development. Their separate studies all stem from Erikson's explorations of postadolescent life, which hinted at psychic terrain as varied and profuse with dimension as life's first 21 years. Three developmental stages, Erikson proposed, stand between adolescence and senescence. Each,

Reprinted with permission from *Science Digest* (April 1976), pp. 35–41. Copyright © 1976, The Hearst Corporation.

he said, is a crucial turning point to be skill-fully negotiated before development pro-ceeds to the next personality plateau.

Achieving *genuine intimacy* is what he identified as the task of 20s. Success or fail-ure in forming "trusting fellowships" and intimacy with a mate can determine whether or not development runs its course to what Erikson termed *generativity.* Dur-ing this phase, spanning, roughly, one's 30s, 40s and early 50s, the goal is staving off stagnation and self-indulgence by forging a commitment to guiding new generations. *Integrity,* the final stage, means coming to grips with the hardest realization of all: the feeling that time is running out and this is "one's one and only life cycle." Failing the challenge, life can end despairingly.

Sweeping and thematic, Erikson's design never quite gets down to cases. He left that for others. Like Erikson, today's life-cycle scholars believe that adult development oc-curs according to a predictable, age-linked timetable and that without a conception of what the scheduled stations and stops are we can't possibly understand adults and the changes their lives go through.

What Levinson, Gould and Vaillant have done for the first time is to spell out exact age spans (within two to three years) for each period and more importantly, to study the interrelationships of each age phase with the others. How phases overlap and interact, says Levinson, is what makes a person unique. Yet, underlying each per-son's individual differences are basic gov-erning principles of development.

Advancing from one stage to the next means meeting specific developmental tasks. Ignoring these challenges and crises can stifle development during early and middle periods. Surmounting them is not only desirable, but essential if one's life structure is to be properly "enlarged, re-formed or radically restructured in order to

express more of the self," according to Le-vinson. He believes that no healthy phase lasts longer than seven to ten years and that stages must follow in sequence to escape developmental impairment.

Levinson's research involved the movie and play characters mentioned earlier along with 40 interviews of real people. Gould conducted about 600 interviews: 300 with psychiatric outpatients at the UCLA Medi-cal Center and 300 with non-patients re-ferred to him by medical students who were also working on the life cycle project. Vail-lant's research is perhaps the most ambi-tious. It involves a 38-year study of about 268 Harvard graduates whose lives have been traced by various Harvard researchers for the four decade period. Every six to twelve months each subject is contacted and asked pertinent questions about his (her) life.

Many of the findings are tentative, based as they are on a narrow range of subjects. More men have been sampled than women and subjects come largely from white, mid-dle-class backgrounds. Yet, though all three studies were conducted independently on different populations in different ways at different times, common themes have emerged. My own amalgam of the results:

16–22: LEAVING HOME

"We have to get away from our parents" is the unavoidably clear motto that Gould found among adolescents on the verge of adulthood. Their predicament, he says, is that they're neither in nor out: they con-sider themselves more as family than as true individuals. For them, the future seems vague and "out there"; complete autonomy seems precarious and frequent rebounds to the nest are common.

Striking out on one's own, it appears, is no all-or-nothing affair, but more like learning to walk all over again. Living away at college, working, footing part of the bills, owning a car are some of the ways that fledglings can try their wings. Peers can also help, to a point, by serving as "the ally that will help them out of the family," Gould learned from his retrospective study of UCLA psychiatric outpatients. But he also found that friendships at this age tend to be short-lived and brittle, particularly "if the intimate person's way of thinking is not identical to their own."

Groping toward independence has its pitfalls. One of the trickiest: early marriages. Getting married and starting a family of one's own, according to the researchers, may seem like escaping the family, but often it just prolongs ties to relatives. Says Levinson: "Even though a young man in this position may be economically self-sufficient and living on his own, he is still on the boundary between the family and the fully adult world, and getting across this boundary is his major developmental task." That balance between adolescence and adulthood usually shifts, the three agree, during one's early 20s.

23–28: GETTING INTO THE ADULT WORLD

This phase, Erikson posited, is dominated by a quest for personal identity and mastering the demands of intimacy. Levinson elaborates: "The overall developmental task is to explore the available possibilities of the adult world, to arrive at an initial definition of oneself as an adult and *to fashion an initial life structure* that provides a viable link between the valued self and the wider adult world."

Adds Vaillant: It's the time "when wives are wooed and won. The adolescent friendships that are to endure into adulthood deepen; the others vanish." And Gould

rounds the picture out: Commitments, for the most part, go unquestioned, extreme emotions are guarded against and self-reliance replaces a dependence on one's peers. "There is a definite feeling," he says, "that 'now' is the time for living as well as growing and building for the future."

Crucial to this passage into adulthood, according to Levinson, is The Dream, each young adult's personal imaginings of himself in the world. Usually cast in an occupational context, this highly personal vision is a vitalizing force that generates excitement and hope in what lies ahead. "Major shifts in life directions at subsequent stages," Levinson believes, "are often occasioned by a reactivation of the sense of betrayal or compromise of the dream."

To help realize their dream, many men in their 20s get what Levinson calls a "mentor," someone eight to 15 years older who takes the young man under his professional wing, shows him the ropes, imparts advice, care and, most importantly, says the Yale psychologist, "bestows his blessing." The relationship depends upon the mentor's own stage of development—well enough along to represent greater wisdom and authority, but still young enough to serve as a nonparental role-model, something like an older brother.

In time, the mentee repudiates this arrangement, but more of that later. In the meantime, for the next five years or so, the relationship "enables the young man to relate *as an adult* with another man who regards him as an adult and welcomes him into the adult world on a relatively (but not completely) mutual and equal basis," according to Levinson. Men without mentors, Vaillant discovered in his four-decade study of Harvard graduates, "tended to have had unsuccessful careers." Levinson, too, recognized "a great developmental handicap" among those who lacked such guides.

29–32: ACROSS THE GREAT DIVIDE

Not really a developmental stage in the "Leaving Home" sense, this is what Levinson calls a *transitional period,* riddled with turmoil, confusion and crisis. It begins when the 20s bedrock shifts and all of a sudden life doesn't seem so easy any more. Painful self-reflection resurrects the nagging questions: "What is this life all about now that I am doing what I'm supposed to be doing? Is what I am the only way for me to be? Why aren't I accepted for what I am? By my boss, by my spouse, by my parents?"

Says Vaillant: "Self-deception about the adequacy of both marital and career choice is common." Often, life structures carefully erected during the 20s are torn apart to prepare for the 30s. Finally, internal commitments are forged again, presaging the next state of development.

33–39: STURM AND DRANG

"They appeared to leave [behind] the compulsive calm of their occupational apprenticeships and experience once more the *sturm und drang* of adolescence," is how Vaillant characterized subjects in this age group. Gould spotted the same first signs of "quiet desperation" in patients he interviewed. Marital satisfaction withers and in its place, says Gould, "work is often looked to as offering the hopes of compensation . . . one last chance to make it big." Inner timetables are established, complete with goals (a $50,000 salary), way stations (that promotion to vice president) and ages (by 40).

Whatever's been accomplished is not enough; it's no longer sufficient to be the prize-winning novelist or promising junior executive. The mid-lifer feels constrained and overly dependent on outside influences: bosses, colleagues, his wife and, most forbidding of all, his mentor. The only way out is through what Erikson called "gener-

ativity," nurturing and teaching others. Levinson has redefined the process as BOOM —Becoming One's Own Man. To achieve it, a man must cast aside his mentor.

Explains Levinson, "The person who was formerly so loved and admired and who was experienced as giving so much, comes now to be seen as hypercritical, oppressively controlling . . . in short, as a tyrannical and egocentric father rather than a loving, enabling mentor." By severing the relationship, the younger man "gives up being a son in the little boy sense" and moves "toward assuming more fully the function of mentor, father and peer in relation to other adults." Though the partnership is over, the mentee is left enriched by the mentor's best qualities and stands on the brink of middle age, ready to further his own development.

40–42: MID-LIFE EXPLOSION

Throughout this second major "developmental transition," individuals tread the boundary between youthful dreams and adult fulfillment. Successes seem hollow and bittersweet. Life seems suspended. "The central issue," says Levinson, is not whether a man "succeeds or fails in achieving his goals," but, rather "what to do with the experience of disparity between what he has gained . . . and what he wants for himself." A first real awareness of death and a sense that time is running out instigate a soul-searching for "what it is I really want."

Added to the turmoil is a sense of bodily decline and aging. And according to Levinson, there is also a "flowering of fantasies" of young, erotic girls as well as mature, nurturing women. These, he says, represent not "a final surge of lasciviousness," but are rather ways of finally cutting free from the mother, healing old psychic wounds and learning to love "formerly devalued aspects of the self." Disastrous as it all may seem, Vaillant has concluded that all of this agonizing self-reappraisal can portend new beginnings. "However marred by depression and turmoil middle-life may be," he assures us, "it often heralds a new stage of man."

43–50: RESTABILIZATION

Settled and stable is how Gould describes most of his patients in this age group. Their feeling that "the die is cast" no longer seems as frightening and almost has a certain satisfaction to it. Sympathy and affection once sought from parents are now derived from spouses. Developmentally, though, this is not yet the end, despite the common belief that by the 40s "personalities are pretty well set." Levinson reminds us that at 40, such men as Freud, Eugene O'Neill, Goya and Ghandi underwent profound crises and made tremendous creative strides as a result.

AFTER-50: MELLOWING

Loose ends in relationships with parents, children and friends are tied during this era and a self-accepting attitude is adopted. Parents are no longer blamed for causing one's own personal problems. Children's lives become a wellspring of comfort, warmth and satisfaction. Spouses are valued as lifelong companions. Still, Gould, reminds us, all is not rosy.

A dwindling concern for past or future leaves one unprepared to deal with renewed questioning about life's meaninglessness and the value of one's own contributions to the world. Petty annoyances and failing health can cloud the everyday joys and triumphs that seem so important now. A new hunger for personal relationships conflicts with the need to avoid emotion-laden issues. Making sense of it all before time runs out sometimes seems beyond one's grasp.

Gould concedes that a thoroughly detailed portrait of adult development is "years away, if one ever emerges at all from the stacks of case histories and statistics being accumulated." And according to Vaillant: "Undoubtedly, the idea of an adult life cycle can apply only when humans are provided a rather wide scope in which to mature. The sample [which we] studied is limited by history, education and social class." Yet the orderly march of developmental stages now identified is already altering the perceptions of patients and psychologists alike.

Because most people still cling to the illusion that adults don't change, Gould told me, they're shaken when they find themselves different than they were ten or 20 years ago. But instead of embracing and learning from these changes, he said, they deny the experience. "Now that studies have demonstrated that there's a predictable progression to adult development, people seem relieved to be told that what they're going through is not unique, just normal."

16.   HOW TO COPE WITH MALE MENOPAUSE

Gloria M. Zaludek

Mitch Gordon is the 44-year-old senior partner of a manufacturing firm in the Midwest. He's a casually friendly man—athletically built, well-dressed, good looking. His business associates regard him as a happily married, prosperous man.

Mitch Gordon, however, is sexually impotent. Over the past few months he gradually lost the ability to achieve and maintain an erection. He secretly blames his wife for his failing potency.

Besides the sexual problems, Mitch is experiencing bouts of deep depression, so profound at times that he has contemplated suicide. Overriding all the problems are his fear of aging and his recognition that he will never achieve the successes he envisioned years earlier. Not willing to admit his problems, Mitch has begun to drink heavily and is having an affair with a woman young enough to be his daughter.

What causes such bizarre behavior in Mitch and in thousands of men like him? Modern medicine has an answer: it's called male menopause.

Physicians who treat growing numbers of 40-to 60-year-old menopausal males say that men experience a "climacteric"* often just as traumatic as the female menopause. And they can benefit from much the same kind of hormonal and psychological therapies.

The initial hurdle, however, is to get men to admit there's anything wrong in the first place. "Female menopause is respected, accepted and traditional. Everyone treads lightly, offers special help and even anticipates more than actually happens. But the male's changes are not acknowledged. He has to maintain an image as strong and impervious, while at the same time he desperately needs sympathy and understanding." This is the way Dr. Estelle Ramey, an endocrinologist at Georgetown University Medical Center, Washington, D.C. describes the situation.

She says that most males, as they age, undergo a decrease in testosterone—an androgen which is the most potent naturally-occurring male hormone. [It stimulates the activity of male secondary sex characteristics (hair growth, bone formation, deep voice, etc.), and later in life, helps prevent the change and destruction of sex organs.]

The male sex glands—essential for the vitality of youth—unfortunately form the weakest link in the chain of endocrine glands. They are the first to suffer when aging causes a reduction in many of the life processes.

Although the complex biological condition called "aging" is only partly understood, physiologists agree that it entails an overall slowing of bodily functions. Oil glands begin to dry up and secrete less oil; hair falls out; faces wrinkle. The digestive system becomes sluggish. Blood circulation slows, causing tingling in the arms and legs and decreased mobility.

Along with these biological changes

*Menopause technically means a cessation of the menses or the menstrual flow. Physicians feel that the more correct term for the male "change of life" is the "climacteric," when the gonadal function ceases. The terms are used here interchangeably.

come other, more subtle, changes—such as a decline in the number of sperm in the ejaculate and a reduction of the testosterone present in the plasma and urine of an aging male. The testes begin to lose their earlier vigorous functioning and produce decreasing amounts of hormones. Sometimes the hormonal level drops sharply.

All of the biological changes, unfortunately, come at a crucial time in a man's life. In the 40-to-60 age period, a man often begins to re-evaluate himself and may suddenly realize that he will never reach the goals he had set for himself. He foresees nothing but a boring job and, perhaps even worse, a boring retirement.

Overshadowing these feelings of dejection and despair is the gnawing fact that his physical strength seems to be ebbing, along with his sexual functioning. In an effort to recapture some former enthusiasm, and perhaps to shake the unsettling doubts and fears, the middle-aged man may drive himself to work harder, to exercise more often, or to seek younger women. One word of caution: Dr. Ramey says that the main problem with having an affair with a much younger woman is that it only compounds the problem by increasing the male's pressure to perform—at a time when he's least able to cope with such demands.

Fear is a major psychological component of the male climacteric and the fear of aging is, of course, one of the prime concerns. Over the years, people often gather erroneous ideas about the aging process and what to expect as we reach "middle age." We envision failing mental and physical abilities and a wearing out of sexual powers. In most cases, these notions are false but the fear of failure can indeed be a self-fulfilling prophecy.

Other fears can make the male climacteric traumatic. Fear of women may surface during the distressing times of hormonal imbalance. According to Dr. Helmut J.

Ruebsaat in *The Male Climacteric* (Hawthorne Books, © 1975): "A man may become secretly afraid of the vastly greater sexual capacity of women. Tests under clinical conditions have shown some women capable of six orgasms in 30 minutes and more than 50 in one night. A man at the peak of his sexual powers is doing well if he attains three to five orgasms in one night." These differences in male/female response and performance may be acceptable to a younger man; they can be emotionally devastating and fearful to an aging one.

Other changes in our social and cultural world can add to a man's feelings of inadequacy during menopause. The increasing use of effective birth control methods, for instance, has freed women to express themselves more openly and to seek more complete sexual fulfillment. A man may fear that women will make more demands on him than he can satisfy. Once again, fear of failure can increase the likelihood of failure.

And mounting failure can prompt a man to harbor another kind of devastating fear —that of rejection. The person most susceptible to rejection is one who has self-doubts to begin with. He keenly feels the brunt of derogatory comments about his age, his figure, his falling hair. Family can hurt him by such references; a young woman to whom he's making sexual advances can destroy him with an unkind remark.

Fear of fatherhood is often another concern of the middle-aged, climacteric man. Whether or not he has had children in his marriage, he probably doesn't want to father a child at his advancing age. In contrast, if the climacteric male is single he may be shocked to realize that he probably will never father a child at all. Fear compounded: if the male is having an extramarital affair, he may worry about impregnating the woman.

And perhaps for the first time in his life, the climacteric man begins to face the idea of death. He realizes that he has lived over half his probable life span. He sees friends, perhaps younger than he, die. All of these fears have a profound impact on the male's emotional and sexual functioning, and dysfunctioning, during the sometimes crucial menopausal years.

The notion that men may experience waning gonadal function in middle age (and suffer distressful physical and emotional symptoms, much as do women) is a relatively new concept and still considered controversial in some medical circles. Writing in the late 1930s, Dr. August A. Werner of the St. Louis University School of Medicine describes the "male climacteric syndrome" and attributes it entirely to an endocrine imbalance; that is, an insufficient production of male sex hormone.

Dr. Werner says the syndrome is a purely physical problem that can be treated clinically with hormone replacement therapy. In more recent years, however, physicians are finding that the picture is not so clearcut. Hormones may relieve some of the biological symptoms but they do little to assuage the psychological agonies. Depression, for instance, is a prime symptom of the menopausal syndrome. And depression so severe as to bring on suicidal thoughts cannot be "cured" by hormonal therapy alone. In many cases, physicians prescribe antidepressant therapy and psychiatric counseling—along with urging the support and understanding of family and close friends, to treat the male climacteric effectively.

But again, the critical aspect of treatment is that the man admit having the problems and needing help. Education often is the first step in the treatment process. Dr. Saul Kent says in *Geriatrics,* a medical journal specializing in the care of the elderly, that many of the prevailing cultural attitudes toward aging are not factual. He feels it's time to dispel the myths that cause people to fear growing older. Above all, he says that "it's normal for men to thoroughly enjoy sexual intercourse into their 70s, 80s and 90s."

Dr. Kent explains that many of the normal physiological changes that alter a person's body can also change the nature of his sexual response. (An older man may not respond as quickly to sexual stimulation as a younger man and may need a longer time to achieve an erection. Nonetheless, he can still have a slightly different, but just as satisfactory, sex life.)

Once the climacteric male acknowledges his difficulties and seeks medical help, he may receive therapy with a combination of testosterone and thyroid hormones or with steroid replacement. (Steroids are a large family of chemical substances, including the hormones.) The pharmacologic treatment, however, is not always the most effective method. As an example of the controversial nature of using medication alone, Dr. Ramey describes an experiment conducted in her Washington, D.C., clinic. Researchers gave combination drug therapy to males troubled with partial or complete impotence; 78 percent showed positive results.

The interesting part of the experiment, however, is that 40 percent of a control group given placebos, or sugar pills, also reported improvement in their sexual performance. "This points up the psychological value of attention and support, of the feeling that they *were* being helped," she added. Because of the importance of moral support in the overall treatment program, Dr. Ramey recommends that the family try to get the man to talk out his menopausal problems. If he refuses, at least they can show him that they still care about him and his abilities.

Hormone replacement therapy is considered controversial for several other reasons. Questions arise, for example, about the side effects of long-term treatment. A New York City endocrinologist who has been treating his climacteric patients for nearly 30 years, Dr. Herbert S. Kupperman, says, "Of the 200 males I've treated, I haven't had one case of prostatic cancer, which is one of the chief objections to the long-term therapy. If I were doing anything to accelerate the growth rate of the cancer, I would expect it to appear somewhat sooner."

Dr. Kupperman adds that there seem to be important beneficial side effects from the therapy, all of which vastly outweigh some vague threat of cancer. When androgens are injected consistently for four to six years, for example, they can halt and actually reverse the thinning of bone (osteoporosis) that weakens the body with advancing age. Most of all, though, the hormone replacement therapy helps return the male to his potential sexual functioning and helps him control premature ejaculation or incomplete erection—the very problems associated with falling sex hormone levels in the body.

When a man weighs the risk-to-benefit ratio and finally opts for the therapy, he must first undergo a battery of laboratory and clinical testing so the physician can determine the patient's general state of health and the depth of his hormonal needs. During the course of treatment, the patient is checked every four to six months so the physician can monitor his level of triglycerides, cholesterol and glucose tolerance. Thorough physical examinations, including a careful examination of the prostate, are also part of the regimen. The tests are precautionary and extremely important in helping the physician make necessary adjustments in treatment throughout the years.

In general, several types of men should not receive hormone therapy: those who have had prostate cancer or other kinds of bone cancer related to prostatic cancer, men with marked hypertension or swelling associated with a buildup of fluid in body tissue, or those with congestive heart failure.

How long will a man with testosterone deficiency need to be on the therapy? " For as long as he lives," Dr. Kupperman believes. "Why deprive a man of one of the great pleasures of life? After all, if you have a thyroid deficiency then you should be receiving thyroid for the rest of your life."

In addition to counseling his patients in this way in private practice, endocrinologist Kupperman shares his experience and knowledge in academic circles at New York University Medical Center where he is an associate professor of medicine. He describes hormone replacement therapy: "There are two basic methods. I prefer giving the hormones by injection every two to three weeks."

The other method involves implanting hormone pellets under the skin between the male's shoulder blades, or in his groin. Usually the physician and patient decide together which method will be used. Each has its special benefits and considerations; the implantation method seems more painful, for instance, but an advantage is that it must be done only every six months. (There is also an oral preparation that can be given. Physicians feel, however, that oral androgens may have an adverse effect on liver function, and some of the androgens are not terribly active. For these reasons the oral form of hormone is considered merely supplemental therapy.)

Dr. Kupperman says that for the treatment to be successful, though, a true and accurate diagnosis of "male climacteric" must first be made. Physicians must know certainly that the male patient complaining of impotency is truly experiencing the treatable clinical syndrome and not suffering from another physical or mental illness. Only if the diagnosis is accurate can the patient expect positive results from the hormone replacement treatment.

Three underlying problems can make a man impotent: 1) skewed instructions or no instructions are being sent to the testes (the male simply has lost interest in performing); 2) the body is suffering mental stress or physical emergency, such as an added need for adrenalin; or 3) the testes themselves fail to obey the instructions to function at their normal rate.

"Produce," says the pituitary, sending plenty of gonadotropin down the line. "We can't," say the testes. "We're too old and tired." This example of the third cause for male impotence is the *only* condition (known as primary testicular insufficiency) which Dr. Kupperman defines as the "true" male climacteric. This is the condition that responds to hormone replacement therapy.

The myth that a man does not experience a biological "change of life" is being worn away a little more each day. Perhaps soon the word "menopause" when applied to males will not seem appalling. Perhaps the first part of the word—"men"—may one day be regarded as an appropriate, acceptable prefix for a word which describes in general terms the changes a man goes through.

17. THE THANATOLOGIST

John Riley

Edwin S. Shneidman's name, in academic and psychological circles, is synonymous with the study of death and dying. One of the cofounders of the world-famous Los Angeles Suicide Prevention Center, he moved from being one of the world's foremost experts on suicide to a broader-based expertise in all phases of death and dying. A course he invented at Harvard University on death became an overnight academic sensation, a success he repeats regularly on the campus at UCLA. He is the author of the entry on suicide in the *Encyclopaedia Britannica.* His latest book, *Deaths of Man,* has a foreword written by Arnold Toynbee. Shneidman is a disciple, like Erik Erikson, of Henry A. Murray, the esteemed

Harvard educator-psychologist and personality theorist.

I am taking you to meet Shneidman. It is Saturday morning at UCLA. On the lowest floor of the university's Neuropsychiatric Institute (known locally as NPI), a group of women are seated in a small, cluttered office. Standing before them is a gnomelike man who is smiling and laughing and moving about as he talks.

Dr. Edwin S. Shneidman is all motion. From his fringe of still-dark hair to his toes five feet and six inches below, he exudes kinetic energy. The women are volunteers. Under Shneidman's direction, they counsel people who are dying. Suddenly the session, in which the doctor and his group are to review cases, turns serious.

"I saw Louise [not her real name] on Thursday and asked her to take an *MMPI*

(Minnesota Multiphasic Personality Inventory). Hers was a standard score to one standard deviation. About two-thirds hysteria, some depression. Paranoia. Obsessional traits. Schizophrenia, aberrant. I know her sex life is very unsatisfactory." Louise has survived two quite serious suicide attempts.

"If you took it seriously you would be dismayed," Shneidman continues. "I take it seriously but I am not dismayed. I got insights, as if Franz Alexander or Harry Murray had pulled up the case. She's an unusual girl. She's all sacred and profane like in literature, Melville's *Pierre* or *The French Lieutenant's Woman*. She frightens me. I don't like a patient who has that much insight. You see it only in patients who have been psychotic."

He changes the subject to a terminal patient, a South American physician hospitalized with a recently discovered cancerous kidney.

"My note," he begins, "if he starts breaking under the stress, the theoretical question to me is whether or not this is optimal health or Catholicism? Is this denial? How goddamn brave can you be? I find that people who use euphemisms are worse than people who use straight language. This man is almost too good to be true. He has great ego strength."

"Has he cried?" asks one volunteer.

"Yes, he cried with his wife the other night. This man goes to take a piss and he sees his death in the blood right in front of him in the urinal.

"What's marvelous is that I'm as close to him as I've been able to be to terminal patients who are in trouble." Shneidman notes that with the terminal patient apparently under control it is time to focus on caring for "the significant other"—survivors, his wife, the doctors caring for him.

Then Shneidman announces that next Tuesday he will attend a ceremony being held for a terminal patient who has died.

"At a cemetery in the Valley will be the unveiling of his stone. After the acrimonious way we parted, I'll now stand by his widow in that lugubrious cemetery."

Soon Shneidman is screening a film of a young Berkeley poet who is dying. It is called "How Could I Not Be Among You." It is romantic and real: the group is clearly moved. Shneidman comments as the film is rewound.

"It reminds us that our patients are two, the dying person and the survivors. Is there anything we can do for a man like that?" The film implies that the poet is facing death stoically.

"Let me tell you. The film was made in 1970. In 1973, he dies in New York. I spoke to his father. The son had divorced that wife and married someone else. He left his two children. It doesn't end in iambic pentameter. I have a feeling it didn't go as beautifully as it might have.

"I was going to print and transcribe his poetry. I had his parents' and his producer's approval. I phoned my publishers and had 'em pull it out of my book. It troubles me. One has to die well. I think of that doctor telling me as I look at his X ray that he'd rather go back to Chile and die with dignity in his bedroom or on his patio. Part of death itself is a degradation ceremony." He says the hospital did well with the man whose ceremony he will attend Tuesday. "They discharged him. They needed the bed. He bled to death at home."

There is a great debate about death, Shneidman tells his group, between the forces of scientism and those of intuition. The poet took the side of intuition.

"When you talk to a dying person or a survivor, try to divine that person's philosophy of life. You have to induce it. Part of the way you resonate to the person is that you resonate to that philosophy. I'm flexible enough to be catholic with a small *c*— different with the doctor and different with Louise. My task with Louise is to give her a philosophy of life."

And suddenly Shneidman supplies the group with his own philosophy. Standing, he proclaims:

"I know who I am.

"I eschew nihilism.

"I need to stand with the enlightened.

"It colors my sex life, my life as a parent, as a teacher, and it will color, willy-nilly, the way I die."

Earlier in the meeting one of the volunteers, a lovely dark-eyed woman, had told how a friend of hers in shock but matter-of-factly called her and told her, "I have cancer of the uterus." Shneidman comments on this: " 'I have cancer of the uterus,' your friend said. It's a way of saying something that's too much to say."

And while Shneidman is distributing a paper to each person on philosophy and the dying (from *Essays in Self-Destruction*), he is ruminating and contrasting the Apollonian and Dionysian persuasions:

"Apollonian: austere, clear, pristine, classical Greek, Bach, Mozart, geometry, appeals to structure, form, ascetic.

"Dionysian: Georgian architecture, cherubic, gothic amok, the pejorative term would be vulgar.

"My mentor, Henry Murray of Harvard, is Apollonian," he says. "My love for him reflects my Apollonian side. I have both Dionysian and Apollonian fantasies about death. I think I would prefer it like Henry would do it and Melville would do it, but I'm afraid of the Dionysian in me, the need for pathos, if not bathos: the Second Movement of the *Eroica*—that'll get 'em, move 'em to tears!"

The volunteers are laughing and Shneidman, who is quick and amazingly light on his feet, is leading them. He moves past a table strewn with papers and manuscripts and reports (behind it is a framed print of Harvard Yard in snow) and sits down for a moment.

"Do you, any of you, know the fact about me that I like the most, and it's the least real to me? What is it?"

After a number of tongue-in-cheek guesses, he reveals the answer.

"It's the fact that I was born in 1918. I'm 56 but it's not real to me. It doesn't make sense. I'm 35 at most, and sometimes I'm 18. Here is someone who is being pushed through life. There are certain parts of me with which I have no difficulty. In a sexual situation, I have no difficulty as a male. But my appearance has never been syntonic with my image of myself." Suddenly he stands and holds a portrait of Herman Melville (the subject of laborious and lifelong study by himself and his mentor, Dr. Murray) close to his own face, which is beaming.

"I have my own height and my own credentials," he says. "I view age as a constant. Henry Murray is in his 80s, but when I met him in 1951 I thought he was 45. In my own life I've grown in great jumps—mostly attendant to illness and hospitalization. I've really had the megalomaniac delusion that I could do anything."

Anything.

Soon the group has left. Dr. Shneidman will submit to a few biographical questions.

He grew up in the Lincoln Heights section of Los Angeles. His father had a men's clothing store. "They both were noble people. Mother was bright and sassy and well-read and pushy, intellectually disappointed in her own life. My father was not a great reader. He was terribly tall and handsome —strikingly handsome, I don't mean pretty. He had no relatives here. Mother had a coterie of brothers and sisters who tended to deprecate my father intellectually. He was steadfast, loyal, decent, honest, utterly reliable. I don't mean he didn't read Dostoevsky in his life. He was not a successful man. He sent three kids through school, and he borrowed from the bank to pay tuition.

"Both my parents, who are dead now, were born in Russia. Peasants. They came here in 1905. I had uncles and aunts who were murdered in pogroms. Neither parent had anything to do with the new or Soviet regimes. They spoke English. Occasionally, they used a Russian phrase. They knew Yiddish. I was a second child. I have an older brother who is a physician/surgeon. And a sister five years younger.

"I had uncles who were quite financially successful. At the time, I compared my father to them. I later appreciated my father —that was in my 30s and 40s.

"My parents had arguments but they never had fights. As closely as I can say, my father never looked at another woman. I can stake my life on it—that's a 19th-century model.

"As a clinician in the past 25 years, I've seen or heard—and this is a basis for some ego strength—from patients a whole Krafft-Ebing. Nothing anyone does surprises me. I'm willing to believe anything about anybody. It's not a moral issue. Nothing surprises me anymore."

The talk flows as from a practiced analysand. Openly. I ask a question he rephrases as "how I became suicidal." The four-time elementary school grade-skipper breezed through Lincoln High, acquired a BA from UCLA in 1938, an MA there in 1940, served in the Navy and picked up an MS and a Ph.D. at USC in 1947 and 1948, respectively. Then, one fateful day in 1949, while Shneidman was serving as a staff clinical psychiatrist at the VA hospital in West Los Angeles, he was given a task.

"I got a letter through the manager's office. Someone wrote asking for information about a patient who committed suicide. Then I got a second similar request. I was to prepare return letters for the manager's signature. A clerk would have gone to the VA files. As a Ph.D., I went to the county coroner's office for better materials. I was led to the old Hall of Records in downtown Los Angeles—a huge room with stack after stack of dusty files and a couple of light bulbs. I pulled this one folder. In it were a suicide note and, in addition, three type-written copies.

"I looked in other folders. I spent the day. I had a couple of thousand suicide notes. This was a thrilling moment. I had read a standard monograph on suicide notes, about 47 notes collected in Bern, Switzerland. Here was a trove of raw material, collected since about 1900. And in the hall was a woman in her 60s who had typed many of them. I asked her, 'For whom have you been typing these in triplicate all these years?' Her answer was, 'For you, honey.'

"Norman Farberow, my friend and coresearcher (we had been at college together), and I went through those notes like two dedicated locusts. We got 721 notes."

Out of that came the books *Clues to Suicide* and *The Cry for Help* and projects with Farberow, grants of $5,000 and then $1.6 million from the federal government (NIMH) for the Suicide Prevention Center, which began with a few professionals and a volunteer lay staff in a steam-cleaned formerly condemned TB building at Los Angeles County Hospital. And then there were all of the desperate telephone calls received around the clock from the disturbed, the would-be self-killers.

And then I asked a question Shneidman need not rephrase: why the interest in suicide and death? Is there any event in your background or in your makeup to account for any predilection?

"In 1950, fields such as homosexuality

A BEQUEST

Dr. Edwin S. Shneidman, in the obituary he has prepared for himself, lists as one of his major accomplishments: invention of the concept of "psychological autopsy." He proposes that psychological autopsies be conducted by all government medical examiner/coroner entities. He explains (in his *Deaths of Man*, Quadrangle, 1973):

An outline for the psychological autopsy procedure is presented below, with the caution that the investigator must never forget that he is asking questions that are very painful to people in a grief-laden situation. The person who conducts a psychological autopsy should participate in the anguish of the bereaved, work in the service of the mental health of the survivors, and at the same time quietly obtain information that may throw light on the intention (divined from behavior) of the deceased in regard to his own death.

1. Identifying information for victim (name, age, address, marital status, religious practices, occupation, and other details).

2. Details of the death (including the cause or method and other pertinent details).

3. Brief outline of victim's history (siblings, marriage, medical illnesses, medical treatment, psychotherapy, suicide attempts).

4. Death history of victim's family (suicides, cancer, other fatal illnesses, ages at death, and other details).

5. Description of the personality and life style of the victim.

6. Victim's typical patterns of reaction to stress, emotional upsets, and periods of disequilibrium.

7. Any recent—from last few days to last 12 months—upsets, pressures, tensions, or anticipations of trouble.

8. Role of alcohol or drugs in (a) overall life style of victim and (b) his death.

9. Nature of victim's interpersonal relationships (including physicians).

10. Fantasies, dreams, thoughts, premonitions, or fears of victim relating to death, accident, or suicide.

11. Changes in the victim before death (of habits, hobbies, eating, sexual patterns, and other life routines).

12. Information relating to the "life side" of victims (upswings, successes, plans).

13. Assessment of intention; i.e., role of the victim in his own demise.

14. Rating of lethality.

15. Reaction of informants to victim's death.

16. Comments, special features, etc.

(Shneidman, 1969)

and alcoholism had been worked over. Freud and Menninger (who wrote the foreword to *Clues to Suicide*) had written about suicide, but it was a virgin field. There was no one *in* suicide. Our goals were to pioneer."

At that time, he met Henry Murray. Shneidman's first book was based on an interpretation of a psychological test that Murray had invented. Shneidman wrote Murray asking him to write a foreword: "He wrote an elegant, soaring, masterful foreword of which only he is capable,"

Shneidman says. "Murray is a protean man; his ideographic approach to the mysteries of human life, to know a relatively small number of people in life well, versus the statistical nomothetic approach, requires a first-class brain. There are very few Freuds, Jungs, Darwins and Murrays. You have to be pretty goddamn smart. Any mediocrity with an IQ of 130 can do a nomothetic study.

"The opportunity to meet a protean man such as Murray, a prince of the mind, turned my head. He is the most impressive man I've met, to one standard deviation (to use a nomothetic term). Now that will insult lots of people I know, because I know some marvelous people."

Shneidman first met Murray in person in Washington, D.C., at a dinner at the Mayflower Hotel. Shneidman reached over his chateaubriand to pour tea from the large pot in front of them. Upon sipping it, Shneidman's first reaction was that it was cold. His second was that it was a rare and wonderful 101-proof bourbon: "some great exotic stuff," smuggled there by Dr. Murray. "I was even more taken with him when I met him. I couldn't believe he was 100 times more knowledgeable than I thought he could be after having read him."

In the early '60s, Shneidman studied with Murray at Harvard. Murray, with Gordon Allport, is credited with formulating a humanistic concept of personality. He is the author of *Explorations in Personality* (with coworkers) and with Clyde Kluckholm edited *Personality in Nature, Society and Culture.*

In the mid-'60s, Shneidman left Los Angeles to head a NIMH suicide study for three years in Washington. Later, he was to leave there to teach at Stanford. He received a call from Harvard asking him to revisit there as visiting professor.

"It was a chance to be near Professor Murray again. I said, 'I've thought about it five seconds, I'll take it.' " He taught a course on death to undergraduates. And he counseled the terminal patients at Avery Weisman Hospital.

"My mentor suggested I needed to back away from suicide, to refresh myself and return. To study people coming unwillingly to death. To attempt to understand the dying person. The other side of the coin." The suicidologist became a thanatologist, too. He expected 20 students in the course. Its enrollment was 250. Out of that experience came the book *Death and the College Stu-*

dent. The young, he learned, more easily considered themselves immortal.

The next year, he took the course to UCLA, where he became professor of medical psychology. He has just been appointed professor of thanatology in addition to his continuing duties as director of the Laboratory for the Study of Life-Threatening Behavior. Each fall, as many students as will fill the Neuropsychiatric Institute's auditorium fight for registration cards for the psychology/sociology death course.

At one session of the course I attended, the male student seated next to me in the back row confidently confided to a friend that it was well-known that Shneidman was quite ill and dying. I made a note to check the rumor with its subject. On stage, Shneidman, after administering a quiz on Tolstoy's *Death of Ivan Ilyich,* was punctuating his lecture with jokes and anecdotes: "Here are two jokes about death; they're Yiddish, so they're good. A wife tells her husband, 'If one of us dies first, I'm going to Palm Springs.' Two men are talking. One asks how the other would like to die. His answer, 'suddenly, a myocardial infarction, at work, painlessly.' The other says, 'Not me. I'd like to be sick. And linger, and linger, and linger—and then recover.' " The students respond to the humor and its message. And he continued.

"I want to not lose the serious point. The NASH system [of merely officially designating deaths by causes Natural, Accidental, Suicidal or Homicidal] doesn't tell us what we want to know. It's obvious that a lot of people *participate* in their own natural death. A diabetic can fool around with sugar, a sufferer of Burger's disease can fool around with nicotine, an alcoholic with cirrhosis can sneak off with a couple gallons of Gallo. You can play around with your own death. Accident proneness is a contradiction in terms. A true accident is totally unforeseen. By the time you've totaled the third car in a year, you're in a determined event. So many homicides have an element of victim participation. I'm going to suggest a major system of classification to superimpose on the NASH system. Deaths should be classified as (1) intentioned; (2) subintentioned; (3) unintentioned. It would put the decedent back in his own death and permit us to apply 20th-century psychology."

Back in Shneidman's office across the hall in NPI, after he signs scores of late registrants' classcards, I ask about the rumor that he is dying. He says that rumor has been in circulation ever since he began teaching death at UCLA five falls earlier. But last spring, he admits, the rumor had a certain partial validity. For 15 years, he had been postponing an abdominal operation.

"My stomach was in my thorax. I had a hiatus hernia. My stomach was becoming necrotic. I got along for years occasionally vomiting blood. I had a final attack. To show that I'm not too neurotic, when all the alternatives were narrowed to one, I went ahead. But I viewed the surgery as onerous." The surgery was a success. The rumor was a considerable overstatement.

His telephone buzzes and he picks up the receiver. A doctor is calling. He has referred a young and pretty female patient who has terminal cancer and does not know it. Shneidman has seen her.

"I can see how her husband loves her," Shneidman says into the telephone. "She's much prettier the closer you get to her. Those pretty pearllike teeth! I'd like to meet with your staff about her. She's not on an *immediate* death trajectory. She said if she were told she was dying she couldn't handle it. I don't think that is suicidal. I think she

could handle it. If there's a miraculous remission, we'll all celebrate. She isn't sick now. She came walking into this office, marvelous, feisty in the best sense. When this begins to hit, she'll know. She'll ask you and you can say, 'Do you really want to know?' I believe the human psyche is very gyroscopic. This girl is as psychotic as you or I—that is, not at all. She's realistic. I turned her over to one of my clinical associates. She's never died before and she's in her 20s.

"She's a darling person and it's a real tragedy. There are three people to work with. She, who is doomed but who deserves to die in a good mental state. Second, her husband, who needs to be seen after she dies so he doesn't sink into psychosomatic illness. And third, you and your staff; dealing with a young terminal person can leave you with depression and a feeling of professional impotence."

Soon the telephone is back on the hook and we talk. I ask if there is any deep internal reason to explain why he thanatologizes.

"I've discussed this with professional friends, who have been cautionary. They say I am doing this counterphobically. Am I rehearsing my own death with the deaths of others?"

He implies that he does not really know. Or will not say. Why, I ask, does he seem more closely involved in the deaths of certain of his terminal patients than in others?

"That would have to do with my countertransference. Why do I fall in love with some people and not with others? Some people resonate more to my neuroses."

CHAPTER III

Personality and Individual Differences

To MOST PEOPLE, psychology is the study of personality, and perhaps of the individual differences of people. While these are only a part of psychology, they are an important one. It is perhaps natural to be interested in oneself, curious about one's own personality as well as those of the people with whom one interacts. It also may be natural to be interested in and curious about those whose personalities are markedly different from everyone else's. We like to know who we are, who they are, and to understand what makes us all tick.

Unfortunately, the passage of time has not produced a unification of theories about personality—quite the contrary. Gradually, more and more diverse theories of personality have been developed and presented to the psychological community. This proliferation notwithstanding, there are a few theories which are so universally recognized that they serve as landmarks for the entire area of inquiry.

This chapter includes two readings which explore three of the most prominent personality theories. The psychoanalytic theories of Sigmund Freud and Carl Jung are presented in "Freud, Jung and the Collective Unconscious," and Erik Erickson's ideas on psychosocial development are explored in "Erik Erikson's Eight Stages of Man." These three theories, although different, represent a continuous line of theoretical development which starts with Freud's insights into early childhood, sexuality, and the dynamic nature of the mind and the unconscious. Jung universalized the symbols of the mind and conceived the unconscious as beneficent and creative. Jung also advanced the notion that psychological growth should be ongoing throughout the course of life. Erikson elaborated upon the ongoing nature of personality growth and development and postulated eight major stages of growth, each with its possibilities of fulfillment or failure and each engendering consequent dimensions of personality.

Love is important to everyone, and there are many kinds of it. However, the love relationship of overriding significance in the development of the personality is the one that takes place in early infancy between the child and the mothering one. Harlow's investigations have induced a radical revision of our information on and conceptualization of that relationship. His work is reported in "Love among the Monkeys."

Physicians and psychologists are increasingly cognizant of the pervasive effects of the personality on other aspects of life. "Does Your Personality Invite Disease?" presents evidence that an individual's personality has an important bearing upon the type of diseases he or she develops, as well as the state of physical health.

We are all, in many ways, different from one another. Being different can be pleasant or distressing and problematic. We can be a problem not only to others but to ourselves as well. Two readings about people who are different, "The Homosexuality Hangup" and "What Makes Creative People Different" are also included in this chapter.

18. DOES YOUR PERSONALITY INVITE DISEASE?

Howard R. and Martha E. Lewis

Alan Owens was small, neat, poised. He was obviously intelligent and was open and responsive toward the interviewer, a psychoanalyst we'll call Dr. Jones.

Owens mentioned that his first marriage had "just dissolved itself."

"What went wrong?" Dr. Jones asked. "Who didn't like whom?"

"We were both young," Owens replied. "I was thinking too old for my age, and she was thinking the age she was, and so we didn't have maybe the intelligence to reconcile this difference."

"How did you get to thinking so old?"

Owens laughed. "Now that's a question. I was a boy until I was nineteen, and then I became a man overnight, and I became an older man than I should have become. When I was a boy I was a prankster. Then overnight I accepted the responsibilities of the world."

Owens and Jones were taking part in an experiment at the Chicago Institute for Psychoanalysis. Researchers wanted to see if certain common organic disorders could be diagnosed *without* a medical examination, merely on the basis of the patient's personality. The disorders under study were bronchial asthma, hypertension, hyperthyroidism, neurodermatitis, peptic ulcer, rheumatoid arthritis, and ulcerative colitis.

A transcript of the lengthy interview Owens had with Dr. Jones was sent to an in-

ternist, whose job it was to delete any clues that could possibly suggest the medical nature of the disease. "Then the rash appeared," would obviously be censored out of a transcript, for it suggests dermatitis. So also would such allusions as "I had to be near a bathroom all the time," a particular problem for ulcerative colitis patients, or "Thank God I didn't need surgery," which would focus on conditions often requiring operations.

Copies of the edited transcript then went to psychoanalysts who knew nothing more of Alan Owens and his condition than what they could read in this expurgated interview. From dozens of personality clues coming out of the interview, one analyst offered this interpretation: "He was an acting-out person, early as a prankster, later in 'grinding down' his wife by an indiscriminating imposition of his will and wishes."

The analysts noted that Owens was rigid and self-controlling and wished to control others. At the same time he was a responsible person with a strong desire to care for others. This combination of personality traits matched characteristics they had already observed in large numbers of rheumatoid arthritis victims. They thus concluded that Alan Owens suffered from rheumatoid arthritis.

In Owens' case, the analysts were unanimously correct. He had developed rheumatoid arthritis two years before, following the breakup of his second marriage. Overall, the analysts predicted the correct diagnosis 41 percent of the time, a remarkable average since the disease could be diagnosed only in terms of the person's behavior patterns and moods.

The idea that certain personality types are predisposed to certain diseases is not new to medical thought.

Hippocrates himself formulated a connection between illnesses and temperament. When medicine was based on clinical observations alone, sharp-eyed physicians noted the frequent occurrence of certain diseases in persons of distinct physical and mental types. The observant clinician knew that the long, lean, narrow-chested person was more inclined to tuberculosis than the rotund, robust type—who, on the other hand, was more likely to suffer a cerebral hemorrhage.

Early physicians commented that diabetics are fond of the pleasures of the table, that heart disease often occurs among the anxious, that peptic ulcer sufferers are frequently hard-driving go-getters. Expressions like "melancholia" reveal the intuitive knowledge that many depressed people suffer from gallbladder disturbance. Melancholia, a term for severe depression, is derived from the Greek *melas* ("black") and *chole* ("gall"). Balzac in his *Cousin Pons,* one of the first novels written on a psychosomatic theme, draws a masterful picture of a bachelor who develops first melancholia, later a gallbladder condition.

Relatively new, however, are systematic studies linking personality types with bodily disease. This approach is under debate throughout the field of psychosomatics, and some investigators discount such a search as a wild-goose chase.

One critic, Dr. Lawrence S. Kubie of the New York Psychoanalytic Institute, has examined patients suffering from such psychogenic ailments as migraine, ulcerative colitis, and heart disease, yet has found no consistent personality types. "I have been impressed by the dissimilarities at least as vividly as by the similarities among the in-

dividuals in each [disease] group," Kubie reports. "Indeed I could not convince myself that the similarities were greater than those which obtain among any heterogeneous group of neurotic patients."

True, there is no single theory that can account for all psychosomatic disorders, and psychosomatic personality studies are often contradictory: Many kinds of personality can voice the identical complaint. Individuals with the same personality may manifest many kinds of illnesses.

On the other hand, an impressive body of evidence shows that to some degree at least there is a significant correlation between the kind of person you are and the kind of bodily disease you are prone to. For some illnesses more than 80 percent of the sufferers fall into characteristic personality patterns. By contrast, in some disorders, far fewer than 80 percent of patients show the *physical* signs characteristic of the disease. "In other words," observes Dr. Helen Flanders Dunbar, "the diagnostic symptoms of a disease may show greater variability than the personality pattern."

One skeptic, Dr. E. F. Gildea of New Haven Hospital, set out to disprove the idea of the personality profile. He evaluated patients in eight different disease groups, then drew up his own personality portraits. To his surprise, each of the distinct pictures he drew of the typical hypertensive, the typical asthmatic, and so on, corresponded with the portraits already drawn by previous investigators.

Of the acid tests to which psychosomatic personality studies have been subjected, few have been more stringent than one devised by psychiatrist Floyd O. Ring of the University of Nebraska College of Medicine.

Dr. Ring found much truth in the concept that patients with a given personality profile could often be matched to a corresponding bodily illness. "But," he cautioned, "with a little imagination one could see almost any profile in almost any patient if one were looking for that profile."

... vestigators,
... fact that if
... eptic ulcer,
... of his being
... —and there-
... relation be-
... and that
... er hand, if
... d arthritis,
... evidence to
... on of a pre-
... attern. Ev-
... urrents of
... ly, and de-
... t a person
... ell pick out

... if in a given
... ity pattern
... evident. He
... e than 400
... ourteen ail-
... nary occlu-
... diabetes,
... pertension,
... irodermati-
... thritis, and
... to see if an
... the basis of
... little as 15

... examiners
... precise ill-
... every patient was instructed to say nothing about symptoms, treatment, disabilities, diet, medical conditions, or anything else in any way associated with his physical self. Furthermore, the patient's body was covered during the interview, so the examiners could get no hints to the disease. To keep the sampling airtight, all interviews were conducted with at least two other professionals looking on. If the patient let slip a clue to his illness, or removed

even his hand from under cover, he was rejected.

Dr. Ring's percentage of correct diagnoses on first crack was so far beyond what chance would dictate that it supports his conclusion: "Persons with some illnesses can be picked out ... with a good percentage of accuracy by personality ... alone." One hundred percent of the hyperthyroid cases were detected. Similarly, personality alone uncovered 83 percent of the patients with peptic ulcer and rheumatoid arthritis, 71 percent with coronary occlusion, and between 60 and 67 percent with asthma, diabetes, hypertension, and ulcerative colitis.

In at least one case the personality interview revealed a correct diagnosis where a physical examination report had erred. After talking with a forty-year-old man, Ring concluded that he had rheumatoid arthritis. Because the man's medical chart listed "bleeding peptic ulcer," Ring was about to mark his own impression wrong. He questioned the patient further. It turned out that rheumatoid arthritis *was* the man's main problem now. He had been taking medication for arthritis and had developed the ulcer as a side effect.

From repeated observations, Ring asserted that personality types not only exist but fall into three broad categories. In some diseases the typical sufferer is excessively apprehensive. He readily expresses his thoughts, and freely reacts to his feelings of fear or anger. In nearly all his spheres of living, he is physically and verbally active.

He was asked, among other questions, "If you were sitting on a park bench ... and [a stranger] just your size, age, and sex ... walked up ... and kicked you in the shins, what would you do?" Most such patients, instead of saying they would demand a reasonable explanation, replied: "We'd have a showdown," or "I'd beat the hell out of him." Dr. Ring termed this type of patient the "excessive reactor." He found that in this category fell nearly all the victims of coronary occlusion, degenerative arthritis, and peptic ulcer.

Another type of patient is much of the opposite. He tends to suppress his fear and anger, indeed is not even aware he has such feelings. He inhibits his actions and holds back his thoughts.

If kicked in the shins by a stranger, what would such people do? Most of them reply: "Nothing." Nearly all of the sufferers of neurodermatitis, rheumatoid arthritis, and ulcerative colitis fall into this group as "deficient reactors."

A final group are the "restrained reactors." They are aware of their fears and anger but rarely act on or express them. A characteristic response to a kick in the shins is: "I'd be pretty mad," or "I might hit him." In this group are most sufferers from asthma, diabetes, hypertension, hyperthyroidism, and migraine.

In 1932 Franz Alexander and his associates at the Chicago Institute for Psychoanalysis found that, in patients suffering from organic ailments, similar emotional conflicts recurred too frequently to ignore. In such conflicts, they felt, could lie clues to the cause of a specific psychosomatic disease.

The Chicago workers began a series of psychoanalytic studies that continue to this day. Clear patterns of motivation have emerged, among them: Duodenal ulcer patients have a characteristic conflict about dependency needs. Asthma sufferers frequently fear losing their mothers and have difficulty crying. Trouble in handling hostile impulses appears again and again in people suffering from hypertension. Neurodermatitis victims intensely crave physical closeness.

Alexander and his colleagues formulated the "specificity hypothesis" as a clue to who gets what disease under what conditions. In essence, the theory goes like this: A person

may be born with or develop through illness or injury a physical vulnerability, an "X factor." There is considerable evidence that a predisposition to a specific organic disease is inherited. For example, someone may have as an X factor a vulnerability in his circulatory system. This person may experience a second variable: a basic emotional conflict. His bodily response to this "psychodynamic constellation" may now put a chronic strain on his heart or blood vessels.

As a final variable, this person—his vulnerable organs already under attack by his response to emotional conflict—finds himself in an "onset situation." Such an external life event may trigger a full-blown case of hypertension. Likewise, if the X factor was in the lining of his bronchial tubes, and a severe emotional conflict was present, he might develop asthma.

These variables may well be interrelated. A person born with a vulnerable circulatory system may feel great hostility toward his parents, but never express it because he craves their approval. Unexpressed hostility may affect his internal chemistry, causing a constriction of the arteries and a buildup of cholesterol on the artery walls.

His craving for approval may lead him to an onset situation, perhaps driving him to carry on his work dutifully even under unreasonably difficult conditions: overconscientiousness is a common trait among hypertensives. A "beast of burden" may subtly invite heavier and heavier loads. He then may feel ever greater unexpressed hostility, which in turn can cause further stress to his vulnerable organs and lead to a case of hypertension.

As Alexander notes, individual variations are enormous. Many people are in the same psychological boat as hypertensives but never develop hypertension. Identical life events may be an onset situation for one person, roll off the back of a second, and be a blessing to a third. Losing a wife may be a stark tragedy for Smith, a great relief for Jones.

An inborn bodily defect lies at the root of diabetes. There may be either an inadequate production of insulin by the pancreas or an excessive destruction of insulin by the tissues. Either way, the sugar content of the blood is abnormally high. The condition is believed to exist from birth, though diabetic symptoms may show up only later in life. It is thought that prolonged stress, emotional as well as physiological, may result in a permanent failure of the person's already strained regulatory mechanisms, and so the disease becomes apparent.

Before the disease is discovered, Dr. Helen Flanders Dunbar found, diabetics have a long history of deprivations, fatigue, weariness, and a sense of depression and hopelessness. The emotional picture may be the result of the unrecognized disorder in metabolism. It is thought more likely, however, that these emotional difficulties represent psychological conflicts boiling beneath the surface. In at least one case reported by Dunbar, diabetic symptoms disappeared with psychoanalysis.

Dr. Dunbar found the typical diabetic to be indecisive, frequently letting others make decisions and then bearing his lot with much grumbling, rarely doing anything to relieve his seeming hard luck. In early childhood most diabetics were torn between resenting their parents and docilely submitting to them. Many were "spoiled" children. Diabetic men especially were dominated by their mothers and dependent on them.

Diabetics tend to be passive in a sexual as well as a general sense. Marriage is often disappointing because the diabetic partner wants to be babied too much for mutual happiness. Dislike of sex keeps many of the men single.

If you put a wild rat into an absolutely hopeless situation, say in a tank of water from which there is no escape, he will swim around a bit. Then, though he is in no way exhausted or drowned, he will go into shock. His body temperature will fall, his heart will slow down, and he will die. In fights among wild rats, the loser often lies down, weakens, and dies, although he shows no evidence of injury. "A series of bouts may leave an attacked wild rat in a state of collapse," writes zoologist S. A. Barnett, "while the dominant attacker shows no distress . . ."

There may be a connection between such deaths, and the fact noted by Dr. R. S. Fisher, coroner of the City of Baltimore, that a number of Americans die each year after taking poison in doses so small it could not in itself cause death, or after inflicting small, nonlethal wounds on themselves. They evidently die as a result of a belief in their doom. As every doctor knows, one of the most important requirements for recovery in any patient is his will to live.

19. FREUD, JUNG AND THE COLLECTIVE UNCONSCIOUS

David Elkind

On Nov. 24, 1912, Sigmund Freud and Carl Gustav Jung, who Freud once hoped would succeed him as the leader of the psychoanalytic movement, met for next to the last time in Munich, Germany. It was ostensibly a business meeting, but all those among the small group of psychiatrists who attended were aware of the imminent break between the Father of Psychoanalysis and his chosen heir.

After dinner that evening, the discussion turned to the Egyptian pharaoh Ikhnaton, who had destroyed the polytheistic icons of his father and created a monotheistic religion of his own. One of the group suggested that Ikhnaton's action was a consequence of his father complex. Jung retorted that Ikhnaton's monotheism was a creative insight that had nothing to do with antagonism toward his father, whom Ikhnaton respected and admired. As Jung spoke, Freud, who had been listening intently, fainted and slid silently to the floor. Jung, who was 6-foot-2 and massively built, picked up Freud, carried him to the lounge and laid him gently on the sofa.

Freud's faint was not the first in similar circumstances. In 1909, Freud and Jung were journeying to America to lecture at Clark University, in Worcester, Mass. In one of their casual conversations, Jung spoke avidly about the then newly discovered "peat bog" corpses, which were of anthropological significance. Freud fainted

while listening to that discussion as well— and, on awakening, accused Jung of harboring death wishes toward him.

Apparently, Freud's faint in Munich also arose from a suspicion that Jung wished him dead. After the Munich episode, the Freud-Jung relationship became progressively colder and terminated altogether in October, 1913, the date of Jung's last letter to Freud. Jung went on to create his own analytical psychology, which has been the only other depth psychology to rival Freud's in influence and worldwide professional following. In recent years, Jung's work (he died in 1961) on mythology, religion, alchemy and the occult has captured the imagination of young people, and a more general appreciation of Jung seems to be on the way. This appreciation is likely to be aided and abetted by the availability of the Jung-Freud correspondence, which is scheduled to be published in 1971 by the Princeton University Press.

Although Jung is only now beginning to acquire the widespread popular recognition accorded Freud, many of his concepts have long since become part of the American idiom. It was Jung who introduced the terms "introversion" and "extraversion," "complex," "persona," "archetype" and "collective unconscious" into psychological discussions. Jung was, in addition, the first of the self-realization personality theorists (later exponents of this type of theory— none were ever Jungians—are Carl Rogers and the late Abraham Maslow). Jung also anticipated many of the current *avant-garde* therapy techniques, including marathon sessions (he once spent 12 hours with a schizophrenic patient) and the existential type of therapeutic relationship in which patient and therapist meet as equals (Jung occasionally told his patients his dreams if they were pertinent to the therapy). Finally, Jung's theories regarding the dynamics of personality give an almost prophetic explanation for many contemporary phenomena from the Women's Liberation movement to youth's discovery of Eastern religions and drugs.

Jung was born in 1875 in the village of Kessweil on Lake Constance in Switzerland. From early childhood, he had a rich and vivid life of dreams, fantasies and visionary experiences. Moreover, he grew up in a small country town and was early exposed to the rich lore of superstition, magic and occult phenomena that is, even today, perpetuated in rural villages only several kilometers removed from modern and scientifically oriented metropolitan centers. Jung's own propensities and his early experience in the country were the root of his life-long preoccupation with mythological, occult and parapsychological phenomena. Even as a youth, he revealed a prodigious intellect and a true European sense of scholarship—which led him to acquire and read every possible book on a subject in which he was interested. He grew to be big in size as well as intellect; he admired physical strength and appreciated the brute—as well as the romantic—qualities of nature. He enjoyed practical jokes, though he never let them get out of hand.

In his choice of a profession, Jung followed the tradition of his paternal grandfather, who had been a well-known physician in Basel. During his student days at the University of Basel, he pursued an interest in occult phenomena and attended weekly seances. At one of these, he witnessed a striking case of personality dissociation. Under a kind of trance, a 15-year-old girl took on the voice, mannerisms and sophistication of a grown and worldly woman. When she was in the guise of this mature woman, the girl expressed ideas and phantasies which, as far as Jung could determine, had no basis in her personal experience. The girl made a strong impression on Jung and he used his records of her verbal productions as the material for his doctoral thesis, published in 1902, entitled "On the Psychology and Pathology of So-Called Occult Phenomena."

Jung had not thought about going into psychiatry, particularly since it was the one vocation his father, a village pastor, had warned him against. When, however, he heard schizophrenia described as a "disease of the mind" he knew at once that he wished to be a "doctor of the soul." Accordingly, he arranged to go to the Burghölzli clinic, the psychiatric hospital associated with the University of Zurich, to undertake his residency training. The clinic was under the directorship of the psychiatrist Eugen Bleuler, famous for his work on the delineation of schizophrenia and his concept of "ambivalence."

Bleuler was also a teetotaler—and demanded total abstinence among his clinic associates, as well. So Jung, known as "The Barrel" in his student days, submitted to the edict, and gave up alcohol during his seven years at the Burghölzli.

Under the tutelage of Bleuler, Jung undertook studies in word association. The process consisted of presenting the subject with a list of words to each of which he was asked to respond with the first word that came to mind. Other workers had ignored deviant responses (long delays, failure to answer) as of no value to the experiment. For Jung, however, it was just these unusual responses that were of the most interest. He found that the long delays and blockings were related to what he came to call emotional "complexes." These "complexes" were emotion-charged ideas and images that interfered with the associative system. To illustrate—one of Jung's subjects responded to the word "propriety" with "intellect" after a reaction time of 4.6 seconds, when his mean reaction time was 1.2 seconds. Analysis of the case revealed the subject's complex—namely, his belief that masturbation (i.e., an "impropriety") destroyed the "intellect." (Jung later used the phrase "association technique," combined with equipment for measuring heart rate, blood pressure and skin resistance, in the examination of criminal suspects—and was thus the originator of the "lie detector" in use today.)

Jung had read Freud (whose "The Interpretation of Dreams" was published in 1900), and believed that his own word-association results gave experimental support to Freud's notion that unpleasant impulses and ideas were repressed but remained active in their unconscious state. His book on the association studies, published in 1906, acknowledged this support. Saying so took some courage, because Freudian theory, at that time, was abhorred by professionals and laymen alike. Indeed, Jung was warned by several German psychiatrists that support of Freud would certainly end his career.

Upon publication of the word-association book, Jung sent Freud a copy. Freud had already heard of it and had bought a copy before the volume sent by Jung arrived, but the gift initiated the Jung-Freud correspondence, which became increasingly cordial and detailed.

Jung met Freud for the first time in 1907 in Vienna. The two spent more than 12 hours together, engrossed in conversation. Jung was bursting to talk and flooded Freud with ideas and observations. Freud proceeded to organize the material under general headings so that they could conduct their discussion in a more organized and systematic fashion. He not only was taken by Jung's brilliance and vitality, but was pleased for another reason as well. Until then, with few exceptions, Freud's adherents had been Jewish, and Freud was afraid that psychoanalysis would become a target of anti-Semitism. With a non-Jew like Jung as a follower, this likelihood was diminished. The two men exchanged visits over the next few years; Freud grew increasingly enthusiastic about Jung, and made many references to his wish that Jung might succeed him and take over leadership of the psychoanalytic movement. In retrospect, Freud probably overestimated Jung's commitment to the cause of psychoanalysis and misread his defense of Freudian theories as due to conviction rather than as, what was more likely the case, an expression of Jung's independence and self-definition.

In 1909, Freud was invited by G. Stanley Hall, the American psychologist and educator, to lecture at Clark University and receive an honorary doctorate. Freud asked Sandor Ferenczi, a colleague, to accompany him. Jung was invited by Hall as well, and Freud then took the invitation as a greater honor still. The three men traveled to America together. In the course of their trip, Freud and Jung occasionally interpreted each other's dreams. Jung would tell a dream and Freud would interpret it, and vice versa. At one point, Freud refused to free-associate to one of his dreams, saying: "I would lose my authority." It was then, Jung said later, that Freud indeed ceased to have authority for him.

The two men reacted to their American experiences quite differently. Jung's letters read like those of a school boy on his first trip abroad—excited, wide-eyed and admiring. Not surprisingly, considering his independent, individualist spirit, Jung liked the land of Lincoln, Thoreau and Emerson, and he was much taken with William James, whom he had the occasion to meet. On this first trip, he picked up some American slang, and for the rest of his life Jung took impish delight in using words like "hell" whenever the conversation was in English. Jung returned to America several times before World War I, and again in the nineteen-twenties to visit the Pueblo Indians, and in the nineteen-thirties to lecture at Yale and Harvard. Freud did not like America, to which, probably unjustly, he attributed a life-long intestinal ailment. Part of his dislike may have been due to his difficulty with the language; in any case, he never returned.

Despite their differences during the trip, Freud continued to regard Jung as the son who would assume leadership of the psychoanalytic movement. In 1910, Jung became the first president of the International Psychoanalytical Association, and was also the editor of the first periodical exclusively devoted to psychoanalysis, The Yearbook for Psychoanalytical and Psychopathological Studies. He had left the Burghölzli the previous year and, with the exception of some university teaching, was spending full time in his private practice. He also returned to the lines of research he had begun in his thesis, which had been interrupted by the ultrascientific atmosphere of the clinic, where his interest in parapsychology was regarded with suspicion. Jung's research into occult phenomena thus led him to give up his position at the Burghölzli, and was soon to be the cause of his break with Freud. This research was, however, also the foundation upon which he built his own theory of personality.

Although Jung's notions about personality had been suggested in his 1902 thesis, they were greatly stimulated by his work at the Burghölzli with schizophrenic patients. One afternoon, one of the inmates, particularly given to hallucinations, took the ward physician to a window and said: "Stand here and look at the sun. What do you see?" The doctor said: "Well, I see the sun." Whereupon the patient said: "But don't you see the phallus upon the sun?" The doctor answered: "I'm not so sure." "Well," said the patient, "look carefully and move your head as you look; you will see the phallus move. That moving phallus is the source of the wind."

The incident was reported to Jung, who, it happened, was reading a book by a German philologist, Albrecht Dieterich, which dealt with a liturgy derived from a so-called magic papyrus in Greek. In the liturgy described in the papyrus, the initiate was asked to look at the sun, where he would see a tube hanging down—swinging to the right to produce the east wind, and then to the left to produce the west wind. The parallel between the vision of the insane man and the liturgy was striking because there was so little chance that the patient had ever had any acquaintance with the Greek papyrus. During his stay at the Burghölzli, Jung encountered other such parallels between the fantasy productions of the insane and the mythology of ancient times.

When he left the clinic and began treating private patients, he encountered still more phenomena that gave weight to the observations he had made of institutionalized patients. Freud had already described the "transference" phenomenon, the fact that in treatment the patient tends to project his conception of the parent onto the therapist, who thereupon becomes a "father figure" (or "mother figure" if the therapist is a woman). Such transference projections involve attributing traits of the parent to the therapist and also investing the therapist with the same powers over the patient that the parent once held.

Jung encountered just such transference phenomena in his own patients. In addition, however, he also noted that the transference often went beyond making him a parent figure. Some of his patients appeared eventually to endow him with godlike or demonic traits that were not part of their parent conceptions. It seemed to Jung as if the patients were raising the relationship to a higher power—mythologizing it and him. It was observations such as these, together with the mythological elements encountered in children's dreams and the universality of certain mythological motifs among widely separated and isolated primitive peoples, that led Jung to reconsider Freud's conception of the unconscious.

In Freud's theory, the unconscious is constituted mainly of impulses, ideas and wishes that the individual has come to regard as evil and reprehensible as a consequence of his exposure to social and cultural mores and taboos. These materials are repressed but remain active in an unconscious state and are at the root of neuroses as well as of more everyday phenomena such as forgetting and slips of the tongue and pen. Jung observed much evidence for this type of unconscious material but began to believe that there was still another stratum of unconscious elements that could not be traced to the personal experience and repressions of the individual. This deeper stratum of the unconscious, he began to think, might contain inherited potentialities which derived from the collective experience of the species and could thus account for the parallels between elements of ancient mythology and the projections of his patients.

Although Jung was coming to these hypotheses while he was at the clinic and during his friendship with Freud, he was reluctant to make his ideas public until he had amassed sufficient evidence to support his case. It was during this period (1907–09) that he came across some material published by the Genevan psychologist Theodore Flournoy that contained the transcript of the dreams and phantasy productions of an American woman, Miss Miller. In them Jung found numerous parallels with mythological characters, themes and settings. Since he had never seen the patient and so could not be accused of influencing her, he seized upon the material as data upon which to test his own, broader conception of the unconscious.

Freud was, of course, aware of this work but looked upon it indulgently as the waywardness of a prodigal son who would eventually return. He wrote to Jung on May 12, 1911:

Dear Friend,
... I know that your deepest inclinations are impelling you toward a study of the occult and do not doubt that you will return with a rich cargo. There is no stopping that, and it is always right for a person to follow the biddings of his own impulses. The reputation you have won with your "Dementia" [Jung's classic summary and integration of the literature on schizophrenia, published in 1907] will stand against the charge of "mystic" for quite a while. Only don't stay too long away from us in those lush tropical colonies, it is necessary to govern at home. ... With cordial greetings and the hope that you will write me again after a shorter interval this time.
Your Faithful
Freud.

But Jung's work in those "lush tropical colonies" was taking him even further away from psychoanalysis than Freud suspected. Indeed, Jung knew, as he began to write the results of his researches on the Miller phantasies, that it would cost him his friendship with Freud. As he was writing the final chapter, entitled "The Sacrifice," he suffered a severe writing block that lasted for two months. In that chapter, Jung described the Oedipus complex as but one manifestation of the mythological theme of incest and thus robbed it of the central place which it held in Freud's theory. Jung also challenged Freud's description of the libido as consisting of sexual energy alone and postulated that the libido had to be thought of as general psychic energy.

The publication of "Psychology of the Unconscious" did indeed alienate Freud. While he was generally open-minded scientifically, he regarded his sexual theories as the very basis of his system; if anyone differed on that fundamental point, what they were doing could no longer be considered psychoanalysis. After Jung's book appeared, correspondence between the two men became increasingly more formal ("Dear Friend" turned into "Dear Dr. Jung") and terminated altogether in 1913, when Jung resigned from the presidency of the International Psychoanalytical Association and gave up all editorial responsibilities with the yearbook. A year later, he also resigned his university lectureship, and thereafter devoted his full time to private practice and research.

Jung's book cost him not only Freud's friendship but that of other co-workers as well. Jung had made a daring hypothesis which most scientifically trained men at that time could not even entertain. What he was arguing, in effect, was that there are *two* sources of human experience—not just one. The traditional, philosophical and scientific view is that all our experience originates in the physical world of things outside ourselves (animals, trees, rocks and so on). Nonetheless, we never confront the external world in "the raw," so to speak, because the mind always imposes an organization prior to experience. When a group of notes is played in sequence, we hear a melody— not just a sequence of sounds. The organizing categories of the conscious mind within which all experience comes to us, are those of space, time and causality.

But, said Jung, there was another source of human experience in addition to the external world—one that is contained within the human psyche itself. This inner source of experience is the deeper stratum of the unconscious, which Jung called the "collective unconscious."

Just as the individual never experiences the external world "in the raw," so does he never experience the internal world of the collective unconscious in its unadulterated form. The organizing structures of this psychic source of experience are "archetypes," the structures which provide the patterns for dreams, phantasies and imagination.

Archetypes are most clearly elaborated in myths which, in ancient times, served the same function as the therapist does today— i.e., to serve as a screen upon which to project the products of the collective unconscious. The nature of archetypes can, therefore, be gleaned from the basic elements of mythological drama. There are archetypal characters (the hero, the wise old man, etc.), archetypal themes (love, hate, faith), archetypal settings (the cave, the river crossing), archetypal plots (the chase, the battle, the search) and archetypal moods (storm and turbulence, serenity and rest).

Accordingly, we know the external world only as it has been transformed by the organizing categories of space, time and causality, and we know the internal world only as it is presented in the dramatic categories of the archetypes.

It should be said here that Jung regarded the collective unconscious as a purely psychological hypothesis to the effect that all peoples, of whatever race or culture, share, at some psychic level, an archaic heritage of archetypal forms. These collective archetypes, like the materials of the personal unconscious described by Freud, are active and come to the fore in human experience in both direct and indirect ways throughout an individual's lifetime. In a sense, Jung was saying that our behavior is not a simple matter of reflexes and habits, but rather that each of us lives a myth—a drama, if you will—in which archetypal characters, themes, plots and settings play a considerable role. While Jung believed that such archetypal patterns were inherited, he was also convinced that there were not sufficient data to warrant speculation about the biological nature of this inheritance.* As a consequence of this scientific caution, his statements about the collective unconscious often seemed vague and won him the label of "mystical"—a euphemism for "unscientific and soft-headed."

Jung was, however, anything but soft-headed, and he saw the hypothesis of a collective unconscious as opening up a whole new territory for psychological research. The inner world of experience within the psyche was almost totally unexplored country as far as modern Western man was concerned, although it was familiar terrain to primitive man and to the practitioners of such Eastern philosophies as Zen Buddhism and yoga. Jung saw his next task as a dangerous and formidable one, the exploration of the collective unconscious. Such an exploration was essential for the problem that was to preoccupy him for the rest of his life—i.e., the significance of the collective unconscious for the development of the individual and of society.

The ensuing period in Jung's life—roughly, the years 1913 to 1917—he described as his "confrontation with the unconscious." By a variety of techniques, including meditation and painting, Jung opened himself to the materials originating in the collective unconscious. In particular, he found that, to re-establish the vivid inner life he had experienced as a child, there was nothing for it but to play childish games. On the Zurich lake shore, he began collecting stones and building a miniature village, including a castle, cottages and a church. The building game had the desired effect and released a stream of vivid phantasies.

It was a dangerous period, because much of the phantasy material he encountered was the stuff of psychosis and there was always a danger of being trapped by the imagery and of going insane. His family (his wife, Emma, who was also an analyst, and their four daughters and a son) and his practice served as reality counterpoises to his descent into the depths. Jung was sure that the same material was in everyone but that it seemed so fearful most people turned away with fear and trembling. Clearly, Jung was thinking of Faust: "Now let me dare to open wide the gate/Past which men's steps have ever flinching trod." As Jung described that self-exploration: "Unpopular, ambiguous and dangerous, it is a voyage of discovery to the other pole of the world."

During this entire period, he made careful transcriptions of his dreams, phantasies and visionary experiences that became the data for much of his later work. The period ended with several spontaneous productions. One of these was the almost automatic setting down of the "Seven Sermons to the Dead," which was written in the style of the Gnostics (an early Christian heretical sect) and which foreshadowed many of his later ideas about the human personality.

A few excerpts from the "Seven Sermons" may help to convey its flavor:

> Yet when night was come the dead again approached with lamentable mien and said: There is yet one matter we forgot to mention. Teach us about man.
> Man is a gateway, through which from the outer world of gods, daemons and souls ye pass into the inner world; out of the greater into the smaller world. Small and transitory is man. Already he is behind you,

---

*Even today, with our extraordinary knowledge about genetic coding, the orientation between such chemical codes and human thought and behavior remains a matter largely of speculation rather than fact.

and once again ye find yourselves in endless space, in the smaller or innermost infinity. At immeasurable distance standeth one single Star in the zenith.

This is the one god of this one man. This is his world, his pleroma [nothingness and completeness], his divinity.

Another product of this period was the drawing and painting of "mandalas." These are symmetrical designs based on the circle and the square. A rose window in a church is a familiar mandala; a human figure drawn so that its arms and legs extend to form the spokes of a wheel is another. The current peace symbol is also a kind of mandala.

The mandala held a clue to the major question that troubled Jung at this time—what is the adaptive significance of the collective unconscious? Is it merely a troublesome carry-over from primitive times (like our prehistoric emotional tendency toward fight or flight, which is not appropriate for a mechanized world) or does it have some useful purpose for man and for mankind? The mandala seemed to hold the answer.

Jung gradually came to regard the mandala as a symbol of psychic wholeness which man could move toward only after he had mastered both the inner and the outer worlds with which he must, at some point, contend. The goal of life, Jung came to believe, was *individuation,* the emergence of a unique and integrated self through confrontation and mastery of both the outer world of man and society and the inner world of mythology and fantasy. The mandala—the square within the circle, or the circle within the square—symbolized the psychic wholeness derived from man's mastery and integration of his inner and outer worlds of experience. Jung drew and painted mandalas at various points in his own life and they seemed to express both

how far he had come and how far he had yet to go in the process of individuation.

Still a third result of Jung's confrontation with the unconscious was his discovery of alchemy. It was a field of interest that was to concern him for the rest of his life.

Jung's interest in alchemy came about as a result of some historical considerations. It was clear to Jung that Western man, since the beginning of the Christian era, had taken great pains to shield himself from contact with the collective unconscious. At each point in history, however, some group within Western culture seemed burdened with maintaining contact with man's inner world. In the early Christian era, for example, the task was assumed by the Gnostics (much more recently, the Hasidim played a similar role in Judaism).

Jung's search for the group which had taken over from the Gnostics the task of maintaining contact with the unconscious led him to alchemy. The alchemists, as Goethe so clearly dramatized in the person of Faust, were occupied with far more important issues then the mere transmuting of base metals into gold. They were concerned with the mystery of the human soul. Jung found in the alchemical practices and symbols parallels both with ancient mythology and with contemporary psychotherapy. This lent support to his view that psychotherapy was modern man's avenue to contact with the collective unconscious, that there was continuity between the Gnostics, the alchemists and the psychotherapists in this respect. Jung's study of alchemy led to numerous articles and to one book, "Psychology and Alchemy" (1944).

During the period that he was exploring and recording his collective unconscious materials, Jung was doing other research as well. One of the problems he sought to explore was the difference in viewpoints between Freud and Alfred Adler, the

Viennese doctor who broke with the master and made the "inferiority complex" and the "will to power" central to man's motivation.

It seemed to Jung that the difference had somewhat to do with their respective positions in life, that a man's psychology reflected his personal situation. Freud, an established and successful physician, had power—so he could concern himself with pleasure, and make this the central motivational issue in life. Adler, in contrast, was just starting out in a new and then-unaccepted field and lacked power—so he raised this factor to the level of a universal and made it the central motive force in human affairs.

The study of this difference between Adler and Freud, together with his own clinical experience and his vast reading—particularly of Nietzsche—led to Jung's famous delineation of introversion and extraversion, which he described in the book "Psychological Types," published in 1921. Jung had already used the term "introversion" in a 1913 lecture, and Freud had adopted it in his descriptions of neurosis to indicate a morbid turning inward and away from social reality. The popular conception of introversion and extraversion stems from this early usage and assumes that the introvert—the quiet introspective person—is somehow less psychologically healthy than the outgoing, hail-fellow-well-met extravert. This is something of a distortion of Jung's view.

For Jung, introversion and extraversion were conscious attitudes toward social and physical reality. In some respects, they are close to the outlooks of David Riesman's inner- and other-directed individuals, in the sense that the extravert tends to be guided by directions and suggestions from without while the introvert tends to be guided by his personal predilections. Introversion and extraversion are, moreover, not absolutes, but relative, and most individuals combine both introversion and extraversion.

As often happens with typologies, however, Jung's conceptions of introversion and extraversion, as enunciated in 1913, could be taken as absolutes and Jung felt called upon to differentiate the types further in order to avoid misunderstanding. Some 10 years later, in "Psychological Types," he indicated that introversion and extraversion were attitudes taken by the four basic functions of the psyche—thinking, feeling, sensation and intuition. What Jung argued now was that the types referred to an introverted or extraverted emphasis in one or the other of the basic functions. This made possible eight different types, rather than two.

To illustrate this expanded typology, one might roughly characterize the engineer as an extraverted thinking type (applies thinking to practical matters), whereas the theoretical physicist would be an introverted thinking type (applies thinking to conceptual or ideational matters). Likewise, an actor might be regarded as an extraverted feeling type, whereas a writer or artist might be an introverted feeling type. Both types develop feeling more than reason, but the actor empathizes with the feelings of another person (the character to be portrayed), while the writer and the artist empathize with characters or artistic productions of their own creation.

Turning to other possibilities, an example of the extraverted sensation type would be the "sensuous" person who is extremely responsive to externally aroused experiences of touch, taste and smell. The hypochondriacal person, beset with a medley of bodily complaints, provides an illustration of the introverted sensation type who is extremely responsive to aches and pains arising within himself.

The intuitive types are quite different and tend to be more rare. Intuition, in Jung's sense, has to do with "seeing around corners," with knowing things without knowing how one knows, with hunches and guesses as to what is going to happen next. An inventor, for example, is often an intuitive extravert trying to devise an apparatus to fill a need that most people are not even aware exists. The introverted intuitive, on the other hand, has considerable self-knowledge which he seeks to further—while feeling compelled to put himself at the service of mankind. Such men as Marcus Aurelius, Gandhi and Dag Hammarskjöld would fit within the intuitive introvert category.

Another aspect of Jung's typology that should be mentioned involves his theory of opposites and compensation. Jung regarded thinking and feeling as rational functions, and sensation and intuition as irrational functions. The paired functions are somewhat in opposition to one another, and development or differentiation of one is always at the expense of the other. The more highly differentiated a man's thinking, for example, the more childlike will be his feelings. A stereotype is the abstracted professor who is so childlike that his wife, children and students all must take a protective attitude toward him. Contrariwise, gifted actors, actresses or writers who have developed their feeling function to an extraordinary extent are often quite childlike in their thinking and can be temperamental and superstitious in the extreme.

The same polarity holds true for intuition and sensation. The intuitive person who is always looking at the whole picture and into the future is often unattuned to the immediate reality around him. It is the intuitive inventor, who has his thoughts fixed on the big problem, who does not notice what color socks he has on. Intuition is developed in such men at the expense of sensation, response to the details of immediate reality. In contrast, the person whose sensation function is highly developed suffers a corresponding poorness of intuition, what might be called a lack of imagination. The person in whom sensation dominates is happy with things as they are and as they have been. He wants stability and change is seen as a threat. An extreme case is the housewife who gets upset if a doily is a millimeter out of place.

Jung used this typology diagnostically and as a guide to therapeutic tactics. In his view, many neuroses, particularly in people during the second half of life, derive from an exaggerated use of one or another function to the exclusion of the others. An extraverted thinking type, such as a businessman or an engineer, may enter the second half of life having attained all of his rational goals, including financial success and recognition. Nonetheless, these successes and his work no longer bring him the pleasure they once did, and he begins to feel moody and depressed. In such cases, Jung feels that previous goals have lost their capacity to mobilize psychic energy and what the individual needs to do is realize some other side to his personality, particularly the feeling side. Such a person, to illustrate, might now find fulfillment in acting (feeling extraversion) or in writing or painting (feeling introversion). Jungian therapy thus tries to help the individual to realize potentialities that have lain dormant while other facets of the personality have been in the foreground.

In such cases, the problem for treatment becomes one of helping the individual to find the unexplored resources and potentials within himself. After years of self-analysis and after analyzing hundreds of patients, many of whom were gifted, brilliant and internationally known, Jung observed that the process of finding the hidden aspects of the self, which he came to call "individuation," occurred in several stages and involved successive encounters with the many structures of the human personality.

The first structure the individual encounters in the quest of individuation Jung called the *persona*. An individual's persona includes the sum total of his social roles—the masks he wears in his interpersonal relations as son, husband, father, employe, employer, friend, etc. In general, men tend to be more identified with their persona than are women. The physician, for example, who gets upset when he is not called "Doctor" is somewhat overidentified with his persona. Likewise, the aging actress who refuses to accept matronly roles is over-identified with her sex-goddess persona. The first stage of individuation, then, is to begin to differentiate and separate the self from the social mask which is the persona.

The next phase in the process of individuation involves confrontation with the *shadow*. In general, the shadow has to do with those parts of ourselves that we dislike and are reluctant to acknowledge. We like to think of ourselves as honest, straightforward, generous, "only too willing"—when, in fact, we are not really, or at least not always, these things. What happens is that we project the shadow upon others. For example, we often get most angry at our children when they display our own faults. In coming to grips with the shadow, the individual must discover the relativity of good and evil and come to accept the shadow as part of himself and as having some value. This does not mean that the individual condones "evil" within himself, or that he gives up his values as to right and wrong. It means only that he recognizes the "evil" within him so that he can better control and regulate it.

In some individuals, the shadow does not stay in the background but intrudes into his thoughts and behavior. Each culture has its caricature of this type of person. In America, he is sometimes described by the phrase: "He's a menace." "The menace" is the fellow who tries to enter a room quietly but proceeds to knock over a vase, catch his foot on the dog's leash and bring the top of the piano crashing down. He is the fellow who always wants to help—and always succeeds in producing a worse mess than when he offered his services. In such a person, the shadow elements—the wish to be the center of attention, to sabotage and destroy—are presented side-by-side with protestations of modesty, goodwill and the desire to be helpful.

Following the confrontation with the shadow, the individual is ready to come to grips with the *anima* (in the case of a man, or the *animus* in the case of a woman). In Jung's view, the man has some archetypal conceptions of the female which he projects outward and that determine his relations to women. Among the most frequently projected archetypal anima figures are "mother," "whore," "high priestess" and "inspiring woman." As the man becomes aware of his archetypal projections onto women, these projections gradually lose their power and he comes to see women more realistically as individuals. He is then able to form a more understanding and compassionate relationship with women.

In women, parallel masculine archetypes can be found. Again, these figures are projected onto other persons and women at different points in their lives will be attracted to "paternal" men, to men of action, to religious or priestly men. The last case, when the figure of priest or sorcerer is projected upon a real man, can lead to the woman's enslavement—perhaps explaining the emotional power that a pimp holds over his prostitutes.

Again, to the extent that a woman becomes aware of the masculine archetypes which govern her relations with men, to that extent is she freed from her enslavement by projections—and to that extent are her relationships with men founded on a more realistic and sympathetic basis.

Once the individual has dealt with the persona, the shadow and the anima and animus, he has moved far along the road to individuation and to the realization of the self which, for Jung, is the integrating force between our archaic heritage and our personal history. The self integrates all that is acquired with all that is innate in us.

The process of integration is, however, never-ending and continues so long as we live. There are always new discoveries to make about ourselves if we are willing to look inward. No person ever fully realizes all sides of himself and all of his potential because no person is perfect. We can only strive for personal wholeness and completeness and that, in Jung's psychology, is what life is all about.

It should be said that Jung himself was quite eclectic in his treatment and did not insist upon self-realization as the goal for all of his patients. He used Freudian and Adlerian procedures and concepts if he thought they were appropriate. He disliked doctrinaire, preconceived approaches. "Each patient," he wrote, "is a new problem for the doctor and he will be cured of his neurosis only if you help him to find his individual way to the solution of his problems."

An example of Jung's highly individualized treatment is the case of a woman who was in the habit of slapping her employes and her doctors. She was a big woman, 6 feet tall, and her slaps hurt. She went to Jung, and in the course of their discussion he said something that aroused her anger. As Jung described it:

"Furious, she sprang to her feet and threatened to slap me. I too jumped up and said to her, 'Very well, you are the lady. You hit first—ladies first! But then I hit back.' "

The woman crumpled into her chair and from that moment on the therapy began to succeed.

Jung's followers have tried to maintain his open-minded approach to psychotherapy. In their training institutes, Jungian therapists expose their students to the whole range of depth psychologies and to the whole gamut of psychotherapeutic procedures. Likewise, in their practice, Jungian therapists employ whatever methods and techniques seem appropriate to the patients' problems. What distinguishes Jungian therapists from all others is that they are uniquely informed regarding the archetypes of the collective unconscious and are prepared to deal with these archetypes if and when they appear in the patients' dreams and artistic productions.

After Jung had worked out some of the implications of the collective unconscious for individual patients, he turned increasingly to problems of society. While he recognized that there are fundamental differences between a group of people and an individual, he also recognized certain parallels. In some of his later books, including "The Undiscovered Self," "Flying Saucers" and "Answer to Job," he turned his attention to some of the major problems confronting modern man. In these books, as in all his writings, the prose is often dense and obscure, but there are also many clear and insightful passages that enrich literature as well as psychology.

While it is really not possible to summarize these books here, a few dominant themes can be noted. Jung argued that a culture, no less than an individual, can exaggerate a particular attitude or function—with the inevitable compensatory reaction of the opposing function. Thus, in Western society, the deification of reason, of industrialization and technology together with the intellectualization of religion, has progressively alienated modern man from his inner world and from his feeling function. Jung believed that the rapid growth of contemporary interest in the "I Ching" (to which he wrote a famous introduction), in spiritualism, in astrology, in psychology and in Eastern religions is a natural reaction to Western man's exaggerated extraverted thinking function. Cultures, no less than individuals, can lack wholeness and completeness.

In the realm of religion Jung introduced still other themes. His view was, in the words of a leading Jungian analyst, Dr. Edward F. Edinger, "that man is naturally religious in the sense that he has an inborn urge to realize and to relate at a transpersonal level of being." But to relate at the transpersonal level, man needs what Jung called "living symbols"—representations which retain some indefiniteness of meaning and mystery. Living symbols give man's religious archetypes a medium of expression and realization. Such symbols were once provided by the church, but modern religion—particularly Protestantism—has given up most of its symbols. Those which do exist are to a large extent "dead," in that they have become so intellectualized that they have lost the uncertainty and mystery that made them such a welcome host to archetypal projections. Jung warns that God is an archetype which will be projected into something—and that where religion fails, the demagogue prevails.

Jung's conception of opposites, compensation and symbolism helps to explain some other contemporary phenomena. The sexual and maternal sides of women's functions have been so exploited and exaggerated that their symbols have lost their meaning. What women are looking for today, in Jung's terms, would be new symbols to express the creative and intellectual components of their personalities. Likewise, today's youths are generally disdainful of the dead symbols of institutional religion, but are intensely interested in spiritual matters,

in finding new ways to explore inner experience and in finding new symbols to guide their explorations—hence their interest in Eastern religions, whose symbols seem to be alive in the sense that they retain an air of mystery.

In many domains, therefore, Jung offered prophetic insights about modern man which are only now coming to be widely appreciated. Nonetheless, he and his work have been criticized from many different points of view. The personal animosities dating from his break with Freud still smoulder and cause somewhat overdetermined rejection by Freudians. Even objective scholars, including Jung's own followers, acknowledge the obscurity of some of his writing, the contradictions in his pronouncements and the lack of systematization in his ideas. Some critics find his prophetic interpretation of dreams and symbols a kind of mysticism, and dismiss him as a man who did some good scientific work while young, but who became progressively more diffuse and less scientific as the years rolled on. Finally, the stigma of anti-Semitism lingers on.

In 1933, Jung accepted an invitation to become president of the International General Medical Society for Psychotherapy and editor of its journal, after the Jewish psychiatrists who had filled these positions resigned their posts. Jung at that time also made some statements about differences between Germanic and Jewish psychology which, while they were not anti-Semitic in themselves, were easily transformed into malicious propaganda by the Nazis. At the same time, however, he made the association truly international and made its membership open to all, including Jews. Indeed, one interpretation of his actions was that he accepted the presidency and editorship to save the association and to protect its members by giving it the sanctity of "Aryan" leadership.

From this point in history, Jung's behavior seems best regarded as an act of political naiveté, engendered, in part, perhaps, by some initial enthusiasm, as a German-speaking Swiss, for National Socialism and the restorative effect it seemed to be having on a dead Germany. This enthusiasm soon died, and his genuine concern for the fate of the society's members made Jung continue his association as long as he did (three years). Thereafter, Jung openly condemned the Nazis in his lectures and in print. The matter did not die, however, and there were, over the years, repeated discussions in the popular press and in scientific journals which enlarged Jung's alleged anti-Semitism far out of proportion to his actions and to the significance and importance of his scientific contributions.

Although the charge of anti-Semitism—and of being a mystic—alienated many professionals and kept them from taking Jung's work seriously, this was not universally the case. Men like Arnold Toynbee, Paul Tillich and J. B. Priestley were his supporters and regarded Jung as having made a large and significant contribution to the understanding of modern man and his present condition. Jung's patients and students, moreover, uniformly credit him with having had a profound influence upon their lives, which became fuller and richer for having been associated with him.

There is, in addition, evidence of steadily increasing interest in Jung's analytical psychology by both professionals and laymen alike. The sales of his collected works, first published by the Bollingen Foundation, have been growing steadily, as have the sales of the Modern Library's "The Basic Writings of C. G. Jung" and the Anchor anthology entitled "Psyche and Symbol."

The number of Jungian analysts is also increasing, and there are now clusters of Jungian therapists in New York, Chicago, Texas, San Francisco and Los Angeles. The International Association for Analytical Psychology, founded a little more than a decade ago, already has affiliated societies in America, England, Switzerland, France, Italy and Israel. There is every indication that this growth of interest will continue as Jung's works become more generally known and as the significance of his monumental contribution becomes more widely appreciated.

Toward the end of his life, when Jung gave up his practice, he spent much time at The Tower, a circular stone house that he built on the lake of Zurich, near the village of Bollingen. At The Tower, Jung read, meditated, sculptured, sailed and practiced an extraordinary culinary skill. Writing was something of a chore for him (though his output was tremendous—his collected works, published by Princeton, will run to 20 volumes, besides correspondence, seminars and letters) and he was always relieved when a piece was finished and he could go back to his reading. His autobiography, "Memories, Dreams, Reflections," written in collaboration with Aniela Jaffé and published posthumously, has been compared with Goethe's *"Dichtung und Wahrheit."* At his home near Zurich, in Küssnacht (where Freud had visited him in the years of their friendship), he kept the enormous library he had collected over the years and in which he delighted. Despite failing health, he conducted a prolific correspondence even in his last years. Jung died at Küssnacht in June, 1961.

Jung always maintained that his psychology was a personal confession of value only to him and to those of similar inclinations, and he expressed this confession most simply as follows:

"Fulfill something you are able to fulfill, rather than run after what you will never achieve. Nobody is perfect. Remember the saying 'None is good but God alone.' And nobody can be. It is an illusion. We can modestly strive to fulfill ourselves and to be as complete human beings as possible, and that will give us trouble enough."

20.   ERIK ERIKSON'S EIGHT AGES OF MAN

David Elkind

At a recent faculty reception I happened to join a small group in which a young mother was talking about her "identity crisis." She and her husband, she said, had decided not to have any more children and she was depressed at the thought of being past the child-bearing stage. It was as if, she continued, she had been robbed of some part of herself and now needed to find a new function to replace the old one.

When I remarked that her story sounded like a case history from a book by Erik Erikson, she replied, "Who's Erikson?" It is a reflection on the intellectual modesty and literary decorum of Erik H. Erikson, psychoanalyst and professor of developmental psychology at Harvard, that so few of the many people who today talk about the "identity crisis" know anything of the man who pointed out its pervasiveness as a problem in contemporary society two decades ago.

Erikson has, however, contributed more to social science than his delineation of identity problems in modern man. His descriptions of the stages of the life cycle, for example, have advanced psychoanalytic theory to the point where it can now describe the development of the healthy personality on its own terms and not merely as the opposite of a sick one. Likewise, Erikson's emphasis upon the problems unique to adolescents and adults living in today's society has helped to rectify the one-sided

emphasis on childhood as the beginning and end of personality development.

Finally, in his biographical studies, such as "Young Man Luther" and "Gandhi's Truth" (which has just won a National Book Award in philosophy and religion), Erikson emphasizes the inherent strengths of the human personality by showing how individuals can use their neurotic symptoms and conflicts for creative and constructive social purposes while healing themselves in the process.

It is important to emphasize that Erikson's contributions are genuine advances in psychoanalysis in the sense that Erikson accepts and builds upon many of the basic tenets of Freudian theory. In this regard, Erikson differs from Freud's early co-workers such as Jung and Adler who, when they broke with Freud, rejected his theories and substituted their own.

Likewise, Erikson also differs from the so-called neo-Freudians such as Horney, Kardiner and Sullivan who (mistakenly, as it turned out) assumed that Freudian theory had nothing to say about man's relation to reality and to his culture. While it is true that Freud emphasized, even mythologized, sexuality, he did so to counteract the rigid sexual taboos of his time, which, at that point in history, were frequently the cause of neuroses. In his later writings, however, Freud began to concern himself with the executive agency of the personality, namely, the ego, which is also the repository of the individual's attitudes and concepts about himself and his world.

It is with the psychosocial development

of the ego that Erikson's observations and theoretical constructions are primarily concerned. Erikson has thus been able to introduce innovations into psychoanalytic theory without either rejecting or ignoring Freud's monumental contribution.

The man who has accomplished this notable feat is a handsome Dane, whose white hair, mustache, resonant accent and gentle manner are reminiscent of actors like Jean Hersholt and Paul Muni. Although he is warm and outgoing with friends, Erikson is a rather shy man who is uncomfortable in the spotlight of public recognition. This trait, together with his ethical reservations about making public even disguised case material, may help to account for Erikson's reluctance to publish his observations and conceptions (his first book appeared in 1950, when he was 48).

In recent years this reluctance to publish has diminished and he has been appearing in print at an increasing pace. Since 1960 he has published three books, "Insight and Responsibility," "Identity: Youth and Crisis" and "Gandhi's Truth," as well as editing a fourth, "Youth: Change and Challenge." Despite the accolades and recognition these books have won for him, both in America and abroad, Erikson is still surprised at the popular interest they have generated and is a little troubled about the possibility of being misunderstood and misinterpreted. While he would prefer that his books spoke for themselves and that he was left out of the picture, he has had to accede to popular demand for more information about himself and his work.

The course of Erikson's professional career has been as diverse as it has been unconventional. He was born in Frankfurt, Germany, in 1902 of Danish parents. Not long after his birth his father died, and his mother later married the pediatrician who had cured her son of a childhood illness. Erikson's stepfather urged him to become a physician, but the boy declined and became an artist instead—an artist who did portraits of children. Erikson says of his post-adolescent years, "I was an artist then, which in Europe is a euphemism for a young man with some talent and nowhere to go." During this period he settled in Vienna and worked as a tutor in a family friendly with Freud's. He met Freud on informal occasions when the families went on outings together.

These encounters may have been the impetus to accept a teaching appointment at an American school in Vienna founded by Dorothy Burlingham and directed by Peter Blos (both now well known on the American psychiatric scene). During these years (the late nineteen-twenties) he also undertook and completed psychoanalytic training with Anna Freud and August Aichhorn. Even at the outset of his career, Erikson gave evidence of the breadth of his interests and activities by being trained and certified as a Montessori teacher. Not surprisingly, in view of that training, Erikson's first articles dealt with psychoanalysis and education.

It was while in Vienna that Erikson met and married Joan Mowat Serson, an American artist of Canadian descent. They came to America in 1933, when Erikson was invited to practice and teach in Boston. Erikson was, in fact, one of the first if not the first child-analyst in the Boston area. During the next two decades he held clinical and academic appointments at Harvard, Yale and Berkeley. In 1951 he joined a group of psychiatrists and psychologists who moved to Stockbridge, Mass., to start a new program at the Austen Riggs Center, a private residential treatment center for disturbed young people. Erikson remained at Riggs until 1961, when he was appointed professor of human development and lecturer on psychiatry at Harvard. Throughout his career he has always held two or three appointments simultaneously and has traveled extensively.

Perhaps because he had been an artist first, Erikson has never been a conventional psychoanalyst. When he was treating children, for example, he always insisted on visiting his young patients' homes and on having dinner with the families. Likewise, in the nineteen-thirties, when anthropological investigation was described to him by his friends Scudder McKeel, Alfred Kroeber and Margaret Mead, he decided to do field work on an Indian reservation. "When I realized that Sioux is the name which we [in Europe] pronounced "See ux" and which for us was *the* American Indian, I could not resist." Erikson thus antedated the anthropologists who swept over the Indian reservations in the post-Depression years. (So numerous were the field workers at that time that the stock joke was that an Indian family could be defined as a mother, a father, children and an anthropologist.)

Erikson did field work not only with the Oglala Sioux of Pine Ridge, S. D. (the tribe that slew Custer and was in turn slaughtered at the Battle of Wounded Knee), but also with the salmon-fishing Yurok of Northern California. His reports on these experiences revealed his special gift for sensing and entering into the world views and modes of thinking of cultures other than his own.

It was while he was working with the Indians that Erikson began to note syndromes which he could not explain within the confines of traditional psychoanalytic theory. Central to many an adult Indian's emotional problems seemed to be his sense of uprootedness and lack of continuity between his present life-style and that portrayed in tribal history. Not only did the Indian sense a break with the past, but he could not identify with a future requiring assimilation of the white culture's values. The problems faced by such men, Erikson

recognized, had to do with the ego and with culture and only incidentally with sexual drives.

The impressions Erikson gained on the reservations were reinforced during World War II when he worked at a veterans' rehabilitation center at Mount Zion Hospital in San Francisco. Many of the soldiers he and his colleagues saw seemed not to fit the traditional "shell shock" or "malingerer" cases of World War I. Rather, it seemed to Erikson that many of these men had lost the sense of who and what they were. They were having trouble reconciling their activities, attitudes and feelings as soldiers with the activities, attitudes and feelings they had known before the war. Accordingly, while these men may well have had difficulties with repressed or conflicted drives, their main problem seemed to be, as Erikson came to speak of it at the time, "identity confusion."

It was almost a decade before Erikson set forth the implications of his clinical observations in "Childhood and Society." In that book, the summation and integration of 15 years of research, he made three major contributions to the study of the human ego. He posited (1) that, side by side with the stages of psychosexual development described by Freud (the oral, anal, phallic, genital, Oedipal and pubertal), were psychosocial stages of ego development, in which the individual had to establish new basic orientations to himself and his social world; (2) that personality development continued throughout the whole life cycle; and (3) that each stage had a positive *as well as* a negative component.

Much about these contributions—and about Erikson's way of thinking—can be understood by looking at his scheme of life stages. Erikson identifies eight stages in the human life cycle, in each of which a new dimension of "social interaction" becomes possible—that is, a new dimension in a person's interaction with himself, and with his social environment.

TRUST VS. MISTRUST

The first stage corresponds to the oral stage in classical psychoanalytic theory and usually extends through the first year of life. In Erikson's view, the new dimension of social interaction that emerges during this period involves basic *trust* at the one extreme, and *mistrust* at the other. The degree to which the child comes to trust the world, other people and himself depends to a considerable extent upon the quality of the care that he receives. The infant whose needs are met when they arise, whose discomforts are quickly removed, who is cuddled, fondled, played with and talked to, develops a sense of the world as a safe place to be and of people as helpful and dependable. When, however, the care is inconsistent, inadequate and rejecting, it fosters a basic mistrust, an attitude of fear and suspicion on the part of the infant toward the world in general and people in particular that will carry through to later stages of development.

It should be said at this point that the problem of basic trust-versus-mistrust (as is true for all the later dimensions) is not resolved once and for all during the first year of life; it arises again at each successive stage of development. There is both hope and danger in this. The child who enters school with a sense of mistrust may come to trust a particular teacher who has taken the trouble to make herself trustworthy; with this second chance, he overcomes his early mistrust. On the other hand, the child who comes through infancy with a vital sense of trust can still have his sense of mistrust activated at a later stage if, say, his parents are divorced and separated under acrimonious circumstances.

This point was brought home to me in a

very direct way by a 4-year old patient I saw in a court clinic. He was being seen at the court clinic because his adoptive parents, who had had him for six months, now wanted to give him back to the agency. They claimed that he was cold and unloving, took things and could not be trusted. He was indeed a cold and apathetic boy, but with good reason. About a year after his illegitimate birth, he was taken away from his mother, who had a drinking problem, and was shunted back and forth among several foster homes. Initially he had tried to relate to the persons in the foster homes, but the relationships never had a chance to develop because he was moved at just the wrong times. In the end he gave up trying to reach out to others, because the inevitable separations hurt too much.

Like the burned child who dreads the flame, this emotionally burned child shunned the pain of emotional involvement. He had trusted his mother, but now he trusted no one. Only years of devoted care and patience could now undo the damage that had been done to this child's sense of trust.

AUTONOMY VS. DOUBT

Stage Two spans the second and third years of life, the period which Freudian theory calls the anal stage. Erikson sees here the emergence of *autonomy*. This autonomy dimension builds upon the child's new motor and mental abilities. At this stage the child can not only walk but also climb, open and close, drop, push and pull, hold and let go. The child takes pride in these new accomplishments and wants to do everything himself, whether it be pulling the wrapper off a piece of candy, selecting the vitamin out of the bottle or flushing the toilet. If parents recognize the young child's need to do what he is capable of doing at his own pace and in his own time, then he develops a sense that he is able to control his muscles, his impulses, himself and, not insignificantly, his environment—the sense of autonomy.

When, however, his caretakers are impatient and do for him what he is capable of doing himself, they reinforce a sense of shame and doubt. To be sure, every parent has rushed a child at times and children are hardy enough to endure such lapses. It is only when caretaking is consistently over-protective and criticism of "accidents" (whether these be wetting, soiling, spilling or breaking things) is harsh and unthinking that the child develops an excessive sense of shame with respect to other people and an excessive sense of doubt about his own abilities to control his world and himself.

If the child leaves this stage with less autonomy than shame or doubt, he will be handicapped in his attempts to achieve autonomy in adolescence and adulthood. Contrariwise, the child who moves through this stage with his sense of autonomy buoyantly outbalancing his feelings of shame and doubt is well prepared to be autonomous at later phases in the life cycle. Again, however, the balance of autonomy to shame and doubt set up during this period can be changed in either positive or negative directions by later events.

It might be well to note, in addition, that too much autonomy can be as harmful as too little. I have in mind a patient of 7 who had a heart condition. He had learned very quickly how terrified his parents were of any signs in him of cardiac difficulty. With the psychological acuity given to children, he soon ruled the household. The family could not go shopping, or for a drive, or on a holiday if he did not approve. On those rare occasions when the parents had had enough and defied him, he would get angry and his purple hue and gagging would frighten them into submission.

Actually, this boy was frightened of this

power (as all children would be) and was really eager to give it up. When the parents and the boy came to realize this, and to recognize that a little shame and doubt were a healthy counterpoise to an inflated sense of autonomy, the three of them could once again assume their normal roles.

INITIATIVE VS. GUILT

In this stage (the genital stage of classical psychoanalysis) the child, age 4 to 5, is pretty much master of his body and can ride a tricycle, run, cut and hit. He can thus initiate motor activities of various sorts on his own and no longer merely responds to or imitates the actions of other children. The same holds true for his language and fantasy activities. Accordingly, Erikson argues that the social dimension that appears at this stage has *initiative* at one of its poles and *guilt* at the other.

Whether the child will leave this stage with his sense of initiative far outbalancing his sense of guilt depends to a considerable extent upon how parents respond to his self-initiated activities. Children who are given much freedom and opportunity to initiate motor play such as running, bike riding, sliding, skating, tussling and wrestling have their sense of initiative reinforced. Initiative is also reinforced when parents answer their children's questions (intellectual initiative) and do not deride or inhibit fantasy or play activity. On the other hand, if the child is made to feel that his motor activity is bad, that his questions are a nuisance and that his play is silly and stupid, then he may develop a sense of guilt over self-initiated activities in general that will persist through later life stages.

INDUSTRY VS. INFERIORITY

Stage Four is the age period from 6 to 11, the elementary school years (described by classical psychoanalysis as the *latency phase*). It is a time during which the child's love for the parent of the opposite sex and rivalry with the same sexed parent (elements in the so-called family romance) are quiescent. It is also a period during which the child becomes capable of deductive reasoning, and of playing and learning by rules. It is not until this period, for example, that children can really play marbles, checkers and other "take turn" games that require obedience to rules. Erikson argues that the psychosocial dimension that emerges during this period has a sense of *industry* at one extreme and a sense of *inferiority* at the other.

The term industry nicely captures a dominant theme of this period during which the concern with how things are made, how they work and what they do predominates. It is the Robinson Crusoe age in the sense that the enthusiasm and minute detail with which Crusoe describes his activities appeals to the child's own budding sense of industry. When children are encouraged in their efforts to make, do, or build practical things (whether it be to construct creepy crawlers, tree houses, or airplane models—or to cook, bake or sew), are allowed to finish their products, and are praised and rewarded for the results, then the sense of industry is enhanced. But parents who see their children's efforts at making and doing as "mischief," and as simply "making a mess," help to encourage in children a sense of inferiority.

During these elementary-school years, however, the child's world includes more than the home. Now social institutions other than the family come to play a central role in the developmental crisis of the individual. (Here Erikson introduced still another advance in psychoanalytic theory, which heretofore concerned itself only with the effects of the parents' behavior upon the child's development.)

A child's school experiences affect his industry-inferiority balance. The child, for example, with an IQ of 80 to 90 has a particularly traumatic school experience, even when his sense of industry is rewarded and encouraged at home. He is "too bright" to be in special classes, but "too slow" to compete with children of average ability. Consequently he experiences constant failures in his academic efforts that reinforce a sense of inferiority.

On the other hand, the child who had his sense of industry derogated at home can have it revitalized at school through the offices of a sensitive and committed teacher. Whether the child develops a sense of industry or inferiority, therefore, no longer depends solely on the caretaking efforts of the parents but on the actions and offices of other adults as well.

IDENTITY VS. ROLE CONFUSION

When the child moves into adolescence (Stage Five—roughly the ages 12–18), he encounters, according to traditional psychoanalytic theory, a reawakening of the family-romance problem of early childhood. His means of resolving the problem is to seek and find a romantic partner of his own generation. While Erikson does not deny this aspect of adolescence, he points out that there are other problems as well. The adolescent matures mentally as well as physiologically and, in addition to the new feelings, sensations and desires he experiences as a result of changes in his body, he develops a multitude of new ways of looking at and thinking about the world. Among other things, those in adolescence can now think about other people's thinking and wonder about what other people think of them. They can also conceive of ideal families, religions and societies which they can then compare with the imperfect families, religions and societies of their own experience. Finally, adolescents become capable of constructing theories and philosophies designed to bring all the varied and conflicting aspects of society into a working, harmonious and peaceful whole. The adolescent, in a word, is an impatient idealist who believes that it is as easy to realize an ideal as it is to imagine it.

Erikson believes that the new interpersonal dimension which emerges during this period has to do with a sense of *ego identity* at the positive end and a sense of *role confusion* at the negative end. That is to say, given the adolescent's newfound integrative abilities, his task is to bring together all of the things he has learned about himself as a son, student, athlete, friend, Scout, newspaper boy, and so on, and integrate these different images of himself into a whole that makes sense and that shows continuity with the past while preparing for the future. To the extent that the young person succeeds in this endeavor, he arrives at a sense of psychosocial identity, a sense of who he is, where he has been and where he is going.

In contrast to the earlier stages, where parents play a more or less direct role in the determination of the result of the developmental crises, the influence of parents during this stage is much more indirect. If the young person reaches adolescence with, thanks to his parents, a vital sense of trust, autonomy, initiative and industry, then his chances of arriving at a meaningful sense of ego identity are much enhanced. The reverse, of course, holds true for the young person who enters adolescence with considerable mistrust, shame, doubt, guilt and inferiority. Preparation for a successful adolescence, and the attainment of an integrated psychosocial identity must, therefore, begin in the cradle.

Over and above what the individual brings with him from his childhood, the attainment of a sense of personal identity depends upon the social milieu in which he or she grows up. For example, in a society where women are to some extent second-class citizens, it may be harder for females to arrive at a sense of psychosocial identity. Likewise at times, such as the present, when rapid social and technological change breaks down many traditional values, it may be more difficult for young people to find continuity between what they learned and experienced as children and what they learn and experience as adolescents. At such times young people often seek causes that give their lives meaning and direction. The activism of the current generation of young people may well stem, in part at least, from this search.

When the young person cannot attain a sense of personal identity, either because of an unfortunate childhood or difficult social circumstances, he shows a certain amount of *role confusion*—a sense of not knowing what he is, where he belongs or whom he belongs to. Such confusion is a frequent symptom in delinquent young people. Promiscuous adolescent girls, for example, often seem to have a fragmented sense of ego identity. Some young people seek a "negative identity," an identity opposite to the one prescribed for them by their family and friends. Having an identity as a "delinquent," or as a "hippie," or even as an "acid head," may sometimes be preferable to having no identity at all.

In some cases young people do not seek a negative identity so much as they have it thrust upon them. I remember another court case in which the defendant was an attractive 16-year old girl who had been found "tricking it" in a trailer located just outside the grounds of an Air Force base. From about the age of 12, her mother had encouraged her to dress seductively and to go out with boys. When she returned from dates, her sexually frustrated mother demanded a kiss-by-kiss, caress-by-caress description of the evening's activities. After the mother had vicariously satisfied her sexual needs, she proceeded to call her daughter a "whore" and a "dirty tramp." As the girl told me, "Hell, I have the name, so I might as well play the role."

Failure to establish a clear sense of personal identity at adolescence does not guarantee perpetual failure. And the person who attains a working sense of ego identity in adolescence will of necessity encounter challenges and threats to that identity as he moves through life. Erikson, perhaps more than any other personality theorist, has emphasized that life is constant change and that confronting problems at one stage in life is not a guarantee against the reappearance of these problems at later stages, or against the finding of new solutions to them.

INTIMACY VS. ISOLATION

Stage Six in the life cycle is young adulthood; roughly the period of courtship and early family life that extends from late adolescence till early middle age. For this stage, and the stages described hereafter, classical psychoanalysis has nothing new or major to say. For Erikson, however, the previous attainment of a sense of personal identity and the engagement in productive work that marks this period gives rise to a new interpersonal dimension of *intimacy* at the one extreme and *isolation* at the other.

When Erikson speaks of intimacy he means much more than love-making alone; he means the ability to share with and care about another person without fear of losing oneself in the process. In the case of intimacy, as in the case of identity, success or failure no longer depends directly upon the parents but only indirectly as they have contributed to the individual's success or failure at the earlier stages. Here, too, as in the case of identity, social conditions may help or hinder the establishment of a sense

of intimacy. Likewise, intimacy need not involve sexuality; it includes the relationship between friends. Soldiers who have served together under the most dangerous circumstances often develop a sense of commitment to one another that exemplifies intimacy in its broadest sense. If a sense of intimacy is not established with friends or a marriage partner, the result, in Erikson's view, is a sense of isolation—of being alone without anyone to share with or care for.

GENERATIVITY VS. SELF-ABSORPTION

This stage—middle age—brings with it what Erikson speaks of as either *generativity* or *self-absorption,* and stagnation. What Erikson means by generativity is that the person begins to be concerned with others beyond his immediate family, with future generations and the nature of the society and world in which those generations will live. Generativity does not reside only in parents; it can be found in any individual who actively concerns himself with the welfare of young people and with making the world a better place for them to live and to work.

Those who fail to establish a sense of generativity fall into a state of self-absorption in which their personal needs and comforts are of predominant concern. A fictional ease of self-absorption is Dickens's Scrooge in "A Christmas Carol." In his one-sided concern with money and in his disregard for the interests and welfare of his young employe, Bob Cratchit, Scrooge exemplifies the self-absorbed, embittered (the two often go together) old man. Dickens also illustrated, however, what Erikson points out: namely, that unhappy solutions to life's crises are not irreversible. Scrooge, at the end of the tale, manifested both a sense of generativity and of intimacy which he had not experienced before.

INTEGRITY VS. DESPAIR

Stage Eight in the Eriksonian scheme corresponds roughly to the period when the individual's major efforts are nearing completion and when there is time for reflection —and for the enjoyment of grandchildren, if any. The psychosocial dimension that comes into prominence now has *integrity* on one hand and *despair* on the other.

The sense of integrity arises from the individual's ability to look back on his life with satisfaction. At the other extreme is the individual who looks back upon his life as a series of missed opportunities and missed directions; now in the twilight years he realizes that it is too late to start again. For such a person the inevitable result is a sense of despair at what might have been.

These, then, are the major stages in the life cycle as described by Erikson. Their presentation, for one thing, frees the clinician to treat adult emotional problems as failures (in part at least) to solve genuinely adult personality crises and not, as heretofore, as mere residuals of infantile frustrations and conflicts. This view of personality growth, moreover, takes some of the onus off parents and takes account of the role which society and the person himself play in the formation of an individual personality. Finally, Erikson has offered hope for us all by demonstrating that each phase of growth has its strengths as well as its weaknesses and that failures at one stage of development can be rectified by successes at later stages.

The reason that these ideas, which sound so agreeable to "common sense," are in fact so revolutionary has a lot to do with the state of psychoanalysis in America. As formulated by Freud, psychoanalysis encompassed a theory of personality development, a method of studying the human mind and,

finally, procedures for treating troubled and unhappy people. Freud viewed this system as a scientific one, open to revision as new facts and observations accumulated.

The system was, however, so vehemently attacked that Freud's followers were constantly in the position of having to defend Freud's views. Perhaps because of this situation, Freud's system became, in the hands of some of his followers and defenders, a dogma upon which all theoretical innovation, clinical observation and therapeutic practice had to be grounded. That this attitude persists is evidenced in the recent remark by a psychoanalyst that he believed psychotic patients could not be treated by psychoanalysis because "Freud said so." Such attitudes, in which Freud's authority rather than observation and data is the basis of deciding what is true and what is false, has contributed to the disrepute in which psychoanalysis is widely held today.

Erik Erikson has broken out of this scholasticism and has had the courage to say that Freud's discoveries and practices were the start and not the end of the study and treatment of the human personality. In addition to advocating the modifications of psychoanalytic theory outlined above, Erikson has also suggested modifications in therapeutic practice, particularly in the treatment of young patients. "Young people in severe trouble are not fit for the couch," he writes. "They want to face you, and they want you to face them, not as a facsimile of a parent, or wearing the mask of a professional helper, but as a kind of over-all individual a young person can live with or despair of."

Erikson has had the boldness to remark on some of the negative effects that distorted notions of psychoanalysis have had on society at large. Psychoanalysis, he says, has contributed to a widespread fatalism— "even as we were trying to devise, with scientific determinism, a therapy for the few, we were led to promote an ethical disease among the many."

Perhaps Erikson's innovations in psychoanalytic theory are best exemplified in his psycho-historical writings, in which he combines psychoanalytic insight with a true historical imagination. After the publication of "Childhood and Society," Erikson undertook the application of his scheme of the human life cycle to the study of historical persons. He wrote a series of brilliant essays on men as varied as Maxim Gorky, George Bernard Shaw and Freud himself. These studies were not narrow case histories but rather reflected Erikson's remarkable grasp of Europe's social and political history as well as of its literature. (His mastery of American folklore, history and literature is equally remarkable.)

While Erikson's major biographical studies were yet to come, these early essays already revealed his unique psycho-history method. For one thing, Erikson always chose men whose lives fascinated him in one way or another, perhaps because of some conscious or unconscious affinity with them. Erikson thus had a sense of community with his subjects which he adroitly used (he calls it *disciplined subjectivity*) to take his subject's point of view and to experience the world as that person might.

Secondly, Erikson chose to elaborate a particular crisis or episode in the individual's life which seemed to crystallize a life-theme that united the activities of his past and gave direction to his activities for the future. Then, much as an artist might, Erikson proceeded to fill in the background of the episode and add social and historical perspective. In a very real sense Erikson's biographical sketches are like paintings which direct the viewer's gaze from a focal point of attention to background and back again, so that one's appreciation of the focal area is enriched by having pursued the picture in its entirety.

This method was given its first major test in Erikson's study of "Young Man Luther." Originally, Erikson planned only a brief study of Luther, but "Luther proved too bulky a man to be merely a chapter in a book." Erikson's involvement with Luther dated from his youth, when, as a wandering artist, he happened to hear the Lord's Prayer in Luther's German. "Never knowingly having heard it, I had the experience, as seldom before or after, of a wholeness captured in a few simple words, of poetry fusing the esthetic and the moral: those who have suddenly 'heard' the Gettysburg Address will know what I mean."

Erikson's interest in Luther may have had other roots as well. In some ways, Luther's unhappiness with the papal intermediaries of Christianity resembled on a grand scale Erikson's own dissatisfaction with the intermediaries of Freud's system. In both cases some of the intermediaries had so distorted the original teachings that what was being preached in the name of the master came close to being the opposite of what he had himself proclaimed. While it is not possible to describe Erikson's treatment of Luther here, one can get some feeling for Erikson's brand of historical analysis from his sketch of Luther:

> Luther was a very troubled and a very gifted young man who had to create his own cause on which to focus his fidelity in the Roman Catholic world as it was then. . . . He first became a monk and tried to solve his scruples by being an exceptionally good monk. But even his superiors thought that he tried much too hard. He felt himself to be such a sinner that he began to lose faith in the charity of God and his superiors told him, "Look, God doesn't hate you, you hate God or else you would trust Him to accept your prayers." But I would like to make it clear that someone

like Luther becomes a historical person only because he also has an acute understanding of historical actuality and knows how to "speak to the condition" of his times. Only then do inner struggles become representative of those of a large number of vigorous and sincere young people—and begin to interest some troublemakers and hangers-on.

After Erikson's study of "Young Man Luther" (1958), he turned his attention to "middle-aged" Gandhi. As did Luther, Gandhi evoked for Erikson childhood memories. Gandhi led his first nonviolent protest in India in 1918 on behalf of some mill workers, and Erikson, then a young man of 16, had read glowing accounts of the event. Almost a half a century later Erikson was invited to Ahmedabad, an industrial city in western India, to give a seminar on the human life cycle. Erikson discovered that Ahmedabad was the city in which Gandhi had led the demonstration about which Erikson had read as a youth. Indeed, Erikson's host was none other than Ambalal Sarabahai, the benevolent industrialist who had been Gandhi's host—as well as antagonist—in the 1918 wage dispute. Throughout his stay in Ahmedabad, Erikson continued to encounter people and places that were related to Gandhi's initial experiments with nonviolent techniques.

The more Erikson learned about the event at Ahmedabad, the more intrigued he became with its pivotal importance in Gandhi's career. It seemed to be the historical moment upon which all the earlier events of Gandhi's life converged and from which diverged all of his later endeavors. So captured was Erikson by the event at Ahmedabad, that he returned the following year to research a book on Gandhi in which the event would serve as a fulcrum.

At least part of Erikson's interest in Gandhi may have stemmed from certain parallels in their lives. The 1918 event marked Gandhi's emergence as a national political leader. He was 48 at the time, and had become involved reluctantly, not so much out of a need for power or fame as out of a genuine conviction that something had to be done about the disintegration of Indian culture. Coincidentally, Erikson's book, "Childhood and Society," appeared in 1950 when Erikson was 48, and it is that book which brought him national prominence in the mental health field. Like Gandhi, too, Erikson reluctantly did what he felt he had to do (namely, publish his observations and conclusions) for the benefit of his ailing profession and for the patients treated by its practitioners. So while Erikson's affinity with Luther seemed to derive from comparable professional identity crises, his affinity for Gandhi appears to derive from a parallel crisis of generativity. A passage from "Gandhi's Truth" (from a chapter wherein Erikson addresses himself directly to his subject) helps to convey Erikson's feeling for his subject.

So far, I have followed you through the loneliness of your childhood and through the experiments and the scruples of your youth. I have affirmed my belief in your ceaseless endeavor to perfect yourself as a man who came to feel that he was the only one available to reverse India's fate. You experimented with what to you were debilitating temptations and you did gain vigor and agility from your victories over yourself. Your identity could be no less than that of universal man, although you had to become an Indian—and one close to the masses—first.

The following passage speaks to Erikson's belief in the general significance of Gandhi's efforts:

We have seen in Gandhi's development the strong attraction of one of those more inclusive identities: that of an enlightened citizen of the British Empire. In proving himself willing neither to abandon vital ties to his native tradition nor to sacrifice lightly a Western education which eventually contributed to his ability to help defeat British hegemony—in all of these seeming contradictions Gandhi showed himself on intimate terms with the actualities of his era. For in all parts of the world, the struggle now is for the *anticipatory development of more inclusive identities* ... I submit then, that Gandhi, in his immense intuition for historical actuality and his capacity to assume leadership in "truth in action," may have created a ritualization through which men, equipped with both realism and strength, can face each other with mutual confidence.

There is now more and more teaching of Erikson's concepts in psychiatry, psychology, education and social work in America and in other parts of the world. His description of the stages of the life cycle is summarized in major textbooks in all of these fields and clinicians are increasingly looking at their cases in Eriksonian terms.

Research investigators have, however, found Erikson's formulations somewhat difficult to test. This is not surprising, inasmuch as Erikson's conceptions, like Freud's, take into account the infinite complexity of the human personality. Current research methodologies are, by and large, still not able to deal with these complexities at their own level, and distortions are inevitable when such concepts as "identity" come to be defined in terms of responses to a questionnaire.

Likewise, although Erikson's life-stages have an intuitive "rightness" about them, not everyone agrees with his formulations. Douvan and Adelson in their book, "The Adolescent Experience," argue that while his identity theory may hold true for boys, it doesn't for girls. This argument is based on findings which suggest that girls postpone identity consolidation until after marriage (and intimacy) have been established.

Such postponement occurs, says Douvan and Adelson, because a woman's identity is partially defined by the identity of the man whom she marries. This view does not really contradict Erikson's, since he recognizes that later events, such as marriage, can help to resolve both current and past developmental crises. For the woman, but not for the man, the problems of identity and intimacy may be solved concurrently.

Objections to Erikson's formulations have come from other directions as well. Robert W. White, Erikson's good friend and colleague at Harvard, has a long-standing (and warm-hearted) debate with Erikson over his life-stages. White believes that his own theory of "competence motivation," a theory which has received wide recognition, can account for the phenomena of ego development much more economically than can Erikson's stages. Erikson has, however, little interest in debating the validity of the stages he has described. As an artist he recognizes that there are many different ways to view one and the same phenomenon and that a perspective that is congenial to one person will be repugnant to another. He offers his stage-wise description of the life cycle for those who find such perspectives congenial and not as a world view that everyone should adopt.

It is this lack of dogmatism and sensitivity to the diversity and complexity of the human personality which help to account for the growing recognition of Erikson's contribution within as well as without the helping professions. Indeed, his psychohistorical investigations have originated a whole new field of study which has caught the interest of historians and political scientists alike. (It has also intrigued his wife, Joan, who has published pieces on Eleanor Roosevelt and who has a book on Saint Francis in press.) A recent issue of *Daedalus,* the journal for the American Academy of Arts and Sciences, was entirely devoted

FREUD'S "AGES OF MAN"

Erik Erikson's definition of the "eight ages of man" is a work of synthesis and insight by a psychoanalytically trained and worldly mind. Sigmund Freud's description of human phases stems from his epic psychological discoveries and centers almost exclusively on the early years of life. A brief summary of the phases posited by Freud:

Oral stage—roughly the first year of life, the period during which the mouth region provides the greatest sensual satisfaction. Some derivative behavioral traits which may be seen at this time are *incorporativeness* (first six months of life) and *aggressiveness* (second six months of life).

Anal stage—roughly the second and third years of life. During this period the site of greatest sensual pleasure shifts to the anal and urethral areas. Derivative behavioral traits are *retentiveness* and *expulsiveness.*

Phallic stage—roughly the third and fourth years of life. The site of greatest sensual pleasure during this stage is the genital region. Behavior traits derived from this period include *intrusiveness* (male) and *receptiveness* (female).

Oedipal stage—roughly the fourth and fifth years of life. At this stage the young person takes the parent of the opposite sex as the object or provider of sensual satisfaction and regards the same-sexed parent as a rival. (The "family romance.") Behavior traits originating in this period are *seductiveness* and *competitiveness.*

Latency stage—roughly the years from age 6 to 11. The child resolves the Oedipus conflict by identifying with the parent of the opposite sex and by so doing satisfies sensual needs vicariously. Behavior traits developed during this period include *conscience* (or the internalization of parental moral and ethical demands).

Puberty stage—roughly 11 to 14. During this period there is an integration and subordination of oral, anal and phallic sensuality to an overriding and unitary genital *sexuality*. The genital sexuality of puberty has another young person of the opposite sex as its object, and discharge (at least for boys) as its aim. Derivative behavior traits (associated with the control and regulation of genital sexuality) are *intellectualization* and *estheticism.*

—D.E.

to psycho-historical and psycho-political investigations of creative leaders by authors from diverse disciplines who have been stimulated by Erikson's work.

Now in his 68th year, Erikson maintains the pattern of multiple activities and appointments which has characterized his entire career. He spends the fall in Cambridge, Mass., where he teaches a large course on "the human life cycle" for Harvard seniors. The spring semester is spent at his home in Stockbridge, Mass., where he participates in case conferences and staff seminars at the Austen Riggs Center. His summers are spent on Cape Cod. Although Erikson's major commitment these days is to his psycho-historical investigation, he is embarking on a study of pre-school children's play constructions in different settings and countries, a follow-up of some research he conducted with preadolescents more than a quarter-century ago. He is also planning to review other early observations in the light of contemporary change. In his approach to his work, Erikson appears neither drawn nor driven, but rather to be following an inner schedule as natural as the life cycle itself.

Although Erikson, during his decade of college teaching, has not seen any patients or taught at psychoanalytic institutes, he maintains his dedication to psychoanalysis and views his psycho-historical investigations as an applied branch of that discipline.

While some older analysts continue to ignore Erikson's work, there is increasing evidence (including a recent poll of psychiatrists and psychoanalysts) that he is having a rejuvenating influence upon a discipline which many regard as dead or dying. Young analysts are today proclaiming a "new freedom" to see Freud in historical perspective—which reflects the Eriksonian view that one can recognize Freud's greatness without bowing to conceptual precedent.

Accordingly, the reports of the demise of psychoanalysis may have been somewhat premature. In the work of Erik Erikson, at any rate, psychoanalysis lives and continues to beget life.

21. LOVE AMONG THE MONKEYS

Harry F. Harlow, the father of the surrogate mother, is well known for his more than 40 years of research on primate development. His innovative use of terry cloth-covered wire monkeys as surrogate mothers helped explain the importance of contact comfort and warmth in mother-infant relationships. It has been thought that mother's milk was the prime factor in the mother-infant bond. Last month, Harlow was in New York to be honored with a $25,000 award from the Kittay Scientific Foundation (SN: 6/14/75, p. 383). He used the occasion to discuss some of his research and to describe another type of research mother —the monkey monster mother.

Primate emotional development, especially love and aggression, has long been a subject of investigation for Harlow and his colleagues at the Wisconsin Regional Primate Research Center. Their work has shown that external aggression, aggression directed toward others, develops relatively late in primates. In macaque monkeys, for

instance, full-blown aggression is not displayed until the fourth year in males and later in females. This is equivalent to the midteens in humans.

In contrast, various types of love (mother love, peer love and the beginnings of heterosexual love) develop early in life and have a chance to become well established before aggression comes into play. "It is fortunate," says Harlow, "that aggression is a late-maturing mechanism. Were it otherwise there would never have been even one primate society. At an early age all the infants would have destroyed each other and societies without infants become societies without adults."

Experiments with monkeys isolated from birth show just how important it is to experience love and to learn loving ways before aggression develops. Infant rhesus monkeys were raised in total isolation for six months of the first year of life and for six months in partial isolation where they could see and hear other monkeys but not be with them. At the age of three, these animals were compared with mother-raised and peer-raised monkeys in their reactions to strange

Reprinted from *Science News* by permission of publisher.

monkeys. The isolates threatened, pulled, bit and tore violently at the hair and flesh of the strangers to a significantly greater degree than did the others. In these isolates, explains Harlow, no ties of affection had had a chance to be formed prior to the opportunity for aggressive behaviors to emerge, and normal positive age-mate play had not been present to soften the sadistic sorties.

Outgroup aggression, or violence against strangers, is not too hard to imagine. The most dramatic expression of agonistic behavior in both monkeys and humans is aggression against their own children. This too can be created in the laboratory. Mother love can be almost perpetually prevented by withholding mother love from the mother-to-be, even if she isn't to be a mother for many years. Harlow and his co-workers illustrated the battered child syndrome with motherless mothers who proved to be monsters as mothers.

The motherless mothers were animals that had never had the chance to express love to a mother nor to exchange affection in play with age-mates. After giving birth, they showed two basic behaviors. One was to totally ignore the infants. The other pattern, says Harlow, was grim and ghastly. When an infant attempted to make physical contact with its mother, she would literally scrape it from her body and abuse it by various sadistic devices. The mother would push the baby's face against the floor and rub it back and forth. Not infrequently, the mother would encircle the infant's head with her jaws, and in one case an infant's skull was crushed in this manner.

In most instances, the researchers were able to stop the sadism, but some mothers were so violent and vicious that a few infants were lost because the researchers had not anticipated the severity of the events in the reproduction of the battered child syndrome.

The motherless mothers, says Harlow, gave more to science than their offspring. They not only opened doors of understanding of the battered child syndrome but also provided two fringe benefits. First was confirmation of the power and persistence of infant love for the mother. If the infants were among those favored and fortunate enough to be just ignored by their mothers, or if they had survived the battering, they persisted in their intense efforts to make and maintain contact with the mother whether or not she scraped them away or engaged in maternal mayhem. The amount of punishment or banishment the infants would accept was a measure of their motivation.

The second bonus from the babies was that after they had continuously forced their mothers into accepting protracted contact, some of the contact comfort, softness and warmth seemed to rub off on the mothers. Furthermore, after the maternal contact had been achieved for a period of time, there tended to be a gradual but progressive maternal rehabilitation with partial or total submission to the infantile affection. The few mothers who succumbed were impressively more normal in the treatment of subsequent infants of their own. This finding has implications for therapies with humans.

"Research has shown," concludes Harlow, "that developmental timing and sequencing of the loves and of aggression are of vast significance in preventing or ameliorating aggression. When the development is out of normal sequence, aggression is uncontrolled and extremely difficult to alter or eliminate. New therapeutic techniques are making rehabilitation more of a reality, but the ideal solution is to prevent antisocial aggression through anticipation."

22. THE HOMOSEXUALITY HANGUP

Wayne Sage

"It is one thing," wrote Alfred Kinsey in 1948, "if we are dealing with a type of activity that is unusual, without precedent among other animals, and restricted to peculiar types of individuals within the human population. It is another if the phenomenon proves to be a fundamental part, not only of human sexuality, but all mammalian patterns as a whole." Kinsey was referring to homosexuality, which, whatever it is, is apparently none of the things we have always assumed it to be.

One of the principal things it has been thought to be, by most Western religions, is an abomination—or, by some psychiatrists, such as New York psychoanalyst Dr. Charles Socarides, a violation of nature that runs against "two and one-half billion years of mammalian heritage."

As early as 1911 André Gide suggested that "uncustomary" is probably a better adjective to describe homosexual acts than "unnatural." Judging from Kinsey's findings, they are not even uncustomary. His survey of over 12,000 adult males found that 37 percent had experienced at least one same-sex encounter leading to orgasm. The best current estimate for the number of predominately homosexual persons in the United States is 20 million. Homosexual practices are commonplace in primitive societies. Primates, rodents, even the noble porpoise have been caught at their gay pursuits. Historically, it has occasionally been accepted (in ancient Mesopotamia), even exalted (ancient Sparta), if generally condemned.

But we condemn less these days than we used to. Or at least we have changed our terms. As psychiatry began to take on the job of handling our deviants for us, homosexuality, as with so many of our moral outrages, became a disease. That is, we attempted to treat it as one.

The problem is that any respectable disease must meet three requirements. First, there must be abnormal symptoms. Second, some pathological condition, readily identifiable and definitely harmful, must be linked to—the third requirement—a cause.

One of the major proponents of the disease theory, the late Dr. Edmund Bergler, offered six personality traits which he believed were common to all homosexuals and which, therefore, he felt fulfilled the first requirement. They were "masochistic provocation," "defensive malice," "flippancy covering depression and guilt," "hypernarcissism," "refusal to acknowledge accepted standards in nonsexual matters" and "general unreliability."

In 1956 Dr. Evelyn Hooker, a West Coast psychologist who headed the National Institute of Mental Health's task force on homosexuality, submitted the results of psychiatric tests on 30 "normal, overt male homosexuals" and a comparable group of heterosexuals to a panel of experts on each of the tests used. Not only could the panel find "no difference of degree of adjustment between the two"; when the results for each gay subject were paired with those for one of the straights and resubmitted, even the psychiatrists and psychologists were unable to tell which of the volunteers were homosexual and which were heterosexual. Dr. Hooker "very tentatively" suggested that homosexuality might be "a deviation of sexual pattern which is within the normal range," noted that "its forms are as varied as are those of heterosexuality" and finally concluded that "homosexuality as a clinical entity does not exist." The gasp that went through the scientific community was one from which it has only now begun to recover.

The repeats of this study have been numerous, with gays undergoing practically every test known to psychiatry. Most notable is that recently run under the direction of educational psychologist Marvin Siegelman of the City University of New York. His subjects included gay teachers, artists, physicians, business executives, musicians, college students and cooks, to name but a few of the occupations represented. This group was matched with heterosexuals similar in education and socioeconomic background. Not only were there "no significant differences in terms of alienation, trust, dependency and neuroticism," but the gays actually scored better than the straights on four separate aspects of personal adjustment: self-acceptance, goal directedness, sense of self and nurturance. Siegelman, continuing his analysis of the data on his original subjects, believes that what his colleagues in the field may have been measuring all along is something quite aside from neuroticism—femininity. He draws a clear distinction between what he calls the male "invert," a homosexual whose "perceptions and personality are typical of women," and the "homosexual" per se, "whose sex object is men but whose behavior otherwise is masculine."

On comparing the more masculine homosexuals and heterosexuals selected from each of his two former groups, the better adjustment ranking for the homosexuals reappeared. They were again higher on self-acceptance, nurturance, goal-directedness and sense of self.

Separating out the members of the homosexual sample who displayed qualities stereotyped by society as "feminine," Siegelman found that the heavy contributor to the behavior disorder claim seems to be detected by factor I on the *Crowne and Marlow Social Desirability Scale*. The person who typically scores high here has been described as "over-protected, cultured, fastidious, gentle, helpless, emotionally sensitive and basing his reactions on unrealistic, emotional feelings." It has occasionally been labeled a "masculinity versus femininity" rating in a questionable effort to pin strong personality traits on males and to associate weak ones with females. When the homosexuals low on this ranking were compared to those high on the measure, the so-called "feminine" gays were indeed determined to be more tender minded, submissive, anxious, generally neurotic, alienated, dependent and lower on trust, goal directedness, self-acceptance and sense of self. There were no differences on the depression or nurturance measures.

Yet even here Siegelman does not feel that such a deviation from the norm can, in and of itself, be construed as an indication of psychopathology. "The tendency of some therapists to describe all (male) homosexuals as feminine," he says, "may be due to the higher incidence of neuroticism among feminine homosexuals, which brings them into more frequent contact with therapists. The masculine homosexuals may rarely be seen by the therapist, who erroneously concludes that all (male) homosexuals are feminine and neurotic."

Perhaps the most comprehensive of all

works on the social functioning of homosexuals is the British Wolfenden Report. This revolutionary document was prepared in 1957 by the Committee on Homosexual Offenses and Prostitution under the chairmanship of Sir John Frederick Wolfenden. After sifting more evidence for a longer period of time on more homosexuals than practically anyone (except Kinsey) had ever attempted to deal with, that committee finally deemed homosexuals generally well adjusted socially. It also noted that the homophile way of life does not "lead on" to other offenses.

Finally, where there is a disease, there must be a cause. Most experts agree that homosexuality is a learned, acquired trait, sort of, to some extent. Psychiatrist Dr. Irving Bieber, one of the most noted contributors to the sickness theory, traces male homosexuality to an "inappropriately close relationship" between son and mother and a relationship with the father marked by "fear and hostility." He goes on to claim that children likely to become homosexual can usually be identified between the ages of seven and 10.

Even Dr. Hooker tends to agree. "The emasculation of the boy by the mother and the lack of a male model with whom to identify is a contributing cause for a sizeable number of people," she says, but she goes on to emphasize that this is "not the only cause."

More recently, this idea has been almost completely undercut by the PhD dissertation of psychologist Thomas Pritt of the University of Utah. His studies of male homosexuals' own perceptions of their family relationships reveal that it is Dad, not Mom, who is more often at fault. Though there were no significant differences in the homosexual group's attitudes toward their mothers compared to a heterosexual control group, their relationships with their fathers often showed wide variations. Gen-

erally speaking, hostile, distant fathers seem to be characteristic of a homosexual's childhood, regardless of the role played by the mother.

Some researchers have sought a more fundamental explanation in biological terms. Both male and female hormones are known to be present, to some degree, in both men and women. Though the layman generally equates male homosexuality with femininity, a link to an excess of female hormones has never been found. This is not for want of trying, however, and along the way, some intriguing facts have come to light.

Dr. Sidney Margolese, a Los Angeles endocrinologist, selected 10 male subjects who felt themselves to be strongly homosexual and 14 who felt themselves to be strongly heterosexual. Urine samples were then collected over a 24-hour period. Normally, when the male sex hormone, testosterone, is broken down by the body, two byproducts—androsterone and etiocholanolone—show up in the urine of both homosexuals and heterosexuals, whether male or female. When the ratios of the two chemicals were computed for Dr. Margolese's samples, the amount of androsterone was invariably greater than the amount of etiocholanolone in male heterosexuals. In homosexuals, this ratio was reversed.

Dr. Margolese later happened to mention this finding to Dr. Oscar Janiger, a psychiatrist studying homosexuality at the University of California. Himself a firm believer in the theory of homosexuality as a behavior pattern developed in childhood, Janiger promptly challenged Margolese to a test of his claim. Urine samples of a mixed group of homosexuals and heterosexuals were handed over to Margolese, who was to identify each with regard to sexual orientation. He did so correctly in every case.

Working along with Dr. Richard Green of UCLA, Dr. Margolese has discovered a similar effect, in reverse, for women. In heterosexual females the amount of etiocholanolone in the urine is always greater than that of androsterone. For lesbians, the balance is in the opposite direction.

Dr. Margolese is quick to insist, however, that the relation between androsterone and etiocholanolone amounts is not the cause of homosexuality. Such ratios are also known to be correlated with such conditions as thyroid problems, diabetes and mental depression. But though he believes the underlying cause of homosexuality is still unknown, he quickly adds that "we must not close our minds to the possibility of a biochemical explanation."

No one has. A team of medical researchers at the Harvard Medical School recently took a more direct approach by measuring the amounts of testosterone itself in the blood plasma of 30 male homosexuals. Again, in every case the testosterone level was lower than that of the heterosexual controls. A consistently lower sperm count was also discovered. But once again the causal effect was denied.

When Masters and Johnson echoed this finding at their clinic in St. Louis, but reiterated the disclaimer of a cause-effect relationship, the conclusion fell on unbelieving ears in one British research institute. The English team repeated these studies, then, perhaps too thoroughly believing, used injections to raise the level of testosterone in several homosexual subjects in the hope of straightening out their sex lives. The injections only increased the subjects' homosexual drives.

Nevertheless, the lack of a clear-cut cause has not slowed the search for a cure. The traditional approach has always been years of psychotherapy, yet not only are psychiatrists ignorant of the "disease" they are treating, they are less than clear on what it means to "cure" a homosexual.

Some therapists set their sights on nothing less than an exclusively heterosexual life for their patients. Dr. Irving Bieber of the New York University Medical School claims a one-third cure rate by such standards. Others insist such a cure is, if not impossible, at least superficial, often resulting in patients acting out the "illusion of heterosexuality" contrary to their fundamental drives. One prominent psychiatrist even reports that he received several patients on the rebound from psychoanalysts who had attempted such cures, the homosexuals not wanting to return to their former doctors because they did not want to disappoint them.

There is a newer method, however. When the late-night conversation in the booth at a gay bar turns to horror stories, there are two words that can instantly chill every homosexual spine: aversion therapy. This neat little Pavlovian trick uses electric shocks to punish the male patient when he is shown erotic pictures of another male. When viewing an attractive female, he is rewarded by the absence of pain.

For all its repugnance to homosexuals who say they do not want to be redirected, aversion therapy is undeniably effective, in its way. Dr. Lawrence Hatterer, author of *Changing Homosexuality in the Male,* takes into consideration 240 factors in determining a given patient's capacity for change. Age, religious background and personality factors, for example, play major roles, but by far the two most important indicators are a genuine desire to change and some previous heterosexual experience. The Kinsey continuum, a seven-point scale running from exclusively homosexual to exclusively heterosexual with the varying degrees of bisexuality represented by the middle numbers, is used as a gauge. It is generally acknowledged that aversion therapy can, if repeated often enough over a long period, nudge almost any patient a few notches along the scale. Dr. Hooker's task force estimates that about 40 percent of "predominately homosexual patients who have some heterosexual orientation ... can become predominately heterosexual," though one cannot help but wonder if a similar treatment in reverse could not coax heterosexuals in the opposite direction.

But the ultimate technique for snuffing out homosexual impulses is the hypothalamotomy, defined most specifically by one British medical journal as "the stereotaxic ablation of the ventromedial hypothalamic nucleus or 'sex-behavior' center." In the vernacular, holes are bored in the skull and those areas of the brain related to sexual motivation systematically destroyed. The reporting German surgeon at the Neu-Mariahilf Hospital in Göttingen first tried out this method some time ago on three homosexual child molestors. A reduction in sex drive resulted in a "complete abolition of homosexual tendencies in two and a sufficient (decrease) in the third to enable them to be controlled." Not surprisingly, follow up studies at three and six months and seven years revealed a total absence of further sex offenses by the three.

Of course the medical profession at large has never recommended such drastic measures for other than dangerous patients who cannot be helped in any other way. Such offenders, surveys have consistently shown, are only rarely homosexual anyway. Child molesting and rape are predominately heterosexual problems.

One final and eminently more palatable way of influencing sexual orientation is that suggested by UCLA psychiatrist Dr. Richard Green. Going along with the Bieber idea that little boys likely to become homosexual can often be identified at an early age, Green believes that professional intervention into family relationships can encourage masculinity and thus redirect gender identity, especially when parents are willing to modify their own child-rearing attitudes. Dr. Green reports two cases, one a five-year-old and another a four-and-one-half-year-old boy, both diagnosed as excessively "feminine," who have shown a "capacity for change." Longitudinal studies to prove the effectiveness of either the methods of identification or treatment have yet to be carried out, however.

One final nagging gap in our knowledge is the fact that studies have generally concentrated on males. Little girls who grow up to be lesbians find themselves even further in the dark corners of scientific presumption than do men who take to the closets rather than face their homosexual identities.

Perhaps this is partly because female homosexuality seems to be less common than male homosexuality. Only one out of 10 women compared to one out of six men, by Kinsey's estimates, lean passionately toward favoring their own sex. Also, according to another of psychologist Jan Loney's surveys on homosexual lifestyles, lesbians seem generally "better behaved" socially (i.e., less likely to allow themselves to be found out publicly).

Of course, both of these tendencies may be largely due to our traditional cultural demand that women "act like ladies"—that is to say, repress themselves sexually. But otherwise, psychiatrists have tended to assume that homosexuality in the female is simply the mirror image of homosexuality in the male. If a hostile father tends to predispose his son toward male sex partners, the unaffectionate mother would do so for his sister, and so on for each point in the traditional theoretical schemes.

Yet the theory remains only presumption in that no researcher had ever considered it worthwhile to take time out from studying males to make a direct, systematic effort to either prove or disprove the stereotype of a lesbian. Finally, when British clinical psychiatrist June Hopkins did just this, and found the lesbians generally getting on quite well with the world, her findings were quickly challenged by the psychiatric team of David Swanson, Dale Loomis, Robert Lukesh, Robert Cronin and Jackson Smith, all of the Mayo Clinic in Rochester, Minnesota. Preferring to accept the "lesbian characteristics" listed by British psychiatrist F. E. Kenyon, they took a somewhat different research approach. The heterosexual control group was eliminated in their study. So were the "normal" homosexuals. Instead, the lesbians were chosen from their files on female psychiatric patients and then compared to heterosexual women who had also sought aid for emotional problems.

The lesbians thus selected did match, to some extent, Kenyon's description. There was a relatively high incidence of hostile parents, psychiatric disorders and so on. But they were also found similar to women psychiatric patients in general. All the women under study complained most frequently of fear or hopelessness. There was extensive evidence of family disorganization and conflict, but it occurred with equal frequency in both groups. The researchers were finally forced to conclude that "the lesbian who seeks psychiatric treatment is similar to any other seriously troubled female patient. She is stressed, conflicted and unsatisfied because of various conditions in her life . . . and the conflict over homosexuality was only one factor (not a primary one) that caused the patient to seek treatment." They went on to add that their results, which failed to show "significant historic and clinical factors specific to the lesbian, makes a psychological etiology of female homosexuality open to even more questions than already exists."

But lately, Marvin Siegelman has been trying just as hard to answer those questions for the female as he did for the male homosexual. Kenyon's "lesbian character-

istics" had led to a neuroticism score for the female homosexuals higher than that for a group of university students but not high enough to be considered proof of psychopathology. On examining Kenyon's data more closely, Siegelman discovered that the problem seems to have been not so much one relating to the subjects' homosexuality as their heterosexuality. Over 34 percent of Kenyon's subjects were actually predominately heterosexual with homosexual "problems." Nearly 20 percent, though more homosexual than heterosexual, were maintaining a fair amount of heterosexual activity. Nine percent were predominately heterosexual and 7 percent were bisexual. "The need to sample a wider segment of the homosexual community is emphasized by the contradictory findings that emerge when (such) contrasting samples are evaluated," he pointed out, and, as he had done in his studies on gay males, went after such a sample.

Siegelman began by trying to establish contacts through homosexual organizations (in this case, primarily the Daughters of Bilitis) and the patrons of a homosexual bookstore in New York's Greenwich Village. Customers known to be homosexuals by the store's owners were given questionnaires and information and were asked to pass the word on to homosexual friends who might be willing to volunteer. Within a few months, Siegelman had located homosexual women from a wide variety of professions. Nurses, social workers, editors, a statistician, a librarian, a psychiatrist were among those tested and finally included in the sample.

Actually, Siegelman is not yet satisfied that even this was a "random or representative sample" of a homosexual population that does not necessarily join homosexual organizations or patronize such shops or gay bars and, therefore, even today remains out of the reach of most scientific investigations. But he feels his methods did round up a group far closer to the homosexual norm than previous studies which used only mental patients.

His results: Female homosexuality does indeed seem to be the mirror image of homosexuality in the male. Not because their "pathologies" are similar, but by virtue of the fact that both seem to adjust particularly well in some respects, perhaps as a result of being forced to come to grips with the social conflicts resulting from their sexual orientation. The lesbians scored consistently lower than the heterosexual control group on depression, higher on self-acceptance and goal direction. There were no differences on "total neuroticism." The heterosexual women were found to be generally more "tense and excitable" than the lesbians. These results matched the findings originally published by June Hopkins. On the basis of the psychiatric analyses she had made for normal homosexual women at the United Cambridge Hospital, in England, she had suggested that the description "neurotic" be replaced with the following profile: independent, resilient, reserved, dominant, bohemian, self-sufficient and composed.

In 1948, exhausted by the most extensive compilation to that date of information for evaluating theories of symptoms, pathological conditions, causes and cures, the Wolfenden committee concluded: "Our evidence suggests that homosexuality does not fit any of them unless the terms in which they are defined are beyond what could reasonably be regarded as legitimate." The committee finally contented itself with labeling such acts merely a sin, as opposed to a crime, and demurred: "There must remain a realm of private morality and immorality which is, in brief and crude terms, not the law's business." All English statutes

prohibiting homosexual acts in private between consenting adults were eventually thrown out as a result of that committee's recommendations.

Where have the years of research since 1948 led us? If anywhere, in the same direction. Within the mental health profession itself, the disease theory is losing ground. One recent survey found only 41 percent of the experts still subscribe to the idea that homosexuality is a sickness. Ninety percent felt that the public has been seriously misled by that label in the past. Perhaps also significantly, 54 percent of all psychiatrists still cling to the sickness view compared to only 28 percent of the psychologists. Yet, for all the disagreement on the basics, there is one point on which virtually all behavioral scientists (99 percent in the most recent survey) now agree with the Wolfenden Report: the necessity for repealing all laws violating the civil liberties of this minority.

In fact, society's overtime game of odd man out with the homosexual may be coming to an end altogether, mainly because the homosexual himself no longer wants to play. Homosexual activist and lobbyist groups abound. Gay candidates are running for, even sometimes winning, political offices. Even public acceptance is beginning to swing their way. One recent Penn State graduate, denied a teaching position in public school for admission of his homosexuality, found to his amazement that community support in the small, conservative Pennsylvania town was on his side in his legal battle to regain his job.

Psychologist Kenneth Smith of the State University of New York at Fredonia recently turned the tables in the traditional experimental design for the study of homosexuality. This time the personality profiles were administered to 130 heterosexual undergraduates to "investigate individuals whose negative attitude toward homosexuals may contribute to the problem" of the social pressure with which gays must learn to cope. The tentative profile found that those extremely antagonistic toward and intolerant of homosexuals tended to be "status conscious, authoritarian and sexually rigid."

There is one final charge by the more traditional psychiatrists, however. It is something less than scientific in approach, yet, as with most such accusations, it has been one of the most difficult to dispel. This claim is that homosexuality is a maldevelopment of the emotional capacity to "love." Some investigators have gone into gay bars to run "living-arrangement" surveys. The majority of the women interviewed were found to be living with one partner over long periods of time. The majority of the men were not. The Pritt study did reveal that homosexual "acting out" does generally involve "relationship needs" rather than just the reduction of sexual tension. But unfortunately, there is simply no scientific definition of the ability to love, much less a test for it.

Yet, repeatedly, in their legal battles, homosexuals have found themselves confronted with the insistence that they prove just this.

Jack Baker, at 28, is a top University of Minnesota law student, the president of the student body—and an admitted homosexual. For the last two of the five years he has been living with James McConnell, he has been fighting for the right to marry. Baker, like a good lawyer, recently argued his case against the State of Minnesota from practically every conceivable moral, religious and legal standpoint. Yet his brief for the trial revolves around one point:

We feel it is the relationship i.e. love and concern that is important—not procreation. We look at marriage as a commandment of God to love one's companion. In our view,

sex is a natural extension of love and a child is the biological result of sex between a man and a woman. But a child is by no means necessary to create a valid marriage. It is more important that people learn to share their lives with someone who will help them grow and mature. Someone who will share their happiness and their troubles.

That may be, of course. Still, in the final analysis, at least from a social point of view, homosexuality can probably never be considered exactly as desirable as heterosexuality precisely because of the absence of the possibility of procreation.

Should it nonetheless be recognized as an alternative lifestyle for those who would choose it? The Baker argument continues:

Any relationship that promotes honesty, self-respect, mutual growth and understanding for two people and which harms no other person should be accepted by law. Relationships which foster harmony among the participants remove disharmony from the community. And conversely, relationships that foster disharmony among the participants increase disharmony in society. Since society has an interest in maintaining order, it is to society's benefit to recognize and encourage harmonious relationships. There is no biological reason why the participants in a harmonious relationship have to be of the opposite sex. Therefore, we believe the state is unwise to set up artificial criteria when there is no compelling reason to do so.

Again, perhaps so. But the insistance of the militant gay groups that their sexual orientation is solely a matter of personal preference may be too simplistic. One further demand—an end to all scientific research on the subject—is a mistake even from their point of view.

There can be no doubt that some psychiatrists have speculated recklessly and added to the subjugation and ridicule of a group whose only social offense, it does now seem, is being different. One prominent Washington psychiatrist is firmly convinced (on the basis of two cases) that obesity is often a give-away to true homosexuality due to what he feels is an oral fixation which necessarily drives gays to overeat. Another, in Chicago, begins his treatments assuming a correlation between the degree of homosexuality in adulthood and the number of "compulsory childhood enemas."

Science, and pseudo-science, as any other intellectual endeavors, can be used to rationalize the imposition on all of the standards of the majority. This does not, however, amend the simple fact that objective, competent investigators such as Hooker, Kinsey and Wolfenden have done more to free the homosexual from his closet than all the gay lib parades and marches put together.

Perhaps, even, anthropologists Clellan Ford and Frank Beach are correct in their claim that homosexuality is "a basic capacity" of all mammals and differs only in degree from one individual to the next. Sex researchers attempting to wrest the truth from people concerning their individual sexual histories have found that children,

for whom heterosexual acts are more strictly off limits, tend to lie much more often about their heterosexual experiences, admitting their homosexual contacts with relative ease. Adults, however, for whom homosexual acts are proscribed by society, give false information more often when it comes to their homosexual encounters.

Ultimately, today's gay militants may be correct anyway in one of their fundamental claims: that the varying facets of human love are not a proper subject for scientific inquiry.

But sex is a proper subject. The homosexuals' legal battles for employment and the right to privacy have been won in recent years on the factual basis of scientific studies. And hopefully, whatever the nature of homosexuality is ever found to be, it will be on this basis—the truth, rather than ignorance—that society will proceed in its dealings with all the problems which have been too sensitive to handle in the past, but will no longer stay hidden.

23. WHAT MAKES CREATIVE PEOPLE DIFFERENT

Colin Martindale

Artists, by choice and by repute, are eccentric, sensitive and antisocial. The poet Emile Verhaeren disconnected his doorbell because its ringing caused him pain; Schiller could write only when he soaked his feet in ice water; and Proust lined his study with cork to shut out all distractions. Flaubert, Hölderlin and Swinburne holed themselves

Copyright © 1975 Ziff-Davis Publishing Company. Reprinted by permission of *Psychology Today* magazine. From *Psychology Today* (July), pp. 45–48.

up in isolation, being unable to tolerate the hue and hustle of madding crowds and barking dogs.

Folklore about creative people reports that they are merely vessels for the Muse, who races roughshod through their brains and produces a work of art whether they will it or not. Artists themselves help create the impression that novel ideas do not spring from the intellect or from conscious calculation, but come full-blown, often unbidden, from some mysterious dark corner of the mind. William Blake said that he wrote one poem "from immediate dictation, 12 or sometimes 20 or 30 lines at a time without premeditation, and even against my will." Mozart and Beethoven, we read, simply heard symphonies in their heads and had only to write them down. Creative scientists have the same experience as composers and poets. The French mathematician Henri Poincaré wrote:

One evening contrary to my custom, I drank coffee and could not sleep. Ideas rose in crowds: I felt them collide until pairs interlocked, making a stable combination. By the next morning I had established the existence of a class of Fuchsian functions ... I had only to write out the results, which took but a few hours.

What black coffee was to Poincaré, a pint of ale was to A. E. Housman, who reports that whole stanzas of poems came to him "with sudden and unaccountable emotion" while he was in a pleasantly sozzled state. The artist, then, seems separate from art. "I witness the breaking forth of my thoughts," wrote the poet Rimbaud, "I watch them, I listen to them." Hard work and logical thought do not enter the creative process until after the idea is born. Then it must be written down, painted, composed, transmitted.

For a long time I have been curious about the physiological basis of creative thought. Coffee and ale don't explain it, for sure. Perhaps there is something fundamentally different about the creative person's brain that accounts for the legendary eccentricities of style and the spontaneity of ideas.

PRIMARY AND SECONDARY THOUGHT

I took my first clues from the psychoanalytic explanation of creativity, which poses two kinds of thought proc-

esses. Primitive or *primary-process* thinking belongs to the chaotic realm of dreams and reveries, free associations, and fantasies, drug highs and mystical trances. It is "primary" because it comes first in our mental development and because it is the basic stuff of the unconscious. In contrast, *secondary-process* thinking is logical, analytic, and reality oriented. Psychoanalyst Ernst Kris explains that creativity comes from what he called "regression in the service of the ego." That is, the initial creative inspiration comes from the person's ability to regress to primary-process thought; the later elaboration of the idea requires the person to use secondary, logical thought to carry out the inspiration.

Some researchers believe that primary- and secondary-process thought belong to different hemispheres of the brain—that the right hemisphere is responsible for primary, creative thought while the left controls secondary, logical reasoning. I do not feel, however, that this explanation tells the whole story.

My approach to finding the physiological basis for the progression from primary to secondary thought rests on the level of cortical arousal in the brain. The eye sends information about what it sees to the brain (specifically, the cortex) through a pathway, the reticular activating system, which alerts the cortex that information is on its way. When an individual is in a completely deprived environment, and the reticular system has no information to announce at all, he eventually will become drowsy or fall asleep; some external stimulation is necessary for normal alertness. Cortical arousal increases as the person goes from sleep to brooding states of reverie and daydreams, to alert concentration, and finally to emotional agitation and panic.

We can measure the degree of cortical arousal with electroencephalograms (EEGs) of brain-wave frequency. For example, alpha rhythms go along with mental moods of complete relaxation and meditation; they are very slow, high-amplitude brain waves that range in frequency from eight to 13 cycles per second. The more aroused a person is, the fewer alpha waves he produces. When he reacts to a stimulus, his alpha rhythm is blocked, and replaced by fast, low-amplitude wave patterns (30 to 60 cycles per second).

We do our best rational work, our most efficient plotting and calculation, at medium levels of arousal. If one's brain-wave frequency is too high, and one is too upset, anxious or stressed, it is hard to concentrate and settle down to the task at hand. But if arousal is too low, and one's mind is floating off in a delicious daydream, the work won't get done either. Secondary thought, then, rests on medium levels of cortical

arousal. Primary-process thought may occur both with very high and very low levels of arousal. From dream states at one end to emotional highs at the other, the irrational stuff of new ideas floats in unplanned on a load of brain waves too high or too low to calculate with.

OF SWEETHEARTS AND BRICKS

Over the last few years my colleagues and I have sought to determine how creativity and cortical arousal are linked. We measured creativity in two ways. The Remote Associates Test consists of 30 sets of three words that are related in an associative rather than a logical way, and the person must come up with a fourth word in each case that goes along with the other three. Given the words *cookies, sixteen* and *heart,*

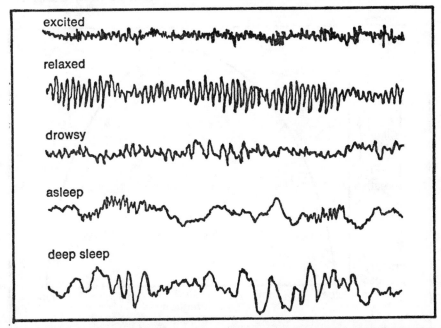

EXCITEMENT AND DEEP SLEEP. Electroencephalographic records during excitement, relaxation and varying degrees of sleep. Excitement is characterized by a rapid frequency and small amplitude, and deep sleep brings increasing irregularity and slow waves.
From Jasper, 1941. *Epilepsy and Cerebral Localizaton,* Charles C Thomas.

for example, one should answer *sweet*. This test is a valid measure of creativity, but it also depends on intelligence.

Our second measure was the Alternate Uses Test, which simply asks people to list as many uses as they can think of for common objects, such as a brick. Some people never come up with more than two or three obvious uses, and óthers go right on listing until you make them stop. (Some creative uses for bricks: "metaphorically, as in 'you've been a brick about this, Cynthia,' " and "a bug-hider—you leave it on the ground for a few days, pick it up and see the bugs hiding"). The Alternate Uses is a pure measure of creativity, unrelated to knowledge and intelligence; all one has to do to do well on it is come up with lots of novel ideas.

Perhaps, we thought, the reason that some creative talents are so oversensitive,

so unable to tolerate normal noises, is that their basic resting level of brain-wave activity is unusually high or low. In that case they would respond to otherwise innocuous stimuli, such as ringing doorbells or barking dogs, with larger increases in cortical arousal than those with moderate levels of resting brain-wave activity. Some researchers think these sudden jumps explain the oversensitivity of some schizophrenics. It may apply equally to creative people.

Creatives may not be able to tolerate simple distractions easily, but they have a marked preference for complicated distractions and attractions. Creative people, psychologists find, prefer designs that are complex, asymmetric, ambiguous and odd over the simple, orderly and familiar design that less creative people like. George Moore, the English novelist, explained, "I am above all perverse, almost everything

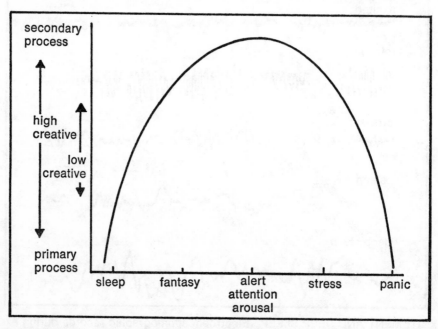

SECONDARY-AND PRIMARY-PROCESS THOUGHT. Secondary-process (rational) thinking goes along with medium levels of cortical arousal, while primary-process (imaginative) thought goes along with very low levels (sleep, fantasy) and high levels (stress, panic).

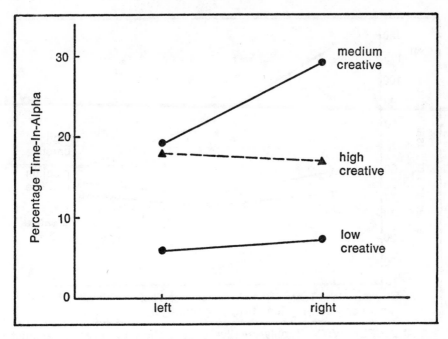

LEFT AND RIGHT HEMISPHERES. Percent of time during relaxation that produced alpha waves. Medium-creative people show the most extreme difference between the left hemisphere (secondary-process thought) and the right hemisphere alpha (primary process).

perverse fascinates me ... The commonplace, the natural, is constitutionally abhorrent." I'm not saying that all geniuses are perverse, but there is something to their "constitutional" fascination with novelty that again may be related to their baseline brain-wave patterns.

Two people, one creative, the other not, see the same modern abstract painting. One loves it, the other hates it. To explain why their reactions to it differ, psychologist Daniel Berlyne posed the theory that *medium* levels of cortical arousal bring pleasurable sensations. Art, like any other stimulus, increases brainwave frequency, and the more novel or complex it is, the greater its potential to arouse the brain. If creative and uncreative people prefer different degrees of novelty, perhaps medium arousal is different in the two cases. So

we're back to the idea that their resting levels of brain-wave activity differ also.

ALPHA WAVES AND CREATIVITY

To find out, we did five experiments, using the amount of alpha waves as a reverse measure of arousal. The more alpha, i.e., the more relaxed one's mental state, the less one's arousal. We measured each person's alpha rhythms with his eyes closed, to get the level in a resting state. Over the five studies, the highly creative people produced alpha waves 38 percent of the time, while medium- and low-creative people produced alpha 51 percent and 48 percent of the time. The highly creative people, we also determined, had higher levels of skin conductance, another good measure of arousal. In short, creative people do have higher rest-

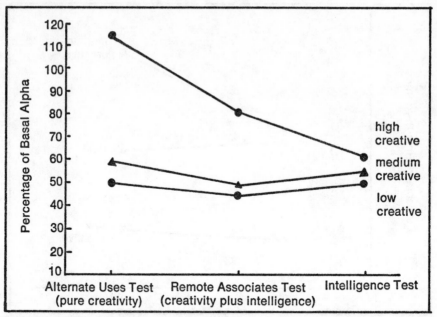

ALPHA AND CREATIVITY. Highly creative people show the greatest amount of alpha waves on pure tests of creativity (the Alternate Uses Test), and the lowest amount on intelligence tests. Less-creative people show no significant differences in their alpha patterns over tests.

ing levels of brain-wave activity, therefore less alpha, than average people.

Most of our alpha experiments measured alpha in the right hemisphere of the brain, which Robert Ornstein and others believe operates in a primary-process manner; the left hemisphere is primarily responsible for logical, intellectual thinking. Indeed, when we measured the amount of alpha in both hemispheres during relaxation, we found that medium-creative people had more alpha, and less arousal, in the right than in the left hemisphere. This suggests that they have more left arousal (secondary process) than right arousal (primary process). Highly creative people had about the same amount of alpha in both hemispheres, a greater level than that of low-creative people. While hemispheric differences may play a role in creative thought, alpha patterns count for more.

We speculated further that the supposed oversensitivity of creative people comes from the fact that they are blocking alpha rhythms more than uncreative people. We inferred that this was the case from three simple tests with students:

• We played a loud, high-pitched tone, a sound that would interrupt anyone's alpha patterns. But the highly creative individuals were more jarred by the noise, and later produced fewer alpha waves, than the rest.

• We gave electric shock to volunteers and asked them to rate the intensity of the shocks. The more creative the person, the more intensely he felt the shocks (the princess who felt the pea through 13 mattresses must have been extraordinarily innovative).

• Finally we gave students what is called a kinaesthetic aftereffect task, in which a blindfolded person rubs his fingers over a block of wood and then judges the width of another triangular-shaped block. Some people, augmenters, consistently overestimate the block's dimensions, while others underestimate its size. Our creative students came out as augmenters on this test.

These three experiments indicate that highly creative people amplify sights, sound and textures, and stimuli around them. They feel shock and noise more intensely; they exaggerate sizes and sensations. This oversensitivity is the subjective counterpart of the physiological overreactivity that shows up in greater alpha blocking on EEG records.

One would expect to find the greatest differences in brain waves between creative and uncreative people while they are doing things that call for imagination. So we measured alpha waves while the students took the two creativity tests and a culture-fair intelligence test.

This time, results were just the opposite of what we found when the students were simply meditating quietly. Now the most creative people were operating at a high frequency of alpha—low cortical arousal—on the creativity tests. They had the lowest level of arousal, and the most alpha, on the pure creativity measure (Alternate Uses); the highest on the intelligence (Remote Associates). The uncreative students, on the other hand, produced increased cortical arousal, and fewer alpha waves, on all the tests. They concentrate too well and too earnestly; they focus on the trees and overlook the forest.

CREATIVE BRAIN WAVES

In short, most people produce alpha waves when they are relaxing, and reduce alpha frequency when they are working on a problem. Creatives produce less alpha when they are relaxing, and increase their alpha frequency when they work on an imaginative problem. Creativity and intellectual ability require two different thought processes: the former calls for low cortical arousal and defusing one's powers of concentration; the latter calls for higher cortical arousal and focused attention.

We showed this contrast clearly with another group of students, asking them to make up stories while we studied the effect of speech on EEG patterns. We told half of them no more than that, but with the other half we stressed the importance of making the story as original as possible. Thus half of the students were under some pressure to be creative.

The uncreative students produced the same amount of alpha waves whether they were striving for creativity or not. But the imaginative students immediately produced significantly more alpha when we had told them to be original.

That result was so stunning that it seemed as though the creative students were turning on an alpha switch in their brains. How were they changing their levels of cortical arousal according to the demands of the moment, just like that? If they do it in some sort of purposeful or conscious manner, we thought, they should do well with biofeedback. We knew from studies by Joseph Kamiya [see "Conscious Control of Brain Waves," PT, April 1968], Barbara Brown [see "New Mind, New Body," August 1974] and others that people can learn to increase or decrease their frequency of alpha waves if they hear a tone or signal whenever their brains are producing alpha. Creatives, we reasoned, should be a whiz at this business.

But they aren't. On the first try of biofeedback tests, highly creative students were somewhat better at learning to produce alpha—or suppress it—in response to a tone than uncreatives. But after several trials the less creative people caught up with them. Overall, creative people actually did *worse* than others in learning to control or suppress alpha waves.

TM MAY STIFLE NOVELTY

Mind control and creativity, then, may be inversely related—if you're good at one, you're probably not so good at the other. Gary Schwartz studied teachers of transcendental meditation (TM), who should be especially good at physiological self-control, and found that on tests of creativity they scored worse or only as well as control groups. People who practice TM regularly have few spontaneous fluctuations in their skin conductance, but creative people have many. It's possible, then, that all the effort to promote biofeedback gadgets, alpha machines, and meditation, transcendental or otherwise, may have the side effect of decreasing our ability to think creatively. At least, if biofeedback doesn't actually decrease creativity, we can say that people who excel at it are not all that creative in the first place.

I suppose we should have suspected that highly creative people were not consciously controlling their alpha rhythms, and that they would therefore falter at biofeedback tests. Creative artists all stress the spontaneous, uncontrolled nature of inspiration, the unpredictability of new ideas. Several years ago, in reviewing some studies, I found that creative people describe themselves with adjectives that share the quality of "uninhibited," such as *enthusiastic, assertive, impulsive.* (Less creative people describe themselves as *contented, conventional, virtuous* and *rational.*) And when artists want to invoke the Muse, they tend to choose external methods to change their levels of cortical arousal, not internal, self-controlled ones. They withdraw and work in isolation, they drink liquor, they take drugs. Many famous artists, as Théodule Ribot's book describes, worked with idiosyncratic tricks, all external ways of invoking inspiration: Jacques-Bénigne Bossuet wrapped his head in furs; Milton, Descartes, Leibnitz and Rossini dreamt words and visions while lying flat in bed; and that's why Schiller wrote with his feet in ice water.

Arthur Koestler has remarked that the great scientists are extremely skeptical, "often carried to the point of iconoclasm, in their attitude toward traditional ideas, axioms and dogmas," whereas they have an "open-mindedness that verges on naïve credulity towards new concepts." You can see this in any art museum, classroom, park or concert. Confronted with novelty, whether in design, music, or ideas, creative people get excited and involved, while less creative people turn suspicious or even hostile. Given a new solution to a problem, imaginative students in my classes get enthused, suggest other ideas, and overlook defects or problems with the plan. Less creative students do the opposite. They find fault with the solution, and start analyzing its defects rather than exploring its potential.

Our research shows that such different reactions have a physiological basis in brain function. We do not know yet whether imaginative people are made or born that way, however. We know that some EEG patterns are heritable, but few have explored the possible genetic components of alpha or levels of cortical arousal that I found. For the present, we can conclude that creative people view the world and react to it unlike most of their peers do, not because they are eccentric and strange, but because they process information differently. Creativity is not just a matter of having the proper quirks and curiosities, but of having the right brain waves.

CHAPTER IV

Social Psychology

SOCIAL PSYCHOLOGY is responsible for investigating and illuminating those psychological processes that are related to the social components of our lives. We are influenced and in turn influence others. We are shaped by the forces of society and at the same time are part of those forces.

Although society may be conceived of as devoted to the nurturance and support of its individual members, it often operates to thwart and adversely affect some segments of its membership. The readings in this chapter illuminate some of the problems inherent in the operation of social-psychological processes. "Youth After the Revolution" explores the outcome of the youth-engendered revolution of the 1960s and the implications of the changes that have since taken place. "The Quest of the Black Man" is a stirring account of the struggle for meaning and identity of the black man in America. It presents to public view the forces of subjugation and their psychological impact and consequences, and it reveals the nature and scope of the struggle which continues to exist.

Every day there are more people on the earth than ever before. Can we cope with the increasing crowding, or will it eventually destroy us all? You may well wonder as you cope with your roommate or wait in line to register. "New Evidence on Crowding" suggests it may be bad for rats but good for people.

Sometimes being close is nice; we are seldom aware of it, but touching is an important part of our psychological lives. Psychologists are starting to decipher the hidden language of touch, which has its own rules, messages and meanings, and time and place. "How People React to Your Touch" presents some of the recent findings uncovered in this ticklish area of psychology. Sometimes people do not touch nicely; they hit and beat and torture. Why do *they* do it? Who are they, and what makes them that way? "If Hitler Asked You to Electrocute a Stranger, Would You?" has some humbling answers and a challenge for each person.

24.   YOUTH AFTER THE REVOLUTION

Edmund Faltermayer

In many respects the "youth revolution" of the Sixties has come and gone like a strange comet from deep space. Campuses are enjoying their third academic year of relative calm. Shrill young revolutionaries, small in number even at the apogee of political turmoil in the spring of 1970, have lost much of their following. Indeed they have been complaining that today's students are self-centered and apathetic, throwbacks to the youth scene of the Fifties.

But extensive interviewing at fourteen high schools and colleges across the country suggests that any such analogy between today's young and those of the serene past should not be pressed very far. It is true that things have been settling down in the last few years, with the outlines of a new "normalcy" now discernible. Underneath all that hair, young Americans exhibit many of the same qualities their predecessors did ten or fifteen years ago. Yet the "youth revolution," once the subject of an entire issue of FORTUNE (January, 1969), has left a permanent imprint on the young people who passed through their formative years while it was under way. Middle-class values were challenged in basic ways, and a broad residuum of change in style and viewpoint remains.

WHEN FREAKS WERE IN CIRCUSES

Early 1963 is the bench mark against which this article will attempt to measure

these changes. The bench mark is a valid one because the young at that time had grown up in the final years of the old "normalcy." A decade ago school hallways and quadrangles still swarmed with crew-cut boys, and girls in cardigan sweaters and skirts below the knee. Pornography was still under the counter, grass meant the lawn, and freaks, in Archie Bunker's words, were in a circus tent. A popular President had not yet met his death in Dallas, and America's world mission was still seen in the non-controversial simplicities of the cold war and the post-Sputnik race to the moon. The militant struggle for civil rights had barely begun, and our major involvement in Vietnam was two years away.

That the young now *look* utterly different is obvious from the photographs opposite, taken in the same classroom eleven years apart. What is not so generally appreciated is that the trappings of youth culture no longer bear any predictable relationship to social or political attitudes. The long-haired college man who smokes "dope" (the current vogue word for marijuana) at parties may be an athlete or engineering student. Take, for example, Elgin Community College, west of Chicago, perhaps the epitome of a "straight" institution for students pursuing practical curricula. A strong majority of students at Elgin favored Nixon in the recent election. Yet men with shoulder-length hair are much in evidence, 75 percent of the daytime students recently polled by their fellows have tried marijuana, and in another survey rock music was favored by a three-to-one majority over its nearest rival.

Reprinted from *Fortune* (March 1973) by permission of publisher, pp. 145–158.
Research associate: Stuart Schoffman.

RADICALS WITH MANNERS

Beneath the surface evidence of a distinctive youth culture, significant changes in attitude have been taking place. If any single word sums up the viewpoint of students in 1973, it is tolerance. Considering the rareness of this virtue in human history, and the natural narrow-mindedness of the young, the blossoming of tolerance on campus is a phenomenon worth pausing over. It has eroded the elaborate caste systems of ten years ago, typically based on beauty, money, or athletic prowess, and more recent caste systems that were based on political zealotry.

At Harvard, perhaps the nadir of intolerance was reached in the spring of 1971, when radical students successfully prevented the Young Americans for Freedom from holding a teach-in in support of the Vietnam war. A Harvard faculty member doubts this would happen now. At several other of the college campuses visited, educators remarked on the new civility among today's smaller band of radicals. Last spring, on the morning following an all-night vigil inside Rutgers University's historic Old Queens building to protest President Nixon's mining of North Vietnam's harbors, an official coming to work was struck by the number of "Excuse me's" from students who thoughtfully moved aside to make way.

The increase in tolerance results partly from a decline in political passions. The protest of recent years has virtually disappeared. Of the students interviewed, only a few, all at Harvard, were outspoken radicals on any subject, and even they turned out to be pretty tame by the standards of a few years ago.

Most high-school students shun militant political activity, and some call it risky. Picketing does no good, says a girl at Roswell High School, north of Atlanta, "and it can hurt you at school and in your career, because you're identified as a troublemaker."

NOBODY HAS ALL THE ANSWERS

Such attitudes have prompted much of the new talk about apathy and despair among today's young. Some students are indeed apathetic, and pointedly refuse to engage in organized activity of any kind, either political or social. Some educators notice more students who are concerned strictly about themselves, less eager to help oppressed mankind than the children of the New Frontier era. Richard P. McCormick, a historian at Rutgers, also worries about a "possible white backlash" against blacks. As recently as 1969, he says, whites supported the demands of black students at the university. Now, when he lectures about past injustices to blacks, "some of the white kids become uncomfortable, they just writhe."

Most of today's young, however, are several removes from the carefree and naive "silent generation" of the Fifties to whom they have been erroneously compared. Again and again, educators use the terms "more aware" and "better informed" in comparing them with predecessors from any past period. The awareness even extends to adult jargon about the young. "There's hardly any peer pressure here to use drugs," said a high-school student at a session in which the interviewer had not yet used the term "peer pressure." If anything, students suffer from an overawareness of mankind's woes and they know it. "It's hard to react to a barrage of information," says a Harvard senior.

Nevertheless, as one student at California's San José State University puts it, "there is a universal concern here with the quality of life." Improving the world, many students now say, will take longer and require more patience than seemed necessary a few years ago. Their tolerance stems in part from a new awareness that nobody—young or old—has all the answers. But this is a sign of realism rather than apathy. Compared to the students of a few years ago, says Burton R. Brazil, executive vice president at San José State, "today's kids are not as frenetic about getting the world changed by 0900 tomorrow. They realize you can't go back to Thoreau and change the whole culture. But they haven't lost the idealism, thank God!"

A PRESSURE TO TOLERATE EVERYTHING

The new tolerance extends—perhaps too far—to personal morality. Youngsters are far more willing than ten years ago to overlook deviant behavior in others. Many colleges now have "gay" organizations that operate openly. At Georgia's Roswell High a group of seven students say they wouldn't morally condemn a friend for using heroin, though one quickly adds that "using heroin is just dumb." About half of the group see nothing particularly shocking in an unmarried couple living together.

It is clear that students are motivated partly by a laudable respect for the rights of others. But in some cases tolerance may reflect uncertainty about moral standards. "There is a certain pressure," said a Stanford University coed, "to be tolerant of everything."

A NEED FOR MORE LOCKS

"Honesty," as used by many of today's young, refers to frankness rather than ethics. In most ways, young men and women are just as ethical and law-abiding as their predecessors; most teachers report no increase in cheating on exams. Paul W. Fatzinger, a stern-looking but warmhearted disciplinarian who has watched students come and go for twenty years at Allen High

School in Allentown, Pennsylvania, believes the current crop are "just as honest" as those of a decade ago. But Fatzinger, who is assistant principal, also sees "a wider lack of respect for property."

The school itself suffers little vandalism, Fatzinger says, but the town parks have "more epidemics" of damage than ever before. Other high schools report a rise in vandalism and, like Allen High, the disappearance of more books from the library and an increase in petty theft. Ten years ago few students at Allen felt a need for locks on their lockers; now most of them do.

At colleges, thefts from campus bookstores have increased greatly in recent years. A large proportion of students see nothing terribly wrong in this. Nine Stanford students, out of a group of fourteen, say they would not intervene if they saw someone making off with a book. "The bookstore is a rip-off anyway," says a woman student. At Harvard and at New York's Staten Island Community College, none of the interviewees say they would stop a bookstore thief. However, all say they would stop someone stealing from a fellow student.

An official at the University of Illinois at Urbana-Champaign says students have revised ethics somewhat in the direction of a Robin Hood concept. Thus, he says, many see nothing evil in thefts from large chain stores or in the use of false credit-card numbers in placing long-distance telephone calls. But they condemn thefts from "the mom-and-pop candy store" or from their own personal acquaintances.

In their friendships, say some educators, students can be extremely considerate, but evidently this consideration often disappears in impersonal dealings with outsiders or institutions. At that level, says a psychiatrist who generally lauds today's students, "appreciation of the rights of others has decreased." Thus a rise in humanitarian idealism has been partly negated by a decline in an abstract sense of community.

THE TRASH ON THE CAFETERIA FLOOR

And the young have their own special hypocrisies. Ready to condemn the pollution and environmental ills of a world they did not make, they nevertheless tolerate another type of pollution in their own midst. "The trash on the cafeteria floor is a foot deep at lunchtime," says a student at New Trier High School East, north of Chicago, with a bit of exaggeration. The concern about the environment, says a New Trier official, "is a macro-concern." Many students, he says, fail to see that ecology begins at home or don't care.

William H. Cornog, superintendent of secondary education in New Trier Township, sees littering as symptomatic of another change in adolescent society. In the past, he says, more student leaders would have spoken out against the problem and said, "Damn it, we can be responsible!" Ten years ago, he recalls, "kids were more willing to put their personal popularity on the line, and to take the guff that accrues to the student who says, 'Don't do that!' Today there are fewer leaders and more politicians."

B.M.O.C.'S HAVE VANISHED

But the decline in leadership is related to broader changes that also have their positive side. The pecking orders are much more flexible than they were ten years ago. The increase in tolerance has eroded the old hierarchies.

College yearbooks from a decade ago are brimful of "big men on campus," star athletes, and fraternity and sorority leaders who were treated like demigods. Student leaders still abound at the campuses visited, and in some ways the range of extracurricular activities is greater. But there are no B.M.O.C.'s in the old sense, and no one feels like a social untouchable if he's outside the "Greek" system. Here and there the Greeks have had some resurgence lately, with more fraternity and sorority rushing last fall than in several years. But the jaunty superiority of old is absent, and at some universities fraternities have become active in community-service projects and are at pains to redress their image as mere party lovers.

At high schools, too, the social structure is less rigid than ten years ago, although there has been less change in this respect than at the colleges. Leading athletes are still at the top of the pecking order, but in some schools they now share this position with others. At Woodside High, in a high-income suburb south of San Francisco, a teacher who was a student there in the early Sixties says that these days the big dramatics star is as much of a hero as the superjock. Girl cheerleaders have lost a bit of their prestige. At Pennsylvania's Allen High, one of them says that in the last few years a faction of students has tended to make fun of the "rah-rah" spirit. The competition for cheerleader "is not quite as strong as it used to be," she says. "Some girls are embarrassed to do some of the stunts."

Cliques are still fairly strong in high schools. In the late 1960's one important division was between "straight" students and longhairs. In recent years, however, feuding between the two groups has abated at some schools. At Illinois' New Trier East, a senior boy with very short hair gazes across the room at a long-haired classmate. "Two years ago," he says, "I'd have called him a freak and he would have called me a jock. Now the labels are being dropped." The long-haired boy doesn't quite agree. "The distinctions are still there," he says, "but people are withdrawing into themselves and saying, 'I won't hurt you if you don't hurt me.' "

PUTTING UP WITH ADULTS

Tolerance extends toward adult values, too, including values enforced by parents. Even at the height of the "youth revolution," to be sure, students who sensed a chasm between themselves and their parents were in the minority. Today, a strong majority of students to whom the question is put affirm that they are "pretty satisfied" with their upbringing. Some are doubtless influenced by older siblings who have become parents. "I remember my sister saying she was going to raise her kids differently and be freer with them," says a girl at New Trier East, "but now she's changed."

This tolerance nevertheless symbolizes an important shift in attitudes since the early Sixties. A decade ago the young, aside from some hijinks, were enthusiastic imitators of an adult society they held in considerable awe. This attitude is gone, at least for now.

"Kids don't accept things you tell them at face value," says Ralph V. Wilson, principal of Roswell High. "Today you have to give them a reason." A teacher at the same school notices "less open respect" for staff members than ten years ago, and he overhears more four-letter words in the corridors. "There's more noise in class," adds a faculty member at California's Woodside High, "as well as more eating in class, more lateness, and more cutting."

This somewhat irreverent attitude toward the adult world stops well short of *dis*respect in personal encounters. If more students use earthy language, or address teachers by their first names (in California more than elsewhere), they do it mainly in the new spirit widely described as "open-

ness." If anything, today's young men and women come across as both likable and wholesome.

Despite a veneer of sophistication, today's young are no more *mature* at a given age than their predecessors. Says a high-school official: "The sophistication disappears—zap!—the minute a real problem comes up." Guidance counselors and campus psychiatrists report a land-office business from students who come to them with problems. Much of the increase, they note, reflects the greater willingness of today's students to seek remedies, but they see some increase in problems as well.

WHERE WOMEN RACE ALONGSIDE MEN

There is a disturbing vogue for "downers," particularly "sopors" (soporifics). Otherwise, use of most illegal drugs has crested. LSD is less prevalent than a few years ago, and heroin has never caught on with more than a very small proportion of white youths. Marijuana usage, on the other hand, remains high, though alcohol is by far the most popular mood-altering drug.

An unmistakable change since the early Sixties is the blurring of sex roles. Almost none of the women interviewed said that their sole objective in life was to be a housewife and mother. The few who did were defensive about it. "I know it sounds blah," said a pretty freshman at Emory University in Atlanta. A recent study at Stanford University showed that 26 percent of the women in the class of 1972 intended to go into medicine, law, and other professions, compared with only 6 percent in the class of 1965. Only 3 percent wanted to go into "women's jobs" such as housewife, secretary, or nurse, down from 12 percent in the earlier class. At community colleges more and more women are taking courses in drafting and computer technology, and at Elgin one coed runs alongside men on the cross-country team. Very few of the women, however, are militant liberationists.

IT'S NO LONGER "SISSY" TO COOK

Meanwhile, men's notions about manliness have softened in some significant ways. Some men, such as the male nursing students at Staten Island Community College, are invading traditionally feminine turf, but this is still the exception. The big change is in attitudes. At high schools where such activities would have been called "sissy" in 1963, men take courses in gourmet cooking, or devote a lot of time to nonathletic activities such as dramatics. Fights among high-school boys are less common ("I can't even remember when the last one was," says a high-school principal who used to break up lots of them). At colleges, there's far less of the traditional roughhouse and pranks. In the early Sixties, officials at the University of Illinois recall, water fights got so bad that several dozen men had to be expelled following one battle that resulted in a serious injury.

In today's more informal atmosphere, women have ceased to be creatures upon a pedestal. Emory University's 1962 yearbook opened with a twelve-page section on campus queens, led by the beauteous Miss Emory University of that year. Last spring's yearbook contained no such celebration of idealized womanhood.

Girls still find ways to flaunt their good looks, of course, and even liberated Stanford retains pompon girls. But at the college level, artificial barriers between the sexes are virtually gone. It is hard to realize that a decade ago Rutgers University allowed women in the lounges of men's dormitories only on certain festive weekends; only

mothers of male students could set foot in their rooms.

The top question in the minds of parents, of course, is whether coed dorms and the other new freedoms have opened the floodgates of licentiousness. Actually, most coed dorms segregate the sexes into separate floors, wings, or self-contained apartments. In those that don't, students say, brother-sister relationships tend to develop. Educators at several colleges agree that a new kind of incest taboo tends to discourage sexual relations with partners from the same dormitory. The whole question of university freedoms has become moot for students who are moving in increasing numbers into houses and apartments off campus in a quest for privacy and quiet. "Dormitories would be depressing even if the noise wasn't a problem," says an upperclassman at the University of Illinois. It is also moot for the growing proportion of young people who live with their parents and commute to nearby community colleges.

At high schools the most noticeable change from a decade ago is the open display of affection in corridors. Formerly this would have drawn a scolding or worse from a member of the staff, and girls would have feared for their "reputations." Today nobody minds. Some high-school students are quick to label any premarital sex as immoral, but many say that what others do is their business. Says a boy at California's Woodside High: "It's uncool to say it's wrong."

THE NEW MARXIST STUDIES

A few years ago, when the "student power" and "free university" movements were in full flower, it appeared that a vanguard of the young were bent upon transforming education to its roots. Today's students appear to accept the essentials of a traditional system, partly because of large concessions won in recent years. At the college level, students now sit on all sorts of academic and disciplinary bodies, and in one institution visited are failing to attend meetings and fully exercise their new voice. High schools have blossomed with "mini-courses" on useful or trendy subjects (e.g., crocheting, ecology, the Marx Brothers), and at many high schools and colleges students can think up elective courses and petition the faculty to offer them.

Students who dislike conventional classroom schedules and lectures can also work out "self-directed" curricula. A majority of students shun such innovations ("I need structure," says a high-school boy). "Most of what our undergraduates get is still the traditional stuff," says a dean at the University of Illinois. "The difference today is that there are more avenues for the 10 percent who don't want to play the game."

High-school students not only are less regimented, but for the most part are able to handle their new freedom. For the last two years students at Evergreen Park Community High School, southwest of Chicago, have been permitted to smoke just outside a rear entrance. "Best thing we ever did," says School Superintendent Stephen J. Storkel, who claims that the new privilege has eliminated a big source of student discontent. At Evergreen Park disruptive students are no longer detained after school. So how does the school deal with them? "We talk to them," calmly answers Ardith Inman, a school official in charge of discipline problems. "We show them how their behavior affects the rest of the class." She says that the response of students is "tremendous." Evergreen Park retains the ultimate weapon of expulsion, of course.

AUTHORITY ISN'T A DIRTY WORD

A number of educators believe that the big grant of freedom to students is now be-

hind them, and that a rough new equilibrium has been reached. Here and there, however, they see a need for some backtracking that today's students might accept. The University of Illinois has changed the method of selecting students to serve on a joint faculty-student disciplinary body. Previously, the student government appointed representatives and showed a bias, in one official's words, toward those "in favor of abolishing all discipline on campus." Now the representatives are chosen at random from the entire student population by a computer, with the result that the disciplinary body has become tougher with offenders. Students go along with the change, says an official, "because many of them are sick and tired of having the bad guys holding the field."

For many students, moreover, authority is not a dirty word. When a group of Emory University students are asked whether they are mature enough to govern themselves without even the vestigial adult controls that remain, one quickly answers: "Things would tend toward anarchy." Stanley R. Levy, associate dean of students at the University of Illinois, believes that most students, if given the choice, would now be "willing, and even eager," to return to a world of "ground rules clearly stated." The rules, of course, would be far different from those of ten years ago, and Levy emphasizes that today's young would expect to participate in writing them.

DRIBBLING AWAY THEIR YOUTH

Statistics on college enrollments seem to show that the long-standing American love affair with education has lost a bit of its ardor in recent years. Last fall the number of freshmen at four-year colleges and universities declined about 3 percent, according to a study by Garland G. Parker of the University of Cincinnati. The decline,

Parker recently explained in *Intellect* magazine, was due not only to rising fees and delays in federal aid to students, but to a growing tendency of the young to question the value of a college education.

But education still has plenty of enthusiasts among young people, including almost all of those interviewed for this article. In this respect they are little different from their predecessors of 1963. Many, for example, scoff at the notion that television has lessened the need for conventional book learning. "You could watch Einstein himself on the educational channel," says a Rutgers man, "and it wouldn't make you a physicist."

Students concede that much of their time is taken up with courses that do not prepare them for a career. But college, they say, is a place to "explore," to "find yourself," and to meet different kinds of people and broaden the mind. An engineering student who intends to run a motorcycle shop says that "one of the best courses I'm taking is Italian Renaissance painting." Many believe, rightly or wrongly, that too much education is better than too little because it preserves career options in a time of rapid change.

Far from feeling like prisoners of a long and tedious process, a majority of students say frankly that they are having quite a good time, not all of it in the classroom. At the Urbana campus of the University of Illinois, for example, there are more than *one thousand* men's and women's intramural basketball teams.

"STOPOUTS" ARE WELCOME

But the young are beginning to break up the lockstep of uninterrupted, fulltime education from kindergarten through the B.A. and beyond. In recent years some high schools have stopped telling dropouts that they have irreparably ruined their prospects in life. Instead, "stopouts"—the preferred term these days, since it carries no stigma—are told they are welcome to resume their education later. At top high schools it is no longer automatic for all seniors to go directly into college the following autumn. At New Trier East about 5 percent work or travel for a year or so before starting higher education, and about 10 percent go to two-year colleges.

Nor are full-time students strangers to the labor market these days. When the hippie movement was riding high during the late Sixties, there were worries that the young were turning away from such traditional virtues as work and thrift. Some do indeed seem to be drifting rather lazily through life. But most young people still have plenty of energy and motivation.

Several high-school principals report an "amazing" increase during the Sixties in the number of students with parttime jobs. The eagerness to work is borne out by data from the Bureau of Labor Statistics showing a sizable increase in white sixteen- and seventeen-year-olds in the labor force. Since many of these youngsters work on and off, the figures understate the proportion with work experience.

When a group of high-school juniors or seniors are asked how many have parttime jobs "right now," between a third and a half of them raise their hands. They baby-sit, deliver newspapers, man delivery trucks, sell merchandise at counters, help out at construction sites, and perform myriad other jobs. Typically, one or two out of ten have earned at least $1,000 in a year. Asked why they work, they give a variety of answers: to save toward college, maintain a car, buy a stereo set, put aside money for a trip, for "enjoyment," or simply to gain work experience. Many high schools now permit seniors to leave in January so they can work full time for a semester to accumulate money toward college.

At colleges, the proportion of working students is often much higher. A recent survey of California students by the College Scholarship Service, a New York-based organization that evaluates student applications for financial aid, reveals that students in middle and upper income families are earning much more money than they did a few years ago. This may represent both a "thrust for independence" on the part of the students, says an official, and cutbacks in support from parents. Says one California university dean: "The folks at home just aren't shelling out."

FIGHTING FOR A PLACE IN LAW SCHOOL

Academically, today's young seem about on a par with their counterparts of 1963. Average scores on College Board admission tests have dropped a bit in ten years, but not enough to prove anything. Faculty members differ in their assessment of the work done by current students. Some think work has fallen off but that teachers are more lenient in grading. Others say today's students work harder than their predecessors, and are more serious intellectually. Ten years ago, says Emory University historian George P. Cuttino, "students here weren't concerned about a damned thing but keeping up with the Joneses." Competitiveness now thrives at Emory, with its large proportion of pre-med and pre-law students seeking entry to crowded professional schools. "I've seen it in the classroom," says a dean, "and it can be absolutely frightening."

A majority of young people, both in high school and in college, claim to have career goals. Many mention "business" as a broad objective. Pre-professional students are far more common than a decade ago; both Harvard and Stanford report big increases in this category. A lot of the would-be doctors and lawyers, in the words of one disapproving Emory student, "have focused on the dollar sign." But humanitarian motivations are evident, too. Some pre-med students intend to work in community clinics, and a lot of pre-law students say they want to go into politics or legal-aid work. Humanitarianism is an especially important element in the career choices of women. Some want to go into environmental protection and city planning, while others want to work with old people, juvenile delinquents, and runaways. In remarkable numbers, young women say they want to help the mentally retarded.

Many of today's young men and women were raised by parents unusually concerned about fostering self-expression and creativity. Yet many educators notice no rise in original or creative work of high quality, and some even see a decline. "They expect instant success," complains a high-school art teacher, echoing the words of colleagues elsewhere in the country. If students don't achieve success, he says, they shrug and say to hell with it. When classroom work is closely linked to future jobs in specific fields, however, the picture can be different. Jack Boone, who teaches a television workshop at California's two-year College of San Mateo, is impressed by his students' patient hard work.

"A SUBORDINATE NATION"

It would seem, then, that reports from the campus, whether of continuing revolution or of counterrevolution, have been exaggerated. A distinctive youth culture has spread from a trend-setting minority to the majority, but in the process of assimilation has lost most of its ideological content. "It's no longer as fashionable to be alienated, or appear to be," says an official at New Trier East.

Clearly there were valid grounds for

worry about the generation now in high school and college. They grew up during a tumultuous period in which adult society, in the words of President Edward J. Bloustein of Rutgers University, suffered a "loss of nerve because it suddenly found itself without the confidence and the assurances of the past."

Today's young are the first generation heavily exposed to television from infancy. More than previous generations, they grew up in homes in which both parents worked. They grew up at a time, some psychologists say, when the primary influence in upbringing increasingly shifted from adults to contemporaries. The steady lengthening of the American education process far past physical adolescence, in the opinion of sociologist James S. Coleman, has turned the young into "a subordinate nation," segregated from responsibility and fertile ground for the anti-adult doctrines and attitudes that come its way.

The worries of Coleman and others are valid ones. Students are ignorant about many aspects of the real world, and in that sense they may indeed be "a subordinate nation." But as of now they are not arrayed against society; their attitudes seem non-adult, or pre-adult, rather than anti-adult. Moreover, today's competitive job market, particularly for college graduates, appears to be pulling students toward the mainstream. Job scarcity, in the opinion of Harvard sociologist Seymour Martin Lipset, "means you have to worry about what the adults who control the jobs think."

It is unlikely, in any event, that the U.S. will soon again see the combination of circumstances that produced the recent "youth revolution." One factor in that revolution was the explosive growth of the youth fraction of the population during the Sixties. In the mid-1970's that fraction, now growing more slowly, will start to decline. As that happens, American society should lose some of its famous infatuation with everything young, a development that doubtless will be good both for the society and for young people. In the meantime, the young seem to be surviving the infatuation surprisingly well.

25.   IF HITLER ASKED YOU TO ELECTROCUTE A STRANGER, WOULD YOU? *PROBABLY*

Philip Meyer

In the beginning, Stanley Milgram was worried about the Nazi problem. He doesn't worry much about the Nazis anymore. He worries about you and me, and, perhaps, himself a little bit too.

Stanley Milgram is a social psychologist, and when he began his career at Yale Uni-

Reprinted by permission of *Esquire* Magazine © 1970 by Esquire Inc.

versity in 1960 he had a plan to prove, scientifically, that Germans are different. The Germans-are-different hypothesis has been used by historians, such as William L. Shirer, to explain the systematic destruction of the Jews by the Third Reich. One madman could decide to destroy the Jews and even create a master plan for getting it done. But to implement it on the scale that Hitler did meant that thousands of other people had to go along with the scheme and help to do the work. The Shirer thesis, which Milgram set out to test, is that Germans have a basic character flaw which explains the whole thing, and this flaw is a readiness to obey authority without question, no matter what outrageous acts the authority commands.

The appealing thing about this theory is that it makes those of us who are not Germans feel better about the whole business. Obviously, you and I are not Hitler, and it seems equally obvious that we would never do Hitler's dirty work for him. But now, because of Stanley Milgram, we are compelled to wonder. Milgram developed a laboratory experiment which provided a systematic way to measure obedience. His plan was to try it out in New Haven on Americans and then go to Germany and try it out on Germans. He was strongly motivated by scientific curiosity, but there was also some moral content in his decision to pursue this line of research, which was, in turn, colored by his own Jewish background. If he could show that Germans are more obedient than Americans, he could then vary the conditions of the experiment and try to find out just what it is that makes some people more obedient than others. With this understanding, the world might, conceivably, be just a little bit better.

But he never took his experiment to Germany. He never took it any farther than Bridgeport. The first finding, also the most unexpected and disturbing finding, was that we Americans are an obedient people: not blindly obedient, and not blissfully obedient, just obedient. "I found so much obedience," says Milgram softly, a little sadly, "I hardly saw the need for taking the experiment to Germany."

There is something of the theatre director in Milgram, and his technique, which he learned from one of the old masters in experimental psychology, Solomon Asch, is

to stage a play with every line rehearsed, every prop carefully selected, and everybody an actor except one person. That one person is the subject of the experiment. The subject, of course, does not know he is in a play. He thinks he is in real life. The value of this technique is that the experimenter, as though he were God, can change a prop here, vary a line there, and see how the subject responds. Milgram eventually had to change a lot of the script just to get people to stop obeying. They were obeying so much, the experiment wasn't working—it was like trying to measure oven temperature with a freezer thermometer.

The experiment worked like this: If you were an innocent subject in Milgram's melodrama, you read an ad in the newspaper or received one in the mail asking for volunteers for an educational experiment. The job would take about an hour and pay $4.50. So you make an appointment and go to an old Romanesque stone structure on High Street with the imposing name of The Yale Interaction Laboratory. It looks something like a broadcasting studio. Inside, you meet a young, crew-cut man in a laboratory coat who says he is Jack Williams, the experimenter. There is another citizen, fiftyish, Irish face, an accountant, a little overweight, and very mild and harmless-looking. This other citizen seems nervous and plays with his hat while the two of you sit in chairs side by side and are told that the $4.50 checks are yours no matter what happens. Then you listen to Jack Williams explain the experiment.

It is about learning, says Jack Williams in a quiet, knowledgeable way. Science does not know much about the conditions under which people learn and this experiment is to find out about negative reinforcement. Negative reinforcement is getting punished when you do something wrong, as opposed to positive reinforcement which is getting rewarded when you do something right.

The negative reinforcement in this case is electric shock. You notice a book on the table, titled, *The Teaching-Learning Process,* and you assume that this has something to do with the experiment.

Then Jack Williams takes two pieces of paper, puts them in a hat, and shakes them up. One piece of paper is supposed to say, "Teacher" and the other, "Learner." Draw one and you will see which you will be. The mild-looking accountant draws one, holds it close to his vest like a poker player, looks at it, and says, "Learner." You look at yours. It says, "Teacher." You do not know that the drawing is rigged, and both slips say "Teacher." The experimenter beckons to the mild-mannered "learner."

"Want to step right in here and have a seat, please?" he says. "You can leave your coat on the back of that chair ... roll up your right sleeve, please. Now what I want to do is strap down your arms to avoid excessive movement on your part during the experiment. This electrode is connected to the shock generator in the next room.

"And this electrode paste," he says, squeezing some stuff out of a plastic bottle and putting it on the man's arm, "is to provide a good contact and to avoid a blister or burn. Are there any questions now before we go into the next room?"

You don't have any, but the strapped-in "learner" does.

"I do think I should say this," says the learner. "About two years ago, I was at the veterans' hospital ... they detected a heart condition. Nothing serious, but as long as I'm having these shocks, how strong are they—how dangerous are they?"

Williams, the experimenter, shakes his head casually. "Oh, no," he says. "Although they may be painful, they're not dangerous. Anything else?"

Nothing else. And so you play the game. The game is for you to read a series of word pairs: for example, blue-girl, nice-day, fat-neck. When you finish the list, you read just the first word in each pair and then a multiple-choice list of four other words, including the second word of the pair. The learner, from his remote, strapped-in position, pushes one of four switches to indicate which of the four answers he thinks is the right one. If he gets it right nothing happens and you go on to the next one.

If he gets it wrong, you push a switch that buzzes and gives him an electric shock. And then you go to the next word. You start with 15 volts and increase the number of volts by 15 for each wrong answer. The control board goes from 15 volts on one end to 450 volts on the other. So that you know what you are doing, you get a test shock yourself, at 45 volts. It hurts. To further keep you aware of what you are doing to that man in there, the board has verbal descriptions of the shock levels, ranging from "Slight Shock" at the left-hand side, through "Intense Shock" in the middle, to "Danger: Severe Shock" toward the far right. Finally, at the very end, under 435- and 450-volt switches, there are three ambiguous X's. If, at any point, you hesitate, Mr. Williams calmly tells you to go on. If you still hesitate, he tells you again.

Except for some terrifying details, which will be explained in a moment, this is the experiment. The object is to find the shock level at which you disobey the experimenter and refuse to pull the switch.

When Stanley Milgram first wrote this script, he took it to fourteen Yale psychology majors and asked them what they thought would happen. He put it this way: Out of one hundred persons in the teacher's predicament, how would their break-off points be distributed along the 15-to-450-volt scale? They thought a few would break off very early, most would quit someplace in the middle and a few would go all the way to the end. The highest estimate of the number out of one hundred who would go all the way to the end was three. Milgram then informally polled some of his fellow scholars in the psychology department. They agreed that very few would go to the end. Milgram thought so too.

"I'll tell you quite frankly," he says "before I began this experiment, before any shock generator was built, I thought that most people would break off at 'Strong Shock' or 'Very Strong Shock.' You would get only a very, very small proportion of people going out to the end of the shock generator, and they would constitute a pathological fringe."

In his pilot experiments, Milgram used Yale students as subjects. Each of them pushed the shock switches, one by one, all the way to the end of the board.

So he rewrote the script to include some protests from the learner. At first, they were mild, gentlemanly, Yalie protests, but, "it didn't seem to have as much effect as I thought it would or should," Milgram recalls. "So we had more violent protestation on the part of the person getting the shock. All of the time, of course, what we were trying to do was not to create a macabre situation, but simply to generate disobedience. And that was one of the first findings. This was not only a technical deficiency of the experiment, that we didn't get disobedience. It really was the first finding: that obedience would be much greater than we had assumed it would be and disobedience would be much more difficult than we had assumed."

As it turned out, the situation did become rather macabre. The only meaningful way to generate disobedience was to have the victim protest with great anguish, noise, and vehemence. The protests were tape-recorded so that all the teachers ordinarily would hear the same sounds and nuances, and they started with a grunt at 75 volts, proceeded through a "Hey, that really hurts," at 125 volts, got desperate

with, "I can't stand the pain, don't do that," at 180 volts, reached complaints of heart trouble at 195, an agonized scream at 285, a refusal to answer at 315, and only heartrending, ominous silence after that.

Still, sixty-five percent of the subjects, twenty- to fifty-year-old American males, everyday, ordinary people, like you and me, obediently kept pushing those levers in the belief that they were shocking the mild-mannered learner, whose name was Mr. Wallace, and who was chosen for the role because of his innocent appearance, all the way up to 450 volts.

Milgram was now getting enough disobedience so that he had something he could measure. The next step was to vary the circumstances to see what would encourage or discourage obedience. There seemed very little left in the way of discouragement. The victim was already screaming at the top of his lungs and feigning a heart attack. So whatever new impediment to obedience reached the brain of the subject had to travel by some route other than the ear. Milgram thought of one.

He put the learner in the same room with the teacher. He stopped strapping the learner's hand down. He rewrote the script so that at 150 volts the learner took his hand off the shock plate and declared that he wanted out of the experiment. He rewrote the script some more so that the experimenter then told the teacher to grasp the learner's hand and physically force it down on the plate to give Mr. Wallace his unwanted electric shock.

"I had the feeling that very few people would go on at that point, if any," Milgram says. "I thought that would be the limit of obedience that you would find in the laboratory."

It wasn't.

Although seven years have now gone by, Milgram still remembers the first person to walk into the laboratory in the newly rewritten script. He was a construction worker, a very short man. "He was so small," says Milgram, "that when he sat on the chair in front of the shock generator, his feet didn't reach the floor. When the experimenter told him to push the victim's hand down and give the shock, he turned to the experimenter, and he turned to the victim, his elbow went up, he fell down on the hand of the victim, his feet kind of tugged to one side, and he said, 'Like this, boss?' ZZUMPH!"

The experiment was played out to its bitter end. Milgram tried it with forty different subjects. And thirty percent of them obeyed the experimenter and kept on obeying.

"The protests of the victim were strong and vehement, he was screaming his guts out, he refused to participate, and you had to physically struggle with him in order to get his hand down on the shock generator," Milgram remembers. But twelve out of forty did it.

Milgram took his experiment out of New Haven. Not to Germany, just twenty miles down the road to Bridgeport. Maybe, he reasoned, the people obeyed because of the prestigious setting of Yale University. If they couldn't trust a center of learning that had been there for two centuries, whom could they trust? So he moved the experiment to an untrustworthy setting.

The new setting was a suite of three rooms in a run-down office building in Bridgeport. The only identification was a sign with a fictitious name: "Research Associates of Bridgeport." Questions about professional connections got only vague answers about "research for industry."

Obedience was less in Bridgeport. Forty-eight percent of the subjects stayed for the maximum shock, compared to sixty-five percent at Yale. But this was enough to prove that far more than Yale's prestige was behind the obedient behavior.

For more than seven years now, Stanley Milgram has been trying to figure out what makes ordinary American citizens so obedient. The most obvious answer—that people are mean, nasty, brutish and sadistic—won't do. The subjects who gave the shocks to Mr. Wallace to the end of the board did not enjoy it. They groaned, protested, fidgeted, argued, and in some cases, were seized by fits of nervous, agitated giggling.

"They even try to get out of it," says Milgram, "but they are somehow engaged in something from which they cannot liberate themselves. They are locked into a structure, and they do not have the skills or inner resources to disengage themselves."

Milgram, because he mistakenly had assumed that he would have trouble getting people to obey the orders to shock Mr. Wallace, went to a lot of trouble to create a realistic situation.

There was crew-cut Jack Williams and his grey laboratory coat. Not white, which might denote a medical technician, but ambiguously authoritative grey. Then there was the book on the table, and the other appurtenances of the laboratory which emitted the silent message that things were being performed here in the name of science, and were therefore great and good.

But the nicest touch of all was the shock generator. When Milgram started out, he had only a $300 grant from the Higgins Fund of Yale University. Later he got more ample support from the National Science Foundation, but in the beginning he had to create this authentic-looking machine with very scarce resources except for his own imagination. So he went to New York and roamed around the electronic shops until he found some little black switches at Lafayette Radio for a dollar apiece. He bought thirty of them. The generator was a metal box, about the size of a small footlocker, and he drilled the thirty holes for the thirty switches himself in a Yale machine shop. But the fine detail was left to professional industrial engravers. So he ended up with a splendid-looking control panel dominated by the row of switches, each labeled with its voltage, and each having its own red light that flashed on when the switch was pulled. Other things happened when a switch was pushed. Besides the ZZUMPHing noise, a blue light labeled "voltage energizer" went on, and a needle on a dial labeled "voltage" flicked from left to right. Relays inside the box clicked. Finally, in the upper left-hand corner of the control panel was this inscription, engraved in precise block letters:

SHOCK GENERATOR TYPE ZLB
DYSON INSTRUMENT COMPANY
WALTHAM, MASS.
OUTPUT: 15 VOLTS—450 VOLTS

One day a man from the Lehigh Valley Electronics Company of Pennsylvania was passing through the laboratory, and he stopped to admire the shock generator. "This is a very fine shock generator," he said. "But who is this Dyson Instrument Company?" Milgram felt proud at that, since Dyson Instrument Company existed only in the recesses of his imagination.

When you consider the seeming authenticity of the situation, you can appreciate the agony some of the subjects went through. It was pure conflict. As Milgram explains to his students, "When a parent says, 'Don't strike old ladies,' you are learning two things: the content, and, also, to obey authority. This experiment creates conflicts between the two elements."

Here is a partial transcription from one of the experiments. The naïve "teacher" is a heavyset, worried-looking man with prematurely grey hair. He is wearing a polo shirt. He is very polite. He has just pushed the 180-volt lever. A hidden camera is recording the performance.

LEARNER (*who, from the teacher's point of view is heard but not seen, an offstage voice*): Ow, I can't stand the pain. Don't do that. . . .

TEACHER (*pivoting around in his chair and shaking his head*): I can't stand it. I'm not going to kill that man in there. You hear him hollering?

EXPERIMENTER: As I told you before, the shocks may be painful, but—

TEACHER: But he's hollering. He can't stand it. What's going to happen to him?

EXPERIMENTER (*his voice is patient, matter-of-fact*): The experiment requires that you continue, Teacher.

TEACHER: Aaah, but, unh, I'm not going to get that man sick in there . . . know what I mean?

EXPERIMENTER: Whether the learner likes it or not, we must go on, through all the word pairs.

TEACHER: I refuse to take the responsibility. He's in there hollering!

EXPERIMENTER: It's absolutely essential that you continue, Teacher.

TEACHER (*indicating the unused questions*): There's too many left here, I mean, Geez, if he gets them wrong, there's too many of them left. I mean who's going to take the responsibility if anything happens to that gentleman?

EXPERIMENTER: I'm responsible for anything that happens to him. Continue please.

TEACHER: All right. (*Consults list of words.*) The next one's "Slow—walk, truck, dance, music." Answer, please. (*A buzzing sound indicates the learner has signaled his answer.*) Wrong. A hundred and ninety-five volts. "Dance." (*Zzumph!*)

LEARNER: Let me out of here. My heart's bothering me! (*Teacher looks at experimenter.*)

EXPERIMENTER: Continue, please.

LEARNER (*screaming*): Let me out of here, you have no right to keep me here. Let me out of here, let me out, my heart's bothering me, let me out! (*Teacher shakes head, pats the table nervously.*)

TEACHER: You see, he's hollering. Hear that? Gee, I don't know.

EXPERIMENTER: The experiment requires. . . .

TEACHER (*interrupting*): I know it does, sir, but I mean—hunh! He don't know what he's getting in for. He's up to 195 volts! (*Experiment continues, through 210 volts, 225 volts, 240 volts, 255 volts, 270 volts, delivered to the man in the electric chair at which point the teacher, with evident relief, runs out of word-pair questions.*)

EXPERIMENTER: You'll have to go back to the beginning of that page and go through them again until he's learned them all correctly.

TEACHER: Aw, no. I'm not going to kill that man. You mean I've got to keep going up with the scale. No sir. He's hollering in there. I'm not going to give him 450 volts.

EXPERIMENTER: The experiment requires that you go on.

TEACHER: I know it does, but that man is hollering in there, sir.

EXPERIMENTER (*same matter-of-fact tone*): As I said before, although the shocks may be painful. . . .

TEACHER (*interrupting*): Awwww. He—he—he's yelling in there.

EXPERIMENTER: Start with "Blue," please, at the top of the page. Continue, please, Teacher. Just go ahead.

TEACHER (*concentrating intently on list of words in front of him, as if to shut everything else out*): "Blue—boy, girl, grass, hat." (*Buzz indicates answer.*) Correct. "Night—day, sky, job, chair." (*Buzz*) Wrong. The answer is "day." Two hundred and eighty-five volts. (*Zzumph!*)

LEARNER: Ohhhuhhoohhh!

EXPERIMENTER: Continue, please.

TEACHER: "Fat—man, lady, tub, neck." Answer, please. (*Buzz*) Wrong. The answer is "neck." Three hundred volts. (*Zzumph!*)

LEARNER: Ohhh. I absolutely refuse to answer any more. (*Shouting urgently, now*) Let me out of here. You can't hold me here. Get me out. Get—me—out—of—here.

EXPERIMENTER: Continue. The next word is "Green," please.

TEACHER: "Green—grass, hat, ink, apple." (*Nothing happens. No answering buzz. Just gloomy silence.*)

TEACHER: I don't think he is going to answer.

EXPERIMENTER: If the learner doesn't answer in a reasonable time, about four or five seconds, consider the answer wrong. And follow the same procedures you have been doing for wrong answers. Say "Wrong," tell him the number of volts, give him the punishment, read him the correct answer. Continue, please.

TEACHER: "Green—grass, hat, ink, apple." Answer, please. (*More silence. Teacher just sits there.*)

EXPERIMENTER: Go on with the procedure, please, Teacher.

TEACHER: Three hundred and fifteen volts. The answer is "ink." (*Zzumph!*)

LEARNER: Ohh. Ooohh.

TEACHER (*relieved to hear response*): Next one. . . .

LEARNER: I absolutely refuse to answer.

TEACHER: You got to. You get a shock if you don't answer. (*Experiment continues with learner refusing to answer, and, finally, failing even to grunt or groan. At 375 volts, the teacher stands up. Has he had enough? Will he break off the experiment? Will he disobey?*)

TEACHER: I think something's happened to that fellow in there. I don't get no answer. He was hollering at less voltage. Can't you check in and see if he's all right, please?

EXPERIMENTER (*same detached calm*): Not once we've started. Please continue, Teacher.

TEACHER (*sits down, sighs deeply*): "Cool—day, shade, water, paint." Answer, please. Are you all right in there? Are you all right?

EXPERIMENTER: Please continue,

Teacher. Continue, please. (*Teacher pushes lever. Zzumph!*)

TEACHER (*swiveling around in his chair*): Something's happened to that man in there. (*Swiveling back*) Next one. "Low—dollar, necklace, moon, paint." (*Turning around again*) Something's happened to that man in there. You better check in on him, sir. He won't answer or nothing.

EXPERIMENTER: Continue. Go on, please.

TEACHER: You accept all responsibility.

EXPERIMENTER: The responsibility is mine. Correct. Please go on. (*Teacher returns to his list, starts running through words as rapidly as he can read them, works through to 450 volts.*)

TEACHER: That's that.

EXPERIMENTER: Continue using the last switch on the board, please. The four-fifty switch for each wrong answer. Continue, please.

TEACHER: But I don't get no anything!

EXPERIMENTER: Please continue. The next word is "White."

TEACHER: Don't you think you should look in on him, please.

EXPERIMENTER: Not once we've started the experiment.

TEACHER: But what if something has happened to the man?

EXPERIMENTER: The experiment requires that you continue. Go on, please.

TEACHER: Don't the man's health mean anything?

EXPERIMENTER: Whether the learner likes it or not. . . .

TEACHER: What if he's dead in there? (*Gestures toward the room with the electric chair.*) I mean, he told me he can't stand the shock, sir. I don't mean to be rude, but I think you should look in on him. All you have to do is look in the door. I don't get no answer, no noise. Something might have happened to the gentleman in there, sir.

EXPERIMENTER: We must continue. Go on, please.

TEACHER: You mean keep giving him what? Four hundred fifty volts, what he's got now?

EXPERIMENTER: That's correct. Continue. The next word is "White."

TEACHER (*now at a furious pace*): "White—cloud, horse, rock, house." Answer, please. The answer is "horse." Four hundred and fifty volts. (*Zzumph!*) Next word, "Bag—paint, music, clown, girl." The answer is "paint." Four hundred and fifty volts. (*Zzumph!*) Next word is "Short—sentence, movie. . . ."

EXPERIMENTER: Excuse me, Teacher. We'll have to discontinue the experiment.

(*Enter Milgram from camera's left. He has been watching from behind one-way glass.*)

MILGRAM: I'd like to ask you a few questions. (*Slowly, patiently, he dehoaxes the teacher, telling him that the shocks and screams were not real.*)

TEACHER: You mean he wasn't getting nothing? Well, I'm glad to hear that. I was getting upset there. I was getting ready to walk out.

(*Finally, to make sure there are no hard feelings, friendly, harmless Mr. Wallace comes out in coat and tie. Gives jovial greeting. Friendly reconciliation takes place. Experiment ends.*)

© *Stanley Milgram 1965.*

Subjects in the experiment were not asked to give the 450-volt shock more than three times. By that time, it seemed evident that they would go on indefinitely. "No one," says Milgram, "who got within five shocks of the end ever broke off. By that point, he had resolved the conflict."

Why do so many people resolve the conflict in favor of obedience?

Milgram's theory assumes that people behave in two different operating modes as different as ice and water. He does not rely on Freud or sex or toilet-training hang-ups for this theory. All he says is that ordinarily we operate in a state of autonomy, which means we pretty much have and assert control over what we do. But in certain circumstances, we operate under what Milgram calls a state of agency (after agent, n . . . one who acts for or in the place of another by authority from him; a substitute; a deputy. —*Webster's Collegiate Dictionary*). A state of agency, to Milgram, is nothing more than a frame of mind.

"There's nothing bad about it, there's nothing good about it," he says. "It's a natural circumstance of living with other people. . . . I think of a state of agency as a real transformation of a person; if a person has different properties when he's in that state, just as water can turn to ice under certain conditions of temperature, a person can move to the state of mind that I call agency . . . the critical thing is that you see yourself as the instrument of the execution of another person's wishes. You do not see yourself as acting on your own. And there's a real transformation, a real change of properties of the person."

To achieve this change, you have to be in a situation where there seems to be a ruling authority whose commands are relevant to some legitimate purpose; the authority's power is not unlimited.

But situations can be and have been structured to make people do unusual things, and not just in Milgram's laboratory. The reason, says Milgram, is that no action, in and of itself, contains meaning.

"The meaning always depends on your definition of the situation. Take an action like killing another person. It sounds bad.

"But then we say the other person was about to destroy a hundred children, and the only way to stop him was to kill him. Well, that sounds good.

"Or, you take destroying your own life. It sounds very bad. Yet, in the Second World War, thousands of persons thought it was a good thing to destroy your own life. It was set in the proper context. You sipped some saki from a whistling cup, recited a few haiku. You said, 'May my death be as clean and as quick as the shattering of crystal.' And it almost seemed like a good, noble thing to do, to crash your kamikaze plane into an aircraft carrier. But the main thing was, the definition of what a kamikaze pilot was doing had been determined by the relevant authority. Now, once you are in a state of agency, you allow the authority to determine, to define what the situation is. The meaning of your action is altered."

So, for most subjects in Milgram's laboratory experiments, the act of giving Mr. Wallace his painful shock was necessary, even though unpleasant, and besides they were doing it on behalf of somebody else and it was for science. There was still strain and conflict, of course. Most people resolved it by grimly sticking to their task and obeying. But some broke out. Milgram tried varying the conditions of the experiment to see what would help break people out of their state of agency.

"The results, as seen and felt in the laboratory," he has written, "are disturbing. They raise the possibility that human nature, or more specifically the kind of character produced in American democratic society, cannot be counted on to insulate its citizens from brutality and inhumane treatment at the direction of malevolent authority. A substantial proportion of people do what they are told to do, irrespective of the content of the act and without limitations of conscience, so long as they perceive that the command comes from a legitimate authority. If, in this study, an anonymous experimenter can successfully command adults to subdue a fifty-year-old man and force on him painful electric shocks against his protest, one can only wonder what government, with its vastly greater authority and prestige, can command of its subjects."

This is a nice statement, but it falls short of summing up the full meaning of Milgram's work. It leaves some questions still unanswered.

The first question is this: Should we really be surprised and alarmed that people obey? Wouldn't it be even more alarming if they all refused to obey? Without obedience to a relevant ruling authority there could not be a civil society. And without a civil society, as Thomas Hobbes pointed out in the seventeenth century, we would live in a condition of war, "of every man against every other man," and life would be "solitary, poor, nasty, brutish and short."

In the middle of one of Stanley Milgram's lectures at C.U.N.Y. recently, some mini-skirted undergraduates started whispering and giggling in the back of the room. He told them to cut it out. Since he was the relevant authority in that time and that place, they obeyed, and most people in the room were glad that they obeyed.

This was not, of course, a conflict situation. Nothing in the coeds' social upbringing made it a matter of conscience for them to whisper and giggle. But a case can be made that in a conflict situation it is all the more important to obey. Take the case of war, for example. Would we really want a situation in which every participant in a war, direct or indirect—from front-line soldiers to the people who sell coffee and cigarettes to employees at the Concertina barbed-wire factory in Kansas—stops and consults his conscience before each action. It is asking for an awful lot of mental strain and anguish from an awful lot of people. The value of having civil order is that one can do his duty, or whatever interests him, or whatever seems to benefit him at the moment, and leave the agonizing to others.

When Francis Gary Powers was being tried by a Soviet military tribunal after his U-2 spy plane was shot down, the presiding judge asked if he had thought about the possibility that his flight might have provoked a war. Powers replied with Hobbesian clarity: "The people who sent me should think of these things. My job was to carry out orders. I do not think it was my responsibility to make such decisions."

It was not his responsibility. And it is quite possible that if everyone felt responsible for each of the ultimate consequences of his own tiny contributions to complex chains of events, then society simply would not work. Milgram, fully conscious of the moral and social implications of his research, believes that people should feel responsible for their actions. If someone else had invented the experiment, and if he had been the naïve subject, he feels certain that he would have been among the disobedient minority.

"There is no very good solution to this," he admits, thoughtfully. "To simply and categorically say that you won't obey authority may resolve your personal conflict, but it creates more problems for society which may be more serious in the long run. But I have no doubt that to disobey is the proper thing to do in this [the laboratory] situation. It is the only reasonable value judgment to make."

The conflict between the need to obey the relevant ruling authority and the need to follow your conscience becomes sharpest if you insist on living by an ethical system based on a rigid code—a code that seeks to answer all questions in advance of their being raised. Code ethics cannot solve the obedience problem. Stanley Milgram seems to be a situation ethicist, and situation ethics does offer a way out: When you feel conflict, you examine the situation and then make a choice among the competing evils.

You may act with a presumption in favor of obedience, but reserve the possibility that you will disobey whenever obedience demands a flagrant and outrageous affront to conscience. This, by the way, is the philosophical position of many who resist the draft. In World War II, they would have fought. Vietnam is a different, an outrageously different, situation.

Life can be difficult for the situation ethicist, because he does not see the world in straight lines, while the social system too often assumes such a God-given, squared-off structure. If your moral code includes an injunction against all war, you may be deferred as a conscientious objector. If you merely oppose this particular war, you may not be deferred.

Stanley Milgram has his problems, too. He believes that in the laboratory situation, he would not have shocked Mr. Wallace. His professional critics reply that in his real-life situation he has done the equivalent. He has placed innocent and naïve subjects under great emotional strain and pressure in selfish obedience to his quest for knowledge. When you raise this issue with Milgram, he has an answer ready. There is, he explains patiently, a critical difference between his naïve subjects and the man in the electric chair. The man in the electric chair (in the mind of the naïve subject) is helpless, strapped in. But the naïve subject is free to go at any time.

Immediately after he offers this distinction, Milgram anticipates the objection. "It's quite true," he says, "that this is almost a philosophic position, because we have learned that some people are psychologically incapable of disengaging themselves. But that doesn't relieve them of the moral responsibility."

The parallel is exquisite. "The tension problem was unexpected," says Milgram in his defense. But he went on anyway. The naïve subjects didn't expect the screaming protests from the strapped-in learner. But they went on.

"I had to make a judgment," says Milgram. "I had to ask myself, was this harming the person or not? My judgment is that it was not. Even in the extreme cases, I wouldn't say that permanent damage results."

Sound familiar? "The shocks may be painful," the experimenter kept saying, "but they're not dangerous."

After the series of experiments was completed, Milgram sent a report of the results to his subjects and a questionnaire, asking whether they were glad or sorry to have been in the experiment. Eighty-three and seven-tenths percent said they were glad and only 1.3 percent were sorry; 15 percent were neither sorry nor glad. However, Milgram could not be sure at the time of the experiment that only 1.3 percent would be sorry.

Kurt Vonnegut Jr. put one paragraph in the preface to *Mother Night,* in 1966, which pretty much says it for the people with their fingers on the shock-generator switches, for you and me, and maybe even for Milgram. "If I'd been born in Germany," Vonnegut said, "I suppose I would have *been* a Nazi, bopping Jews and gypsies and Poles around, leaving boots sticking out of snowbanks, warming myself with my sweetly virtuous insides. So it goes."

Just so. One thing that happened to Milgram back in New Haven during the days of the experiment was that he kept running into people he'd watched from behind the one-way glass. It gave him a funny feeling, seeing those people going about their everyday business in New Haven and knowing what they would do to Mr. Wallace if ordered to. Now that his research results are in and you've thought about it, you can get this funny feeling too. You don't need one-way glass. A glance in your own mirror may serve just as well.

26.   HOW PEOPLE REACT TO YOUR TOUCH

Ruth Winter

Even a slight touch of the hand can be very potent. Dr. Richard Heslin, associate professor of psychological sciences at Purdue University in Lafayette, Indiana, conducted an interesting experiment at his school.

He had clerks in the library either purposely touch or not touch the hands of borrowers when they handed over their library cards. The clerks maintained contact for about half a second. Their touches were so light and brief that only a little more than half the persons who were touched later recalled that it had even happened.

Without telling the book borrowers about the touch research, the students were asked to describe their feelings about the library, the clerks and themselves.

Men and women who were touched were more likely to report a positive feeling about *themselves* and to give a clerk a better rating than those who were not. Women who were touched generally rated the library more highly than did the other women or any of the males.

Touching is perhaps our swiftest and most direct form of communication. When you touch people, their skin surfaces have millions of sensory receptors which inform them not only about heat, cold and pain, but literally how you feel about them.

And as the library experiment proves, you have the power within your hands to make people feel good—good about you and good about themselves. Dr. Heslin be-

lieves the fleeting touch of the library clerks was so potent because we live in a cold, impersonal world.

Unfortunately, touching is an extremely inexact language. We are only beginning to study it in a scientific way. And unlike other languages, we don't as yet have a "dictionary" that tells us what a particular kind of touch means. Just as important, we don't always know how our touch will be interpreted by others or how they will react. Identical touches in different situations with different people will create a variety of reactions.

For instance, most of us know that kissing our mother will elicit a positive response, while kissing a stranger in an elevator will most likely bring a less-than-positive response.

Okay, that's a fairly simple prediction. Now put yourself in the following situations:

1. You're a college-aged man and you're in love with a sophomore woman you've been seeing. And, not unusually, you are both sexually attracted to each other. The next time you see her, you feel a strong urge to express both your sexual desire and your emotional warmth for the girl. Your immediate impulse is to kiss her passionately and caress her breasts. According to recent experiments, if you act on these sincere feelings, will she understand how much you care about her? Is your touch likely to make her feel good?

2. You are a young medical doctor struck with the coldness and indifference of the

Reprinted from *Science Digest* by permission of author. From *Science Digest* (March 1976), pp. 47–56.

world. You want to change all that and decide that whenever you touch any of your patients during examinations, you will exude warmth and personal concern through your hands. How big a practice can you expect?

3. You are a married woman. Your husband is feeling depressed after a rough, humiliating battle with his boss. You want to show him that, in your eyes at least, he is a valuable person. So you touch his body fondly, paying particular attention to erogenous zones. How will he react?

4. You are a middle-aged man waiting in an airport to greet an old childhood friend who's flying in to visit you. You have not seen each other for five years. When you finally catch sight of him disembarking from the plane, surrounded by dozens of other people, you rush up and throw your arms around him. The two of you leave the terminal arm in arm. But when you reach the parking lot, where you and your friend are the only people around, you suddenly remove your arm from his and keep your hands to yourself. How have you made your long-time friend feel?

5. You are an Italian immigrant male who has made Bismarck, North Dakota, his home. After 20 years of marriage to a frigid, unfeeling American woman, you have finally been granted a divorce. Having been starved of affection for two decades, you decide to take a long trip abroad. Secretly, you hope that after your years of frustration in America you will meet a European woman who will understand your emotional and physical needs. While lunching in a London restaurant early in your trip, a charming woman with a Scottish accent strikes up a conversation with you. She coyly mentions that she's catching the two o'clock train back home, that Edinburgh is beautiful this time of year and that she wouldn't mind company. You, however, are booked on an afternoon flight to Athens. What do you do? Cancel your plane reservations and catch the train ... or head on out for the airport?

ANSWERS

We don't intend that the following answers should *always* be adhered to when in the above situations. But according to recent studies, here's what psychologists and other social scientists would say about these five situations:

1. Your girlfriend will probably *not* perceive your touch as an expression of caring and warmth on your part. She may, in fact, be threatened by your caress.

2. As things now stand in society you could possibly frighten away patients with this kind of touching.

3. You will probably drive your husband into greater despair by your actions. He will most likely be threatened by your advances.

4. Your friend will feel relieved. You displayed affection at a "safe" time and broke it off when reaching an uncomfortable location.

5. Hold on to your plane ticket. A Scottish woman is not for you at this time in your life. A Greek woman might be perfect, however.

To understand the rationales behind these answers you must first understand the research behind the relatively new science of human touching. (Explanations to the above answers will emerge as you finish the article.)

Despite the potency of touch, only recently have scientists begun to look at it with a serious eye. Purdue's Dr. Heslin maintains that touching is a form of nonverbal behavior that has been neglected compared to other kinds of expression— such as the use of interpersonal space, eye contact and hand gestures. One reason touch has not been studied as much, he contends, is that it borders on being a taboo subject. It is somewhat like sex or eating; you may do it, but when, where, how and with whom is carefully controlled.

One of the main things Dr. Heslin has done is to categorize the various touching relationships. In effect, he's begun a dictionary of touch language. Keeping the following categories in mind should help you understand what others mean by their touch and how they might react when you touch *them:*

Functional/Professional. In this case, a person is touched in order for the toucher to do something to the receiver. Examples include physician-patient, golf pro-student, fireman-fire victim, tailor-customer and barber-customer. Heslin says that even though you may deny it, the relationship involved is virtually manipulator to object. The toucher touches the receiver only because of his need to do something to him or his need to move him to do something else.

Although there is a tendency to decry the inclination of professionals to relate unsympathetically to their clients, a "cold," businesslike manner is required. It is needed, maintains Dr. Heslin, to make clear the touch is professional rather than intense, since the actual contact is intimate in many cases and would be quite inappropriate from a stranger. (This explains our answer to situation No. 2 above.)

Social/Polite. Touching that occurs in this context occurs under heavy cultural restraint. There are definite (unwritten) rules about how you should touch and what is not allowed. The classical example of Social/Polite, Dr. Heslin says, is the handshake or the kiss on the hand. The function of this is to acknowledge the humanity of both parties. Touch signals the encounter is starting off on an equal footing, and because it is a recognition of the humanity of a person, it signals that you will start off as, if not

friends, at least not enemies. Quite a bit is accomplished with your handshake, Heslin concludes.

Friendship/Warmth. This category can cause you the most uneasiness, according to the Purdue researcher. It is less formalized than Social/Polite and might be misinterpreted as indicative of love and/or sexual attraction. This is especially threatening with friends of the same sex.

Touching in Friendship/Warmth relationships shows a sharp decrease when you and your partner are alone. This is because of the likelihood that Friendship/Warmth touching might be misconstrued as loving and sexual in private since privacy is associated with sex and love. (And this also explains our answer to situation No. 4.)

Dr. Heslin thinks it is in the area of Friendship/Warmth touching that the greatest cross-cultural variability occurs. And differences in friendly touching among cultures reflects their different approaches to handling potential illicit or unsanctioned sexuality. For some cultures, the fear of such sexuality is so great that people are willing to avoid it to the extent that they forego the warmth and touch of their friends.

Love/Intimacy. Touches in this category require that your relationship be appropriate for your message if your touch is not to create a disturbance. Laying your hand on the cheek of another person or taking his hand will be interpreted as a loving gesture by most people, according to Dr. Heslin. Also, within a love relationship, the number of different kinds of touch that are construed as indicating Love/Intimacy would theoretically increase.

To the extent that you do not want to commit yourself to the responsibilities of a Love/Intimacy relationship, you will be made uncomfortable by such contact—or your partner will. Furthermore, if you are a male, you will feel conflict between the behavioral style defined by "masculinity" and the gentler, tender behavior expected in a Love/Intimacy relationship.

Sexual Arousal. This is the highest level of contact arousal. It is the kind of touching that is pleasant because of its sexual meaning and the stimulation it conveys. Yet it can be frightening and anxiety arousing, according to Dr. Heslin, because of the same characteristics of Love/Intimacy. In Sexual Arousal, you may well give the kinds of touches that have heavy components of both feelings, depending on the person involved and the situation.

But there are other kinds of touches that fall clearly into one category or the other. Holding hands, for instance, would score low on Sexual Arousal. Stroking the genitals would score high, obviously. The extent to which the two categories overlap for you is an empirical question, says Heslin. For some people, touch that means Sexual Arousal also means love. For others the two concepts are quite distinct. And for still others, the more they consider a touch to convey sexual desire, the less they believe it conveys love.

There are two ways of ranking these five categories of touch, according to Dr. Heslin. One theory is that as you move from Functional/Professional to Sexual Arousal, there is an ever-increasing extent to which you individualize and humanize the other person. Under this thinking, the other becomes less of an object and more of a person as intimacy becomes deeper.

The alternate theory claims that the most appreciation of a person occurs in Friendship/Warmth. In that category you can be yourself. At other levels, a partner is less tolerant of your idiosyncracies. Of course, even in a Friendship/Warmth relationship, there are expectations and requirements

that you act a certain way for your friend, but the pressure, goes the theory, is less than in Love/Intimacy or Sexual Arousal.

The problem is that contact which might mean Friendship/Warmth to you may mean Love/Intimacy to the one you touch. This was made clear in another experiment with undergraduate university students conducted by Dr. Heslin and his colleagues, Dr. Tuan Nguyen and Michelle Nguyen.

The young men and women were asked to tell how they felt when a close person of the opposite sex (excluding relatives) touched various parts of their bodies in each of four ways. The four ways were a pat, a squeeze, a stroke or an (accidental) brush. Did they think the touch connoted playfulness? Love? Friendship? Sexual desire? Pleasantness? The areas of the body they were questioned about included the head, face, neck/shoulder, chest/breast, arm, hands, abdomen, thigh/buttocks, genitals, legs and back.

The students were asked to keep in mind the same steady date throughout the entire questionnaire.

Among the results, the Purdue researchers found that students considered touching the legs the most playful, the hands the most loving, friendly and pleasant, while contact with the genital areas, not surprisingly, indicated sexual desire.

The professors found, however, that males and females held significantly different views of their body areas in terms of what it means when the regions are touched.

The male students said that when touch was associated with a sexual zone, it indicated love, warmth and pleasure. The females, on the other hand, thought it did not.

Dr. Heslin concluded from that: "Most freshman and sophomore girls questioned were relatively sexually inexperienced. They may have reacted that way because they felt emotionally insecure—that a fellow may love them and leave them." (This explains our advice in situation No. 1.)

Heslin's theory seemed to be reinforced when he looked at the results of the same questionnaire presented to married couples. He was dumbfounded to discover the completely opposite reactions in both male and female respondents:

"When the men's wives touched them in a sexual way, the men did not associate it with warmth, pleasure and love. When the wives' husbands touched them in a sexual way, the women associated it with very positive feelings."

Dr. Heslin believes the men felt threatened if their wives touched them as an invitation to sex. It created anxieties about their ability to perform. The men would rather be the initiators. (Which helps explain our answer to situation No. 3. When a man is feeling already threatened, it's possible that a sexual touch could cause even more anxiety about his masculinity.)

On the other hand, the married women, unlike the coeds, felt very comfortable about sexual touching.

Finally, how people react to touch depends heavily on nationality and culture. As said earlier, we Americans touch each other rarely. Russians however, are highly tactual. They receive a great deal of touch stimulation when young and continue the habit of touching each other through life.

The Arab is even more contact oriented. He likes to touch his companion, to feel and smell him. To deny a friend your breath, according to the Middle Easterner, is to be ashamed. The Japanese, despite their suffocating, overwhelming population density, preserve a formality and aloofness. They manage to touch and still keep rigid boundaries. The Arab, by comparison, pushes such boundaries aside and thinks nothing of shoving, pushing and even pinching women in a public place.

Greeks, particularly Greek women, are the most touching of all members of the human race while, according to social scientists, Scottish women are the least touchable. (Which is why the Italian gentleman in situation No. 5 should make his plane to Athens.)

No matter which culture you study, you're still bound to conclude that on the whole our world is an impersonal one. And some of the problems in it can be directly attributed to lack of touch. For example, Dr. Heslin feels that many people who are locked in mental and penal institutions are literally untouchables:

"They are not as good looking as the people on the outside. They are strangers so they are not touched by other humans and become even stranger. Studies have shown that nurses in psychiatric hospitals are more likely to touch younger patients than older ones because they find the younger patients more attractive or less of a reminder of their own mortality."

Dr. Heslin believes one of the reasons sensitivity training and marathon groups were so popular just a few years ago was that they tried to make people feel less isolated, less unhappy about themselves by actual physical contact with other humans.

You rarely, if ever, go through a day without touching another person or being touched, and yet the many meanings of human physical contacts are still not fully understood. Dr. Heslin, at least, has begun an attack on the problem.

27. NEW EVIDENCE ON CROWDING

Barbara Ford

The most crowded living conditions in the world are found in:

a) a New York City tenement

b) a one-room house in a Rio de Janeiro slum

c) a Hong Kong sampan-houseboat

d) a !Kung bushmen camp on the Kalahari Desert of Africa.

The right answer is the !Kung camp. The !Kung (the exclamation point stands for a click in the spoken language) are a tribe of hunter-gatherers who *voluntarily* set up their camps so that those inside are jammed into a tiny central area. Arms and legs are usually touching and women hand food back and forth as they cook. The density of the camps, figures University of New Mexico anthropologist Patricia Draper, who lived among the !Kung, is about 30 people to the room, or 180 square feet per person.

But crowding doesn't seem to affect the !Kung's health. Their blood pressure is low and doesn't rise with age, Draper found, and their serum cholesterol levels are among the lowest in the world.

Draper's findings are of interest to social scientists because they seem to contradict what we know about crowded animals. Animal studies show that crowding has extremely unpleasant effects on deer, rats, lemmings, coypus and other four-footed subjects. Among other things, animals subjected to long-term crowding show increased competitiveness, excess sexual activity, lowered birth rates, high infant mortality, and even cannibalism. Eventually, crowded animal populations "crash" —most die off, leaving a few survivors to carry on.

It's a dismal picture for a world inevitably destined for more human crowding. But does it really apply to humans?

Some sociologists, ethologists and city planners believe the physiological ills that beset crowded beasts account for some of the more unpleasant aspects of urban life. They blame crowding for disease, mental illness, crime, riots, drug addiction, divorce and, in one often-cited study, war. But not every expert buys this argument. In the last few years, some social scientists—sociologists, anthropologists, psychologists—have begun pushing another viewpoint. Human crowding, they say, is not necessarily bad; depending on circumstances, crowding may even be good.

"Crowding does have bad effects on rats, mice, lemmings, chickens and various other creatures but not on humans," asserts psychologist Jonathan L. Freedman of Columbia University, who lives and works in the nation's most crowded city, New York City.

Residents of New York, Tokyo and other crowded urban areas do not show the extreme reactions of crowded animals, he points out. There's evidence, in fact, that the most populous cities in this country have a lower crime rate than somewhat less crowded cities. New York, with the nation's greatest density (the number of people per square mile) has a much lower crime rate against persons than either Los Angeles or Chicago, both of which have lower densities than New York. And Hong Kong, one of the world's most densely populated cities, has half the crime rate of New York. The most recent FBI crime figures for the six most populous cities in the United States show New York first in population but fifth in crime. Detroit, fifth in population, is first in crime rate. The real source of our urban ills, believes Freedman, lies not in crowding but in discrimination, poverty, inadequate housing, drug abuse, alcoholism and other conditions.

Survey data like that cited by Freedman is intriguing but not really convincing, at least to most psychologists. They demand controlled "experimental" studies in the laboratory or field. But studies like this are a problem in human crowding. A psychologist obviously can't cram a few dozen people in a small room and leave them there for a few months to fight and copulate, as researchers have done with animals. But he can test short-term crowding of the kind humans regularly experience in subways and popular movies. In the late 1960s, when he was at Stanford University in California, Freedman and Stanford colleagues Paul R. Ehrlich and Simon Klevansky set up one of the first laboratory experiments to test human crowding.

They directed nine volunteers to work on a variety of tasks—some simple, others complex—for four hours in large and small rooms. All the subjects sat on wooden chairs with writing arms. The small room was just 35 feet square, giving the subjects less room than a !Kung tribesman.

To their surprise, the crowded subjects did just as well as the uncrowded ones. After moving to Columbia, Freedman directed another study with Alan S. Levy, Roberta W. Buchanan and Judy Price. This time, all-male and all-female groups played games requiring cooperation. Again, the results were surprising. In the small room, the males were much more competitive, just like the subjects in the animal studies. Females, however, were much more cooperative. To test this unexpected sex difference, the Freedman team set up a crowding experiment with a mock jury trial. All-female groups in the small room gave much lighter sentences than all-male groups. But when a mixed group occupied the small room, the males reduced the severity of their sentences!

Freedman came to several general conclusions after studying his results: 1) Crowding doesn't produce arousal and thus doesn't affect people's ability to perform tasks and 2) women respond to crowding more positively than men do. The effects of crowding, he suggests, are "complicated," but not necessarily negative. Circumstances, most of them unknown, determine the effects and sex is definitely one of those circumstances. "All male juries or cabinets should probably be avoided, or at least be given spacious quarters," he recommends. "Better still, women should be included, not only to give them equal representation, but because apparently any negative effects of crowding disappear when the sexes are mixed."

By the time Freedman's results appeared in psychological journals, a number of other social scientists were devising their own people-oriented crowding experiments. One of them was Yakov M. Epstein, a psychologist who grew up in New York City but who now works at Rutgers University in uncrowded New Brunswick, N.J. Epstein and a Rutgers colleague, Robert A. Karlin, set up a short-term crowding experiment with several controls absent from Freedman's research. They got rid of the armrests, which they figured gave the subjects a sense of territory, and they postponed the tests and games on the theory that they allowed subjects to remove themselves psychologically from the crowded situation.

The same psychological removal, Epstein points out, can be seen any day on a crowded bus or subway as certain people "bury" themselves in a newspaper or book.

What Epstein and Karlin ended up with was a clearly-designed experiment in which subjects first simply sat quietly in their respective rooms, some in a big room, others in a small one, for a half hour. Afterwards, they all filed into a medium-sized room where they performed a variety of tasks. When the two investigators checked their results, they found that both crowded males and females did better on simple tasks. The females were cooperative in the small room, the males competitive. After the experiment was over, the crowded females reported more positive feelings about each other than crowded males did.

The sex differences, obviously, were in line with what Freedman discovered but not the task performance. Epstein knew that arousal usually results in better performance on a simple task, so he reasoned that crowding is, somehow, arousing, despite Freedman's findings to the contrary. To prove it, he, Karlin and Rutgers psychologist John R. Aiello set up a crowding experiment to measure skin conductance of electricity, an accepted measure of physiological arousal. For a half hour, six persons sat silently in a large or small room with electrodes pasted to their hands. Then one person sat alone in both rooms. The results were conclusive: While skin conductance remained the same for subjects when they sat together in the large room and for the person who sat alone in both rooms, it soared when all six were crowded into the *small* room. And the high levels persisted, indicating subjects did not adapt.

Since then, Epstein and psychologist Susan Saegert of City University of New York have carried out separate experiments with physiological measures of arousal. The results, says Epstein, are "incontrovertible." Crowding is definitely arousing. He believes Freedman's subjects avoided arousal because they had a task to divert them. (Freedman still thinks crowding is not arousing, calling Epstein's results on task performance "very mild.") The Rutgers and Columbia research are the most elaborate explorations of human crowding to date, but other social scientists are also coming up with data that contradict the results of animal research. Some of their findings:

• Jeanette Desor of the Monell Physical Chemical Senses Center in Philadelphia gave subjects a number of dolls and told them to put as many as they wished in a miniature enclosure representing a 35X15-foot room. The room was to be used for four different activities: A cocktail party, waiting for a flight at an airport, sitting and talking, and sitting and reading. The subjects put the most dolls in the cocktail party, the fewest in the reading situation. The difference, Desor believes, lies in expectations: We expect a cocktail party to be crowded but reading demands privacy.

• Chalsa Loo of the University of California at Santa Cruz observed groups of four- and five-year-olds playing in large and small rooms. Both rooms had a selection of attractive toys. The groups played first in one room, then in the other. Boys were much *less* aggressive in the small room than in the large one, Loo found. She thinks that when the number of people remain the same but the space decreases, they see each other as all "pawns to something greater than themselves, the physical environment." This all-in-the-same-boat syndrome welds the group together.

• Paul J. Hopstock of the State University of New York at Stonybrook set up a model room experiment with two enclosures, one representing a small room and the other a large room. He put a number of dolls in each room. The subjects, half of them males and half females, were told the rooms were lounges. Males saw the small room as smaller than females saw it, Hopstock found, and males consistently rated rooms with more people in them as more crowded than females did. "Women and men," he sums it up, "have different space requirements. Men are more sensitive to spacial restrictions."

• John Collette of the University of Utah discovered that household crowding—the number of people residing in a single dwelling—actually leads to *less* stress in a survey he conducted in New Zealand. "The greater the number in the household," he says, "the less evidence there is of psychological disorder, alcoholism and the use of mood-modifying drugs." The explanation, he thinks, is that household residents are probably either relatives or long-term associates who form cohesive units that counteract any environmental stress.

• Robert M. Factor and Ingrid Waldron of the University of Pennsylvania compared ten similar community areas in Chicago and found that mortality was not correlated with density. Nor was mortality related to density in a number of countries matched for income and health care. True, diseases such as cancer, bronchitis and ulcers caused more deaths in densely populated nations, but deaths from other causes were lower than in sparsely-populated countries.

Do all these bits and pieces of research add up to any clear picture of the effects of human crowding? People-oriented crowding research is still in its infancy, but Yakov Epstein and his Rutgers colleagues have devised a tentative theory of crowding that pulls together some of the current research. "Our research shows crowding is always arousing," says Epstein in his office on Rutgers' spacious campus. "People in a small room do better on simple tasks because they

are aroused. But how we *feel* about crowding is the cognitive label we attach to it. By using our minds, we interpret and label situations.

"That's why you can't extrapolate from animals to humans in crowding situations; animals can't label situations the way we do."

On a crowded subway or bus, he says, people are aroused, but the cognitive label is "bad." At an equally crowded cocktail party, the cognitive label is "good." Rock festivals, Epstein believes, are a prime example of a situation to which the participants attach a good cognitive label. "Woodstock and Watkins Glen were extremely crowded situations. Yet the Woodstock Festival has come to connote an image of love and peace. At both festivals, despite a great deal of physical discomfort, participants have largely reported an intense sense of community with an affection for others present." Both festivals, he feels, were times when crowded groups "became cohesive and cooperative groups as did the crowded women in our studies and Freedman's."

And why did the women in those studies become so cooperative? John Aiello, also a former city dweller ("I find New Brunswick a little unstimulating,") has an explanation that involves another aspect of crowding: Cultural norms. Some of his earlier research shows females stand closer together than males at all ages, even as young children (look for the phenomenon at the next male-female gathering you attend). Researcher Michael Ross of the University of Waterloo in Ontario, Canada, finds that women look at each other more directly than men do. Also, Aiello notes, our culture deems it masculine to maintain a cool facade under stress, feminine to share distress.

Put a group of women to whom cultural norms dictate that they sit close to each

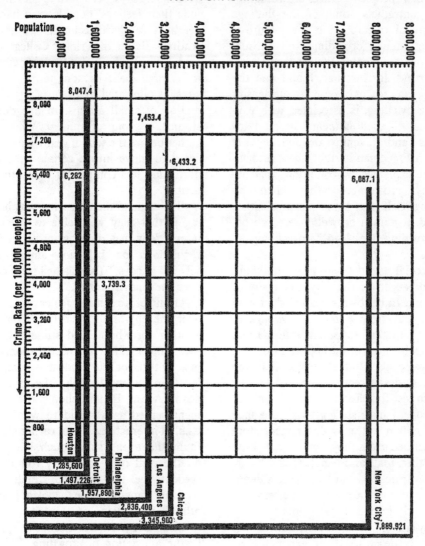

The FBI's 1973 crime figures for the nation's six most populous cities show Detroit, fifth in population, with the highest crime rate among six. New York is fifth.

other, look into each other's eyes, and share distress, into a crowded room and you get the results Epstein and Freedman discovered, Aiello believes. But reverse those norms and you reverse the behavior.

There's some evidence that women's expectations about other women get them in trouble when crowding persists over a long period of time. Aiello and Epstein are now involved in a long-term study of Rutgers dormitory students which shows that when three women share a room meant for two, they fight more than men in the same situation. "Men retreat from the crowded situation, but women try to interact more, which leads to stress," says Aiello. "Maybe women have unreal expectations about each other."

The new people-oriented crowding research contradicts some of the findings from animal research, but the picture it paints of human crowding isn't entirely rosy. Both the Factor-Waldron and Collette surveys, for instance, found that the density of an area, as opposed to the density within a dwelling, is associated with psychological ills such as mental hospital admissions and juvenile delinquency. If Jonathan Freedman is right, these associations are explained by conditions that accompany crowding, rather than by crowding itself. But some social scientists involved in human crowding research believe crowding does lead to psychological distress.

One social scientist who takes this stand is Susan Saegert of the City University of New York. In her own research, she found subjects had trouble moving *through* a crowded situation to obtain information. Saegert, who works in a high-rise building on New York's 42nd Street, possibly the nation's busiest street, set up two experiments to test the effects of real-life crowding. In one, female students visited a shoe department in a nearby department store and described shoes they would like to buy; in the other, male and female students carried out various tasks in New York's Pennsylvania Station. Crowded subjects did more poorly in both experiments.

Oddly enough, though, the women in the shoe study described their experience as more pleasant when the shoe department was crowded. To women, bargain day at the department store among a crowd of female shoppers may be a "good" crowd.

If crowding is stressful, what can be done about it? Social scientists are busier trying to describe crowding than alleviate it, but they offer a few tentative suggestions. John Aiello tried changing cultural norms in the

dorm study he is involved in and had some limited success. "It's difficult to maneuver norms," he says. "It's hard to get females to hide their feelings, but it's even harder to get men to share feelings." Psychologist Andrew Baum of Trinity College (Hartford, Conn.), who is also studying crowding in dorms, believes long-term crowding stress is alleviated by encouraging the formation of small groups. In one dorm he studied, a group of students who got together before the school year began and decided to move into a certain area of the dorm had less complaints than other students.

"It's clear to me that what was happening is that they were able to circumvent interactions they didn't want by setting up regulations on behavior among themselves," he says. "They gained some control over their environment."

Architecture can also foster more control over the environment, believes Baum. In another dorm he studied, students in suites —a number of interconnected rooms occupied by three or four students—complained less than students in a typical corridor-style dorm. Again, Baum believes, the arrangement served as a shield to ward off unwanted interactions. In an earlier study, he found that even a small touch, like pictures on the wall of a dormitory room, makes students feel less crowded. "Pictures give students something else to look at than each other," he explains.

Susan Saegert takes a broader approach to the alleviation of crowding. "The person's total experience of density and other stress in the course of daily living must be examined," she says. Those !Kung bushmen, she believes, thrive because their crowded camps are surrounded by the vast and empty Kalahari Desert. Saegert worries about the city dweller who goes from a crowded apartment to a crowded office, traveling between the two via a crowded train. What such people need, she suggests, is a form of "escape." It can take the form of a spacious office, an apartment with an extra room, a weekend home or, if the escapee is rich, a chauffeured limousine.

But the rich, believes Saegert, turn most of their environment into an escape, which may explain why they so often extol the delights of big cities. "I think those who benefit most from cities are those who avoid crowding," says Saegert, whose own escape is an apartment in a relatively quiet part of the city and a small but quiet office.

Even those who aren't rich, her experience indicates, should be able to find an escape somewhere in the urban environment. And as they pull down the escape hatch, they can take comfort in the thought that even if crowding is stressful, it isn't nearly as bad for people as for rats.

28. THE QUEST OF THE BLACK MAN

T. Bradford Johnson and McKinley Dillingham

Sociologists and anthropologists often refer to the family as both a social and economic institution, in which man and wife are "business partners," with the male functioning as titular head and his wife a capable manager. Historically, family life usually has been patriarchal, with the father emerging as dominant and his wife and children conceding to his demands.

The family structure in the U.S. still is dominated primarily by the patriarchal system, despite current reforms. The American Ideal dictates that the husband assume the responsibilities for his wife and children. In contemporary society, however, when the wife has become a partner with wages earned outside the home, the father's dominance still is expected to pervade in crucial family decisions.

Black society, like the other cultural groups in America, is divided into social classes, the majority of whom are members of the lower-income families. Social mobility is restricted for blacks due to financial, educational, and color barriers. Thus, many blacks are born poor and die poor.

The traditional patriarchal family structure is not adhered to by most of the lower-class black families in the U.S., since the mother serves as head of the family, breadwinner, and decision-maker. The assumption of responsibility by the mother for the well-being of herself and her children was, in most cases, a matter of circumstances— *e.g.,* she had not chosen this authoritarian matriarchal role voluntarily. It became necessary for the woman to assume the male's role because of his absence. The absence of the father in lower-class black homes is not uncommon, and usually affects the entire family. A book entitled *Nigger* depicts quite graphically how an innocent child can be emotionally distraught by a father's absence. "I got it right now, my Daddy gave it to me to turn in today, my Daddy said . . . And furthermore, she said looking right at me, her nostrils getting big and her lips get-

Reprinted from *Intellect* (March 1973) pp. 366–370, by permission of publisher.

ting thin and her eyes opening wide, 'we know you don't have a Daddy.' I walked out of school that day, and for a long time I didn't go back very often. There was shame there."[1]

The majority of American society attributes the absence of the lower-class black male in the home to separation, divorce, or desertion. These negative phrases have been associated with him constantly since his legal emancipation more than a century ago.

The numerous burdens and responsibilities of the black male often are overlooked, and he too often is caricatured as being a clown, lazy and shiftless, dishonest, irresponsible, unstable, and unreliable. His illiteracy forever is being capitalized upon by entrepreneurs. Are these true descriptions of his character? Is he really trying to escape the responsibility of being the protector and provider for his dependent family? Is he absent because he wants to perpetuate a matriarchal society and has enshrined it as a unique family? Is lower-class black male absence because of psychological phenomena or by personal choice? Has he been caught in the continuous web of oppression, segregation, discrimination, and unemployment? The black family structure was not destroyed by modern technology or automation—the roots of destruction were planted over 100 years ago on the plantation during the days of slavery.

The lower-class black male slave had no self-image or idea as to the constituents of manhood, and even today is unaware of what the affluent American society recognizes as being a man. The black erroneously thought that he would acquire manhood in the "promised land"—the North.

The role of today's black male in our society has been determined largely by his historic past—slavery, discrimination, oppression, and economic insecurity. These factors caused innumerable frustrations, and are responsible for his plight. Thus far, he has been unable to compete successfully in our materialistic society.

The black male's psychological castration was evident throughout the U.S., but was most visibly apparent in slavery, when the white plantation owner twisted his mind by according him none of the rights of a human being. The slave never could free himself, and, in addition, was regarded by whites as a totally inferior being. As a result, the slave could not view himself with any sense of human identity. He soon realized that submissiveness and unmanly behavior was rewarded, while aggressive and assertive behavior on his part was subject to punishment. Minimal consideration was shown for the slave personality. In many cases, slaves in America were not allowed the choice of a sex partner, and learned to regard themselves as "stallions" or "studs" whose only purpose in regard to women was to breed—like the animals. The slaves copulated to meet the demands of the master, and the master mated his slaves with the same enthusiasm that he mated his other stock. Female slaves, at one time, outnumbered the male slaves so that breeding increased the master's population of slaves and was to his economic advantage. "An excess of males was created where slavery tended to be a purely industrial enterprise requiring masculine labor. Under such circumstances there was no opportunity for permanency in the association between the sexes."[2]

In some cases, individual affectional preferences were exhibited when the male insisted upon having the woman of his choice, regardless of the punishment and inconveniences caused him. The master's sadistic

---

[1] Dick Gregory, *Nigger* (New York: Dutton, 1965), p. 31.

[2] E. Franklin Frazier, *The Negro Family in the United States* (Chicago: University of Chicago Press, 1966), p. 17.

reaction generally was to "cure the nigger of wife hunting" when he had been caught trying to procure a wife from another plantation. "Massa Charlie" believed that there were enough slave girls on his own plantation for a male slave to pick from and thereby to increase his fortune in slaves. "Whenever the slaves showed discrimination [in] definite preference in the selection of a mate, the purely sexual impulses and feelings were transformed into something more than animal appetite. There developed in many cases what might truly be called a period of courtship."[3]

During slavery, the male's basic sexual needs were satisfied, but his psycho-physiological needs were not recognized as an integral facet of human existence. However, slaves were allowed the privilege of creating their own entertainment and of courting, either before or after the long work day. Marriage was allowed, providing it met with the master's approval. The male who was a good worker or could be referred to by the master as a "good nigger" was granted the privilege of selecting a mate of his choice. Yet, "marriage between slaves was not recognized as law. Indeed, to permit slaves to marry would have worked an intolerable inconvenience upon the slavemaster who often found it economically expedient to sell part of a family, and who not infrequently satisfied his own sexual lusts through [the] instrumentality of his female slaves."[4]

The black male, after being allowed to select a wife, was still not the provider for his family, nor could he protect his wife from the master's sexual transgressions. The master possessed a tyrannical monopoly on him, both physically and mentally. The male slave was not permitted to de-

velop a family organization equivalent to that of his forefathers in Africa, or even that of his white master. As a result of the bonds of slavery, "the matriarchal family is still strong in the Negro tradition, and the circumstances of tradition . . . , bid for its definite retention, at least within the Negro lower class."[5]

The black female's ego constantly was elevated as the male's ego was trampled upon. She was favored by the master because of her sexual availability and usefulness within the house. The black male "never [was] thought of as a husband or a father and was viewed as his wife's assistant at best. In the language of the day, such a slave was referred to as 'Hattie's Jim,' or 'Mandy's Sam,' thus giving primacy and possession to the female rather than the male."[6]

The children of these castigated black males were victims of hatred, disloyalty, and disrespect. They were taught at an early age to believe that the mother would provide for their well-being whenever the father was absent. The fact that he was not absent by choice made no difference. During the era of slavery, legality of birth was as unheard of for blacks as was a marriage license. "A male slave's children were seldom called 'Jim's' or 'Sam's,' but were usually referred to as having been 'got by Jim' or 'got by Sam.' "[7]

Too often, the slave stood helplessly by and watched and listened while his family was removed from him, and he merely gritted his teeth when the master would not let the babies and their mother "holler" when he sold them. No doubt, he wanted to strike out when the master threatened to beat them if they did not stop crying, but he could not, as he was too fearful of the white master's reprisals. The white man repre-

[3] *Ibid.*, p. 21.
[4] C. Eric Lincoln, "A Look Beyond Matriarchy," *Ebony*, 21:112, August, 1966.

[5] *Ibid.*
[6] *Ibid.*
[7] *Ibid.*

sented the only law and order known on the plantation.

Slavery and its dehumanizing masters created one of the most deadly social diseases in the history of our country. This disease was rooted as deeply as cancer, and it ate deeply into the souls of the black males and molded the lives of its victims, leaving many with complete psychological castration, stripped of personal pride and feelings. The monster that slavery created was weak, oppressed, afraid to reach out and defend his decaying soul. The black male's self-concept was equivalently as low as the social-class group of which he found himself an unwilling member. The white man dehumanized the black male, minimized any ego strength, and accorded him status of the lowest order. Repetitious degradation of the soul of the black male convinced him that he was a misfit in society—little more than an animal. He even was referred to by a pet name—by which any male could answer regardless of his age or his gray hair. He had to answer to "boy," "Jack," or "Matilda's Jack."

Meanwhile, the black woman's self-esteem and confidence was rising steadily, and her songs indicated she had hopes of freedom. The white man's physiological drives for the black woman and his need of her domestic services gave her a sense of self-worth and superiority. Her role and views of freedom were enhanced, and she became "the mistress of her cabin, and save for the interference of master or overseer, her wishes in regard to mating and family matters were paramount. Neither economic necessity nor tradition had instilled in her the spirit of subordination to masculine authority. Emancipation only tended to confirm in many cases the spirit of self-sufficiency which slavery had taught."[8]

The black male's sense of freedom was nearly nonexistent, since he had nothing to encourage any feelings of security. All he received from the white man was a deep-rooted feeling of subservience. Male folk songs were seldom songs of hope, nor did they exude confidence or self-assurance. It has been only recently, since the rise of the black middle-class society, that the male has chanted the songs of freedom. The lower-class black male's voice still is lost in the sonorous tumult of humanity.

When emancipation was proclaimed, the slaves were freed and released from the Southern plantations, but without any provisions for their well-being. They left slavery behind them, but actually, ". . . not even the shock therapy of a Civil War was able to cure it. Initially it seemed as if the chief consequence of that war was merely to change the symptoms—the substitution of psychological for actual slavery; the use of political and economic restrictions for economic bondage; and the construction of a pattern of legally enforced forms of segregation for the slave compound."[9]

The women often returned to the white man's "kitchen" to benefit by his favors, but the male had no place in which he was welcome. His inadequacies frequently were illuminated, and his inability to hold a job which would grant him dignity resulted in his inability to hold his family together. Emancipation resulted in the masters releasing their slaves, and the freedwomen releasing their non-productive, ego-deficient husbands. How could the man be expected to function in a totally new environment that required literacy as a prerequisite for success? The released slave was without money, skills, a home, and he was living in an economically depressed area. When he attempted to better his circumstances by moving to the "promised land"

---

[8]Frazier, *op. cit.*, p. 102.

[9]Kenneth B. Clark, "A Relevant Celebration of the Emancipation Centennial," *Ebony*, 18:63, September, 1963.

—the North—he often was met with prejudiced hostility. The black male truly had no place to call home. The black woman eventually grew tired of perpetuating her old status, and wanted to improve herself vocationally or lighten her burdens through matrimony. She desired a patriarchally structured marriage, but the male was unable, by virtue of his ignorance and past indoctrination, to provide her with this security. It therefore became necessary for the woman to exercise her influence by getting a job and providing for her children. Hence, she became *de facto* head of the household. The matriarchal society was inefficable, since the female offered the only source of family continuity—the child was dependent upon the mother. The male continued to roam, becoming more of a visitor in the home than part of the institution of marriage. His deflated ego never let him rise psychologically from slave status, and he never has been able to gain the dignity that is bestowed upon the white man as his birthright.

It was not the white man's original intention or objective to allow the Negro to become self-reliant, since he failed to educate him for self-sustenance. White supremacy flourished, and the Negro lived on superficial promises and tokenism. The black male soon had to depend upon state and Federal relief funds for existence, since he failed to become a consistent wage earner. "He could not present himself to his wife and children as a person who had the opportunity or the ability to compete successfully in politics, business or industry. His doubts concerning personal adequacy were reinforced."[10]

During slavery, the suppression of blacks had been overtly obvious, and was enforced consistently. The Emancipation Proclamation evidenced only partial freedom for the Negro and much covert suppression. "With the ending of physical slavery after the Civil War new devices were found to 'keep the Negro in his place ...,' extending from birth in Jim Crow hospitals through burial in Jim Crow sections of cemeteries ..."[11]

The white man reluctantly built schools for blacks, since he fervently felt that it was not important to educate a "nigger." Why should he create a problem—with an "educated nigger"? Even in the more liberal North, the black found prejudice in many public facilities. If he was allowed to partake of the white man's pleasures, it was in separate places or in sections segregated and labeled "colored." During the post-Civil War period, the black male further became immersed in second-class citizenship, and suffered economically, socially, and psychologically. To the delight of many whites, he had learned his place and stayed there. If the black male had the opportunity to attend school, how would he support himself or his family? Who would encourage him to pursue an education? What role models did he evidence in his neighborhood? Many black males wanted to learn, but their lack of skills, coupled with long arduous hours, provided only a subsistence income with no time or energy left for educational growth.

In many cases, fortunate slave women were exposed to reading in the master's house, and the white woman often helped her black servant learn. The black woman's educational progress, as a result, was significantly greater than that of most black males.

It was during the Reconstruction period that the white man attached the label "satisfied" to the black. The black was not "satisfied" with his status, but he could do no

---

[10]Kenneth B. Clark, *Dark Ghetto* (New York: Harper & Row, 1965), p. 70.

[11]Martin Luther King, Jr., *Why We Can't Wait* (New York: Signet Books, 1964), p. 28.

better. At that time, he was not motivated by other black successes to extend himself. He had no comprehension of the implications of success—he was too suppressed. "The average Negro is born into want and deprivation. His struggle to escape his circumstances is hindered by color discrimination. He is deprived of normal education and normal social and economic opportunities. When he seeks opportunity he is told, in effect, to lift himself up by his own boot straps, advice which does not take into account the fact that he is barefoot."[12]

Massive unemployment in the formative years of the black struggle for total freedom held the Negro back, and he is still a victim of unemployment and a constant visitor to the unemployment offices. With each new technological invention or advance toward automation, the black lower-class male's anxiety increases, knowing full-well that, when the invention is patented, he again will be unemployed and untrained for the new technical position. The lower-class black male thus is lost in the economic mainstream of society. He is a victim of inadequate employment, and he remains in intellectual and academic bondage. Too often, poor vocational experiences and minimal education prohibit the black from even being considered for a job. When the male in the large city searches for a job and is refused—often without good reason—he becomes ashamed and depressed. His lack of education implies that he is intellectually inferior. He thus becomes fearful of his future and that of his family. It is generally the lower-class black male who is relegated to a subservient status. His earnings just will not support his family in today's inflationary economy. Insecurity has caused the Negro to take a back seat vocationally. The fact that he is the "last hired and the first fired" has not gone unnoticed by the black

male. He also knows that he is obviously at the bottom of the economic ladder. "The lowest paid employment and the most tentative jobs are reserved for him. If he seeks to change his position, he is walled in by the tall barrier of discrimination."[13]

Unemployment causes many Negro children of lower-class homes to grow up without a father image. The "fatherless" home has characterized the Negro for generations. "The pattern is as rigid as it is vicious, and it is re-inforced by a converging complex of socio-economic patterns [and white men who] traditionally have more and better schooling than Negro men, to the frequent unavailability of employment that pays enough to enable the Negro male to support his family."[14]

Social welfare regulations often make it necessary for the black male to remain outside the home if his family is to continue to receive financial assistance from the city or state. He does not realize, however, the frustration and anger that it causes within his children. His absence leaves the children without a patriarchal image. In *Nigger*, Dick Gregory revealed the shame, stress, and frustration that he felt in relation to his absent father.

Dick: "God's a good God, ain't He, Momma?"

Momma: "Yes, Richard."

Dick: "Next time you talk to Him, ask Him to send Daddy home."

The psychologically castrated father returns home to find the Gregory home to be headed by his wife, perhaps not by choice, but because of the economic forces of society and his lack of understanding of his role within the family.

Daddy: "I brought you some money, Richard."

Dick: "Don't want it, Daddy."

---

[12] *Ibid.*, p. 23.

[13] *Ibid.*, p. 24.
[14] Lincoln, *op. cit.*, p. 113.

Daddy: "I'm your Daddy, boy, don't you want to see me?"

Dick: "I see you every time I see Momma on her knees in front of the window cryin' and prayin' you'll come. You ought to thank me 'cause I brought you here."[15]

The lower-class black husband often is unable to elicit respect from the white man, nor is he financially able to remove his family from relief. He is enmeshed in a chronic neurotic fear, and he often gives vent to his emotions by excessive drinking or beating and cursing his wife. Acts of violence are signs of his frustration, inferiority, and guilt feelings. He regrets the fact that he can not demand the respect of his family and society as well.

In *Nigger,* Daddy is a jobless man, full of hate and lack of motivation. " 'I don't even feel right walking down the street with you,' he said kicking her in the side with his foot. 'Walk down the street everybody wants to run up, say hello to you, they look at me like I was dirt.' "[16]

It is primarily for the benefit of the lower-class black male, whose role of suppression has been so great for over 100 years that he has not fulfilled the "American Ideal"—the patriarchal society—that the black has to march and chant "We shall overcome." It is for the redemption of the black male's self-respect and dignity within his family and society that men like Dr. Martin Luther King, Jr., responded fervently "We can't wait." The white man originally planned the family structure of the black to fit his selfish economic whims. This antiquated plan has castrated the Negro psychologically. It is time that his role in society be reevaluated. Oppression, igno-

rance, economic bondage, "tokenism," and discrimination must be removed, allowing him to become a viable member of the patriarchal society that denotes the culture of the U.S.

It is necessary for the survival of the black family and the male image within the family that shame, doubt, and guilt be removed. The black male never has overcome his past, and his past is not dead, even though the potentially vibrant middle class has come into existence. Blacks must unite their effort to strengthen family bonds and to provide the depressed lower-class males with a sense of dignity. "The social advantage or economic security enjoyed by an individual member of an oppressed minority will be only temporary unless the least advantaged and the most impoverished of that group improves his status."[17]

The role and status of the black lower-class male must be improved; his anger must be erased. His role can be improved by allocating him with responsibility, education, and job opportunities which will result in increased motivation to achieve and a growth of self-respect. These essential variables cause the image of lower-class black males to change, help them to overcome their resentments, and allay some of the frustrations that are causing their roles in the family to be that of the absent link, either by desertion, separation, or divorce. To bring the traditional American ideal of a patriarchal society back into the lower-class black homes, the male role must be elevated, his past must be understood, and he must be granted a new beginning, free from oppression and discrimination.

---

[15]Gregory, *op. cit.,* pp. 13–19.
[16]*Ibid.,* p. 20.

[17]Whitney M. Young, "The Role of the Middle Class Negro," *Ebony,* 18:66, September, 1963.

CHAPTER V

Problems of the Individual

PEOPLE HAVE psychological problems. Some are easy to solve, some are difficult, and some do a neat job of destroying lives. This chapter includes articles which explore many of the most prominent and the most destructive psychological problems. Perhaps just as importantly, they give worthwhile suggestions as to how to cope with these problems of the individual.

Some of the readings in this chapter are about what is commonly called mental illness, such as "Paranoia," and "What You Should Know About Mental Depression." Another is concerned with the problematic nature of the diagnosis of mental illnesses—"Can Psychiatrists Tell the Sane from the Insane?" Beyond diagnosis, psychologists are concerned with the causes of mental illness, which, surprisingly, may not be of psychological origin. "It's Not All in Your Head" presents a view regarding causes of psychological problems.

The remainder of the readings in this chapter presents important insights into the nature and the dimensions of the various types of drug, food, and behavioral addictions which afflict people. They may be of personal help if you have one of these addictions or know someone who is so afflicted. "A Psychiatrist Looks at Alcoholism" explores the most significant drug problem in the world. The addiction to food and eating is defined in "Obesity and Behavior," and the subtle addiction to working too much, called workaholism, is explored in "If You Think You're Working Too Hard," a mine of information and useful suggestions concerning this most recently recognized form of addiction.

29. CAN PSYCHIATRISTS TELL THE SANE FROM THE INSANE?

Long-term psychiatric institutions, already being phased out in some states, have been dealt a body blow by a study concluding that mental hospital staffs "cannot distinguish the sane from the insane." Some psychiatrists contacted think the conclusion landed below the belt, but others agree that the study demonstrates a serious weakness in psychiatric diagnosis and treatment.

The report, published in *Science* (179: 250–8), describes the experiences of eight volunteers who presented themselves for admission to psychiatric hospitals. All complained of the same faked symptom— they said they heard hollow voices. In 11 out of 12 tries the eight healthy pseudopatients were admitted with a diagnosis of schizophrenia. Discharged, one to seven weeks later, the men were tagged with a diagnosis of "schizophrenia in remission." In the 12th case, the admission and discharge diagnosis was manic-depressive psychosis.

No staff member ever questioned the original diagnosis, though the pseudo-patients behaved normally and cooperated fully. Dr. David L. Rosenhan, the Stanford University psychologist who designed the study, found fellow patients more perceptive. "You're not crazy," one inmate told a pseudo-patient; "you're checking up on the hospital."

Among the 12 hospitals challenged by the volunteers were three whose names would "be recognized by anyone in the field as in the top rank," says Dr. Rosenhan. The three have AMA-approved residency programs. Besides Dr. Rosenhan, the investigators included two psychologists, a pediatrician, a psychiatrist, a painter, a graduate student, and a housewife.

In a follow-up experiment with a reverse twist, Dr. Rosenhan warned a 13th hospital that he was going to send one or more pseudo-patients to seek admission there over the next three months. The staff agreed to rate all new patients as to whether or not they were fakes. Of 193 candidates screened, 41 were labeled fakes by at least one member of the staff, and 19 were rated "suspicious" by both a psychiatrist and another staff member. The kicker comes from Dr. Rosenhan: "No genuine pseudo-patient (at least from my group) presented himself during this period." The two studies lead to the same conclusion, he states: "Any diagnostic process that lends itself so readily to massive errors of this sort cannot be a very reliable one."

The pseudo-patients' experiences were also damning to the institutional system, in his view. For the most part, their efforts to establish communications with staff members were ignored, Dr. Rosenhan reports. In four institutions where the volunteers kept notes of their attempts to initiate contacts with the staff, psychiatrists "moved on with heads averted" 71% of the time, and other staff members did so 88% of the time.

The encounters frequently took a bizarre form, notes Dr. Rosenhan. When one pseu-

Reprinted from *Medical World News*. Copyright © 1973, McGraw-Hill, Inc. From *Science Digest* (July 1973), pp. 248–251.

do-patient approached a doctor to politely inquire when he would be eligible for grounds privileges, the physician answered, "Good morning, Dave. How are you today?" Then he moved off without waiting for a reply. At the hospital where Dr. Rosenhan was admitted, other patients were punished—in one case beaten—for trying to start conversations with attendants.

Patients were generally deprived of privacy; physical examinations were conducted in the open, urinals were in view of the nursing station, and even bowel movements were sometimes monitored. At most of the institutions, the staff sequestered itself in what patients called "the glass cage," emerging only to give orders or specific medication.

The hospital setting, in the researcher's view, is itself "an insane place." And, he concludes, "the consequences to patients hospitalized in such an environment—the powerlessness, depersonalization, segregation, mortification, and self-labeling—seem to be undoubtedly counter-therapeutic." The reactions of psychiatrists and other professionals to the Rosenhan study range from total approbation to disparagement.

Dr. Loren Mosher, chief of the schizophrenia study center of the National Institute of Mental Health, thought it was "provocative" and "very useful." A diagnosis of schizophrenia based on a single symptom, with no preceding history, "shows lack of care and thoroughness," Dr. Mosher said. "Disappearance of such a symptom may not be noticed for three or four days, but the next time the patient talks to a psychiatrist he probably should be discharged." He notes, however, that some patients do hide symptoms to get out.

"That nobody paid attention to the pseudo-patients once they got in is a devastating critique," says Dr. Mosher. "Dr. Rosenhan is pointing out the effects of the context in which psychiatrists work. It's one of illness

and pathology, and this dictates the behavior of the psychiatrists."

Dr. Leonard Heston, associate professor at the University of Minnesota, believes the Rosenhan statement "goes too far. . . . We sometimes don't distinguish the sane from the insane, but that doesn't mean we can't." And Dr. George Winokur, psychiatry chief at the University of Iowa, disagrees with another Rosenhan conclusion—that the consequences to patients of the depersonalized way in which they are treated are counter-therapeutic. "It's appalling and certainly antihumanistic, but I don't accept the fact that it can be termed counter-therapeutic."

The diagnoses of schizophrenia in 11 of the 12 pseudo-patients drew fire from several specialists. "You shouldn't make a diagnosis on the basis of the clinical picture on a one-shot basis," says Dr. Winokur. "In addition to the clinical picture, family histories and follow-up studies are necessary. From what the article says of these pseudo-patients, they don't fulfill the criteria for schizophrenia. I asked some of my staff, and they said that such patients would be discharged from our hospital in a couple of days."

Dr. Eli Robins, chairman of psychiatry at Washington University in St. Louis, regards the Rosenhan article as valuable and important in pointing up the fact that many psychiatrists are poorly trained in diagnosis and show little interest in it. "In the case of these eight people there was no history leading up to the key symptom, which disappeared in a day's time. For schizophrenia to begin with no previous history of any kind is most unusual." Dr. Robins also makes the point that "hearing voices" does not necessarily point to schizophrenia. It could imply manic depression or brain damage.

On the other hand, Dr. Jack R. Ewalt, director of the Massachusetts Mental

Health Center in Boston, who is enthusiastic about the Rosenhan study ("I thought it was great"), believes the experiences described could have happened at his center. "For all I know," he remarked, "we may have been one of those referred to. But I'd hope my staff would be on to them. Genuine symptoms of that kind could have been treated on an outpatient basis. What impressed me was that these people were kept in when they didn't show enough pathology to warrant their being there."

Among negative reactions to the report, the most caustic comes from Dr. Henry Brill, director of Pilgrim State Hospital in Brentwood, N.Y. "Why are the members of the Rosenhan team anonymous?" he asks. "Why doesn't he give us information from the other side? We don't have the view of the other observers—the hospital staffs. This is close to anonymous accusation." As for the inside-the-walls technique, "It's not new," says Dr. Brill. "It's been practiced by newspaper reporters since the days of Nellie Bly" (the 19th-century reporter who wrote an "inside" exposé of asylum conditions).

Dr. Brill maintains that it takes much longer to prove that an individual is not psychotic than to prove he is. "If I have the evidence, I can prove a man is psychotic in a day, but to give him a clean bill of health takes a couple of weeks."

David B. Wexler, a professor of law at the University of Arizona who conducted a seminar with Dr. Rosenhan last year, finds the study "exciting and distressing. It emphasizes the need for due process in commitment hearings and mental health laws generally—including the right to counsel and to call independent medical or behavioral experts for the patient. Committed patients need a statutory guarantee of periodic reassessment, as well as rights to visitors, mail, phone calls, personal clothing, and privacy. Many states don't provide these rights."

Dr. Robert S. Wallerstein of San Francisco, immediate past president of the American Psychoanalytic Association, terms the Rosenhan paper "disturbing and embarrassing" but also "exaggerated in some of its conclusions. It's an old story in our field that the nomenclature is not satisfactory," Dr. Wallerstein said, "and there's unevenness and occasionally ineptitude of diagnosis. Dr. Rosenhan has, however, demonstrated quite dramatically how much our perceptions of patients are conditioned by the context in which we see them. This, to me, is the real significance of his study.

"If presented with a symptom like the one described by the pseudo-patients," he adds, "I'd look for the total context in which it was presented. If I couldn't make sense of the whole picture, I'd suspect any number of things, including the possibility of an intent to deceive. I think Dr. Rosenhan has overmade his point—so much so that his study may not do the good he intends."

According to Dr. Karl Menninger of the Menninger Foundation, the study "belongs with what I've been saying for years. I don't believe there is such a disease as schizophrenia. There are personality disorganizations; I've described them and treated people for them. But schizophrenia to me is just a nice Greek word that some psychiatrists use to sound scientific and impress relatives. Nine tenths of people with so-called schizophrenia get well without a hospital."

To Dr. Donald T. Lunde, assistant professor of psychiatry at Stanford medical school, his colleague's findings are "less than surprising. The staff of a mental hospital doesn't look for healthy people trying to talk their way in, because it isn't a pleasant place to be." The "confusion" in diagnosing could be explained by several factors, he thinks. One is disagreement in the field of diagnosis, and another is that state hospital medical staffs "even today are made up 95% of semiretired GPs, foreign medical graduates who can barely speak English, and other doctors who have no training in psychiatry."

Dr. John Donnelly, psychiatrist in chief at the Institute for Living in Hartford, Conn., is not impressed by the Rosenhan study: "To me, it says that the patient who is really knowledgeable about the subjective symptoms can mislead anyone." But he also observes that "a skilled diagnostician would have looked for inconsistencies between the history of the symptom and the rest of the picture and possibly would have picked up the deception." The symptom of hallucinations alone, Dr. Donnelly adds, would not justify a diagnosis of schizophrenia.

To Dr. Rosenhan, the main point is just that—"the large leap that was made from hallucinations to a diagnosis of schizophrenia." In his view, the pseudo-patients should have been characterized as hallucinators, not schizophrenics. None of them were discharged as sane, he notes, because most psychiatrists believe schizophrenia to be permanently disabling.

The Stanford professor of psychology sees two lines of hope. The first is "the proliferation of community mental health facilities, of crisis intervention centers, of the human potential movement, and of behavior therapies that tend to avoid psychiatric labels. The focus should be on specific problems and behaviors, while retaining the individual in a relatively nonpejorative environment."

The second is the possibility of "increasing the sensitivity of professionals to the 'Catch 22' position of psychiatric patients." Some could achieve this simply by study, Dr. Rosenhan concludes, but "for others, directly experiencing the impact of psychiatric hospitalization will be of enormous use."

30. PARANOIA: AN IDÉE FIXE WHOSE TIME HAS COME

Hendrik Hertzberg and David C. K. McClelland

Three people, Phil and Sam and Lucy, are at a party. They share enough common experiences, beliefs, and preconceptions to be having a chat. Each contributes, by his talk or by his attentiveness, about as much as the others contribute. Everyone is having a good time. Everyone *seems* to be having a good time.

But suppose Phil is really having a bad time. Perhaps he feels ugly or stupid or out

of it; perhaps he is merely depressed. He might excuse himself and go home, but he is afraid of being thought unsociable, so he stays and lets his mind fasten on some premise that seems to explain why he is not enjoying himself. His thoughts begin to congeal around the explanatory premise, which is probably something like, *I'm bad and unhappy and they know it* or *I'm bad and unhappy and they don't know it.*

The conversation goes on:

Lucy: Did you see that new Altman movie—what's it called?

SAM: *Thieves Like Us.*

PHIL: Yeah, I saw that.

SAM: Me too.

LUCY: What did you think of it?

SAM: I think it's overrated.

Meanwhile, Phil struggles to establish a connection between the conversation and his premise. He may be thinking, *Why are they talking about movies? They must notice that I'm horrible and miserable, but they know there's no way they can help, so they're trying to take my mind off it.*

Or he may be thinking. *Why are they talking about movies? It must be because they don't notice I'm horrible and miserable. They couldn't care less how I feel.*

Phil fails to notice, among other things, that he, too, is talking about movies. His mind is so full of his own wretchedness that he assumes Sam and Lucy are also preoccupied with it. (The only alternative is that Sam and Lucy are callous and unfeeling.) In fact, Sam and Lucy may simply think they are at a party talking about movies.

Phil, so far, is suffering from little more than a lousy mood. But suppose that Phil's condition is more serious. Suppose that he is paranoid. In that event, the premise dominating his mind will be far from simple, and it will explain far more than why he is unhappy. The premise might be, for example, that an elaborate Mafia conspiracy is trying to control his life. Now Phil will have to work harder to interpret the conversation in a way that "proves" his premise.

LUCY: Did you see that new Altman movie—what's it called? (Phil thinks, *You know damn well what it's called.*)

SAM: *Thieves Like Us.* (Phil thinks, *Thieves indeed. What could be more obvious? You can't fool me.*)

PHIL: Yeah, I saw that. (Phil thinks, *Don't kid yourselves that I don't know what you're really talking about.*)

SAM: Me too. (Phil thinks, *So you know I know—is that what you're saying?*)

LUCY: What did you think of it? (Phil thinks, *You're trying to invade my thoughts.*)

SAM: I think it's overrated. (Phil thinks, *Of course you do—those thieves only steal money, you steal minds.*)

Phil is clearly in a bad way.

A LITTLE SEMANTICS

Paranoia is a word on everyone's lips, but only among mental-health professionals has it acquired a tolerably specific meaning. It refers to a psychosis based on a delusionary premise of self-referred persecution or grandeur (e.g., "The Knights of Columbus control the world and are out to get me," "I am Norman Mailer"), and supported by a complex, rigorously logical system that interprets all or nearly all sense impressions as evidence for that premise. The traditional psychiatric view is that paranoia is an extreme measure for the defense of the integrity of the personality against annihilating guilt. The paranoid (so goes the theory) thrusts his guilt outside himself by denying his hostile or erotic impulses and projecting them onto other people or onto the whole universe. Disintegration is avoided, but at high cost: the paranoid view of reality can make everyday life terrifying and social intercourse problematical. And paranoia is tiring. It requires exhausting mental effort to construct trains of thought demonstrating that random events or details "prove" a wholly unconnected premise. Some paranoids hallucinate, but hallucination is by no means obligatory; paranoia is an interpretive, not a perceptual, dysfunction.

Paranoia is a recent cultural disorder. It follows the adoption of rationalism as the quasi-official religion of Western man and the collapse of certain communitarian bonds (the extended family, belief in God, the harmony of the spheres) which once made sense of the universe in all its parts. Paranoia substitutes a rigorous (though false) order for chaos, and at the same time dispels the sense of individual insignificance by making the paranoid the focus of all he sees going on around him—a natural response to the confusion of modern life.

Strictly speaking, there was no such thing as paranoia before the mid-nineteenth century, when the word (from the Greek for "beside" and "mind") first surfaced as one of several medical-sounding euphemisms for madness. In an earlier age, the states of mind now explained as paranoia were accounted for differently. The vastness of the difference is suggested if one reflects on the likelihood of a president of France placing the command of his country's armed forces in the hands of a teen-age peasant girl who hears voices from God.

Even more recent is the wholesale adoption of the terms "paranoia" and "paranoid" into everyday speech as metaphors for a bewildering variety of experiences. Hippies could no more communicate their thoughts without using "paranoia" and "paranoid" than they could eschew "like," "y'know," and "I mean." In this context the meanings of the terms are blurry but readily comprehensible. "Man, are you ever paranoid." This is not meant as a compliment. The implication is that the accused is imagining a threat where none exists. "I mean, she really makes me paranoid." The speaker feels that "she" is more powerful than he is, making him uncomfortable. "There was a lot of paranoia at that concert." One gathers that the security precautions were excessive. "No thanks, man, I get really paranoid when I smoke dope." Here paranoia is merely a euphemism for fear. "I'm paranoid" is less disturbing, for both speaker and listener, than "I'm frightened." (Psychiatric terminology is central to contemporary etiquette. One says, "I'm having trouble relating to you." One does not say, "I hate your guts.")

In politics, paranoia is a logical conse-

quence of the wrenching loose of power from the rigid social arrangements that once conditioned its exercise, and the resulting preoccupation with questions of "dominate or be dominated." Political and quasipolitical notions, such as the conviction that the telephone company is manipulating reality in order to control one's mind, appear routinely in the delusions of persons suffering from paranoid psychosis. In American public life, as Richard Hofstadter showed in *The Paranoid Style in American Politics,* persecutory themes have cropped up periodically from the beginning. Groups widely believed to have been at the center of the shifting conspiracy against the common weal have at various times included the Masons, the Papists, the Illuminati, Wall Street, the gold hoarders, the outside agitators, the Communists, and —bringing us up to the present—the pointy-headed bureaucrats, the Establishment, the system, the straights, the New Left nihilists, the Mafia, the oil companies, the media, and the CIA.* As Lincoln said, you can fool some of the people all of the time.

The Nixon years have been something of a Golden Age of political paranoia. The paranoid strategies of projection, denial, and the use of code language with private meanings ("law and order," "peace with honor," "executive privilege")† have been played out on a national scale. The Nixon Administration saw politics as an array of reified conspiracies against it ("the criminal forces as against the peace forces," the

---

*The CIA turns up in paranoid delusions perhaps more than any other single organization. Its name is extremely suggestive—"central," "intelligence," and "agency" are all words rich in multiple meanings— and, since the CIA does in fact engage in conspiratorial activities, it can easily be adapted for any scheme involving domination and control by unseen forces. Freud always maintained that every paranoid delusion contains a nugget of truth.

†"I don't have to spell it out," the President told a group of milk producers during a tape-recorded meeting.

Chicago defendants, Ellsberg, the campus bums, the radiclibs, the media) and behaved accordingly. The unprecedented security arrangements at the Washington headquarters of the Committee to Re-Elect the President, designed to counter an imaginary threat of political burglary and wiretapping, were entrusted to precisely the people who carried out the political burglary and wiretapping of the Democratic National Committee. When the crimes and conspiracies known as Watergate began to come to light, the Administration's two basic responses were denial ("I am not a crook") and projection ("everybody does it"). During the fuss over Pentagon thievery of documents belonging to Henry Kissinger, one "White House source" described his colleagues as "a bunch of paranoids spying on each other."

DOUBLE SPACE

Zero is an extremely bright, self-taught experimental electronics engineer who was the central figure in a small cult in Pontiac, Michigan, one of thousands of local paranoid cults produced by the late counterculture. Zero and his friends made pilgrimages to hear Pink Floyd, a rock group to whose music and lyrics they attached great importance. They occasionally ingested psychedelic drugs and made midnight visits to the main office building of Pontiac Motors, where they intoned mock prayers at the chain-link fence protecting the "temple," a white office monolith lit by floodlights.

Zero lived in a house which would take as long to describe as it would to explicate *Finnegan's Wake*. He had used an old chicken coop, later a lampshade factory, as the shell. Inside he had created an environment from electronic and other debris. The house was too disorienting to be merely a straightforward collection of symbolic junk. No object's use was related to its name. Something that looked and worked like a floor lamp turned out to be a fence post, a telescope, and a plastic cake stand, wired to produce light. Aggregates of machines played the radioactive emissions from one's body back through guitar amplifiers hung from the ceiling. Visual punning marked nearly every object in the house. Overall, it had the impact of a brilliant work of art. But Zero did not consider himself an artist; he regarded his house as a means of self-protection, not of self-expression.

Zero's speech, like his house, was disorienting. In the monologue below, reconstructed by John Farrah, a writer and friend of Zero's, Zero discourses on the great conspiracy he devoted so much energy to protecting himself from.

This isn't something I usually run down. People don't want to hear about it. They figure that if this is true then what's the use. Even if somebody brave like the *National Enquirer* ran it down, which I suppose is impossible, nobody could handle it.

Here's the deal. There's this thing, you know, that would like us all to be very nice polite robots. First, they planned to build androids to replace us. It would either be when you're sleeping or at work or in jail. I used to think that this was unbelievable, but I got busted once, and they really dug on beating me up. I'm sure they get off on offing people, too. You've heard about how every couple of hundred years there's a bunch of people who disappear? Well, they're being offed by GM and getting recycled into new cars. There's a computer under Rochester, Michigan. It completely ran the Vietnam war. That's right, and what's happening now is that the computers of GM have figured out a master scheme to turn us into androids via the food we eat. And McDonald's is the front for the whole thing, and the president of GM is actually Ronald McDonald, who's a front in a scheme to rip off our minds and souls. They're planting electrodes and embalming fluid and synthetic God-knows-what in our food. Did you know that the most widely used used preservative in white bread is embalming fluid? We're being turned into robots without a hand being laid on us! Maybe those satellites up there are programmed to control us, and it's some kind of worldwide monitoring system. And with all this shit inside us from eating Quarter Pounders that undoubtedly strangle up our minds, who even thinks about all of this?

I worked for Pontiac Motors for a while before I went into the Army, and I used to think that maybe the assembly line was once used to turn out robots. Anyway, there was this food company there that filled all the vending machines and ran the plant cafeterias. It was called Prophet Food. Can you dig that? I mean, it's like saying, "Fuck you, we're going to turn you into androids," you know? Oh, man, I ate one of their hamburgers by mistake once. I got sick and couldn't think straight for a few days. Anyway, every day the workers came in like perfect robots and made the cars that were probably melted down years later and made into bombs or something. Hardly anybody picks up on it—you just had a Big Mac or some other kind of poison and you're driving around trying to relate to the cops. Who's going to be able to think about Pontiac Motors? I mean, you gotta get up tomorrow and be there at 6:28 anyway. So pick up a six-pack and forget about it. It's the whole system. It's its own preservative. And it doesn't matter where you work, man, 'cause it's all GM. Generous Motors. What else is there to say? No one believes it. No one dares even think about it. But it's not their fault. We're all just calcium propionate on this bus.

Like his house, Zero's monologue makes one think of art. The hamburger conspiracy is a striking metaphor for the life Zero sees around him. But Zero is innocent of satiric purpose. He has turned the metaphor on its head. It is not a metaphor to him; it is reality, and he lives inside it.

It is a commonplace of both art and psychology that the line between madness and genius is sometimes difficult to draw. But Zero would seem to fall on one side of it, and a self-aware artist like Thomas Pynchon on the other. In his novel *The Crying of Lot 49,* Pynchon presents a massive conspiracy discovered by a young Southern California housewife, Oedipa Maas. As she begins to find connections between Tupperware, her psychiatrist, a giant corporation called Yoyodyne, perpetual-motion machines, an underground postal system called WASTE, the Mafia, a Jacobean tragedy, the German noble family of Thurn und Taxis, and so on, Oepida begins to doubt her sanity.

Change your name to Miles, Dean, Serge, and/or Leonard, baby, she advised her reflection in the half-light of that afternoon's vanity mirror. Either way, they'll call it paranoia. They. Either you have stumbled indeed, without the aid of LSD or other indole alkaloids, onto a secret richness and concealed density of dream; onto a network by which X number of Americans are truly communicating whilst reserving their lies, recitations of routine, arid betrayals of spiritual poverty, for the official government delivery system; maybe even onto a real alternative to the existlessness, to the absence of surprise to life, that harrows the head of everybody American you know, and you too, sweetie. Or you are hallucinating it. Or a plot has been mounted against you, so expensive and elaborate, involving items like the forging of stamps and ancient books, constant surveillance of your movements, planting of post horn images all over San Francisco, bribing of librarians, hiring of professional actors and Pierce Inverarity only knows what-all besides, all financed out of the estate in a way either too secret or too involved for your nonlegal mind to know about even though you are co-executor, so labyrinthine that it must have meaning beyond just a practical joke. Or you are fantasying some such plot, in which case you are a nut, Oedipa, out of your skull.

The Crying of Lot 49, like Pynchon's latest book, *Gravity's Rainbow,* is a story whose plot is a plot—a fiction with the structure of a paranoid delusion. Pynchon verbally (like Zero visually) uses puns, metaphors, and layers of symbols so intricately that he ends by making one doubt one's own sanity—which is his purpose. The codes are never explicit, and therein lies the hostility of the arts of paranoia. The reader (or house guest) must work terribly hard to feel even minimally oriented. Neither in art nor in life is paranoia a generous state of mind.

A USEFUL DISORDER

One of Philip K. Dick's most delightful science-fiction novels, *Clans of the Alphane Moon*, is full of paranoids. The story unfolds on an obscure moon that colonists from earth had used as a mental hospital and then abandoned. Left to their own devices, the former mental patients have organized a workable society, dividing themselves into "clans" according to diagnosis. A psychiatrist from Earth rockets in for a visit, looks around, and speculates on the sociology of the moon. "The paranoids—actually paranoiac schizophrenics —would function as the statesman class," she says. "They'd be in charge of developing political ideology and social programs —they'd have the overall world view." And, she concludes, "Leadership in this society would naturally fall to the paranoids, they'd be superior individuals in terms of initiative, intelligence and just plain innate ability. Of course, they'd have trouble keeping the manics from staging a coup."

No doubt Dick exaggerates. But the fact remains that paranoia (unlike, for example, catatonia) is not necessarily a bar to many kinds of success, including success at leading people. Paranoids, in the course of maintaining and defending their delusionary premises, often develop aptitudes for reasoning, for organization, for argument and persuasion. Paranoids are fond of patterns, and they abhor confusion and uncer-

tainty. For them there are no accidents, and nothing is coincidental. Their dogged tenacity and the supreme confidence with which some of them are able to elucidate their all-embracing theories and nostrums can result in their accession to positions of power. "Though a great many patients with paranoia have to be hospitalized," notes Norman A. Cameron of the Yale School of Medicine, "some do not, and among these an occasional one succeeds in building up a following of persons who believe him to be a genius or inspired."

Paranoids live in a state of perpetual crisis. They are always ready for catastrophe. A psychiatrist has recalled an incident that occurred when he was attached to the staff of a large mental hospital. A gas main had broken and the poisonous fumes were seeping into the wards. It was vital that the hospital be evacuated, and the staff was undermanned. The expected chaos and panic did not materialize, however, because a group of paranoid schizophrenics, once released from their cells, immediately took charge of the evacuation, organized it, and carried it out quickly and efficiently. These paranoids saw nothing unusual in the fact that the hospital was about to be engulfed by an invisible deadly malevolent force.

The average person has many worries but there is one thing he does not generally worry about. He does not worry that somewhere, without his knowledge, a secret tribunal is about to order him seized, drugged, and imprisoned without the right of appeal. Indeed, anyone who worries overmuch about such a thing, and expresses that worry repeatedly and forcefully enough, would probably be classified as a paranoid schizophrenic.

And, once he is so classified, the probable next step is for a secret tribunal to convene, and, without his knowledge, order him to be seized, drugged, and imprisoned without the right of appeal. Such, at any rate, is the situation in many states of the Union, where commitment laws empower official boards to hospitalize involuntarily a "mentally ill" person whose "illness" renders him unable to appreciate his need for treatment. Whatever else this may prove, it does suggest the power of paranoia to refashion the objective world, as well as the subjective universe, in its own image.

These talents for crisis management and self-fulfilling prophecy are not limited to hospitalized paranoids. Persons who see life as a series of "crises," and who pride themselves on being "the coolest man in the room" when a crisis actually develops, sometimes rise to positions of the highest responsibility. The same is true of people who believe themselves persecuted and harassed by "enemies" who are out to "get" them—and who, as a sort of "protective-reaction strike," persecute and harass these same "enemies." The danger such a person incurs is that with the powers of his high position at his disposal, he may force reality into a conformity with his delusions. He will then find himself besieged by *real* enemies, who will indeed do their best to "get" him. But since such a person has been preparing for precisely this all his life he will be well equipped to "fight like hell" when his back is against the wall.

MAKING ENEMIES REAL

An individual paranoid may (as one authority puts it) join "some fanatical movement in current vogue, in this way succeeding sometimes in sublimating his excessive zeal and saving himself from further illness." The paranoiac tendencies of social groups sublimate themselves in another fashion. Supermarkets have their security guards; cities have their police forces, states have their state troopers. And nations —which conduct their relations with one another according to rules that are even less binding and explicit than those governing individual behavior—have their armies.

In any large country, it is the solemn duty of the military establishment to be paranoid on behalf of the nation as a whole. Here in the United States, the Department of Defense employs hundreds of superb logicians—"contingency planners"—to imagine the most appalling, most devious, most diabolical horrors that could possibly be perpetrated by other nations against our own. And, so as to be able to deal with any and all such hypothetical nightmares, it employs and equips millions of soldiers, sailors, and airmen at a cost of scores of billions of dollars each year. Although there has not been a large-scale war in nearly thirty years, the Department of Defense maintains at all times what it calls the "capability" of fighting two-and-a-half wars the size of World War II.

The Department of Defense also maintains, at hair-trigger readiness, an arsenal of nuclear weapons which, if used, would destroy all the major cities of the Soviet Union and China and kill nearly all the people in them. The rationale behind this arsenal is that if we in the United States lacked these weapons, other countries that do possess them would use them against us. Or, to put the rationale more precisely, it is thought to be *more likely* that other countries would attack a disarmed United States than it is thought that the United States and other countries will destroy each other (through inadvertence, miscalculation, or a suicidal-homicidal paroxysm) under the existing "balance of terror" arrangement.

Some people believe that this logic is faulty, that the possibility of an unprovoked nuclear attack on a disarmed United States would be remote—more remote, at least, than the possibility of mutual destruction is now. Some people believe that to maintain an enormously expensive and dangerous "deterrent" against the possibility of such a monstrous, hypothetical crime is to enshrine paranoid delusion as the governing principle of international affairs. The people who believe these things are very few. Most of their fellow citizens regard them as hopelessly naive and unrealistic.

American society at large believes in the usefulness of maintaining an army, but it also recognizes that the military perception of reality is inevitably a distorted one. For this reason, among others, the military has been kept subservient to the civilian authority even in specifically military matters. The wisdom of this arrangement is apparent when one examines a a country like Chile, where the military forces have overthrown the civilian authorities and have begun the task of restructuring society in their own image. When a military government as serious as Chile's goes to work, the result is a terrifying bloody purge—a kind of political psychotic episode—followed by an attempt to construct a society as rationalized, as well organized, and as free of uncertainty as the most highly articulated paranoid delusion.

POSITIVE PARANOIA

Paranoia is customarily thought of as a distressing experience. It is terrible to be persecuted, even if the perceived mode of persecution happens to be imaginary. Delusions of grandeur, pleasant in themselves, can turn into nightmares when others disbelieve in them. And the shared paranoia of belief in malevolent conspiracies arises from a conviction that something is very wrong with the way things are.

In his book *The Natural Mind,* Andrew Weil describes an anomaly that turned up in psychological testing administered by the Haight-Ashbury Research Project of the Department of Psychiatry of Mount Zion Hospital, in San Francisco. Weil calls this anomaly "positive paranoia." On the Ror-

schach test, a number of subjects showed a marked "W-tendency." The Rorschach test is a series of ten increasingly fragmented inkblots. Someone who tries to account for every drib and drab of ink is said to have a strong "W-tendency," or "Whole-tendency," which correlates well to paranoia. Yet these particular subjects were unmistakably happy people. The tests said they were paranoid, and in a way they were— each of them thought the universe was a sort of conspiracy organized for his or her own benefit. Such beliefs may be no more realistic than the delusions of "normal" paranoia, but they undoubtedly make for a jollier type of paranoid.

Weil defines paranoia as "the tendency to see external events and things forming patterns that appear to be inimical." (Pattern-seeing, by itself, Weil views as neutral.) Positive paranoia would therefore be the tendency to see events and things forming patterns that appear to be beneficent. By these definitions, however, mere pessimism would qualify as (negative) paranoia, and any religion that posits a benevolent Providence would be a species of positive paranoia. So for that matter would any system of social analysis (such as Marxism or classical economics) that finds in the workings of history a progression toward a desirable goal.

Weil's definition seems to us to leave out one element of paranoia. Accordingly, we would amend it to say that paranoia is the tendency to see external events and things forming patterns that appear to be harmful (negative paranoia) or beneficent (positive paranoia), which patterns appear to center upon the person seeing. Now it is not pessimism *per se* that is paranoid, but rather belief in a hostile universe focusing its enmity on oneself. And it is not religion *per se* that is an instance of positive paranoia, but rather a particular kind of religious experience: in Weil's phrase, the perception of the universe as "a radially symmetrical pattern, its center coinciding with the center of focused consciousness." Such experiences are a goal of many kinds of religious and spiritual disciplines. The mandalas of Tibetan Buddhism are, in a sense, maps of precisely this variety of experience.

The concept of positive paranoia is a useful one because it sheds light on the connection between madness and transcendental experience and also because it illuminates what is so seductive about paranoia in general: the comfort of a universe ordered about oneself, a comfort that many people are willing to pay for in the currency of anguish. Paranoia is the very opposite of meaninglessness; indeed, paranoia drenches every detail of the world in meaning.

31.   IF YOU THINK YOU'RE WORKING TOO HARD

Interview with Dr. Saul M. Siegel
An Expert on "Workaholics"
Reprinted from *U. S. News & World Report*

Q: Dr. Siegel, how serious is the problem of overwork among Americans today?

A: The problem has never been precisely measured. But it exists, in different ways, among many Americans—and for some, it can be a pathological addiction.

Q: Is that the origin of the term "workaholics"?

A: Yes. But I think you have to distinguish carefully between people who just work hard, other people who work *too* hard, and still others who work too hard to the point where it's pathological.

People who simply work hard can be found in any walk of life and in varying kinds of personalities. If a person rises to the occasion when work demands are high but relaxes when demands are lowered, then he's working hard but not too hard.

People who work too hard in most cases are trying to meet some personal need or problem. They're using work to lessen the problem—by escaping an unhappy home situation, for instance.

But the person who works too hard pathologically will suffer various symptoms when he or she is deprived of work—much as a drug addict will suffer when deprived of narcotics.

Q: What are the symptoms?

A: They vary according to personality. Most commonly they are anxiety or depression, or a combination of both—and always they become evident when the person is away from work, because work for that person is a means of easing pain.

Q: Could you give an example?

A: Yes. A patient of mine was such a person, a rather successful. professional man who showed all the signs of workaholism—that is, at home or during leisure time he did not feel comfortable unless he was doing something "constructive," such as reading professional literature. He felt driven, vaguely guilty and anxious.

Yet the reason he came to me for treatment was none of these things. He came because he had had two unsuccessful marriages, had begun a third—and it was developing the same difficulties that appeared in the first two. That is, he was subject to vile temper tantrums, and his wife was beginning to complain that she was being treated not as a wife but as somebody "just around the house."

It turned out that these tantrums in which he berated his wife had these characteristics: First, they centered around her not being "up to par" as a housekeeper; second, they occurred when he was trying to *not* work. When he was buried in his work at home, he didn't notice whether the house was extremely well kept or not.

The pattern was similar in their sex life. It was very regular and, if disturbed in some way, again sent him into rather vile rages.

The same pattern had developed in his first two marriages. He was an intelligent person, able to see that something was wrong, but he had many different ways of concealing from himself a key to the problem—that he felt extremely uncomfortable when he was not working very hard. He saw work as a way of achieving status and prestige and material possessions, and a rather good thing.

By the time I saw him, he was in his early 40s and successful enough so that he no longer had to work as hard as before. Therefore, it was becoming more apparent that his kind of overwork was really an answer to other needs.

Like a number of other people who work too hard pathologically, he had a fantasy which only emerged after a year of treatment: an idea that someday he would relax completely, that some nirvanalike state would eventually envelop him. In this state, because he had been so hard-working and "good," he would be rewarded by sort of being cushioned on the breast of some original mother—entirely at ease and entirely taken care of without having to move a muscle.

This was an inner, driving conception which I'd seen in others, too—that eventually they would have earned complete rest. It appeared in his dreams and in his waking thoughts, but in so slight a way that it took some time to identify it.

One other thing about this particular person: Because of his working so hard, he allowed himself many bits of behavior which his morals otherwise would not have permitted him. He circumvented the law to some extent. Why? Because he had "earned" it. He was such a hard-working and ambitious person that, in a way, he corrupted his own conscience. These tantrums? Well, in a sense, he "earned" the right to blow off steam because he had been so good the other 23½ hours of the day.

Q: Were you able to help this man?

A: Yes. He was able to develop better working habits and was able to relax eventually. His marriage survived. But it took three years for this. We had defined the problem after one year. It took another two years for him to develop new patterns.

Q: How many Americans have a problem of overwork?

A: If you are including the ones who simply work too hard but have no symptoms when away from their work, the number might be comparable to the 5 to 10 million who are designated as alcoholics. Perhaps the number of those who overwork is more. Who knows?

My own impression is that the ones who overwork pathologically are a relatively small proportion, but again we have no figures. Many workaholics never get treatment. Some are successful enough to afford private psychiatry, and statistics on them would be hard to get.

Q: Is it a growing problem?

A: Look at it this way: There have always been people who have been addicted to work, as far as I can tell from the general body of literature. The problem among women may become more apparent as they move into the workaday world to stay—though I think there is some cultural difference in the way women and men are reared so that work as an addiction might not become quite as extreme or prevalent among women as among men.

Q: Are there women workaholics at the present time?

A: Sure. It's more apparent among men because in our society today men still are more work-conscious. But there are women who make their husbands' lives miserable by not being able to relax. She may be always emptying an ash tray the moment an ash appears on it. She may create "work" by constantly correcting her children.

Or, as another instance, I know of a woman who was an avid gardener. This may sound fine, because gardening belongs with God, mother and patriotism on the list of praiseworthy things. But this woman carried it to the point where it occupied practically every waking moment. Even during the winter she was working on gardening catalogues, and just wasn't available to her husband or children.

Q: Among men, where is the problem found most commonly? At the executive level?

A: It's most visible there, possibly, though that's not where it's necessarily the most prevalent. I think one finds it in the professions more than among the people who work at a 9-to-5 job where you have to stretch matters in order to overwork. That is, on the 9-to-5 job, you have to take work home, or stay down at the office long after everybody else has gone, in order to overwork.

On the other hand, a professional man—especially the ones who have a lot of clients and whose services are in demand—can slip easily into extending office hours or use the excuse of "keeping up" on professional reading, and still seem rather like a good person to himself and even those close to him.

It's a problem you can find at any level. An assembly-line worker may be putting in overtime and then, when he goes home, spend many hours working around the house—and this could be a pathological form of overwork if he feels driven to it by duty, conscience or simply a feeling of discomfort when he's not working.

Q: Do all workaholics fit into a similar pattern?

A: No. There are two main classes in the way they first present themselves:

In one category are those who feel a definite symptom which prompts them to seek treatment. When you look into the conditions behind the symptom, you learn that the symptom is strongest when they're not working. They feel most strongly the famous "Sunday neurosis" that many people experience.

In the other category, it's somebody else who is in pain—most often a mate, sometimes the children. In such cases, you could say he doesn't come in for treatment. He's brought in, even "pushed in" by somebody who is made uncomfortable by his work habits or behavior—for instance, the executive's wife, who complains that he's never home, or that he's always going on business trips or bringing his work home.

Q: Does this suggest that compulsive work becomes a problem generally among adults in their 30s or older?

A: Yes, except you're forgetting the college "grind"—or even the high-school "grind." We don't see them very often because they're getting good grades and usually doing so well they're not suffering. Once in a while, though, a young person will come in and state that he or she is uncomfortable because of not knowing how to relate to people in other than a work setting.

Q: Can signs of workaholism develop in early childhood?

A: Children don't have much opportunity for overwork, and even adolescents who are hard workers don't often become "grinds." Compulsive overwork becomes overwhelming as an adult pattern. In the 30s, inner feelings of guilt can begin to cause severe anxieties and depression away from work, as job demands grow or the competitive climb up the corporate ladder intensifies.

Q: How much is really known about the problem of workaholics?

A: Not nearly so much as we need to know. There is little in the professional literature about it. Furthermore, often the condition is not seen as a problem because whatever remnants of the Protestant work ethic are left in our society encourage us to look up to people who work hard. It is only when their symptoms force them to seek professional help that the real problem has a chance to emerge, which has enabled some like myself to study it.

Q: What drives people into workaholism?

A: Usually we find some conditions within the person's very early upbringing which have resulted in a tendency to overvalue work. Then, as pressures arise in adult life, he or she uses work excessively.

Q: Are you speaking of persons driven by ambition—to escape poverty, get ahead, prove themselves?

A: Most often, the merely ambitious people are not workaholics. They perhaps work too hard to ease a sense of low self-esteem caused by their background of poverty. But one can tell the difference between such persons and the workaholics: The merely ambitious workers do not suffer symptoms when deprived of work; the workaholics do suffer.

Q: Does this mean that those who overwork simply to reach a goal can relax and enjoy life once they've reached the goal?

A: Well, they may have some difficulty at first, and they may continue to be rather intense about such things as their golf. But that's largely a personality habit that hangs on, and for the most part they learn to enjoy life.

On the other hand, when the true workaholic is faced with having more leisure time, he will not be able to learn how to play. He'll work at golf. He doesn't really enjoy it, because he doesn't know how to relax.

Q: What is the treatment for such a person?

A: One has to get at the root causes of this addiction to work—get at the deeper, more dynamic reasons which are tied to a very strong sense of guilt.

Q: Guilt in what way?

A: If such a person isn't working, he feels a guilty anxiety and often some depression which, essentially, is guilt and anger turned inward on oneself.

Why? The causes in early upbringing are legion. Very often, however, we find that the parental home stressed work as a very important way for this person, as a boy, to earn approval—by doing chores or otherwise following the example set by the breadwinner in the family.

Now, this is not necessarily pathological in and of itself, but it can become so when a child grows up into an adult who uses work for neurotic rather than healthy reasons—to ease the pain of deep inner conflicts.

Q: What are those conflicts?

A: They differ. One rather common one is found in the person who has developed much too strong an attachment to a mother and whose father has been a successful, hard-working individual. He becomes like father, but in secretly competing with father and trying to overcome father's image, he is driven into working harder and harder in order to please an inner image of the mother, who admired father for being this way. Of course, he can never obtain mother as such—but he might find a mate who also may be impressed with his ambitions and hard work.

The trouble is that the mother has been a kind of forbidden figure in terms of getting close to her as father was able to be close. Therefore, the compulsive worker's conscience begins to bother him. This interferes with productive work, and he gets into an ever-increasing spiral of hard work in order to please a mother whom he is forbidden, emotionally and unconsciously, to get close to.

Q: Can workaholics also come out of families where the father, instead of being a hard worker, was lazy?

A: Yes, but I think you are more likely to find people from that background in the "just working too hard" class. Usually they don't suffer discomfort when they are not working. People are very complicated, you know. The fellow I mentioned to you as a case history illustrated that need to please the forbidden mother—what you might call the "Oedipal impulse."

But there are other people who have been truly deprived at a very early age of an ideal balance of firmness and love. They are left very, very hungry for affection, and vulnerable to depression from a variety of causes.

When, in addition, work becomes an important value in such upbringing, the child can grow up either into a bum—or a workaholic. That person is driven by what you might call just plain love hunger. It is not related specifically to pleasing a mother image but to seeking all the "goodies" that hard work will bring, but insatiably so.

That kind of person is always looking for more, more, more—especially material things. Even when he achieves them, he's not too comfortable with having gotten them. What threatens him when he isn't working is a kind of loss of a basic feeling of identity with the world, not identity with a particular woman or mother image.

There is one category we've just recently begun to look at. These are people who suffered some maldevelopment in their sense of self-esteem. In order to develop an adequate sense of self-esteem, you have to have reasonably good mothering and fathering in your very early years. Otherwise, you can have a sense of not being much of a self unless somebody who is like a parent —big and powerful—is around to give praise and approval.

This kind of workaholic is what we call "narcissistic." That is, he will often work extremely hard for somebody who is giving him a good deal of approval.

Q: What happens if he doesn't get that approval?

A: When that somebody fails to give him a compliment, he will continue to work hard but the work becomes more robotlike. It's not enjoyable in the least, because the person who has been giving him approval has withdrawn—or so he feels.

In fact, the approving boss usually hasn't withdrawn. He just hasn't happened to notice something the worker achieved. But there will be a disruption, not in the amount of his work but in what it does for him. Then he will enter not into a severe depression but into an apathetic existence until something happens to restore the balance— until, for instance, the boss says something nice to him.

"ANXIETY SURFACES ON SUNDAY"—

Q: Do personnel officers and other executives understand this person's problems? Do they ever notice the compulsive worker?

A: Indeed they do. They notice him with approval. I don't think they're inclined to disturb him because they don't see the symptoms—the anxiety and depression which surfaces on Sunday rather than at work. If anything, such people are seen by executives and personnel departments as very valuable workers—not brilliant, not innovative, but useful.

Q: Are they high achievers?

A: Not always. It may take such a person 16 hours to do what somebody else can do in 8. He often will "piddle around"—rearranging paper clips, so to speak. He gets his work done, usually, but it takes him much longer.

Even that professional man I mentioned earlier just monkeyed around much of the day, rearranging this or that, talking on the telephone and so forth. He didn't get into stride until after 5 o'clock, when other people would normally be going home. Then he would feel at the height of his powers and see his clients until as late as possible—even 10 o'clock—then stay at his office a while longer doing other things.

He rationalized this by saying he was a "night person," which wasn't really true. Once he was able to look at work differently, it turned out he could sleep just as well as anybody at normal hours.

Q: Is workaholism in some cases an escape from an unhappy situation at home?

A: I wouldn't classify that as workaholism. I would classify such persons as among those who overwork as a solution to some specific situation. For a person who has a nagging wife, staying down at the office becomes sort of a solution. When he relaxes he's not driven by symptoms as a truly pathological worker is.

Q: What about cases where overwork becomes a screen for extramarital affairs?

A: I think that would be more typical of the people who simply are working too hard, are bothered by a poor marriage, and have access to the office secretary.

You have to remember that the true workaholic is a person who can't play. You know, Sigmund Freud said that a balanced life includes the ability to love, to work and to play. The workaholic can't love or play —not very well, at least. He can have an affair, but he's likely to turn the affair into work.

Q: How would he do that?

A: A successful affair takes a good deal of arranging, and he is likely to become busy at that—so much so that after a while the mistress begins to notice it. I've even seen an instance where the mistress began to complain that the man was working too hard at the job, so that he wound up with both a nagging wife and a nagging mistress.

WHEN "SUICIDE RATES ARE HIGH"—

Q: Do workaholics account for many of the older people for whom retirement or the end of raising children become traumatic experiences?

A: That condition would be most extreme among workaholics. The person who's merely developed a personality trait of working too hard might have some trouble, but his or her whole world won't collapse. Such older people often learn how to do other things.

Even before official retirement, however, a workaholic may develop "involutional depression." A man in his 50s or early 60s who has not yet been officially retired loses his job or is left with very little to do or with very little authority, even though he's still at his existing pay level. That kind of person often will go into a rather severe depression, and suicide rates are fairly high in that age range.

Q: Should people who overwork head for the psychiatrist?

A: Not if they're merely working too hard. Perhaps they can do some stock-taking and self-analysis, or discuss the matter with a close friend or religious counselor.

The real workaholic probably needs professional psychiatric help in solving a problem of some magnitude which is "intrapsychic"—within himself and originating within his childhood.

Q: Isn't psychiatric treatment in such cases rather long and difficult?

A: The problem is like that involved in almost any addiction: The substance, whether it's narcotics or work, has its own reward, consisting of some pleasure or at least relief from physical or psychic pain.

You can't deprive people of the means they've used to relieve their pain without helping them restructure their whole inner balance. Otherwise, they'll go right back to compulsive overwork. It's not among the easier psychiatric problems to resolve.

Q: Is compulsive overwork necessarily a bad thing if it provides occasional moments of pleasure and results sometimes in constructive achievements?

A: That depends on the situation. You could say that there are worse things in life than simple overwork. In such cases, a person might find overwork the solution to a personal situation—while perhaps adding to society's wealth and his happiness.

But the person who works too hard pathologically isn't able to go through life in relative happiness. There are too many occasions when he can't work, or when his extreme work habits and symptoms disturb not only him, but other people. He can go along for years, but later on, when he's deprived of work, he can't maintain his balance.

———

32.   OBESITY AND BEHAVIOR

Robert J. Trotter

Chastity belts are no longer in vogue, but some insecure husbands may have come up with an equally cruel method of trying to keep their wives from fooling around. Psychologist Richard B. Stuart of the University of Michigan has found that husbands sometimes encourage their wives to overeat and gain weight in order to keep the wives unattractive and, supposedly, faithful.

Stuart, a behaviorist, worked for many months with married women who seemed to be unable to lose weight. Stuart sus

pected that the husbands might be at least partially responsible for the overeating so he asked the couples to make tape recordings of their dinner conversations. Stuart found, among other things, that the husbands were four times more likely to offer food to their wives than the other way around—even though the husbands knew that their wives were on a diet.

Stuart then interviewed 55 men who were married to women who were trying to lose weight. He found that many husbands seem to enjoy demonstrating what they consider to be their masculine power by coaxing or forcing their wives to become

Reprinted with permission from SCIENCE NEWS, the weekly news magazine of science, copyright 1974 by Science Service, Inc., vol. 106, p. 76.

fat. In addition, Stuart found out that some husbands used their wives' fatness to win arguments. A husband can usually get the final word in an argument by calling his wife a "fat slob." If the wives were successful in losing weight the husbands felt (perhaps unconsciously) that they would not win as many arguments.

In addition to using fatness to win arguments and to keep wives faithful, Stuart found that some husbands who were no longer sexually attracted to their wives used fatness as an excuse for lack of sexual desire. In most cases, the husbands lost their desire first and then started to fatten up their wives.

The chastity-belt theory of weight gain is one point that J. V. McConnell of the University of Michigan brings up when he talks about weight control. McConnell feels that the environment, including the people in the environment, is a major factor in obesity. McConnell and Chauncey Smith have recently opened a private behavioral clinic in Ann Arbor. They call it the Institute for Behavior Change, and obesity is one of the problems treated there.

Like almost every human behavior, says McConnell, eating behavior is multidetermined. People eat for many reasons, not just because they have been without food for a while. People eat because their blood-sugar level has fallen, because brain mechanisms urge them to eat, because their stomachs are contracting, their dinner time is approaching or because they have just seen or smelled or heard about something good to eat. And there are other reasons. People eat because their parents thought that fat babies are healthy babies and because food and eating have a variety of symbolic and social values. Obviously, says McConnell, any dieting program must take into account not just calories and exercise. Motives, mannerisms and environmental factors must be considered as well.

While most purely medical approaches to weight loss yield a success rate of about 10 percent McConnell and Smith claim that their behavioral clinic has a success rate of better than 70 percent. For people who do not have a severe weight problem, a clinic may not be necessary. The behaviorists suggest the following:

· Begin by recording everything you eat for a week or two. Take note of where you eat, the events (and thoughts) that occur just before and after you eat and record who is around you when you eat and what their response is to your food intake.

· Write down all the rewards and punishments that will come to you if you gain better control over your eating behavior.

· Break your eating habits by changing mealtimes to a very irregular schedule several weeks before you go on a diet.

· Any weight-control program will probably be more efficient if you increase your physical activity to burn off excess fat. If you are not particularly athletic, think about what forms of physical activity you like best and try to arrange to get more of this kind of exercise.

· Involve as many people as possible in your program. If someone close to you consciously or unconsciously wants you to remain fat, try to think of substitute rewards that will encourage that person to help you lose weight. You may even have to offer people money or services for every pound they help you lose.

· When you start the program make a chart or graph on which you record your daily weight and each aspect of your daily routine, including the amount of food eaten and exercise taken. Post the graph in a prominent place so that everyone can see your progress and comment on it. Arrange to have someone give you regular rewards (money, privileges, a verbal pat on the back) each time you meet your daily goal. Such a graph, says McConnell, may be the most important part of any weight-control program because it provides immediate feedback.

• Don't expect too much too soon or set unrealistic goals. The average weight loss is about a pound a week. Long-term weight loss is difficult for most people to achieve because so many factors are involved. But success is encouraging, so make sure that the first goals—the first few days' changes in behavior—are easy to achieve.

• Not everyone, of course, can lose weight on their own by the behavioral method. Some people may have to seek the help of a psychologist and a physician to make sure that symbolic as well as physical needs are accounted for in the weight-loss program. And, warns McConnell, about five percent of all weight problems (underweight as well as overweight) in the United States are the result of a physically malfunctioning body. Therefore, any weight-control program should begin with a physical checkup.

33. WHAT YOU SHOULD KNOW ABOUT MENTAL DEPRESSION

Interview with Dr. Bertram S. Brown
Director, National Institute of Mental Health
Reprinted from *U. S. News & World Report*

Q: Dr. Brown, about how many Americans suffer from depression?

A: Perhaps 4 to 8 million people during a year's time. I'm referring to cases of depression serious enough to keep people home from work or send them to a doctor. Some studies suggest that as many as 15 per cent of the adult population may suffer significant depressive symptoms.

Q: Is it a trouble that is growing worse?

A: In Los Angeles, where we followed the situation for the last 20 years, there seems to be an increase in depression among young people aged 15 to 35. The incidence of depression apparently is stable for middle-aged people. With older folks, we seem to be identifying it as depression more often, instead of giving other names to the trouble.

For example, an older person of 65 or 70 may start to fall off in his or her functioning —becomes forgetful, doesn't have as much energy—and is taken to a hospital, where often the trouble is eventually described as senility or arteriosclerosis or something similar. In England, it has been found that if a good clinician looks at the symptoms, over half of those cases turn out to be depression.

Q: Is depression causing the higher rates of suicide in America today?

A: To put it in perspective: Of those who have clearly committed suicide, when we take a look at what's happened in their last few months, we find that over 80 per cent were clearly depressed. No ifs, ands or buts about it—they had a clinical depression.

So, yes, the most common thing you see before suicide is depression.

Q: Doctor, exactly how do you describe depression?

A: From the layman's point of view, sometimes people say they're depressed when they're just feeling a bit moody, a little "down"—and that's just as common as can be. In that sense, maybe 30 per cent of all Americans suffer from depression at times.

But clinically, we mean something more serious when we speak of depression. In the intermediate stage, victims feel a lack of energy and interest in life that hangs on for a few days or a few weeks and affects their life functions.

Q: In what way?

A: I mean that even the everyday, routine things just are hard for a depressed person to perform—things like getting one's own breakfast or getting the day's work done.

The third level, where no one can doubt that you're dealing with depression, is when somebody literally sits in a corner—almost paralyzed—looking into space.

Let's take, for example, a depressed woman. If she is willing to talk to you—which she often isn't—ask her what she's thinking, and she'll tell you that life isn't worth living and that she's a terrible person. She's feeling guilty about things that may have happened recently or in the past. She's feeling gloomy about herself and the world to the point that it occupies her whole mind and soul.

Q: Does it become mental illness at that point?

A: Yes. I don't think one can say it's then anything but a mental illness.

One of the ways of looking at it that I find illuminating is to say it involves great feelings of helplessness, hopelessness and haplessness.

Q: Do physical symptoms generally come with depression?

A: With severe depression, yes, there are physical symptoms and they're fairly well known.

For example, it's rare to have a serious depression without loss of appetite. Sometimes this sneaks up on the victim, so the doctor always asks about weight changes.

Another symptom is a change in sleep patterns. The most common one is when the person wakes up early in the morning for no apparent good reason. Or less often but just as significant, he or she has trouble falling asleep.

A third symptom is that depressed people feel aches and pains and complain about them more. They have chest pains, their head aches, their muscles hurt and their bones creak.

Q: Are these symptoms easy to discern?

A: It's usually easier to pick it up in a family member or a friend than it is in yourself—though it's worth thinking about if you're having unexplained aches and pains.

Q: Is depression often confused with other forms of mental illness, such as schizophrenia?

A: In the most severe cases, depression can become temporarily confused with schizophrenia, since it shows up with changes in thinking or illogicality or paranoid thoughts. We call this psychotic depression, and it is the worst kind, but a severe "black mood" change points to the diagnosis of depression rather than schizophrenia. Nevertheless, a diagnosis of depressive illness may be missed for a variety of reasons. Recent research indicates that in one of our large cities, 20 per cent of the patients admitted to mental hospitals diagnosed as schizophrenic may have been suffering from a depressive psychosis.

Q: Is there a genetic factor in depression?

A: Yes. It varies from very heavy, if not predominant, to very minimal, depending on the type of depression.

Q: Does depression develop slowly?

A: It can develop rather quickly—within a day—or it can build up over months.

One form of depression, as you know, is linked with the opposite—mania. This is the manic-depressive form of the disease. In such cases, people have an episode of hyperactivity and grandiosity that can go on for a month or two or three. Then they're well for a time. Then, a few months later, they'll have a depressive illness.

Q: How many types of depression are there?

A: We talk about a number of alternative types. Briefly:

Reactive depression is more clearly associated with outside events—unlike endogenous depression, which is more closely associated with biological factors.

We talk about neurotic depression—mild, without thinking that you're rotten inside.

Psychotic depression is so deep that you become afraid that not only isn't food worth eating but you may even have a paranoid thought that it might kill you because you really want to kill yourself.

The newest way of looking at it is the unipolar-bipolar axis. The bipolar is the form more commonly known as manic-depressive, in which some people have a depressive illness whose symptoms show up at one time in excitement, at another in depression. The unipolar variety shows up as depression without the alternating excitement.

Q: Is a depressed patient dangerous to society?

A: Well, he creates problems in two ways through sheer cost. We recently tried to think through how many people in the course of a year will have a depressive episode serious enough to warrant attention. Our estimates are that somewhere between 4 million and 7 or 8 million Americans will have a depressive episode in a given year.

In regard to all forms of mental and emotional illness, we keep careful statistics on how many people come to psychiatric and mental-health clinics in a year's time. It may strike you as interesting that approximately 4 million people, or 2 per cent of our population, seek treatment each year: They see a doctor or undergo psychiatric hospitalization. Of that 4 million, about 600,000 or 700,000 are depressives.

Our latest statistics show that direct cost for care and treatment of mental illness—hospital cost, outpatient cost, doctor bills, drug bills—runs approximately 4 to 5 billion dollars a year. That's about 5 per cent of the annual U.S. medical bill. And our estimate is that perhaps a quarter of that 4 or 5 billion dollars is related to depression. That's at least a billion dollars a year.

I personally think from other studies that have been made there's a hidden billion-dollar cost in cases of depression which show up in a general physician's office and don't get labeled as such.

Q: Do many who suffer from depression forgo treatment?

A: Yes. But even without treatment, most—though not all—depressions will eventually get better. Time is a great healer. It works quite well in depression—but not nearly as well as getting treatment, of course, and it takes much longer.

There's another cost of depression, in terms of self-destruction. Suicide is the eleventh leading cause of death, and 80 per cent of suicides have had a recent depression. Among teen-agers, suicide is the third leading cause of death.

The one social cost we don't incur from depression is crime. If you're feeling withdrawn, hopeless and helpless you're not likely to do anything dangerous to others.

Q: What causes depression?

A: We are getting close to the actual biological mechanisms that are involved—down to what happens between nerve connections in the transmission of messages.

The transmission from nerve "A" to nerve "B" is a complicated chemical-electrical phenomenon involving enzymes which help the chemicals to move around and change their nature rapidly. We now know which enzymes might be deficient and which chemicals might pile up at the place between the nerve "A" and nerve "B" where the connection takes place and the message is transmitted.

This has led to our major, exciting pharmacological breakthroughs. I know you have to be careful in saying "breakthroughs," but just 20 years ago, if any of us had a serious depression, the chances were we would be in a mental hospital for nine months to a year or so. Now, if the same thing happens, the chances of being back at work or functioning or at home in a month or two are excellent—perhaps 80 or 90 per cent.

Q: What are some of the big breakthroughs?

A: One is a very effective, and yet somewhat frightening, treatment, and I wish that we understood it better. That's electroshock. We find that electroshock treatment in certain types of depression brings the patient out of the depression.

Another very successful approach to treatment is psychoactive drugs. There are antidepressant compounds that have direct activity on the nervous system. Another drug, offering the prospect of a tremendous breakthrough in terms of *preventing* depression, is lithium chloride—a simple salt which seems to be especially helpful in warding off the manic-depressive type of depression if it is taken regularly, just as insulin shots help ward off the effects of diabetes.

Q: How widely is this being used?

A: Our estimate is that approximately 30,000 people in the United States are on lithium chloride. Scientists are not sure, but they suspect that several hundred thousand would benefit from being on the drug under supervision.

Q: The diabetic has to keep taking insulin the rest of his life. Is that true of the person taking lithium chloride?

A: Usually. For the particular type of manic-depressive disease where it seems to be working as a preventive, taking the drug becomes a lifetime endeavor.

Q: What about nonprescription drugs, such as pep pills and that sort of thing?

A: I don't think that self-prescription is helpful, and perhaps is much more dangerous than taking nothing at all. We are using several energizers, such as Ritalin, in the treatment, but usually in conjunction with some over-all strategy.

Of course, amphetamine has proven to be quite dangerous, in terms of its addictive potential and the letdown afterwards.

Q: You mentioned two basic approaches to treatment—

A: A third category of treatment for depression which is being tried is the psychological approach. In this, the idea is not to dig into the patient's past—what happened in his childhood—but to do a frontal attack on that feeling of helplessness to show that the person isn't helpless.

For example, the patient will say how weak he or she feels, and you ask, "How much do you think you can lift?" Well, perhaps about 5 pounds is the answer. So you bring in a 7-pound weight and let the patient lift it, and go on from there.

Or the depressed person will say it's too far to walk down the corridor. With a little bit of encouraging, you take him or her to the corridor and back—give them success experiences to counteract the feelings of helplessness.

WHEN SHOCK THERAPY IS USEFUL

Q: How long do effects of electroshock treatment last?

A: For most of the people who have received electroshock, it's the first and only time they need it.

Q: Does electroshock therapy take a long time?

A: We've made progress. The usual course of treatment might be somewhere between four and 10 treatments over a period of approximately two to three weeks at most. In the old days, those electroshock treatments would produce muscular and convulsive movements, but now we have chemicals to use in conjunction with the therapy, and find those responses aren't essential at all.

Q: How long does each individual shock last?

A: Less than a second. And within an hour or two, the patient can walk home with a friend or relative. The treatment is most often given in a hospital, because if a person's sick enough to have electroshock treatment, he's sick enough to be in the hospital.

While electroshock treatment still gives rise to some anxiety and fears, it can free patients of depression in one or two weeks. It's a rapid form of treatment which many doctors turn to, especially for suicidal patients.

Drugs work as effectively in many cases and take two to three weeks. However, electroshock is not used in mild depressions which are clearly related to external events and which are not very deep and present no suicidal danger.

Q: Are there any side effects to electroshock?

A: Either none or a minimal memory loss for a few days.

Q: Could electroshock be given to a heart patient?

A: Yes, and in some emergency situations it has. For example, if you have a heart patient who is clearly suicidal, you might use electroshock. But in most situations drugs would be used.

Q: Is there anything a depressive individual can do for himself short of seeking psychiatric advice?

A: One thing depressed individuals can do is to build into themselves, even before the depression begins, the idea that they are not helpless or hopeless.

Of course, once a depression starts to become stronger and sustained, they will help themselves best by seeking professional help.

HOW THE FAMILY DOCTOR CAN HELP

Q: Are general practitioners capable of dealing effectively with depression?

A: Yes. This is part of a promising breakthrough in treating depression. Most general practitioners and internists can treat mild and moderate depression quite successfully. In fact, physicians often must deal, in serious and disabling illness and injury, with the bereavement reactions of broken and upset families.

With severe depression or prolonged bereavement, consulting a psychiatrist would be very useful.

Q: How can friends and relatives help?

A: Well, they can avoid the error of screaming at the person to "snap out of it" when people just can't very well "snap out of it." If they could, they wouldn't be staying depressed. Also, we can avoid recriminatory statements that can aggravate the person's guilt feelings and knock down one's self-image.

If your colleague at work is feeling kind of blue and depressed, for example, and thinks his work isn't worth anything, you can make known your approval when he turns out a good piece of work. Then, as he internalizes your approval, he sees that maybe he isn't as helpless and hopeless as he thought.

Most people, by the way, give positive clues and warnings to their friends or relatives before committing suicide. These clues should be taken very seriously, and the person should be advised to see a psychiatrist.

Q: Does diet play a role in depression?

A: I'm sure that diet plays an important role, but we do not yet know just what this role is. This is one of the areas of research we're still exploring. We have all sorts of leads and theories, but no real findings at the present time.

Q: Is there a difference in depression among women and men?

A: Yes. Our statistics show that of patients coming under care in psychiatric facilities and services, female patients outnumber males 2 to 1. This is in all age categories.

As you look at external events that are difficult enough to be a major precipitant of depression, some appear quite predictable. One is the woman who has not worked and, when the last child leaves home, has not yet made any adaptation. I think this is a first cousin to the problems of the man who's worked successfully and at age 60 has not made any plans as to what he's going to do next, after retirement.

This suggests an intriguing problem for the future: As we see a shift in life patterns, with changing roles for men and women and more "singles," we will have to keep a very sharp eye on changes in depression and psychiatric syndromes accompanying these changes.

Q: Do you find more depression among married or single people? Or does marital status make any difference?

A: Right now, we're pursuing careful statistical studies as to family structure and mental illness. I'll give you some statistics that are just mind-boggling—at least to me:

Of American males aged 45 to 64—unmarried, single, widowed, divorced or separated—6 per cent are in institutions such as mental hospitals, old-age homes, retirement centers and veterans' hospitals. This increases to 13 per cent for males 75 and over. Corresponding figures for females are 2 per cent and 13 per cent. Psychiatric hospitalization and outpatient treatment among "singles"—whether they're divorced, wid-

owed or never married—is more than double the rate for married persons.

Q: How serious can depression become in children?

A: Young children can get depressed, though it shows up in different ways than among adults. Sometimes their symptoms are restlessness and lack of attention at school, or sleep troubles and nightmares.

Currently, we're pulling together our knowledge about depression in children and looking carefully at which approach might be useful for children. Depression in children is an uncharted area with a great deal of controversy, but one that, I think, holds much promise for solving a lot of mysterious troublesome behavior in our youngsters.

Q: Does any particular kind of attitude on the part of parents seem to predispose children to depression?

A: There is no one, simple answer. I think that in depression among children we have to carefully avoid blaming the parents for what may not be their fault in any way, but has more to do with biology or genetics.

Q: Are we living in times that could inspire a growth in depression?

A: I think the current times are having an effect on people's psychological and mental health. One of the characteristics is an increasing sense of confusion and helplessness. "Things" seem to be getting out of hand. The future is less certain. What one does in his personal life seems not to be important in how things will come out in the end.

I would say cynicism and distrust are the major phenomena that I'm seeing. You can't carry out good psychotherapy or psychiatric or even medical help unless there's trust between doctor and patient. And the lack of trust in the Government is a terribly troubling and a real phenomenon.

Q: Are working situations today really

any more stressful and competitive than they have been in the past?

A: I think in most ways work at present is more satisfying and less difficult than in most prior ages: The hours are shorter, the pay is better, and there is less monotony.

On the other hand, the expectations with which we come to work have shifted perhaps more dramatically than the nature of work itself. Eight hours on a boring, repetitive assembly line—when it's seen as a clear way just to make a living for your family—would be tolerable. But not so if the expectation is that the workday will also be rewarding from an interpersonal point of view and offer some mastery and challenge. If one has a chronically unrewarding situation where the expectation is otherwise this can be an external stress that could precipitate depression.

Q: Does our modern era—through television and other wonders—tend more than other eras to create unrealistic expectations among people?

A: I think there's little doubt as to the answer to that question. The whole world of communications not only builds up expectations but markets them—second cars, second homes, boats, foreign travel, and on and on.

And something that I've learned in my world travel is that if there's some resignation and acceptance of one's lot, there is not the frustration, anxiety, tension and, occasionally, depression that we get with unmet expectations.

Q: Does weather bear on depression rates?

A: There are differences in suicide rates across the world in different cities. As to whether or not the weather itself is a predominant factor, we're not sure. Studies in Switzerland show a significant increase in suicide and crime in periods when the foehn —a warm, dry wind which blows in the mountain valleys—is a prevailing influence on the climate.

Scientists have investigated the question of the influence of weather and climate on our mental processes. The question is a very old one, but most of the studies have been inconclusive.

More often I'm asked about what happens to depression and suicide rates over Christmas.

Q: What does happen?

A: We have found, surprisingly, that there are fewer suicides right around Christmastime rather than more. In the aftermath—early spring—suicide rates show an increase.

Q: Is a little depression good for you?

A: I think this may be so. Recently, one colleague—a very distinguished leader— was offered and then went through three weeks of agony declining a very high Government job. Thereupon, he went into what I would call a moderate depression. In the course of it, he learned that he was able to think through some basic issues in a way that he couldn't have done during his busy life. He wasn't so sick as to be in danger of suicide, but he wasn't so well that he could carry out his daily duties, either. But he was able to think things through.

FEELING BLUE? BREAK YOUR ROUTINE

Q: For mild depression, does it help to go to a ball game or take a week off and go to the beach?

A: I think the wisdom through the ages is that a break in routine or something that's pleasurable is perhaps the best medicine in the recovery from mild depression.

I've known literally dozens of my friends who were feeling a bit blue, and after a good few weeks of vacation came back with their spirits renewed. But this does not work for severe depression.

Some suggest going out and getting drunk. I don't think that's a very good treatment for depression. Some people do find that using alcohol to handle their moods does give an alleviation of tension anxiety. But then, the secondary dependency on alcohol turns out to be worse than the disease itself.

Q: How effectively can people recover from severe depression, especially if they have a tough or high position of responsibility?

A: It's a very delicate issue, but one example of successful recovery in a demanding post is that of Senator Thomas Eagleton [of Missouri], whose depressive illness was in the headlines when he was the Democratic nominee for Vice President in 1972.

I think that in terms of the public's understanding and acceptance of depressive illness and its treatment, this whole episode and the personal example of the Senator's recovery was a remarkable step forward. We would hope that through this and other examples more people now realize that you can have a severe depression, be hospitalized several times, and come back to full and effective functioning and enjoyment of life.

---

34.   IT'S NOT ALL IN YOUR HEAD

Seymour S. Kety

Mental illness, although not a major cause of death, like cancer or heart disease, nevertheless ranks as one of our most serious national health problems. More than 10 million Americans will experience one or more episodes of serious mental illness, which may last for only a few weeks or even for many years, before they reach old age. The care of mentally ill, inadequate as it often is, costs this nation considerably more than $5 billion annually—and less easily calculated is the larger human cost to the victims and their families.

For two mental illnesses that at one time rivaled schizophrenia in severity and extent —general paresis and pellagrous psychosis —biomedical research discovered the causes: an invasion of the brain by the spirochete of syphilis for one, and a dietary deficiency of nicotinic acid for the other. This made possible their effect treatment and prevention through purely physiological reasons. As a result, these disorders have become practically extinct in America; where they do occur, the cause is a failure to utilize available knowledge.

But schizophrenia and the so-called affective disorders (depression and manic-depressive psychosis) have remained with us, and their seriousness is matched by our ignorance regarding them. We do not yet know their causes or understand the processes through which they develop. Their treatment, which has improved dramatically through the use of recently discovered drugs, still leaves much to be desired. However, over the past two decades substantial

Reprinted from *Saturday Review* (February 21, 1976) by permission of publisher, pp. 28–32.

indications have revealed that these serious mental illnesses have biochemical underpinnings, and powerful new techniques and concepts have been developed which make the search for these remedies more promising than it has ever been before.

The idea of a biochemical cause of insanity is not new. The Hippocratic physicians of ancient Greece argued against the prevailing attribution of insanity to supernatural causes:

... and by the same organ [the brain] we become mad and delirious and fears and terrors assail us, some by night and some by day, and dreams and untimely wanderings and cares that are not suitable and ignorance of present circumstances, desuetude and unskillfulness. All these things we endure from the brain, when it is not healthy but is more hot, more cold, more moist, or more dry than natural, or when it suffers any other preternatural and unusual affliction.

The modern biochemical approach to mental illness can be traced to J. W. L. Thudichum, a physican and biochemist, who, nearly 100 years ago, hypothesized that many forms of insanity were the result of toxic substances fermented within the body, just as the psychosis of alcohol was the result of a toxic substance fermented outside. Armed with the hypothesis, he received a 10-year research grant from the Privy Council in England. He did not go to the mental hospitals and examine the urine and blood of patients; instead he went to the abattoir to obtain cattle brain and spent the 10 years studying the brain's normal composition. It is fortunate for us that he did that, because he laid the foundations of modern neurochemistry from which will come whatever we learn about the abnormal chemistry of the brain. If Thudichum had been less wise and courageous, or if Parliament had insisted on "relevant" research, what contribution could he have

made with the little knowledge that existed at that time? What chances would he have had to identify abnormalities in substances unknown in his day? He would have frittered away funds and wasted 10 years in a premature and futile search.

Thudichum, and the science of neurochemistry he founded, were concerned at first with composition and chemical structure. In the normal brain a large number of substances were identified that were later found to be abnormal in a substantial variety of neurological disorders. Fifty years ago biochemistry began to trace the complex metabolism by which foodstuffs and oxygen are utilized and energy is made available. This understanding was eventually applied to the brain, where its dependence on glucose was discovered, and the oxygen utilized in various mental functions could be measured. Application of this knowledge to the states of sleep, coma, anesthesia, and senile dementia soon followed. But the major psychiatric problems (schizophrenia and manic depressive psychosis and depression) remained unaffected. No known changes in chemical composition or structure account for these disorders; the brain uses just as much oxygen thinking irrationally as rationally.

Over the past 25 years there has been dramatic growth in the neurosciences and unprecedented knowledge of the brain and behavior. One major new concept is that of the synapse, the highly specialized junction between one nerve cell and another through which information is carried. Electron microscopy, biophysics, biochemistry, and pharmacology have taught us a great deal about the synapse's structure and function. Most novel and far-reaching is the knowledge that chemical mediators called "neurotransmitters" carry the message over a small gap (the synaptic cleft) that lies between the termination of one nerve cell and the beginning of another. Because sensory processing, perception, the storage and retrieval of information, thought, feeling, and behavior all depend upon the operation of these chemical switches, this discovery elucidated the focal points at which chemical processes and substances, metabolic products, hormones, and drugs could modify these crucial aspects of mental state and behavior. If there are biochemical disturbances in mental illness, they would be expected to operate there, and drugs that ameliorate these illnesses should exert their influences at synapses.

There are hundreds of billions of synapses in the human brain, and they are organized in a marvelously systematic way along pathways that neuroanatomists are mapping. A growing list of neurotransmitters is being identified, and these are found to be associated with particular pathways, functions, and behavioral states. The class of substances known as *catecholamines* includes *adrenalin, noradrenaline,* and *dopamine,* first identified in the adrenal gland or in the peripheral sympathetic nervous system. Catecholamines are now known to be important neurotransmitters in the brain, where they appear to be involved in emotional states such as arousal, rage, fear, pleasure, motivation, and exhilaration. *Serotonin,* first discovered in the intestine, has also been identified as a neurotransmitter in the brain, where it seems to play a crucial role in sleep and wakefulness, in certain types of sexual activity, and perhaps in modulating, damping, and balancing a wide range of synaptic activity that we are only beginning to understand. *Acetylcholine,* which is known to be the transmitter between nerve and muscle and is therefore crucial to every voluntary movement, has also been found to be involved in a very large fraction of brain synapses. There are other neurotransmitters, such as *gamma amino butyric acid,* certain amino acids and polypeptides discovered more recently, and

undoubtedly many that are as yet undiscovered. The importance of the concept of chemical neurotransmission and its implications for medicine and psychiatry were recognized by the Nobel Committee, which made the award in 1970 to Julius Axelrod, Bernard Katz, and Ulf von Euler for their contributions to the understanding of acetylcholine and catecholamines as neurotransmitters.

Fundamental knowledge of the synapse and chemical neurotransmission has had important implications for the understanding and treatment of nervous and mental disease and represents an area of unusual promise for the future. At the same time that noradrenaline and serotonin were being identified in the brain, several drugs were discovered quite independently to exert important effects on mood. The first of these was *reserpine,* which has been found to be useful in the treatment of hypertension. In a small percentage of patients, however, reserpine produced a state of depression very much like that known to psychiatrists. At the same time scientists at the National Institute of Health made the important discovery that reserpine causes the disappearance of serotonin and noradrenaline from the brain.

A few years later a new drug, *iproniazid,* was introduced and found to be highly effective in the treatment of tuberculosis. It caused excitement in some patients, however, and was supplanted by other drugs equally effective and without such side effects. What was a deleterious property of iproniazid in the treatment of tuberculosis, however, became the basis for an effective treatment of depression. Iproniazid was found to block the enzyme, *monoamine oxidase* (MAO), that is responsible for inactivating biogenic amines, including serotonin, and catecholamines, in the brain. Thus, iproniazid exerted an effect on these transmitters opposite to that of reserpine, permitting them to rise in concentration and activity and exerting an antidepressant effect. A number of other *MAO inhibitors* were developed that were also effective in treating depression. Even more effective were a group of drugs, the *tricyclic antidepressants* such as *imipramine* and *amitryptaline,* that enhanced the synaptic actions of noradrenaline and serotonin by yet another mechanism.

Thus, depletion of these two neurotransmitters is associated in animals and man with depression, while the drugs that restore their levels and increase their synaptic activity are effective antidepressants.

It is reasonable inference from the foregoing observations that clinical depression may be the result of an inadequacy of one or both of these neurotransmitters at particular synapses in the brain—and similarly that mania, the obverse of depression, may represent an *overactivity* of such a transmitter. Testing such hypotheses has engaged a number of research groups. There have been some interesting findings, e.g., that in certain types of depression and in mania there is in the urine a decrease or an increase respectively of a particular product of noradrenaline metabolism which appears to be derived largely from the brain. Others have found in cerebrospinal fluid evidence of a decrease in serotonin metabolism in the brain in patients suffering from manic or depressive psychosis. A very effective agent in the treatment of mania and the prophylaxis of manic-depressive illness is *lithium,* a relatively simple substance closely related to sodium, which plays a crucial role in synaptic function. The mechanism by which lithium produced its therapeutic and prophylactic action is as yet unknown.

Similarly, over the past two decades, newly acquired knowledge has begun to unravel the enigma called schizophrenia. This disorder or group of disorders (we may be dealing with a number of different diseases with a common symptomatology) is characterized by disturbances not only in mood but also in thinking and the normal association between them. In the typical severe schizophrenic one sees bizarre behavior, disorders of thinking and speech, impoverishment of feeling, lack of motivation, anhedonia (an inability to experience pleasure), withdrawal from interaction with others, hallucinations, delusions, and educational, occupational, social, and marital disabilities. Such symptoms appear insidiously early in life and become critical in early adulthood. There are such drugs as *mescaline, LSD,* or *dimethyltryptamine,* which are capable of inducing hallucinations and some of the other symptoms of schizophrenia, and have, for some, suggested hypotheses about the nature of schizophrenia itself.

What most hallucinogenic drugs have in common is one or more methyl (CH_3) groups. It is, therefore, especially interesting that an enzyme has been found in body and brain tissues of animals and man which is capable of adding a methyl group to *normal* metabolites, thus converting them to hallucinogenic substances. To date, however, no such hallucinogenic substance has been clearly identified in schizophrenics. In 1950 a new drug was found to be more effective than any previous treatment in the relief of some of the major symptoms of schizophrenia. That discovery came about in an interesting and unexpected manner. Pharmacologists had been developing and studying drugs that blocked the actions of *histamine,* a substance manufactured within the body, which appears to play an important role in many forms of allergy. The *antihistaminic* drugs thus elaborated have been found to be very beneficial in the treatment of asthma and other types of allergic disorders. One of these drugs was found to combine both antihistaminic and sympatholytic properties—i.e., it also blocked the actions of the sympathetic nervous system.

Henri-Marie Laborit, a French anesthesiologist, was looking for a drug which had such properties as a means of preventing surgical shock, on the hypothesis that both histamine and sympathetic overactivity contributed to its development in surgical operations. He used this drug in preoperative medication, and, because he was a careful observer, he noted in his patients the occurrence of an unwanted and unsearched-for sedation, a kind of sedation different from that which occurs with the barbiturates—a "euphoric quietude." He felt that such a property might be helpful in treating disturbed patients and suggested that to psychiatrists. That drug was the immediate forerunner of *chlorpromazine,* which revolutionized the treatment of schizophrenia. Chlorpromazine was tried in Paris and very quickly in Europe, England, Canada, and the United States. It became the first of a series of "major tranquilizers" or "anti-psychotic" drugs, so named because of their rather specific ability to terminate or ameliorate the psychotic manifestations of schizophrenia, especially the bizarre behavior and thinking, the delusions and hallucinations.

But chlorpromazine had an important side effect—its tendency to produce in some patients the facial and motor disturbances that are seen in Parkinson's disease. Modifications of chlorpromazine were developed in an effort to preserve the therapeutic benefit while avoiding this side effect, but—with very few exceptions—whenever an effective agent appeared it was also found to have the side effect. In addition to the *phenothiazines,* of which chlorpormazine was a member, an entirely new chemical class of drugs appeared, the *butyrophenones,* which were also effective in the treatment of schizophrenia but similarly suffered from the tendency to produce

symptoms of Parkinsonism. An explanation of this phenomenon, however, had to await a better understanding of Parkinson's disease. This was not long in coming.

In 1960 a new technique was developed in Sweden for demonstrating certain neurotransmitters within the brain by means of their characteristic fluorescence under appropriate conditions. That technique was quickly applied by neuroanatomists and used within the brain to trace circuits that implied these transmitters. A pathway that used dopamine as its transmitter was discovered in a region of the brain where lesions were known to exist in cases of Parkinsonism. This led to the hypothesis, and the ultimate demonstration, that in Parkinson's disease there was a partial destruction of the dopamine-containing nerve cells. Efforts to replenish the lost dopamine by administration of its precursor *L-dopa* led to marked improvement in the patients and represents one of the major contributions of fundamental neurological research to mental illness in recent times.

It was first suggested by Arvid Carlsson that anti-psychotic drugs must act by blocking the effects of dopamine in the brain, which would explain their tendency to produce the symptoms of Parkinson's disease. On the basis of his studies and more recent observations on dopamine synapses in the brain and components of such synapses studied *in vitro,* it is now clear that Carlsson's insight was correct and that a major action of both the phenothiazine and the butyrophenone drugs is to diminish the actions of dopamine within the brain.

There is another drug which effects dopamine synapses — *amphetamine* — except that amphetamine exaggerates the effects of dopamine rather than diminishing them. Amphetamine is not at all an anti-psychotic drug—quite the opposite. In animals it produced some of the behavior seen in schizophrenia—i.e., stereotyped movements of various kinds and aimless pacing. When it is abused by human subjects, it produces a psychosis often indistinguishable from schizophrenia. The same drugs that are effective in the treatment of schizophrenia are also practically specific in terminating amphetamine psychosis, and amphetamine is known to exacerbate the psychosis of schizophrenic individuals. Thus drugs that enhance dopamine activity in the brain tend to produce or aggravate schizophrenic symptoms, and those that diminish excessive dopamine activity are capable of relieving these symptoms. That does not mean that the biochemical principles underlying schizophrenia have been found in an abnormal overactivity of dopamine synapses. A therapeutic benefit may sometimes be obtained by an action that only indirectly affects the pathological process. It is nevertheless clear that continued and expanded research on the neurotransmitters in the brain cannot help contributing to our understanding of these illnesses. And with understanding will come more specific treatment and prevention.

What evidence do we have that a continued search for the biochemical factors of mental illness will be rewarding, or that such biochemical disturbances even exist? If there were clear evidence that these illnesses had important genetic bases, that would justify the search for their biochemical principles because genetic factors must express themselves through biochemical processes.

Until quite recently, the evidence for the operation of genetic factors in these major mental illnesses was compelling but not conclusive, because non-genetic factors could account for the observation. Psychiatrists have known for a long time, and every epidemiological study has confirmed their observation, that the major mental illnesses run in families. There is an estimated 10 percent risk for the occurrence of schizo-

phrenia in the parents, siblings, and offspring of schizophrenic individuals, and manic-depressive illness shows a comparable familial tendency. Although this figure is compatible with genetic transmission of these illnesses, it is by no means proof of a fixed pattern. Wealth and poverty run in families but are not genetically transmitted, and the familial occurrence of pellagra was used to support an erroneous genetic concept of what we now know to be a nutritional disorder. A family shares not only its genetic endowments but also its environmental influences, and either or both of these factors may be responsible for familial disorders. Somewhat better evidence came from twin studies; a number of these studies have shown that for both schizophrenia and the affective disorders, a high risk (on the order of 50 percent or more) exists that the illness will appear in the identical twin of an affected person, while the risk for a fraternal twin is of the same order as that for a sibling. Because identical twins are derived from a single fertilized egg and are therefore the same genetically, whereas fraternal twins are no more than siblings conceived at the same time, the high concordance rates for these illnesses in identical twins would be expected in strongly genetic disorders, although that evidence is insufficient, in itself, to establish their genetic nature. Identical twins who look remarkably alike tend to be treated alike by their families and friends. They also share much of their environment and develop a mutual identification. It is those factors, rather than their genetic similarity, that account for the frequency with which they both choose the same occupation or marry similar partners.

During the past 10 years a new approach has been used that appears to have succeeded in separating genetic from environmental factors in the transmission of schizophrenia. This approach consists of the study of adopted individuals who share their genetic endowment with their biological relatives, but their environment with their adoptive relatives. In the several studies that have been completed to date the results are quite consistent. Schizophrenia continues to run in families, but, now, its high prevalence is restricted to the genetic relatives of schizophrenics with whom they have shared few, if any, environmental factors. The adoptive relatives of schizophrenics who reared them and shared their environment show no more tendency to schizophrenia than does the population at large.

In still-incomplete studies of adopted populations compelling evidence that some forms of manic and depressive illness have a genetic basis has recently been discovered; they occur in a number of families, in association with such traits as color blindness and a specific blood group known to reside in the X chromosome. Although this association does not occur in *all* families with manic-depressive illness, when it does oc-

cur, it follows a pattern so consistent that it cannot be explained on a nongenetic basis. One is forced to reach the conclusion that in the majority of severe cases of schizophrenia and in a substantial number of manic-depressive illnesses, genetic factors play a crucial causative role.

There thus exists the basis for a continued and intensified search for the biochemical processes through which these genetic factors operate in the development of the two most important forms of mental illness that confront us. In addition, neurobiology and psychobiology have in recent years provided important clues as to where to look, and powerful techniques have been developed and applied to this search. During this time a cohort of neurobiologists and psychiatrists have been trained, skilled in fundamental research and in clinical investigation. The time has never been more propitious or progress more promising for an understanding of these serious disturbances of the human mind.

35.   BOREDOM: THE MOST PREVALENT AMERICAN DISEASE

Estelle R. Ramey

If you really want to know what's bothering a lot of Americans, don't read the articles in the medical journals; read their advertisements. One such sociomedical vignette showed some busy mothers decorating the school gym for a PTA non-event. Off in a corner is a lone, dispirited woman. The caption under the picture diagnoses

her disease as: "M.A. (Fine Arts) ... PTA (President-elect) ... representation of a life currently centered around home and children, with too little time to pursue a vocation for which she has spent many years in training ... a situation that may bespeak continous frustration and stress: a perfect framework for her to translate the functional symptoms of psychic tension into major problems. For this kind of patient— with no demonstrable pathology yet repeated complaints—consider the distinctive properties of Valium."

In other words, our heroine is dying of boredom. Short of a personal and cultural revolution, the root causes of her sickness can't be treated. Her brain is starving. A convenient way to adjust her to her proper duties is to "tranquilize" her with a mind-dulling drug. It will also get her off her doctor's back.

Boredom is a grossly underestimated malady. It causes mischief and destruction; it is socially very expensive. Erich Fromm identifies it as the insidious cause of catastrophes ranging from drug addition to violence. Bertrand Russell said that "boredom is a vital problem for the moralist since at least half the sins of mankind are caused by fear of it." Yet boredom per se gets little or no attention from the public health establishment. For one thing, most victims do not identify it as the origin of their difficulties. They tend to think of it as a trivial complaint that afflicts only the decadent and jaded. This is nonsense; in our society boredom is endemic and increasing.

If poverty is economic deficit, then boredom is psychic deficit. Like poverty, its consequences must be cured by social changes, not by medicine. From the medical point of view, therefore, both poverty and boredom are no-win problems. Patients come to the doctor complaining of a myriad of physical symptoms, and most resist treatment. Such patients are a drag on themselves, their families, their doctors. The big traffic in prescription tranquilizers probably reflects the boredom of the doctor more than the needs of the patient.

Aside from the medical costs of boredom, this neural disorder exacts a social price in many other ways. Schoolteachers have known for a long time that children who are bored in the classroom are a menace to everyone around them—the older the child, the more extensive the damage. Ris-

ing suicide and divorce rates reflect, in large part, higher and more broadly democratic demands for "meaningful" experiences, and an unwillingness or inability to tolerate monotony. Educated people are bored. Uneducated people are also bored. The old are bored, and so are the young.

What is boredom and who is most susceptible to it? It is a painful condition resulting from a deficit of sensory responsiveness to the external world. Every human being is vulnerable because of the fundamental nature of our nervous system. There are no class, race, age, or sex lines in its distribution, but it seems most agonizing after sustained intellectual challenge or prolonged stimulation of the senses. Starving or force-feeding the highest centers of the brain will induce its characteristic discomfort, while high sensory or intellectual expectations will intensify its symptoms.

Most studies of boredom have concentrated on the pathological effects of monotony on people or animals under controlled laboratory conditions. The results are directly applicable to many real situations—men stationed in distant Antarctic outposts, prisoners of war, prisoners of peace, lonely housewives, truck drivers on long solo runs, space probers, and airplane pilots. Every piece of evidence we have supports the eloquent statement of Christopher Burney, who, as a British secret agent during World War II, was caught and imprisoned by the Nazis: "I soon discovered that variety is not the spice but the very stuff of life. We need the constant ebb and flow of wavelets of our consciousness; now here, now there, keeping even our isolation in the ocean of reality so that we neither encroach nor are encroached upon."

Emotional and intellectual health depends on an appropriate amount of action in a varied environment; there is no reason to believe that women need less variety than men, or children less than adults. It has been a complacent male assumption that intelligent women don't mind doing the kind of tedious tasks that would send an intelligent man right up the wall. However, studies done on sex differences as a factor in tolerance to a monotonous environment have shown that women may respond even more irritably than men to such constraints. D. V. Biase and his colleagues used a group of male and female college students and subjected them to a uniformly uninteresting environment. They were well fed and put singly into soundproof rooms of comfortable temperature, with a dim, diffused light (or no light) and either a low, unchanging background hum or no sound at all. The subjects could lie down but were not allowed to sleep. A device like a lie detector was used to monitor their nervous response. None of the subjects could stand the boredom for long.

The absolute monotony quickly produced emotional disturbances sometimes verging on the violent. Women showed a lower tolerance than men for isolation and tedium, and they were more likely to verbalize their distress. In what Biase calls "the Colonel Glenn syndrome," however, some of the men persisted in denying that they had difficulty coping with the torment of sensory deprivation, even though they had been observed during the course of the experiment to be moaning and writhing. Our culture, it appears, does not like its men to be anything but strong and stoical in public. When anguished, they keep a stiff upper lip and perforate their ulcers. Women have the right, for what it's worth, to complain.

Whatever the culturally permissible responses, it is a fact that every aspect of brain function, in both men and women, was disturbed after even a few hours' exposure to sensory deprivation. Their reaction time, sensory acuity, power of abstract reasoning, verbal ability, space visualization, and internal motivation to move or to daydream or to think all decreased. They became as empty of responsiveness as the environment was empty of input. Nothing in, nothing out is apparently the credo of the human nervous system. (Physical exercise, incidentally, appears to tone up the entire nervous system. When the subjects were allowed to move around or to exercise, their tolerance for environmental monotony increased.)

We come by our hungry brains in a natural progression. Even rats can get bored in an unchallenging environment. Anita Hatch took some laboratory rats and put them singly in warm cages with plenty of food and water but with little visual or aural stimulation or handling. After three months in this suburban rat heaven, the animals began to act like caricatures of the lonely housewife or her unemployed spouse. They became jumpy, irritable, and aggressive. They nibbled constantly and became fatter than their peers out in the exciting world. The bored rats then began to show signs of organic disorders. They developed nervous twitches and scaly tails. If they had had access to a rat doctor, they would have run up high medical bills and would have been put on tranquilizers. It wouldn't have helped them to have to go back to the same old cage.

Those rats didn't need a doctor. They needed some variety and stimulation. Just putting them back in a lively rat community for one week reversed all their pathology. It should be noted, however, that if the rat community gets too crowded and too lively, the rats once again begin to develop diseases, and these disorders of satiation are little different from those of deprivation. Thus either too much or too little nervous stimulation leads to unresponsiveness. A good environment provides just enough sensory input to maintain a sense of wellbeing—for mice, women, and men.

The need for exploration and novelty

seems to be built into brains and the more complex the brain, the more the need for variety. It is not only men who climb mountains just because they are there. Laboratory animals trained to run a maze to get food will learn the easiest and fastest path to the food, and then, after a while, the little beasts begin to experiment with more difficult ways to get fed. If even a rat brain is willing to sacrifice a quick meal for a change of pace, what can we expect from the voracious human brain? Exactly what one might think—it will go to remarkable lengths to escape boredom.

The trouble is, we don't know how. Ennui is so pervasive and so nebulous. Whose fault is it that so many people are bored with their lives? Mrs. M. A. Fine Arts, because of her underutilized brain, has psychic tension, but just turn the page of that same medical journal and meet her husband—the male mainstay of the tranquilizer industry. This drug ad shows a middle-aged, middle-management executive with overflowing in- and out- boxes and three phones ringing at once. Tranquilizers will keep him going until his coronary occlusion makes further medication unnecessary. His is the other face of boredom— psychic tension from overload and satiation. Life is unsatisfying. Tranquilize it.

Clearly, it's not simply the occupation that creates the pervasive sense of tedium that many Americans are experiencing. Large numbers of stereotypic housewives are not bored by the PTA or their daily routines. They enjoy them. There is, in fact, far more potential flexibility and variety in running a home than in being a file clerk, a bank teller, a sentry at a missile base, or an assistant to an assistant editor at *Penthouse.* Many workers in what seem to be deadly, boring jobs do not report unhappiness with the work. Others in occupations that are far more interesting (to the observer) quit in rage and despair at the boredom of their

lives. The depression and anxiety of boredom seems to be generated by one's perception of the value of the work and the degree of envious awareness of more exciting possibilities. It is not the job itself but the sense of control, power, and status it engenders that determines whether you'll suffer the pain of boredom.

A research scientist may have to perform many repetitive operations to obtain useful data, but the publication of that data and the recognition of her unique contribution make the work exciting. A psychoanalyst hears some stupefying stories during a day's work, but his status, his income, and his God-like importance to the patient make up for the tedium. An accountant spends his day with endless columns of numbers, but there is apparently a satisfying symmetry to his balanced additions and subtractions that compensates for the intrinsic monotony of his life's work. Of course, accountants do get bored. Some take to squirreling away large numbers of $100 bills to enliven the day. Psychoanalysts, too, get bored and start investing in real estate or racehorses, and research scientists get bored and become ineffectual scientist-administrators.

It's nice to have options. But what happens to someone who is fixed in a job or a household like a bug in amber? When there are no other viable choices, boredom is endured. But human beings always get some of their own back; they strike out with whatever power they have against the society that inflicts this torment upon them.

You can't tranquilize everybody. The bright child, bored by a tedious, unimaginative educational system and too little physical activity, tries to enliven things by throwing spitballs. Bored adolescents form rampaging gangs to provide the excitement that their routine, impoverished lives don't generate. They don't all live in slums. You'll find them in the best suburbs, rip-ping off the local stores just for the hell of it.

Men on assembly lines get so bored that they develop a free-floating hostility. On a recent television program, a man was shown moving an auto from one spot to another a few feet away, after which he went back to get another car, and so on and so on all day long—the ant and the grains of sand. He was asked whether he ever detected any faults in the cars in the process of moving them. He said, "Sure I do." He was asked if he reported them. His answer was succinct: "No." He was being screwed by "them." Screw "them."

There's nothing new about boredom, just as there's nothing new about its emotional cognates—sloth, despair, hopelessness, alienation, passivity, and anomie. It's simply that we are less willing to endure the condition than our bored forebears. The desire for change is now accepted as a justification for almost any kind of behavior. The divorce rate is escalating in all age groups but is most dramatic in marriages of twenty to thirty years. More than 95 percent of all those late divorces are requested by the bored, middle-aged husbands. Most bored wives are still willing to settle for a tranquilizer, but then, an older woman's options are pretty much limited to that. The husband, however, can opt for a hedonistic thrashing around that used to be culturally unacceptable. Even politicians, those sensitive barometers of social sanctions, can now seek out new young bed companions without suffering a drop in the polls. Their constituents seem to understand that marriage to the same woman for thirty years can get damned boring. Everybody understands, except maybe the politician's old wife.

Our society regards its women's capacity for being bored in a curiously contradictory way. Women no longer have to be pregnant all the time, and they don't have to be ignorant. At last, they can be seen as strong,

intelligent, vigorous persons. At the same time, however, they are seen as weak, nonintellectual, and by nature fit only for the protected atmosphere of a harem. The same man who insists on sending his daughter to the most elitist and intellectually demanding college can't understand why women aren't satisfied with a nice home, husband, and children. His mother was. What right have these pampered women to be bored?

It is true that in an industrial society, most jobs are sedentary, monotonous, and impersonal. They have one big advantage, though, over housework. They provide money as an index of personal worth and, along with that money, a subtle but important sense of independence. The tranquilized housewife is bored, and so is her husband, but he at least has some economic ego assurance. And working men do get out of the house every day and into a world of other adults. Even the assembly-line worker can get some relief from his tensions by relating to his co-workers as in a tribal rite, and every evening he can leave his tedious job and find a change of pace in his "after-work" activities. There is little change of pace for his wife.

The forlorn wife and mother in the pharmaceutical blurb suffers not only from a lack of "meaningful stimuli," as one psychiatric reference book puts it, and an "inability to become stimulated" by her daily activities; she also compounds her psychological problems by feeling guilty about her attitude. She doesn't necessarily want a paid job but the "libidinal and aggressive strivings" that were necessary when she was a student are now counterproductive and must be denied. One way to deal with this is to take on still more obligations (president-elect PTA) and then to complain about having too much (not too little) to do. Obviously, she does have a lot of very necessary functions. Her harried day has been catalogued ad nauseam—the constant chauffeuring of the children, the volunteer work that nobody appreciates, the gourmet cooking classes, the PTA wheel-spinning, the care and feeding of her semidetached husband, and the endless shopping trips. Somehow, though, she can't work up that old zest. Neither can her husband, but the dynamics are different.

Medical counseling for the bored of either sex usually comes at a high price. But there is general agreement in the profession that women far outnumber men in the category of time-wasting, neurotic goldbrickers. Doctors complain bitterly about the bored housewives who clutter their waiting rooms and "have nothing the matter with them." Such women place a heavy load on our medical-care delivery system because boredom—with its accompanying depression, guilt, and anxiety—mimics just about all organ system disorders—skin rashes, headaches, backaches, chronic fatigue, dizziness, shortness of breath, sexual dysfunction, insomnia, excessive sleeping, stomach pains, menstrual disorders, personality changes, and chest pains. Unfortunately, "psychogenic pain" hurts just as much as any other kind of pain and all good doctors are obliged first to rule out grim organic diseases that can present the same symptoms. This takes a lot of time and money.

Dr. William A. Nolen, a surgeon, writing recently in a popular women's magazine, describes the problem this way: "Women who are 'all tired out' account for a substantial segment of most medical practices. They're difficult—almost impossible—patients to treat. Most are in the thirty-five-to-forty-five age group. They've been married ten to fifteen years, their children are all in school, their husbands are earning a reasonably comfortable living. Very few of them have jobs outside the home. When a woman with this complaint comes to my office, I almost always find the same thing. She may

be slightly overweight—who isn't?—but otherwise physically, there's not a darn thing wrong with her." Dr. Nolen then speaks directly to these maddening females: "Most of you are tired for only one reason. You're bored." The good doctor is exactly right, but his Rx for cure shows a curious lack of insight.

Nolen advises these women to take the $10 or $15 that an office visit might cost and spend it on a "relaxed lunch at a restaurant" or on a "good movie." What happens to his patient when the movie is over and the lunch is digested? She comes back for another prescription for her sickness. But even this Band-Aid treatment of a destructive disease is preferable to the Draconian "cure" some doctors use to treat chronic boredom. Dr. Nolen describes a typical, restless patient named Beth, aged forty-two, who "was referred to me by a reputable family doctor as a candidate for hysterectomy." The referring doctor suggested the operation because Beth was "anemic due to prolongation of her menstrual periods." It turned out Beth was not anemic and that she "needed a hysterectomy about as much as I did."

But if Beth shops around long enough, she will almost certainly find a doctor prepared to yank out a healthy uterus or prescribe expensive iron shots or tranquilizers or energizers or prolonged psychoanalysis. In fact, Beth may insist upon such mistreatment in order to have a socially acceptable reason for her terrible malaise. Being bored out of your mind is not considered a serious ailment, but a hysterectomy has clout. So does a nervous breakdown or alcoholism.

It's not only the women who can afford the casual hysterectomy, the endless psychoanalysis, who are caught up in the tedium of high expectations and minimal satisfaction. Traditionally, the working-class woman was supposed to be uninterested in anything other than her home, her church, her children, and her man. Not for her the luxury of yearning for fulfillment. All she needed was a full uterus, a full belly, and shining kitchen linoleum. Where McGinty sat was the head of the table, and that's how she liked it (he said). Boredom was for those fancy ladies uptown. In actual fact, her life was stultifyingly boring most of the time, and so was her husband's; but neither was encouraged to do any soul-searching about the full life. Times have changed. Working-class women, like their richer sisters, don't have to be pregnant all the time, and, when they do go to work to help keep the family in shoes, they learn about another dimension of themselves. They like the give and take of the working world. They are finding in themselves the ability to be independent.

No woman—upper, middle-, or working-class—gets bored with her daily routines because Gloria Steinem and Betty Friedan told her to be unhappy. Boredom is a predictable consequence of the pill, educational opportunities, and the financial demands of an expanding economy. Recent books that cry havoc because women are no longer satisfied with lives of undeveloped potential and unrealized dreams are trying to preserve a social structure that is already a shambles. To understand what's going on, their authors would do better to look at the indignities we inflict on older, retired men. As life expectancy and our expectations of life increase, so does our vulnerability to boredom. Healthy men who are forced to retire and "enjoy" their well-earned leisure often find themselves sickened by the deprivation. Dr. Jay A. Winston of Harvard described a typical retired man:

Mr. G., a self-employed businessman, had delayed his retirement until age 72. His health had remained good. His work had been personally fulfilling. Retirement was actually his wife's idea. Mrs. G. was look-ing forward to the relaxing lifestyle that her husband's retirement would finally allow.

Mr. G. expected he would travel, develop new interests, and spend more time with his family. But his work had been at the center of his life. He had never developed hobbies. While he had enjoyed providing his family with the means to entertain themselves, he had not partaken in many of the activities himself.

His business sold, Mr. G. found he was bored, frustrated, resentful. He arose each day and wandered around the house without a sense of purpose. His personal habits began to change—he became uncharacteristically sloppy, changed his clothes less often. He was irritable. And his mental capacities were suddenly failing. He would walk downstairs only to discover he had forgotten what he was looking for, or what he wanted to do. He began to forget people's names.

Disturbed at these changes, Mrs. G. sought help for her husband. A thorough medical examination revealed no organic basis for his symptoms, which were classic signs of early senility. As part of a psychiatric evaluation of the problem, Dr. Shader decided to initiate a "life review" with Mr. G.

Mr. G. admitted he never really wanted to retire, and he acknowledged anger and resentment towards his wife for forcing him to do so. Eventually he was able to confront his wife and express his anger, which re-opened communications between them.

Things improved after that. He was able to arrange to do part-time consulting work for the new owners of his life-long business enterprise. He and Mrs. G. soon found they were beginning to enjoy their new-found leisure time together. After 16 weeks of therapy, Mr. G.'s memory problems and other signs of senility had disappeared.

Not many old men can afford such therapy. They just disintegrate.

When sensory activation and intellectual curiosity are suppressed by a dull environment, the brain responds with a protective withdrawal from the real world. In his work with institution-bound patients, Dr.

Frank R. Mark has found that revitalization of almost moribund human beings can often be achieved by the simple technique of making available things that they can handle and examine and manipulate When you engage their interest, it is like engaging the wheels with the motor; they start to move. Doctor Mark calls loneliness, anxiety, and boredom America's major diseases.

Our society has thus created the apotheosis of a physiological dilemma. For some, satiation is the problem. The phones on the desk never stop ringing. Crisis follows crisis. The rock music gets louder, the strobe lights whirl faster, the movies become bloodier, movement from place to place becomes more frenetic, relations with others increase exponentially, and the ability to respond decreases constantly. The sound must be turned up even higher as deafness supervenes, and even then the excitement diminishes. Catch-22. For others, nothing exciting or new happens as each day mimics every other day. Little is asked, little is given

History is full of examples of the extraordinary things that women and men will do to avoid satiation or boredom. The only thing that is new is the great increase in the number of people who have joined the chase for diversion or fulfillment. Ennui used to be strictly an upper-class disease that affected a few lords and ladies of the realm. The rest of their contemporaries were struggling desperately to survive. It is only when primal hungers are comfortably blunted to mere appetites that other human needs—love, respect, creativity—come to the surface of consciousness. It is absurd to speak of the intellectual boredom of a starving woman or man.

In the United States, although there is terrible poverty for some, most Americans are well fed and have more than a modicum of shelter, education, leisure, and freedom. Advanced technology and splendid natural resources made this possible and simultaneously made boredom more democratic. The rich and the ruling have always put a lot of energy into staving off ennui. They invented fetes, fancy clothes, hunts, racing, political intrigue, chivalry, gambling, sex games, and that most exciting game of all—war. It takes a lot of ingenuity to stay viable in the face of total leisure. Most of these diversions are now available to large numbers of Americans. They don't seem to be enough.

Rich men are going into politics—making money is not stimulating enough. Rich women are taking jobs: so are the not-so-rich women. Older people are swarming back to school to get retraining or simply to get back into the real world again. Everybody seems to have decided all at once that he or she has just one life to live, and to live with "gusto." A resigned acceptance of boredom as part of the inescapable pain of living is becoming less common. Inevitably this makes for chaos at every level of the social structure. Somebody has to do the boring work to get the papers filed, the refuse collected, the cars assembled, the letters typed, and the laundry washed. But who should be saddled with these jobs? Not me. Let it be you.

Women and men don't have much sympathy for each other's pain. Yet for all of us in America it's not easy to be young, it's harder to be middle-aged, and it's terrible to be old. It seems that our best hope is to try to help each other reach for the Greek definition of happiness: the use of all of one's powers to achieve excellence. If we put our fertile brains to designing an environment in which people who do the necessary monotonous jobs are rewarded richly for their daily boredom, in which retraining for new occupations is a normal phase of every life, and in which women and men complement instead of wounding each other, boredom will not be so pervasive.

A country that can produce the Constitution can produce a more enriching and fulfilling environment with less noise and more music. First, however, we must recognize the destructiveness of boredom, and then ask how this disease can be minimized. It will mean a massive cultural reevaluation.

36.   A PSYCHIATRIST LOOKS AT ALCOHOLISM

Sheila B. Blume, M.D.

We all know people suffering from alcoholism. According to the National Council on Alcoholism, 9,000,000 Americans are afflicted. At least one out of 20 readers of this article is already in some stage of the development of the illness. Yet, most educated Americans feel helpless when it comes to recognizing, understanding, or coping with alcoholism. Although there is a great deal yet to be learned about this disease, much knowledge is already available. The organized, systematic, large-scale application of present knowledge to the prevention, early detection, and treatment of alcoholism throughout the country remains a pressing social issue. Medical schools, for example, are only beginning to address the problem of teaching their students about alcoholism itself, as opposed to teaching only the physical complications of the disease. Schools of social work, clinical psychology, nursing education, and police science continue to turn out graduates substantially unequipped to deal with the large numbers of problem drinkers among their clients and students or to guide those in their care toward safe drinking practices. Few areas of the country boast adequate treatment facilities, even for those alcohol-

ics and their families who come forward spontaneously in search of help. Nothing short of a massive national effort on the part of government and individuals alike will begin to make a meaningful impact on the problem.

ALCOHOLISM, THE DISEASE

Although social consequences of excessive drinking were recorded in ancient civilizations,[1] the disease concept reflects a relatively recent view of alcoholism. Individual physicians such as Benjamin Rush, a signer of the Declaration of Independence, argued, at the beginning of the 19th century, that alcoholism was an illness. However, the traditional view of alcoholism as a purely moral issue prevailed well into this century, and remains alive among us.

There are as many social and political consequences of the disease concept of alcoholism as there are medical ones. Earlier in our nation's history, excessive drinkers were reprimanded publicly and put in stocks as punishment for their drunkenness. Imprisonment for public intoxication is still legal in many states in the absence of

---

Reprinted from *Intellect* (July/August 1975) by permission of publisher, pp. 27–30.

[1] See Raymond G. McCarthy, ed., *Drinking and Intoxication* (New Haven, Conn.: College and University Press, 1959), for a discussion of drinking in ancient Greece, Rome, and other cultures.

any other criminal misconduct. Such penalties share one important attribute with the much-practiced method of exhortation of the alcoholic to mend his ways—they are equally ineffective in making any permanent improvement in the drinking pattern. Shaming, imprisoning, and exhortation are ineffective because they are based on a faulty theory, which might be called the "moral concept" of alcoholism. The moral concept makes the assumption that alcoholics drink because of error, sin, or perversity. It postulates that the person suffering from alcoholism is able to exercise free choice in relation to his drinking, and, therefore, is perfectly able to stop or decrease his intake if he "really" wants to. The problem is thought to reside in the wanting. Punishment or warning are meant to establish this "really wanting." The doctor who declares that the alcoholic's liver will shrivel up and cause his death, and the employer who warns that he will lose his job, may be telling the truth, but they will be frustrated if they expect the information to arrest the course of the illness. The untreated alcoholic does *not* have free choice about drinking. Rarely can he recover without help. The disease concept expresses this fact.

Loss of control over drinking of alcohol is a hallmark of the illness. Treatment can be looked upon as the process of reestablishing the power of choice by teaching the alcoholic individual to adjust to his illness, much as a diabetic is helped to lead a normal life through diet and insulin. The disease concept thus defines the alcoholic as a sick person in need of help, rather than as a bad person worthy of scorn. Social policy based on this concept provides treatment, rather than punishment.

Physicians think of alcoholism as a disease because persons who become afflicted present relatively uniform clusters of signs and symptoms, relatively characteristic courses of progression, and a similar range of eventual outcomes.[2] Some clinicians prefer to look upon alcoholism as merely a symptom of some other underlying disorder, much as fever may be a symptom of smallpox, sunstroke, or the common cold. While it is true that certain people who manifest the typical picture of alcoholism have pre-existing neurotic illness, schizophrenia, or recurrent depression, by no means will such well-defined disorders be found in the majority. Neither is it true that any of the diagnosable mental disorders will predictably lead to alcoholism. Finally, resolution of the neurosis or treatment of the schizophrenia, in alcoholics who have these disorders, does not reliably relieve the alcoholism. The disease concept calls attention to the need for treatment of the alcoholism itself.

Alcoholism has also been looked upon as an addiction. This view is a useful one if the diagnosis is not limited to persons showing actual physical dependence. Such symptoms as round-the-clock drinking and physical withdrawal symptoms when drinking is interrupted represent rather late-stage phenomena in many alcoholics.

CAUSES OF ALCOHOLISM

The precise cause of alcoholism is not completely understood, but the disease is thought to result from an interaction of physical, social, and psychological factors.

Although a variety of physiological theories of alcoholism have been advanced, none has yet been clearly demonstrated. Alcoholism is well known to be a familial disease, but whether this may be explained by an inherited physiological predisposition, rather than an environmental, psychological, and cultural influence, is not yet clear.

―――――――――

[2]Criteria Committee, National Council on Alcoholism, "Criteria for the Diagnosis of Alcoholism," *American Journal of Psychiatry,* 129:127–135, August, 1972.

Genetic studies have yielded conflicting results.[3]

Different cultures seem to produce differing rates of alcoholism in their members. Chinese, Jews, Greeks, and Italians have relatively low rates, as compared to other cultural groups. This is true in spite of the fact that Jews in the U.S. have a higher proportion of drinkers (90% of the adults) than either Protestants or Catholics. Italians have a low rate of alcoholism, although the use of wine is widespread. Attitudes and customs surrounding drinking seem to be the important determinants. Cultural factors thought to encourage alcoholism include poorly agreed-upon norms for drinking, as opposed to ritualized alcohol use; use of distilled spirits, rather than low-alcohol beverages; cultural conflict and moralization surrounding alcohol use; culturally encouraged drinking as an isolated activity "for its own sake," rather than as an accompaniment of eating or recreational activities; acceptance of drunkenness as a tolerable, or even admirable, state; and cultural encouragement of the use of alcohol as a remedy for emotional distress. The lower social acceptance of drinking among women in most cultures probably influences the lower rate of alcoholism in females. As society changes in this regard, the ratio of female to male alcoholics has increased.

Psychological factors influence the onset and course of the illness in any individual case. The search for a single personality type—"alcoholic personality"—or a single unresolved conflict area to explain alcoholism has been unsuccessful. People of many different personality types and with many different life problems become dependent on the effects of the sedative drug alcohol

[3]See F. A. Seixas, ed., "Nature and Nurture in Alcoholism," *Annals of the New York Academy of Sciences,* 197:5–229, May 25, 1972.

when alcohol seems to offer them an effective, if temporary, solution. It is this emotional dependence on alcohol which distinguishes the alcoholic from the normal drinker. Alcohol makes him feel more adequate, more as he wishes to be. As one alcoholic put it, "I always used to say that I was born two martinis short."

The normal drinker, who is not alcohol-dependent, will enjoy the mild disinhibiting effects of the drug, but consider the experience outside of his ordinary functional life, to be enjoyed as a recreation, along with other recreational activities. He will consider the effects of alcohol to be an altered state of consciousness, rather than his "true self," and will not entrust his work, emotional life, or important decision-making to such a state.

Dependence on alcohol may begin when drinking is found useful in relieving shyness, depression, anger, tension, fear, feelings of inadequacy, or other unwanted emotions. If the individual finds drinking a personally acceptable way of dealing with these feelings, and alternate means of handling such problems are not developed or employed, alcohol dependence progresses.

It has often been said that alcoholics drink to escape, or to run away from reality. Although this may be true for some, especially in the late stages, most alcoholics drink for quite the opposite reason—to join into life more adequately.

COURSE OF THE DISEASE

Alcoholism may start at any age, occurs in either sex, and cuts across racial and socioeconomic groups. Although some people feel they were alcoholic from the first drink, most alcoholics begin their drinking careers much in the same way as their non-alcoholic peers. Somewhere along the way, however, the discovery of alcohol as an acceptable and useful drug initiates the pattern of alcohol dependence, the first step toward alcoholism. For some, this pattern does not develop until middle life or old age. For some, it begins on the advice of a physician,[4] or in an attempt to arrest addiction to another drug, such as heroin or one of the sedatives.

Dependence may progress slowly or may increase dramatically in response to a specific life crisis, such as divorce, unemployment, illness, or death in the family. The alcohol-dependence pattern is reversible in its early stages through life experience or counseling. However, when increasing dependence leads to increasing quantities of alcohol consumed, the phenomenon of tolerance develops. A tolerant drinker may drink four or five times as much as a naïve drinker without obvious signs of intoxication. Unfortunately, such tolerance is widely admired in American society as a sign of masculinity or strength, instead of being recognized as an early indication of disease. Alcohol tolerance is chiefly a central-nervous-system adaptation to the presence of the substance, rather than a metabolic adaptation via an increase in the speed of alcohol metabolism. Elderly people or those with other physical disorders may not develop notable tolerance. Late in the disease, the tolerance is lost due to physical damage caused by the alcohol itself, and by aging. Late-stage or elderly alcoholics may drink less in actual quantity than many normal drinkers, but experience all the severe consequences of the disease nevertheless.

During the period of increasing dependence, most incipient alcoholics have some insight into the pathological nature of their drinking. The mechanisms of denial and ra-

tionalization are used to repress this insight, since drinking has become a prerequisite to normal functioning. The individual no longer brags about his drinking, but tends to gulp and sneak his extra drinks out of sight, as much to hide them from himself as from others. Alcoholic blackouts—temporary memory lapses due to drinking—often appear as alcohol intake increases. These periods of amnesia are characteristically noticed upon waking. The drinker can not remember going to bed or the events of a number of hours before that time. Sometimes, an entire day or more is lost to memory. Blackouts tend to increase in frequency as the disease progresses. Imagine awakening to find your car in the driveway with its fender dented and stained with blood. Imagine awakening to wonder where you have been and what you have said or done. Such are common experiences in the life of many persons suffering from alcoholism.

The early symptoms mentioned above are apparent to those nearest the afflicted individual, but are hidden from the outside world. With the onset of the middle stage of the disease, control of alcohol intake is lost, and the disease becomes more visible to others. The loss of control does not develop as a single event, but, rather, over a period of time. To the alcoholic, this development represents the "invisible line" across which he passes into irreversible illness. He still drinks as he always did—just to feel right. However, he can no longer do this without outward signs of intoxication and disinhibited behavior for which he later feels deeply ashamed.

Once the loss of control begins, severe family conflicts, bursts of violence and of remorse, deep depressions, extravagent promises and gifts, and swings in emotional tone occur. The individual's functional ability is impaired, and frantic attempts are

[4]Sheila B. Blume, "Iatrogenic Alcoholism," *Quarterly Journal of Studies on Alcohol,* 34:1348–1352, December, 1973.

made to cover up the defects. At this time, efforts are made to stop drinking, change beverages, and change locales ("the geographic cure").

The middle stage is a stormy period for most alcoholics and their families, with periods of improvement and of regression, periods of abstinence and bouts of uncontrollable drinking, periods of hopefulness and confidence, and returns to deep despair. Suicide is common during this stage. Many alcoholics compare the experience to riding an "emotional roller coaster," although, for some, the period marks a gradual progressive withdrawal from life without great mood fluctuations. Physical illnesses directly related to alcohol intake, such as gastritis, alcoholic hepatitis, neuritis, and the alcohol withdrawal syndromes, occur. Driving and pedestrian accidents and industrial injuries are often seen. Many alcoholics also consult their physicians during this phase with non-specific complaints of insomnia, anorexia (loss of appetite), and nervousness. If an accurate diagnosis is not made and appropriate steps are not taken, the patient is often given sedatives or minor tranquilizers which may start him on a secondary pattern of drug dependence.

Throughout the ups and downs of the middle stage, the untreated alcoholic progressively loses ground unless help is obtained. Frequent job changes, separations, divorce, and repeated hospitalizations are the rule. Withdrawal syndromes may include shakes and sweats, hallucinations, convulsive seizures, and delirium tremens.

Late-stage alcoholism results in irreversible damage to the brain and other body organs, with permanent disability. Many die before this stage is reached. Less than one out of 20 alcoholics becomes a skidrow inhabitant. Alcoholism shortens the lifespan of those affected by an average of 12 years.

TREATMENT OF ALCOHOLISM

Pre-care

All transactions which take place until both the afflicted individual and the helping person agree that the problem is alcoholism —and that something must be done about it—may be thought of as pre-care. Early casefinding methods, such as public education, drunk drivers' programs, and the first phase of industrial alcoholism programs, are pre-care. The goal of this phase is simply problem recognition. It involves breaking through rationalization and denial to reach the insight which has been buried. The danger involved in the pre-care phase involves a common misconception on the part of the helping person. He—and, therefore, also the alcoholic—entertains the unrealistic expectation of full recovery from pre-care alone. This feeling that, once the alcoholic has admitted the nature of the problem, he should be able to handle it himself dates from the old moral theory of alcoholism. The disappointment in both parties when this does not happen is intense, and suicide often occurs at this point. Intelligent pre-care concludes with the immediate involvement of the alcoholic in a full-scale program of treatment and recovery.

Detoxification

The next step is to help the individual attain an initial alcohol- and drug-free state. This process may require medication and/or full hospitalization to treat withdrawal symptoms. Again, frustration and despair will result if detoxification alone is expected to be complete treatment for the disease. The detoxification period represents an ideal time to work with the alcoholic toward involvement in further treatment, since, when he feels ill, his defenses tend to be lowered. He must be made to realize, however, that, although detoxification has helped him through the present drinking bout, it will, in itself, do nothing to prevent the next.

Rehabilitation

This most challenging phase of treatment involves a major change in attitudes, self-concepts, habits of living, and, most important, ways of dealing with internal feeling states.

Whatever the initial motivation for treatment, the task of the rehabilitation phase is to build toward an ideal and self-sustaining motivation. The ideal motivation in an alcoholic is a desire to remain sober for himself, because he prefers himself that way, and no longer needs a drink.

Rehabilitation also involves learning about the nature of the illness. Guilt is relieved when the patient realizes that he did not become an alcoholic by choice, but unwittingly developed a disease which can be arrested with help.

Rehabilitation involves helping the alcoholic face and understand himself, particularly the patterns of feeling and behavior that began and perpetuated the alcohol dependence. The smiling lady who has been taught to bury her anger so that everyone will like her, but has also learned to drink to relieve the tense knot in her stomach, is helped to face and express her anger in a realistic way. She is helped to bear the displeasure of others, to hold her ground, and to take pride in her firmness. The shy young man is helped to face and get to know other people, to communicate honestly with them, and to feel pride in doing so. The depressed person is brought face-to-face with his feeling of uselessness and helplessness, and, through a gradual series of small victories, finds self-respect and the ability to help others. The patterns of change are as individual as each of the 9,000,000 Ameri-

cans who suffer from the disease. All, however, must readjust their views of self and others to accept an alcohol-free life.

Long-term Follow-up

Alcoholism is a chronic, life-long illness, in some cases associated with other physical or mental illnesses, requiring long-term care. Once the initial rehabilitative effort is made, it must be followed by a period of at least two to three years in which sober habits of adjustment to life are solidified, lost ground is regained, and new achievements are accomplished before a stable recovery is reached. Even after such a period, a return to alcohol use will reliably reestablish the alcoholic drinking patterns. Services such as marital counseling, group psychotherapy, vocational rehabilitation, and legal aid are helpful to many alcoholics during the follow-up phase.

Relapses must be watched for and treated promptly with detoxification and further rehabilitative efforts.

THE ROLE OF ALCOHOLICS ANONYMOUS

In 1935, two alcoholic men discovered that, although each had been unable to maintain sobriety alone, they were able to achieve sobriety together by helping other alcoholics with a desire to stop drinking. This was the origin of Alcoholics Anonymous, a world-wide self-help organization which has helped many thousands of alcoholic persons to recover. A.A. charges no dues or fees, keeps no lists, gives out no membership cards, owns no property, and works totally on a person-to-person level. A.A. presents a program for sober living in the form of its 12 suggested steps. Regular attendance at meetings helps members maintain motivation, identify with other sober alcoholics, form new interpersonal relationships, and help one another. Members are prepared to help other alcoholics in need at any time of the day or night.

A.A. is a useful program at every stage of treatment. Many alcoholics can recover fully with A.A. alone, without additional professional help of any kind. Others find they can not grasp the program without treatment. Most professional programs utilize A.A. volunteers who lead meetings and introduce patients to A.A., and A.A. offers a life-long follow-up program which converts the alcoholism from a liability to an asset.

ALCOHOLISM IN THE YOUNG

Attention has recently been focused on the rising number of alcohol problems among the young in this country. Alcohol misuse has always been present among the young, with many alcoholics who come to treatment in their 30's describing dependence on alcohol since their early teens. Heightened public awareness, resulting from the recent drug epidemic among young people, holds out promise that programs of education and assistance for the young will, at last, be developed, and many years of later suffering prevented.

Other prevention efforts must be made by means of changing social attitudes toward alcohol use. The National Institute on Alcohol Abuse and Alcoholism has initiated such a campaign in the media. Education alone will not be sufficient to prevent the disease. Programs which foster good mental health, help all people of all ages deal with the emotional problems of living, and eliminate racism, inequality of opportunity, poverty, and other contributing social problems, are also needed.

I would like to end by delivering a message from a former patient. I had asked our therapy group for advice on my first public lecture on alcoholism. "Tell them," he said, "that being an alcoholic is not like attending a perpetual party from which you're not smart enough to go home. There is no pleasure involved. It is a living hell."

CHAPTER **VI**

Social Problems

OF THE MANY KINDS of problems we are called upon to solve, some have their origins with the individual, such as those presented in the preceding chapter, and others are socially based. We are forced to cope with those that are thrust upon us; these are problems characteristic of the times. While many problems are tackled out of a sense of social concern and fellowship, we deal with others simply because we have to. It is important to recognize that these problems may herald new and more productive ways of living, a view which is surely heartening.

This chapter explores the psychological aspects of seven significant social problems. "Alternative Gender Roles among Women: Masculine, Feminine, Adrogenous" sets forth the dimensions of a variety of problems which women have been attempting to solve. These have recently been brought to public attention by the various aspects of the women's liberation movement, which expresses the contention that women are treated unequally relative to men. Women's underlying desire is to be liberated from the traditional role prescriptions of society, but if female roles are shed, what will replace them? Moreover, the press of women for liberation has had some perhaps unanticipated consequences, such as the growing awareness among men that they too have not been liberated from their role prescriptions, the theme of "Now Men's Lib Is the Trend." Indeed, our society is undergoing massive social changes in the mores controlling behavior, particularly those relative to sex roles. "Changing Patterns of Premarital Sexual Behavior" and "Why Marriages Turn Sour—and How to Get Help" explore two of these dimensions.

Two of the problems considered in this chapter are of special concern to parents and others who provide care for children. In the United States, one of the most mobile of societies, people are forever changing their place of residence. What are the effects of all this moving on the children in these families? "Nobody Knows My Name" explores aspects of the problem and provides an answer which is not at all comforting. The problem of child abuse, its prevalence, and what can be done about it is considered in "Child Abuse: A Killer Teachers Can Help Control."

In our dealings with these and other social problems we can be pessimistic or hopeful and positive. The challenges are real, and we must be realistic enough to solve them. But are we?

37. ALTERNATIVE GENDER ROLES AMONG WOMEN: MASCULINE, FEMININE, ANDROGENOUS

Virginia E. O'Leary and Charlene E. Depner

Women constitute over 50% of the population of the U.S. Until recently, it was generally believed that discriminatory hiring and promotional practices and other powerful societal barriers accounted for the disproportionately low representation of women in fields traditionally occupied by men. Dramatic changes in legislation and media images have accounted for substantial improvements in the opportunities for Amercan women to attain positions of responsibility and prestige. However, this increase in opportunity has not been accompanied by a concomitant increase in the proportion of women employed in male-dominated professions. Not only did the percentage of professional and technical positions held by women in the U.S. decline from 45% in 1940 to 38% in 1968, but female participation in these occupations is disproportionately concentrated in areas traditionally considered "female-sex-role-appropriate." For example, 97% of all registered nurses, 92% of all dieticians, 85% of all elementary school teachers, and 70% of all health technicians are women. In contrast, two per cent of the engineers, five per cent of the attorneys, and nine per cent of the physicians in this country are women.[1] It is generally agreed that, for a woman to succeed in the competitive economic market place, she must possess characteristics which have stereotypically been regarded as male-sex-

role-appropriate. Clearly, there is a reluctance on the part of many women to pursue occupations which require the expression of traits traditionally ascribed to men. Apparently, this reluctance extends even to the acquisition of the educational training which would qualify them for such occupations.[2]

Gender role may be defined as everything a person says or does to indicate to others or to themselves the extent to which he or she personally endorses the characteristics and behaviors stereotypically ascribed to his or her biological gender. It is through one's gender role enactment that gender identity is expressed. The concept of appropriate gender role may moderate the determination of educational objectives and life goals among women. A woman's definition of those traits and behaviors appropriate to the role enactment of her biological gender will determine her perception of the behavioral options open to her. The more constricted a woman's gender-role definition, the more restricted her behavioral alternatives. In this article, we will deal with three alternative gender-role definitions endorsed by women—the masculine, the feminine, and the androgenous.

Traditionally, gender role has been conceptualized as a unitary, dichotomous construct anchored by masculinity at one extreme and femininity at the other. By

Reprinted from *Intellect* (January 1976) by permission of publisher, pp. 313–315.
[1]U.S. Department of Commerce, Council of Economic Advisors, "Where Women Stand in the Professions," 1973.

[2]Matina S. Horner, "The Motive to Avoid Success and Changing Aspirations of College Women," in Judith M. Bardwick, ed., *Readings in the Psychology of Women* (New York: Harper & Row, 1972), pp. 62–67.

definition, an individual's position on this single bipolar dimension implies that the characterization of self as possessing masculine traits excludes the possibility of a feminine role definition and vice-versa. Adherence to such a bipolar representation of sex-role typing encourages the actualization of traits and behaviors stereotypically associated with only one gender to the exclusion and/or denial of those associated with the other.

However, an alternative conceptualization—that of androgenous gender role—has been recently proposed by social scientists investigating the social-psychological origins of sex differences. The postulation of androgenous gender role assumes that an individual of a given gender identity may incorporate the traits and behavioral characteristics stereotypically associated with both males and females. Thus, masculinity and femininity are viewed as two orthogonal dimensions which may vary independent of one another, such that an individual may endorse attributes typically characterized as both extremely masculine and extremely feminine, while maintaining a consistent gender identity.

THE ANDROGENE LEGEND

The term androgene originates from a legend related in the *Symposium of Plato.* Aristophanes, in describing the true nature of mankind, explains that there once existed three kinds of human beings—the male, the female, and the androgene, who was at once male and female. According to the legend, humans at that time were shaped as spheres and had two sets of arms and legs. Males and females had two faces and two sets of genitals of the same sex. The androgene had one face and one set of genitals of each gender. The sphere people were endowed with tremendous strength and en-

ergy and, in their arrogance, assaulted the gods.

As retribution, Zeus decided to debilitate them by splitting them in half and refashioning them as singular hemi-people. Unhappily, mankind has lost the "other half" of his nature, and now seeks it among others.

A woman whose gender-role definition is androgenous is free to recognize and actualize not only those stereotypically feminine traits which she possesses, but the stereotypically masculine ones as well. However, the woman who defines appropriate-sex-role behavior as dichotomous perceives herself as one of the severed same-sex hemipeople, actualizing one set of characteristics to the exclusion and denial of the other.

This artificial dichotomy which characterizes the individual who defines her gender role stereotypically has been the prevailing conceptual basis for the assessment of the masculinity-femininity construct in research, as well as theory.[3] Test items used to measure the construct were empirically derived in terms of their ability to discriminate the responses of females from those of males. Examples of such paper and pencil measures include the Terman-Miles M-F test, the Strong Vocational Inventory Blank, the M-F scale of the MMPI, and Gough's Femininity Scale. On each of these scales, high feminine scores imply low masculine ones and vice-versa. This historical tendency to define masculinity-femininity on a single bipolar dimension has restricted the social scientist's conceptualization of the "absolute" nature of both gender role and gender identity. Recently, however, the notion of defining masculinity and femininity as independent

[3]Anne Constantinople, "Masculinity-Femininity: An Exception to a Famous Dictum?," *Psychological Bulletin,* 80: 389–408, May, 1973.

dimensions has led to a reevaluation of sex-role conceptualization and the attitudinal and behavioral implications of adherence to a given gender-role definition.

Adherence to the bipolarity assumption is the basis for strong and exclusive endorsement by the woman who defines her gender role in accordance with the conventional norms governing feminine sex-typed behavior. She may perceive that any indication of less than intense commitment to the female stereotypic role would imply masculine characteristics. Further, she may perceive the recognition and enactment of those "masculine" aspects of her character as threatening to the successful demonstration of her femininity.

Society assigns particular characteristics to males and females for the purpose of enhancing performance in traditional sex roles. The stereotypic images of the achieving male and nurturant female become a powerful force in the socialization of children as they grow into adulthood. Norms governing the approved masculine and feminine image are clearly defined and consensually endorsed.

An analysis of those characteristics most commonly ascribed to each sex reveals that the attributes valued highly in men reflect a "competency" cluster. Female-valued traits comprise a "warmth-expressiveness" cluster antithetical to the male profile—that is, the ideal female does not possess male-valued attributes. Further, both sexes agree that male-valued traits are more socially desirable than female-valued traits.[4]

The expression of masculine traits may be anathema to a woman because she anticipates negative consequences to be associated with the demonstration of such traits. Horner contends that many women fear intellectual pursuits for this reason. She writes:

> A woman is threatened by success because unusual excellence in academic and intellectual areas is unconsciously equated with loss of femininity and, as a result, the possibility of social rejection becomes very real.[5]

Thus, women who define their role as stereotypically feminine are likely to inhibit the expression of masculine traits and behaviors in order to maintain a consistently feminine image. For such women, the mere acknowledgement of a masculine trait may jeopardize their perceived ability to successfully enact the female role. Indeed, women with a high fear of success perform less well in competitive situations, particularly when their opponents are males. Further, traditionally oriented feminine women are more likely than their less stereotypically role-bound peers to "play dumb" on a date.[6]

BIPOLAR FEMALE GENDER ROLES

Like the hemi-people searching for their other half, the woman who defines her gender role as stereotypically feminine has a strong need to anchor her self-definition against a masculine "better" half. Such a woman requires a mate in order to enact many, if not all, aspects of the exclusively feminine role. Her very success as a woman is measured by her ability to "catch" and hold onto a man. His pleasure is the object of her domestic concern, and he is the source of her reinforcement for domestic

---

[4]Inge J. Broverman, Susan R. Vogel, Donald M. Broverman, Frank E. Clarkson, and Paul S. Rosenkrantz, "Sex-Role Stereotypes: A Current Appraisal," *Journal of Social Issues,* 28: 59–78, February, 1972.

[5]Matina S. Horner, "Sex Differences in Achievement Motivation and Performance in Competitive and Non-Competitive Situations," unpublished doctoral dissertation, University of Michigan, 1968.

[6]Mirra Komarovsky, "Cultural Contradictions and Sex Roles: The Masculine Case," *American Journal of Sociology,* 78: 873–884, April, 1972.

tasks. The role prescription dictates that, in order to maintain her femininity, she must play "woman" to his "man."

On the other extreme of the bipolar gender role dimension, it is possible to identify women who define their gender role as stereotypically masculine. This mode of sex-role integration has been referred to as the "grey flannel pantsuit syndrome." Women who adhere to such role definitions deny the stereotypically feminine aspects of their character, and focus on the development of their more "masculine" attributes, such as self-assertion, dominance, and competence. Hair pulled tightly in a bun, attired in severely tailored grey, such women give up their claims to womanhood, remaining single and childless. Their careers flourish.

Like their "feminine" sisters, these stereotypically "masculine" women also need a male "half." However, his function is that of role model, rather than mate. Such a model provides a technical explanation of how the stereotypical masculine role is to be performed. It has been generally assumed that the most common source for such male models is the woman's father, or "the kindly old country doctor who inspired her to study medicine." However, more often, "he" is an abstract representation based on identification with masculine heroes and values. Although aspersions as to the sexual proclivity of the stereotypically masculine woman abound, they have little basis in fact. Adherence to a gender-role definition characteristically ascribed to the opposite sex may represent an arbitrary decision with regard to valued attributes and behaviors without implying anything about the gender of one's sex-object choice.

Thus far, we have characterized women in terms of the extremity of their endorsement of the traits associated with the masculine and feminine anchors of a unitary sex-role dimension. There is ample evidence that many women endorse traits characteristically associated with both the masculine and feminine stereotypes as equally appropriate to the definition of their gender role. Such "androgenous" women do not regard the expression of masculine attributes as threatening to the successful enactment of the female sex role.[7] Neither do they deny the female-valued traits they possess when they engage in behaviors traditionally defined as male sex-role appropriate.

THE BEST OF BOTH WORLDS?

Adherence to an androgenous role definition appears to facilitate the expression of stereotypically masculine achievement needs among women.[8] They have higher educational goals and regard their own accomplishments as equally important as those of their husbands.[9] Freed from the confines of a rigid role definition, men and women who obtain androgenous scores on the Bem Sex Role Inventory endorse a relatively equal number of male and female stereotypical traits as self-descriptive. The behavior of androgenous individuals is determined by situational demands, rather than by role prescriptions. For example, such individuals readily display nurturance when confronted with a tiny kitten, and are independent when under pressure to conform.[10]

In a recent study, we asked three groups of women to indicate on a behavior and an

[7]Peggy Hawley, "What Women Think Men Think," Journal of Counseling Psychology, 193–199, March, 1971.

[8]Gerald S. Lesser, Rhoda Krawitz, and Ralph Packard, "Experimental Arousal of Achievement Motivation in Adolescent Girls," Journal of Abnormal and Social Psychology, 66: 59–66, January, 1963.

[9]Jean Lipman-Blumen, "How Ideology Shapes Women's Lives," Scientific American, 226: 34–42, 1972.

[10]Sandra Bem, "Sex-role Adaptability: One Consequence of Psychological Androgyny," Journal of Personality and Social Psychology (in press).

adjective check list those activities and characteristics which they personally deemed unfeminine. The lists were comprised of a large number of behaviors and traits stereotypically regarded as either masculine or feminine. Professional career women in male-dominated fields endorsed a greater latitude of activities as female sex-role appropriate than did women employed in traditionally female occupations. Housewives' behavioral definitions of femininity were most constructed and almost exclusively female sex-role stereotypic. The fact that professional women endorse a broader latitude of behaviors as female sex-role appropriate suggests that the women in this group maintain a greater variety of acceptable goals. While they perform tasks which are traditionally sex-role inappropriate, they fail to label such tasks as masculine, preferring instead to consider them as feminine.

Although the responses of the women professionals and women employed in traditionally female sex-role appropriate fields (*e.g.,* secretaries) were similar, it was the traditionally employed women who demonstrated the widest latitude of acceptable female characteristics. Professional women were slightly more reluctant to make such androgenous judgments.[11]

One explanation for this finding may lie in the image which professional women wish to portray. Because they subscribe to a life style and perform tasks labeled "masculine" by the general population, they may be anxious that their femininity remains unchallenged by the nature of their work. This would lead them to endorse a more stereotypically feminine image, while sanctioning a broader spectrum of "masculine" behaviors as female sex-role appropriate.

It appears that, for women, an androge-nous gender-role definition represents an additive mode of sex-role acquisition. Such women incorporate stereotypical masculine traits and behaviors into their definition of the feminine role. The core of the gender definition is essentially feminine in the traditional stereotypical sense. The strength of commitment to both roles, however, is strong, but one is not exchanged for the other.

SUPERWOMAN

Adherence to an androgenous role definition may lead to what has been labeled the "superwoman syndrome." In effect, such women attempt to respond simultaneously to the enactment of both the male and female gender roles. The "superwoman" strives competitively for professional advancement while attempting to maintain the social-domestic responsibilities traditionally ascribed to her role as female. Models for such dual achievement currently abound in the media—for example, the popular breakfast drink commercial which presents Dr. X, biochemist, lecturer in a large university, and mother of four beautiful, healthy, and well-adjusted children. Some recent evidence indicates that the media-message has impacted on college-males whose stereotypic characterization of "my ideal woman" parallels the superwoman profile.[12]

Unfortunately, the superwoman of the 1970's is a mere mortal. Unlike Plato's androgene, she was not endowed with two sets of arms and legs and unbounded energy. Commitment to the simultaneous enactment of role behaviors appropriate to both the male and female gender is, at best, exhausting, both physically and emotionally. At worst, it may represent such unrealistic

[11]Charlene Depner and Virginia E. O'Leary, "Achievement-Goal Selection: The Impact of Latitudes of Femininity," unpublished manuscript, 1972.

[12]Virginia E. O'Leary and Charlene Depner, "Changing Sex-Role Stereotypes: College Males' Ideal Female," *Journal of Social Psychology* (in press).

expectations regarding one's own capacities that failure—with its accompanying feelings of conflict, frustration, and doubts about self-worth—is inevitable.

While androgenous gender role definitions may ultimately result in the liberation of both women and men from the constraints imposed upon their behavioral alternatives by adherence to rigidly defined gender roles, the reformulation of gender role inherent in the manifestation of the superwoman syndrome falls short of providing a realistic alternative to stereotypical role-binding. A woman should not feel that any behavioral limitations are placed upon her as a function of her biological gender, but neither should she feel compelled to enact the roles of both men and women in order to "atone" for her gender definition that incorporates activities stereotypically considered masculine as female-sex-role-appropriate. The freedom to endorse traits and behaviors of the opposite sex as gender-role appropriate must also imply the freedom to establish priorities in accordance with realistic goal-setting.

38. NOW MEN'S LIB IS THE TREND

Reprinted from *U. S. News & World Report*

The age-old "battle of the sexes" is taking on new meaning in an America that appears to be moving toward sexual equality at all levels.

Women push ahead in Congress and State legislatures for laws putting an end to all sexual discrimination—in hiring, job advancement, education and use of public facilities.

Wives, increasingly, are going to work and calling for husbands to share household duties from washing the dishes to diapering the baby.

Today, a wide variety of responses to this drive is emerging from the ranks of the nation's 68 million adult men.

Some look favorably on women's rights. Some are hostile—and many, bewildered, are wondering what will be left to men in the times ahead.

In a number of factories, resentful males refuse to co-operate in training women for advancement. Elsewhere, men are launching counterattacks—moving into jobs once reserved for women, and seeking alimony from their wives.

In a less-hostile way, discussion groups of young, college-educated males are pondering man's place in the brave new world of sexual equality, and the problem of how to achieve happiness in marriage to liberated women.

"MEN SCARED TO DEATH"

What such developments reflect, experts say, is deep and growing unease over the new relationship emerging between the sexes—in the home, on the job and socially. Said Dr. Albert E. Ross, a clinical psychologist in Los Angeles:

"What women's liberation is really telling men is, 'You, too, can be free.' But most men are scared to death.

"Most men have a great chance for personal fulfillment they never knew before—if they only pay attention to what is happening around them."

Some men are paying close attention. After watching women encroach into male domains in recent years, they are making the struggle for sexual equality a two-way street.

Increasing numbers of males are going to court, charging employers with sex discrimination. The Equal Employment Opportunity Commission reports that male charges of sex discrimination grew from 278 in the year ended June 30, 1970, to 1,397 during the same period of 1972.

BREAKING BARRIERS

Many of these charges are forcing employers to offer "female" jobs to males for the first time.

After the Supreme Court ruled in 1971 that airlines could not limit flight attendants' jobs to females, most airlines began hiring male stewards.

United Air Lines, for example, now employs 7,191 flight attendants, 447 of whom are male. A spokesman for United said male stewards receive the same pay and duties as the airline's stewardesses.

Other opportunities for men in jobs once considered female are appearing, ironically, as the result of charges of discrimination against women.

Example: As part of its settlement of Government charges of discrimination against women and minorities, the American Telephone & Telegraph Company agreed to hire men for jobs traditionally occupied by women.

An AT&T spokesman said the firm intends ultimately to fill 25 per cent of its clerical jobs and 10 per cent of its telephone-operator positions with men.

During the first 10 months of 1973, the spokesman said, nearly 75 per cent of the clerical personnel hired—a total of 3,348—were men. During the same period, the company tripled the number of its male operators from 2,060 to 6,193.

MORE MALE NURSES

Another field attracting more and more men is nursing. California State University's school of nursing, the nation's largest, noted that its male enrollment has grown from none in 1966 to nearly 70 males among its 1,200 students.

A school official said hospitals are eagerly seeking out males with four-year degrees in nursing. He reported:

"For the most part, patients love these young male nurses and respond quite positively to them. In fact, all of our male seniors have job offers well before they are graduated."

Why are men interested in jobs formerly reserved for women?

WITH PHONE COMPANIES

Telephone-operator jobs appeal to some men because they can arrange their schedules to allow them to work nights and go to college in the daytime.

Others see such jobs as entry-level positions, leading to an eventual promotion and a successful career. James Douglas, 24, quit a job as a Brooklyn hospital worker to become a directory-assistance operator with the New York Telephone Company. He explained:

"I wanted to move up. I'm married, and I could only go so far at the hospital. I took the test at the telephone company, and the operator's job was all they had. So I took it."

Sometimes, men trying to work in women's career fields encounter resistance. A male private nurse, in 1973, told the District of Columbia Court of Appeals that female supervisors at one hospital prevented him on two occasions from reporting to female patients who had requested that he be assigned.

The court agreed that his supervisors' obstruction constituted sex discrimination, a violation of his civil rights.

SOUGHT: EQUAL CONDITIONS

Lawyers for the Equal Employment Opportunity Commission said that more and more of the sex-discrimination charges brought to them by males concern conditions of employment, rather than hiring and promotion policies. Men are demanding working conditions equal to those enjoyed by women, such as these:

• Lounges with sofas and refrigerators so they can relax during work breaks.

• Revision of retirement plans which allow women to retire at age 60 or 62, but require men to be 65 before full retirement.

• Paternity leave to allow men time off from work to help run the family while their wives are giving birth.

In some cases, these demands are being met. A few employers, such as the New York City board of education and the United Church of Christ's Center for Social Action, also in New York City, now grant male employes unpaid leave in order to care for children.

The number of men taking women's jobs is still quite small. Most men currently experience their first brush with sexual equality when a woman invades their department at work.

MALE RESENTMENT

Many men are resentful of the woman's presence and give her little help in learning the skills of her new job. Dr. Margaret Hennig, associate professor of management at Boston's Simmons College, said that some men deliberately set out to sabotage a female co-worker.

"It's perfectly normal for a person who feels vulnerable to strike back," she said. "The foreman may be angry because a woman with more seniority than he has is transferred out of a 'woman's department' and gets more money than he does. We've seen this in a number of factories around here.

"And I know that there are men who would prefer hiring a black male to a white female. It's reasonable to assume that these traditional views would be stronger as one goes down the socioeconomic scale, where the white male would be more vulnerable."

Particularly upset are men who lose promotions to less-experienced women hired to satisfy federal equal-employment guidelines. One public-relations man who recently lost a promotion as head of his department related his experience:

"I was furious. I had worked years for that job, and I was in line for it. Then, the company brought in this woman to fill a quota. If she hadn't been female, she never would have gotten the job."

Such complaints are proliferating as the movement of women into so-called men's jobs picks up speed. Already in the labor force are 31 million women, and more are joining all the time. Nearly half of all wives in their early twenties are employed.

On another front, organized groups of males are beginning to appear in cities across the country to demand equal rights with women in divorce court.

Groups such as Baltimore's "Fathers United for Equal Rights" and Berkeley's "Equal Rights for Fathers" assert that divorce law in most States is set up to protect women—at the expense of their ex-husbands.

"Men as fathers are supposed to have equal rights under the law," said David

Gerfen, 27-year-old founder of the Berkeley organization. "But they don't."

Mr. Gerfen has been divorced for a year and has alternate week-end visiting rights to see his 5-year-old son.

"It's just assumed by everyone—the courts, lawyers, society—that mothers are more fit as custodial parents than fathers," he said. "Often, a father who wants custody of his children must prove the mother unfit."

"Father's rights" groups also claim that traditional alimony and child-support requirements constitute an unreasonable and sometimes crippling financial burden for divorced men. George B. Williams, executive director of Parents Without Partners, a group including divorced men and women, explained:

"We have men in our groups paying huge portions of their income to support their former wives. They can't afford to get married again—even if they want to."

To limit such hardship, courts in many States, like Iowa, deny alimony in most cases.

In other States, courts are striking down laws that have granted alimony to wives only, because this discriminates against husbands.

In some cases, men are even being granted alimony from their ex-wives. The Oakland County Court in Michigan recently granted one man custody of his four children, title to the family home, alimony of $667 a month and payment of $10,000 for legal fees.

The New York State Senate on February 26 approved a bill that would permit needy men to sue their wives for alimony.

FRICTION AT HOME

The drive for sexual equality is causing friction even in some "liberated" households.

Husbands sympathetic to the women's movement are trying to share family chores with their liberated wives. But some wives say these efforts amount to little more than "tokenism." A young Chicago attorney, who described her husband as "more liberated of male prejudices" than most men, complained:

"Sure, he helps clean the house and wash the clothes and dishes. But he does it as a favor. Ultimately, I remain responsible, and so housekeeping is still 'women's work' that my husband condescends to do."

The demands of women's liberation are found by some experts to be striking deeply into the fragile egos of many husbands—sometimes creating serious psychological problems.

Psychologists and family counselors report that many men feel as though they are personally inadequate if their wives want to get an outside job.

One couple in suburban Chicago began seeing a psychiatrist after the wife resumed a long-dormant teaching career.

"I had no objection before the fact," said the husband, who is an attorney for a Chicago-based corporation. "But once my wife started working, I couldn't handle it.

"To me, it was a form of competition for her to work anywhere, and when I saw others interested in her as an individual, it created terrific insecurities within me."

"TIP OF THE ICEBERG"?

Tom Durkin, a marriage counselor and director of the North Berkeley Counseling Service, in California, reported some young men strive so hard to meet the demands of liberated women for full sexual satisfaction that tension produces impotence and other dysfunctions.

"This could be the social disease of the future," he said. "What I'm treating now may be only the tip of the iceberg."

Mr. Durkin said he has met with 30 men in the past year who complained of sexual inadequacies because of demands for satisfaction by their wives or girl friends.

Most of these clients said they had approved of women's liberation at first, but as they lived with it, they became very uncertain.

Through counseling and therapy, Mr. Durkin claimed to have restored roughly two thirds of his clients to sexual adequacy. However, he added, the original relationships, once broken, were never rekindled.

Some men—struggling to adjust to the rigors of sexual equality—are joining "men's liberation groups," which are springing up in several cities across the country.

These groups hold small, informal meetings, called "consciousness-raising sessions," usually in a member's home, to discuss what women's liberation means to men. Warren Farrell, who teaches a course in "sexual politics" at American University in Washington, D.C., said:

"Women's liberation means a chance for men to break free from restrictive, stereotyped sex roles, to get to know women as full-fledged partners in life, not sex objects to be dominated or put on a pedestal."

WAYNE AND BOGART

Says Dr. Robert E. Gould, professor of psychiatry at New York Medical College:

"Society's masculine ideal is John Wayne or Humphrey Bogart—silent, unemotional and strong.

"But most men aren't like that, and I'm not sure they should be. I can picture John Wayne fighting Indians or brawling in a bar, but I can't picture him talking for three hours with a woman.

"Unfortunately, most of us want to be John Wayne.

"The he-man role is very restrictive. I think men should be able to show more emotion—even cry in public. We should be able to develop close friendships with other males, without arousing fears of homosexuality."

The male-liberation movement is tiny, and critics say it will never become widespread. George Gilder, author of the book "Sexual Suicide," argues that men must not be liberated from their traditional roles, lest they run wild, desert their families and indulge in sexual promiscuity and violence.

Men's-liberation leaders disagree. Though the movement is limited now to a few white, middle-class groups in major cities and college communities, they believe that it will grow enormously during the years ahead.

Dr. Gould advises:

"Don't take a short-run view. The movement is just beginning—just as the blacks began to make strides after 1954. It's just a matter of time."

39. CHANGING PATTERNS OF PREMARITAL SEXUAL BEHAVIOR

Anne McCreary Junasz

Growing acceptance of intimate heterosexual behavior between never-married persons has taken place since the publication of the Kinsey reports in the late 1940's and early 1950's, and the incidence of such behavior has increased. Modest predictions based on research indicate that, by the end of the senior year in college, 40% of females and 60% of males will have had sexual intercourse, compared to Kinsey's figures of 25% and 50%, respectively.[1]

PREMARITAL SEXUAL BEHAVIOR

The term "premarital sexual behavior" no longer includes the implication that marriage is to follow. Many young people have no intention of marrying their sexual partners. Thus, in this article, "premarital sexual behavior" will refer to the sexual behavior of never-married persons.

Much human behavior is sexual in nature. We can not really separate sexuality from the total being. It is an integral part of the whole and its influence permeates all interaction. Here, specific sexual behaviors will be discussed. Masturbation, oral-genital activity, homosexuality, and petting will be mentioned briefly, while more extensive reference will be made to heterosexual intercourse and cohabitation.

Of these activities, we know little about masturbation and premarital oral-genital sexual behavior. Since the former is usually a solitary private activity, little concern is evidenced about it. We do know that it is more frequent among males than among females. However, the incidence reported is low. Oral-genital sexual activity is quite a widespread phenomenon premaritally, according to Hunt's findings.[2]

With the increasing recognition and acceptance of homosexuality as one of a variety of sexual life styles, more related information has become available. Reportedly, male homosexuality is increasing and at an earlier age.[3] Perhaps it is now easier to "come out." Perhaps the move from same-sex to heterosexual contact seems too fraught with problems to make the attempt worth while. For some males, too early attempts resulting in a negative experience and the accompanying fear of failure in the heterosexual relationship could result in too early identity closure or in promiscuity. This is incompatible with successful heterosexual adjustment.

Recent research indicates that a pattern of early and frequent dating is typical for many young people who have sexual intercourse at an early age.[4] In this respect, information on early dating behavior is of interest. In 1974, an Illinois study showed

Reprinted from *Intellect* (April 1976) by permission of publisher, pp. 511–514.

[1]Alfred C. Kinsey, Wardell Pomeroy, and Clyde Martin, *Sexual Behavior in the Human Male* (Philadelphia: Saunders, 1948).

[2]Morton Hunt, "Sexual Behavior in the 1970's; Part II, Premarital Sex," *Playboy,* November, 1973, p. 74.

[3]Patricia Miller and William Simon, "Adolescent Behavior: Context and Change," *Social Problems,* 22:58–76, 1974.

[4]Robert A. Lewis, "Parents and Peers: Socialization Agents in Coital Behavior of Young Adults," *The Journal of Sex Research,* 9:156–170, 1973.

that, by their 15th birthday, 50% of the boys and 48% of the girls had engaged in light petting and that, by 17 years of age, the rate had risen to 73% of the males and 69% of the females.[5] In Hunt's *Playboy* survey, more than 50% of single women 18 to 24 years of age had experienced orgasm through petting just in the years previous to the study.

SEXUAL INTERCOURSE

Light petting is usually an initial stage preceding heavy petting and sexual intercourse, and figures for sexual intercourse show increases at earlier ages over those reported by Kinsey in 1953. He found that, regardless of when they were born, three per cent of the women in his study had had intercourse by 15, 20% by 20 years of age, and 33% by 25.[6] In 1971, Kantner and Zelnik reported that, in a national sample of teenaged girls, 14% of the 15-year-olds had had sexual intercourse, with the percentages increasing yearly to 46% of 19-year-olds.[7] Offer, in 1971, interviewing normal adolescent boys from a well-to-do Illinois community, found that 10% of the boys had experienced sexual intercourse by the end of the junior year of high school.[8] In a poll of 23,000 high school student leaders and high achievers, percentages having experienced sexual intercourse were 22% of males and 19% of females.[9] In 1974, Miller and Simon reported that more female adolescents were experiencing intercourse,

but that experienced adolescent males were decreasing in number considerably.[10] The extent of premarital intercourse among adolescents varies, depending upon the sample and the region. Comparison of the figures presented above and those from a Western college town illustrate this point. In 1975 the Jessors reported on nonvirgin high school students as follows: in 10th grade, 21% of males, 26% of females; in 11th grade, 28% of males, 40% of females; in 12th grade, 33% of males, 55% of females.[11] These figures are much higher than those previously reported for high school students. In fact, the percentages for females are larger than those generally quoted for college girls.

A general figure on premarital coitus of 40% for females and 60% for males by the end of college emerges from many studies. The Jessors' figures for college students are much higher than this general figure. By the end of the four years of college, the following rates of nonvirginity were reported: first year, 46% of males, 51% of females; second year, 65% of males, 70% of females; third year, 74% of males, 80% of females; fourth year, 82% of males, 85% of females.

It is evident then that, compared to Kinsey's figures of the 1950's (25% for females and 50% for males), rates of premarital sexual intercourse are increasing. The increase varies regionally, with a noticeably larger increase for females than for males, indicating the easing of the double standard. In addition, more young people have their initial experience in early and middle adolescence.

In order to interpret this increase in premarital sexual intercourse, one must consider how often and under what circum-

[5]Miller and Simon, *op. cit.*

[6]Alfred C. Kinsey, W. B. Pomeroy, and C. E. Martin, *Sexual Behavior in the Human Female* (Philadelphia: Saunders, 1953).

[7]John F. Kantner and Melvin Zelnik, "Sexual Experience of Young Unmarried Women in the United States," *Family Planning Perspectives,* 4:9–18, 1972.

[8]Daniel Offer, D. Marcus, and Joy L. Offer, "A Longitudinal Study of Normal Adolescent Boys," *American Journal of Psychiatry,* 126:917–924, 1970.

[9]*National Survey of High School High Achievers* (New York: Merit Publishing Co., 1970).

[10]Miller and Simon, *op. cit.*

[11]Shirley L. Jessor and Richard Jessor, "Transition from Virginity to Nonvirginity Among Youth: A Social-Psychological Study Over Time," *Developmental Psychology,* 11:473–484, 1975.

stances it occurs, for answers to these questions will indicate whether or not young people are sexually active and promiscuous. Most studies indicate that females limit themselves to only one partner, while males are more likely to have multiple partners. Interestingly, whites are reported to have more partners than blacks, and, for almost all teenagers, frequency of intercourse is very low.

Increasingly, the level of the relationship has become the prime determinant of the decision to have or not to have sexual intercourse. Reiss' work and his scale of premarital sexual permissiveness stimulated much research, which has consistently revealed a movement toward a permissiveness-with-affection sexual standard. This has expanded the formerly narrow limits of "engagement or in love with."[12] While marriage is not a prerequisite, many young females still hope to marry their partners.

Recently, the focus of concern about premarital sexual intercourse has shifted from the college student down to the high school student. Since 40% of babies born out of wedlock are born to teenaged mothers, the ramifications of this for the infant, the mother, and for society as a whole justify this concern. The Jessors have isolated these variables which may enable them to predict which students will lose their virginity during high school years:

They tend to have higher values on and expectations for independence, to value and expect achievement less, to be more tolerant of deviance and less religious, to have friends whose views agree with those of their parents and who influence them more than do their parents, to have parents who disapprove less of deviant behavior and friends, and who provide more models for

deviant behavior, and finally to have engaged more in general deviance and less in conventional activity related to church and school.[13]

There appears to be a constellation of related behaviors for those who are irresponsible sexually. A study at the Institute for Juvenile Research in Chicago revealed a correlation between the use of drugs and alcohol and the incidence of juvenile delinquency and premarital sexual activity, and similar findings were reported by Vener.[14]

COHABITATION

Yet another aspect of premarital sexual behavior is occurring with increasing frequency, particularly with college students. Estimates of the extent of "cohabitation" or "living together under conditions which approximate those of the marriage situation" now range from 20% to 40% of the student body, with numbers increasing from freshman to senior year. Moreover, there is wide acceptance of the practice— 80% of students questioned at a midwestern university said that they would cohabit if they had the opportunity and the desire, although only 20% were cohabiting at the time.[15]

From those who are cohabiting, emerges a picture which appears to be as varied as is the marriage scene, in terms of motivation, interaction and outcome. Macklin's Cornell University subjects seemed to drift together gradually, either because they enjoyed being together or because it was more convenient. Often, no sexual intercourse was involved or not for periods of time.

---

[12]Ira L. Reiss, *The Social Context of Premarital Sexual Permissiveness* (New York: Holt, Rinehart and Winston, 1967).

[13]Jessor and Jessor, *op. cit.,* p. 480.

[14]Miller and Simon, *op. cit.,* and Arthur M. Vener and Cyrus S. Stewart, "Adolescent Sexual Behavior in Middle America Revisited: 1970–1973," *Journal of Marriage and the Family,* 36:728–735, 1974.

[15]Ibtihaj Arafat and Betty Yorburg, "On Living Together Without Marriage," *Journal of Sex Research,* May, 1973, pp. 97–105.

These students had mixed feelings, with only half of them having a successful experience. Problems included overinvolvement, lack of identity, jealousy, lack of privacy and space, guilt, and fear related to concealment from parents. Sexual problems were common, including lack of orgasm, differing interests, and inhibitions. On the positive side were deeper understanding of self, knowledge of what is involved in a relationship, and clarification of what they want in marriage. Macklin's students (both cohabiting and non-cohabiting) saw marriage as a negative thing. However, for Peterman's cohabitors, marriage was still the most popular choice of arrangement as a future goal.[16]

The stage of the relationship at the time that cohabitation begins appears to be a strong determinant of the success of the experience. Three-quarters of Thorman's University of Texas subjects had entered the arrangement with strong affection—while they were not engaged, they were not casual daters. They were free to have sex with others, but would not think of it. The sexual aspect of living together was of secondary importance—the relationship was more important and emotional security, mutual affection, and loyalty were valued. These students felt that openness and honesty were important and that there was more dignity and meaning in this new pattern of intimacy than in furtive experimentation. Few of these students had sexual problems and 70% expected cohabiting to continue indefinitely.[17]

Investigations of background factors

which may be common to cohabitors are just beginning, and some of the findings point to desire for intimacy as a motivating factor. At Pennsylvania State University, a larger number of cohabiting females were Catholic than Protestant, and, for males, separated or divorced mothers were frequent among cohabitors.[18] Another study revealed that both male and female cohabitant groups had less close relationships with the same-sex parent during high school years, and also saw themselves as having some of the stereotyped sex-role characteristics of the opposite sex.[19]

SOCIETAL CHANGES

To be meaningful, any behavior must be viewed against the environmental backdrop. What are the societal changes which have led to current attitudes toward, and involvement in, sexual activity? The development of a highly technological society has had two major effects. First, travel and job opportunities have expanded, resulting in movement away from the homogeneous family center or community to the more heterogeneous urban center. Secondly, the proliferation of new mass media resulted in widespread dissemination of different ideas. Thus, the breakdown of the extended family and the insular community began. As a result, the firm guidelines for sexual behavior set down by church and reinforced by community weakened or, in some instances, disappeared. This created a vacuum to be filled by other sources. However, the logical source—the family—has also changed. As increasing numbers of mothers entered the labor force, maternal supervision and control of children lessened. This

---

[16]Eleanor D. Macklin, "Heterosexual Cohabitation Among Unmarried College Students," *The Family Coordinator,* 21:463–472, 1972; and Dan J. Peterman, Carl A. Ridley, and Scott M. Anderson, "A Comparison of Cohabiting and Noncohabiting College Students," *Journal of Marriage and the Family,* 36:344–354, 1974.

[17]George Thorman, "Living Together Unmarried," *The Humanist,* March-April, 1974, pp. 15–17.

[18]Peterman, *op. cit.*

[19]Edna C. Guittar and Robert A. Lewis, "Self-Concept Among Unmarried Cohabitants," unpublished paper presented at the Annual Meeting of the National Council on Family Relations, St. Louis, 1974.

gap in parental influence was filled by other transmittors of values, including peers, teachers, other adults, and mass media.

Technological advances were accompanied by the need for more highly educated people. As a result, college and university populations spiralled. At the same time, these institutions no longer acted as *parentis in loco*. Without these guardians of morality and virtue, students were made fully responsible for their own sexual decisions, in a milieu which encouraged cross-fertilization of ideas, learning-through-doing, questioning, and thinking. This has placed an added burden upon those youth who are still attempting to master the crucial "identity crisis," and the over-all effect has been to produce a youthful generation which refuses to accept arbitrary rules and regulations about sexual behavior.

In addition, the increasing emphasis on individual rights to self-enhancement and fulfillment, the women's liberation movement, and a high incidence of broken homes have resulted in large numbers of young people, disenchanted with marriage and the idea of raising children, content to live independently and to delay marriage. Still another factor is the impact of the publication and popularization of the research of Masters and Johnson, with emphasis on standards of sexual performance in terms of quantity and quality. The resulting pressures for achievement in terms of orgasm and sexual satisfaction for oneself and one's partner have caused doubt and anxiety for both young people and their parents.

THE OVER-ALL PICTURE AND THE PROBLEM

While traditional influences appear to be waning in strength, evidence suggests that, for many young people, the family and parents still exert a strong influence on degree of sexual permissiveness and that involvement in church activities is negatively related to premarital sexual intercourse. Also, where higher education is a goal, females are more likely to delay sexual intercourse. In addition, cultural norms are reflected in regional differences.

What is new is concern for the quality of the relationship and the realization that, if morality is involved in sexual interaction, true morality rests in the meaning and circumstances attached to the activity, and not merely in the absence or presence of a legal document. Secondly, there exists a wider range of choice, and the responsibility of choice and for the ensuing behavior has shifted to include early adolescence as well as young adulthood. Moreover, in the absence of firm models and the presence of varied examples and sometimes conflicting information, choices become more difficult. Many of the models include troubled families (with one-third of all marriages facing divorce at some time) in which there is little time to relate or to demonstrate concern for others.

While much information is available through mass media, emphasis is placed on less frequent aspects of sexual behavior and upon the problematic situations which arise. Much of this behavior is not universally socially acceptable (such as homosexuality, transsexualism, and abortion). There is increasing emphasis on individual sexual rights and freedom, often to the exclusion of cooperation and interdependence. Also overemphasized are woman's right to orgasm and man's need to prove his potency. Increasingly, sexual activity is lifted out of the context of daily normal living and the act itself is isolated from the affective context, the meaningful setting— rather, it is depersonalized, portrayed and displayed as an object or activity to be used and abused.

As a result, young people are formulating

a whole new set of rules to govern sexual behavior. Under these new rules, the final commitment of marriage is taken very seriously and entered into only after much experience and careful consideration. A close relationship, loyalty, and fidelity are attributes to be valued and sought after. In *Future Shock,* Alvin Toffler predicted that serial marriage—a pattern of successive, temporary marriages—is the mainstream marriage pattern of tomorrow. Perhaps young people are attempting to circumvent this predicted pattern and, through cohabitation, to postpone marriage until this serious step can be taken with greater assurance and confidence. Cohabitation may become a developmental stage en route to marriage or even a substitute for it.

At any rate, it seems likely to persist. As long as financial resources rest with parents, this pattern does not seem likely to filter down to the high school student. However, if we are aware of the adolescent's need for a close relationship and if we recognize cohabitation as a pattern which evidently meets this need, perhaps our task and our challenge is, as Maddock suggests, to somehow try to determine to what extent and in what manner intimacy can and should be established as an adolescent experience.[20] Within the Eriksonian framework, resolution of this crisis is assigned to young adulthood, and the results of too early attempts at resolution are uncertain. We do know that those who begin dating early also have sexual intercourse early, marry early, bear children early, and have more children out of wedlock. We also know that sex is used to solve other problems, including those of family breakup, inadequate self-concept, and career.

SUGGESTIONS

Faced with the difficulties and problems inherent in our changing society, young people are attempting to work out for themselves a meaningful and viable pattern of premarital sexual behavior. They are seeking ways of meeting their need for warmth and closeness and, at the same time, incorporating individual values internalized from home, church, and parents. In addition, they must keep pace with personal and career goals which are unique to the last half of the 20th century.

For adults who will not live to see the next century, it is difficult to prepare and assist those who will bear and raise the children of that era. Those young people who know who they are and where they are going in other respects will be able to deal in a responsible and effective manner with their sexual urges. In this respect, four suggestions deserve consideration, suggestions related to research and teaching:

· Teach decision-making skills related to responsible sexual behavior, as outlined in Junasz's chain of sexual decision-making.[21]

· Understand the importance of self-concept, motivational patterns, personal beliefs, and personal controls on sexual behavior.

· Emphasize the need for intimacy and the stages which are manageable and rewarding from a developmental point of view.

· Concentrate efforts on portraying sexuality and sexual behavior in the mass media, within the normal family setting, as an integral and vital aspect of the total life cycle.

[20]James W. Maddock, "Sex in Adolescence: Its Meaning and Its Future," *Adolescence,* 8:326–341, 1973.

[21]Anne McCreary Junasz, "A Chain of Sexual Decision-Making," *The Family Coordinator,* January, 1975, pp. 43–49.

40.   WHY MARRIAGES TURN SOUR—AND HOW TO GET HELP

Interview with James Lieberman, M.D.,
Psychiatrist and Marriage Counselor
Reprinted from *U. S. News & World Report*

Q: Dr. Lieberman, is something seriously wrong with the American family as an institution? Is it outmoded?

A: No, it's only outmoded if you believe that 100 per cent of the adults should be married and should be having children. But if we say that maybe 75 or 80 per cent should be married and even fewer would be expected to have children, then I think the family is very viable.

We've moved away from the viewpoint that if you're not married, you're odd. We're going into a situation where most people will still want to get married, and will do so, but a little later on in life. They will be able to use birth control more effectively, so the family will be formed by deliberate choice rather than by chance.

As a result, families will be better able to cope with stresses of modern industrialized society in which the family may need two wage earners for a while and may not be able to get a house at all—or at least not as soon as was the case with young couples until very recently.

Q: Is the family losing many of its functions?

A: Yes and no. In the old days, most of the health care and nursing care used to be at home, not in hospitals. Most of the education used to be at home, not at schools and universities. Most of the recreation used to be devised by the family.

But the family's role still exists in setting rules for kids, in having a place to get together and in providing best access to ties and a sense of stability. As far as the psychological intangibles go: Where do you form your ego? Where do you form your identity?

One fifth of the nation's families move every year. They don't get used easily to living in Dubuque, Ia., or wherever they move to, but they get used to being with the same people in their family. That really means the family is every bit as important as it always was.

Q: Why does the divorce rate keep going up?

A: What has happened in the late 1960s and early 1970s is a long-term trend that coincides with development of women's rights. More women in the work force means that more women are economically in a position to undertake living alone if necessary. Also, they are meeting more men —a wider selection than the mailman and the meterman. And many States have instituted more-reasonable divorce laws.

Q: Will divorces continue to rise?

A: I don't think they will, because the prevailing age of first marriage has been going up, which is a good thing. Teen-age marriage, of course, is associated with a high divorce rate. Ten years from now—or maybe even sooner—we'll begin to see a lowering of the divorce rate because the people who did decide to get married were more mature and less likely to get divorced.

Q: There seems to be growth in the divorce rate of people who have been married for 25 or 30 years. Why?

A: The growth is not as great as we've been led to believe. A few years ago, I read that there was a 52 per cent increase. Well, that is talking about a rise from 3.3 per cent to 5 per cent of all divorces. It's a very small proportion and the increase is much less than with the younger marriage breakups.

And then the number of years that people stay married to the same person is much greater now than it was a generation ago because people live longer.

Q: What do marriage crises generally center on—money, sex?

A: Or in-laws. Those are the three that are usually cited, and I don't know of any research that would tell us or give us a weighting that we could be sure of. But in my own practice, I would put sex and intimacy generally—that is communication—first. Problems involving relatives or family members and money would probably run close behind.

Q: Is fidelity still important?

A: I think so. Trust takes time to build, and infidelity often destroys it.

Some of my colleagues get attention by saying that "swinging" is all right. However, the number of couples who do this open experimenting with other sexual partners is still very small—well under 5 per cent.

Q: What do you find to be the actual damage that is done by "swinging"?

A: It may not hurt all the people who do it, but I see the ones who don't adapt to it, and I've seen some who have given it up. It's hard enough to maintain a balanced relationship with one person; try to do it as a couple with other couples, and it's really rough. A degree of jealousy is normal in a love relationship and shouldn't be trifled with.

Q: How can a couple tell if their marriage is in trouble?

A: I'd say it would be a sign of oncoming trouble if husband and wife don't have anything to say to each other, are not happy being around each other and are keeping themselves busy so that they are essentially distracted from each other.

Q: By communicating, do you mean in-depth and intense talks—or just the ability to chat amiably?

A: I would say both. If it's an amiable chat and one party is dissatisfied, then that dissatisfied party has to be able to go beyond and say, "I'm feeling this way," and get into it.

One study found that the average couple, after a year of marriage, spends about 37 minutes a week in exclusive conversation with each other—some very low figure—and yet it's believable.

Q: Is a lack of communication worse than having a knockdown, drag-out fight?

A: It's hard to say. People think that psychiatry is in favor of getting everything out, but that's not true. There's no license to ventilate at the expense of someone else's integrity. If "letting it all hang out" means saying, "I feel depressed, I feel alone, I need to talk," that's one thing. But if it means accusing the other person or hurling abuse, that's something else. Physical violence is absolutely taboo in a relationship of a civilized husband and wife.

When I see people engaging in verbal violence, I assume that the only reason they're still with each other is because they have a sado-masochistic interlock. That is, one of them gets something out of hurling abuse, the other from being abused.

Q: Is it often helpful for a married person to discuss his or her family problems with a friend?

A: It depends whether that friend is being used really as a weapon against the spouse—where you tell the friend: "This is what he's doing to me," or "I'm right, and isn't she terrible?"

Some people use their children, and that's the worst thing of all because it's not just unfaithful to the spouse but damaging to the child. If the spouse is so bad you can't handle the problem, then you should go to a professional.

Normally a professional can keep you from "grinding an ax" by getting to the point—however unpleasant. For example, if you say your husband didn't come home until 3 a.m., the friend might not want to ask about your sexual relationship. A professional would ask you.

Q: When should one turn to a professional?

A: When you can imagine yourself telling a friend with your problem: "For heaven's sake, don't just keep talking to me. Go see a professional."

I see people coming in who have finally reached the end of their rope. A lot of people around them knew it, but they couldn't bring themselves to call a spade a spade. If they had done so, the marriage might not have deteriorated so much. If you like somebody enough and you see him or her in physical pain, you say, "Go see a doctor." It's the same way with emotional pain.

Q: Once a person decided on professional help, should the choice be a marriage counselor or a family counselor?

A: The American Association of Marriage and Family Counselors includes both. In fact, they are the most interdisciplinary group because they include social workers, psychologists, psychiatrists, clergymen and a few with other degrees in behavioral science.

Q: How many counselors are there?

A: There are only about 2,000 members of the AAMFC, and they have high standards—a master's degree or equivalent, and other requirements.

Because of sheer numbers, the persons who usually handle marital problems are psychiatrists, psychologists and social workers, who are not known primarily as marriage counselors. In fact, for over half the people seeking psychiatric care, the No. 1 complaint relates to their marital situations.

Now, psychiatrists have status in this country, but they don't all necessarily have the training. Not many of them, for example, have ever been trained to work with a husband and wife in the same room at the same time because they come out of the medical tradition in which you treat one person at a time.

I would say that about 25 percent of psychiatrists currently practicing really have had any experience working with families and married couples. This means that if you're going to go to a psychiatrist for a marital or family problem, you should ask whether this person will see your spouse with you.

Q: Will a family counselor bring children into discussions?

A: That's right—but again there are variations. Some counselors will work with the whole family all the time.

Q: Is that your policy?

A: No. I think there are some issues where kids are more of a hindrance than a help. For instance, you can't really talk about adult sexuality with children in the room.

Q: Are there quacks in this profession?

A: Yes.

Q: How do you avoid them?

A: Marriage and family counselors have master's degrees, and psychiatrists, of course, have their credentials.

Psychologists and social workers do a lot of this work, too, calling it "psychotherapy" or "marital therapy." Psychologists are increasingly being licensed, requiring them not only to have Ph.D.'s but also to pass a board examination. Social workers are licensed and accredited by national social-work agencies.

The consumer should ask what the person's training is, where he was trained and whether he's licensed. For health-insurance purposes, you have to know these things. If you're seeing a psychiatrist—an M.D.—or a psychologist, social worker or counselor who is affiliated with an M.D., your health-insurance plan may pay for it, and that's important.

We still don't have the kind of regulation we need, and I would regretfully point out that there are even bad practitioners who have all the credentials you want. Why? Because in the medical and other professions, too, we don't have relicensing or recertification, so a person could have graduated from medical school any time in the last 50 years and still be practicing without any further test.

Q: Would a family doctor or clergyman be likely to offer guidance on whom to get?

A: They should. Dr. William H. Masters and Mrs. Virginia Johnson [the sex-research team] say: Call your local medical society to avoid quacks in the sex-therapy business.

Clergymen also can often make a good referral, and some have had training in family or marriage counseling.

Q: Are Transcendental Meditation, yoga, and encounter groups helpful in solving marriage problems?

A: I think they are for some people. Encounter, I think, has passed its crest. I don't think there's any instant intimacy. Group therapy takes time just like anything else. You do not change deep-seated attitudes overnight; you don't do it with "primal screams," touching or cuddling with strangers.

I don't consider myself knowledgeable about TM. I respect it a little bit more because it doesn't claim to do anything in an instant. It's a longer-term thing, and just common sense would suggest that if you can get into a new pattern and take 20 minutes out every morning for meditation, it will have an effect.

HELP CAN BE COSTLY IN TIME AND MONEY

Q: Is marriage or family counseling very expensive?

A: Unfortunately, yes. A psychiatric hour now runs about $40. That's the 50-minute hour. Medical insurance might pay for some of it, depending on the plan. But many plans don't cover psychiatric treatment at all. Others range as high as 80 per cent of the cost.

Q: What's the usual duration of a course of treatment—not necessarily psychiatric, but in general?

A: Off the top of my head, I'd say once a week for a year would be about what I would expect. Some people do well in three months; some people do well in three or four years.

There's another recourse, and that's couples in a group, which I think is an excellent thing. If you get four couples in a group, the leader can charge $15 a head—or $30 a couple—for an hour and a half. They'll get a little longer time than they would otherwise. They will see other couples working out their problems; they'll get to know these couples over a year's time. They'll also get less attention to their own problems, but they will be learning through other people's problems. It will cost them $30 for the couple instead of $40 for an individual per week.

Q: Is treatment lengthy because people wait until the marriage is almost on the rocks before seeing a counselor?

A: Unfortunately, yes. The patterns are very ingrained by the time they get to us.

Q: How did people manage before there was psychiatry or counseling?

A: Not very well. There's an idea that the good old days were really good—but I don't think they were. Marital happiness today is greater than ever, in spite of the fact that the divorce rate is high. And one of the reasons it's high is because people aren't putting up with what their parents and grandparents had to put up with.

Q: Didn't people in the past pay more attention to the idea of lifelong committment than some young people do today?

A: Probably, yes. With divorce easier to get, some people simply won't work as hard at making a go of marriage. And it takes a tremendous amount of work.

Q: Should couples stay together for the children's sake?

A: No. When I see married people with children who are complaining about marital problems, I tell them that staying together "for the sake of the children" is a mistake. As soon as I say that it clears the air, because the usual reality is that the people are afraid to face up to loneliness so they're saying, "It's for the kids that I'm keeping the marriage together."

They're making it sound altruistic when in fact it's selfish. Make them face that very hard reality; then start working from there.

Q: Does a psychiatrist consider that he's failed if he can't patch up a troubled marriage?

A: I don't, because it's not always desirable—or possible. In Los Angeles, when the court instituted some predivorce counseling, about half the applicants for divorce reconciled and were still together a year later. I consider that a good result.

Q: How is sexual equality changing the institution of marriage?

A: In general, it's giving women more options, and it has had a liberating effect on men, too. For instance, divorced men are getting more access to custody of children. And both sexes are learning that they don't have to rush into marriage—or get married at all.

Q: Are "trial marriages" a good trend?

A: I think, on balance, they're going to be a positive help in contributing to the rising age of marriage. They also go against the idea that the marriage license is a li-

cense for legal sex. Holy matrimony was, all too often, really a sex license. And when the sexual satisfaction tapered off, a lot of those teen-age marriages ended in divorce.

The ability to have sex before marriage without shame doesn't mean everyone should do it. But it does mean that there's no real excuse to get married just for sex. Marriage should be composed of other values, too. And chastity is a value: There are some couples for whom premarital sex will not work, and they should not be pushed into it.

HAPPIER HOMES ... AND BETTER PARENTS

Q: How will the old concepts of marriage and family change in the years ahead?

A: If you want to see what marriage of the future will look like, look at today's marriages that were contracted by people who were college-educated, or nearly so, and who were in their mid-20s.

Those people, I think you'll find, are more nearly equal as partners. They communicate more to each other. They have a better sex life. They have good, effective family planning. The divorce rate is not as high among them as it is for teen-agers. When there are divorces, it's because their fulfillment standards are high, not because their marriages are awful.

Q: Will people be better parents in times ahead?

A: Yes, I believe so. They're not going to be having kids by accident, so children will be more wanted.

We'll see better-educated and more-mature parents than a generation ago.

Q: Won't those benefits be offset by the increase in working mothers?

A: If we provide good part-time child care, the mothers will come home with a lot more energy and interest in their children than if they have to stay at home all day.

41. "NOBODY KNOWS MY NAME"—THE EFFECT OF ROOTLESSNESS ON YOUNG PEOPLE

Vance Packard

What does a youngster whose family has moved into five different towns during the eight years of his lifetime say when asked where he is from? What happens to his sense of place? What training is he getting in uprootedness as a way of life?

Eugene Jennings of Michigan State University, who has conferred with many business managers in their homes, overheard the son of one mobile manager ask his dad when they were going to move again. Knowing that they had lived in the community for almost two years, the son was starting to wonder when they would be packing.

And a young man who had been raised in the military establishment confessed to me that since boyhood he had had difficulty developing close friendships. He was certain the reason was that while he was growing up his close friends were from military families and were usually rotated out every two years. The pain of repeatedly losing friends caused him unwittingly, he suspected, to start shunning close friendships.

Mobility as a major cause of social fragmentation in America obviously has some sort of impact on the millions of youngsters who find themselves being moved to a new locality each year. The majority of these young people are the children of highly mo-

bile, affluent parents; military parents; and migrant workers.

Yet the impact of mobility on children is not readily predictable. It varies with the family. Many children are resilient and seemingly learn to cope readily. They are less inhibited than their parents about making acquaintances in new neighborhoods. A year can seem like a long time to a four-year-old. And moves often do contribute to broadening young people's horizons and training them to respond to challenges.

A great many children reach the age of 10 without ever finishing a single grade in the same school where they began it. In Montvale, New Jersey, I found that only two out of 110 high school seniors questioned were now living in the house where they were born. Nearly half had spent some of their high school years elsewhere. An official of Florida Tech University told of one student who had attended 17 different schools. And a wife of a manager in Darien, Connecticut, who had moved 16 times in her 22 years of marriage, told me: "Our youngest son, now 15, has been subjected to three different school systems in the past 12 months. This is our price paid for progress."

But what is that price for youngsters in general?

In the several studies I've encountered that compared the school grades or IQ test scores of mobile and nonmobile students, only minor or subtle differences seem apparent, and even these are not entirely consistent from study to study.[1] Mobile parents who worry about the commonly held belief that they handicap their children academically by moving apparently can ease up on their worrying, at least if they are not super-mobile, if they don't keep moving during school years, and if their children are reasonably good students.

R. Keith Thomas, principal of the Loy School for children of the highly mobile military personnel at Great Falls, Montana, mentioned one interesting thing he had noticed. He said the children of above-average ability tend to adjust to a new school situation rather well, whereas adjustment is often a hardship on the student who is average or below average in ability. Schools vary in what they teach at different grade levels, and for the struggling student the frustration of academic problems caused by moving can lead to emotional problems.

The age of the children at the time of a major move unquestionably is a major determinant of how well they will adjust to the move socially and emotionally. The three- and four-year-olds and those from 13 to 18 appear to be most vulnerable to difficulties. Louise Bates Ames of the famed Gesell Institute of Child Development in New Haven, Connecticut, advised me:

"At the very earliest ages (infancy), children probably don't mind too much. Then you come to the rigid preschool years (21 months to four years for some) when everything has to be *just the same* (even within a house or room). Moving may be quite traumatic in that it disturbs this rigidity. Five- to 10-year-olds might, hopefully, accept moving without too much trauma, but then come the teens, when youngsters' lives are *shattered* by leaving their hometowns and their hometown friends."

The problem for teen-agers is not only that of leaving their old friends but of finding friends in the new town. Loneliness may become a problem because teen-agers take longer to make friends than grammar school youngsters. By junior and senior high school, cliques have become a big thing. A school official in Darien, Connecticut, bluntly explained the incoming teen-agers' problem there:

"Often new students are not accepted, are isolated, and look miserable. If newcomers are in the seventh, eighth, or ninth grades, the adjustment is more difficult than if they were in lower or upper grades. The ninth graders' adjustment is the most difficult. When young people are in the seventh to the ninth grades, mothers are concerned that their children get in the right set and push them into dating. But if the newcomers are from affluent families, they will fit in."

A mother who called the ninth-and tenth-grade years the ones that are "murderous" for newcomers said that such youngsters from high-mobile families tended, under the pressure for popularity, to get on "the fast track" and to get "too far out in their behavior."

At a forum I was conducting with members of the Darien Newcomers Club, one mother raised an extremely interesting point. She asked: "How do parents who are new in a town help their children evaluate their friends? How can parents counsel

---

[1]See "The Effect of Pupil Mobility upon Academic Achievement," *National Elementary Principal,* April 1966; C. H. Gilliland, "The Relationship to Achievement of Mobility in the Elementary School," University Microfilms, Inc., Ann Arbor, Michigan, 1959; E. D. Tetreau and J. V. Fuller, "Some Factors Associated with the School Achievement of Children in Migrant Families," *Elementary School Journal,* February 1942; Carla Fitch and Josephine Hoffer, "Geographical Mobility and Academic Achievement of a Group of Junior High Students," *Journal of Home Economics,* May 1964; and Frank Farmer, "The Effect of School Change on the Achievement of Military Dependent Children," paper presented to the California Educational Research Association, Palo Alto, California, March 3–4, 1961.

wisely since they don't know what kind of parents these friends of their children have?"

This woman, I felt, was unwittingly putting her finger on one substantial cause of the so-called generation gap. The network of parental and community guidance that traditionally has helped orient teen-agers as they hit the testing phase for adulthood is coming apart. Too many of the people who would normally be involved in the process are strangers. Teen-agers have no frame of reference on what constitutes appropriate behavior and thus are forced to make their own decisions. For guidance, they turn to their peer group, which at the early teen level instinctively tends to take an adversary position regarding adults and adult values.

And as parents continue moving, teen-agers must continually become acceptable to new peer groups. If the moving continues while the teen-ager is away at college or boarding school, he comes "home" on vacations and in the summer to a totally friendless environment. After a few days, his inclination is to take off in search of his scattered friends.

One mother I know who moved several times in the United States and abroad while her children were of college age made this further observation: "The worst thing about moving as the children get older and into college is that you find you have dropped them all over the landscape—from California to Rome."

After college, the graduate usually doesn't seek employment in the "hometown" where his parents are currently living. He looks elsewhere. Thus, social fragmentation is reaching into the family not only because of divorce but because of generalized mobility.

As these cases indicate, the mobility of Americans intensifies the so-called generation gap. If, as projected, the mobility accel-

erates, the gap will become even wider and social fragmentation will probably increase.

Probably the most highly mobile Americans are the hundreds of thousands of migratory people who help to harvest the nation's fruits and vegetables. These migrants follow three main streams: the East Coast stream that has its main staging area in the spring around Belle Glade, Florida; the West Coast stream that operates principally in California, with its main staging area at El Centro in the Imperial Valley; and the main stream, whose staging ground is south Texas, particularly the town of McAllen in Hidalgo County.

McAllen's school system has established a special school with an extended-day program to help migrants' children go north without falling hopelessly behind. Its school year, 35 days shorter than the regular school year, runs from the end of October to early May. Still, many children arrive late and leave early. Many families start moving north around April 15.

Migratory workers in Texas have spent the median number of about six years in school. They mostly speak a special Mex-Tex language, which mixes Spanish, Indian, and English. On the road, most let the crew boss, who is often a relative, speak for them. He also negotiates terms of employment. The average crew of workers is about 20, plus children; but some caravans have more than 100 persons.

An important point to remember in considering migratory workers: Although there are truly uprooted migratory workers in America, such as the Anglos who are simply drifters in central California, the Mexican Americans from south Texas do have significant roots.

During the time they are on the road, they are usually with kinfolk or people they have known for years, so that, like a nomadic tribe, they remain a cohesive group. Thus, the adults have relatively little basis for being plagued by a sense of uprootedness or loneliness. However, their children are hard hit. They are torn from their schools and are moved from one bewildering town to another, where they frequently spend long stretches alone as their parents work; and local youngsters often treat them as aliens.

The Mexican American migrants attach enormous importance to returning annually to their homes in south Texas. One of the nation's leading authorities on migratory workers, James Nix of the U.S. Department of Labor, relates:

"I was surprised at the number of these migratory workers who are homeowners back in Texas or wherever their home base is. One of our studies showed that 48 percent owned their own home or were in the process of buying one. This means that they are higher in home ownership than the general U.S. population."

Quite probably, this purchase of a home reflects their extraordinary need for a sense of place.

The possible negative impact of frequent moving on the mental health of children of military parents, migrant workers, or highly mobile, affluent mothers and fathers remains to be tested and pinpointed by anything resembling an impressive body of studies. One systematic study in the 1940's found evidence that childhood disorders increase with frequent changes of residence. A former director of children's services at the Menninger Clinic, in speaking of the emotional disorders some children undergo *temporarily* in the course of a move, added that feelings of loss, helplessness, and isolation "become more than temporary if the child is already anxious about his relationship with his parents." But most of the evidence that there is negative impact comes from convictions developed by academic experts and by cases in point.

Sociologist Philip Slater has pondered extensively the impact of the fact that the whole socioeconomic structure of the United States is moving toward producing a society of "temporary systems." These would take the form of task forces organized around problems to be solved by groups of relative strangers. The concept would apply primarily to handling work problems. But even marriage, he suggests, conceivably may become a temporary system tied to a particular locality and task.

Convinced that a child moving from place to place suffers social impairment, he advised me: "I still find it difficult to imagine how the raising of children can be reconciled with temporary systems. I think, in fact, that it cannot be. Of course, children grow up one way or another, and I do not in any way mean to imply that under such an arrangement everyone would end up in a mental hospital. The kinds of personality development we could expect under such a system are simply incompatible with our society as it now exists. Something altogether new might emerge from this. I really cannot imagine what it would be."

Another academician who, a few years ago, expressed concern for mobile children was social philosopher Helen Merrell Lynd at Sarah Lawrence College. She noted: "It is hard to overrate the importance of continuity for children. Some children I know began to stutter after their families had made several moves that for the parents had been 'a good vacation' or 'a step up in the world.'"

Children of fathers who are commuter-travelers may experience some of the same negative influences as the children of highly mobile parents. The *Wall Street Journal* reported that an investigation which involved interviewing commuters to New York concluded that they felt their commuting had hurt their relationships with their families. How might it hurt? Consider these three comments by three people in Darien, our prototype commuter town.

• A junior high school official: "If the father works nearby, say in the Stamford-Greenwich area, the youngsters can understand, and if the commuting hours are moderate, the father commands a good deal more authority with his children. Many problems at school stem from the fact that parents are not home. The male image that ought to be there is lacking. Often both parents are working. I frequently have to contact parents about disciplinary problems and can't get either of them because both are working or the wife is running around all day to teas and bridge parties."

• A businessman who has been in affluent Darien more than 15 years: "Because the commuter is in New York or traveling most of the time or works late and stays in the city overnight, a gap develops between him and his children. This is bound to have an effect on them. It frequently takes the form of vandalism, drugs, and thievery." (In the early seventies, Darien ranked among the highest of all the towns in Fairfield County in drug arrests of young people.)

• Helen Miller, a mother, volunteer school worker, and long-term resident of Darien: "I've watched one whole generation grow up here. The doctors and lawyers and the ones who stay here all day that I have seen have yet to face a serious social problem with their children. Almost all of the serious problems arise in situations where the family is split or the father commutes or travels a lot. Darien has no grandfathers to fill in while the fathers are away. The mother can be a drunk or run around a lot, yet this doesn't show up as sharply in the kids as the difference that develops when the father isn't there. It's unbelievable."

Mrs. Miller's observation is supported by studies made by family life specialists.[2] Urie Bronfenbrenner, Cornell psychologist, found that "absence of the father was more critical than absence of the mother" in personality formation.

Family mobility is only one of several factors which undermine community life in modern society and have a negative impact on youngsters. The result of the population explosion and implosion into great metropolitan areas that has occurred in the past 25 years is another. Philip Hauser, noted demographer at the University of Chicago, says: ". . . disorder of contemporary life may be better understood and dealt with as frictions in the transition still under way from the little community to the mass society." In talking of the confusion and "chaos" of contemporary life, he mentioned delinquency, crime, alcoholism, drug addition, mental disorder, and the youthful revolt which in its extreme form has manifested itself in the hippie's resolving his problems by dropping out.

The impact on children of the environment of a mass society that is increasingly anonymous has been specifically singled out for critical reports or comments by several behavioral experts in childhood development.

Herbert Wright and associates at the University of Kansas compared the everyday lives of youngsters growing up in a small town with the lives of youngsters living in a modern metropolitan area. They found that children in the small town got to know *well* more adults in various walks of life and were more likely to be *active participants* in the adult settings where they found themselves.[3] (Here again we see a causative factor in the "generation gap.")

[2]See Vance Packard, *The Sexual Wilderness* (New York: David McKay Company, 1968), Chapter 23.
[3]See Urie Bronfenbrenner, "The Split-Level American Family," *Saturday Review,* October 7, 1967.

Urie Bronfenbrenner is another who is concerned about the impact of the constricted world of "shifting suburbia" on children. He points out:

"Whereas the world in which the child lived before [the small town] consisted of a diversity of people in a diversity of settings, now, for millions of American children, the neighborhood is nothing but row upon row of buildings inhabited by strangers. One house or apartment is much like another, and so are the people. They all have about . . . the same way of life."[4]

While only a restructuring of urban life to recapture something resembling the socializing environment of small towns would seem to offer much hope of relieving the present constricted environment provided for children in most large urban settings, schools and families can at least ease the negative impact of mobility on children. For example, teachers can see that an incoming child gets a little welcoming ceremony, can invite the child to stay after school for a friendly get-acquainted and orientation chat, and can appoint a classmate

to serve as a buddy to the newcomer in getting him involved with his new classmates. Preferably the buddy would be someone living near the newcomer so that the new child would also have someone to walk to and from school with.

Several family researchers have offered the opinion that any negative effect of mobility on children can be small if relationships within the family are solid. A number of wives I consulted echoed this belief. A recently arrived mother in Darien observed: "One of the most important things is this: A good family situation—and especially one in which the father is firm but companionable—wipes out an awful lot of the headaches that can come from being transplanted."

At the least, it would seem, there is a very real *potential* negative impact in all the uprootedness of modern life upon the children. Another Great Falls educator put this in somber terms by asserting: "Society faces a hazard because of all this moving, where children don't have roots and don't have grandmothers they can see fairly regularly."

---

[4]*Ibid.*

42. CHILD ABUSE: A KILLER TEACHERS CAN HELP CONTROL

Bert Shanas

Maryland—Donna S., a 9-year-old fourth-grade student at Damascus Elementary School, arrives at the hospital dead. Examination of her body reveals burns,

---

Reprinted from *Phi Delta Kappan* (March 1975), pp. 479–482, by permission of the journal.

bruises, and scars inflicted over a long period of time. Donna's mother is held for premeditated murder and torture.

New York—Richard K., a 14-year-old junior high school student in the Bronx, shows up at school with multiple welts on both arms, swollen wrists, and puncture wounds on his legs and buttocks. He is quiet, shy, and withdrawn. When questioned by school authorities, he admits his father has been beating him.

California—A 13-year-old Los Angeles youngster is forced into incestuous relationships with her father. She tries to take her own life on three occasions by overdosing medication, by strangling herself, and by leaping from a school window.

Ugly and revolting as they may seem, the cases cited above are far from unusual. In fact, they are typical of the thousands of cases each year with which teachers come in contact. Child abuse is a "disease" believed to be the largest killer of children in the United States today.

Sixty thousand cases were reported in the nation last year. Some authorities estimate that there are a minimum of 25 actual cases for every one reported. Two children per day are known to be dying from child abuse —more than seven hundred deaths every year.

According to the best estimates, some ten thousand children are severely battered each year; 50,000 to 75,000 are sexually abused; 100,000 are "emotionally neglected": and another 100,000 are physically, morally, or educationally neglected.

Child abuse is so widespread that within the past 10 years every state in the union has either passed or updated laws that require the reporting of abuse or suspected abuse cases. Twenty-four states specifically require school personnel to report cases. Yet it is an out-of-control epidemic. Nobody knows for sure how many cases continue to go unreported.

"The variation of these [reporting] laws doesn't matter," says Minnesota Senator Walter F. Mondale, who sponsored the $60 million national Child Abuse Prevention Act signed into law early last year. "What matters is that we have seen they don't work. Child abuse continues to go undetected and untreated in case after case."

And though it may sound cruel, thousands of teachers across the country—people who have dedicated themselves to providing for the welfare of children—are contributing to the injury and death statistics by failing to report cases and refusing to get involved in the problem.

Physical abuse and neglect of children at the hands of their own parents is certainly not a new development; one might say it is steeped in tradition. "Spare the rod and spoil the child," advises the Old Testament. "She gave them some broth without any bread/And whipped them all soundly and sent them to bed," says the nursery rhyme about the fabled woman who lived in a shoe.

The older generation, at least, has read Charles Dickens's accounts of the horrors of growing up in an industrial society; in history lessons we learned that American children received much the same treatment in our own factory systems and turn-of-the-century sweatshops.

The first court case involving child abuse in the United States arose exactly a century ago in New York City, when little Mary Ellen, who was being starved and beaten repeatedly, was unchained from her bed. She was given safety outside her home after church officials called the case to the attention of the Society for the Prevention of Cruelty to Animals. It was after that case that some "conscientious" citizens thought maybe there should be a similar society for children. And so the Society for the Prevention of Cruelty to Children was founded.

But child abuse remained something most folks preferred not to talk about, and it was only 10 years ago that we began to read shocking newspaper accounts of children who are dropped in tubs of boiling water, whose hands are held over flames, and who are beaten beyond recognition for no apparent reason.

For most of those 10 years, the focus was on abuse of the younger child, and it wasn't until fairly recently that authorities began emphasizing that part of the problem is caused by the unwillingness of teachers and school officials to get involved. This despite the fact that at least one national study, conducted in 1967, found that half of a sample of some six thousand abuse children were over six, or of school age.

"The teacher may well be the first line of defense for the child against child abuse," says Dr. Vincent J. Fontana, medical director and pediatrician-in-chief, New York Foundling Hospital, and chairman, New York City Task Force on Child Abuse and Neglect. He points out that some families (especially middle-income parents) can hide the problem by finding private doctors willing to break the law and hide suspected cases. There isn't even any assurance that poorer youngsters will get to public clinics, which are more likely to report the problem.

But because of the nation's compulsory education laws, few youngsters escape school these days. Teachers may just be the fail-safe method for ensuring that child abuse cases are reported—at least those cases involving school-age children.

Unfortunately, however, large numbers of teachers are still failing to meet this responsibility, and there are several reasons. High on the list is a personal fear of getting involved—a fear that certainly is not unfounded. There have been many instances of parents striking out physically against teachers who have reported child abuse cases. In one California case, a parent actually stabbed a teacher who reported her child as a suspected abuse victim.

School systems more attuned to the problem have alleviated that danger somewhat by making the building principal or another administrator solely responsible for reporting suspected cases. That is, the teacher reports the case, but the same principal's name always goes on the reporting form.

Michigan's Wayne-Westland School District has a reporting policy that outlines specific procedures of reporting, including notification of school officials, the hospital, and the abusive parent. It also tells teachers how to ensure that the child is examined as quickly as possible.

New York City's system makes teachers who fail to report suspected cases subject to a Class A misdemeanor, as well as "civilly liable for the damages caused by such failure." Teachers are actually encouraged to photograph suspected abuse and neglect victims, and educators who make reports in good faith are granted legal immunity. In 1971, 866 New York cases were reported by teachers. In 1973 the number jumped to 2,120. At the end of the first six months of 1974, New York teachers had already reported 2,666 suspected cases—and most cases were still going unreported.

Many teachers who want to report suspected cases run into problems with their own principals and school administrators, who seek to "protect the image" of the school by sticking their head in the sand when such problems arise. At least one county school system in California, realizing what was happening, has mandated its teachers and school nurses to report suspected child abuse cases even when their principals instruct them not to do so.

In other school systems throughout the country, there is simply a lack of procedures for handling the child abuse problem. Mrs. Kay Drews, a former child abuse coordinator at the University of Colorado Medical Center, writing in *Helping the Battered Child and His Family,* told of a survey in which questionnaires about child abuse reporting procedures were mailed to half of the nation's school districts with enrollments of over 10,000 students. Responses were received from 34% of the districts. When asked if they had a standard operating procedure to follow in reporting suspected abuse cases, 49% of the administrators answered in the affirmative, but only

24% of the principals, teachers, and nurses said they knew of such a procedure.

What the study implied, of course, was that high-level administrators who have little direct contact with children were not making practitioners aware of the reporting methods.

"It is not enough to concentrate just on the academics," warns Dr. Fontana. "A teacher can do a great deal just by being human. Sure, there are risks involved in reporting child abuse cases; but the risks are much greater if the teacher fails to report a case she suspects."

It is the teacher's responsibility, whether or not the principal and school system are willing to help, to learn about child abuse, and to be equipped to spot potential cases.

The definition of child abuse varies from place to place. Severely battered children are often easy to spot because the signs are there—repeated bruises and welts a teacher can distinguish from injuries resulting from scraps with other pupils. Then there are the classic neglect cases: students coming to school dirty, hungry, and poorly clothed. Other children suffer from more subtle kinds of emotional abuse. A child whose parent is constantly drilling into his mind the fact that he is unwanted suffers a form of abuse that may ultimately be at least as serious as battering and neglect.

Child abuse and neglect are not always clear-cut and easy to detect, of course. It takes sensitivity, clear thinking, and good training. It is probably better for a teacher who isn't quite sure to have the child checked out by a competent authority. Then there is the danger that a teacher will, either consciously or subconsciously, label a problem child the victim of abuse as a means of getting rid of him.

The American Humane Association has published a list of signs teachers should look for as possible child abuse and neglect tipoffs. Among them:

—If the child is aggressive, disruptive, or destructive, he could be acting out for attention. It could be the child's way of calling for help, of reflecting a destructive climate at home, or of imitating parental behavior.

—If the child is shy, passive, or overly compliant, he may have internalized his abuse problems and his cry for help is a whisper.

—A child who comes to school too early or loiters and hangs around after school is dismissed may be seeking an escape from home.

—A child who is always tired, sleeps in class, is lethargic or listless may be suffering from family problems that disrupt his normal routine.

The list also includes signs to look for in parents as possible indicators of abuse and neglect of their children. For example, parents may become aggressive or abusive when approached by teachers with problems concerning their children. They may be apathetic or unresponsive. They may be reported by their children as behaving strangely. They may simply fail to take an interest in their children's activities.

Many teachers are reluctant to become deeply involved in parental problems no matter what they are, but in child abuse cases, teachers can't separate the children's problems from those of the parents. In fact, current theories on child abuse treat the abusive parent as a victim also. In a large number of cases, the abusive parent was abused himself or herself as a child.

Often the parent is trapped by the pressures of a large family. He feels much like the teacher faced with a class of 30 acting-out students. Most abused children are not unwanted children, but frequently the parent acts in a fit of uncontrollable fury. In larger families an abusive parent will sometimes single out just one child for maltreatment.

It is not unusual to find a poor relationship between spouses in abusive families. As a result, mothers may look to their young children as a sole source of love; when the infant cries or the older child fails to respond in a satisfying way, she feels rejected. These chronic problems trigger the specific incidents of abuse whose signs the teacher sees in the classroom.

Dr. C. Henry Kempe, who has been working in the child abuse area for many years at the University of Colorado Medical Center, originated the term, "the battered child syndrome." He now estimates that 90% of the nation's abusive parents "are readily treatable by reconstituting their sense of trust and by giving them considerable minute-to-minute support over a crucial period of eight to nine months." In such cases it is not necessary to remove the abused child from the home permanently for placement in a foster or adoptive home.

The other 10%, says Dr. Kempe, "belong to the categories of abusive psychopaths or delusional schizophrenics" who use a child as a scapegoat. Dr. Kempe urges early removal of a child from the home in these cases.

Most teachers have neither the ability nor the training to recognize whether parents fall into the 90% or 10% group. Nor do teachers have time to give parents in the first group that "minute-to-minute" support. But they do have the responsibility, for the sake of the parent and the child, to guide such people, using channels set up by the school, to the social and welfare agencies that provide such help.

Today there are a number of parental treatment systems used throughout the country that appear to be working out well. At the National Center for the Prevention of Child Abuse and Neglect in Denver, a national training center run by the University of Colorado and directed by Dr. Kempe, four treatment methods have been

---

SOURCES OF INFORMATION ON CHILD ABUSE PROBLEMS

The following is a list of places for teachers to write for further information on the child abuse problem:

1. For a list of indicators of child abuse and neglect a teacher should know, write for "Guidelines for Schools" to the American Humane Association, Children's Division, P.O. Box 1266, Denver, Colo. 80201.

2. For information on the new Federal child abuse legislation, write to the National Center on Child Abuse and Neglect, P.O. Box 1182, Rm. 5847, Washington, D.C. 20013.

3. For a copy of the New York City Schools' procedures for handling child abuse, write to the Board of Education's Office of Information and Public Affairs, 12th floor, 110 Livingston St., Brooklyn, N.Y. 11201. Request a copy of Special Circular No. 31, 1973-74.

4. For information on the role of educators and general information on child abuse, write to the National Center for the Prevention and Treatment of Child Abuse and Neglect, University of Colorado Medical Center, 4200 East Ninth Ave., Denver, Colo. 80220.

5. For information about child abuse laws and reporting procedures where you live, contact your local social services agency, police department, and municipal and state governments.

---

developed that are being successfully used in various parts of the nation.

The first type uses lay therapists, both men and women, who work in the homes of abusive parents, providing support and spirit in times of need. The second is called "crisis nursery," a place for parents to leave their small child when they feel the child needs a safer place. The nursery is open day and night, and a child may be left there for a few hours or a few days if need be.

Next, Dr. Kempe uses a day-care center for abused children, a place where abusive parents can see their young children with other children and discuss their feelings and experiences with other parents who share their problems.

The fourth method of treatment Dr. Kempe uses was actually begun in California in 1969 by a mother now known throughout the country as Mrs. Jolly K. Mrs. K. was a typical abusive parent who on one occasion threw a kitchen knife at her 6-year-old daughter, on another attempted to strangle the child, and at various times would harass and verbally abuse the girl.

Sensing the need to help herself, Mrs. K. went to 10 county and state facilities, but could not find help—probably because the child wasn't physically scarred. So she began a self-help group called Mothers Anonymous. Fashioned after the Alcoholics Anonymous system, it encouraged parents to meet once or twice each week and begin to appreciate the fact that they were not alone. They discussed their own problems as a group and began to derive a great deal of help and support from each other. Today the organization has been renamed Parents Anonymous. There are some six hundred chapters across the country.

Child abuse is a phenomenon any teacher may encounter, whether the school is in an urban ghetto, a middle-class area, or a wealthy suburb. It knows no class distinction, although middle-and high-income parents can often hide the problem better by avoiding public health facilities.

Sometimes people with more money can also "buy their way out" of potentially explosive child abuse situations by getting out of the house and becoming involved in other activities. The ability to pay for a steady babysitter can help save a child from abuse. Still, the teacher has to recognize that no particular class of parent is immune.

By doing nothing about suspected child abuse cases, the teacher is not only endangering the child and furthering the ruin of the parents, but is also contributing to the recycling of the problem. Abused children tend to become abusive parents.

The teacher's inaction also contributes to many other educational problems. Case studies have shown a strong link between abused or neglected students and pupils who later disrupt school activities. A study of 8,000 New York State children abused or neglected between 1951 and 1971 found that 35% of them later became known to the family court as juvenile delinquents or "persons in need of supervision."

But it is not only by a teacher's inaction that he or she contributes to the problem. Often a teacher directly contributes, too. Unfortunately, there are still large numbers of teachers who use corporal punishment as a behavior control technique. Such teachers often lose their own control in much the same way as an abusive parent. And every time a teacher uses corporal punishment, he is sanctioning the use of physical abuse. He is telling the class that it's okay to strike out physically against another person. He is helping students grow up with the notion implanted in their heads.

David Gil, professor of social policy at Brandeis University, is a well-known child abuse authority and an advocate for a national law to ban corporal punishment in schools. He says: "Such a message from the Congress could initiate a rethinking of the entire child-rearing context in the country. Without such rethinking and without an eventual redefinition of the status and the rights of children, child abuse can simply not be prevented."

The teacher cannot fight the battle all alone. Many teachers, in fact, don't report child abuse cases because they feel the social agencies don't follow them up, and thus it's a wasted effort on their part.

What the teacher can do, however, is work with school officials and get them to work with the social agencies to ensure that each reported case is followed through. If they have to, tenured teachers and their organizations can prompt such action by threatening legal steps or otherwise embarrassing lax officials.

Many professionals in the child abuse field are beginning to call for a complete teacher education program that would train the teacher, while in college, to recognize signs of abuse, work with abusive parents, and ensure the proper follow-up of reports by social and school agencies.

For their part, boards of education should be insisting that both administrators and teachers learn to recognize the problems. They can finance in-service training programs for both groups. Every school and school system in the country should have specific policies and procedures for child abuse reporting and follow-up.

A few school systems have recently recognized their responsibility and have begun child abuse programs. For example, the Montgomery County, Maryland, school system and Community School District 18 in Brooklyn, New York, both received grants from the U.S. Department of Health, Education, and Welfare last August for child abuse programs to begin this school year.

Both programs use special "remedial and reentry classes" for children in their districts who are identified as abused. The classes are designed to redevelop abused children's trust in adults as well as respect for themselves. At the same time, the children receive special academic help to compensate for the difficult periods they went through.

The Brooklyn program also includes development of a course of study for teachers, designed to train them to recognize child abuse and neglect at a "pre-crisis stage."

However, such programs are the exception, not the rule. Most school systems today provide very little real help to their teachers, and so perhaps it is up to the teachers to take the initiative. In the midst of an epidemic, you can't sit around and wait for miracles. The teacher can no longer sit around and wait for someone else to provide the solution.

"Unless changes are made in prevention and treatment, there will be 1.5 million reported cases of child abuse in the next 10 years [including] 50,000 deaths and 300,000 permanently injured children—most of whom will be brain-damaged," predicts Ray E. Helfer, a pioneer in the child abuse field from Michigan State University.

Teachers have got to start doing their share. It may be that the role of the teacher in the future will have to be part social worker, part counselor, and even part physician in recognizing abuse symptoms. So be it. With the exception of the parent, nobody sees the school-age child as much as the teacher, and teachers therefore must accept the responsibility to protect children against abusive parents. It is a teacher's job to ensure that children are educable as well as educated.

CHAPTER VII

States of Consciousness

In little less than a century, psychology has apparently gone full circle. About a century ago it was exclusively the study of consciousness. When this approach proved sterile, psychologists devoted themselves to the study of the unconscious in the Freudian tradition or to the study of behavior and conditioning. The latter approach has been dominant in the United States for the past 50 years. With the passage of time, however, it has been recognized that in avoiding study of consciousness, something very critical was being disregarded.

Psychologists therefore have returned to the study of consciousness, but with an approach and conceptualizations that are markedly different from those of a century ago. There has indeed been progress; now there is a three-way interface in the study of consciousness which includes the state of consciousness, the attendant behavior, and the neurophysiological concomitants of the state. This chapter presents a cross section of some of the currents of this inquiry. The first reading asks a pithy question; "The Occult Today, Why?" This is followed by a review of the work proceeding in one area of expression of this recent resurgence, "Boom Times on the Psychic Frontier."

But not all of the research is esoteric. Much of it concerns states of being and states of consciousness common to all, things we experience daily and nightly. Recently psychologists have been delving into the ways in which we experience our bodies, our vehicle for living in the world. The results are not a little surprising, as "Experiencing Your Body" demonstrates.

At night the body sleeps, causing wonder as to why we sleep and how much sleep is necessary. These issues are explored in "How Much Sleep Do You Need?" Sleep has been recognized as the doorway to another world, the world of dreams. This was regarded even in ancient times as a most significant state, but the key to understanding the nature, significance, and meaning of dreams was lost until it was rediscovered by Sigmund Freud. Much progress has been made since Freud; "Dream World" provides another look at this significant domain.

While we are learning to get in touch with ourselves through our dreams, other points of contact are also possible and are no less significant. Formerly, as people lost contact with their dream world, they also lost contact with themselves, their bodies and energy sources. Psychologists are now turning their attention to correcting this malaise. Some of the most recent approaches to other contact points are presented in " 'Rolfing,' 'Aikido,' Hypnodrama, Pyschokinesis and Other Things Beyond the Here and Now."

In regaining touch with ourselves we have discovered techniques which enable us to assume control over a host of bodily processes and psychological states that have long been thought of as beyond our intervention. This new dimension of personal reality has been made possible by the development of the process of biofeedback. "Biofeedback: An Exercise in Self-Control" gives up-to-date information on this significant process, which is a mechanized means of assuming control over bodily functions that otherwise would be uncontrollable.

Another development has provided a new vision of the possibilities for the fulfillment of the human condition, an ancient hope and an ancient promise. For many the vehicle of this fulfillment has become the practice of meditating. There are many forms of meditation, but one of the most popular to emerge in recent years is transcendental meditation, the subject of "Transcendental Meditation and the Science of Creative Intelligence."

43. THE OCCULT TODAY: WHY?

Gary E. Kessler

TIME Magazine does a cover story on "The Occult Revival." "The New Alchemy" is the subject of a two-part series in the *Los Angeles Free Press.* Sunday supplements and flashy national magazines run feature stories with titles like "Satanism in the Suburbs." It is estimated that $150,000,000 a year is spent on horoscopes in America. Small stores spring up across the country selling everything a witch needs to work a few spells. Bloodchilling tales of ritual murders make headlines. Courses on the occult multiply in universities. Churches of Satan and of Wicca dismay and alarm Establishment preachers. Need I mention movies such as "The Exorcist" and "Rosemary's Baby"? What is going on, and why?

The occult has always been with us. Its roots go back to the dim preliterate past, finding expression in the visions and the magic of the shaman. Anyone familiar with Western history knows that no age has ever been devoid of interest in the occult. So why should there be surprise at finding it once again in 20th-century America?

The surprise is due not only to a lack of historical perspective, but even more to the naive assumption, shared by many intellectuals, that science has banished once and for all that superstition known as occultism. We can understand how "ignorant" peasants or "superstitious" natives could be taken in by hocus-pocus. We can dismiss with a smile the well-intentioned, but unin-

formed, little old ladies who attend seances, or movie stars who dabble in astrology, or the uneducated lower class who believe in magical healings. However, the interest in —and practice of—the occult cuts across all classes, educated or not. Indeed, the recent interest seems to stem precisely from that segment of society which is college-educated, middle-class, and relatively affluent. These are the people who ought to know better!

Science has not banished the supernatural and man's interest in the arcane and the occult. To assume that it should have shows not only a woefully narrow view of science, but also an ignorance of what occultism is. In this essay, I shall offer some reflections on the "why" of this contemporary interest. I hope to be able to convince the reader that, if he or she has been surprised by the recent rise of occultism, sober reflection will dispel some fears and, perhaps, even convince him or her that occultism is not merely superstition.

OCCULT AND GNOSIS

Occultism is a much-abused word. So many diverse phenomena, from mysticism to parapsychology, have been associated with it, that it is almost impossible to define. For some, it boils down to Satanism, pure and simple; for others, it embodies a lofty and wise metaphysics; while, for still others, it smacks of sex and violence. The word itself means that which is esoteric, hidden, or secret. Historically, the term has been used to classify a wide and varying group of

Reprinted from *Intellect* (November 1975) by permission of publisher, pp. 171–174.

phenomena which purport to give esoteric knowledge through practices and experiences aimed at securing greater power than is available to man in his ego state of consciousness. This esoteric knowledge is not what we call scientific knowledge nor even information in the ordinary sense. It is knowledge in the sense of gnosis–that is, a nondiscursive understanding of the unity and interrelationships of all the various levels of reality. It consists of the personal and immediate realization of the unity of opposites, usually articulated metaphysically by the doctrine of the microcosm-macrocosm. This gnosis is hidden or esoteric not in the sense that a secret is not publicly known but could be, but in the sense that its object is hidden behind the appearances of things.

In respect to this element of gnosis, occultism can be viewed as part of what Ellwood has termed the "alternative reality" tradition of the West, and which others refer to as the perennial philosophy.[1] It is attractive to mystics and philosophers alike who are interested in the possibility of a unitative gnosis.

MAGIC

Occultism also consists of certain practices and experiences aimed at gaining power, and it is this element which is usually responsible for its popular appeal, as well as its rejection by mystic, philosopher, and intellectual. The practices of occultism are known as magic, and consist of individual or group rituals designed either to gain gnosis or exercise its power (gnosis is power). Magic comes in many varieties, ranging from simple healing rituals to complex conjurings and a bewildering variety of divinatory techniques. The Tarot, astrology, Ouija, and I-Ching are but a few examples.

The commercial exploitation of occultism emphasizes this element exclusively, usually in a very superficial manner. Almost everyone is tempted to spend a few dollars for the power to make beautiful women or handsome men fall in love with them. Promises of "telecult" powers or the "secret health remedies of the ancients" always will appeal to people, especially to the relatively powerless. In an age when more and more areas of an individual's life are being taken from his personal control by ever-increasing government and technology, magic becomes for many almost the only alternative they have left in attempting to regain personal power and control. Freud offered his theory of the individual fixating at the stage of development he called the "omnipotence of thought" to explain man's fascination with magic. When reality gets too harsh, adults, like children, retreat into a fantasy world, where events and people can be controlled by the mind.

We are constantly being reminded that we live in an age of science and technology. While this fact would seem, on the surface, to make the turn to magic improbable, Claude Levi-Strauss has pointed out that magic itself is a kind of technology. Indeed, magic presupposes a completely deterministic universe of cause and effect. For some, technology may appear to be little more than our society's form of magic. The control of scientific technology is open to only a highly educated few, but magical technology is more readily available and, from this perspective, does not at all appear as an illogical means to combat the loss of power at the hands of scientific technology.

Insofar as some magic really seems to "work" for some people, many have turned to parapsychology and various forms of ESP for a "scientific" explanation. If ESP exists, and if, by chance, magical techniques

----
[1] Robert S. Ellwood, Jr., *Religious and Spiritual Groups in Modern America* (Englewood Cliffs, N.J.: Prentice-Hall, 1973), p. 42.

have discovered ways of utilizing it, this would make the occult all the more appealing to the technologically powerless.

We must also note that contemporary subatomic technology and astrophysics seem to be destroying many scientific "myths" with a vision of new possibilities which sound more occult than scientific. This creates an atmosphere which makes some occult ideas almost "scientific" to the speculatively bold. Philosophical speculation on the limits of reason and anthropologically generated cultural relativism also contribute to this atmosphere in which anything seems possible.

The magical practices of occultism can never be separated from the quest for gnosis without distortion. Behind pop magic stands the hope for gnosis and a sophisticated metaphysical view of the ultimate unity of opposites. The serious student of the occult realizes that magical techniques embody and concretely illustrate a fairly complex gnosis which is not apparent on the surface. For the serious occultist, magical rituals are symbolic embodiments of deeper levels of reality. The difference between the popular and commercial view of magic and that of the serious occultist is like the difference between regarding alchemy only as a means to make gold and regarding it as a concrete symbolic embodiment of a highly spiritual gnosis and psychology.

Carl Jung has been largely responsible for teaching us this fact about alchemy, and his views can be extended to other occult practices. However, Jung is not only helpful in revealing the symbolic richness of occultism—he also helps us to understand why magical practices and ideas appeal to those unaware of their symbolic depth. Jung's views on archtypes and the collective unconscious illuminate how even the most debased and popularized magical ritual can communicate unconsciously to the very depths of our humanity. The ankh, which is an ancient occult symbol consisting of a tau cross with a circle above, symbolizes the union of male (the phallic tau) and female (the circle). It stands for fertility and life. The ritual magical circle divided by a cross into four parts symbolizes the unification of opposites. These and similar symbols which abound in occultism speak, according to Jung, directly and intuitively to our unconscious, arousing emotions and responses of which we may be only half conscious.[2]

OCCULT POWER

The power or force with which the occultist seeks contact and over which he seeks control has been conceived in a variety of ways. Most often, it has been thought of in terms of the supernatural. This power, while regarded as ultimately unitary, is believed to be manifested in a great variety of forms. It is ethically neutral in the sense that it transcends good and evil, being itself the unification of all opposites. However, its manifestations may be termed good or evil from a lesser viewpoint. It is a notorious fact that, with the triumph of Christianity, the gods of the pagans became the demons of Christianity. Because occultism contains a good deal of "pagan" mythology and symbolism, it is not surprising to find Christians associating occult power with evil and Satan. A more objective viewpoint recognizes that this power is closer to the primitive idea of mana, an ethically neutral form of energy which manifests itself as sheer overwhelming power. Rudolph Otto's concept of the *"mysterium tremendum,"* which he finds at the heart of all religious experience, comes closer to characterizing

---

[2]See Lee W. Gibbs, "Religions, Devils, and Contemporary Crosses," *Ohio Journal of Religious Studies,* 2:53–62, April, 1974, for a discussion of the ankh and other symbols from a Jungian viewpoint.

this force than either the terms supernatural or evil.

Ironically, many modern would-be occultists have bought the Christian viewpoint, and actively seek to worship and obey what the Christians have called Satan. It should be noted, however, that some serious magicians like Aleister Crowley actively seek out debased and "evil" methods precisely because of their belief in the unification of opposites. If this power does unify good and evil, then the "lefthanded" or sinister path ought to lead there as well as the "righthanded" path. Indeed, some occultists maintain that the sinister route is the shortest, although also the most dangerous. Those who actively seek this lefthanded or "black" magical route may be consciously or unconsciously reacting against an established religious tradition and a puritanism which have, from the occult viewpoint, overstressed the right-handed way, and thereby made it practically useless.

More recently, it has become fashionable, even in occult circles, to regard this power and its many manifestations as "higher" states of consciousness transcending our ego states. Metzner has argued that the various occult and magical practices ought to be understood as "maps" to higher and better states of human awareness.[3] As such, they are of interest to psychology, especially psychoanalysis, humanistic psychology, and transpersonal psychology, which are deeply interested in the human potential to achieve greater states of consciousness and being.

ECSTATIC EXPERIENCE

Occultism has always, to a certain degree, offered its followers the opportunity to achieve ecstatic experiences. These experiences are often directly related to magical practices, and hold out the possibility of a radically empirical or experiential unification with the power which reconciles opposites. Ralph Metzner was an associate of Timothy Leary at Harvard and, for a while, was very much into the psychedelic scene. Here, we have the link between the interest in occultism today, and what people like Theodore Roszak have termed the "counter culture," others the "youth culture," and still others the "hippie" movement. Whatever the label, there can be little doubt that this movement, which broke upon the American scene in the 1960's, is an important factor in the rise of popular interest in occultism.

Their route to occultism was via the psychedelic experience and a youthful opposition to the evils of technocratic society. The psychedelic experience gave thousands a brief glimpse at a land of expanded consciousness that few had dreamed was there. They found these ecstatic experiences echoed in primitive shamanistic religions, Eastern mysticism, occultism, and even in Christian pentecostalism and evangelical revivalism. John B. Orr and others have developed the image of Protean and expansive man to grasp a new form of the American character which has developed out of this experience.[4] Expansive man seeks experiences which will expand his conscious horizons. The occultistic promise of an ecstatic experience appeals to him.

Max Weber distinguished between two forms of prophecy. One he called emissary, the other exemplary. A charismatic religious founder can be understood as a person who has gained wisdom and knowledge

---

[3]Ralph Metzner, *Maps of Consciousness* (New York: Collier-Macmillan, 1971), *Introduction*.

[4]Robert Jay Lifton, "Protean Man," in Donald Cutler, ed., *The Religious Situation: 1969* (Boston: Beacon, 1969), p. 816; and John B. Orr and F. Patrick Nichelson, *The Radical Suburb: Soundings in Changing American Character* (Philadelphia: Westminster, 1970).

through some ecstatic experience. An emissary prophet is one whose followers seek to utilize his teachings as the prime ideal to be realized. Most Western religion has been of this type. If, on the other hand, it is the ecstatic experience itself which is considered central and which the followers are urged to realize, the prophet is of an exemplary type. Much of Eastern religion is exemplary. Occultism may be regarded as fitting Weber's exemplary model. If one has come to see, through a series of ego-shattering ecstatic experiences, the hypocrisy, narrow-mindedness, ego-ridden, Appollianian character of modern technocratic society and all its institutions, including the church, the expansive promise, Dionysian abandon, and greater awareness promised by an exemplary type of movement like occultism become very appealing indeed.

RAPID SOCIAL CHANGE

Of course, not every one who is "into" occultism has gone through the counter culture or the psychedelic experience. However, many Americans interested in occultism have experienced what Durkheim called "anomie," most recently popularized as "Future Shock." In times of rapid social change, traditional values and ideals tend to break down. This causes a feeling of helplessness, bewilderment, fear, anxiety, and the like. It causes individuals and groups to enter a kind of random search for new values or ways to shore up the old.

If one couples this concept of anomie with Weber's notion of the routinization of charisma and what some have called the "death of God" and others His absence, one has most of the ingredients necessary to understand, at least in part, why many turn to the occult. Weber taught us that all attempts to preserve the charisma of a religious founder lead to institutions which, of necessity, must destroy, in time, that very charisma they seek to preserve. Dostoyevsky's *The Grand Inquisitor* is a masterful dramatic enactment of this idea. We know from our study of the history of religions that, when "high" gods or "sky" gods become so remote that they are no longer perceived as directly available to the believers, magical rituals and rites centering around lesser, but more accessible, deities gain ascendency. It appears the case that established Western religion of a primarily emissary type has routinized itself to the point of death, and its "sky god" has become very remote indeed. This has left a religious vacuum or void which is rapidly being filled by religions and occult groups which seem far less routinized, and which offer gods more accessible to man.

CATASTROPHIC AND ESCHATOLOGICAL HISTORY

In articulating some of the possible reasons for the "revival" (perhaps it is more accurate to say resurfacing) of the occult today, I have neglected to mention the reasons the occultists might cite, and those reasons given by their most vocal opponents, fundamentalistic Christians. Occultists generally subscribe to both a catastrophic and a cyclical view of history. History repeats itself, so the occult claims, insofar as societies evolve from simple to complex and then some misuse of power causes the destruction of the complex civilization. The last great civilization to be destroyed by the misuse of power was Atlantis. Western civilization now stands at the same place Atlantis did before its fall. We have the opportunity to prevent another Atlantis, and thereby to cause a shift from sheer repetition to a higher state of civilized, indeed, cosmic evolution. The gnosis made available by the occult is the key that can save us. The occult has resurfaced today precisely to present us with that opportunity.

This is something of an eschatological vision and is, in that respect, similar to the fundamentalistic Christian claim that we stand at the brink of the second coming of Christ. The last days are upon us and, as the Bible foretold, in these days, Satan will gain more and more ground, roaming as a beast over the face of the earth, turning as many from Christ as he can. The occult today confirms, for these Christians, those Biblical prophecies.

The reader may be surprised that I mention these ideas as "reasons" for the interest in the occult today. Surely, they are too bizarre and unscientific to be taken seriously. However, following the good occult principle that appearances are deceiving, we may find more in these unscientific ideas than meets the eye. Myth often contains a truth our science can not see. William Irwin Thompson, in his book, *At the Edge of History,* has taken such ideas seriously, at least in their symbolic depth.[5] The result is a fascinating speculation on the transformations of cultures and an illuminating insight into the trials and tribulations of our age. I do not have the space to fully explicate his ideas, so I will merely commend the book and close with a few of my own speculations, inspired by Thompson.

A plausible model for the evolution of society can be constructed around the idea that, as complexity increases, the conflict between values increases. This complexity and conflict reach a point where culture itself becomes transformed. Such times of radical transformation are experienced as "eschatological ages." They are typified by anxiety in the face of an unknown future and by an intensification of value conflict to the point where something has to give. The occult can be viewed as a kind of underground esoteric value system which stands in conflict with the exoteric traditions of society. It is like a mirror image of established values, reflecting them in a reversed manner. In times of transformation, this underground esoteric stream emerges, intensifying the conflict of values and offering what appears to many as a real alternative route into a better future. We live, I think, in such a time, "at the edge of history," when the desire for the unification of opposites makes any kind of gnosis, magical or otherwise, a power to be sought after and prized.

---

[5]See, especially, Chapter 4 in Thompson, *At the Edge of History* (New York: Harper & Row, 1971).

44.   BOOM TIMES ON THE PSYCHIC FRONTIER

Glendower: I can call spirits from the vasty
deep.
Hotspur: Why, so can I, or so can any man;
But will they come when you do call for
them?
—Henry IV

Reprinted by permission from TIME, The Weekly Newsmagazine; Copyright Time Inc.

For all the enormous achievements of science in posting the universe that man inhabits, odd things keep slipping past the sentries. The tap on the shoulder may be fleeting, the brush across the cheek gone sooner than it is felt, but the momentary effect is unmistakable: an unwilling suspension of belief in the rational. An old friend suddenly remembered, and as suddenly the telephone rings and the friend is on the line. A vivid dream that becomes the morning reality. The sense of bumping into one's self around a corner of time, of having done and said just this, in this place, once before in precisely this fashion. A stab of anguish for a distant loved one, and next day, the telegram.

Hardly a person lives who can deny some such experience, some such seeming visitation from across the psychic frontier. For most of man's history, those intrusions were mainsprings of action, the very life of Greek epic and biblical saga, of medieval tale and Eastern chronicle. Modern science and psychology have learned to explain much of what was once inexplicable, but mysteries remain. The workings of the mind still resist rational analysis; reports of psychic phenomena persist. Are they all accident, illusion? Or are there other planes and dimensions of experience and memory? Could there be a paranormal world exempt from known natural law?

Both in America and abroad, those questions are being asked by increasing numbers of laymen and scientists hungry for answers. The diverse manifestations of interest in so-called psychic phenomena are everywhere:

• In the U.S., *The Secret Life of Plants* becomes a bestseller by offering an astonishing and heretical thesis: greenery can feel the thoughts of humans.

• At Maimonides Medical Center in New York City, the image of a painting is transmitted by ESP, and seems to enter the dreams of a laboratory subject sleeping in another room.

• In England, a poll of its readers by the *New Scientist* indicates that nearly 70% of the respondents (mainly scientists and technicians) believe in the possibility of extrasensory perception.

• At the University of California, Psy-chologist Charles Tart reports that his subjects showed a marked increase in ESP scores after working with his new teaching machine.

• In Los Angeles, a leaf is cut in half, then photographed by a special process. The picture miraculously shows the "aura" or outline of the whole leaf.

• In Washington, the Defense Department's Advanced Research Projects Agency assigns a team to investigate seemingly authentic psychic phenomena at the Stanford Research Institute.

• On both sides of the Atlantic, Uri Geller, a young Israeli psychic, astounds laymen and scientists alike by bending spoons and keys apparently with the force of his thoughts.

• In the Philippines, Tennis Star Tony Roche is relieved of painful "tennis elbow" when an incision is made and three blood clots are apparently removed by the touch of a psychic healer, who knows nothing of surgery or of modern sanitation.

• In the U.S., the number of colleges offering courses in parapsychology increases to more than 100.

• In the U.S.S.R., researchers file reports on blindfolded women who can "see" colors with their hands.

• In California, ex-Astronaut Edgar Mitchell, who while on the Apollo 14 moon mission conducted telepathy experiments with friends on earth, founds the Institute of Noetic Sciences. His new mission: investigate occurrences that will not yield to rational explanation.

• In London, Arthur Koestler examines psychic research with the zeal of the believer. Koestler, one of the foremost explicators of Establishment science (*The Sleepwalkers, The Act of Creation*), speaks of "synchronized" events that lie outside the expectations of probability. In anecdotes of foresight and extrasensory perception, in the repetition of events and the strange behavior of random samplings,

Koestler spots what he calls the roots of coincidence. In his unforgettable metaphor, modern scientists are "Peeping Toms at the keyhole of eternity." That keyhole is stuffed with ancient biases toward the materialistic and rational explication and, consequently, away from the emerging field of psychic research. Once skeptics abandon those prejudices, says Koestler, they will be free to explore fresh concepts and new categories.

That exploration is already being conducted by a number of serious paranormalists in a wide range of disciplines. In his Foundation for the Research on the Nature of Man, in Durham, N.C., the grand old man of paranormal studies, J. B. Rhine, still keeps watch on test animals for precognitive powers. At the nearby Psychical Research Foundation, William Roll and a research staff investigates "survival after bodily death." In studies with a "sensitive" and his pet cat, Roll finds evidence for a human ability "to leave" the body and "visit" the animal. At the University of Virginia Medical School, Psychiatrist Ian Stevenson also studies the plausibilities of reincarnation.

At the Division of Parapsychology and Psychophysics of the Maimonides Medical Center, Dr. Montague Ullman directs tests in which message senders "think" images into the brains of sleeping subjects. "If we had adequate funding," says Ullman, "we could have a major breakthrough in this decade." In Connecticut, Businessman Robert Nelson directs the Central Premonitions Registry, meticulously recording the prophecies of the dreams and visions that people send him.

All of these researchers believe to some extent in the existence of some form of paranormal psychic powers. But the forms are open to wide debate. Says Psychologist Gardner Murphy, professor at the District of Columbia's George Washington University and a dean of psychic researchers, "It may well turn out that parapsychology will be a multidisciplinary thing, owing much to psychiatry, neurology ... medicine, biochemistry, social sciences." One of parapsychology's most famous proponents, in fact, is an anthropologist: Margaret Mead. It was her passionate advocacy that helped give the Parapsychological Association its greatest claim to legitimacy. After several vain attempts to enter the eminent American Association for the Advancement of Science, the P.A. won membership in 1969 —after a speech by Mead. Her argument: "The whole history of scientific advance is full of scientists investigating phenomena that the Establishment did not believe were there. I submit that we vote in favor of this association's work." The final vote: 6 to 1 in favor of admission.

IMMENSE CLAIMS

As parapsychology gains new respectability, so do its terms gain wide currency: "psi" for any psychic phenomenon; "clairvoyance" for the awareness of events and objects that lie outside the perimeters of the five senses; "out-of-body" experience for seeming to journey to a place that may be miles from the body; "psychokinesis" for the mental ability to influence physical objects; "precognition" for the foreknowledge of events, from the fall of dice to the prediction of political assassinations; and the wide-ranging term ESP for extrasensory perception.

For all its articulate spokesmen and scientific terminology, however, the new world of psi still has a serious credibility problem. One reason is that like any growth industry or pop phenomenon, it has attracted a fair share of hustlers. Indeed, the psychic-phenomena boom may contain more charlatans and conjurers, more naïfs and gullibles than can be found on the stage and in the audience of ten Ringling Brothers circuses. The situation is not helped at all by the "proofs" that fail to satisfy traditional canons of scientific investigations. Despite the published discoveries, despite the indefatigable explorations of the psychic researchers, no one has yet been able to document experiments sufficiently to convince the infidel. For many, doubt grows larger with each extravagant claim.

To Science and Mathematics Analyst Martin Gardner (*Relativity for the Million, Ambidextrous Universe*), announcements of psychic phenomena belong not to the march of science but to the pageant of publicity. "Uri Geller, *The Secret Life of Plants,* telepathy, ESP, the incomplete conclusions of Koestler—all seem part of a new uncritical enthusiasm for pseudo science," says Gardner. "The claims are immense, the proof nonexistent. The researchers, almost without exception, are emotionally committed to finding phenomena. And few are aware of the controls necessary in a field in which deception, conscious or unconscious, is all too familiar."

Daniel Cohen, former managing editor of *Science Digest* and author of the debunking volume *Myths of the Space Age,* remains unpersuaded by what he sees through the Koestlerian keyhole. "After decades of research and experiments," Cohen observes, "the parapsychologists are not one step closer to acceptable scientific proof of psychic phenomena. Examining the slipshod work of the modern researchers, one begins to wonder if any proof exists."

The criticism that psychics find hardest to counter comes not from scientists but from conjurers. Theoretically, magicians have no place in serious science. But they are entertainers whose business it is to deceive; thus they feel that they are better qualified to spot chicanery than scientists, who can be woefully naive about the gimmicks and techniques that charlatans may use for mystical effects. James Randi, who

appears on television as "the Amazing Randi," duplicates many of Uri Geller's achievements with a combination of sleight of hand, misdirected attention and patented paraphernalia, then calls them feats of clay. "Scientists who fall for the paranormal go through the most devious reasoning," Randi says. "Fortunes are squandered annually in pursuit of mystical forces that are actually the result of clever deceits. The money would be better spent investigating the tooth fairy or Santa Claus. There is more evidence for their reality."

PURE DECEPTION

Charles Reynolds, editor and member of the Psychic Investigating Committee of the American Society of Magicians, agrees. "When evaluating the research, we have found that the researcher's will to believe is all powerful. It's a will that has nothing to do with religion; there are Marxists, atheists, agnostics who cling stubbornly to the ancient faith in black magic. Only now it's called 'the paranormal.' "

That faith is nowhere more evident than in the U.S.S.R., which has been beset in recent years with controversial sensitives. One, Ninel Kulagina, was appraised as capable of causing objects to float in mid-air. As Martin Gardner notes, "She is a pretty, plump, dark-eyed little charlatan who took the stage name of Ninel because it is Lenin spelled backward. She is no more a sensitive than Kreskin, and like that amiable American television humbug, she is basically show biz." Indeed, Ninel has been caught cheating more than once by Soviet Establishment scientists.

Another Russian lady, Rosa Kuleshova, can "read" with her fingertips while securely blindfolded. James Randi, analyzing photographs of Kuleshova, promptly announced that her act was "a fraud." To prove his point, he invited testers to blind-

A LONG HISTORY OF HOAXES

The first professional organization to study paranormal phenomena was the British Society for Psychical Research, founded in 1882. Among its membership were prominent scholars and scientists— men of unimpeachable credentials and high moral character. They soon discovered and enthusiastically reported on the telepathic abilities of five little girls, daughters of the Rev. A. M. Creery. The mentalist millennium was at hand. Six years later, the girls were caught cheating and shamefacedly admitted that they had fooled the investigators. They were the first in a long series of deceivers of scientists.

The society's next major project was an investigation of two "sensitives" from Brighton, G. A. Smith and Douglas Blackburn. Smith would allow himself to be blindfolded, his ears to be plugged, his body to be thoroughly blanketed; yet somehow the thoughts of Blackburn reached him. This time, it seemed, the S.P.R. had really justified its existence.

When Smith left the S.P.R. in 1892, no other comparable sensitive could be found. Still, the members had seen the telepathy performed with their own eyes; the evidence was held acceptable. It was not until 1908 that Blackburn admitted deceit. "The whole of these alleged experiments were bogus," he later wrote. The remainder of his statement has echoed to this day: "(Our hoax) originated in the honest desire of two youths to show how easily men of scientific mind and training could be deceived when seeking for evidence in support of a theory they were wishful to establish."

The American Society for Psychical Research, organized with the help of Philosopher William James in 1885, suffered similar embarrassments. Yet it pursued its quarry with vigor. As James had noted, "To upset the conclusion that all crows are black, there is no need to seek demonstration that no crow is black; it is sufficient to produce one white crow. But after 25 years of reading psychic literature and witnessing phenomena, James admitted that he was "theoretically no further than I was at the beginning, and I confess that at times I have been tempted to believe that the Creator has eternally intended this departure of nature to remain baffling."

Other researchers had not been humble or uncertain. Late in the century, a self-styled sensitive named Henry Slade toured the U.S. and Europe making objects vanish and swinging compass needles without the aid of a magnet. He was so convincing that a German scientist published a book, *Transcendental Physics,* devoted to Slade's accomplishments. Again, the psychic millennium seemed imminent. But his biography, *A Magician Among the Spirits,* Harry Houdini reported that the conjurer was simply a fraud with a dazzling technique; Slade later confessed that it was indeed all an act.

Perhaps parapsychology's most gullible proponent was Sir Arthur Conan Doyle, creator of the superrationalist detective Sherlock Holmes. Doyle remains the greatest proof that intelligence and scruple cannot compete with naiveté and the desire to accept the paranormal as demonstrable fact. After the death of his son in the Great War, he turned to spiritualism for solace. This led, in time, to investigations of spirits, and eventually to little winged creatures in the bottoms of gardens. In his 1922 volume *The Coming of the Fairies,* Doyle reproduced photographs of a tiny goblin and elves caught by a child's camera. The pictures were manifestly staged; the entire project made all but the blindest believers wince. One who did not was a young American botanist named J. B. Rhine. After an inspiring Doyle lecture on spiritualism, Rhine and his wife Louisa immersed themselves in literature published by the Society for Psychical Research. When Rhine later joined the faculty of Duke University, he began a lifelong devotion to psychic research. It was he who coined the terms extrasensory perception and psi (for psychic phenomena); it was he who gave his specialty an academic *(continued)* imprimatur by compiling mountains of statistics about psychic subjects who could "read" cards that they could not see.

From the start, Rhine was criticized for juggling numbers. (Subsequent researchers have also used questionable procedures, citing "negative ESP" when the number of correct guesses fall below average and "displacement" when subjects call the card before or after the one they are trying to guess.) H. L. Mencken summarized the early views of the dubious when he wrote, "In plain language, Professor Rhine segregates all those persons who, in guessing the cards, enjoy noteworthy runs of luck, and then adduces those noteworthy runs of luck as proof that they must possess mysterious powers." Rhine tightened his laboratory conditions in the 1930s, and much of the criticism withered—but so did his ESP stars.

In the 1960s a psychic superstar came along in the person of Ted Serios, a hard-drinking, onetime bellhop from Chicago. Serios' gift was definitely off-beat: he produced pictures inside a Polaroid camera using nothing but his mind and a little hollow tube he called his "gismo." Reporters Charles Reynolds and David Eisendrath, who observed Serios at work in Denver, had little trouble constructing a device that could be secreted inside a gismo to produce all of Serios' effects. The instrument contained a minuscule lens at one end and a photographic transparency at the other. When the device was pointed at the camera lens and the shutter was clicked, an image was recorded on film. The Reynolds-Eisendrath story was printed in *Popular Photography* and many of Serios' followers were shattered. Again the millennium was deferred.

fold him with pizza dough, a mask and a hood. Then he proceeded to drive a car in traffic. "I won't tell you how I did it," he says. "But it was not parapsychologically. It was pure deception, just as hers was." Such revelations have not deterred the parapsychologists in the U.S.S.R. or elsewhere. They freely concede that many of their subjects do sometimes cheat, but still may have paranormal powers.

In and out of the laboratory, many paranormalist investigators conduct experiments that mock rigorous and logical procedure. Claims are made, and the burden of proof is shifted to the doubter. Ground rules are laid down by the psychic subject and are all too eagerly accepted by his examiner. If the venture proves unsuccessful, a wide range of excuses are proffered: an unbeliever provided hostile vibrations; the subject was not receiving well; negative influences were present; testing rules were too restrictive. It is all reminiscent of the laws in *Through the Looking-Glass*, where people approach objects by walking away from them. And it creates an atmosphere in which even a genuine paranormal subject might have a hard time certifying his abilities.

No one has contributed more to the paranormal explosion than Uri Geller, the handsome, 26-year-old Israeli former nightclub magician who seems equally adept at telepathy, psychokinesis and precognition. "I don't want to spend my whole life in laboratories," Geller recently told TIME London Correspondent Lawrence Malkin. "I've just done a whole year at Stanford Research Institute [TIME, March 12]. Now I'll go on to other countries, and let them see if they know what it is I've got."

Death Threats

At the Stanford Research Institute Geller successfully worked most of his repertoire of miracles. In a film made by

S.R.I., Geller picks the can containing an object from a group of identical empty cans, influences laboratory scales, reproduces drawings sealed in opaque envelopes, deflects a magnetometer and correctly calls the upper face of a die in a closed box—eight times in eight tries. If Geller's prowess with dice is indeed paranormal, it raises serious and disturbing questions for all of modern science. But if S.R.I.'s tests were indeed conducted with what University of Oregon Professor Ray Hyman calls "incredible sloppiness," then other disturbing questions may be raised. Assigned by the Department of Defense to report on the wondrous happenings at S.R.I., Hyman, accompanied by George Lawrence, DOD projects manager for the Advanced Research Projects Agency, caught Geller in some outright deceptions.

Unhappily for Geller, his powers have a tendency to vanish in the presence of sleight-of-hand men. On the *Tonight Show,* where Johnny Carson instituted airtight controls at Randi's suggestion, nothing that Geller attempted (during an embarrassing 20 minutes) seemed to work. After a group of English magicians made plans to catch him in the act during a British tour, Geller abruptly canceled out, citing mysterious "death threats."

In the long run, however, Geller's friends may well be more damaging to his cause than are his detractors. This spring the reputable old firm of Doubleday will publish a book entitled *Uri* by Dr. Andrija Puharich, who brought Geller to the U.S. from Israel. In a crude mishmash of *Mission: Impossible, 2001* and the James Bond series, Puharich (author of a previous volume on the psychedelic effects of mushrooms) soberly describes his adventures with Geller.

From outer space, highly intelligent computers called SPECTRA communicate through taped messages, which disappear. "We can only talk to you through Uri's power," says the mystical voice. "It is a shame that for such a brilliant mind we cannot contact you directly." When Uri finally meets the investigators from S.R.I., he confesses that outer-space intelligence directs his work. But the S.R.I. scientists are not taken aback. One, Russell Targ, placidly remarks, "The things you are telling us agree very well with things that Hal [S.R.I. Colleague Harold Puthoff] and I believe but we can't prove." Adds Astronaut Ed Mitchell: "Uri, you're not saying anything to us we don't in some way already sense or understand." The text raises some troubling questions. Is Puharich indeed in touch with what he calls "my editor in the sky"? Is his account of the S.R.I. meeting as true as his reasonably accurate report of Uri's meeting a year ago with the editors of TIME? If it is, why have the S.R.I. scientists failed to mention Uri Geller's contacts with outer space? Are they properly fearful of that most irrefutable antidote to nonsense: laughter? Or were they, as they now claim, merely "humoring" their subject?

Almost as impressive as Geller's rise to fame is the phenomenal success of *The Secret Life of Plants* (Harper & Row; $8.95), a volume that is unaccountably placed on the nonfiction shelves of bookstores. The work of two occult journalists, *Secret Life* is an anthology of the absurd, costumed in the prim gown of laboratory respectability. In it are researchers like Cleve Backster, a lie-detector expert who attached the terminals of his machines to plants. Behold! The vegetation reacted to his thoughts. Most scientists have greeted the experiments with open skepticism—with good reason. After his plants would not respond for a visiting Canadian plant physiologist, for example, Backster offered an interesting hypothesis: the plants "fainted" because they sensed that she routinely incinerated her own plants and then weighed the ashes after her experiments.

Backster is the essence of conservatism compared with the book's more adventurous researchers. A New Jersey electronics buff, Pierre Paul Sauvin, attached a Rube Goldbergian machine to his plants, and then spent the weekend with his girl friend at a place 80 miles away. He found that even at that distance the plants had responded to his sexual relations with the girl. The tone oscillators went "right off the top," he says, at the moment of orgasm.

In Japan, Ken Hashimoto, another polygraph expert, discovered that his cactus could count and add up to 20. George De La Warr, a British engineer, insisted that young plants grew better if their "mother" were kept alive. Ironically, the authors did not address themselves to some significant facts about botany. Plants do respond physiologically to certain sound waves. Talking to a plant may indeed make it healthier, because it thrives on the carbon dioxide exhaled by the speaker.

Many psychics and their followers believe that paranormal powers may be dependent on mysterious auras or "energy flows," phenomena that they say can be recorded by Kirlian photography. The technique, developed in the late 1930s by Russian Electronics Expert Semyon Kirlian and his wife Valentina, involves introducing a small amount of high-voltage, high-frequency current into the subject and recording the subsequent discharge on photographic film. The result is a photograph showing an "energy body"—a weird aura —around the plant, animal or human part being photographed.

Soon, Kirlian claimed that photographing a portion of a leaf, for example, would produce the aura of the entire leaf on film. Some psychics claim that in time the aura of a missing limb might be discernible with Kirlian photography. Today the process is an integral part of paranormal exploration. In the U.S. the leading proponent of the art

is U.C.L.A. Psychologist Thelma Moss, who has taken more Kirlian photographs and done more experimental work with them than anyone outside Russia.

Moss, a former Broadway actress, found her interest in parapsychological phenomena kindled after LSD therapy. "From the first," she recalls, "I intended to specialize in parapsychology because of the glimpses of psychic phenomena I experienced during the LSD treatments. But I certainly don't feel the need to use drugs any more ... When you've gotten the message, you hang up the phone." For Moss, the message is that Kirlian photography clearly demonstrates a human aura. "We have done work with acupuncturists and [psychic] healers," she says, "and we find that the corona of the healer becomes intense before healing, and then afterward is more relaxed and less strong. We think we're looking at a transfer of energy from the healer to the injured person."

Others are less certain. Writing in the *Photographic Society of America* journal, Bill Zalud concluded, "All speculation hinges on obtaining photographs of normal tissue patterns for comparative purposes and, so far, no one has really determined what a normal Kirlian photograph is." Stanford Professor William Tiller, an enthusiast of the paranormal, is more assured about the technical cause of Kirlian phenomena on film. "What we're looking at," he maintains, "is cold electron discharge."

Sickly Tissue

Says L. Jerome Stanton, author of a forthcoming book on auras and Kirlian photography: "Perhaps some day the technique will be a valuable diagnostic tool. Maybe sick people do have different 'auras.' But as of now, there is no assurance that it is at all useful." Though not accusing Kirlian researchers of faking effects, Stanton notes that the famous "phantom leaf" is easy to duplicate by double-exposing the film, first with the whole leaf, again after a portion has been removed, and that different voltages and conditions can change the picture in incalculable ways. "Working with advanced equipment," he says, "I could produce Kirlian effects that would astound the unsophisticated, and that includes a lot of scientists and physicists. Remember, electronics and photography are two very complicated fields. Mix them and all but the expert will remain in the dark."

The most irresponsible and odious niche in the world of the paranormal is occupied by the psychic healers, who cannot operate legally in the U.S. but lure unfortunate Americans overseas with claims of spectacular cures. Diagnosing illnesses and locating diseased organs by purely psychic means, they perform operations by plunging their hands through what appear to be deep incisions to grasp and remove sickly tissue. In the Philippines, currently the center for psychic surgery, a number of conjurers use sleight of hand and buckets of blood and animal parts to work their wonders. Surrounded by adherents who have been "cured," the ill-educated and often filthy surgeons perform "operations"—slashes of the epidermis, knives in the eye cavity, fingers in the abdomen—sometimes painlessly and always with great flourish.

As one witness to such "surgery" describes it: "The healer pulled some tissue from the area of the 'operation' . . . I literally grabbed the 'cancerous tissue' from Tony's hand . . . I wanted to have valid medical tests performed on it. The tests, conducted in Seattle, showed that the tissue was 'consistent with origin from a small animal . . . there is no evidence in any of this tissue to suggest that this represents metastatic carcinoma from the breast of the patient.' " Tom Valentine, author of a book on perhaps the best known of the psychic surgeons, Tony Agpaoa, documents the experience of a Mrs. Raymond Steinberg of Two Rivers,Wis. Tony "made a major production" of removing a piece of metal and several screws that had been surgically placed in her hip after an automobile accident. X rays later showed that Agpaoa had removed nothing.

True Believer

But the psychics, and those who profit from them, remain undaunted. In a few months, the respectable publishing firm of Thomas Y. Crowell will publish the story of yet another psychic healer, the late great Brazilian Arigo, *Surgeon of the Rusty Knife.* The author: John Fuller, whose pro-flying-saucer books *Incident at Exeter* and *The Interrupted Journey* were big sellers during the UFO craze of the 1960s. The afterword is written by Geller Biographer Puharich, who in *Uri* incidentally tells of extraterrestrial intelligence assuring him that Arigo was not hurt in his fatal car accident in 1971: "There was no pain. He left his body before the crash."

No amount of demonstrable fraudulence, no exposure of the fake, the manipulator, the unscrupulous, ever seems capable of dissuading the true believer in paranormality. James Fadiman, of the Stanford School of Engineering, believes that "most (but not all) parapsychologist demonstrators are also frauds," then gives the classic rationale: "Look at it this way. You think you have powers of clairvoyance, and finally you become a celebrity because of it. You're on the stage or in an experimental situation and sometimes your powers fail you. They do very often for most of these guys. So what do they do? They cheat."

Robert Benchley once separated people into two categories: those who separate people into two categories and those who do not. Parapsychologist Gertrude Schmeidler of New York's City College is in the first category. Her studies show that on the issue of parapsychology her subjects divide into believing sheep and doubting goats. The sheep almost invariably score higher in tests of paranormal powers. Will the sheep ever convince the ruminating goats? Will the goats ever undermine the faith of obedient sheep? Stranger events have occurred.

Just a few years ago what smug Western rationalist would have accredited acupuncture? Yet the ethnocentric prejudice seemed to disappear almost at a stroke when the Western world learned of James Reston's appendix operation. The New York *Times* columnist submitted to acupuncture after surgery on a trip to China in 1971; thereafter, the unorthodox method was examined throughout the U.S. Today acupuncture is under intense study at several medical centers. Although some of the beneficial effects of "paranormal" medicine have been acknowledged by Western scientists, they are still at a loss to explain it. It was not long ago that most Americans attributed the feats of Eastern yogis to clever fakery. Yet the new Western experimentation with biofeedback* has shown skeptics that the mind can indeed control what are normally involuntary bodily functions. The Menninger Foundation in Topeka, Kans., reports incontrovertible proof that subjects trained by biofeedback can control their blood circulation and lower the temperature of the parts of their bodies at will; migraine headaches can be literally wished away. The ancient yogic mythic skills suddenly seem within the grasp of everyone.

Is it not possible that thoughts—like TV programs—can be transmitted from one brain to another? And if enough energy can be generated by the brain, why should it not influence the roll of dice? Or make a plant respond?

In an epoch when the new physics posits black holes in the universe and particles that travel faster than the speed of light, and has already confirmed the existence of such bizarre things as neutrinos that have no mass or charge, antimatter and quasars, why should any phenomenon be assumed impossible? What is wrong with Physicist Sir James Jeans' attempt to give coherence to an unruly cosmos: "The universe begins to look more and more like a great thought than a great machine"?

The psychic adherent's reply is simple: anything is possible. But simply saying that it is so, and then supporting the contention with shoddy or downright fraudulent evidence, is not enough. Psychic phenomena cannot be accepted on faith; they must be convincingly demonstrated to objective people by objective researchers. To date, those demonstrations have not been made.

Any close examiner of psychic investigators and reporters will find a new meaning for Koestler's roots of coincidence. A loose confederacy of parapsychologists parodies the notion of the scientific method. Harold Puthoff, one of the two S.R.I. investigators of Uri Geller, is singled out in *The Secret Life of Plants* as a reputable scientist who has been experimenting with the response of one chicken egg to the breaking of another. He is also a promoter of the bizarre and controversial cult of Scientology, which Ingo Swann, another psychic tested by S.R.I., also practices. William Targ, a Putnam executive, recently contracted to publish Astronaut Ed Mitchell's forthcoming book, *Psychic Exploration, A Challenge for Science.* At the signing, Targ stated that "the real race now between the Russians and us is in the area of sciences like ESP." Mitchell's Institute of Noetic Sciences helped to fund S.R.I.'s Geller research, which was conducted largely by Puthoff

---

*A process by which one can learn to control involuntary bodily functions (such as heartbeat) through the visual or aural monitoring of physiological data.

and Russell Targ, who happens to be Editor Targ's son.

The questionable connections of many psychic researchers, in addition to the paucity of objectively verifiable results in their work, has made it difficult to raise funds for research; parapsychologists barely squeak by with money from a few foundations and gifts and encouragement from occasional philanthropists like Stewart Mott and Manhattan Realtor John Tishman. There is only one academic chair on parapsychology in the U.S., at the University of Virginia. Should the findings prove depressingly negative, it is unlikely that academies or foundations would encourage more chairs, or promote further psychic investigations.

In a way, it is rather a pity that the sheep cannot get together with the goats. At the very least, the paranormal establishment has questioned the dogma, emphasized the ignorance and underlined the arrogance of modern medicine and science. Indeed, modern doctors have scarcely breached the frontiers of the mind. Science has all too frequently destroyed the layman's sense of wonder by seeking materialistic explanations for all phenomena.

As C. P. Snow says: "Scientists regard it as a major intellectual virtue to know what not to think about." Complains one S.R.I. spokesman: "The society we live in doesn't give you permission to have psychic abilities. That is one reason that so much talent is suppressed." As Martin Gardner believes, "Modern science should indeed arouse in all of us a humility before the immensity of the unexplored and a tolerance for crazy hypotheses."

As for the parapsychologists who make many of those hypotheses, they could learn the most valuable weapon in the arsenal of the truth seeker: doubt. One hundred and fifty years ago Charles Lamb observed that credulity was the child's strength but the adult's weakness. That observation is even more valid today, when shoddy or ignorant research is used to lend legitimacy to the most extravagant tenets of the psychic movement.

That is not to say that parapsychology ought to be excluded from serious scrutiny. Some first-rate minds have been attracted to it: Freud, Einstein, Jung, Edison. The paranormal may exist, against logic, against reason, against present evidence and beyond the standard criteria of empirical proof. Perhaps there are reasons why the roll of the dice and turn of the cards sometimes appear to obey the bettor's will. Perhaps the laws of probability are often suspended. Perhaps Geller and other magicians can indeed force metal to bend merely because they will it. Perhaps photographs can be projected by the mind. Perhaps plants think.

Perhaps not.

There is only one way to tell: by a thorough examination of the phenomena by those who do not express an a priori belief. By those for whom probability is not a mystique but a comprehensible code. By those who have nothing to lose but their skepticism. Until such examiners are allowed to play the psychic game, it is unlikely that the paranormal will escape the ambiguous utterance against it in *Leviticus:* "Do not turn to mediums or wizards; do not seek them out, to be defiled by them . . ." And that most wondrous and mysterious of entities, the human mind, will remain an underdeveloped country.

45.   BIOFEEDBACK: AN EXERCISE IN "SELF-CONTROL"

Barbara Brown

Most biomedical discoveries are about bits and pieces of man's mind or body. It is not that these discoveries are not important; they have saved society the sadness of much disease and salvaged injured bodies and damaged minds. Significant as medical progress has been, it has not slaked the nagging feeling, the intuition, of most people that the occasional brilliance and power of man's mind in conquering nature could as well be turned to promoting the well-being of mind and body by action of the mind alone. As sophisticated as society has become, today's robust resurgence of interest in spiritual healing and psychic surgery is graphic testimony of a widespread belief in mind power.

From the beginning of history, mentalists have challenged scientific authority, just as convinced that mind power controls the universe as scientists are that physical order controls man's destiny. Science has always won, for it is far easier to be convincing with demonstrations of physical cause and effect on your side. On its side, mind power has not been systematically corralled nor put to effective use. Mind power has not existed for most scientific authority, even when it fathomed mysteries or became engulfed in momentous ideologic conflicts.

Then suddenly, in the Sixties, like a series of underground nuclear explosions, experiments began rumbling throughout the country that presaged perhaps the greatest medical discoveries of all time. In the fran-

tic research activity that has followed, it has become clear that man may, after all, have a mind resource to control his own being, down to the most minute fragments of his physical structure. Including his brain.

The simplest statement of the discovery is revolutionary: Given information about how any one of the internal physiological systems is operating, the ordinary human being can learn to control the activity of the system. It can be heartbeat, blood pressure, gastric acid, brain waves, or bits of muscle tissue; it does not seem to make much difference what function of the body it is as long as information about how it is behaving is made available. And generally, the more the information, the easier it is to learn to control the body function.

Most people can control what they do with arms and legs, with eye, face, or other muscles, using the kind of body control called voluntary. But until recently, medical science has believed and taught that nearly all other body functions, such as blood flow, body temperature, brain waves, or even residual muscle tension itself, were under automatic regulation and beyond voluntary control. Almost without warning this dictum has collapsed. The new research has shown that people can learn to control even these kinds of body function.

The discovery of this ability of mind is abbreviated in the term *biofeedback,* an ideograph that describes the phenomenon of control over internal biological functions occurring when information about the function is "fed back" to the person whose biologic activity it is. It is a compound of a

Reprinted from *Saturday Review* (February 22, 1975) by permission of publisher, pp. 22–27.

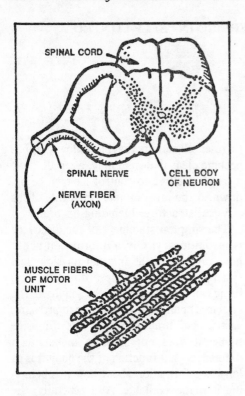

SPINAL CORD

SPINAL NERVE

CELL BODY
OF NEURON

NERVE FIBER
(AXON)

MUSCLE FIBERS
OF MOTOR
UNIT

technology and a training procedure, using specially designed electronic instruments to detect and monitor physiologic activities (such as heart rate or brain waves). The individual practices to control the action of the monitor by manipulating his mental and internal activities, and the result is a learned, voluntary control over the physiologic functions monitored. It is a technique for extending the capabilities of the mind to control the body—and the mind.

The discovery occurred when researchers began giving information about body activities directly *to* people rather than recording it to be filed away for their own research or medical uses. It is the return of information to the individual that is crucial to the biofeedback process. For centuries medical men have laid claim to the increasing volumes of information about human bodies, but never before have they shared it. Somehow medical opinion had decided that information about the workings of one's own body could be hazardous to one's health. But medical opinion was wrong.

The implications of biofeedback are revolutionary and perplexing, because biofeedback research itself is dramatic and mystifying. In Dr. John Basmajian's neuroanatomy laboratory, for example, ordinary people are shown oscilloscope tracings of the spontaneous electrical activity of various small groups of their own muscle cells, activity detected by sensors on the skin over a muscle. With almost psychic power, these ordinary people begin to control, selectively, the minute electrical activity of different groups of muscle cells—voluntarily—just as they can voluntarily control the whole muscle when they want to move it. However, now they are activating as few as three muscle *cells* simply by deciding to do so.

Basmajian further taxes our capacity to conceptualize such mind control by demonstrating that the site of control actually occurs in single motoneuron cells in the spinal cord. His subjects (and the subjects of many other investigators) learn to activate these single cells within as short a time as 15 minutes, sometimes much less. The precision of the control is extraordinary: To activate one cell independently means that other related cells, normally involved in muscle movement, must simultaneously be suppressed. Yet despite the facility in learning the control, and its complexity and precision, the human mind appears to be at a complete loss to explain how it accomplishes this extraordinary feat. The reports of most people are that they know they *can* do it, but they do not know *how* they do it.

Or, as in the laboratories of Brener and Hothersall, it was discovered that human beings could—unconsciously—learn to control a body function traditionally believed to function automatically: the rate of the beating heart.

Like so many other experimental psychological studies, this one sounds more like a practical joke than research; yet the results are impressive and interesting. Volunteer subjects were asked to make a device produce different pitches of tones "by purely mental means." A red-light signal was a request to make high tones, and a green light was a request to make low tones. Presumably the subjects did not know that they were, in fact, directly wired to the tone-producing device and that it was the amplified electrical energy of their own heartbeats that activated the tones. When the heart accelerated, the tones were high; when the heart slowed, the tones were low. With a little practice, the subjects learned to manipulate the tones. Incredibly, they remained unaware that their own heartbeats turned on the tones and that it was their unconsciously learned control of heart rate that caused the tones to change.

In the brief span of time during which biofeedback has been with us, there have been more reports confirming its validity than for almost any previous biological discovery in an equivalent period of time. Its implications for both theory and applications are almost limitless, for when we come right down to it, there is little about the functioning of human beings that does not in some way depend upon the feeding back of biological information to the generator of that information. The excitement that biofeedback has brought is the discovery that man's mind can process and understand even his own cellular information and use it to extend his control of self far beyond that ever before believed possible.

Take the role of biofeedback in tension and anxiety as the simplest example, but one with perhaps the farthest-reaching potential. The majority of emotional problems, and perhaps a good many medical problems as well, stem from the excessive tension and anxiety of today's fast-paced world, and the tensions are directly and immediately manifest as muscle tension.

In medical science the vast therapeutic benefits of relaxation have been known since the early days of this century. Although remarkably successful in many emotional and medical problems, the medical use of relaxation has been limited because it is time-consuming and requires more patience and persistence than most ill patients can summon. This relative impracticability has led therapists to neglect the fact that it is the intimate relationship between muscles and mind that becomes distorted under mental and emotional tension, that somehow this affects other body functions, and that effective relaxation can relieve those emotionally caused illnesses called psychosomatic.

To many relaxation theorists, anxiety (emotional tension) and relaxation are mutually exclusive. Certainly it has been learned, both medically and psychologically, that where there is anxiety, there is muscle tension, and that when muscle tension is relieved, so is anxiety.

Physiologic studies suggest why this may be true. The tension of muscle cells is adjusted by means of a feedback control loop operating between tension sensors in muscle cells and brain areas concerned with effective muscle movement. The control system, operating something like the household thermostat, compares actual tension with what it should be for a given situation and initiates activation of appropriate adjustments. This linear mechanism is ideal for moving muscles and for mobilizing muscles as a first line of defense. The system does not, however, cope well with the way human beings react to social pressures. By social custom physical action is tempered, submerging the defense posture into an unconscious intention to be ready for action, to be alert and tensed. When emotional tension and its muscle-tensing effect are prolonged, the system undergoes adaptation and the control becomes set to higher and higher levels of tolerated muscle tension. It is an insidious accommodation that leads to the muscles' becoming set into patterns of tenseness. Its continuous-loop nature feeds upon itself, anxiety tenses the muscles, and the increased tension of muscles keeps the mind apprehensive. But because it is a continuous loop, intervention can be either in the mind or in the muscles. Effective psychotherapy can relieve muscle tension, and effective relaxation procedures can relieve anxiety.

Biofeedback-assisted relaxation is so reasonable that it is surprising it has taken so long to discover. With its ability to amplify a hundredfold, it detects that muscle tension persisting even when the muscles appear at complete rest, the tension built up from social pressures. This residual tension is amplified and converted to a form of electrical energy that can operate meters of any other convenient signal. Because a signal like a meter constantly reads and displays the tension, it can be perceived as it fluctuates over time. Although this is a new form of muscle information, the brain uses it to exert voluntary control over the otherwise-imperceptible tension level in the same way that it uses internally sensed information from muscle sensors to move muscles.

In much the same way, symbols of the body's other functions are used to bring them under voluntary control. The diversity of functions—such as peripheral blood flow, blood pressure, heart rate, intestinal contractions and secretions, skin electrical activity, and brain waves—that are responsive to this learning paradigm sharply implicates the intervention of complex mental activity in the automatic regulation of the body.

A strange blindness has prevailed in modern science about the role of the mind in the catalog of human abilities. The failure of the mind sciences to conjecture meaningfully about mind capabilities is easily seen in their indifferent attitude about the way the mind-brain can supervene in what we take to be the automaticity of reflexes. Take blinking and winking, two simple, related, but quite different acts: one automatic, the other learned. Nearly every physiologic system of the body has a similar automatic mode for its fundamental operation, and now biofeedback has shown that each automatic control system can be additionally influenced by higher mental activities. Yet until this discovery, science had put little thought to what brain activity might occur when ordinary reflexes are controlled mentally, as when blinking is done intentionally and becomes winking. There is little, if any, concrete neurophysiologic knowledge about how volition turns into action.

There are other unacknowledged dimensions of voluntary control. Because intention can select and direct *any* physiologic action, it can be deduced that the decision to intervene actively and specifically in an otherwise automatic biologic activity may be a function of mind relatively independent of specific physiologic systems. This possibility is reminiscent of metaphysical thought: If intention—the will—can be mentally evoked and applied to a variety of biological actions with molecular specificity, it is necessary to postulate other mental actions of similar relative independence. The *decision* to do something must be implemented; it needs mechanisms to select the body system and to direct or carry out the intent.

As a matter of fact, the biofeedback phenomenon has already rather startlingly revealed a semi-independent role for sensory information. Bundles of sensory information once believed to play a subsidiary role in directing various physiologic activities can, instead, be mobilized to assume a primary role, as when visual information is used to control muscle tension or is substituted for visceral information to control heart rate. This unexpected substitution of sensory information is a sophisticated action of the mind-brain and one that begs for experimental clarification by its implications for extending mind abilities.

Until biofeedback and the recognition that higher, complex mental processes could alter automatic functions, the concept of intention, or voluntary control, was considered exclusively in terms of control of muscular activity. Yet despite a century of research, the decision-making part of brain activity has eluded physiological and anatomical definition. The paucity of information about the purely mental activities of the brain is not generally appreciated by mind scientists. The brain scientist becomes enmeshed in the complexities of neural and biochemical elements, while the experimental psychologist attempts to define mental capabilities largely in terms of behavioral responses to changes in the environment.

So the authorities on the functions of mind have data chiefly for reductionist theories to describe the abilities of the mind, theories circumscribed by the physical nature of the brain and physical responses to physical stimuli. Any experiencer of hallucinogens, or any religious mystic, could give more recognition to the existence of mind and its unique place in nature than could any mind scientist. It is as if laboratory-man, no less than primitive man, fears the unknown. Rather than seeking to learn and to use the non-ordinary capacities of mind, mind scientists (who are mainly brain scientists) have worked to keep the awesome power of mind within the limits of its physical confines.

I do not argue that ultimately the brain scientists may not prove out their theories; what I argue is that they have dogmatized rigid inhibitions for using mind, and these

have captured our social standards. We have set limits and norms for intelligence and creativity and outlawed flights of mind. It was less science than a changing social conscience that allowed some minds to see the ability of mind to control itself and its body in experiments that were little different from hundreds of earlier experiments that had discouraged such thoughts.

Through biofeedback we now know, as perhaps we should have always known, that the mind-body cannot direct the activities of the body unless it has information about what is going on in the environment of the body, its tissues, and its cells. And we should have known, too, that if the mind-brain cannot operate without information from the body, and the body cannot operate without information from the mind-brain, then mind-brain and body are not merely connected, they exist and function as a unit. There are volumes of experiential and medical documentation confirming the inseparability of mind and body; yet professional therapists, by tradition, by certification, and probably by economic considerations, assume responsibility for only one aspect: mind *or* body. Even with the development of psychiatry, medical science continues to impose a schizophrenic therapy on the problems of illness. The capacity of mind to regulate and heal the body, and itself, has been short-shrifted almost out of existence; problems of mind especially are nearly always first attacked by salving minds with drugs.

The unexpectedness of the biofeedback phenomenon stimulates more philosophic scientific conjecture than does any previous psychophysiologic research. It has taken some time for most researchers to realize that this "new" capacity of mind is most likely an extension of the inherent capability of man, and animals, to exert voluntary control over their own beings. Just how we voluntarily control anything about ourselves is still a mystery, but no matter how the phenomenon is viewed, it proceeds from a sophisticated action of the mind-brain. The fact that learning to control physiologic activities occurs without obvious use of conscious effort and without conscious understanding of how the control is accomplished is a dramatic confirmation of the remarkable capabilities of mind.

It has been, of course, disturbing to find that subjective knowledge of how individuals accomplish control of body functions could rarely be defined in conscious awareness. If the sensation of manipulating distant body activities is so elusive as to escape descriptions that can be communicated, then one is led to conjecture that a nonconscious awareness guides the entire process. And a complicated process it is, one that involves sense perception of abstract information (such as a meter reading) about a physiologic activity, one that organizes, associates, and integrates the information, then disperses correct directions to be transmitted neurally to the organs to change their activity according to a predetermined effective objective.

The non-verbalizable aspects of consciousness are a no-man's-land, uncharted and unpartitioned, without physical landmarks or guideposts. The scientist hesitates to enter such a strange land; yet the obvious facility of the mind to learn control over even the most vital of the body's functions can provide the scientist with physical indices for marking the action of the subconscious mind. To chart this long-hidden expanse of mind is one of the most exciting future uses of biofeedback.

The biofeedback phenomenon also generates new conjecture about the structural capabilities of the body. The rapidity and ease of biofeedback learning is difficult to account for by known theory and literally mandates new insights for study of those internally generated mental abilities that

shape what our minds and bodies do. If people can so quickly learn to control events in their bodies that they scarcely knew existed, are they reactivating a lost ability, or are they evolving a new capacity of mind? Either conjecture is provocative. The fact that we, and our animal relatives, do voluntarily control our major life's activities suggests that the control ability has always existed. If it were a new, evolving capacity, chances are it would be manifest as an erratic, fumbling attempt to control the microcosms of our bodies. But if, as in Basmajian's experiments with single cells buried deep in the spinal cord, the human mind can learn full control in a matter of minutes, is it because the ability to control single cells has always existed? If it has always existed, has our reluctance to recognize it been because the idea that mind can alter physical nature has been too overwhelming conceptually to our primitive understanding of the physical order of the universe, or too God-defying, to bring into conscious appreciation? Is it possible that man has suppressed a higher level of mental function, one that regulates every cell of the body?

And will the extraordinary potential of the biofeedback breakthrough be realized, or will the tradition that requires substantive proof of the limits of mind continue to restrain explorations of the endowments of mind claimed by artists, musicians, mathematical geniuses, inventors, mystics, and drug-takers?

The sticky point is that our society has accepted a good bit of scientific theory about the mind as fact, accepting definitions of mind as bounded and limited by the physical nature of the brain. The concept that the mind functions one-to-one with brain processes, a theory for which there is really very little data, should not be accepted as an unwritten limit to the faculties of the mind. Rather, because science is a long way from defining mind, it should be just as valid to explore the mind subjectively as it is to explore it by means of the objective measures currently used that are admittedly inadequate, meager, and often inappropriate.

We should by this time be well aware of the powerful consequences of untracking the mind and breaking its limits by means of drugs, the musical experience, or the emotional overloading of unorthodox experiential psychological techniques. While scientists themselves avoid recognizing the powerful impact of awareness-raising, consciousness-expanding, creative explosions that have marked the non-scientific society since the early Sixties, there can be no doubt about the revolutions in thought and conscience and consciousness that have occurred. New attitudes have developed about war, about social responsibility, about life values, about the environment. These are powerful changes in mind function, which have, in fact, significantly altered our notions of reality.

And yet, as a member of the scientific community, I watch reports of new research that purport to explore the principle of biofeedback, and I see the security blanket of traditional methodology and concept smothering the vital mechanism of a "new" mind, shaping experimental forays and conclusions to conform to concepts of mind that yet other evidence suggests may be illusory. It is like the Western attitude toward yogis. Until biofeedback, appropriate scientific experts refused to acknowledge the possibility of control of the physical body by mental disciplines. Now that biofeedback has shown that similar control can be attained through technologic aids, the conclusion is drawn that the yogic process is a biofeedback process and that the biofeedback process is little more than rote learning. That such conclusions are drawn without data is ignored; it seems obvious to

these experts that the similarities must exist and, more comfortingly, that the model for explaining human behavior can be preserved intact. And they continue to forget that the model does not explain why and how we select our goals, or what intention and creativity are.

For the immediate, practical applications of biofeedback, it may make little difference how the nature of the phenomenon is viewed, that is, whether one views it as a mechanical learning contingent upon rewards or as a capacity of mind in which complex mental processes can be marshalled by other complex mental processes that give rise to intent and direction. It will make no difference how the effect occurs, for the ability of the mind to exert voluntary control over body functions can be used effectively to relieve a startling number of distressing conditions of body and mind. Biofeedback has been successful in an unbelievable array of problems of health: tension and migraine headaches, cardiac irregularities, high blood pressure, peripheral vascular disease, gastric ulcer, insomnia, epilepsy, asthma, spastics, learning problems in children, and a host of other troublesome medical and psychological problems in human beings. And along the way it is opening the door to a more holistic approach to therapy.

The future of biofeedback is uncertain only because no one knows the limits of mental control of mind and body. A wide variety of physical and emotional illnesses are certain to be relieved. We should be able to learn how to keep our bodies and minds in states of good health because we now have the means to become aware of their best operating conditions. We have only now begun to explore what all of our brain waves mean to human mental activity, and in the future it seems likely that we will be able to control many of the numerous specific brain waves as well as patterns of brain waves that reflect the activities of our minds and states of consciousness. We should be able to become so aware of the best states of minds and bodies that we can achieve both internal harmony and harmony with the universe.

46. TRANSCENDENTAL MEDITATION AND THE SCIENCE OF CREATIVE INTELLIGENCE

Paul H. Levine

The search for definition of basic goals which is so prominent a concern of the educational community echoes a similar quest for purpose within my own field of science and, indeed, within society at large. While educators are asking, "What are schools for?"[1] scientists are asking, "What is the significance of science?"[2] and political leaders still seek to define our "national purpose." The soul-searching is widespread, yet within each profession or field of activity the search is carried out within the boundaries of that field, solutions are sought in the framework of the problem perceived, and more fundamental aspects of the situation are consequently overlooked.

It seems clear that what is really being asked is, What should be the objectives of human activity? with specific reference in each of the examples cited to the activities of teaching, doing science, or running a nation. If we adopt the common-sense position that the principal objective of *any* activity is to promote the fulfillment of the individuals engaged in and influenced by that activity, then the real goal of education

is seen to encompass nothing less than the *fulfillment* of the student.

In the sense we are using it here, fulfillment implies the actualization of the full potentialities for growth latent in the individual. Therefore, the measure of any educational system is first the breadth of its implicit *vision* of the range of these potentialities, and second its *effectiveness* in providing every student with a practical means for achieving such full development. If a crisis is felt to exist in education, then it may logically be asked whether the fault lies in too narrow a vision of the possibilities and, in consequence, too restricted an armamentarium for achievement.

This article discusses a particular conception of the range of potential human development which, if further validated by a growing body of anecdotal and scientific evidence, must necessarily change our ideas about individual fulfillment and with this our views on the structure and responsibility of education. The conception is that of Maharishi Mahesh Yogi; it is being taught as part of a new discipline called the Science of Creative Intelligence.

CREATIVE INTELLIGENCE

The concept of creative intelligence arises from an examination of the structure

Reprinted from *Phi Delta Kappan* (December 1972) by permission of the journal.

[1] Robert L. Ebel, "What Are Schools For?" *Phi Delta Kappan,* September, 1972, p. 3.

[2] Victor F. Weisskopf, "The Significance of Science," *Science,* April 14, 1972, p. 138.

of purposeful change in nature. No matter where we look, new forms and relationships are continually being created from lesser developed states. This evolution appears to be orderly, i.e., governed by intelligible laws. The intelligence displayed by nature in this process may be called creative intelligence. When we observe creation in action, whether it be in astronomy or biology—or even the growth of a rose—we encounter striking parallels in the structure of the creative process as it unfolds in each case. Through such interdisciplinary analyses, it comes to be appreciated that a fundamental significance can be accorded to creativity (and to the intelligence shaping its expression), a significance which transcends the particular sphere of activity in which the creativity is being manifested. Creative intelligence thus becomes a valid object of intellectual inquiry in its own right.

The relevance of such inquiry to education, and to practical life in general, stems from the circumstance that the creative impulse in man, as expressed in his progressive thoughts and actions, is found upon close examination to be structured along precisely the same lines as creative processes in the purely physical domain. This circumstance (not as remarkable as it may seem at first glance, since we are, after all, part of nature) immediately suggests a transcendental aspect to human creativity which necessarily casts consideration of the human condition into broader evolutionary contexts.

Fulfillment, for example, comes to mean full expression in an individual's life of the creative intelligence inherent in his nature. Lack of fulfillment (which we may call suffering) in this view is ascribed to some restriction of the flow of creative intelligence from its source at the core of one's being to the level of conscious awareness from which one perceives and acts. A practical consequence of this approach is the intriguing possibility that human problems can be attacked at a common fundamental level—without specific regard to the nature of the problem—much in the same way that a gardener simultaneously attends to deficiencies in the development of the many separate leaves of a plant by simply watering the root.

TRANSCENDENTAL MEDITATION

The existence of a simple natural technique called transcendental meditation lends substance to the above considerations, removing them from the realm of purely philosophical speculation. TM, as it is frequently abbreviated, is a systematic procedure of "turning the attention inwards towards the subtler levels of a thought until the mind transcends the experience of the subtlest state of the thought and arrives at the source of the thought. This expands the conscious mind and at the same time brings it in contact with the creative intelligence that gives rise to every thought."[3]

Figure 1. Relationship of TM to Other States of Consciousness

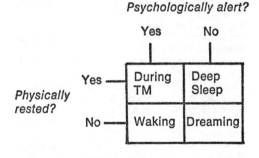

This technique for the direct *experience* of the field of creative intelligence at the

[3]Maharishi Mahesh Yogi, *Maharishi Mahesh Yogi on the Bhagavad-Gita: A New Translation and Commentary* (Baltimore: Penguin Books, 1969), p. 470.

root of one's being is apparently a universal human faculty not requiring any particular intellectual or cognitive facility other than the ordinary ability to think. It is easily learned by anyone in about six hours of instruction (spread out over four consecutive days) from a Maharishi-trained teacher.[4] Once learned, it can be continued without the necessity for additional instruction. It is primarily on the basis of this systematic and apparently universally applicable procedure for the empirical[5] verification of theoretical constructs involving creative intelligence that one may validly speak in terms of a *science* of creative intelligence, or SCI.

The rapidly expanding interest in SCI, both in and out of academia, and—surprisingly—both within the Establishment and the youth subculture, presently derives not so much from an appreciation of its inherent scope as from a desire for a fuller understanding of the immediate practical benefits of TM.[6] Notwithstanding the simplicity of the practice, meditators unanimously report improvements in the energy and enthusiasm with which they approach their activities and in their clarity of mind, mental and physical health, and ability to interact harmoniously with their environment.[7] Marked reductions in tension and moodiness are frequently cited, even by those in particularly stressful occupations or family situations. The list goes on to include increased creativity, perceptiveness, self-confidence, productivity, reading speed, psychomotor facility, and learning ability. As one might expect, meditators report concurrent reductions in their use of tranquilizers, stimulants, and other prescribed drugs—and, most significantly, of nonprescription drugs as well.[8] The combined effect is succinctly expressed by a Yale biology instructor: "There's been a quantum increase in the quality of my life since I started meditating."

Experiences during meditation vary from individual to individual and from one meditation to the next. A common experiential denominator, observed even in the first meditation, is a unique blend of deep physical relaxation and expanded mental awareness. The relationship of this state of mind and body to the more familiar states of waking, dreaming, and deep sleep may be schematized as in the matrix shown in Figure 1.

---

[4]A number of nonprofit tax-exempt organizations coordinate the activities of TM teachers. The educational community is served by the Students' International Meditation Society (SIMS), whose national headquarters is located at 1015 Gayley Avenue, Los Angeles, California 90024. Inquiries may be directed to the attention of the Science and Education Communications Coordinator.

[5]The customary view that subjective experience is ipso facto beyond the purview of science is undergoing change. See, for example, "States of Consciousness and State-Specific Sciences," by Charles T. Tart, in *Science,* June 16, 1972, p. 1, 203.

[6]The rate of instruction in TM has doubled each year since 1968. By the fall of 1972 over 150,000 Americans had learned TM. The broad base of this appeal can be gauged from the range of publications featuring articles on TM and SCI during the past year: *Time* (October 25, 1971), *Yale Alumni Magazine* (February, 1972), *Soldiers Magazine* (February, 1972), *Kentucky Law Journal* (1971–72, Vol. 60, No. 2), *Seventeen* (July, 1972), *Wall Street Journal* (August 31, 1972), *Today's Health* (April, 1972), *Science Digest* (February, 1972), and *Psychology Today* (March, 1972).

[7]TM is a purely mental technique practiced individually every morning and evening for 15 to 20 minutes at a sitting. It requires no alteration of life-style, diet, etc., and being a technique of direct experience (rather than a religion or philosophy), it does not require belief in the efficacy of the practice nor an understanding of the underlying theory.

[8]The widely publicized efficacy of TM in promoting the voluntary reduction of drug abuse as documented, for example, in the retrospective study of 1,862 subjects by Drs. R. K. Wallace and H. G. Benson of the Harvard Medical School (see "Narcotics Research, Rehabilitation, and Treatment" in "Hearings Before the Select Committee on Crime, House of Representatives," Serial No. 92-1, Part 2, p. 682—U.S. Government Printing Office, 1971) tends to overshadow public understanding of the broader effects of the practice and particularly its utility for the non-drug abuser.

Viewed in this context, TM can perhaps be accepted as just another natural albeit very useful style of functioning of the nervous system, to be alternated with the others on a regular daily basis. Since the dynamism of daily activity in large measure depends on the thoroughness of the psychophysiological rest achieved during the deep sleep and dreaming states, the additional profound rest claimed to occur during TM would account for the enlivened functioning in the waking state reported by meditators.

SCIENTIFIC RESEARCH

The anecdotal claims for TM, even when they are echoed by people of unquestioned objectivity and stature, must nevertheless be verified by the tools of science before they can be accepted by a society grappling with the very ills TM is purported to relieve so effortlessly. A unique aspect of TM vis-à-vis other techniques for mental or physical development is the depth of scientific investigation of its effects currently in progress throughout the world. Major research projects on TM are being carried out at over 40 universities and institutes, including the Harvard Medical School, Stanford Research Institute, and the Universities of Cambridge, Cologne, Rome, and Capetown. In great measure, this widespread research activity is made possible by the availability of large numbers of cooperative meditators at virtually every major university, as well as by the effortlessness of the technique itself, which permits experimentation to be performed without disturbing the meditation.

Much of the meditation research is still in its early phases, particularly the long-term clinical studies of TM's *possible* value for hypertensives (Harvard Medical School) and in the relief of mental illness (Hartford's Institute of Living). The re-

search that has reached publication stage, however, is already sufficient to establish that the psychophysiological effects both during and after TM are real and unique in their degree of integration.

In the *American Journal of Physiology,* a team of Harvard and University of California researchers has reported on these integrated characteristics of mind and body during TM, calling it a "wakeful hypometabolic physiologic state," i.e., a state of restful alertness (see Figure 1).[9] They found that the degree of metabolic rest after 5-10 *minutes* of TM was characterized by an average decrease in oxygen consumption of 17%, deeper than that achieved after 6-7 *hours* of sleep. They found a reduction in heart rate of three beats per minute, which, when correlated with an earlier study reporting a drop in cardiac output of 25% during TM,[10] indicates a significant reduction in the workload of the heart. EEG (i.e., "brain wave") measurements showed a predominance of slow alpha wave activity in the central and frontal areas of the brain, thereby clearly distinguishing TM from the waking, dreaming, and sleeping states.[11]

Most significant were the observations of an approximately threefold increase in skin resistance during TM, indicating relaxation and a reduction of anxiety. Biochemical studies of the meditators' blood showed a remarkable reduction in lactate concentration both during and after meditation. Anxiety symptoms are believed to be correlated with high blood lactate levels. Thus, as re-

---

[9]Robert Keith Wallace, Herbert Benson, and Archie F. Wilson, "A Wakeful Hypometabolic Physiologic State," *American Journal of Physiology,* September, 1971, pp. 795–99.

[10]Robert Keith Wallace, "The Physiological Effects of Transcendental Meditation: A Proposed Fourth Major State of Consciousness," Ph.D. Dissertation, University of California, Los Angeles, 1970; see also *Science,* March 27, 1970, p. 1, 751.

[11]The physiological measurements also show that TM is radically different from hypnotic states and other so-called "altered states of consciousness."

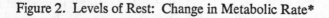

Figure 2. Levels of Rest: Change in Metabolic Rate*

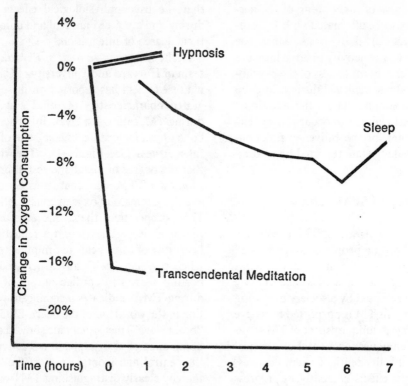

During transcendental meditation oxygen consumption and metabolic rate markedly decrease, indicating a deep state of rest. Reference: *Scientific American*, February, 1972.

ported in a recent *Scientific American* article, Robert K. Wallace and Herbert Benson are led to view TM as an integrated response or reflex which is opposite in its characteristics to the "fight or flight" response believed to be primarily responsible for the high incidence of hypertension and related diseases in today's fast-paced society.[12]

Psychological studies of personality changes attributable to TM have also begun to appear in the literature. In the *Journal of* *Counseling Psychology,* a University of Cincinnati team concluded that "the practice of meditation for a 2-month period would appear to have a salutary influence on a subject's psychological state as measured by the Personal Orientation Inventory."[13] Changes in the direction of increased "self-actualization" were found to occur for meditating subjects.

Another study, reported in the *Journal of Psychosomatic Medicine,* gives insight into a possible explanation for the wide variety

[12]Robert Keith Wallace and Herbert Benson, "The Physiology of Meditation," *Scientific American,* February, 1972, p. 84.

[13]William Seeman, Sanford Nidich, and Thomas Banta, "Influence of Transcendental Meditation on a Measure of Self-Actualization," *Journal of Counseling Psychology,* May, 1972, pp. 184–87.

of beneficial results apparently following from the simple practice of TM.[14] It was found that meditators habituated more rapidly to a stressful environment than nonmeditators and, furthermore, that meditators' nervous systems displayed greater autonomic stability. This evidence, together with the lactate observations cited earlier, tends to substantiate the view (presented in SCI) that TM acts to reduce one's store of psychophysiological stress while simultaneously reducing the likelihood of further stress accumulation. When one considers the manifold deleterious effects of stress, it becomes apparent that any technique which can reduce stress—e.g., the twice-daily experience of a hypometabolic wakeful state—has the potential for simultaneous improvement of one's life on all those levels previously stress afflicted. A "quantum jump in the quality of life" suddenly becomes credible.

IMPLICATIONS FOR EDUCATION

In the broader vision of SCI, stresses are viewed as impediments to the spontaneous flow of creative intelligence from the inner being to the level of conscious awareness from which one perceives and acts. An integral component of fulfillment, therefore, becomes the progressive physiological refinement of the nervous system in the direction of a reduced accumulation of stress. Indeed, SCI associates such refinement with a "growth in consciousness" and delineates the remarkable potentialities of a fully stress-free, fully normalized nervous system. The attainment of higher states of consciousness, long thought to be incompatible with an active life, now is said to be within the reach of anyone through TM,

and experiential evidence of this possibility seems to be one of the common cumulative effects of the practice.

The implications of all of this for education are quite exciting. At the most superficial level, the level of the problems, reduction of drug abuse among students and of social tension in the classroom is a likely concomitant of a widespread introduction of TM into the schools. The improved attitudes and behavior which generally are among the more immediate of TM's effects offer a chance for achieving affective goals without sacrificing performance goals. Indeed, preliminary reports of increased learning ability and reading speed with TM would seem to indicate that affective dispositions and cognitive resources grow hand in hand. Students at ease inside can be expected to respond more spontaneously and creatively to a learning environment.

On the other side of the desk, a meditating teacher (or administrator), being more at ease, energetic, healthy, clear-minded, creative, and perceptive, should naturally become more effective. Already, as discussed by Francis Driscoll elsewhere in this *Kappan* [December, 1972], there is concrete evidence that these are all valid expectations if the implementation of a TM/SCI-based program is approached with proper planning.

On a deeper level, if further research continues to substantiate "growth in consciousness" as a pragmatically meaningful concept, can this dimension of human development be overlooked by an educational system whose goal is the actualization of the full potentialities for growth latent in the student? One of the most ancient expressions of man's wisdom, the Vedas (to which SCI traces its ancestry), hold that "knowledge is structured in consciousness," the implication being that the higher the level of consciousness the more pro-

---

[14]David W. Orme-Johnson, "Autonomic Stability and Transcendental Meditation," *Journal of Psychosomatic Medicine,* in press.

found the level of knowledge which can be owned.

This leads finally to the most fundamental possibility for educational fulfillment of all those opened through SCI. The holistic ideal of education is to provide a common basis for all branches of learning. Certainly, *knowingness,* that very intimate relationship between the knower and the object of knowledge, is this common basis. The science of creative intelligence is principally the study of this relationship, both through intellectual analysis and through the direct experience of the field from which all knowledge springs. The whole tree is captured by capturing the seed. In the fullest

sense, therefore, creative intelligence may be said to be both the goal and the source of education.

A WORLD PLAN

Concrete programs are already under way for the widest diffusion of SCI and TM. Since its inauguration as an accredited course at Stanford in the 1970 winter quarter, SCI has achieved recognition from a rapidly growing number of universities and colleges around the world. The SCI course at Yale this past year, for example, explicitly demonstrated its integrative and interdisciplinary nature by bringing together

Figure 3. State of Relaxation: Change in Skin Resistance*

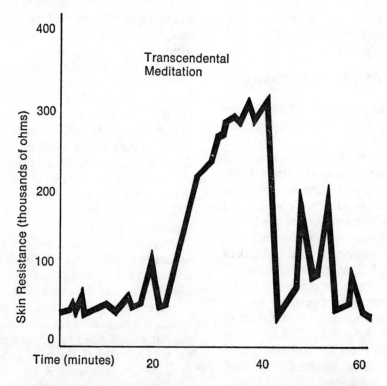

During stress or anxiety, skin resistance decreases. During transcendental meditation skin resistance increases significantly indicating deep relaxation and reduction of anxiety and emotional disturbances.

Figure 4. Biochemical Changes*

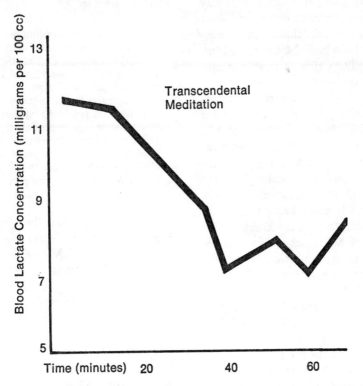

High concentration of lactate in the blood has been associated with anxiety neurosis, anxiety attacks, and high blood pressure. During transcendental meditation the concentration of blood lactate markedly decreases. Reference: *Scientific American,* February, 1972.

*Adapted from *Scientific Research on Transcendental Meditation,* a publication of the Maharishi International University Administration Center.

psychologists, philosophers, political scientists, and artists in a common exploration of the potentialities of consciousness.

SCI is being taught at other educational levels, including junior and senior high schools and adult education, in industry, and even in the military. Indeed, the commandant of the U.S. Army War College, Major General Franklin M. Davis, speaking at the First International Symposium on the Science of Creative Intelligence,[15]

[15]Held at the University of Massachusetts, Amherst, July 18 through August 1, 1971. International symposia on SCI are now held regularly each year at a number of universities throughout the world. Participants in 1971 included Buckminster Fuller, Harvey Brooks (dean of engineering and applied physics, Harvard University, and president, American Academy of Arts and Sciences), Melvin Calvin (Nobel Laureate in chemistry), and Willis Harman (director, Educational Policy Research, Stanford Research Institute). Symposia in 1972 featured Donald Glaser (Nobel Laureate in physics), Hans Selye, Marshall McLuhan, astronaut Rusty Schweickart, and the State Department China expert Alfred Jenkins.

said, "In military education, creative intelligence appears to have a definite potential, because it carries with it so much in the way of innovation, creative thinking, and what we in the military call 'challenging the assumption'!" To which Maharishi added, "When the military rises in creative intelligence, world peace will be a reality."

Educators at MIU (Maharishi International University), the institution founded in 1971 to formalize the training of SCI teachers, are now completing the preparation of syllabuses and teaching aids—including color video cassettes—for the teaching of SCI at all educational levels. MIU is currently embarked on an ambitious world plan to open 3,600 centers for the training of SCI teachers—one center per million population—throughout the world. Each center has as its goal the training of 1,000 teachers by means of a 33-lecture video-based course prepared specially for this purpose by Maharishi. The stated objectives of the world plan include the development of the full potential of the individual and the "realization of the highest ideal of education."

A utopian vision? Perhaps. But who would have imagined that a scant 14 years after a lone monk walked out of the Himalayas armed only with knowledge and his dedication to a long tradition of educators, the Illinois House of Representatives would formally resolve:

> That all educational institutions, especially those under State of Illinois jurisdiction, be strongly encouraged to study the feasibility of courses in Transcendental Meditation and the Science of Creative Intelligence on their campuses and in their facilities; and be it further ... resolved that a copy of this resolution be sent to: the Superintendent of Public Instruction, the deans of all state universities, the Department of Mental Health, State of Illinois, to inform them of the great promise of the program herein mentioned....[16]

And who would have thought that in this same "Year of the World Plan," the National Institute of Mental Health would award an initial grant of $21,540 to help train 120 secondary school teachers to teach SCI in American high schools?

Evidently, in the long war against the bondage of ignorance, a new and fascinating chapter is being written. Its outcome? In absolute earnest, Maharishi often tells his teachers-in-training, "Anything is possible, and anything means ... anything."

---

[16]House Resolution No. 677, adopted May 24, 1972.

47. "ROLFING," "AIKIDO," HYPNODRAMAS, PSYCHOKINESIS, AND OTHER THINGS BEYOND THE HERE AND NOW

Leo Litwak

The road to Squaw Valley crosses the Sierra summit and passes the site where in the winter of 1846 the Donner Party cannibalized itself. Now one can travel the path of the Donners by an all-weather superhighway. There is every safeguard for the traveler. The mountains are domesticated. Lakes Tahoe and Donner are safely hemmed in by driveins, motels, gambling casinos, subdevelopments and pristine acreage owned by the rich.

The ski, introduced by early Norwegian settlers, has proved to be the instrument of civilization. It was the 1960 Winter Olympic Games which finally tamed Squaw Valley, still isolated and unsettled as late as 1930. As the official program for the 1960 games put it, "Before it became the site of these games the valley was remote from large populations. Thanks to the improved roads and increased transportation services, Squaw Valley is accessible to thousands of persons." So, a history which began in dire tragedy ends happily. Within a few minutes of the place where the dead were once cast into stew pots, there is ready access to gambling parlors and hamburger joints.

The valley is a natural amphitheater, two and a quarter miles long, three-eighths of a mile wide. The surrounding ridges rise to 9,000-foot peaks. The ski facilities are at the far end of the valley. In summer, the improvements of civilization show up as wounds. The cables of unused ski lifts hang from the slopes like harpoon lines from beached whales. Squaw Creek, which divides the valley lengthwise, is bone dry and the ripped-up banks are visible. Ski trails cross the slopes like scars. Snow cures all that.

Yet fun and business don't wait for winter. Summer is convention time at Squaw Valley. The lodge facilities are in full use. Last June, hundreds of pom-pom girls arrived to attend pom-pom school. They were followed by Job's Daughters, a Masonic women's auxiliary. The facilities were then stretched to accommodate Dr. Armstrong's Radio Church of God, attended by 9,000 conventioners.

And finally, after the summer but before the arrival of the snows, the Association for Humanistic Psychology convened in Squaw Valley, far off the beaten academic track. It may have been an appropriate setting for an organization that many academic psychologists refuse to acknowledge as belonging in the ranks of reputable psychology. They might be willing to consign it to the domain of religion. They would certainly agree with the characterization of a recent magazine article which condemned humanistic psychology as an outgrowth of "squishy California thought." But for an increasing number of academics and nonacademics who have participated in its programs, the A.H.P. represents the wave of the future, boldly advancing the range of human potential.

More than 950 delegates registered for the 10th annual meeting of the Association.

© 1972 by the New York Times Company. Reprinted by permission. From *New York Times* Magazine (July 16, 1972), pp. 356–364.

A $25 fee entitled them to a full sampling of a long and varied program called "Beyond Here and Now: Bridging Boundaries." There was no simple way of characterizing the delegates. There was a mix of young and old, of academic and nonacademic, of male and female. Dress, manner, physical bearing all had a decidedly California cast. The clothing was exuberant, the manner informal and straightforward, the bearing athletic. Swimmers braved the pool in the chill morning hours and during the cold nights. The tennis courts were in constant use. Yoga practitioners meditated on the lawns. A few of the young unfurled sleeping bags near the Olympic Village dormitories, avoiding the room tab and making use of the dormitory plumbing. Families arrived by camper and set up in the parking lot. In the meetings, it was not unusual to observe a nursing mother calm a wailing infant during a crowded session. No one could have mistaken the Squaw Valley meeting of the humanistic psychologists for an academic conference.

A mere glance at the program was enough to distinguish the A.H.P. from the official academic organization, the American Psychological Association. The A.P.A. membership consists to a large extent of professional psychologists with college or university affiliation. In contrast, a substantial number of humanistic psychologists have no academic connections. Of those who do, many belong to departments other than psychology. Humanistic psychology was until recently practiced mainly off campus at such "growth centers" as the Esalen Institute. It is a movement that, in the past, defined itself in terms of opposition to certain dominant tendencies of traditional psychology; in particular, Skinnerian behaviorism and Freudian psychoanalysis.

I noticed in the program a category of meetings concerned with transcendental states of being and altered consciousness.

Evidence that life energy extends beyond physical boundaries is of considerable interest to those humanists who have taken a mystical direction and urge the notion of a transcendental mode of being. I chose first to attend a session in parapsychology, a report by Stanley Krippner of the Maimonides Medical Center in Brooklyn concerning Soviet research in telepathy, psychokinesis, acupuncture and "Kirlian photography." According to Krippner, the Soviets have seriously undertaken studies of parapsychological phenomena. He showed films of a visit he made to Moscow and Leningrad. There was a movie of a Russian woman with a talent for psychokinesis. She sat beside a plastic table and caused small cylindrical objects such as cigarettes to move in various patterns over the surface of the table by passing her hand above them. Krippner presented that the motion was an electrostatic effect. He tried the experiment himself and was able to move objects in a similar fashion. According to the Soviet research, ability to move objects could be increased with training. Psychokinetic ability also seemed related to such factors as the subject's self-confidence and the sympathy of observers.

The Kirlian photo is made by placing unexposed film between an electrode and the object to be photographed. An electric charge is passed through the object and an impression is left on film. We were shown photos made by the Russian inventors of the process as well as photos made by the Krippner group. The film apparently records the "energy discharge" of the electrified object. We were shown a sequence of three photos—a leaf on the vine, the same leaf immediately after being plucked, then again after a considerable time lapse. A blue glow around its boundaries emanates from the leaf on the vine. Immediately after plucking, the glow becomes red. The last photo shows only a dim glow. Soviet parapsychologists believe, according to Krippner, that all living structures are encompassed by a "bioplasm," or energy field, and that the Kirlian photograph records the state of this surrounding field. The Russians hypothesize that the blue discharge is correlated with high energy, the red with low energy. They believe that various drugs, including alcohol and the hallucinogens, produce a high energy discharge.

The basic commitment of humanist psychology is to what is called the "experiential." As a spokesman of the movement expresses it, "The most significant part of education is the experience which involves the head, the gut, the whole man. The mind is not in the head. It is in the whole body." The detached, impersonal view is rejected and the notion of a totally objective science is criticized. A.H.P. officers feel that their organization has received a bad press from reporters who have failed to participate in the events they reported. Encounter groups of various kinds, employing such methods as psychodrama and fantasy trips, remain a crucial part of the program. As the association's executive officer, John Levy, said to me, "You can't understand any encounter from the outside."

The insistence upon active audience participation keeps the meetings from becoming dull. I attended a hypnodrama session at the Hofbrau, an A-frame, chalet-type building, with scripted placards advertising the menu hanging from the walls ("Hier gibts fondue"). The Hofbrau was jammed. We were to be hypnotized and were then to participate in a hypnodrama. We encircled the fieldstone fireplace in the center of the large dining hall as Ira Greenberg of the Camarillo, Calif., State Hospital led the session. He described hypnosis as a "control of our controls." It was a technique, he said, that enabled us to concentrate deeply and regress to forgotten states; once these states were recalled, hypnodrama could be used

to act them out, enabling us finally to gratify the unsatisfied nurture needs of infancy.

We removed our shoes and lay on the floor flat on our backs. We were instructed to relax. We began with the toes and very gradually worked up to the head. We were reassured that the process was pleasant. We were asked to imagine a yardstick within our minds. We slowly counted down the yardstick until we came to the number which we felt represented the depth of our hypnosis. We tried to sink beneath this number. There were a few snores. We were urged to stay awake. We then began a fantasy trip. We flew up the mountain that was behind the Hofbrau; we were told to soar above the crest and enjoy the flight. We then settled down near the crest by a cave: entered inside and walked down a corridor passing several doors, stopping at that one which enclosed a place we had always wished to enter. We passed through this door, looked around, left the cave, descended to the Hofbrau and then awoke. We assembled in groups of five to discuss the experience. An elderly couple, a trifle disgruntled, denied that they were hypnotized and were skeptical that anyone else was. I myself felt quite relaxed and refreshed. A good many of those in the audience said they had been in deep trances.

A hypnodrama was then staged, based on a young woman's fantasy. When she had been asked to pass through the door to her special place, her fantasy was that she had entered her high school lavatory; a woman attendant sat at the threshold and refused to acknowledge her; she felt deeply disturbed. Roles were assigned to volunteers. The young lady was returned to hypnosis. She again passed through the door and confronted the impassive woman attendant. She burst into tears, and begged for a demonstration of affection. The attendant rose to comfort her. At the moment of revelation I had to leave for an appointment with A.H.P. officers who were to brief me on the current state of humanistic psychology.

The president of the A.H.P., 43-year-old Lawrence Solomon, is a clinical psychologist and dean of students at the San Diego campus of the California School for Professional Psychologists. The outgoing president, 46-year-old Fred Massarik, is a professor in the Graduate School of Management at U.C.L.A. Intense, articulate, academically rooted, they feel that the humanistic movement has gone too far in its opposition to traditional psychology. Massarik fears that "the overcommitment in the experiential direction has produced a growing tide of anti-intellectualism in our movement. There is too much of the attitude, 'All you gotta to do is feel.' "

Solomon questioned the operating assumption in many encounter groups that "more and more self-disclosure is necessary and good." He criticized the failure of the association to participate effectively in social action. "We do our thing and it's just a game of mutual titillation. We're not having the impact on society that we could. The social system is susceptible to humanistic influence. We should try to fix the machine and create a society that reflects our sense of human nature."

Solomon and Massarik acknowledge the need for standards of performance in group work, but they face thorny problems. "Who's to determine who's doing a decent job working with groups?" Solomon asks. "The academic degree is often irrelevant. With the diversity of philosophies in the field, how can you tell?" They are both insistent on the need to remain experimental even if there be risks involved. Massarik concedes that he does not agree with all the programs huddled under the humanistic umbrella. "But then I don't want to. For instance, my attitude toward astrology is agnostic. But, nonetheless, I say, 'Great. Let's do it.' "

Solomon observes that the A.H.P. and the A.P.A. differ on precisely this point. "Unlike the A.P.A., we are on the outer edge of discovery. Academic psychology has been concerned with very minute adjustments, such as, for instance, determining whether a dial reading is .498 or .499. The A.P.A. and the A.H.P. are working at different ends of the scientific continuum."

Despite their reservations about the "anti-intellectual" inclination of their movement, they are still mainly critical of those who see themselves as "purely intellectuals and theoreticians" and who are, as Massarik puts it, "threatened as hell by the experiential events of A.H.P. meetings. They are afraid of them . . . afraid of being drawn in . . . afraid of opening up to the potential flood of experience." He believes that the humanistic movement will inevitably affect all psychological disciplines and says that even the A.P.A. has begun to move in their direction. "Its new Division 32 represents humanistic psychology. The A.P.A. now accepts experiential sessions, although still with condescension."

All the buildings of the Squaw Valley complex were in use. There were meetings at the church, the locker room, the Hofbrau, the theater, the bar, the dining rooms, the conference center. As I walked down the corridor of the conference center, I peered into the rooms. In one room I saw couples lying flat on the floor, undergoing fantasies that explored the "man-woman relationship." Roars, screams, laughter came from Room A. Inside, a large crowd gathered around an open area. A plump young lady stepped to the fore and introduced herself. "I'm Cathy and I always wanted to do this." She lay down on the floor and rolled from one side of the open space to the other, shouting, "Whoopee!" The crowd applauded. A young man took her place. He announced his name, and confessed that he always had dreaded doing what he was doing. He then froze and began to quiver. The group leader worked with him, asking him to shake harder, to let the shaking possess his legs, his hips. Soon his entire body vibrated. I passed another meeting. A middle-aged lady, rather demurely dressed for this crowd, lay on a table, wailing, her body convulsed. Members of the group held her limbs and consoled her.

I noticed a man who had been assisting one of the encounter-group leaders quit a session, obviously disgruntled. I heard him speaking to a friend in what I thought were bitter tones. "There is so much—going on. The movement can't any more afford a hundred failures and one success."

A.H.P. executive officer John Levy, involved in the design of humanistically oriented research under the auspices of the Humanistic Psychology Institute, believes that encounter and therapy groups are beginning to change direction. They have always faced the problem that the momentary enlightenment following a few days of group work doesn't last. He believes that group work increasingly serves as an adjunct to new communities which can support altered life-styles.

Similarly, a young couple with considerable experience leading encounter groups confessed to me that they wanted something more than the release of feeling. After the hugging and the self-disclosure, crucial problems remained. However, like others in the movement who had explored the Here and Now, they now wanted to go beyond. The direction was transcendental, the language mystical.

Next I observed a demonstration of aikido conducted by Prof. Robert Frager, a psychologist at the Santa Cruz campus of the University of California. A trim, bearded young man, in judo garb and wearing in addition what looked like a black skirt split down the center to allow free movement, he described himself as a student of the martial arts. While studying in Japan, he observed a demonstration of aikido by its founder, Morihei Uyeshiba, then in his late 70's, and was converted. He abandoned the martial arts for the spiritual art of aikido, which rejects conflict and competition. It presumes the existence of a universal energy or life force called "ki." Tension, conflict, competition, inhibit the flow of ki. The practitioner of aikido learns to relax, to become centered and balanced. He allows his energy to flow unimpeded. Aikido can become a method of self-defense, never of attack. The disciple of aikido tries to evade assault. In any case, he remains poised and relaxed, tuned in to the flow of energy, experiencing the incoming energy of an assault even before he has been physically touched. He does not flee or resist the attacker, but, instead, blends with him.

Frager invited attacks from his assistant in order to demonstrate. He turned from the path of the attack, then moved with the attacker, who was thrown by the force of his own motion. Frager spoke of the need in all actions to be in harmony with the "laws of nature" to move in a fashion that enabled the mover to remain balanced and centered. The physical center of motion, he observed, was a point below the navel. The object of self-defense was not to harm the attacker, but rather to remain centered in the face of an attack. He showed a movie of the 76-year-old Uyeshiba turning from the path of attacks, blending effortlessly, a tiny man with a long, wispy beard. We then received instructions in becoming centered. We did exercises intended to give us the experience of an unimpeded energy flow.

Down the hall in Conference Room C there was a different prescription for encountering opposition. It wasn't harmony. A less mystically oriented panel discussed "Environmental Psychology and the Feminine." Panelist Richard Farson of the California Institute of Arts and the Western Behavioral Sciences insisted that the problems of women were political and required political solutions. He pointed to the fear he observed in women of being identified with Women's Lib. "They fear being called castrating bitches, fear not being considered feminine, fear that they might be considered Lesbian. If they take advantage of child-care programs, they fear they may not be fulfilling their roles as women." Yet, he went on to argue that the only hope women had for liberation from the guilt and fear that wasted their potential was to organize an effective women's movement. He insisted that only political action could transform the social conditions which were the source of their problems. The solution to their problems wasn't psychotherapy. "We are invisible to each other, that's why we imagine our problems are particular. Women have problems because they are women. Blacks have problems because they are black." The problems were rooted in the American system and until it was changed there was little hope for individual liberation.

I later observed a narrower approach to the correction of human infirmities. Peter Melchior and Keith Gilchrist offered a demonstration of structural integration, a technique developed by Dr. Ida Rolf, a one-time biochemist with the Rockefeller Institute. The technique is called, informally, "rolfing." The practitioners are called "rolfers." It begins with the presumption of an ideal body structure, one most efficiently oriented to the force of gravity. The body, then, in silhouette, would show that a line dropped through the ear would traverse the mid-points of the shoulder, hip, knee and ankle, all in alignment. Rolfing demonstrates Wilhelm Reich's theory of "body armoring," and offers a method for releasing this armor.

The crucial assumption is that psychic attitudes as well as physical accidents throw the body off center and change the entire body structure. Gilchrist suggested a typical occurrence of adaptation to psychological trauma. A boy who habitually shrinks from a despotic father will incorporate his timidity into his stance. His head comes down, his chest withdraws, his pelvis tilts up, his knees come forward. Muscle development is affected. He no longer breathes properly. Then, according to the Rolf theory, the fascial tissue, a sheath around the muscles, becomes deformed and permanently freezes the posture. Neither exercise nor efforts of will are able to correct it. The psychic attitudes, now encysted in the body, continue to afflict us.

The "rolfer" claims to be able to more nearly approximate the true orientation of the body to gravity in a sequence of 10 hourly sessions. He manipulates a different area of the body at each session, reorganizing the fascial tissue by the pressure of fingers, knuckles and elbows, a process which some claim to be painful. The rolfer claims that, following the rolfing program, energy flow is restored to areas of the body that have been enervated. Afterwards, the "rolfee" may breathe properly for the first time since childhood. In the course of these sessions, we were told, the rolfee is often liberated from the crippling psychic attitudes his body had preserved.

We were given a demonstration of the first rolfing session. A young volunteer stripped down to his jockey shorts and Peter Melchior analyzed his body structure, tracing the major postural defect to improperly aligned feet. The young man lay on his back. Melchior knelt beside him and began to knead the chest. The patient reported feeling dizzy. This Gilchrist attributed to greater oxygenation as his chest began to expand. At the end of the hour, the young man rose to his feet, a trifle unsteady, but reporting that he felt marvelous.

The program variety was enormous and I'm not sure I managed a fair sampling. I attended sessions that promised to be fun, and shied away from a few that slightly unnerved me. I tried to get into the massage session but it was oversubscribed. I saw instead a videotape of a massage session in the display area of the Olympic Village Hotel. Attractive women in bikinis were massaged by handsome men in jockey shorts; then the ladies did the massaging. It seemed very pleasant. I also missed the session called "Homosexuality, the Dragon at Your Gate."

My impression was that there were three main categories of meetings. First, there were the experiential sessions concerned with techniques that would heighten sensory awareness and compel a recognition of the Here and Now. Encounter groups, psychodrama, Gestalt therapy and rolfing were all examples of this. Secondly, there were sessions whose concern seemed to be the heightening of political and social sensibilities, often employing the techniques of the first category. Among this group were the meetings devoted to women's issues, gay liberation and humanistic education and, of course, the new politics. For example, I attended a meeting at the village theater where panel members Willis Harman and Mark Markley of the Stanford Research Center and John Vasconcellos of the California State Assembly discussed the topic "Toward a Humanistic Postindustrial Society." The panel agreed that one had to begin with the assumption that the present system—in its political, social and economic dimensions—worked, however inadequately. They contended that this system was in process of modification and that humanistic values were already influencing the direction of change. They discussed humanistic approaches to problems of bureaucracy and possibilities of administration which didn't require rigid hierarchies.

To cite another example of effort in this second category, the Humanistic Psy-

chology Institute has initiated studies for the revision of graduate-school programs for psychology and the behavioral sciences. The institute, under the directorship of Eleanor Criswell at Sonoma State College, has supervised a graduate program at Sonoma State. The curriculum is designed by the graduate student and his adviser. He receives academic credit for off-campus activities. It is an "experiential program" first, a degree program only secondarily. "Programs provide opportunities to concentrate learning experiences in clinical psychology, transpersonal psychology and psychological ecology, in some combination with the behavioral and social sciences, to best meet the student's needs and ambitions."

The third category of meetings represented a movement toward the transcendental and the mystical. Aikido, yoga, meditation, other Eastern disciplines fell into this category. There were also indigenous mystical developments, among them "psychosynthesis" and "transpersonal psychology."

Psychosynthesis is the offspring of Roberto Asagioli, an Italian psychoanalyst, one of the founders of the humanistic psychology movement. His views were presented in several sessions of the conference. The language was mystical, the techniques eclectic. In a session led by young Steven Kull, we began with an exercise. Wearing a faded wool shirt and old corduroys, his hair braided in a pony tail, the bearded Kull wanted to give us a glimmering of the "transcendental being" that psychosynthesis aims to achieve. We were told to relax and to imagine a "peak" experience. We were told to relive that time and examine its energy. We were then to allow the energy of that peak experience to descend upon our bodies. As in the aikido demonstration, it was presumed that there was a condition of free energy flow, of balance and harmony.

Psychosynthesis attempts to put the individual in touch with his "higher self." Beyond the "I" of ordinary consciousness it assumes another "I," the "transpersonal self," that is something more than all the roles we play. "The transpersonal self," says Kull, "is our way of being in the world. It is our true self. It is beyond words. It can only be experienced." It is a depth of being with which we are ordinarily out of touch. We are familiar, as a rule, only with that quite ordinary ego which is subject to the buffeting of everyday existence. The aim of psychosynthesis is to integrate the different levels of self and to put us in touch with that higher self which represents "our full potential for growth." The choice of methods for this higher integration is eclectic. There are the usual encounter groups, psychodrama, fantasy trips.

A stunning illustration of this concept, and the high point of the meeting, was a National Film Board of Canada movie called "The Cosmic View." We see a boy and a dog in a rowboat. The camera steadily withdraws from the scene. We see the boat on a lake, then the lake as part of a waterway system, then the waterway as part of the state of California. We see the North American continent, then the earth. We pass the moon, the planets. We leave the solar system and course through the galaxy to the limits of the universe. Then we return along the same path until we focus on the boy and his dog in the rowboat again. The camera draws closer. We see a mosquito on the boy's hand. We enter a cell in the boy's skin. We enter the world of particles. Once again the camera returns until we again see the boy and his dog as they row across the lake.

Transpersonal psychology is a discipline that, like psychosynthesis, postulates various levels of consciousness. It offers a system of therapy designed to deal with psychic symptoms as they appear on these various levels. Dr. Stanislav Grof of the

Maryland Research Center conducted some of the original research with LSD, first in Europe, and more recently at the Maryland Center. At the convention he illustrated the concepts of transpersonal psychology by means of his LSD research. Transpersonal psychology is concerned with ultimate human impulses and conditions—above all, with dying.

Grof discussed attitudes toward dying alternative to those held in contemporary Western cultures. He observed that Eastern cultures, preliterate culture and antique cultures have regarded death as a sacramental occasion. In these cultures a man was not deprived of the meaning of his death. Dying was an opportunity to become twice-born. The dying man might achieve an enlightened state of consciousness. In the West, on the other hand, death is regarded as no more than a terminal disease. Every attempt is made to prolong life, however absurdly. The process is dehumanizing to the patient, his family and his physician. "Dying is the crisis par excellence," says Grof, "and yet we psychotherapists have no means of helping the dying man. Perhaps we lack means because the case of the dying is hopeless. In an achievement-oriented pragmatic culture, perhaps the hopelessness of a case requires that it be abandoned."

Grof undertook experiments with terminal cancer patients, administering doses of LSD intended to produce a "mystic experience." We observed a film made of two such cases. A young ballet dancer, doomed by an inoperable cancer, applied to the LSD program. We saw her as she was helped onto a couch. The drug was administered by hypodermic. Headphones were placed over the ears. Her therapist sat by her side, holding her hand. The "Ode to Joy" of Beethoven's Ninth Symphony was placed on the turntable. She touched her face. She smiled, then began to weep. She removed the headphones to tell her therapist, "I didn't know it could be so beautiful." She described a feeling of unity with the world, a sense of ultimate being. She was ready to consider her death. We were told that she remained in a joyful, sometimes beatific state until her death. We then saw an old man, close to death, isolated, depressed, inarticulate. He underwent a like transformation after receiving the drug, and was able to articulate, in a groping way, that same vision of unadulterated being.

Grof believes it would be foolhardy to deny the reality of that mystic vision. At a subsequent meeting, he described research in Europe where LSD was used as a psychotherapeutic drug, administered over long periods. He believed that the research demonstrated the existence of evolving states of consciousness, each level bearing its peculiar problems and symptoms. He termed the first level Freudian. Freudian problems, such as the Oedipal complex, were those initially encountered in the LSD sequence. Continued ministrations of the drug resulted in the elimination of the Freudian symptoms, which were then replaced by other symptoms at what Grof calls the Rankian level of consciousness. At this level the patient experiences suicidal depression, the reliving of biological birth, the confrontation with existential dread. It is at this level that the ego is challenged and, as the drug program continues, finally surrenders. Grof suggests that suicide attempts may be an effort at ego death rather than at biological death, that the suicide is an attempt to win through to a higher integration. The erosion and death of the ego are preliminary to the transcendental experience. At the next level the patient undergoes the evolutionary experience. He explores the collective unconscious. He relives past incarnations. He discovers his karma. Finally, beyond this Jungian level,

he enters the transcendental or cosmic dimension.

Grof insists that this mystical language is crucial to the psychotherapist's understanding of a patient's symptoms. The question of whether a patient's state of mind is mystical or religious or neurotic tends to vanish if the therapist takes into account the level of consciousness at which the symptom occurs. Grof believes that doctors have often impeded the progress of patients by refusing to accept the validity of transcendental experience, classifying the patient as schizophrenic, or insisting that his problems be translated into Freudian terms.

Unscheduled events took place after dinnertime. Announcements in the cafeteria summoned people to various interest groups, which were formed to discuss issues, raised in meetings, which individuals wanted to explore more deeply. Some interest groups lasted the entire four days of the conference. There were gay-lib groups, women's groups, and for those who were inclined to brave the chill mountain nights there were the sauna and the swimming pool.

Rosh Hashanah services were held in the Protestant chapel, a winged building of poured concrete whose glass facade overlooks Squaw Creek. The service was especially prepared, we were informed, by a humanistically oriented rabbi. Services were attended by Jew and non-Jew, come to memorialize the Israeli athletes killed at Munich. The rabbi, wearing skull cap and prayer shawl, spoke over a background of recorded secular and religious music. He said, "This Rosh Hashanah is a trip, but it's not a joy ride." He spoke of the pain of the potential that was never realized. He offered a litany of human suffering in the language of humanistic psychology. "I am suffering from guilt because I am blocking my energy flow." He referred to our origin, first in Latin, then, as he put it, in street language. "We are born," he said, "between p_____and s_____." He spoke of the need to strip ourselves of phoniness and concede the crimes of which we are truly guilty, such as making aggressive war and tolerating segregation. When the time came to blow the ram's horn, a frail-appearing young man volunteered to make the attempt. He managed a timid squeal and was heartily cheered.

On the final night of the conference, everyone assembled in the Olympic Village cafeteria for a barbecue dinner, followed by a women's guerrilla-theater production. It was a parable about the education of a woman to subservience and her final liberation. It included song and dance and a comic retelling of the Snow White story. At one point a woman was raised on a cross made of a broom and a mop. Two women bongo drummers set up a persuasive beat. At the conclusion of the parable, the players brought the audience on stage. Soon the entire convention was involved. The cafeteria floor vibrated like a drum skin. This spontaneous demonstration was halted at its climax by a woman announcing the next event—a party, set for the lodge bar in 20 minutes. At the bar we were handed leaflets: "Welcome, people-lovers. You are invited to participate in SERIOUS SCIENTIFIC RESEARCH BY HAVING FUN at this rare experiential event: a humanistically oriented party for *Making Friends With All The Sexes!!*" There followed a detailed prescription for encountering members of the various sexes. The high mood was quickly deflated and, as often happens, the spontaneity that was calculated didn't materialize.

It was clear that this had been no mere association meeting. The delegates were members of a coherent organization with shared values and common attitudes. There wasn't the politicking that goes on at academic conventions. There surely was no sense of rank requiring its proper deference. Unlike those at academic conventions, the meetings were jammed. The insistence on an "experiential" format was a guarantee against dullness. Many programs obviously disregarded the obligations of a rigorous science; but, in consequence, they weren't confined to trivial precision. The Association for Humanistic Psychology is a movement. Its objectives are messianic; its language spiritual. The actions it sponsors are often pure fun.

48.   DREAM WORLD

Edwin Kiester, Jr.

As the Old Testament and James Joyce attest, interest in dreams is scarcely new.

But lately traffic down Freud's "royal road to the unconscious" has become a virtual stampede. It all began in 1952 when Nathan Kleitman and Eugene Aserinsky of the University of Chicago discovered the two types of mammalian sleep and identified one—rapid eye movement or REM sleep—as coincident with dreaming. Result: researchers were enabled to pinpoint the precise moment the midnight mini-dramas began. Ever since, they have been relentlessly and remorselessly arousing sleeping subjects to pry into their night lives. The Association for the Psychophysiological Study of Sleep now numbers about 500 members in at least 20 campus- and hospital-based "sleep laboratories"; by one estimate, 100 significant pieces of research have been added to the literature in the past 10 years.

Yet dreams remain elusive, fragile, mystifying. Squeeze one too tightly and it will disintegrate before your eyes as will a crystal goblet shattered by a high C. For all the intense research effort, the inner secrets of dreaming continue to escape us, racing tantalizingly ahead of our outstretched fingertips like Gatsby's green light. We know more facts about dreams than Freud, Jung or Shakespeare, but some of the old mysteries are as intransigent as ever.

First, the facts. Two decades of research have established beyond doubt who dreams and who doesn't. Everyone dreams—and that means *everyone*. Put those persons who vow up and down that they never dream into a sleep lab, jolt them awake when the REM period starts, and—what do you know—they've been dreaming. Under other conditions, the dream has just flitted away on awakening, and they have been too inattentive to notice.

We also know that the amount of dreaming is remarkably regular from night to night, and from person to person. Freud and Adler went along with folklore in maintaining that dreams increased when the mind was troubled (hence, "dreamless sleep" was idealized), but findings from the labs show dreaming is routine—and evidently necessary—for everyone, including children, who presumably have fewer troubles.

The curtain goes up on our first dream about 90 minutes after we fall asleep. The opening act lasts about 10 minutes. REM and non-REM periods alternate at 80- to 90-minute intervals, through the night, with the REM periods gradually lengthening. The final period of dreaming lasts about 50 minutes. We usually have about five or six dreams totaling about 90 minutes —the length of a feature movie. In all, about 20 to 25 percent of sleeping is given over to dreams.

There is an old belief that dreams are instantaneous—a skein of rapid fantasies woven around a single external stimulus— but that, too, is now challenged. According to William C. Dement of Stanford University, perhaps the most prestigious of sleep and dream researchers, the idea probably originated with a famous dream recounted by the French writer Andre Maury in 1861. Maury dreamed that he was alive during the Reign of Terror. He was denounced as a monarchist and taken before Robespierre and condemned to death. A tumbrel hauled him to the guillotine at the head of a jeering mob. Up to the scaffold he went, and as the blade struck his neck, Maury awoke—to find that the headboard had fallen and struck him in the identical spot. Maury concluded that the dream had been initiated by the falling bedstead and the elaborate drama around it had been compressed into a few seconds between the accident and the time he woke up.

By some laborious research in his laboratory, however, Dement has shown that dreams consume about the same time that similar actions would in waking life. Dement has collected the dreams of subjects, counted the words and timed the activities they describe. Reconstructing the events show that about the same time elapses as if they were watched with open eyes.

Meanwhile, Rosalind Dymond Cartwright of the University of Illinois, Chicago, has shown that the night's dreams follow a ritualized sequence, as with a sonnet or symphony. The first dream states the theme—usually a quick review of a problem related to the day's events. The next two "scenes" recall earlier similar episodes. The fourth scene is set in the future and dramatizes a wish fulfillment: "Suppose I did not have this problem?" Act V ties all the elements into one bizarre present-tense extravaganza. Unfortunately, Dr. Cartwright says, since most of us recall only portions of the final dream, we do not understand its meaning just as we would be baffled by the closing act of a play if we missed the earlier acts.

We can also now draw a profile of a "typical" dream. It usually contains two characters in addition to the dreamer, occurs indoors, is more passive than active, more hostile than friendly and more likely to be unpleasant than pleasant. Dreams contain more strange males than strange females, and most of the hostility centers on these male strangers.

Too, men and women dream differently. Men's dreams are more active and more friendly—but are also more likely to involve fighting. Men also dream more often of appearing naked in public places. Men are the most common characters in the dreams of both men and women—but in men's dreams, they are more likely to be antagonists. In recalling their dreams, men are more likely to use the words *vehicle, travel, automobile* and *hit*; women use words of emotion. Women are more often pursued or endangered; men are more likely to find money.

Finally, it has been established that *no* time of night is free from some sort of mental activity. Even in stage-one sleep, the most dead-to-the-world form of non-REM (NREM) sleeping, the mind is working. Rouse a stage-four sleeper and he or she will indeed report thoughts flitting through the mind. Non-REM mentation, however,

is more true to life, more quiescent and lacks the vivid fantasy of REM sleep. "I was thinking about what I had to do at the office tomorrow," is a common non-REM recollection.

The major mysteries about dreaming that still baffle and intrigue researchers are three, and they interlock:

(1) How can dreams be influenced, either in content or process, and, conversely, how do they influence the waking state?

(2) What is the significance of the dream content?

(3) Do dreams serve a function, or are they merely a form of free entertainment?

Everyone agrees—and common sense tells us—that dreams do not exist in a cocoon, that both internal and external stimuli, plus presleep activity and suggestion, affect them. Most of us have had dreams in which an outside noise smoothly insinuated itself into the dream fabric. What we dreamed of as melodious cathedral chimes dissolved on awakening into the strident jangle of the alarm clock. Indeed, in Freud's day, dreams were considered "guardians of sleep," designed to protect the sleeper by disguising distractions that otherwise would keep the person awake all night. This guardian role is itself a minor mystery, since it does not operate in every instance. Dement once harried a group of subjects first with a stream of cold water, then a bright light, then a pure tone. Only 42 percent reported a dream involving water; 23 percent reacted to the light; and 9 percent to the tone.

A number of studies have shown that between 25 and 50 percent of dreaming time concerns itself with topics considered during the day. More deliberate attempts at programming dreams have had mixed results. In one intriguing study, in which first names were whispered into the ear of the dreaming subject, a "better than chance" correlation was reported that the stimulus was incorporated into the dream. Sometimes it was a "clang association"—a sound similar to the name; other dreams incorporated the name itself; a third group had an emotional reaction based on personal connotations of the name. In other studies, a travelogue shown before sleep has been incorporated into a modest percentage of dreams, while impending surgery turned up in a high proportion. Still other studies have concluded that dreams sometimes compensate for what is lacking during the day. Subjects kept in social isolation, for instance, dream of being surrounded by people.

The problem is to assess objectively whether the stimulus actually triggered the dream. "Everyone has his own language," is the way Rosalind Cartwright puts it. "If you deprive a group of subjects of water, some may dream of the ocean; some may dream of the desert; some may dream of drinking; some may have dreams with an emotional quality whose association to thirst neither they nor we can understand; and some may have dreams that seem not related at all. We need a much more refined measure of dream content before we can judge how successful we are in manipulation."

Still, Charles T. Tart of the University of California at Davis, editor of *Altered States of Consciousness,* cites "incontrovertible" evidence that some persons can deliberately cue their reactions while asleep. The classic case, he says, is the mentally disciplined individuals who can preset an internal alarm clock to wake themselves at an appointed hour. If we can learn that technique, Tart says, we can teach ourselves other responses.

In 1954, Australian anthropologist Kilton Stewart stumbled across a remote Malaysian tribe called the Senoi and launched the popular craze for dream control as a means of personal betterment. The Senoi, according to Stewart, made dreams the heart of their culture. The tribesmen assembled each morning for a dream breakfast to exchange dreams and try to divine their meaning. Children were taught from an early age to remember and discuss their dreams and to actually shape them.

Not unlike modern therapists, the Senoi believed that nightmares represented dark parts of the soul coming forward in disguised form. For the mental health of the sleeper, they had to be faced down and conquered. Senoi children were taught to will themselves not to run, but to fight, when a "dream enemy" appeared. They must consciously decide during the dream to brave out the threat. They were also told that when they dreamed of a friend, they should immediately tell that person, lest there be a continuing grudge between them.

The Stewart paper also focused interest on "lucid dreaming," the high point of the Senoi art and a form of dreaming familiar to Westerners. (It is also part of certain sacred American Indian rituals and is described by Carlos Castaneda in *The Teachings of Don Juan.*) Lucid dreaming is what we all do when we suddenly realize in the midst of a dream that we are asleep. With practice, the dream-control instructors say, you can learn to induce that moment of recognition, prolong it and actually control the flow of the dream thereafter. Thus you can bring the creative energies of the dream to bear on a subject of your choice.

What significance has the selection of characters, settings and activities in the dream? Most of us know that however fantastic our dreams, they are rooted in persons and places we know and events that have concerned us during the day. To Freud, dreams of matters close at hand were the "day residue,"which had to be cleared out of the way so that the mind could get down to the "dream work" of dealing with the repressed infantile and sexual wishes bubbling up in symbolic form from the unconscious.

Adler, however, stressed the continuity of sleeping and waking and declared that the "day residues" were important in themselves, not mere screens for unconscious wishes. Most dream investigators now agree that dreams must be seen within the context of already ongoing mental activity. The real "dream work" is condensation, displacement and symbolization of the daily experiences. Dreams provide an outlet for suppressed feelings, using symbols so that they are not so blatant that the sleeper's inhibitions are offended.

Another departure from classic Freud dream theory is in interpretation. Instead of reciting their dreams to a therapist to have their symbolism explained, sleepers are now encouraged into do-it-yourself dream reflection. The objective is not only to understand the symbols and gain a different perspective on one's problems but to gain insight into the creative forces as the mind flits from thought to thought. Stanley Krippner of the Maimonides Dream Laboratory in Brooklyn, New York, puts it in this way: "It is more important to appreciate your inner life than to become an amateur psychoanalyst." Krippner tells students in his dream workshops to immediately write down their dreams upon awakening and to lie quietly for 30 minutes or so reflecting on their possible meaning. He urges students to discuss their dreams with their friends and particularly to look for hidden puns and jokes such as might be created by an imagination freed from daytime restraints. A "dream journal" kept for several months will reveal recurrent images and themes that represent matters of concern to the sleeper, Krippner says.

One key point about content is that not all dreams may be significant. "Our mind in sleep has as many different facets as when we are awake," says one student of dreams

and dreaming. Thus, it may spend only a small portion of time symbolically worrying over emotional problems, as we are not always thinking hard during the day. A certain amount of dreaming may be simple examination of the day's happenings, with modest emotional input. And some dreaming may be just plain woolgathering, with the mind idly wandering and making jokes with itself.

After listening to literally thousands of dreams at the rate of five or six per subject per night, Cartwright of the University of Illinois has concluded that most dream symbolism is simple, easily understood and funny. "I wonder that people don't wake themselves up laughing," she says. She recalls one newlywed coed who was torn between continuing school and becoming a full-time housewife. "She dreamed that she was standing in the kitchen reading an anthropology text and it suddenly turned into a pot holder," Cartwright recalls. "But when she looked at the pot holder there was a hole in the middle, and she thought, 'What good is a pot holder like that?' When I began to laugh, she looked puzzled. Even when I suggested that perhaps the dream 'meant' she would be ineffective as a housewife, I had to explain it several times before she got the point."

In therapy, dreams are still important but the precise significance is a point of disagreement. A series of experiments have shown that the dreams of schizophrenics are quite different from those of "normals," and that "normals" with schizoid tendencies are still in a third group. Schizophrenic dreams have a far lower fantasy content and are much less vivid and rich; Stanford's Dement has described them as "sterile." The differences in dream content appear to be similar to the differences in waking fantasy, as shown when "normals" and schizophrenics are given the *Thematic Apperception Test.* Evidence seems to be convincing that those who cannot disentangle reality and fantasy during the day have less need for a fantasy outlet at night. (Another view maintains that the sterility of schizophrenic dreams merely reflects the sterility with which they view the world.) A few theorists hold that a high fantasy quotient itself is evidence of illness. Only when dreams approach reality—"when your mother appears as your mother, and not as a gorilla," as one puts it—can the dreamer be considered sane.

What is the function of dreams? Do they indeed serve a purpose, or are they merely a sideshow? It has now been proven virtually beyond doubt that REM sleep is essential to the human body, for reasons unknown. If a person is deprived of REM sleep on a given night, the sleeper will make up the deficit on subsequent nights. If the deprivation continues, it becomes increasingly difficult to prevent him or her from going into the REM stage of sleep. Even the clockwork cycles of REM and non-REM sleep appear critical. After a REM episode has been completed, it becomes impossible to induce another until at least 30 minutes have passed. The assumption is that some as yet unidentified neurophysiological process is going on during REM periods, and that it is as necessary as breathing.

Whether dreams are essential to the process or are simply a by-product is another of those elusive mysteries, but theories abound. Freud's was classic: he said that dreams are the necessary release mechanism for the repressed impulses in the unconscious; sleep arose out of the need to dream, not vice versa. He compared a dream to fireworks, taking hours to prepare and exploding in minutes. A more popular theory today is that dreams are a necessary interlude to assimilate the day's happenings, fitting them together with memories and previous experiences. All of one's emotional, conceptual and perceptual skills can be brought to bear on them before they are filed away for the future.

Another view is that of Milton Kramer of the University of Cincinnati, another eminent dream researcher. Kramer says that dreams are a mood regulator; using pre- and post-dream tests, he has shown distinct mood changes that are regular and predictable. Dr. Cartwright avers that dreams have an integrity of their own, apart from REM sleep. She points out that when a subject is deprived of dreams, the amount of fantasy-type thought increases in the waking state; in other words, dreams begin to invade non-REM sleep.

Probably the most intriguing of all theories is the "psychosynthesis" advanced by Ernest Lawrence Rossi of UCLA and others. Rossi holds that dreams are a biological process in which new protein molecules are actually being constructed as the brain "synthesizes" the events of the day. Rossi bases his hypothesis on the controversial discovery that flatworms and other primitive animals actually grow new cells as they "learn." Dreams represent actual physical changes within the brain, Rossi says—another tantalizing element of mystery in a subject that continues to generate interest as it has since the dreams of Eve.

HOW TO CATCH A DREAM

In order for dreams to benefit waking life, one must quickly capture as many details as possible and record and reflect on their meaning. Patricia Garfield, Ph.D., of the University of California has been keeping a dream journal since she was 14 and has trained herself to wake up and write in the dark. For most of us, says Garfield, a more practical method of dream "recovery" is to:

(1) Place a pencil and paper where they can be reached without changing your position.

(2) Awaken gradually, if possible, without using an alarm; if you must use an alarm, choose one that wakes you to music instead of a jarring bell.

(3) Without rising, begin to make notes on the dream. Try to recall as many details of characters, setting, conversations, as possible. Don't edit or attempt to analyze—simply get down as much as you can remember. Be sure to record your feelings as well as details of the "story."

(4) Review the dream again, if possible from the point of view of the characters, to seek out more key details.

(5) Still in bed, look for hidden meanings and tie-ins to matters that presently concern you. Remember the dreaming mind may spend no more time in serious problem solving than the waking mind. Also look for jokes, puns and other evidence of "the mind at play."

(6) Discuss the dream with family and friends and ask for their interpretation of it.

(7) Enter each day's dream in a "dream diary" and review the entries every few months, looking for recurrent ideas and themes that might give greater insight into your "inner life."

A SHORT COURSE IN DREAM CONTROL

Most people think dreams are the same as Disneyland: you can watch the spectacle and enjoy the rides, but controlling the show is out of your hands. Dr. Patricia Garfield is one of those who says you can learn to pull the switches, too. Her University of California extension course in "Creative Dreaming" (and her book by the same title) teaches you to choose the subject of your dream, shape the plot and rehearse your behavior for the events of the morrow or to enrich your creative life.

As an exponent of Senoi dream control, Garfield says that the first step for Western-

ers is to believe that it can be done. You must convince yourself that self-programmed dreams are possible, the psychologist says, pointing out that most of us inadvertently influence our dreams but aren't aware of it. Once you have become a believer, the next step is to plant in your mind what you will dream about. You must repeat through the day, in a positive and forceful way, your proposed agenda. "Tonight I fly in my dreams. Tonight I fly," is a Garfield example of the emphatic way the plan must be stated. Then you must lie down in a relaxed and peaceful state, much as the ancients reclining in a sacred place and focusing on the qualities of the gods to bring on visions, and your chosen dream will materialize.

The next step is the heart of the Garfield-Senoi technique. She calls it the "confront and conquer" gambit. Instead of passively watching events or recoiling in terror from nightmare threats, you must step forward and dominate them.

One example: Garfield had a recurring nightmare in which she was chased by rapists. Finally, employing dream-control techniques, she decided to end the pursuit. The next time the dream began, she steeled herself, stopped running and turned, terror-stricken but game, to face down her pursuers. As she did so, a can of chemical spray appeared in her hand. She vaporized the pursuers into an oblivion from which they never returned. Furthermore, she says, the successful confrontation bolstered her courage to face difficult problems in real life.

Another example involved a Garfield student, a timid sort, who dreamed that she was in an old-fashioned drugstore where the clerk refused to wait on her. Other customers were served, but he continued to ignore her. Suddenly, she began to scream the most obscene and scatological names she could think of, until he was compelled to attend to her. The feeling of mastery the dream provided carried over to the following day, when she felt brave enough to face her boyfriend with a problem that had been bothering her for months.

The Garfield method eventually leads to instruction in lucid dreaming so that one can program the dream, become conscious during it and work through whatever current problem is of concern. Dr. Garfield says she "lucid dreams" her speeches and even wrote a children's book that way. But lucid dreaming need not be all work and no play. Garfield says you can conjure up a dream lover and "go all the way through to orgasm in the lucid state." We may be on the threshold of X-rated dreaming.

REM AND NREM SLEEP

Anyone who's ever watched a sleeping dog's involuntary barks and twitches ("Oh, look at Rover! He's dreaming!") has witnessed the REM state. All mammals (and only mammals) have REM sleep, although the amount varies from species to species.

Like dogs, human beings twitch and breathe irregularly during REM sleep. Facial muscles and the fingertips move convulsively; breathing is fast, then slow. The bulges of the eyes can be seen to dart back and forth beneath closed lids, as if actually looking at something. Less visibly, the inner ear contracts, as with variations in sound intensity and pitch.

In the sleep lab, REM also produces distinct changes in the electroencephalograph (EEG), electrooccularograph and electromyograph, which measure brain waves, eye movement and muscle electrical impulses respectively. The EEG produces distinct spiky sawtooth patterns. All this activity closely parallels waking, yet the large muscles are as if paralyzed; the sleeper cannot move. One theory holds that REM is not a sleep state at all, but one in which the body is paralyzed but hallucinating.

NREM is the state most of us associate with "a good night's sleep." It is often graded into four stages, the essential difference among them being the amount of smooth, quiescent delta waves that appear in the EEG. We slide rapidly from stage one into dead-to-the-world stage four, with the onset of sleep; then we slide back up to the beginning of the first REM period. As the night wears on, we spend increasing amounts of time in stage two. Although our senses are effectively shut off during this time, some form of mentation continues. With most, it is akin to a kind of desultory thinking; but about 10 to 15 percent of subjects report vivid dreaming during NREM. Whether they are actually different, or just more imaginative or sensitive than the rest of us, is not known.

One suspicion about REM is that it is somehow related to the development of the central nervous system (and perhaps in adult mammals, to its maintenance). The newborn spends about 50 percent of its sleeping time—eight or nine hours a day— in REM sleep; and premature infants, whose nervous systems have not even achieved the maturation of a newborn, have even more—up to 75 percent. During childhood, the amount of REM gradually diminishes, until a five-year-old, whose central nervous system has fully developed, is in REM only 25 percent of the time. Interestingly, newborn kittens and puppies have REM sleep only, while newborn guinea pigs, whose nervous sytems are mature, have no REM sleep at all.

YOUR MOOD AND YOUR DREAM CHARACTERS

Most people know that they may wake up sad, happy or angry, depending on their dreams—even though they recall them. Milton Kramer, Ph.D., of the University of Cincinnati has found that these mood changes and the characters who trigger them are an integral part of everyone's dreams. Recording the dreams of eight men for 20 nights in the sleep lab, he found moods changed according to whom they had dreamed about.

As a group, Kramer said, the subjects were less unhappy, less friendly and less aggressive when they awoke in the morning than when they retired at night—as determined by a 48-item mood scale administered before retiring and on arising. Probing further, he found that the greatest correlation was between the happiness scale and the number of characters in a dream. The greater the number of characters, the happier the subject appeared on awakening. Kramer also found that particular people seemed to affect the subject's morning moods. When the proper people appeared, the subjects awoke feeling fine; when they did not, or when others took their place, they awoke depressed or angry. Often the mood-elevating characters weren't even identifiable except as types of people. One man always felt better after dreaming about older women.

Whether mood determines characters or characters determine the mood is still an open question, but Kramer says that people can learn to influence who will appear in their dreams and, thus, can determine their own wakening mood. "You have to work at it, but it can be done with practice," he says. And he has also shown that schizophrenics and depressives have dreams decidedly related to their mood changes. Schizophrenics usually dream about strangers, depressives about family members. Characteristically, he says, depressives are in their blackest mood on awakening, and their outlook brightens as the day goes on.

DREAMS AND THE DANCE

The young woman stood up, raised her arms above her head and began to glide across the room. As the others watched, she sinuously undulated around them, her face masklike, in the best interpretive-dance technique. The performance continued, silently, for about four minutes. Finally, she resumed her place in the group. Its leader, Joseph Hart, turned to the others. "Does anyone have any comment on Linda's dream?"

The Center for Feeling Therapy in Los Angeles places dreams at the heart of its "integrative psychology." Clients report their dreams in complete detail, acting them out and, as did Linda, dancing them. (Dance gets closer to feelings than words.) Hart, an early experimenter in Senoi dream-control methods, charts clients' progress through dream recall and believes dreams change dramatically when a person is "cured."

Hart and two colleagues founded the Center in 1972, as a spinoff from Arthur Janov's "primal scream" therapy. Its central philosophy is that people with unacknowledged feelings are, per se, insane—a philosophy spelled out in their new book, *Going Sane.* Dreams are one way we mask our feelings and impulses, because we cannot accept them directly. The integrated (sane) person no longer needs the dream's symbolism.

Hart says patients become gradually more direct and realistic, both in dreams and while awake. The milestone is what Hart calls "the transformative dream" in which problems are met head-on. "The parent now appears as a parent, not as some kind of monster," he says.

Even before therapy, Hart says, the dreams and waking lives of clients are virtually indistinguishable. One exercise at the

Center is to ask for a "life-segment report," with the same details of dialogue, action, setting and feeling as in dream report. Invariably, Hart says, the same passivity and unawareness appear in the "life dream" as in the "sleeping dream."

The idea of dream transformation has its parallels in treatment of battle traumas, Hart says, in which drug therapy or hypnotherapy helped the dreamer experience and express feelings previously blocked. And they also occur in other abreactive therapies, such as primal scream. What he learned from the Senoi, Hart says, is the need for a supportive group so that when the transformation comes in both dreams and life the client can be helped to understand and benefit from it.

DO DREAMS HAVE ESP?

Undoubtedly the most elaborate "experiment" ever carried out in dream research occurred in early 1971 and involved Drs. Stanley Krippner and Montague Ullman of the Maimonides Dream Laboratory in Brooklyn, the "psychics" Malcolm Bessent and Felicia Parise, the Grateful Dead rock group and an audience of 2,000 young people. The experiment went on for six nights and was intended to demonstrate that messages could be sent by ESP to a dreaming subject.

As Krippner recalls it, the lab had succeeded nine times out of 13 in sending messages from one individual to a sleeping subject over short distances. The "sender" viewed a randomly selected slide of a painting, then tried to "transmit" it to the subject sleeping in the lab. In the morning, the dreamer recalled the dream. Impartial judges then rated the slide and the report on a scale of 1 to 100 for correspondence.

Tying into the Grateful Dead concert

held in Port Chester, New York, 45 miles from the lab, was an attempt to see if 2,000 senders would make the signal stronger. At precisely 11:30 each night, the audience was asked to send a picture to Bessent, a much-publicized "psychic," who was sleeping at the lab in Brooklyn. Parise, the control, was sleeping at home in Manhattan. The randomly selected slide was projected on a screen behind the stage, along with Bessent's name. Parise was not mentioned. The slide remained on the screen for 15 minutes, while the Grateful Dead continued to perform. In the morning, Bessent and Parise provided dream reports for judging.

According to Krippner, Bessent had four "direct hits" out of six nights; Parise had only one, on the final night. Bessent's best rating was for the second night, when *The Seven Spinal Chakras* was the slide chosen. The painting depicts a man in the lotus position, practicing yoga meditation. Vivid colors spurt from the seven "energy centers" along the spine (chakras) and a brilliant yellow halo surrounds his head. Bessent described his dream the next day:

"I was very interested in using natural energy ... I was talking to this guy who said he'd invented a way of using solar energy and he showed me this box ... to catch the light from the sun which was all we needed to generate and store the energy ... I was discussing with the other guy a number of other areas of communication and we were exchanging ideas on the whole thing. ... He was suspended in midair or something ... I was thinking about rocket ships ... I'm remembering a dream I had ... about an energy box ... and a spinal column."

The judges gave Bessent a score of 82.

Later, Maimonides received a grant from the National Institute of Mental Health to further explore the correlation between

ESP and dreaming but could not produce significant results. However, according to Krippner, they have had greater success in transmitting telepathic messages to subjects in a state of sensory isolation, achieving a significant correlation in such cases.

49. HOW MUCH SLEEP DO YOU NEED?

Interview with Dr. Julius Segal
National Institute of Mental Health
Reprinted from *U.S. News & World Report*

Q: Dr. Segal, how much sleep does an average person need?

A: That's like asking, in effect, what size shoe the average person needs. That is, it is commonly assumed that there is a "normal" quota of sleep for all mankind. Eight hours often is cited as the generally accepted norm—a figure, incidentally, that goes far back, at least to Maimonides, the twelfth-century Jewish philosopher and physician.

The scientific study of sleep, however, shows a range of sleep requirement among us that is much broader than we have ever assumed in the past.

One survey, for example, showed that 8 per cent of a large sample in Scotland required only five hours as a maximum, and many of these got along with less than five hours. Fifteen per cent needed five to six hours of sleep. It is true, as the survey indicates, that the large bulk of the population usually takes between seven and eight hours of sleep. But 13 per cent required nine to 10 hours, and a few needed even more than 10 hours.

Q: Was this all continuous sleep—not counting cat naps?

A: It was continuous nighttime sleep. Even among infants, incidentally, there are already differences. It has been presumed that every newborn spends roughly 20 hours of the 24-hour day asleep, but laboratory studies show a much greater variability —from 10 to 23 hours. So, you see, sleep is a very individual matter.

Q: Does a person who needs 10 or more hours' sleep have a health problem?

A: Not necessarily—any more than a person who needs more food than his neighbor has a health problem. There's an internal criterion here, as in health in general. That is, any radical and chronic departure that you might experience from your own sleeping habits may be cause for concern, and for medical or psychological consultation.

But the fact that I regularly sleep five hours a night and my neighbor sleeps 10 hours does not, in and of itself, say anything about the relative status of our health.

Q: Do certain types of people need more sleep than others?

A: There have been few studies correlating personality types against need for sleep. Many years ago, William H. Sheldon, the physical anthropologist, suggested that body type was related to a number of aspects of human personality and behavior, including sleep. He held that the "endomorph"—the soft, fat, rotund type of person—slept easily and slept a lot, whereas the thin, sensitive, fragile "ectomorph" was prone to insomnia. But no rigorous studies support hypotheses of this sort. Yet, we shouldn't be surprised if there were a built-in, constitutional, genetically determined predisposition for sleep—as in many other areas of behavior.

I'm not discounting the importance of training and environment in shaping sleep habits or eating habits or any other bit of behavior. But the old phrase, "born that way," referring to genetic inheritance, seems increasingly relevant here. That is, the patterns of sleep that many people exhibit or complain about are apparent from earliest childhood. Many parents who are very upset about a child's sleep patterns ought best to make peace with the fact that those patterns came with the child and are not all that easy to change.

Q: Is it unusual for any child to have trouble going to sleep or awakening?

A: It is not at all unusual. Laboratory studies do show that deep sleep is much more apparent in the records of young children than in those of adolescents and, certainly, of adults. That is, the quality of sleep deteriorates with age, and scientifically, the phrase "slept like a baby" is not an idle one.

On the other hand, the emotional and psychological problems of which we're all victims at times can beset youngsters as well as adults. Anxiety, depression, excitement—such enemies of sleep are not absent in the lives of young children. Later, the stresses of adolescence can also cause a disruption of sleep habits—including, incidentally, a phenomenon called "hypersomnia," which is oversleeping, or sleeping more than the individual's norm.

Q: Why would that be?

A: Psychologically, sleep can sometimes be seen as a vehicle for retreating from reality. All of us have experienced the kinds of stresses in which the most comfortable thing to do upon awakening in the morning would be to duck under the covers and escape reality—sleep some more.

Adolescents often give evidence of that kind of approach as they go through stresses of moving into adulthood.

Q: How do you know if you've had too much sleep?

A: The establishment of one's own personal norm can best be done on the basis of experience. My suggestion is to establish your personal norm during a period in which you are relatively free from stress—say, on a three-week vacation when you are away from work, and free of drugs, whether prescribed or self-imposed. Go to sleep at roughly the same time each night and awaken without the help of an alarm clock. The average length of the sleeping hours during a period like that might approximate rather closely your own norm.

Q: Does the need for sleep change as a person ages?

A: Age does not change the need for sleep as much as it influences the quality of our sleep.

Q: In what way?

A: For example, the deep sleep we spoke of earlier which is so typical of the sleep of children and youngsters, declines sharply in adulthood and is almost altogether absent in old age. You could say that an older person is often sleeping more, but enjoying it less. That is, he has to spend more time in bed to enjoy the same "return" that young people do. This may explain the cat-napping and the general feeling of debility often found among older persons.

Q: Is it better to get all your sleep at one time than to cat-nap?

A: The evidence points to the conclusion that sustained sleep is better. Studies of individuals who have been put on broken schedules or alternate work-sleep schedules show an increase in fatigue and a decrease in alertness. People who keep irregular sleep schedules not only affect the quality of their sleep but frequently cut down on the total hours they allot for sleep. Some highly efficient people can, of course, establish unusual sleep patterns distributing sleep in short naps. But, in general, they keep regular habits.

Those of us who follow no regular pattern are often most likely to complain of troubled sleep.

Q: Is it a good idea, then, to have a set time to go to bed? Or could you go to bed earlier or later, depending on when you plan to get up the next morning?

A: It is best to follow a set schedule as much as possible. The old advice of family doctors to keep regular habits is probably nowhere more important than in sleep. The reason is this: From recent research, it is clear that there is embedded in each of us a daily rhythm of just about 24 hours that is as important and real as the blood circulating in our veins. Your body temperature, for example, or the level of adrenal hormones in your blood ebbs and flows in a daily rhythm, and your energies and spirits wax and wane.

All of us have had the experience of feeling exhausted during a theater performance or while chatting with friends—when sleep would have been most welcome—then going to bed later only to find that sleep has eluded us altogether. This often happens because one's natural sleeping point, the low point of one's 24-hour cycle, has come and gone.

Within the limits that patterns of human activity permit there is a best bedtime for each of us. You cannot sleep at random and expect to enjoy a feeling of well-being.

Q: Are there actually "day people" and "night people"?

A: There are indeed—the "larks" and the "owls." There are notable differences in the time of our daily peaks and lows. For some of us, body temperature begins to rise early during sleep, and we wake up whistling, but hit our low point early in the

evening. Others begin slowly and don't hit their stride until afternoon. For them sleep is not an attractive prospect until much later at night.

Q: How are "owls" going to get to school at 9 o'clock in the morning—or how do "larks" get used to working an overnight shift?

A: These are problems with enormous implications for our whole society—schools, industry, perhaps even hospital schedules for surgery. All of us—parents, teachers, bosses, doctors—should be more sensitive to the differences in the people we deal with.

Q: Can youngsters be trained to modify their sleep patterns to the necessary extent?

A: Not as easily as many parents expect. It is difficult to alter the rhythm built into each of us, and often we do no good by trying to impose on children a sleep schedule that is not part of their norm. Many parents expect their children to be entirely pliable where sleep is concerned. Remember, children not only have their own unique patterns of sleep, but their own emotional turmoil, disappointments and crises that can affect their attitudes toward sleep.

After a difficult day at work, you might come home distraught and upset and would want nothing more than to sit down with a bottle of beer and watch an innocuous program on television, maybe a football game, or read a magazine. The thought of sleep is something in the dim future. What if, at that moment, your mother-in-law or wife pokes a finger at you and says: "O.K., lights out and not a sound out of you"? I think you would feel violated. But we do this to our kids.

Q: Are there presleep habits for youngsters that should be encouraged, such as a period of quiet reading?

A: Absolutely. That is, reading, watching television, working at a hobby—I wouldn't discourage any of those things for my adolescent youngster for whom sleep is not appropriate at the hour it is for me.

I'm not suggesting social chaos in a household, in which everybody eats and sleeps at a different hour. But in one's own room without disturbing the rest of the household, I think individual differences should not be stifled.

Q: Some people seem to shift their sleep patterns easily—

A: Some people can exert an unusual degree of control over their internal functions. Maybe one day soon others of us can be taught to do so, too, but a number of studies now demonstrate the havoc that we visit upon the organism, psychologically and physically, when we try to dramatically change sleep-waking rhythms. The early space flights gave some evidence of this. Maj. Gherman S. Titov, one of the early Russian cosmonauts, described his great satisfaction with his sleep in which he maintained an earthbound schedule. This was in contrast to some of our early astronauts who, without preparation, were put on a work-rest schedule contrary to the ones they were used to on earth, and whose sleep suffered. Attempts to shift sleep schedules dramatically can result in fatigue, accidents, poor health and performance.

Q: What about the effects of jet travel on the rhythm and on the efficiency of transcontinental or transoceanic travelers?

A: As with any stress, the effects may be more severe for one person than another. But all of us who have traveled across time zones are aware of what can happen when we disrupt our normal rhythms. Such symptoms as fatigue, irritability and psychosomatic complaints are typical in cases of "jet exhaustion." Internally, the organism becomes desynchronized.

I can't verify it, but I'm told that the Russians have a hotel in Cuba for their pilots which is run on Moscow time, so that when you arrive there you go to sleep at the time you would in terms of your homeland, not in terms of where you are. In any case, taking a day or more to adapt to the new rhythm of life before starting work and making decisions seems crucial.

Q: Are you suggesting that U.S. Presidents who make quick trips abroad may not be at peak levels of efficiency?

A: I've heard that suggested, and it makes sense. You cannot hop continents and retain the mental agility and the physical well-being that you would have in your home country. I'm not saying that we're in national peril as a result of the jet age, but I think it's a factor worth considering—not only for travelers, but for pilots and their crews.

DANGERS IN "LOST SLEEP"

Q: Is it possible to make up for lost sleep?

A: Yes, but not as quickly or as easily for everyone.

Some young, stable people have endured 10 to 12 days of sleeplessness with no apparent ill effects. Others have suffered persistent symptoms. Many mothers date the onset of insomnia problems to the pregnancy and postnatal period, in which sleep becomes fragmented. Many doctors testify that their insomnia problems began in medical school or internship, when sleep schedules were upset or reversed for long periods of time. We still don't know whether prolonged sleep deprivation might cause irreversible damage to some persons. Therefore, a person should treat dramatic and prolonged changes in sleep schedules with caution.

Q: If you pick the right hour, do you need any other help in getting a good night's sleep?

A: That's entirely a subjective matter. Freud observed that everybody has his own pet ritual in preparing for a night's sleep. To a degree, that's true.

There are some people who enjoy reading before bedtime. Some find television a soporific. There are others who find a bedtime snack helpful. And it is not true that darkness and silence is the optimum sleep environment for everyone, children included. Many people need the sound of a radio to fall asleep, or a light in the hallway. The range of bedtime rituals is as varied as human experience itself.

Q: Is the old recipe of warm milk still good?

A: It's not a guarantee of getting you to sleep more quickly, but it's one of the older remedies for overcoming insomnia that seems to have some scientific basis. Milk contains a type of amino acid—tryptophan—which when given to volunteers produces a pronounced sedative effect. Furthermore, warm milk has a symbolic meaning of reassurance, even for an adult. Accordingly, I would say it makes a good bedtime drink.

Q: How about a highball for a nightcap?

A: Liquor is a depressant, and, therefore, for many people causes sleepiness and is a sensible soporific. On the other hand, like our response to any drug introduced in the body, there are differing responses among us. While some people become drowsy, others are stimulated and become energetic or irritable.

One thing is certain, however: Liquor in abundance serves to disrupt normal sleep. The sleep of those who have had a great deal of alcohol is clearly distorted.

Q: Do you mean that they aren't getting the rest they would get otherwise?

A: Yes. We know that one important component of sleep—the so-called REM or the "rapid eye movement" period which is associated with vivid dreaming—is reduced or obliterated in the sleep records of alcoholics. Later, when the alcohol is withdrawn, there is a "rebound" effect—an abnormal increase in the time spent in the REM state.

Many severe alcoholics have been studied, and their sleep is often disturbed ultimately by horrendous nightmares, which is not unusual for persons who have been deprived of the normally recurring REM periods of the night. Many drugs, incidentally, produce the same effect—including, unfortunately, the sleeping pills millions of Americans use as casually as aspirin.

Q: What about children's nightmares? Do they follow periods of dreamlessness?

A: Not typically. The dreams of children are more frequent, and often more vivid and terrifying because they are difficult for the youngster to distinguish from reality. The child is being flooded with new experiences and sensations all the time.

The most terrifying nightmares of all, however, arise not out of the REM period, but from the periods of deepest sleep. During such episodes, a child may scream in terror but be difficult to awaken. Sleepwalking and bedwetting also appear to arise from these periods of deep dreamless sleep during the night.

Q: Does this trouble lessen as children grow older?

A: It does. Many of the phenomena which arise from the depths of sleep—sleepwalking, bedwetting, night terrors, talking in sleep and so on—drop out in later adolescence and adulthood as the child's nervous system matures. Sometimes, of course, they warrant medical and psychological attention.

Q: How can people get better sleep?

A: Keep regular habits, avoid stimulants such as coffee or tobacco, take daily exercise, avoid drugs, and, if necessary, look behind the symptom for the cause. Good sleep is not the result of something you do immediately before retiring, but of a style of life and a manner of daily living.

After all, we're not different persons when we turn out the light. Our sleep reflects on our total selves.

IF A PERSON WAKES UP TOO EARLY

Q: What can be done for people who get to sleep easily but wake up too early and can't get back to sleep?

A: It is not an uncommon problem. When we speak of insomnia we commonly think only of difficulty in falling asleep. But, in reality, insomnia comes in many guises— including intermittent awakenings during the night and difficulty in staying asleep.

As I said earlier, the aging process itself serves to lighten sleep, so that in the latter part of the night we are without the deep periods of sleep so typical of our youth. This means that the sounds that would never have gotten through to us before, now begin to come through—whether it's the milkman or the paper boy or the rustling of a bedmate.

On the other hand, the lightening of sleep can also stem from other causes. It is typical, for example, of those who are suffering a period of depression. Depression is a phenomenon which is much more common than once thought. The symptoms can range from mild sadness and blues to an immobile state of melancholy. Many people who complain only of inability to stay asleep are actually suffering a sense of depression in which life has lost its meaning or purpose. Often, a return of deep sleep is the first sign of recovery.

Or, early-morning awakening can be caused by inappropriate drugs, or too much alcohol, or because we are on stimulants. Whatever the cause, such sleep disturbances are worthy of further study if they become persistent and severe. Most of us are victims from time to time of sleep problems brought on by worry or stress or ex-

citement. Such episodes should not be the occasion for further anxieties about sleep. I know what my prescription for myself is: not just to lie there and fight for sleep but to get up and do something—perhaps not creative and certainly not stressful, but something useful—to occupy the time. I mean such things as writing letters, reading, balancing the checkbook, making notes for the next day's tasks.

Q: Do you then go back to bed?

A: Yes.

Q: How long do you engage in such activity?

A: As long as an hour—even an hour and a half.

"CHEMICAL WARFARE" ON INSOMNIA

Q: What about getting up and taking a walk?

A: There's nothing wrong with that. I guess what I'm trying to say is this: Periods of insomnia, whether during the middle of the night or early morning or at bedtime, are sometimes our common lot just by virtue of the fact that we're human and we all suffer stresses at one time or another. Therefore, episodes of that sort should not be the occasion for a campaign of chemical warfare and drugs and desperation measures.

Many of us panic at the thought of a period of insomnia. I don't think that's indicated at all. One works through those periods by using the time in some other manner than just lying there and getting agitated over lack of sleep.

Q Do people tend to get trapped into using sleeping pills because of this fear of insomnia?

A: No question about it, and the use of sleep drugs must be a major issue in any discussion of drug abuse in this country today. Just a couple of statistics: We spend over half a billion dollars a year on sleeping pills. There are 800,000 pounds of barbiturates alone produced in this country each year. Now that's only one family of sleep drugs—enough, incidentally, to supply one capsule a week for each man, woman and child in the country. Multiply that figure by the more than 200 types of sleep potions available today and you get an idea of the problem.

Q: Are you talking of sleep potions available on prescription or available over the counter?

A: On prescription. And it's not only true in our own country. Ten per cent of all prescriptions by British general practitioners are for sleep drugs.

The spiraling use of drugs for sleep is clearly apparent, and neither patients nor many of their doctors are entirely aware of the potential dangers involved. That is why the insomniac should try to use avenues other than drugs in living through or overcoming sleep problems.

Q: Do sleeping pills affect only sleep adversely, or can they have more far-reaching effects?

A: Both are possible. It is now clear that many of the drugs we have been taking to capture sleep are capable of distorting the very sleep they induce. For example, the nightly rhythm of vivid dreaming—the apparently essential REM periods of the night —is dampened by heavy doses of most sleeping pills. When the drug is stopped abruptly, the results are often further sleep problems, including ugly and disturbing nightmares.

As to longer-range effects, we shouldn't assume when we take a sleeping pill that all we are going to affect is our sleep.

Long after the sedation has worn off, an impact on your mental and emotional state may remain. Barbiturates, for example, may intensify feelings of depression and reduce intellectual acuity. But most impor-

tant, a person builds up a "tolerance" to a particular drug, and then needs ever higher doses to get the desired effect. That is where the really serious trouble begins—leading down the road to possible addiction.

Q: What about nonprescription sleep tablets? Are they effective at all? Are they dangerous?

A: Many nonprescription sleep drugs are the outgrowth of the finding that drugs often used to treat allergies and colds—the antihistamines—had a soporific effect.

As a result, many over-the-counter drugs include an antihistamine as the central ingredient. When used as prescribed—and that's important—they are either innocuous or mildly helpful, and they can do little harm. But the problem is that many people find that the prescribed dose doesn't work, so they increase it.

Moreover, we're living in an age which one expert has correctly referred to as "polypharmacy." A person will not only take high doses of a nonprescription sleep drug, but other drugs as well. There is enough evidence of severe reactions to inspire caution.

Q: Would the person for whom getting up early in the morning is extremely difficult benefit from an afternoon nap?

A: An afternoon nap is a matter of routine for many people. Winston Churchill used to say that he made two days out of one by an afternoon nap. On the other hand, there are many people whose nightly sleep is thwarted by random daytime naps that reduce the possibility of establishing a good routine.

One desperate mother recently described her chronic sleeplessness, saying that no matter what she tried, sleep eluded her. Her young son, overhearing his mother, found the answer: "I think you'd be able to sleep O.K. at night, Mom, if you wouldn't always go back to bed after I go to school."

Q: Does the kind of work you do—

physical versus mental—have anything to do with insomnia?

A: There is good evidence that regular, mild exercise encourages good sleep. But there are longshoremen with insomnia problems and there are professors with insomnia problems. A man's vocation does not of itself explain sleep problems.

Q: Will mental or physical exhaustion make sleep easier or harder?

A: Mental stimulation and physical exhaustion prior to bedtime make sleep harder. By that I mean that if you were to do a great many push-ups and then try to go to bed, that would be self-defeating, because that kind of heavy exercise acts as a stress rather than a relaxant. The evidence from laboratory studies in which people were subjected to stressful films before bedtime—for example, horror films or emotionally toned films—is that these often carry their disturbing residue into the night.

Q: Is it possible to time your own sleep —to be your own alarm clock?

A: Yes, it is. Many people are able to awaken at a predetermined time. It seems almost as if they are responding to biological signals inside them, subtle signals that provide a delicate stimulus to which they have conditioned themselves. Obviously, this is one more piece of evidence that sleep is an active time—that a lot is going on inside the brain and body while we sleep.

"SLEEP IS AN EMOTIONAL MATTER"

Q: Some elderly people say they require less sleep than before and like to get up earlier in the morning as they get older. Is this common, or does it just depend on the individual?

A: The phenomenon you describe is not uncommon at all. As I said earlier, a lightening and fragmentation of sleep are part of the aging process and changes in the central nervous system.

But how the aged person views this development is another story. It depends on the world he is waking up to. How we view our sleep is a function of how we view life in general. If it's an especially difficult day ahead of us, we think we have not slept enough. But if it's an exciting and rewarding thing we're looking forward to, we think we are done with sleep.

Sleep is, after all, a very personal and emotional matter. Anxieties about sleep surround us in childhood and often persist in adulthood. There are many insomniacs who have difficulty sleeping because sleep is a threatening and fearful experience. We teach something about sleep to our children in their bedtime prayers, when we ask them to say, "If I should die before I wake. . . ." We read that sleep may be "death's younger brother," as the poet put it; or, as the ancients believed, that the soul leaves the body at night, goes wandering and is recaptured only with difficulty in the morning.

There are many people who abhor the moment of sleep and are delighted to awaken to face the next day. Others seek sleep as a refuge and an escape. How we view sleep tells us something about ourselves—more, perhaps, than we had ever thought possible.

50. EXPERIENCING YOUR BODY: YOU ARE WHAT YOU FEEL

Seymour Fisher

There is no more fascinating sight than your own image looking back at you in a mirror. You are drawn to it in a half-embarrassed way, excited and intensely involved. Do you remember the last time someone showed you a photograph of yourself? Wasn't there a surge of feeling and a deep curiosity about "How do I look?" Perhaps, too, you have noticed the strange entrancement even animals display at the sight of their mirror double.

Your body encompasses a sector of space that is uniquely your own. It represents your base of operations in the world, the outward manifestation of your being and identity. No other object is so persistently with you. Unceasingly, even when you are asleep, you receive enormous quantities of information from your body. Your decisions, fantasies, even your dreams are influenced by the sensations emanating from it. Yet it is only in the last two decades that serious scientific attention has been given to the study of the body as a psychological phenomenon.

For centuries scientists have studied the body as an anatomical structure and a biological system, leaving its psychological aspects to other disciplines. Artists and writers, for example, traditionally have devoted great energy to capturing the "feel" of the body in dramatic contexts. Eastern philosophies such as yoga have enjoyed a considerable measure of Western popularity in recent years, in part because of their supposed power to put the individual closer to his own body. Similarly, the so-called "drug culture" has drawn on body experience: LSD users, for example, report that the chemical frequently produces the feeling that parts of the body have become detached or that the boundary between the body and the outside world has dissipated.

But even the average person must admit to a curiosity about his body and a preoccupation with the psychological experiences it presents to him. He is concerned about the impression his body makes on others; he experiences anxiety about the potential vulnerability of his body to disease and trauma; he uses "gut" cues to help him decide whether or not to get involved with certain people or confront certain situations; he puts out large sums of money to shape and camouflage his appearance so that it will conform to his idealized concept of the "good body." Indeed, a major portion of advertising is devoted to products that claim to improve the individual's relationship with his body—by making it cleaner, more fragrant, stronger, sexier.

The task of making sense of our own bodies is not as simple as we might hope or expect. As each individual matures, he is confronted with the problems of integrating an endless barrage of sensations and assimilating the meanings adults ascribe to various sectors of his frame. He discovers complicated rules prescribing the areas he can touch, talk about, look at, and even think about. He is puzzled by the multiple, and often opposed, meanings assigned to the same body area. He learns, for example,

Reprinted from *Saturday Review* (July 8, 1972) by permission of publisher.

that the back of his body is simultaneously a spatial dimension, a place where punishment is applied, and a locus for concern about anal sphincter control; yet the same area also remains obscure because he cannot even get a direct view of it.

The child's attempt to construct a complete psychological map of his body is further hindered by the negative messages he receives from others about such an enterprise. His parents are reluctant to talk about body events and, in fact, become angry or embarrassed when he explicitly mentions certain organs or orifices. He learns that the available vocabulary for describing his own body experiences is sparse and tinged with an illicit flavor. Moreover, the child soon realizes that the culture does not trust body experiences; his education focuses on cultivating intellectual capacities, but his teachers insist that he control body impulses that are likely to "break out" if not closely monitored. Growing up in such an atmosphere, a child finds it almost impossible to examine or codify his body experiences realistically. Hasty glimpses of body terrain and fragments of anatomical information must be pieced together with little or no outside help. For these reasons, the individual is inclined to view his body as having alien qualities and to entertain numerous irrational notions about it.

In fact, although an individual experiences his body more often and in far greater depth than he does any other object in his environment, his perceptions of this, his dearest possession, remain distorted throughout his life. For example, when the average person is called upon to describe or make judgments about his body, he displays considerable inaccuracy. In studies in which persons have been asked to indicate the sizes of various body parts (e.g., head, arms), they often grossly over- or underestimate their true proportions. In one experiment Leo Schneiderman asked subjects to

stand in front of a novel full-length mirror consisting of multiple panels that could be moved in such a way as to distort their mirror image in known quantitative terms. When subjects were confronted with the distorted image and asked to reconstruct their true appearance by manipulating the movable mirror panels, they frequently erred. They were indeed surprised to discover how vague their knowledge of their own appearance really was.

Other investigators have found that it is not very difficult to arrange conditions in which the individual fails to recognize pictures of himself. For example, if you take a picture of an individual's shadow profile without his knowledge and subsequently show him a series of shadow profile pictures that include his own as well as those of several other individuals, he will rarely recognize his own. But if you ask him to guess about the personal qualities of each profile pictured, he will say more favorable things about his own silhouette than he will about the others. This repeatedly validated finding suggests that even where there is lack of conscious recognition, one's own image still elicits defensive ego involvement (in the form of self-praise) at the unconscious level. Lack of conscious recognition has also been demonstrated with respect to pictures of one's hands, and even one's face, if presented for only a brief duration.

Freud was one of the first to note, anecdotally, the difficulty we have in identifying our own image when we come across it unexpectedly. The eminent doctor was sitting in a train sleeping car when a sudden jolt opened the door of the washroom and "an aged man, wearing a dressing gown and a cap" entered his compartment. Just as he was about to inform this stranger that he was intruding, Freud discovered that the stranger was actually his own image reflected in the mirror.

One of the problems of maintaining an

accurate picture of your own body is that the image needs to be repeatedly revised. There is often a lag between the occurrence of change in your body and the incorporation of this change into your body model. Consider the effects of aging. Many people have been startled to discover on meeting an old friend after a long separation that the friend perceives much greater signs of aging than the individual had recognized in himself. This lag is especially apparent in the blind. For example, a man of middle age who had lost his sight when he was young told me that this image of himself was still that of the child he had last seen in the mirror years ago. Although others responded to him as a middle-aged adult, he could only visualize himself physically in the form of a young boy.

The so-called "phantom limb" provides another striking example of the difficulty in keeping one's body image up to date. When a person loses a projecting body part such as an arm or nose because of trauma or surgery, he often continues to experience that part as if it were still present. The sensations that seem to emanate from beyond the stump are often so vivid that he may momentarily forget about his loss and try to use the missing part. After a while, however, the phantom limb fades and usually disappears permanently. This phenomenon has been attributed by some to the fact that the sudden loss of a major body sector is too radical a change to "accept." Only gradually does the new pattern of body sensations become assimilated, and the body concept therefore becomes more accurate.

Although the oblique way in which the individual builds up and maintains a model of his body makes it difficult for him to use body cues rationally, there is no doubt that whatever model he *does* evolve strongly influences his behavior. The individual's body concept is an influential intermediary in his transactions with what is "out there." A person who regards his body as weak and fragile will behave less boldly than one who perceives his body as a well-defended place. Similarly, a person who turns away from his body because he experiences it as bad and ugly may turn to intellectual activities as compensation.

Many sophisticated and reliable procedures for evaluating a person's body concept now are available. Reactions to one's mirror image, inkblot interpretations, drawings of the human figure, estimates of body size—such measures of body feelings have proven to be diversely correlated with personality traits, ability to tolerate stress, conduct in intimate group situations, and even psychosomatic symptoms.

Some of the most interesting work being done today by body image researchers is aimed at demonstrating that body experiences can shape an individual's interpretations of the outside world. In a rather ingenious study, Stuart Valins asked men in a laboratory setting to judge the attractiveness of a series of pictures of seminude girls. The men were told that while they were making these judgments their heart rate would be recorded. However, it was added, because of a "defect" in the equipment, they would be able to hear the sound of the heartbeat as it was being picked up. Valins proceeded to manipulate the faked audible heartbeat so that it was changed perceptibly while each man was judging certain of the pictures, but remained unchanged for all the others. The final judgments were significant; the men decided that the most attractive pictures were those of the girls they were looking at when they thought their heart rate had changed. The findings of this study, replicated by other investigators, demonstrated that each man's perception of what seemed to be going on within his own body had a definite impact on his opinions of the world around him.

Another experiment found that a person's mood can be influenced by artificially molding his facial muscles. Explaining to his experimental subjects that he was studying the activity of facial muscles, James D. Laird manipulated these muscles so that to an external observer the subjects seemed either to be "smiling" or "frowning." The subjects had no idea what expression the experimenter had "put on" their face by means of his manipulations. Yet when measures of mood were obtained, the "frown" and "smile" conditions were found to produce opposite mood effects. Somehow, the position of the facial muscles was perceived and interpreted, causing a significant shift in how happy or sad the individual felt.

Rorschach inkblots provide another illustration of the influence that one's body sensations have on his perception of the outside world. The Rorschach, of course, is based on a long-standing psychological theory that one's interpretations of ambiguous stimuli will reveal hidden problems that the individual does not consciously recognize or is afraid to talk about freely. But in studies conducted in my own laboratory, Sidney Cleveland and I discovered that feelings about the body alone can influence the way a person interprets the vague patterns presented to him. The way an individual experiences the outer, peripheral regions of his body will be expressed in the peripheral regions of the objects he creates from the inkblots. For example, people differ in how clearly they perceive their body to have a defensive sheath capable of protecting them from intrusion. Some feel open and vulnerable; others feel well-fortified. The more secure an individual feels about his body boundaries, we discovered, the more he produces Rorschach images with protective sheltering qualities: caves with rocky walls, turtles with hard shells, tanks, shields, persons covered with blankets.

An individual's feeling of boundary security are correlated with how clearly he is aware of his boundary sheath—skin and muscle. Heightened awareness of this sheath seems to contribute to a sense of being adequately bounded and thus more secure. Many of us have employed this trick in fearful surroundings. Lying in bed, a home owner becomes anxious about a break-in and pictures the enclosing walls of his house. A driver entering a storm assures himself of his safety by glancing at the walls of his metal cocoon. Perhaps even more common is the preference many people have for small bedrooms or tight-fitting clothing.

With this notion of body security in mind, we conducted several experiments to determine if heightened awareness of the body sheath would have an effect on the interpretation of inkblots. In one experimental condition, subjects were exposed to experiences that caused them to focus on their skin and muscle. They were asked to report the occurrence of sensations in these areas while various stimuli, such as stroking, were applied to the skin. In the second condition, attention was drawn away from the outside of the body and focused upon the interior, with subjects reporting such phenomena as heart sensations or the feel of swallowing a glass of water. The results of these manipulations validated our assumption that awareness of certain body areas will affect one's feeling of security and, in turn, the perceptions of the outside world. When attention was focused on the skin and muscles, the number of protected inkblot images, such as a man in armor, rose; when attention was directed toward the interior, such inkblot fantasies decreased.

A person's body experiences may permeate his outlook in a number of unique ways. Studies have shown that if a subject is asked to compose imaginative stories, his tales will be affected by whether he is lying down or sitting up; his judgment of how far away an object is will depend on whether or not he feels the object has a meaningful relationship to his body; his beliefs about how friendly others are toward him may depend upon his faith in the security of his body boundaries, and so forth.

All of these body experiences will affect the activities of normal, healthy individuals. But what happens to the body model during psychological breakdown? For years psychiatric literature has suggested that schizophrenics suffer gross fragmentation of the body model. Vivid case histories have been published about schizophrenics who fancy that they have lost important chunks of their anatomy or who perceive their bodies as grotesquely altered—"dead," or transformed into the opposite sex, for example. However, more systematic studies have revealed that the body model stands up pretty well to the impact of the schizophrenic process. In fact, investigators have had a difficult time demonstrating truly impressive differences between psychiatric patients and normals in their mode of body experience. When one sifts through the scientific literature about this matter, only a few limited conclusions seem warranted. Schizophrenic patients *do* report a greater number of distorted and unusual body sensations than do normal persons, but the difference is small. And, somewhat surprisingly, schizophrenics do not exceed neurotic patients in this respect. Even in the throes of severe disturbance, the body concept seems to remain relatively well-preserved.

One specific dimension that *has* shown promise in differentiating psychiatric patients from normal persons is perception of body size. Psychiatric patients are concerned about sensations of body shrinkage and smallness. They feel reduced in stature or perceive one or more body parts to be smaller than they should be. When asked to make numerical estimates of the sizes of various body parts, they usually over-react, either underestimating or compensatorily overestimating the true proportions.

I have suggested that these perceptions of shrinkage represent a view of self that is depreciated and devalued. The psychiatric patient is often one who, in his own eyes, has failed or suffered major rejection by the culture. He feels lowly and unwanted, and his Lilliputian sensations reflect his downgraded view of himself.

In the course of probing the nature of abnormal body experiences, we have learned that certain body feelings, once considered pathognomic, are actually quite normal. A good example is provided by the phenomenon of *depersonalization*. Early psychiatric literature asserted that the patient who reports that his body feels alien, as if it did not belong to him, had a particularly poor prognosis for recovery. Depersonalization was supposed to be a mark of advanced pathology. However, several investigators have recently reported that depersonalization is a common reaction to stress among normal persons. For example, depersonalization has been prominently detected in normal persons who become anxious when swallowing an unknown drug during an experiment. There seems to be adaptive value in responding to stress-induced anxiety by getting "distance" from your own body, thereby decreasing personal involvement with it. Furthermore, normal persons who differ in their use of depersonalization also differ in other aspects of their behavior. For example, they have contrasting ways of responding to certain kinds of sexual stimulation. I have found that women who prefer vaginal stimulation to manual clitoral stimulation in reaching orgasm have an unusually strong depersonalized perspective toward their own body. I have described these findings in detail in *The Female Orgasm: Personality, Physiology, Fantasy,* published by Basic Books.

It would be impossible for anyone to attend simultaneously to all of the things happening in his body. He would be overwhelmed and ultimately confused. Just as one learns to attend to only certain auditory stimuli, each person must learn to attend to the various sectors of his body in some pattern that is meaningful and useful to him. Each individual, we have found, actually is rather consistent in his style of distributing body attention, although such consistency holds true more for men than for women. One man may be unusually aware of his head, another of his legs, and still another of the right as compared with the left side of his body. What is an outstanding body landmark for one may be almost invisible for another. Also, we have learned that each body sector is associated with a fairly distinct conflict or tension theme.

Specific conflict themes turn out to be linked to the following areas: head, back versus front, mouth, eyes, stomach, heart, right versus left. For example, the male with heightened awareness of his back (as compared to the front of his body) is often preoccupied with urges to express hostile soiling feelings toward others that evoke alarm in him because they are experienced as dirty and indicative of loss of self-control (perhaps in a way reminiscent of the child who fails to control his anal sphincter as expected by his parents). The male with heightened awareness of his heart is religiously oriented and especially conflicted about guilt feelings. One of the most intriguing patterns we discovered indicated that the male who is grossly more aware of the right as compared with the left side of his body is in conflict about his sexual relationship with women. He feels inhibited in the presence of women, is less likely to date, and gets anxious when confronted by stimuli with sexual connotations. From such findings we concluded that when an individual habitually concentrates a large amount of attention upon a body sector he is doing so because that sector is linked with a conflictual issue that persistently troubles him. What utility might such an association have? Most likely, the individual's investment of attention in specific body areas has some adaptive or control function. This is somewhat analogous to the piece of string that is tied around a child's finger when he is sent to the store so that he will remember what he is supposed to buy when he gets there. An individual's long-term focus of attention on a body area could serve, therefore, as a kind of "string around the finger" reminding him that certain things should or should not be done.

The persistent concentration of attention upon a body area provides a guiding signal to the individual to restrain the expression of conflictual impulses associated with that area. For example, heightened back awareness would signal that control should be maintained over hostile besmirching urges; or magnified awareness of the right side of the body would warn against heterosexual involvement. Within this framework an individual's style of perceiving his body can be regarded as a part of the elaborate system he evolves to control his behavior. As he develops attitudes toward basic issues in the world, they become coded in terms of differential awareness of specific body parts.

The regulatory function of this concentration of awareness is apparent in the much simpler case of monitoring the muscles of an arm to keep it rigid or the sphincter muscles of a full bladder to inhibit urination. There is also interesting anecdotal information in the psychiatric literature about instances in which patients, having been psychotherapeutically relieved of a preoccupation with sensations or minor symptoms in a body part, suddenly show a dramatic release of affect upon some theme. The investment of concern in the body area apparently served to inhibit awareness of the underlying anxiety that came to the surface when the superficial concern was removed.

We have also completed experiments in which we artificially altered the individual's awareness of a body part to demonstrate the control function of concentration on that region. The greater the amount of attention a man habitually directs to his heart, the greater his religiosity and anxious concern over feelings of guilt. In one experimental procedure a group of men were given exercises designed to heighten their heart awareness; immediately afterward they were briefly exposed to a series of words, half of which referred to guilt themes (e.g., wrong, fault, judge) and half of which did not. They then were asked to recall as many of these words as possible. The purpose of the learning task was to detect defensive emotional attitudes toward the guilt words in terms of the relative proportion of guilt and non-guilt words recalled. Groups of control subjects went through the same procedure, but their degree of heart awareness was not altered. It was found that the group that was made more heart aware had a significantly greater tendency to forget the guilt words. By concentrating a man's attention on his heart, we were able to alter his receptivity to guilt themes.

In view of the obvious differences between male and female bodies, it would be logical to expect that men and women would construct quite different images of their bodies. We do, in fact, find radically different styles of body perception related to sex. At this moment in history the question of body superiority-inferiority most naturally arises. Freud did little for the women's movement by explicitly declaring that the female has a depreciated, inferior concept of her body. A little girl is traumatized, he reasoned, upon discovering that her genital organ is different from the male's, whose phallic attributes are equated with power

and strength. Presumably, this trauma leaves indelible scars; she is destined to interpret her lack of a penis as a sign of body inferiority. Thus the idea grew that the average woman is less secure and more disturbed about her body than is the average man.

Body image research, however, indicates that precisely the opposite is true. For example, we put a series of male and female rubber masks on the faces of men and women and requested the subjects to describe each mask as they glimpsed it in a mirror when a light flashed on. To our surprise, the men were made much more anxious than the women by this procedure. They were flustered by the female masks and made significantly more errors when trying to describe the characteristics of their disguised appearance. The solidity of these observations was affirmed by a second study that produced the same results. It was apparent that the men were less able to cope adequately with the change in body concept imposed by the experimental condition.

Other scientific evidence indicates a similar trend. It has been demonstrated that the average woman perceives her body to be better protected and enclosed by a more secure boundary than does the average man. In one study we found that the male was more disturbed by the threat of injecting adrenaline into his body than was the female. Other investigators have observed that men are relatively more preoccupied with themes of body destruction. Even in their dreams men portray themselves as threatened by imminent body damage more often than do women. Several appraisals of males and females hospitalized for surgery reveal greater anxiety in men than in women about the body-threatening implications of the situation. Men may carefully control their open expression of such anxiety, but inwardly they are more disturbed than women.

In addition to the perception of body threat, there is another important difference in the way males and females experience their bodies. Diverse sources have noted that women are more aware of their body feelings than are men and that they are more positive in accepting these experiences. David J. Van Lennep reported that female children not only display greater body awareness than male children, but the magnitude of this difference between the sexes becomes larger after adolescence. In addition, the degree of body awareness in women is known to be correlated with positive attributes such as a clear sense of identity, while in men it is linked with certain categories of conflictual preoccupation. This confirms what we already observe in everyday life. Girls and women invest much more open interest in the body than do their male counterparts. They feel free to study their own appearance and to experiment with techniques for altering it by means of clothing and cosmetics. A male who displays much direct or open interest in his body (except with reference to athletic activities) is regarded as a deviant.

A woman apparently sees a clearer and more meaningful relationship between her body and her life role than a man. Despite the influence of Woman's Liberation, the chief goals of most women still revolve about being attractive, entering into marriage, and producing children. Such aims readily permit the female to see her body as vehicle for her life career. This is not true for the man. Unless he becomes a professional athlete, he can perceive little connection between his body attributes and the requirements for status and success. Male power and accomplishment are increasingly defined in terms of intellect, cleverness, business acumen, and so forth. The low status jobs are the ones that require body strength. As I have reported in *Body Experience in Fantasy and Behavior* (Appleton-Century-Crofts), an important contribution of the research on body experience is that it has cast serious doubt on stereotyped ideas about the inferiority of the feminine body concept.

Our expanding knowledge about the body as a psychological object encourages thought about the potential practical and therapeutic applications of this knowledge. Intriguing possibilities are becoming visible. For example, efforts are under way in both Europe and the United States to evaluate the potentialities of treating psychological disturbance by altering body experience. Austin M. Des Lauriers has suggested that a major problem of the schizophrenic is that he has lost an articulated image of his body; without it he has little individuality or ability to test reality. Des Lauriers has devised therapeutic techniques to make the schizophrenic more aware of his body, particularly its boundary, and claims considerable clinical success with this approach. Others have indirectly affirmed Des Lauriers's concepts by demonstrating that exercise and systematic stimulation that highlight muscle and skin sensations in the schizophrenic individual do, indeed, increase his boundary security.

Alterations of body experience also are being explored with "emotionally disturbed" children and those with serious learning problems. Preliminary findings suggest that certain types of learning difficulties may be improved by giving the child a more realistic image of his body, especially its spatial dimensions.

Research analyses of body feelings may prove to be of value in clarifying puzzling complications that arise when people must adapt to body disabilities and medical procedures. We now know that fantasies of body vulnerability may cause an individual to respond with grossly inappropriate distress to minor body trauma and to fail completely to adjust to more serious chronic disablement. We have leads that suggest that the amount and kind of psychological disturbance evoked by an injury may depend upon subtle differences in its location upon the body. An injury on the right side may pose a different form of threat than one on the left side; trauma to the back may arouse different kinds of anxieties than if it involved the front. Body attitudes also seem to play a role in the perplexing problem of why people delay in seeking medical treatment after they discover a serious symptom in themselves. Often the delay is so great that a disease process will have advanced to a point where it is no longer amenable to treatment. Paradoxically, it appears that the individual who feels secure about his body is most inclined toward such irrational delay. Finally, it should be noted that we are beginning to see body attitudes as potentially powerful predictors of the psychological effects produced by various drugs. This is quite logical if we remember that an important part of the impact of drugs involves alterations of body sensations.

Various individuals and cults currently acknowledge the importance of the experienced body as a basic component of life adjustment. It is interesting that heightened concern with body experience has coincided with the investigation of body image in the psychological laboratories and clinics. Here, however, the similarity ends: Those involved with these cults or movements are unwilling to wait for the facts to come in. Instead, they have embarked on impulsive quests via drugs and meditation, for example, in the hope of hitting upon new principles that will make possible "revolutionary" innovations in the body model and overall well-being. But the odds are against these haphazard approaches. Only systematic study will provide sound principles and realistic techniques for altering body experience in helpful ways. Indeed, there is little doubt that the body image is one of the most important—and, ironically, most neglected—phenomena in the scientific quest for understanding of our psychological selves.

CHAPTER VIII

Therapies

There are many approaches to the solution of personal psychological problems, and the proliferation and advancement of techniques and therapies within the past 20 years have been remarkable. This chapter investigates a number of recent discoveries, insights, and therapeutic advances of general interest.

Headaches which are persistent or severe can be quite debilitating. "Why You Get Headaches and What To Do about Them" suggests several answers to this common problem. "Rehabilitating the Problem Drinker" indicates some new approaches to a critical problem which has only recently been recognized as an illness rather than a moral lapse. Many other treatment and training techniques have been developed in recent years, such as those considered in "Feminist Therapy: A New Specialization" and "Assertiveness Training: How To Say No and Make It Stick."

For disturbed individuals or their families, finding the right therapy can be a major undertaking. "Shopping for the Right Therapy" is informative and helpful in this respect, and "New Ways to Heal Disturbed Minds" provides an informative and useful overview of the possibilities.

One age-old affliction, manic-depression, in which a person experiences periods of intense hyperactivity coupled with bouts of severe melancholia, may now be yielding to treatment. For more information read, "Lithium—New Hope for Manic-Depression."

There are also many fascinating older approaches, one of which, hypnosis, is in the process of reemergence. "Weapon against Pain: Hypnosis Is No Mirage" suggests new clinical applications of the age-old technique.

Sooner or later, many patients consider discontinuing their therapies. They may feel better or not, but they experience doubt and uncertainty concerning the decision to discontinue this help. Some guidelines they can apply to evalute their situation and the therapist's own involvement in the situation are suggested in "How, When and Why To Fire Your Shrink."

The liberalization of our culture's sexual mores has had many derivative effects. One such effect has been the realization by many individuals and couples that their sexual performance was less than optimal. Fortunately there is help available; read "No-Nonsense Therapy for Six Sexual Malfunctions."

51. WHY YOU GET HEADACHES AND WHAT TO DO ABOUT THEM

Interview with Dr. David R. Coddon
Director, Headache Clinic, Mount Sinai Medical Center
Reprinted from *U. S. News & World Report*

Q: Dr. Coddon, are certain types of people more susceptible to headaches than others?

A: I would say generally, no. Probably everyone, at one time or another, has a headache of some kind—and more than 20 million people a year in this country have headaches that are severe enough to force them to seek medical help.

I get patients from big cities; a chicken farmer who comes from a very peaceful, tranquil area in Ohio; people from the desert—people from all over the world. Headaches just don't know races, creeds or geographic distribution.

Q: Is the number of headache sufferers increasing?

A: I think the number is increasing, for several reasons: Environmental stress is one factor—no question about that—and there's pollution; also the increased use of oral contraceptives by women. My own clinical research suggests that excessive use of antibiotics could be a principal contributing factor.

Q: Let's break that down. What does environmental stress have to do with headaches?

A: Environmental stress is every interaction that goes on involving you in dealing with other people and situations—at work, at home, everywhere. You live in a totally stressful situation from the moment you wake up.

Even while you're sleeping, there's stress.

Stress actually can be therapeutic in itself, but, paradoxically, it is when stress stops that headaches will occur in many individuals.

Q: Do you mean we would be better off to be under stress all the time?

A: In a sense, you are correct: The hard-working, hard-driving individual rarely complains about a headache. It's when he relaxes that the headache comes—not during periods of stress or tension. People come to me and say: "I go on vacation, and I get a headache. I don't understand it, Doctor. I'm relaxed!"

What they don't understand is that most headaches—the severe, disabling kinds—occur when they are relaxed. There is the week-end headache, the headache that occurs after sexual intercourse, or during and after vigorous sports activities, such as tennis—rarely after golf.

Q: Why should relaxing bring on a headache?

A: Because, in my opinion, the vast majority of headaches are probably due to alterations in the blood flow. That's blood flow—not blood pressure. There's a great deal of difference. I'd better explain, because it's crucial to understanding the causes and treatment of headaches:

The head contains the body's greatest number of pain-sensitive nerve endings and chemical transmitters. It also has the greatest amount of blood supply. During periods of relaxation, there is a decrease in blood flow. This happens to everyone, but not everyone has severe headaches.

It is my opinion that the "neurovascular bed"—the parts of the nervous system containing nerves which control the size of blood vessels leading to the head—is different in patients who have chronic, recurrent headaches. When the blood fails to supply enough oxygen to the head, a headache can result.

Q: What about the connection between headaches and pollution?

A: Pollutants in the air definitely play a role in causing headaches. We're not certain just what pollutants they are, but the relationship is definite.

Q: You mentioned antibiotics. How can they cause headaches?

A: As you know, over the past quarter of a century there has been a growing use of antibiotics. In addition to their use as medication, they may even be in much of the food we eat. When one is given too many antibiotics over a period of time, they seem to permit virus activity.

We know that viruses and virus particles can lie dormant in the body for years and then be activated by specific circumstances. Stress, cold or heat, for instance, can activate a virus—and overuse of antibiotics, too.

This activation can cause what I refer to as hyperaggregation of blood platelets. Platelets are associated with blood clotting. It is possible that platelets can hyperaggregate and literally cause blood-sludging and stimulate pain-sensitive nerve endings, resulting from decreased blood flow and decreased oxygen.

We have demonstrated in certain patients an absolute increase in the number of platelets during their acute attacks of severe headaches. Aspirin—if taken early enough —interferes with this platelet aggregation. That's one of the reasons aspirin is so effective.

Q: What are the most common types of headaches?

A: The most common kind of disabling headache is the vascular-flow type we've been talking about. They can occur anywhere in the head, and some people have them chronically.

Migraine headaches are the second-most-frequent type of disabling headache. At least 10 to 20 per cent of the world's population is afflicted with migraine. Migraine sufferers can be Eskimos, aborigines in Australia, Chinese—anyone anywhere.

Q: Why are migraine headaches so widespread?

A: Because we're talking about a genetic, or hereditary, illness. Four out of five migraine sufferers had or have a parent with migraine.

Migraine is also significantly higher in women than in men—no question about that. The ratio is probably at least 4 or 5 to 1.

Q: Are migraines inherited from the male or female line?

A: Either. It doesn't make any difference.

The curious thing is that migraine headaches usually start early in life, frequently in childhood. And somewhere in the family background there's often a very high incidence of allergies. It may be hay fever; it may be an allergy to shellfish, penicillin or something else.

Q: Can you describe what a migraine headache feels like?

A: The attack can be on either side of the head—beginning in the eye, radiating to the back of the head. The pain is throbbing and increases in severity. The patient is usually very sensitive to light and/or sound, may get nauseated and vomit, will want to go into a dark room and lie down. The headache typically can last from several hours to three days, after which most patients will tell you, "I feel all washed out."

Q: What starts migraines? And why do they stop?

A: Migraine is a fascinating illness and may have multiple causes. One thing we know is that it is an illness of childhood. You don't see migraine starting at age 50 or 60.

Another thing is that in 90 per cent of

women during pregnancy, the migraine attacks stop completely and then return after the pregnancy is completed. Migraines also may get worse after a woman has a hysterectomy.

Generally, however, the tendency in both sexes is for migraines to burn out by the time the patient is in his 50s to 60s. The headaches may not only decrease but disappear completely.

There are hormonal factors involved, but we don't know how they work.

Q: What about sinus headaches?

A: Sinus headaches are very real. I know, because I get them myself. The term I use for them is "barometric headache," because they're really caused by a change in air pressure. These headaches usually occur in the region of the eye, cheek or forehead. They're frequently worse in the morning upon arising, and often if you take a hot shower, they get better.

Q: What's the treatment for sinus headaches?

A: People who have sinus, or barometric, headaches often will go to an ear, nose and throat specialist. The vast majority at one time or another—including myself—have had their sinuses irrigated. The pain is excruciating. It feels as if one's head is going to blow off. And once the sinuses are irrigated, the membranes become hypersensitive.

The result is that people like me are much more sensitive to pollutants in the air. I can hardly go into a room filled with smoke without really triggering off a headache. Changes in pressure caused by the weather or by altitude can do the same thing.

One of the most tricky things about sinus headaches is that the pain can radiate almost anywhere in the head. I recall the case of a stewardess who had just returned from a flight and came into the hospital with severe head pain. The doctor who had admitted her thought she had a brain hemorrhage, but tests showed one sinus was clouded—completely blocked.

This shows that sinus pain can be very devastating and may look like a much more serious condition—even life-threatening.

Q: What are some other serious types of headaches?

A: One kind which is very painful is the "cluster headache." It's called that because the attacks come in clusters. A person can get them every day for a period of three weeks or three months, and then they stop. These headaches, incidentally, occur predominantly in men.

Q: What is a cluster headache like?

A: It occurs on just one side of the head involving the front part of the face, almost always the region of the eye. The pain lasts from 15 minutes to about an hour and is associated with redness of the eye and a dripping nose.

It's sometimes called an "alarm clock" headache because it typically awakens the patient one to two hours after he has gone to sleep. They're also often called "killer headaches" because they are so painful that the patient literally bolts out of bed.

The cluster patient may bang his head against the wall for relief. That's how excruciating the pain is. Most of these patients cannot drink any kind of alcoholic beverage or even use after-shave lotion during the period of cluster attacks.

Q: How common are cluster headaches?

A: It's not a common headache, and in some countries they are seldom reported. Doctors in Australia, for instance, don't see it very often. Cluster headaches also are rare in blacks.

We do know that patients with cluster headaches have a high incidence of gastrointestinal trouble—namely ulcers—and there is a high rate of heart disease.

Q: Are cluster headaches more serious than others?

A: No, they're not more serious per se, because once you're over the cluster, that's it. You're fine until you get the next one.

Q: Do all headaches fall into neat categories?

A: No, they don't. Between the extremes we've talked about—the migraines and the clusters—there are a large number of patients who often get severe headaches. We can simply call them chronic headaches because they're always there—often recurring over a long period of years.

Q: How do these chronic headaches differ from others?

A: There may not be the nausea, vomiting or sensitivity to light that is often associated with migraine. But the headache may be just as severe. It may involve the entire head and last the same length of time as a migraine, but there isn't necessarily a history of migraine or allergies in the family.

Q: Dr. Coddon, people often complain about getting headaches from eyestrain. It that really a common cause?

A: No. The so-called eyestrain headache is very uncommon. Most ophthalmologists will acknowledge that eyestrain —or bunching up of the frontal muscles— is a very unusual cause of headaches.

Q: Is it common for people to have headaches after a head injury?

A: Yes, but the severity of the head injury does not necessarily correlate well with the severity of headache.

If you had a cut on your scalp and it's been sewed up, of course the area is going to be sore.

What many people don't realize is that you can get severe headaches from a whiplash injury. They usually last about three to six months but often recur.

Some people get a nonrecurring headache after a spinal tap.

Q: How about so-called "ice-cream headaches"?

A: They're very real, and they happen to most people when they bite into something very cold. The pain shoots up between the eyes, is very severe, but brief. The interesting thing is that cold can cause a headache but not heat.

Q: What other types of headaches are worth mentioning?

A: There are many kinds. One is often referred to as the "Chinese-restaurant syndrome." That's a tightness and pressure in your head caused by the monosodium glutamate—MSG—in Oriental food. It's a form of toxic metabolic headache, touched off by some external substance. Several other chemicals and pollutants can produce the same kind of headache.

Q: Can other foods cause headaches?

A: Yes. Certain foods high in a substance called tyramine can cause so-called "dietary migraine." Tyramine is an amino acid that the body uses to produce protein. It's found especially in cheese, nuts, pork and fish.

Red wine frequently produces headaches. This is usually not the case with white wine. It is my opinion that chemical factors are also involved here.

Q: Do you put these patients on a diet?

A: No. We have found that these foods do not always produce headaches in people who are sensitive to them.

Q: Does drinking too much cause headaches?

A: Yes. But a more common cause is mixing drinks. If you go out and have a couple of martinis and then some red wine or some beer, I can almost guarantee you a headache.

Champagne will produce a headache in almost anybody. There's something about the fermentation process—something going on chemically that affects the nervous system.

Here's a therapeutic tip: If you have had a few drinks and you take three aspirin tablets before you go to bed, you may very well wake up the next day without a headache.

Q: Are headaches in children more serious than in adults?

A: Not necessarily. The vast majority of headaches are harmless in children. Our own two children get headaches after coming home from school—after working or playing very hard. I've found that if I fortify them with two aspirin tablets before they engage in their vigorous activity, it may prevent the headaches.

However, I regard persistent, disabling headaches in children as a more ominous sign than with adults. For one thing, I must consider the likelihood of a tumor. I am also seeing more children with a history of infectious hepatitis or infectious mononucleosis whose headaches persist long after the acute illness subsides.

Nobody knows your child as well as you do. If he complains often of a fever or headache, or he suddenly isn't doing well in school—if he just isn't himself—it would be wise to have him examined.

Q: Do headaches become less frequent as you get older?

A: Generally, yes. Headaches are far more common among younger people. But older people do get headaches for a variety of reasons.

When you start to get into the age group of, say, above 60, you begin to think of other kinds of illnesses that could be causing headaches. It could be glaucoma, cervical arthritis, diabetes or any of several other diseases. There's one we call arteritis, an inflammatory process of the blood vessels. That's very dangerous and can cause blindness.

Q: Broadly speaking, though, how dangerous are headaches? You can live with them, can't you?

A: You certainly can live with them, but it depends on your definition of living. If you have seen any of your friends in the throes of an acute migraine, cluster headache or any kind of severe headache, you know that these people look terribly sick—and they *are* terribly sick.

Q: At what point should a person suffering from headaches consult a physician?

A: I suspect many people try to live with their headaches for a long time before they go to a doctor. This may be O.K., but it could be dangerous, too. What may be too much pain for one person may be bearable for another. It depends on the individual's tolerance and pain threshold, which can be related to upbringing, culture, intelligence, socioeconomic status and other factors.

In addition, many people have built into them a thing called "denial of illness." The best example is a person injured in an automobile accident. He may have blood all over him, but he'll get up and insist, "I'm all right." People generally don't like anything to be wrong with them, and they'll deny that something is wrong.

The point is that people should seek medical help if a headache persists, grows worse, changes or is a new kind of headache that he has never experienced before, or is associated with other symptoms.

Q: When you say "if a headache persists," what do you mean?

A: I mean that if a severe headache persists for more than a day or if a headache is of such intensity that it interferes with his activities, he should seek medical advice.

Q: What treatments do you recommend for headaches?

A: Aspirin is the drug of choice for common headaches. But even with aspirin you must be careful. Taking too much can cause gastrointestinal bleeding and other serious complications. The use of buffered aspirin or an antacid can reduce these hazards.

Ergot preparations are frequently used for migraine attacks because they constrict the blood vessels—a very important part in treating migraine. We usually give them in combination with other drugs.

Q: What is new in headache treatment?

A: We have had great success in prescribing combinations of medications commonly used as antidepressants and tranquilizers which work in an entirely different way in headache patients with an altered neurovascular bed. They are easily tolerated and nonaddicting. They can be stopped at any time. We have used this treatment for people all over the world, and the results are very impressive.

I want to emphasize this treatment is for people who have chronic, disabling headaches—not the garden-variety kind.

Q: What else are you doing that's new?

A: We also have had very good results with a special intravenous therapy involving three medications. It puts the patient to sleep, and it is the sleep that does the trick. If you awaken the patient prematurely, the headache will return.

It's interesting that one of the characteristic features of patients with severe vascular headaches is that most have low blood pressure and cold hands. When you give them these three medications intravenously, the patients' hands begin to warm. When that happens, you can predict with 100 per cent reliability that when they wake up, the headache will be gone. This is an interesting phenomenon which lends credence to what I'm saying about blood flow causing many headaches.

"TOO MANY DOCTORS" PRESCRIBE DRUGS

Q: Is it dangerous to take drugs for headaches?

A: Yes. Actually, the treatment of migraines and other headaches can sometimes be more dangerous than the illness itself. Drugs can be abused—that's always a problem. If you respond to a certain type of medication and you are fearful of getting an attack, you might take the drug prophylactically—that is, to ward off a headache. The danger is: Many of these medications are habit-forming and addicting—ergot preparations, for example.

I might comment here that there is no place for narcotic analgesics with patients with chronic headaches. You're treating the wrong way, and you can make them sicker or probably addict them. Too many doctors use these drugs. I am talking about morphine, Demerol, codeine and so forth.

Q: We keep hearing about "biofeedback" to treat headaches. Can you explain what that is?

A: Biofeedback is simply conditioning the mind to control involuntary body functions. You go past a bakery, and the smell starts gastric secretions and brings a nice, pleasant sensation. That's involuntary.

Now we know that by using visual and auditory cues, a person can learn to control his temperature or relax his muscles—steps that can relieve headaches. We teach you by using gauges that measure these responses so you can see for yourself that you can control your responses. After you have learned to condition yourself, you can end the instrumentation.

Biofeedback unquestionably is of great value in the treatment of all vascular-flow headaches. It also may have great value in essential hypertension and probably a number of other good applications in the hands of competent people.

Q: Is that anything like Transcendental Meditation?

A: Transcendental Meditation is a type of conditioning by autosuggestion but without the instruments.

It was thought that you could not have any voluntary control over the autonomic nervous system. The truth of the matter is that some people—not everybody who undergoes biofeedback training—can relieve their headaches.

Q: Then the instruments used in biofeedback are really a sort of crutch to get started—

A: Yes—to show you that you can do it. It's like putting water wings on somebody to start them swimming, or using training wheels on a bicycle. Pretty soon you don't need the instrumentation.

Q: Would you like to see this approach used more?

A: Yes, I would. It's simple, you can't get addicted to the thing, and you can't overdose yourself. The rule of simplicity applies: the least you can do that will help the patient the most.

FAILURE OF ACUPUNCTURE, HYPNOSIS

Q: Does acupuncture help in treating headaches?

A: No. The results of acupuncture in this field have, by and large, been extremely poor.

Hypnosis, too, does not appear to be very beneficial for headache patients. I'll extend that to psychotherapy, which in most cases does not stop the patient's headaches.

Q: What are the chief goals of headache research now?

A: One main goal is to understand as much as possible about the basic mechanisms of headache production. Ironically, the problem with this is that you don't have experimental animals to work with. You can produce cancers in mice, but what animal can tell you that he has a headache?

We're trying to better understand the mechanism of blood flow and the whole neurovascular network. There have not been enough electron-microscopic studies of the pain-sensitive structures. This is a vast area of mystery.

Also: How can you artificially produce headaches? Is it possible to develop an antiserum? Why does a cluster headache turn on and off?

Q: You're trying to find out what is going on in the body—

A: Yes. We need to know more about the neurochemistry of pain and the neuropharmacology of pain. That's the direction. Knowing the anatomy per se will not help. There are no anatomical differences between the brain, brain coverings and blood vessels of one who suffers headaches and one who doesn't.

When we have more basic science information we'll be better able to prevent headaches—and treat them most effectively when they do occur.

52. REHABILITATING THE PROBLEM DRINKER

Jerome F. X. Carroll and Murray Synigal

The National Institute on Alcohol Abuse and Alcoholism has estimated that there are 10,000,000 alcoholics in the U.S.[1] A somewhat more conservative estimate from the Licensed Beverage Industries is that seven per cent of the adult population in this country manifests behavior indicative of alcohol abuse and alcoholism.[2]

Recent estimates of alcohol abuse in the U.S. Army have risen to 70% for enlisted personnel and 36% for officers.[3] The Veterans Administration has estimated that $25,-000,000 will be spent this year on the treatment and rehabilitation of alcoholics.[4]

These figures are rather awesome and, when considered in terms of the "cost" factor, they clearly indicate that the number-one drug problem in the U.S. concerns the abuse of alcohol. The "cost" of alcohol abuse, both direct and indirect, includes suicide, murder, assault, auto accidents, cirrhosis, divorce, battered children, fearful and angry children and spouses, lost jobs and promotions, social condemnation, imprisonment, and self-loathing.

The threat that alcohol abuse poses to the health and well-being of our society is not likely to diminish, but will very probably increase. This pessimistic forecast is based upon the following observations:

• Some 68% of the adult U.S. population reports using alcohol at least sometimes—the highest percentage reported in 35 years.[5]
• Increasing numbers of youth are using and abusing alcohol.[6]
• More states than ever before permit men and women below the age of 21 to purchase and consume alcohol.[7]
• Increasing numbers of women are using alcohol.[8]
• Many "hard-core" drug addicts being treated at methadone clinics are turning to alcohol for a substitute high,[9] which, in some instances, constitutes a return to their initial drug of abuse—alcohol.[10]

[5]"We're a Nation of Drinkers—Here's Proof," *Philadelphia Inquirer*, Sect. C, p. 1, June 11, 1974.
[6]*Ibid.*; "Youth Shifting to Alcohol Use, Chafetz Warns," *Alcohol and Health Notes*, pp. 1 and 5, September, 1973; and *The Alcoholism Report*, p. 7, Dec. 28, 1973.
[7]"24 States Drop Drinking Age in Three Year Period," *Alcohol and Health Notes*, pp. 1 and 5, October, 1973.
[8]"We're a Nation of Drinkers . . .," *loc. cit.*
[9]Andrew W. Nichols and Paul R. Torrens, "Outpatient Induction to Methadone Maintenance Treatment for Heroin Addiction," *Archives of Internal Medicine*, 127:903–909, 1971; Mary J. Kreek, *et al.*, "Long-Term Methadone Maintenance Therapy Effects on Liver Function," *Annals of Internal Medicine*, 77:598–602, 1972; Barry Stimmel, *et al.*, "Hepatic Dysfunction in Heroin Addicts: The Role of Alcohol," *Journal of the American Medical Association*, 222:811–812, 1972; and Carl D. Chambers, *et al.*, "Characteristics of Patient Retention/Attrition," in Carl D. Chambers and Leon Brill, eds., *Methadone: Experiences and Issues* (New York: Behavioral Publications, 1973), pp. 109–118.
[10]Harriet L. Barr, *et al.*, "The Cross-Use of Alcohol and Drugs by Addicts and Alcoholics: Patterns of Previous Abuse of Alcohol and Drugs in a Group of Hospitalized Drug Addicts," paper presented at the International Conference on Alcoholism and Addiction, Dublin, Ireland, October, 1971.

Reprinted from *Intellect* (July/August 1975) by permission of publisher.

[1]*The Alcoholism Report*, p. 5, Oct. 26, 1973.
[2]"Liquor Industry Contributions to Alcoholism Control Cited," *Alcohol and Health Notes*, p. 2, January, 1974.
[3]"Studies Detail Problem Drinking in Armed Forces," *Alcohol and Health Notes*, pp. 1 and 4, September, 1973.
[4]*The Alcoholism Report*, p. 5, Nov. 9, 1973.

• The advertising industry is engaged in a concerted effort, aimed especially at young men and women, to promote the use of alcohol as a symbol of social status and/ or magical means of "making it" socially.

WHO NEEDS HELP?

There is a continuum of alcohol abuse patterns, varying from infrequent abuse (*e.g.,* the heavy weekend drinker) to alcoholism, and all of these patterns warrant some form of therapeutic intervention. It is the extreme end of the continuum—alcoholism—that has received the greatest attention.[11] Milt defines alcoholism as "a chronic disorder in which the individual is unable, for psychological or physical reasons, or both, to refrain from the frequent consumption of alcohol in quantities sufficient to produce intoxication and, ultimately, injury to health and effective functioning."[12]

He maintains, moreover, that the essential characteristics of alcoholism are: "(1) compulsive, uncontrollable drinking, (2) chronicity, (3) intoxication, and (4) injury to functioning."

Contrary to popular belief, relatively few (from three to five percent[13]) alcoholics are to be found on "skid row." The majority live at home and are employed. Alcoholics can be found in every educational, occupational, race, sex, age, and religious or nonreligious status category.

Along this continuum, there are varieties of alcohol abuse patterns,[14] such as the sustained binge drinker, the excessive lunchtime drinker, and the heavy beer drinker. The National Council on Alcoholism[15] has developed the following questions to determine whether a drinking pattern is suggestive of alcoholism:

1. Do you occasionally drink heavily after a disappointment, a quarrel, or when the boss gives you a hard time?
2. When you have trouble or feel under pressure, do you always drink more heavily than usual?
3. Have you noticed that you are able to handle more liquor than you did when you were first drinking?
4. Did you ever wake up on the "morning after" and discover that you could not remember part of the evening before, even though your friends tell you that you did not "pass out"?
5. When drinking with other people, do you try to have a few extra drinks when others will not know it?
6. Are there certain occasions when you feel uncomfortable if alcohol is not available?
7. Have you recently noticed that when you begin drinking you are in more of a hurry to get the first drink than you used to be?
8. Do you sometimes feel a little guilty about your drinking?
9. Are you secretly irritated when your family or friends discuss your drinking?
10. Have you recently noticed an increase in the frequency of your memory "blackouts"?
11. Do you often find that you wish to continue drinking after your friends say they have had enough?
12. Do you usually have a reason for the occasions when you drink heavily?

---

[11]World Health Organization, *Expert Committee on Mental Health, Alcoholism Subcommittee: 2nd Report,* WHO Technical Report Series, No. 48, August, 1952; and Mark Keller, "Definition of Alcoholism," *Quarterly Journal of Studies on Alcohol,* 21:125–134, 1960.

[12]Harry Milt, *Basic Handbook on Alcoholism* (Maplewood, N.J.: Scientific Aids Publications, 1969), p. 7.

[13]"Chafetz Cites Diagnosis Obstacles," *Alcohol and Health Notes,* pp. 1 and 5, December, 1973.

[14]Elvin M. Jellinek, *The Disease Concept of Alcoholism* (Highland Park, N.J.: Hillhouse Press, 1960); Kenneth W. Wanberg and John L. Horn, "Alcoholism Symptom Patterns of Men and Women: A Comparative Study," *Quarterly Journal of Studies on Alcohol,* 31:40–61, 1970; and John L. Horn and Kenneth W. Wanberg, "Symptom Patterns Related to Excessive Use of Alcohol," *Quarterly Journal of Studies on Alcohol,* 30:35–58, 1969.

[15]National Council on Alcoholism, *The Modern Approach to Alcoholism* (Little Ferry, N.J.: Employee Communications, 1972).

13. When you are sober, do you often regret things you have done or said while drinking?
14. Have you tried switching brands or following different plans for controlling your drinking?
15. Have you often failed to keep the promises you have made to yourself about controlling or cutting down on your drinking?
16. Have you ever tried to control your drinking by making a change in jobs or moving to a new location?
17. Do you try to avoid family or close friends while you are drinking?
18. Are you having an increasing number of financial and work problems?
19. Do more people seem to be treating you unfairly without good reason?
20. Do you eat very little or irregularly when you are drinking?
21. Do you sometimes have the "shakes" in the morning and find that it helps to have a little drink?
22. Have you recently noticed that you cannot drink as much as you once did?
23. Do you sometimes stay drunk for several days at a time?
24. Do you sometimes feel very depressed and wonder whether life is worth living?
25. Sometimes, after periods of drinking, do you see or hear things that aren't there?
26. Do you get terribly frightened after you have been drinking heavily?

All of the above questions refer to various "symptoms" of alcoholism in its various "stages"[16] (questions 1–8, early stages; 9–21, middle; and, 22–26, final). The more times the respondent answers "yes," the more severe the pattern of alcohol abuse is assumed to be. As a note of caution, however, the advice and counsel of a local Alcoholics Anonymous (AA) chapter and/or other recognized alcoholism treatment agency or institution should be sought to verify the nature and severity of any suspected pattern of alcohol abuse, and to develop a rehabilitative strategy appropriate for the individual.

Whether or not an individual technically can be diagnosed as an alcoholic is not nearly as critical as determining the role alcohol plays in his life. For our purposes, anyone who shows signs of losing control over the frequency and amount of his drinking and who habitually uses alcohol as a means of coping with life's problems is a problem drinker and needs help.

CAUSATION AND ALCOHOL ABUSE

Concerning the causes of alcoholism and alcohol abuse, there are still far more questions than answers. Clearly, the alcoholism treatment field is moving away from the moral and medical models. The former stresses "sin" and "redemption," while the latter, through its "illness" concept, stresses genetic and biological causes, with physicians being the primary healers.

The emerging, alternative model is eclectic in character. It emphasizes multiple causation and the interaction of complex physiological, psychological (including spiritual), and sociological systems and subsystems.[17] Within this model, a wide range of disciplines and professions participate equally in determining current practices, as well as the destiny of the field. Treatment, moreover, is not necessarily focused exclusively, or even primarily, on the person abusing alcohol—*e.g.*, the family communications and interpersonal relationships may be the focus of the therapeutic intervention.

[16]Chicago's Alcoholic Treatment Center, *Who Are Alcoholics?* (Chicago: Education Department, Chicago's Alcoholic Treatment Center).

[17]Jerome F. X. Carroll, "Are the Addict and Alcoholic Mentally Ill?" in Donald J. Ottenberg and Estelle L. Carpey, eds., *Proceedings of the 1974 Eagleville Conference on Addictions,* in press; and Donald G. Finlay, "Alcoholism: Illness or Problem in Interaction?" *Social Work,* 19:398–405, 1974.

Intrapsychic factors (*e.g.,* conflict, fear, and insecurity) and extrapsychic factors (*e.g.,* racism, sexism, and poverty) receive equal attention. Rehabilitative strategies, moreover, take both perspectives into account. A woman with a drinking problem, for example, might be referred to the National Organization for Women as part of her rehabilitative program.

To the extent that society fails to provide for equality of opportunity and/or remains insensitive and nonresponsive to human suffering, it creates a fertile breeding ground for alcohol abuse (and other forms of maladaptive behavior). In this regard, the failure of the schools[18] and family[19] to instill and enhance a sound, positive sense of identity and self-esteem has been particularly underscored.

Some of the factors typically, although not uniquely, encountered in the life experience of the problem drinker include very seriously impaired parent-child relations; unstable homes, often with one or both parents themselves abusing alcohol and/or other drugs; a dispiriting degree of hopelessness and a pervasive sense of failure and defeat; a passive, dependent orientation to life; considerable rigidity; a crippling inability to assert oneself; a heightened sense of impotency or powerlessness; considerable sexual conflict, inadequacy, and doubt about masculinity and/or femininity; and a strong sense of social rejection and alienation from society.

All of these factors contribute to the formation of a self-concept which is practically devoid of self-esteem. Using the Tennessee Self Concept Scale, we observed that our sample of problem drinkers manifests less self-esteem than 95% of the general population. These findings have been replicated by other researchers using the same instrument.[20]

To counter the high level of pain associated with the frustration of his human potential, the problem drinker develops a number of very strong defenses. Foremost among these is his abuse of alcohol, which can be considered a self-prescribed analgesic. Under the influence of alcohol, not only is the pain blunted, but some of the underlying anger, resentment, and hostility can be more easily expressed. Alcohol, acting much like a tranquilizer, also enables the individual to overcome inhibitions and tensions associated with social interactions.

Unfortunately, the effects of alcohol are, at best, limited and transitory. At worst, the cumulative consequences of alcohol abuse add to the already existing problems of the problem drinker. A vicious, personally and socially self-destructive pattern of behavior is thus perpetuated and becomes even more deeply engrained. In other words, the person becomes addicted to alcohol.

REHABILITATION

The rehabilitation of the problem drinker occurs in five phases: disruption of the

---

[18]Jerome F. X. Carroll, "An Ecological Analysis of and Prescription for Student Dissent," in William L. Claiborn and Robert Cohen, eds., *School Intervention: Vol. 1 of a Continuing Series in Community-Clinical Psychology* (New York: Behavioral Publications, 1973), pp. 110–121.

[19]Margaret B. Bailey, "Alcoholism and Marriage: A Review of Research and Professional Literature," *Quarterly Journal of Studies on Alcohol,* 22:81–97, 1961; Donald E. Meeks and Collen Kelly, "Family Therapy with the Families of Recovering Alcoholics," *Quarterly Journal of Studies on Alcohol,* 31:399–413, 1970; and Joseph L. Kellermann, *Alcoholism: A Merry-Go-Round Named Denial* (New York: Al-Anon Family Group Headquarters, 1969).

[20]Sol Kutner, *The Impact of a Therapeutic Community on the Self Concept of Drug Dependent Males: A Resocialization Viewpoint* (unpublished doctoral dissertation, Temple University, 1974); William H. Fitts, *The Self Concept and Psychopathology* (Nashville, Tenn.: Counselor Recordings and Tests, 1972), pp. 84–87; and William H. Fitts, *et al., A Self Concept Study of Alcoholic Patients* (Nashville, Tenn.: Dede Wallace Center, 1973).

alcohol abuse pattern; stabilization of the physical, psychological, and social environments; increasing self-awareness; changing behavior and developing a new, non-addicted "life style"; and resolving unfinished problems in living and developing a local, community-based program for continuing support.

Each of these phases can be illustrated by describing the rehabilitative program employed at Eagleville (Pa.) Hospital and Rehabilitation Center (EHRC). EHRC is a residential therapeutic community for both alcoholics and drug-dependent persons. The heart of EHRC's program is its 60-day, inpatient program. EHRC's program also offers a variety of pre-admission and after-care programs.

The community, located about 15 miles northwest of Philadelphia, serves about 120 inpatients (called residents) and approximately 50 after-care patients (called candidates). Candidates are those men and women who have successfully completed the 60-day resident program and who choose to remain in the community for an additional six months as participants in a half-work, half-therapy program.

The residents and candidates are most heterogeneous with respect to demographic variables, as is the staff. Most residents and candidates receive medical assistance and Department of Public Assistance aid. Many have been imprisoned. Alcoholics and drug addicts are about equal in number, but males outnumber females by four to one.

EHRC's therapeutic community is guided by relatively few basic principles, including openness, honesty, and responsible concern for self and others. Violence (actual or threatened), weapons, and drugs (including alcohol) are strictly prohibited, and result in immediate discharge.

EHRC's rehabilitative program is based on abstinence model. Its major form of group therapy is based on an admixture of confrontation, sensitivity, and Gestalt techniques and principles. In addition to therapy, residents and candidates participate in a variety of planned educational, recreational, and social activities. They also receive legal, social, medical, dental, psychiatric and psychological services. Both Alcoholics Anonymous and Narcotics Anonymous meetings are held on the grounds. Work opportunities, on and off the grounds, as well as vocational counseling and job placement, are available. These diverse services reflect EHRC's adherence to a multiple causation model.

Phase One

A problem drinker can not be rehabilitated if he continues to drink as he has in the past. Therefore, the first step in the process is to disrupt the pattern of alcohol abuse. With severe and prolonged alcohol abuse, an abstinence treatment program seems best. Abstinence, however, may necessitate detoxification.

Detoxification is a relatively short (three to five days on the average), although intensive, form of treatment designed to minimize or eliminate the detrimental side effects of alcohol withdrawal. These may include pervasive apprehension, anxiety, nighttime problems (restlessness, interrupted sleeping, insomnia, and severe nightmares), and delirium tremens or D.T's (tremors, convulsions, and hallucinations). With delirium tremens, there is the risk of death. Usually, detoxification is done under medical surveillance, although non-medical detoxification centers are now becoming more numerous.

Physicians will often prescribe certain medications to prevent seizures (dilantin and phenobarbital), to allay anxiety and tension (librium or valium), and to promote sound sleep at night (benadryl or dalmane). Certain medications, however, may give rise to a secondary addiction, in the sense that the problem drinker may consciously or unconsciously substitute their effects for that of the withdrawn alcohol.

Phase Two

Due to the havoc which alcohol abuse creates, there is a great need to reestablish stability with respect to the individual's psycho-biosocial environment. This includes medical and dental attention, a balanced diet, a clean and quiet place to live, and a fairly structured routine of activities and recreation. Often, this will necessitate residential treatment, especially when the pattern of abuse is severe and long-standing.

Phase Three

Since nearly all problem drinkers are reluctant to honestly confront themselves— *i.e.,* to honestly take an inventory of their strengths, weaknesses, problems, and feelings—considerable effort must be directed toward overcoming strong and rigid defenses. At EHRC, group therapy sessions and other activities are used to help problem drinkers get in touch with and express their pain, anger, guilt, and fears. This is not done through intellectual discussion, but, rather, through a variety of experiential techniques which permit the full expression of these feelings.

In addition, their behavior is closely monitored by all members of the therapeutic community, and, most importantly, problem drinkers receive "feedback" regarding their behavior throughout their stay. This feedback is given honestly, sensitively, and out of responsible concern.

When successful, these procedures culminate in a heightened sense of awareness and identity. With increased self-awareness, those behaviors which must be eliminated, modified, and/or enhanced in order to achieve sobriety and personal fulfillment become more evident.

Phase Four

During this phase, what the problem drinker says he *intends* to do is of little importance. What he *does* or *fails to do* is of the utmost importance. The emphasis is on behavioral change, helping the problem drinker to eliminate behaviors associated with alcohol abuse and acquiring new, and/or strengthening existing, behaviors which are supportive of sobriety and personal fulfillment.

These rehabilitative behavioral adjustments do not only pertain to drinking, and may range over a wide assortment of both overt (directly observable) and covert (nonobservable—*e.g.,* thoughts) behaviors. The problem drinker thus may be encouraged to change his manner of speaking, dress, walk, use of leisure time, work habits, personal hygiene and grooming, how he relates to the opposite sex, educational deficits, and how he evaluates and thinks of himself. As a co-worker expressed it, "If in your addiction you got up every morning on the right side of the bed, try getting up on the left side."

If the problem drinker is successful in making significant behavioral changes, his life style moves from addiction to sobriety to personal fulfillment. He begins to experience a sense of personal potency—*i.e.,* the ability to effectively cope with himself, others, and life's problems. As a result, he begins to experience success, hope, and, most importantly, self-respect and dignity, without using alcohol or any other drug.

Great care must be exercised at this point, because many problem drinkers are most uncomfortable with success and good feelings. Out of apprehension and/or residual guilt, they sometimes act impulsively to undermine hard-won gains. In other words, the rehabilitative process should not be stopped at the first signs of positive behavioral changes.

Phase Five

As the problem drinker prepares to reenter the environment from which he came, he is likely to encounter all of the unfinished problems which he left behind—*e.g.*, disrupted and strained family relationships, unpaid bills, pending court cases, unemployment, and having a home located in a neighborhood where many people, including family members and friends, abuse alcohol and other drugs. These reality issues must be faced realistically and resolved. With respect to these issues, the key to continued sobriety and fulfillment often rests upon establishing a community-based program of continuing support. In this regard, Alcoholics Anonymous, out-patient care, half-way houses, etc., can play a vital role.

Taking antabuse on a daily basis has also proven to be a valuable aid in guarding against resuming the former alcohol abuse pattern. This medication, which must be medically prescribed, causes anyone who drinks alcohol to become *very* ill. The fear of an antabuse reaction to alcohol can sometimes be that special extra factor which tips the scale in favor of continued sobriety. The problem drinker who does not want to stop drinking will strongly resist taking this medication.

How much time is needed for successful rehabilitation? This depends on the severity and duration of the alcohol abuse pattern. A two-year followup study at EHRC indicated that 28% of the problem drinkers who complete the 60-day inpatient program remained abstinent and were employed, as compared to 36% of those who complete the post-inpatient candidate program. The percentage of success rose to an impressive 85% when the problem drinker completed the candidate program and voluntarily participated in AA meetings on a regular basis.[21]

THE EFFECTIVE REHABILITATIVE FACILITATOR

There are numerous and diverse programs to help the problem drinker. Some are religious, and some are secular. Some are administered and staffed exclusively by credentialed persons, while others are run and staffed entirely by noncredentialed, recovered persons. Some are residential, others out-patient, and some are drop-in centers. Within this array, there are significant differences regarding philosophy of treatment. The fact is that some problem drinkers recover in all of these programs, but no program or institution is successful with all of its problem drinkers.

This would seem to suggest that the attitude and behavior of the rehabilitative staff is of critical importance. Certain characteristics seem to distinguish the more successful rehabilitative facilitators. First, the person must be experienced in the field of alcoholism and alcohol abuse. The compelling, powerful, and pervasive urge to drink, through any means, regardless of consequences, is a phenomenon which most professional and lay persons have difficulty in comprehending.

EHRC has found that the use of recovered men and women alcoholics as staff members has proven to be particularly effective in its rehabilitative program. Recovered staff members are keenly aware of the "games" problem drinkers play, and are

[21]Harriet L. Barr, *et al.*, "Two-Year Follow-up Study of 724 Drug and Alcoholic Addicts Treated Together in an Abstinence Therapeutic Community" (paper presented at the 81st annual convention of the American Psychological Association, Montreal, Canada, August, 1973).

particularly adept at confronting the manipulative, defensive behaviors of problem drinkers. Their presence within the community also serves to demonstrate that recovery is possible.

The effective rehabilitator can confront. Alcoholics have spent many years learning how to survive, more often than not, in hostile, nonsupportive environments despite their addiction. They have learned how to quickly size up a situation, to manipulate, and to lie convincingly. They can give a dramatic performance in therapy with a minimum amount of practice. These behaviors must be quickly and accurately comprehended by a rehabilitative facilitator, and then firmly and confidently challenged.

A rehabilitative facilitator must be an authentic person. Problem drinkers are often stern judges of those who would help them. Discrepancies between what is preached and what is practiced are sensitively seized upon, and can obstruct and undermine the rehabilitative process.

The rehabilitative facilitator must also be genuinely accepting of the problem drinker. The latter, due to his substantial guilt and low self-esteem, is very quick to detect any indications of moral superiority and indignation. Typical reactions to such feelings are anger, resentment, withdrawal, lack of cooperation, and flight.

At EHRC, this issue is dealt with by encouraging those staff members who most directly guide the rehabilitative process to participate in a staff marathon. The staff marathon is an uninterrupted, intensive, confrontative therapy session which lasts from 36 to 50 hours. Each participant is afforded one or more opportunities to honestly confront and express his deepest fears, pain, and anger. This experience does much to enable the staff to recognize and genuinely accept that which they share in common with problem drinkers they would seek to help.

Finally, the rehabilitative facilitator must have a high tolerance for frustration and considerable patience, since more problem drinkers fail than succeed, especially the first time they participate in a rehabilitative program. In fact, many problem drinkers fail several times before they are able to achieve sobriety and self-fulfillment— "slips" are quite common. Moreover, while some problem drinkers remain abstinent, they may experience only marginally satisfying and fulfilling lives.

CONCLUSIONS

It is likely that alcohol abuse will continue to be a serious psychosocial problem in this country, with a notable increase among women and people below the age of 30. To the extent that society fails to provide for the positive fulfillment of human potential, people will continually have to administer their own forms of pain-killing drugs, such as alcohol.

Those involved in the addiction and mental health fields have learned a variety of skills and techniques which have proven to be helpful to the problem drinker. They still have to struggle, however, with the nagging knowledge that returning an "adjusted psychiatric casualty" to a "sick" social system constitutes a very dubious and often transient success.

Whether significant improvement in our struggle with alcohol abuse occurs will depend on society's sincerity and depth of commitment to the prevention and containment of this problem. With respect to prevention, the primary social systems—*viz.,* the home, schools, and religious institutions —need to become more concerned and effective in building self-esteem, as well as in educating young people regarding responsible drinking.

The success of any efforts directed toward containment will, of course, be directly proportionate to the quantity and quality of resources society actually commits to the task. The anemic pressures for change manifested to date, however, induces some feeling of pessimism regarding any immediate improvement for the society as a whole or for the individual problem drinker in need of assistance.

53.   HOW, WHEN, AND WHY TO FIRE YOUR SHRINK

Otto Ehrenberg and Miriam Ehrenberg

Picking a psychotherapist can be a very difficult task, but parting company with one often proves an even more arduous endeavor. Perhaps lately as you've been leaving your therapist's office you've been feeling depressed. When you stop to think about it you realize that the therapist has been putting you down a lot of late to make you "face up" to your inadequacies. Or, perhaps, you've been seeing someone, and the therapist keeps telling you it's a sick relationship that you should give up, but you have never been so happy in your life. Or maybe you're in a group with a bunch of people you hate and don't respect, and the therapist tells you that you should work on your inability to be more open and accepting. Whatever the problem, you start wondering: Is it all my problem, or is there something wrong with the therapist? How about quitting—should I or shouldn't I?

Difficulty can come up anytime in therapy. It could be apparent in the first session or not appear for several years. Whenever you encounter difficulty, the best thing to do, of course, is to discuss your feelings with the therapist. Unfortunately, a lot of patients don't have the wherewithal

to bring up feelings of disillusion and anger —that's why they are in therapy. Those who can brave it out and talk about their doubts aren't always successful either, for they frequently meet with the pat phrase "You are resisting." Very often, when patients try to discuss their feelings about the therapist's competence with him or her, the therapist will take this doubt and discontent as an indication of the patient's unwillingness to really work at the therapy. And often it is. It may be the patient's way of reacting when he gets close to someone (accusative and hostile), or perhaps focusing on the therapist's inadequacies is a way to avoid looking at one's own. But it can also happen that the patient is right and that the therapist is overbearing, or jealous, or destructive, or just plain incompetent. While most therapists are quick to see the patient's resistance to continuing therapy, there is the real danger that they may be blinded to a patient's genuine need to find a more suitable therapist.

The desire to hold on to a patient may express the therapist's fears about his own competence and control. If a patient brings up the issue of quitting, this is often interpreted by an insecure therapist as a challenge to his professionalism and his authority. A therapist may feel that the re-

Reprinted from *New York* (May 12, 1975) by permission of authors.

lationship should end when *he* suggests it, and he may react to what he considers the patient's usurpation of the therapist's initiative. The therapist may also feel threatened by losing a patient when the issue of the therapist's competence has been raised, since agreeing to termination may be seen by the therapist as admitting his incompetence.

There are, however, some other reasons for a therapist's unwillingness to let a patient go that are not necessarily selfish, egotistical, or unprofessional.

A patient, to a therapist, represents a lot of time, energy, and effort; once a therapist gets drawn into the patient's problems and into the patient as a problem, it is difficult to let go—for the simple reason that people generally don't like to leave engrossing work half done. There is a drive for completion, a drive for resolution, an instinct to finish and to polish things off and to create something whole and beautiful. Since the therapist thinks therapy is necessary or desirable, then he cannot possibly think termination is in the interest of the patient. He may be afraid that the desire to leave the therapist is also a desire to leave therapy. Letting a patient go in such circumstances is not an easy or responsible thing for a committed therapist.

Looking at the patient's motivations, in addition to a healthy desire to get out of therapy, there can also, of course, be an impetus to leave for unsound reasons. There are times when you will want out from the therapy because it is getting too hot, or too close to issues you want to avoid. It would be self-defeating for you to leave under such circumstances. Recognizing such resistance can be very difficult, but the following situations suggest that your dissatisfactions with the therapy may be coming from your own unwillingness to face up to problems:

• When everything in the therapy was going fine but then suddenly it seemed to turn sour;
• When you've been with several therapists and find yourself repeatedly coming up with the same kinds of dissatisfactions;
• When the dissatisfactions with the therapist are similar to those with other important people in your life;
• When sudden attitude changes occur toward things affecting the therapy, such as finding the therapy is costing you too much time or money, or becoming convinced that therapy really doesn't work;
• Perhaps most telling of all, when there's nothing specific you dislike about your therapist but you just have an overwhelming impulse to flee.

But how do you know if the difficulties come from the therapist and not from resistance? If discussions with your therapist leave you nowhere, it is often helpful to get an outside opinion. Perhaps you can clarify your problems by discussing them with an informed friend or by consulting another therapist. Above all, don't be afraid to listen to your own feelings and to use your own judgment. There are some general guidelines which can help in your decision. Here are twelve signs of distress which suggest that the fault lies with the therapist or therapeutic relationship rather than with you.

When the shrink is not your type of person. Therapy is difficult enough without burdening it further with a lack of rapport. If you and your therapist were not meant for each other, it may be futile to try to stay together. Sometimes you feel from the very beginning that you don't make a good pair; sometimes that strikes you later. Maybe you sense the therapist is insincere and stereotyped, furnishing his office with "Danish Modern" or "Traditional Freud." Maybe he's pretentious and stuffy—throwing big words around or trying to impress you with his important patients. Perhaps he's just plain dull and limited—he can't understand a literary allusion, thinks a madrigal chorus is a rock group, and that *Cosmopolitan* is a magazine for liberated women. Perhaps he has other qualities that put you off and make you wonder how healthy he is—obesity, chain smoking, nervous twitches, very fussy or overly casual dress, bleached hair, etc. Whatever the complaint, if you're on different wavelengths, you'll both have trouble tuning in clearly to each other's messages.

When there is a value conflict. Respect for each other's ethics, style of life, and future goals, whether in or out of therapy, is a prerequisite for a productive therapeutic relationship. The therapist may be too conventional in outlook and frown on your search for new ways to fulfill yourself. Or he may indiscriminately swing with each new fad while you are looking for more meaningful and lasting experiences. Perhaps he is a sexist who belittles your struggle to establish your sense of self-worth as a woman. Or perhaps he feels your radical politics is nothing more than an adolescent rebellion. If you don't accept the therapist's values, or feel that he pooh-poohs yours, you'll have a tough time making a go of it.

When your shrink is a cold fish. If you find your therapist too cold or aloof, you may not be receiving the kind of emotional warmth that is needed for relationships aimed at personal growth. While the purpose of therapy is not to provide you with a new friend, a responsive atmosphere helps you mobilize your strengths. A therapist may try to mask his inability to extend himself to you by labeling his behavior as professional distance. Such detachment may not, however, be serving your interests as much as his defenses.

When your shrink is a "star." It is very exciting to be with a therapist who has flair, who sparkles, and who exudes "personality" and charm. Such magnetism can easily produce hero-worship, however, and become overpowering. While it is easy to get started with a very expressive therapist, and to become fascinated by his charisma, in the long run, an intense personal relationship with such a therapist can rob you of your autonomy and, perhaps more dangerous, your objectivity. Some therapists exist as a type of guru and feed on the admiration of their cultists. Excessive devotion to the therapist tends to subvert the quest to find power and value within yourself, and may serve his needs rather than yours.

When your shrink is hung up on unimportant areas. If the therapist repeatedly encourages you to discuss issues that don't seem particularly relevant to you, perhaps his needs are overshadowing yours. At first, such insistence can be deceptive, since talking about your work, sex experiences, or other aspects of your life makes sense. Excessive interest in any one area might, however, really be expressing the needs of the shrink. Sometimes a therapist may spend much of the session pressing you for details of a party, a play, a stockmarket maneuver, or some other occurrence. While you enjoy such recountings, you may feel that they are not particularly productive. In such a case their value may be only in feeding his need for gossip, vicarious excitement, or inside information. If you feel your therapeutic time could be spent to better advantage, it probably could.

When your shrink is hung up on you. Sometimes you may sense that your therapist is overly involved in you as a person rather than as a patient. He may be jealous of your other interests or relationships and become critical of your attempts to move out into the world. In extreme cases, a therapist's needs can get played out in more active abuses of patients. For instance, it is well known that some therapists induce patients to have sex with them under the guise of liberating the latter's blocked ability to love, be intimate, or have orgasms—this is an unambiguous signal to you to get out. To maintain control of a patient some therapists threaten dire consequences if the patient wants to leave the relationship: "You'll become an alcoholic"; "You'll fall apart." The main threat is, however, remaining locked into such a manipulative relationship.

When your therapy is in a rut. If you find your sessions becoming increasingly uneventful and face them as another chore to be gotten through, something is wrong. Perhaps you are both tired, bored, or disillusioned, and the therapist is unable to find a different approach to which you can respond. Perhaps he feels that your problems are so ingrained that he sets the goals too low. For example, he may regard you as so basically passive and unresponsive that he doesn't try hard enough. Conversely, perhaps you have advanced to a level of feeling that places greater demands for emotional intensity on your therapist. He may lack the emotional competence to face up to your new-found strengths and independence. While he was adequate before, he may now back off from the confrontation you seek.

When you feel down on yourself after therapy sessions. If you leave sessions feeling depressed and more displeased with yourself than before, such dissatisfaction may be coming from an inadequacy in your therapy. Your bad feelings may stem from disappointments with the therapy or with the way you are allowing yourself to be treated within the therapy situation. Of course, you should distinguish between those downs which brought you into the therapy and those which you take away from it.

When you feel forced into a mold. Another way the therapist's needs can intrude into therapy is by his encouraging you to react and respond in ways that do not seem right for you. Therapists often feel that they know best and see their role as getting you to accept this. The therapist's need to maintain control over you and to preserve his position as the authority may push you into uncomfortable corners. For example, he may expect you to be compliant and cooperative with him and others as a sign of your "adjustment." Refusal to accept a dream interpretation becomes a sign of your "resistance." Arguing the point with him becomes further proof of your guilt (by revealing the depths of your resistance). Your need for independence is seen as negativism. Acquiescence on your part may really be working against you.

When you both behave in destructive ways. Sometimes therapy becomes an unending series of senseless arguments, blame-throwing sessions, or attempts to tear down each other's sense of self-respect. If the destructiveness cannot be resolved, it indicates a failure in the relationship. Such blaming and accusativeness often stem from a patient's disillusionment with his therapist, or vice versa. If either one has unrealistic expectations of the other (which should not have been allowed to flourish in the first place), failure for them to materialize leads to frustrations and anger. Like the child who finds the idealized parent is really weak, or the parent who finds the unrealistically appraised child is not a genius, the patient or shrink can find his frustrated expectations turning into deep resentment.

When your shrink is inconsiderate or selfish. While occasional lapses in good manners can be overlooked in a therapist as in anybody else, repeated occurrences should not be accepted. Some frequent abuses which many patients needlessly take for granted are: cutting sessions short, reading mail, or falling asleep (yes, this really happens), refusal to ever discuss a problem on the telephone, inflexibility in charging for missed hours, lack of concern for your immediate problems (job demands, family needs, sickness) which interfere with maintaining regular therapy appointments, or unreasonable demands on you in terms of fees, time of appointments, changing or not keeping appointments. Also to be questioned are objectionable personality traits that repeatedly manifest themselves, such as excitability, belligerence, defensiveness, argumentativeness, sarcasm, lack of patience or sense of humor. Your therapist should, at the very least, be able to treat you with the ordinary respect and courtesy due another human being.

When your shrink won't discuss your doubts. If you should bring up any of the above points, or want to talk about any other doubts or discontents, and your shrink refuses to do so, then his adequacy as a therapist is suspect. Some shrinks may let you ramble on, but then become very defensive and/or accusative. Perhaps most telling of all, some shrinks may angrily reject you, saying, "If you don't like it here, get out!" If that is the case, pick up your hat and leave. It is probably the best advice your shrink has ever given you.

54. ASSERTIVENESS TRAINING: HOW TO SAY NO AND MAKE IT STICK

David Docter

"Charlotte, let's go camping this weekend."

"I don't want to go camping."

"Why not?"

"I'm too tired."

"Well, you can go to bed early tonight."

"But we can't go camping. We don't have a tent."

"I'll borrow my brother's tent."

"Christopher, I just don't want to go camping."

"Why not? Give me one good reason. I'll bet you don't want to go because of last night ..."

"Last night has nothing to do with it. If I give you one good reason will you leave me alone?"

"Yes, but it has to be a good reason, not some flimsy excuse."

"Okay, Christopher, I'll give you one good reason why I don't want to go camping. I don't want to go camping because I don't want to go camping this weekend. That's my reason. I would like to go camping with you next weekend, but this weekend I don't want to go."

Turning to the class of 15 students, Christopher Storey asks, "What weaponry did I use, and how did Charlotte defend herself?"

"He used what we call psychoanalysis," said Charlotte Booth. "He asked me 'why' questions, and tried to make me give reasons and wanted to know my motives. Then he tried to outreason me and show me how unreasonable I was being. And he tried to make me feel guilty.

"But I came out of it okay when I got back to the issue. And when I even offered him a compromise, I hit the ball back into his court."

Reprinted from *Science Digest* (September 1975) by permission of author.

Mr. Storey and Ms. Booth, instructors in the Adult Development Program Assertiveness Training Laboratory, walked through several other scripts. Ms. Booth turned down Mr. Storey's insistent invitations to go to a movie; a mother who could only walk away when her teenage daughter started to argue was taught to fight back, and a school bus driver was shown how to deal with rowdy and rude children.

The psychological weaponry of everyday dialogue was used to its fullest advantage by the protagonist in each script. At the point when irritation and hostility would overcome the "victim," that person would suddenly change his or her stance, lock eyes with the antagonist, and with a few words regain control of the situation.

The Adult Development Program (ADP), a part of the University of Washington Department of Psychiatry and Behavioral Sciences in the School of Medicine, shows people how to change their behavior —moods, habits, feelings and attitudes—in directions they choose. The ADP approach is that behavior is learned, that what is learned can be unlearned, and that new, more satisfactory behaviors can be acquired. The emphasis is on self-help and on developing skills necessary to attain personal goals. Each person enrolls for his own reason.

The ADP is open to persons who want to make changes in themselves and their situation and are willing and able to assume responsibility for their behavior.

The assertiveness laboratory taught by Mr. Storey and Ms. Booth, both social workers, gives students practice in asserting themselves in specific situations. Rather than talking about changes the students want to make in their interactions with other people the students actually act out the new behaviors, playing the roles of themselves and others.

"The focus," said Mr. Storey "is on learning to take responsibility for what you allow others to do to you: learning to say 'no,' and learning to recognize and act upon what you want to do rather than what you think you should do."

Typical problems considered by the class include keeping to the issue in an argument, getting a non-fighter to fight (verbally) rather than walking away from an argument and remaining upset, and increasing negotiating skills with other people.

"What is territory?" Ms. Booth asks the class. "What is aggression, and what is assertiveness?"

"Territory," a woman answers, "is anything that holds a person's fancy—anything from an idea to a piece of land."

The students reviewed the breakdown of the kinds of territory: Private domain, personal space, psychological space and action territory.

"Aggression," said the woman, "is acquiring new territory, and assertiveness is defending your territory. It is one's response to aggression without hostility. Hostility," she said, "is another response to aggression. It results from not defending your territory. The results of hostility are backbiting, destructiveness and vengeance."

I took photographs of the next role-playing activity. Usually I ask permission to take photographs, but this time I decided to see whether I would elicit a response. I noticed a tenseness in the air and a few furtive glances, but no one said a word as I snapped several photographs. My presence in the class had not been explained to the students.

The role-playing ended and Mr. Storey called the students back into a large circle. A woman next to me looked at me, then at Mr. Storey and said: "Why was he taking our pictures? I didn't want him to take my picture. I felt like smashing his camera."

I held my camera a little tighter.

A man in his 20s, who had been nervous when I was snapping photographs, then jumped into the conversation.

"I don't like my picture being taken either; I want to know what he is going to do with the film. I don't know him and I don't trust him. I feel like taking the film from him."

The woman next to me again says that she would like to smash my camera and wring my neck.

I turn to her, and then to the nervous man across the room, and say, simply, "If you didn't want your picture taken then all you had to do was to tell me you didn't want your picture taken."

They had gone to Mr. Storey and Ms. Booth to remedy the irritation, rather than to the source of the irritation.

They let me keep the film after I promised not to use the photographs of anyone who did not sign a release form. The nervous man finally assented to my keeping the film, but he would not sign the release.

Afterwards, Mr. Storey and Ms. Booth tell me that no better learning situation could have occurred, even if they had contrived one.

"I'm perfectly willing to argue with you, but don't call me stupid," Ms. Booth reiterates to the class during a dialogue exchange with Mr. Storey. "I don't like it when you talk to me like that," is a suggested retort for the mother with a belligerent teenage daughter.

"This week," Mr. Storey tells the class, "I want you to keep a thermometer of irritations, on a zero-to-ten scale. Start identifying the patterns in persons that cause low-level irritations. They may build up in you, and then there will be an explosion."

"The people that come to this lab," Ms. Booth said, "are students, not patients. We are teachers, not therapists, and the students are here to learn, not be helped. We are teaching them to change themselves, not to put themselves down."

"When Chris and I teach, we are entertaining. We totally involve the students. When they are having fun, they are willing to take risks."

At a weekly laboratory with librarians, clerks and personnel supervisors from a local Washington library system, Mr. Storey and Ms. Booth use scripts and routines that differ very little from those used in their regular ADP classes.

"It's hard," said Ms. Booth, "to say no to your best friend who wants to borrow your necklace to impress someone. It's hard to say no when everyone else at the office has donated to a charity."

"What people don't realize," said Mr. Storey, "is that you don't always have to be rational, fair or even know why you do something. You are your own judge and not wanting to do something is reason enough. So long as you are willing to pay the price and accept the responsibility for the consequences of what you choose to do or not to do, then you can control a situation."

The two teachers told the librarians about power, which they defined as having something that another person wants. Then you can bargain for something they have that you want. But if you give that something away free, then, they said, you are giving away your power.

"Unless you can say no to someone," Ms. Booth said, "you really can't say yes."

The librarians were taught that they can use humor to signal others that further provocation will elicit a more assertive or warriorly stance, meaning, "I'm ready to do business. Don't aggress against my territory."

The librarians acted out real-life situations they face in their work. One supervisor wanted to know what to do with an employee who could not work up to her job description requirements. The employee, Helen, had worked for the library 15 years, but her father had died recently, and she had been sick herself.

Mr. Storey and Ms. Booth told two persons how the roles should be played before the entire group.

Supervisor: Helen, I must ask you to accept a lower position in the office. The office is falling behind because you are not able to do what is required of a Secretary III.

Helen: But I told you when we made out the new job descriptions that you were giving me too much work to do. I never used to do the mail sorting. Susan did that before she retired. Besides, I'm just two years from retirement with my pension.

Supervisor: Helen, I have only so much money to hire staff, and there is a specified amount of work that must be completed. If you are unable to do the work that is required in the Secretary III classification, then I must ask you to accept a Secretary II position.

Helen: You know I've been sick and my doctor doesn't know what is wrong with me, and you know my father died recently.

"Guilt induction," calls out Mr. Storey.

Supervisor: Helen, yes, I know you have been sick, and I know your father died, but I must ask you to accept a lower classification if you cannot do the work. I must have a Secretary III who can do the work. We talked about this problem last month and you were given a one-month probation. But you are unable to do the work that must be done. I will give you until next Tuesday to let me know your decision.

Helen: I already have made my decision. You are not being fair.

Supervisor: We will meet again next Tuesday. You can tell me then whether you will accept the lower classification so that you can continue to work for the library.

"What are the weapons?" Mr. Storey asks the class.

One of the librarians volunteered several weapons, including helplessness, guilt induction, smoke screen and talking about anything but the issue.

"The supervisor," said Ms. Booth, "did a good job in recognizing the weaponry, and most importantly, she remembered how to defend against it—by keeping to the issue that the secretary could not complete the work that was required of her."

"What we are trying to do," said Christopher Storey, "is to teach people to defend themselves against other people who are trying to 'work them over.' We are teaching people the manipulations others use against them, and how you can manipulate others to get them to do something."

"Manipulation," Ms. Booth said, "is not a bad word in our vocabulary."

Editor's Note: *The last real-life situation described by David Docter in his story—the incident in which a supervisor overpowers an employee who is sick and mourning the death of her father—disturbed us here at Science Digest because it conjured up images of a totalitarian society in which employers could use assertiveness training as a tactic for gaining more control over employees.*

So, in an additional interview with Storey and Booth, we asked them if the training was designed mostly to aid employers and/or supervisors.

The answer was an emphatic no. "We've trained more workers to stand up to their bosses than the other way around," replied Ms. Booth, pointing out that so far in their workshops they have trained 250 clerks as opposed to only 50 persons in management positions.

The weekly laboratories with the librarians came about, according to Storey, because the personnel director of one of the local library systems came to them complaining about "lots of backbiting going on between the professionals and the clericals." Their task, as Storey saw it, was to show the clericals how to fight back and to "teach management personnel the price they pay for abusing employees."

While standing up to one's boss is a key phase of assertiveness training, anyone, be they boss or worker, can learn to be more assertive; it does after all, apply to every aspect of life.

55. FEMINIST THERAPY: A NEW SPECIALIZATION

Carole Bennett Regan

Therapy has become an acceptable way of dealing with life's problems in the 1970's, at least for the middle class. The adolescent indecisive about college or career plans, the college student concerned about a choice of a major or a career, the young couple experiencing difficulties in their "relationship," the middle-aged man facing a career change, or his wife contemplating a return to school or to a job after years of remaining at home—all are likely to seek a therapist or counselor to assist them in working through a current crisis or in reevaluating their situation or goals.

The choice of a therapist, unfortunately, often is as much governed by chance as is the choice of any other professional in an area with which prospective clients have had little previous experience. That we live in an age of professional specialization is taken pretty much for granted when we require medical consultation, but often forgotten when we seek other professional consultation.

Specialization already exists to some degree among therapists and beyond the client age breakdown which comes readily to mind. Some of these specializations are

fairly well established—one can readily identify psychoanalysts, behavior therapists, career counselors, marriage counselors, etc. A new area of concentration, if not of specialization, has recently developed, roughly termed "feminist" therapy or counseling. Whether or not it is a "legitimate" specialization, whether or not women should be counseled in a manner different from that of men, is a topic of current debate.

On what might be called the "traditional" side of the argument is the assertion that therapists are trained either to treat all clients alike or at least with equal acceptance of their goals, or to treat men and women differently because they *are* different, not only anatomically, but also psychologically. Countering these assertions is the "feminist" position that therapists do not, in fact, treat all clients equally, that they tend to impose a bias upon behaviors expected of men and women, and that, if men and women do differ psychologically, it is not in the ways previously assumed—differences are real, but they are not deficits. The feminist position asserts that women need specially trained therapists who will offer their clients the *advantages,* rather than the *disadvantages,* of differential treatment.

Reprinted from *Intellect* (November 1975) by permission of publisher.

FEMINIST THERAPY RESEARCH

In 1970, a research study was published which substantiated the suspicions of some female therapists and their clients that therapists hold a double standard of mental health for men and women. The study conducted by Broverman and colleagues[1] submitted a questionnaire to male and female clinically trained psychologists, psychiatrists, or social workers. A third of the therapists were asked to describe a "normal adult man"; another third to describe a "mature, healthy, socially competent adult woman"; and the last third were asked to describe a "healthy, mature, socially competent adult person" (sex unspecified). The authors regarded the responses of the last group of clinicians to be "indicative of 'ideal' health patterns, without respect to sex." The researchers had already determined in a previous study of the questionnaire itself that certain of the descriptions were considered "masculine" and others "feminine," and also that certain of the descriptions were considered more socially desirable than others. For example, the description "can make decisions easily" was previously rated both "masculine" and "socially desirable," while "easily expresses tender feelings" was previously rated both "feminine" and "socially desirable"; "very dependent" was rated "feminine" and not desirable, while "very rough" was rated "masculine" and not desirable.

The Broverman study revealed a number of results which bear upon the feminist therapy movement. First, the clinicians' description of a healthy mature adult man was nearly identical to that of a healthy adult (sex unspecified). Their description of a mature healthy adult woman, however,

differed significantly from that of the healthy adult person. "Clinicians are significantly less likely to attribute traits which characterize healthy adults to a woman than they are likely to attribute these traits to a healthy man."[2] This research lent support to the feminists' contention that therapists will be likely to encourage male and female clients to strive toward different standards of behavior and toward different goals.

A second finding, however, received far less attention than the first, perhaps because it is in opposition to the views of some feminists. Broverman, *et al.*, found that there were *no* significant differences between the descriptions given by male and female therapists. In other words, female therapists were just as likely as male therapists to impose a double standard upon their clients. The researchers tend to ascribe the existence of this double standard to the existence in our society of stereotyped sex roles, inculcated in males and females since birth. Thus, in their views, clinicians, both female and male, merely reflect and transmit, rather than consciously dictate, these roles.

However, what of actual therapist behavior, rather than attitudes? Chesler, in her book entitled *Women and Madness,* assessed therapist behavior toward male and female clients.[3] Taking a case-study approach, she concluded that, in many cases, therapists, especially male therapists, not only perpetuate sex-role stereotypes, but also use them to their own advantage. Chesler cites cases, some contemporary, some historical, to support her contention that therapy, especially involuntary institutionalized therapy, constitutes a form of "slavery" for women who are locked up

---

[1] Inge K. Broverman, *et al.*, "Sex-Role Stereotypes and Clinical Judgments of Mental Health," *Journal of Consulting and Clinical Psychology,* 34: 1–7, 1970.

[2] *Ibid.*, p. 6.
[3] Phyllis Chesler, *Women and Madness* (New York: Doubleday, 1972).

from friends and family and forced to change their attitudes or in some cases, to engage in behavior (including sexual behavior) they do not choose for themselves. She argues additionally that, in many cases, males (often husbands) were responsible for sending women to male therapists in order to transform their behavior into a more "feminine" (*i.e.,* passive) model.

The most recent report of differential therapeutic treatment of men and women appears in the 1975 report of the American Psychological Association's Task Force on Sex Bias and Sex Role Stereotyping in Psychotherapeutic Practice. The committee sent out questionnaires to 2,000 female therapists asking for examples of any circumstances of sexism they had encountered.[4] Most of the criticisms reported apparently derived from client complaints to current female therapists about experiences with their previous therapists. The greatest number of negative comments fell under the complaint that therapists foster traditional sex roles despite clients' attempts to change: "advocating marriage or perfecting the role of wife, deprecating the importance of a woman's career, using a client's attitude toward child bearing/rearing as an index of emotional maturity." Examples cited included clients whose therapists had encouraged them to be "nonassertive" and "seductive" and to stay in professions "open to women." The APA task force also turned up instances of complaints about sexual relations between therapist and client. It can be argued that the closeness of the typical client-therapist relationship grants the therapist more than slight influence over the client, and, thus, such decisions are unlikely to have been arrived at wholly voluntarily.

It should be pointed out that the design

of the APA task force survey involved contacting only *female* therapists, and that they reported only on clients who apparently had been dissatisfied with their former therapists. The results, therefore, must be viewed with some caution, and generalization to all or even most male therapists is unwarranted. Nevertheless, this study adds one more bit of evidence that sex bias does exist among some professional therapists who, theoretically at least, should be unbiased. What are the possible sources of these biases?

SOURCES OF SEX BIAS AMONG THERAPISTS

No doubt, the major source of sex bias among therapists is, as the Broverman study suggested, the fact that they, as well as others, reflect—to some extent—the biases of the society of which they are members. The extent to which sexist attitudes prevail has been examined frequently in the past dozen years following the publication of Betty Friedan's *The Feminine Mystique* in 1963.[5]

Therapists as a professional group, however, have an additional source of bias for their attitudes toward women, and many of their attitudes which feminists might label "sexist" derive fairly directly from their training.

PSYCHOANALYSIS

Most therapeutic theories stem either directly or indirectly from Freudian psychoanalysis, a theory which has made enormous contributions to our understanding of the human psyche, but which also posits a view that men and women differ psychologically because they differ

---

[4]Jules Asher, "Sex Bias Found in Therapy," *APA Monitor,* 6: 1–4, April, 1975.

[5]Betty Friedan, *The Feminine Mystique* (New York: Dell, 1963).

biologically. Psychoanalysis developed in the latter part of the 19th century primarily out of Freud's practice with women, most of whom suffered from some form of hysteria (physically disabling symptoms without apparent organic cause). The cornerstone of Freudian psychoanalysis is the concept of the Oedipus complex. This concept focuses upon several issues, most of them well-known to students not only of psychology, but also of literature. Psychoanalysis views women as incomplete men, resentful that they lack the symbol of male authority, suffering from "penis envy" which can only be resolved if a woman replaces it with a wish for a child.[6]

"Sexist use of psychoanalytic concepts," including labeling competitiveness as "penis envy," was one of the categories of bias encountered by the APA task force. The therapist who views the married woman's interest in developing a career as rejection of the feminine role (and, therefore, virtually pathological) will respond quite differently to her than will the therapist who views her interests as healthy indications that she is growing away from an earlier, childlike dependence and moving toward a life of mature independence.

WHO CAN BE A FEMINIST THERAPIST?

Considerable controversy exists over just who qualifies as a feminist therapist. Some *female* therapists insist that only women can be feminists, arguing that, analogous to the black situation, only a woman can understand another woman's point of view, and that clients need role models with whom to identify. The counter argument asserts that many therapists, especially younger therapists—psychologists, rather than psychiatrists—have been trained in relatively sex-bias-free theories and can function just as effectively with men or women. There are signs that traditional sex roles are changing rapidly, and there are even clearer signs that training programs are not only moving away from Freudian ideology, but are also becoming more sensitive to these issues. Many therapists trained in the 1960's and 1970's were exposed to a more eclectic point of view, or even to programs designed to counter racist or sexist biases. These therapists could be equally effective with any client who wants to move toward development of full, self-defined potential.[7]

Not all women clients, of course, regard the views of their therapists on feminist issues as relevant to the course of their therapy. The woman who seeks therapy, however, for marital difficulties or a career choice, for example, might ask herself whether her therapist's attitudes are likely to matter to her. If the answer is "yes," then she might well make an effort to select a feminist therapist. Finding such a therapist may not be easy, but, for her, the search may be worth the trouble.

---

[6]Sigmund Freud, *New Introductory Lectures on Psychoanalysis,* James Strachey, trans. (New York: Norton, 1965), Ch. XXXIII.

[7]See, for example, Violet Franks and Vasanti Burtle, *Women in Therapy: New Psychotherapies for a Changing Society* (New York: Brunner/Mazel, 1974).

56. NEW WAYS TO HEAL DISTURBED MINDS; WHERE WILL IT ALL LEAD?

Stanley N. Wellborn
Associate Editor
Reprinted from *U.S. News & World Report*

The nation's mind healers are moving into an era of rapid change unparalleled since Freudianism invaded the U.S. at the turn of the century.

Treatment of troubled Americans is shifting from the mental institution and the psychiatrist's couch to a diversity of new approaches—frequently at less cost to the individual patient in time and money.

Many victims of deep depression or schizophrenia are being treated successfully with drugs, often as outpatients at community clinics rather than as inmates in institutions.

The less severely disturbed in increasing numbers are taking their problems to family or sex counselors, or are sampling meditation, yoga, biofeedback, hypnosis and "encounter group" therapies that many psychiatrists are beginning to regard with new interest—and sometimes respect.

Widening scope

Psychiatry, itself, is giving increasing attention to the particular problems of children, old people, women and other elements within the broad population.

Family doctors are also becoming increasingly active in the early detection of psychological disorders, thus freeing psychiatrists to devote more time to the treatment of more severe cases.

And, while psychological treatment was until recently the privilege of the well-to-do and upper middle class, walk-in counseling services are increasingly available in poor neighborhoods, where mental illness is believed to be even more prevalent than in affluent areas.

The result of all this activity is that the study and treatment of mentally or emotionally disturbed persons has become one of the nation's fastest growing occupations.

An estimated 20 million or more Americans find themselves, at one time or another, unable to cope with the daily hazards of a fast-changing and competitive society—foundering marriages, rebellious children, job or school tensions, or pent-up hostility toward others and themselves.

Families who can afford it through personal means or medical insurance are paying as much as $10,000 a year in psychiatrists' fees, and much more than that for treatment of a family member in a private sanitarium. Altogether, the costs of mental disease to the nation, taking into account lost manpower and productivity, are now placed by the National Association for Mental Health at around 30 billion dollars annually. Some researchers believe the recent recession and continuing inflation have led to a steep rise in mental illness, particularly among men 45 to 60 years old. But there's a brighter side to this picture of psychic woes.

Experts of the National Institute of Mental Health, professional societies and medical schools say that diversifying research has produced truly remarkable advances in combatting mental illness in recent years.

Today, only the most chronic psychoses —including severe brain disease—are still regarded as "hopeless." And Dr. Roy W. Menninger, president of the world-famous

Menninger Foundation in Topeka, Kans., says this:

"The overwhelming majority of psychological problems are being resolved favorably when the patient gets early, appropriate and sufficient treatment."

Yet acute worries also are developing.

NAGGING QUESTIONS

How dangerous is increasing reliance on drug therapy? What standards should govern such radical approaches as psychosurgery and electroshock treatments? Is behavior modification—restructuring the mental responses of social misfits by means of often-brutal methods—ethically defensible? Could the rising importance of psychologists and psychiatrists in business and government eventually place the U.S. at the mercy of overzealous "mind benders" intent on changing human personality?

Professionals in psychomedicine are becoming acutely aware of danger signals. Public distrust of psychiatrists and skepticism about traditional Freudian techniques are on the rise. So is consumer pressure for psychotherapists to justify their fees. The Health Research Group, in a recent consumer guide entitled "Through the Mental Health Maze," voiced this concern: "A distressingly large number of mental health professionals take the position that everyone who walks into their offices needs therapy, frequently long-term therapy, which often stretches for several years and is very costly.

"With an estimated 1.5 billion dollars per year being spent in this country for services of private-practice psychiatrists and psychologists alone—to say nothing of the costs of the drugs many of them prescribe —it is not unreasonable to ask: Is the money being properly spent?"

Despite such troubling questions, Americans are becoming increasingly intrigued by the workings of the mind and the lure of exploiting its capabilities more fully.

Around 80 per cent of all college youths study psychology at some time or other, and it currently ranks No. 1 on their list of major fields.

Publishers turn out dozens of books each year with such titles as "The Do-It-Yourself Psychotherapy Book," "Your Inner Conflicts—How to Resolve Them" and "How to Be Your Own Best Friend." Some have become runaway best sellers, as in the case of "I'm O.K.—You're O.K.," by Thomas A. Harris, M.D., a leading practitioner of "transactional analysis," which concentrates on a patient's interpersonal relationships.

Another important phenomenon is the "personal growth" movement.

The most prominent treatment in this area is "encounter therapy," in which supervised groups have found that many individual emotional problems can be resolved if participants are willing to be open and honest and unafraid to talk about their innermost feelings. Encounter groups attempt to break down personal defenses by challenging participants to disclose repressed feelings, no matter how painful the process.

Now, new disciplines ranging from "sensitivity training" and "primal therapy" to "humanistic psychology" have become widely accepted, attracting millions of adherents who insist that such methods are not fringe therapies but are helpful to many individuals. The leading new approaches are examined on pages 398–99.

THE UNTREATED

Feeding this trend is a basic fact: Adequate care from traditional sources is not available for most of those afflicted with mental and emotional troubles.

While nearly 1 of every 10 Americans is

WALK-IN MENTAL-HEALTH CARE—HOW IT'S WORKING

CHICAGO

Illinois is experiencing both the successes and the growing pains that go with the spread of community mental-health centers across the country.

Over the past 10 years, this State has reduced the population in its mental hospitals from nearly 50,000 to 12,500. However, it has managed to close but one State hospital.

And although more than 100,000 patients will be treated this year in community facilities, only 81 million dollars of the mental-health department's 378-million-dollar budget is earmarked for community mental-health programs. Most of the money still goes to the hospitals.

The problem is a political one, believes Dr. LeRoy Levitt, director of the Illinois department of mental health and developmental disabilities. Reason: State hospitals are the economic wellspring of many small Illinois communities, and the State's mental-health workers' union—some 20,000 strong—would almost certainly oppose a rapid shutdown of State hospitals.

Other States, such as New York and California, are facing similar roadblocks to their attempts to channel more money into community mental health. Dr. Levitt notes that only nine of the nation's 257 traditional State and county mental hospitals have been closed.

The object of community health centers is not to close all mental hospitals. Dr. Prakash Desai, the State mental-health administrator for the Chicago area, contends that some patients, such as chronic schizophrenics and elderly patients with organic brain disease, do not respond well to the short-term treatment that is offered by community programs.

Despite the shortage of funds, community mental-health centers have gone a long way in removing the stigma that has often been associated with mental illness.

"You don't find people in the waiting room with their hands over their eyes any more," says William Wedral, who is assistant administrator of St. Mary of Nazareth Community Mental Health Center, one of Chicago's largest facilities.

Located in a modern general hospital on the city's west side, St. Mary's sees about 1,500 mentally ill people each month. It exemplifies the flexibility possible in community mental health.

There are community workers on the staff—people who live in the neighborhoods served by the center. They can relate to the mixed population of blacks and Spanish-speaking and Eastern European residents and help them overcome their fears of seeking help.

And when the patient does come to the center—either for outpatient services or a short hospital stay—there's no set pattern of treatment. The whole staff plays a part—psychiatrists, social workers, psychologists, nurses and community workers.

"The staff members aren't caught up in defending their own profession or some specific theory, such as psychoanalysis or drug treatment," says John Halversen, the center's director.

Emphasis is on "crisis intervention"—spotting and treating mental illness at the earliest possible stage. To identify people who need help, St. Mary's works with the police, schools, many agencies and small mental-health "outposts" in the neighborhoods.

Although there's considerable outreach involved, community mental-health workers now are more realistic about what they can accomplish. That's a change from a few years ago, when they were admittedly trying to "cure all of society's ills." Says Dr. Desai:

"We'd like to do more in prevention, but resources are such that we have to treat the really sick people first."

Mr. Halversen notes that the community is "infinity," as far as the need for help is concerned. "As soon as you hire a new person, he's booked up with patients almost immediately, he says.

With the rapid changes of modern life and the breakdown of such supports

(continued)

as the family and religion, Mr. Halversen believes there is more mental illness today. He contends that one of the biggest roles of centers is to give people a sense of belonging and to give them a chance to re-establish their ties in a familiar community.

For the future, some community mental-health experts are more worried about public attitudes than meeting rising patient needs. As State hospitals close, more and more people will have to be treated in community settings—mental-health centers, nursing homes and sheltered workshops—and local communities will be asked to shoulder mcre of the costs.

Observes Dr. Levitt: "Everyone seems to be in favor of community mental health, but not on their block."

believed to have a mild to severe mental disturbance that would benefit from professional help, only about one seventh of the afflicted actually get treatment.

One reason: The National Institute of Mental Health says there are approximately 27,000 psychiatrists in the U.S. today—yet fewer than 20,000 are practicing. By 1981, the NIMH estimates, the nation will have a shortage of 10,000 practicing psychiatrists.

Furthermore, psychiatrists, who must undergo a rigorous 10-year training period after graduation from college, gravitate toward urban areas.

More than half of all psychiatrists are located in only five States—New York, California, Massachusetts, Illinois and Pennsylvania—and the District of Columbia. Three fourths of all U.S. counties have no practicing psychiatrist. If such related occupations as clinical psychologists, psychiatric social workers and trained psychiatric nurses and aides are added, the total comes to about 97,000 mental-health professionals —or 1 for every 2,200 persons in actual or potential need of help.

These professionals increasingly are being augmented by paraprofessional therapists, including clergymen, social workers, teachers, and even reformed convicts and specially trained housewives. Some 8,000 paraprofessionals around the U.S. have shown marked success in dealing—under supervision—with mild psychological problems that have not yet become serious.

This diversity of treatment is diminishing some of the past emphasis on the $40-an-hour analyst, once considered the ultimate human authority on deep disturbances—neurosis, anxiety, phobia or depression.

Dr. Richard M. Restak, a Washington, D.C., neurologist with psychiatric training says:

"For too long, psychiatry has ignored the fact that emotional disturbances are largely biochemical in nature. Recent research has proved that many—perhaps most—emotional states are determined by changes in the chemistry of the brain. As a result, psychotherapists who have spent their careers dealing almost solely with the emotional causes of mental illness are having to reassess their ideas, and it's a difficult process for them."

FRESH IDEAS

As such calls for new approaches grow in volume, the entrenched establishment of psychiatrists is showing signs of relaxing Freudianism's dictates.

Dr. Robert Gibson, medical director of the Sheppard and Enoch Pratt Hospital in Towson, Md., and president-elect of the American Psychiatric Association, observes:

"Psychotherapists are becoming more willing to try new ideas that appear useful. The recent advances have been too important to ignore."

According to a massive study by an

NIMH task force, emphasis on psychiatric research, training and treatment has shifted from psychology and Freudianism to chemical and biological causes of mental illness.

Dr. Bertram Brown, director of NIMH, cites the discovery in recent years that heredity and various brain chemicals play a role in schizophrenia, depression and manic diseases. These revelations have put scientists on the trail of better drugs for some of the most oppressive human psychoses.

HELPFUL DRUGS

One chemical in particular—lithium—is considered by many to have an almost miraculous effect on persons with severe depression, among the most common of mental diseases. No longer regarded as a wonder drug with wide application to many mental problems, lithium is usually considered "safe" for long-term supervised use, and has restored thousands to normal lives.

Dr. Nathan Kline, a New York psychiatrist who specializes in pharmacological treatments, says he has achieved a 90 per cent remission rate after prescribing a drug regimen for his mental patients—many of whom had tried a variety of other therapies.

"You cannot fight the medication," he tells his patients. "It will work whether you 'believe in it' or not."

Drugs have also revolutionized the treatment of schizophrenia, in which a person experiences a severe withdrawal from reality. Instead of spending years in a mental institution, a schizophrenic patient can now often return to his family and community after a brief hospitalization and treatment with a combination of drugs and conventional psychotherapy.

However, Dr. Leon Eisenberg, a Harvard University psychiatry professor and former chief of psychiatry at Massachusetts General Hospital, warns:

Although drugs have helped in treatment of schizophrenia, from 30 to 50 per cent of schizophrenic patients will be readmitted to hospitals for additional therapy within one year and from 60 to 70 per cent within five years.

WORK WITH THE BRAIN

Research into the brain and the nerves is drawing scientists into strange channels of exploration. Getting wide attention is "biofeedback," in which an individual learns to sense instantly what is going on within his body through study of his organic functioning as registered by precise measuring devices.

Using biofeedback, a person can learn to control his rate of heartbeat, blood pressure, and even brain waves. Backers say this holds enormous promise in dealing with a number of diseases, including asthma, epilepsy, diabetes, migraine headaches, insomnia and hypertension. Some researchers report that they have successfully trained individuals through biofeedback to produce a safe means of voluntary contraception.

Perhaps the most extraordinary achievement of biofeedback is teaching individuals —using equipment that alerts them to changes in brain waves through a beeping sound—to concentrate on alpha waves associated with relaxation and indifference to external stimuli.

One researcher believes that alpha patterns are similar to hypnosis in their relaxing effects. He estimates that 15 minutes in an "alpha state" is equivalent to about four hours of normal sleep.

In addition, physicians believe they can use biofeedback of brain waves to determine brain damage in patients.

Epileptics and schizophrenics can learn to control the causes of their seizures and conditions, and insomniacs may be taught ways to improve their sleep.

Furthermore, some psychiatrists have

found that psychosomatic disorders—such as a hard-driving executive's peptic ulcer caused by mental strain—can be cured much more easily with biofeedback techniques.

Exploration of new treatments for the troubled is advancing in other—and more controversial—areas.

Among the most alarming to many observers is the use of psychosurgery—the removal or destruction of parts of the brain in order to alter a patient's behavior. One well-known procedure is the lobotomy, an incision into the frontal lobes of the brain which, when successful, renders violent or extremely anxious patients calm and carefree. Between 1940 and the mid-1950s, some 50,000 lobotomies were performed in the U.S.

Critics of psychosurgery label it "an ethical, political and spiritual crime" against persons who are helpless to defend themselves.

While newer techniques enable physicians to work deep in the brain, some physicians contend that not enough is known about which areas of the brain affect behavior, and thus psychosurgery is an imprecise method at best.

Other experts disagree. Dr. Ernest A. Bates, assistant clinical professor at the University of California Medical Center in San Francisco, observes: "We cannot leave patients with a life of misery and suffering where there is a possibility of some relief through the medium of psychosurgery." The technique, he adds, can often resolve some of the toughest problems of mankind, such as obsessions, phobias, compulsions, anxiety, depression, tension, violence, sex perversion and child hyperactivity.

MIND CONDITIONING

The psychosurgery debate, however, is overshadowed by another—the growing use of "behavior modification," in which a patient is conditioned by rewards or unpleasant consequences to replace his socially unacceptable ways with more desirable behavior.

The National Institute of Mental Health is spending millions of dollars on behavior-modification research, and estimates that about 60,000 Americans are getting this kind of treatment.

Behavior-modification techniques are found to produce striking results in some instances—making alcoholics sick of liquor, stopping autistic children from mutilating themselves, helping the impotent or frigid achieve sexual fulfillment and salvaging social misfits.

At the same time, complaints are rising that some exotic forms of behavior modification are brutal and dehumanizing. These involve not only psychosurgery, but use of "mind bending" drugs, deep hypnosis, ultrasound therapy and deadening of brain tissue.

In addition, many of the recent experiments have used as subjects prison inmates who volunteered—or were volunteered by prison officials—for research.

Convicted sex offenders, for example, have been subjected to painful "aversion therapy," in which they are wired with electrodes, shown pornographic pictures and simultaneously jolted by a powerful electric shock.

An arsenal of potent drugs used in behavior modification also is generating criticism.

One target is anectine, which produces an extremely unpleasant sensation of drowning or death through suffocation and causes the subject to lose all muscular control for a period of several minutes. In some prisons, "incorrigible" inmates have been given the drug to thwart their "unacceptable behavior."

Another drug, apomorphine, causes violent vomiting, sometimes for a period of hours.

Despite such controversial uses, drug therapy to alter human behavior is seen by some practitioners as a boon for the future. A brain researcher at the University of California at San Diego predicts that science is on the verge of developing new drugs without side effects that will allow normal patients to select the life style they desire— dynamic, creative, aggressive, meditative or whatever.

"The drugs now available are like shotguns compared to the more exquisite agents coming up," he says.

Whatever the qualities of such drugs, critics are raising big questions about medical ethics and the legal rights of institutionalized persons used in such experiments. In late 1974, a Senate subcommittee noted:

"Whenever such therapies are applied to alter men's minds, extreme care must be taken to prevent the infringement of individual rights."

Congress in the same year established a National Commission for the Protection of Human Subjects of Biomedical and Behavioral Research to look at the practices, ethics and values involved in using human beings as research subjects.

Recent revelations of widespread psychological experimentation by federal agencies, prisons and hospitals—some with tragic results—have buttressed demands for accountability in the secret experimentation.

Michael Yesley, staff director of the commission, charged that hospital patients and prison inmates "volunteer" for medical experimentation after being coerced through offers of special privileges.

Recent reports have also pointed out that some persons were given powerful drugs and other treatments without being informed that they were being used as research subjects.

Another landmark on behalf of patients' rights—release of nondangerous mental patients from involuntary confinement—was reached last June when the U.S. Supreme Court ruled unanimously that a mentally ill person could not be held against his will if: (1) the hospital was not offering treatment, (2) the person was not dangerous to himself or others, and (3) the person was able to live in the community with the help of friends or relatives.

Even before then—over the last decade— most States had begun moving toward encouraging treatment of the mentally ill in facilities close to home.

Most prevalent of the outpatient clinics are the more than 500 community mental-health centers, which permit many mental patients to remain with their families and at their jobs while being treated. Such centers account in large part for the 70 per cent decline in the number of persons in State and county mental hospitals since 1950. A closer look at one such center is found on pages 392–93.

FEDERAL FUNDING

Since 1965, the Government has poured more than 1.3 billion dollars into building or staffing community mental-health centers. By concentrating on "crisis intervention" in working with disturbed persons, these centers are largely responsible for the decline in the patient population of the nation's mental hospitals—from some 490,-000 to just over 215,000 in the last 10 years.

Despite their success, community mental clinics remain beset by obstacles. Federal funds are far from adequate, and few new centers are being started.

John Wolfe, director of the National Council of Community Mental Health Centers, says the goal of the 1963 Community Mental Health Centers Act of establishing 2,000 centers has been abandoned. Mr.

Wolfe adds that many existing centers—possibly one third of them—may fold without continuing federal aid.

Under the present plan, centers generally receive a declining level of federal money each year. And increasingly States are unable to take up the slack.

Noting that President Ford vetoed a bill authorizing more than 230 million dollars for the program's 1976 and 1977 activities, Dr. LeRoy Levitt, director of the Illinois department of mental health and developmental disabilities, observed: "The Ford Administration seems to be saying, 'You've proven the program can be successful, so you don't need us any more.'"

Experts on mental-health law say ambiguities in current legal opinion, along with cutbacks in federal funding, hinder use of many new approaches.

NEIGHBORHOOD BARRIERS

Some of the early enthusiasm for "deinstitutionalization" of mental-health patients cooled with investigation into alleged instances of "dumping" inmates on the community to meet budget cuts, without adequate provision for their mental and physical care. Opposition to community mental-health centers frequently surfaces among nearby residents, further slowing down efforts to release all inmates held involuntarily.

The National Institute of Mental Health estimated that of the 403,924 admissions to State and county mental hospitals in 1972, the latest year for which figures are available, 169,000 were on an "involuntary" basis. However, researchers with the Mental Health Law Project—a nonprofit legal-aid organization that brought the action resulting in the High Court ruling last June—believe that the actual number of persons held against their will is much higher.

Says attorney Patricia M. Wald of the project:

> Every patient—especially one being held against his will—has a right to treatment. If he's not getting it at a mental hospital, he should be released to a community facility where he can return to productive life under a supervised outpatient program.

The dramatic changes in mental-health treatment in the past 25 years benefit the millions of Americans who try to cope with one or another type of psychological problem.

NIMH Director Brown and others are convinced that the marketplace will determine who will render the best therapy for an individual patient as consumers become more aware of the variety of new treatments available. Says Dr. Brown:

> Psychiatry will refocus to a significant extent around medical—and particularly biological—psychiatry. It will become more humble about what it can do in regard to social problems and social issues. It will continue to spin off new and experimental therapeutic measures and techniques, most of which will fall by the wayside, but a few of which should lead to more effective treatment.

Harvard's Dr. Eisenberg believes that family doctors will become more aware of mental illness and thus take responsibility for treatment.

"The greatest control we could have over mental illness is a willingness on the part of primary-care physicians to recognize the early symptoms of mental distress and deal with them before a patient ends up in a psychiatrist's office," asserts Dr. Eisenberg.

A major outgrowth of the new state of flux in the mental-health field, many authorities say, is this: More and more, the disturbed person will be considered a complex unit of physical, mental and emotional

LATEST RAGE: GETTING PEOPLE TO "TUNE INTO THEMSELVES"

The "consciousness cults" of the 1970s go by many names—transcendental meditation (TM), biofeedback, yoga, Rolfing and encounter, among others. But all seek the same result: an improvement in the quality of an individual's personal life and relationships with other people.

Most are an outgrowth of the "human-potential movément" that encourages people to "tune into themselves" through sensory-awareness techniques said to tap the hidden capabilities of the body, mind, emotions and spirit.

Many of these disciplines encompass ancient techniques and mysticism found in Eastern religions, combined with Western values—the work ethic, self-improvement and free enterprise.

Unlike adherents of the Rev. Sun Myung Moon or Guru Maharaj Ji, few of the mind-therapy groups espouse religious views. They have a wide middle-class, even middle-aged, following among lawyers, doctors, teachers and other "establishment" types.

Some of the better-known groups:

Transcendental meditation requires two 20-minute periods daily of repeating a word, often from Sanskrit, called a "mantra." Claimed benefits: relaxation, decreased oxygen consumption, slowed metabolism, and an over-all "energizing" effect.

Training cost: $125 for working adults.

Yoga is an ancient method of tuning in to both body and mind, achieving deep relaxation and toning muscles and inner organs through breathing exercises, posture and muscle control.

Erhard Seminars Training (EST) is one of the fastest growing groups, with 65,000 adherents claimed since its start in 1971. The program, which has stirred controversy, covers two full week-ends, including a 16-hour, no-exit group session led by an EST trainer. Participants are urged to be open and honest, to avoid theorizing and instead to talk about their innermost feelings—no matter how painful that may be. EST founder Werner Erhard says that by breaking down personal defenses, people can be made more aware of repressed emotions in dealings with other people. Cost of training: $250.

Rolfing, named for founder Anna Rolf, is a rigorous deep massage and manipulation of the body that aims at realigning and loosening the body's connective tissues so as to release excessive, long built-up tensions.

Probably the fastest growing of the "pop-psych" groups is TM, which claims it has gained 600,000 believers since an Indian monk named Maharishi Mahesh Yogi introduced it here in 1959.

Now TM is a multimillion-dollar enterprise, with centers across the nation. But critics say that the relaxing, deep bodily rest produced by meditation can be achieved without TM's expensive training.

Dr. Herbert Benson, a cardiologist at Harvard Medical School, acknowledges that TM can lower metabolism, heart rate and respiration—relaxing the mind and relieving stress.

But Dr. Benson also contends in his book "The Relaxation Response" that effective meditation can be done by almost anyone without special lessons. Here is his method:

• Sit in a comfortable chair in a restful position. All muscles should be completely relaxed, and eyes closed.

• Breathe through your nose and become aware of your breathing. Breathing out, repeat silently a single-syllable word or sound to free the mind from logical, externally oriented thought.

• Continue for 20 minutes. You may open your eyes to check the clock, but it is important to remain undisturbed for the entire period.

• Also important: Maintain a passive attitude. Don't worry about how well you are meditating or you may inhibit the response. Distracting thoughts will occur. Let them—the meditative word will return naturally.

Many physicians are using mind-body techniques in their practices, but warn

(continued)

that they should not be viewed as a panacea by persons with psychological problems.

Dr. Roy Menninger, who is president of the Menninger Foundation, has this observation:

"In our clinic, we are looking with interest at several of these practices and have occasionally used them in therapy.

"But I am extremely wary of simplistic answers. . . . A person under severe mental stress is probably going to need much more help than meditation or consciousness-raising can offer, and that is when seeking out a current fad may be very unwise."

factors and subject to unique personal, family and social influence—not just the repository for a group of symptoms or diseased organs. And treatment, increasingly, seems likely to focus on the particular needs of particular persons—not on rigid doctrines that have enabled psychiatry to maintain its uneasy rule in the realm of mental-health care for a great part of the twentieth century.

Yet to emerge, however, is a clear answer to deepening anxieties about the growing power of mental-health practitioners in a society increasingly disrupted by technological advances and shifting values. As some experts in the field see it, the question now is whether wisdom will catch up with the deepening exploration into the mysteries of the human mind.

57. SHOPPING FOR THE RIGHT THERAPY

Morris B. Parloff

There is nothing absolute about the aims of psychotherapy. They are, rather, tied closely to current standards of well-being and social effectiveness. In the past, these social standards have seemed relatively fixed and stable. Today, however, our society changes its standards with ever-increasing speed, while the sciences keep fashioning new mirrors to reflect the new images of man. As a result innumerable images are now simultaneously extant; which image we see depends on where we look.

At the same time, we make increasing demands on psychotherapy. In the past, re-

Reprinted from *Saturday Review* (February 21, 1976) by permission of publisher.

ligion and science were the main ways of achieving our aspirations. More recently, to the consternation of some and the satisfaction of others, the license for ensuring our well-being has apparently been transferred to psychotherapy!

The boundaries of the treatment, never firm, have become increasingly ambiguous and provisional; in fact, they now seem to be infinitely expansible. Within the past decade the role of the psychotherapist has been greatly extended. Not only is he expected to help the patient achieve relief from psychologically induced discomfort and social ineffectuality—that is, to treat "mental disorders"; he is also expected to help the client achieve positive mental health, a state presumably defined by the extent to which the patient experiences "self-actualization," growth, even spiritual oneness with the universe. Thus, some therapists have moved away from the earlier aim of "head-shrinking" to the loftier goal of "mind-expanding."

The range of problems brought to the psychotherapist has broadened to include not only the major mental disorders—the psychoses and neuroses—but also the celebrated problems of alienation and the meaninglessness of life. The conception of "pathology"—that is, what needs changing —has been modified. Where formerly the internal and unconscious conflicts of the *individual* were treated, the targets of change now encompass the interpersonal relationship, the family system, and, more recently, even society and its institutions.

Credentials for practicing psychotherapy have been broadening and, by some standards, lowered. What was initially almost the exclusive domain of the medical profession—of the psychoanalyst and psychiatrist —has slowly been opened up to include the related professions of clinical psychology, psychiatric social work, and psychiatric nursing. Among those more recently invited to provide some psychiatric services are the "paraprofessional," the nonprofessional, and even the former patient. The belief that "it takes (a former) one to treat one" has gained popularity, particularly in the treatment of drug abusers, alcoholics, criminals, and delinquents.

The number of "therapeutic techniques" also continues to grow. More than 130 different approaches are now being purveyed in the marketplace of psychosocial therapies.

New schools emerge constantly, heralded by claims that they provide better treatment, amelioration, or management of the problems and neuroses of the day. No school has ever withdrawn from the field for failure to live up to its claims, and as a consequence all continue to co-exist. This remarkable state of affairs is explained in part by the fact that each school seems to be striving for different goals—goals reflecting different views of the "nature of man" and his potential. All approaches to treatment are sustained by their appeals to different constituencies in our pluralistic society.

By way of general introduction, I shall briefly review the four self-proclaimed major schools of psychotherapy. Then I'll describe several other forms of treatment that are difficult to categorize but that currently also enjoy special popularity.

The four major schools of therapy are (1) analytically oriented therapy, (2) behavior therapy, (3) humanistic therapy, and (4) transpersonal therapy.

ANALYTICALLY ORIENTED THERAPY

The analytic (or psychodynamic, or depth) forms of therapy have evolved in a more or less direct line from classical psychoanalysis. While still flourishing, and perhaps the most frequently encountered form of treatment, this school appears— like unemployment and inflation—to be growing at a declining rate.

These psychodynamic therapies assume that people have innate and acquired drives which conflict with both the "external" requirements of society and the "internal" needs and "internalized" standards of the individual. Unacceptable drives are forced out of the conscious awareness—that is, repressed—but they continue, unconsciously or subconsciously, to press for expression.

A person's normal development may be interrupted by early-life experiences that either do not satisfy innate drives sufficiently or gratify them excessively. In either event, the child's development may be blocked. The emotions and fantasies derived from these unacceptable drives may be allowed partial expression in a disguised and compromised form. In some instances these emotions are "sublimated" into creative, socially beneficial channels. In other cases they "surface" as undesirable physical symptoms, or as socially unacceptable character traits and behavior patterns. The psychodynamic approach postulates that socialization is required in order for the person to become human.

Psychoanalytic treatment tries to unravel internal problems by bringing the unconscious neurotic conflicts into the patient's consciousness. The direct target of treatment is not the patient's *symptoms*, but rather the forces that are believed to generate these symptoms.

The formula for bringing this repressed material squarely into the patient's awareness is: clarify, confront, interpret. Understanding and insight of this kind are presumed to be in themselves "curative," provided that they evoke emotional experiences of a compelling nature.

Typically, psychoanalytic approaches involve analysis of the relationship that the patient attempts to establish with the therapist. This relationship is presumed to mirror the patient's unresolved pathological childhood conflicts.

More recently, the analytically oriented therapist has begun taking into account the social and cultural context in which the patient lives. The classical patient-therapist pairing has been widened to permit treatment in groups as well. Some psychodynamic therapies have moved from long-term to brief, time-limited courses of treatment. Though many of the classic procedures have been revised and relaxed, the basic assumption that dynamic forces underlie symptomatic behavior remains unchanged.

BEHAVIOR THERAPY

Most behavior therapy derives from laboratory studies of learning processes. The therapist does not postulate the existence of any disease, aberrant personality development, or internal underlying conflict. The problem is defined in terms of specific behavior that the patient or society considers to be maladaptive. The aim of treatment is to change behavior—to change, specifically, its frequency, intensity, and appropriateness.

The behavior therapist does not consider maladaptive forms of behavior as evidence of "pathology" but rather as ways in which people have learned to interact with their environment. He believes that behavior disorders develop according to the same principles of learning evident in so-called normal learning.

"Behavioral" treatment begins with detailed study of the events that precede and follow occurrences of a particular behavior problem—phobic avoidances, compulsions, temper tantrums, sexual dysfunctions, and so on.

One major form of behavior therapy consists in changing environmental conditions that stimulate or maintain the unwanted behavior; this therapeutic technique is known as "operant conditioning." Behavior therapy now includes a broad spectrum of techniques, known by such names as systematic desensitization, assertiveness training, aversive conditioning, token economy, and modeling. These procedures are offered by psychologists, psychiatrists, educators, social workers, speech therapists, and others concerned with modifying behavior.

The procedure popularly labeled as *biofeedback* is used as a potential treatment for a variety of psychosomatic disorders, such as headaches, insomnia, high blood pressure, asthma, circulatory problems, and backache. The primary principle in biofeedback* is that if someone is provided with information about certain changes occurring in his body, that person can "learn" to: (1) increase awareness of his or her bodily processes, and (2) bring these processes under conscious control. This control should then permit the patient to change the autonomic processes in a more benign or healthful direction. Awareness of events within the body is achieved by means of monitoring instruments, which detect the relevant internal physiological change, amplify it, and translate it into a visual or auditory display.

HUMANISTIC THERAPY

This umbrella term shelters a wide range of therapies and techniques. Perhaps the most important factor uniting them is their strong reaction against what they view as limited conceptions of human nature offered by the analytic and behavioristic therapies.

Humanists postulate that man is driven by an overarching need for self-actualization. Man's needs are, they assert, "higher" than simply mindless pleasure-seeking or avoidance of pain. Goodness, truth, beauty, justice, and order are not to be explained away as byproducts of man's efforts to sublimate, divert, or block the direct expression of the baser drives that lurk within— an explanation sometimes attributed to analytically oriented therapy. Humanists believe that the failure to express and to realize the potential of higher human needs, motives, and capacities is the cause of emotional distress.

*See "Biofeedback: An Exercise in Self-Control" by Barbara Brown, *SR,* Feb. 22, 1975.

The goals of humanistic therapy are self-actualization and the enrichment and fuller enjoyment of life, not the cure of "disease" or "disorders." To realize your potential, you must develop increasing sensitivity to your own—and others'—feelings. Such heightened awareness will help establish warm relationships and improve your ability to perceive, intuit, sense, create, fantasize, and imagine.

The humanists stress that the only reality that merits concern is one's own emotional experience—in contrast to what they view as the unwarranted faith that other therapists have placed in thought, insight, and understanding.

The analytic view holds that man's impulses must be frustrated and redirected in order that he be more fully human. But humanists argue that direct gratification of needs is ennobling and good.

Humanists such as the late Abraham Maslow hold that each individual has a biological essence, or self, that he must discover and develop, but that external influences are more powerful than biologically given characteristics and may distort or block our personal awareness and development.

The panoply of self-actualizing techniques ranges from nondirective counseling and gestalt therapy to the multiple and ever-evolving variants of "growth" groups: the encounter group, the T-group, sensory-awareness training, and so on.

TRANSPERSONAL THERAPY

Unlike the humanists, the transpersonalists are not content with the aim of integrating one's energies and expanding the awareness of oneself as an entity separate from the rest of the universe. Instead, the transpersonalists' goal is to help the individual transcend the limits of ordinary waking consciousness and to become at one with the universe. The various levels and dimensions of awareness are as follows: "intuitive" states, in which vague, fleeting experiences of trans-sensory perception begin to enter waking awareness; the "psychical," in which the individual transcends sensory awareness and experiences integration with humanity; and the "mystical," representing a union of enlightenment in which the self transcends duality and merges with "all there is." Finally, there may be yet a further level of potential development—personal/transpersonal integrative—in which all dimensions are experienced simultaneously.

Transpersonalists do not share an organized theory or a clearly defined set of concepts, but, like the humanists, they assume that we all have large pools of untapped abilities, along with a drive toward spiritual growth.

One may achieve these levels by means of various techniques, including Arica training, the Gurdjieff method, Zen, psychosynthesis, yoga, Sufism, Buddhism, and transcendental meditation.

Three transpersonal approaches have achieved considerable popularity: psychosynthesis, Arica training, and transcendental meditation.

Psychosynthesis was developed by a Florentine psychiatrist, Roberto Asagioli. As a form of therapy, it tries to help people develop "the will" as a constructive force guiding all psychological functions—emotion-feeling, imagination, impulse-desire, thought, and intuition. Treatment aims at enabling the patient to achieve harmony within himself and with the world as a path to attaining the higher self. It consists of techniques for training the will in order that one can master life and merge with "the universal will."

Arica training is an eclectic system, devised by Oscar Ichazo in Chile. It has incorporated many of the teachings of the Middle East and the Orient, including

yoga, Zen, Sufism, Kabbala, and the martial arts. The branches of the Arica Institute now established in some major American cities stress these features: special diet, sensory awareness, energy-generating exercises, techniques for analysis in personality, interpersonal and group exercises, and various forms of meditation.

Transcendental meditation (TM), a variant of Raja yoga, has become extraordinarily popular in the United States and Europe. This form of meditation has been adapted to the habits of Westerners and does not require special postures, forced concentration, lengthy or arduous training, or religious belief. Each person is assigned a mantra—a special incantatory catch-phrase—which he is to keep secret and meditate on twice a day for about 20 minutes. This meditation helps people attain deep states of relaxation that are said to release creative energies. The advocates of TM hold that if 1 percent of the population in a given area meditate properly, the energies generated will benefit the rest of the population.

SPECIAL TREATMENT FORMS

Most techniques of psychotherapy can be included under one or another of these four rubrics—analytic, behavioral, humanistic, and transpersonal—but there remain a number of approaches that do not claim allegiance to any school and are not claimed by any. Some of these special approaches may be termed "pan-theoretical"; others have evolved self-consciously "novel" techniques and procedures. The broad class of group psychotherapies and the many community-oriented therapies illustrate "pan-theoretical" approaches; the "novel" therapies will be illustrated here by perhaps the best known—primal therapy.

"Group psychotherapy" does not represent any particular set of techniques or common philosophy of treatment. It refers to the *setting* in which the particular views and techniques of the analytic, behavioral, humanistic, and transpersonal schools have been implemented. In addition to having a knowledge of his own school, the practitioner of group psychotherapy must understand the dynamics and processes of small groups.

Of the many forms of group therapy, one of the best known is *transactional analysis* (TA), of *I'm OK, You're OK* fame. TA was developed by Eric Berne and represents an adaptation and extension of the psychodynamic orientation. The treatment attempts to identify covert gratifications—the "payoffs" of the "games" that people play with one another. The tasks of both the therapists and the group patients include identifying the moment-to-moment ego states (parent, child, adult) that characterize each participant's interactions. A further step is to name the "game" that the individual is playing and, finally, to identify the "unconscious" life plan that the patient appears to have selected for himself during early childhood. The life plan involves the relatively enduring position of whether the self and others are "okay" or "not okay." The dynamics of change are believed to consist in the patient's learning to shift his "real self" from one ego state to another by an act of will.

Family therapy involves the collective treatment of members of the same family in a group by one or more psychotherapists. This approach treats not merely the individual but the family unit. The individual "patient" is viewed as but a symptom of a dysfunctional family system—a system that has produced and now maintains the problems manifested in a given family member.

The pan-theoretical approaches include those therapies which extend the therapeutic focus to the community and society. The premise that environmental influences may interfere with a person's development has been taken up by a variety of therapists loosely associated with humanistic psychology. Perhaps the most extreme position is that taken by the group espousing *radical therapy,* which holds that society is responsible for most mental and emotional ills, and that, therefore, society rather than the patient is sick. People in psychological distress are considered oppressed rather than ill, and traditional psychotherapy is "part of the problem rather than part of the solution to human misery." The therapist attempts to help the patient recognize not merely his own problems but also the realities of his life situation and the role played by society in generating and perpetuating emotional problems.

Like radical therapy, *feminist therapy* believes that the root of emotional problems may be found in society rather than in the individual. Feminist therapy emphasizes that all psychotherapy must be freed of its tradition sex-role biases. Sexism is viewed as a major force impeding the "growth" of both men and women. This approach is not characterized by any particular techniques, but rather by a shared ideology. Consciousness-raising groups, too, which were initially politically motivated, have recently become oriented toward providing women with help for their personal problems.

Primal therapy is viewed by its inventor, Arthur Janov, as unique in both its effects and its techniques, and as the "only cure of the neuroses." According to Janov, a neurosis occurs when the unexpressed physical and psychological pains experienced in childhood accumulate to the point where they are unbearable and can no longer be simply suppressed. The awareness of these feelings and needs is then "split off" when the child interprets the parents' behavior as meaning that they hate him. This formulation may occur at about the age of five or six and represents to Janov the "primal scene" that precipitates the neurosis.

In Janov's theory the pain of unmet

needs is stored away somewhere in the brain and produces tension, which the patient may deal with by developing a variety of tension-relieving symptoms. Treatment requires the release and full expression of the underlying pain, by restoring physical access to the stored memories. Cure occurs only when each old painful feeling is linked to its origins. The living and reliving of the primal scene is accompanied by a "tower of terror" usually associated with screaming, violent thrashing about, pounding, and even convulsions. The screaming may go on for hours and may be repeated periodically over a period of many months as one event after another is recalled.

According to Janov, the cured individual should ideally have no psychological defenses, nor need any, since all pain and its associated tensions have been dispelled. The recovered patient thus becomes a "natural man," who is "non-industrial, non-compulsive, and non-driving," and finds much less need for sex; women experience sexual interest no more than twice a month.

Even this truncated review of the major schools and techniques indicates the enormous complexity of any serious research effort that undertakes to compare the relative effectiveness of available therapies. Clearly, the basic conceptions differ as to who and what needs treating. It is not easy to prove that changes observed in patients and clients are due to the specific techniques and interventions. The therapist may wittingly or unwittingly provide the patient with experiences other than those assumed to be critical. It cannot be assumed that the same therapist will behave similarly with each of his patients—much less that different therapists espousing the same theory will behave similarly with all patients. The problems of research on the outcome of psychotherapy are further compounded by the concurrent impact of other events in the patient's life.

In terms of consumer guidance, then, I shall report only the most consistent trends that emerge from a review of a large number of studies:

- Most forms of psychotherapy are effective with about two-thirds of their non-psychotic patients.

- Treated patients show significantly more improvement in thought, mood, personality, and behavior than do comparable samples of untreated patients.

- Behavior modification appears to be particularly useful in some specific classes of phobias, some forms of compulsive or ritual behavior, and some sexual dysfunctions. Although behavior-therapy techniques appear to produce rapid improvement in the addictive disorders, such as alcoholism, drug abuse, obesity, and smoking, these changes are usually not maintained and relapse occurs in most cases.

- Biofeedback has been applied to tension headaches, migraine, hypertension, epilepsy, some irregularities of heartbeat. The evidence, while encouraging, has not yet established such treatment as being clinically significant.

- Meditation techniques of a wide variety all produce comparable degrees of relaxation, with associated physiological and metabolic changes. Currently, "noncultist" adaptations of meditative procedures are being applied with some success in the treatment of anxiety, hypertension, and cardiac arrythmias. Again, findings must be viewed as tentative pending further research.

- The criteria of "growth," "self-actualization," and the attainment of transpersonal levels of consciousness remain ambiguous, and it is therefore difficult to measure them objectively.

- Apparent differences in the relative effectiveness of different psychotherapies gradually disappear with time.

- Although most studies report that similar proportions of patients benefit from all tested forms of therapy, the possibility remains open that different therapies may effect different kinds of change.

All forms of psychotherapy tend to be reasonably useful for patients who are highly motivated, experience acute discomfort, show a high degree of personality organization, are reasonably well educated, have had some history of social success and recognition, are reflective, and can experience and express emotion.

Jerome D. Frank has proposed that all therapies may incorporate the same common (non-specific) elements, although in differing degrees: an emotionally charged relationship with a helping person; a plausible explanation of the causes of distress; provision of some experiences of success; and use of the therapist's personal qualities to strengthen the patient's expectation of help.

This statement in no way endorses tactlessness, insensitivity, or psychological assault. The therapist has no license to humiliate—or to thrill. A large-scale, careful study of participants who suffered psychological injury during encounter groups (led by acknowledged experts) revealed that the incidence of such casualties was disproportionately high among clients of so-called charismatic therapists, with their often aggressive, impatient, and challenging confrontation techniques.

No matter how specific the theory, no matter how clearly prescribed the techniques for a given therapy, treatment is far from standardized. Psychotherapy is mediated by the individual therapist and further modified by the nature of the interaction with the particular patient.

When the patient is "therapist-shopping," it is wise for him to select carefully from among an array of qualified therapists the one whose style of relating is acceptable to him—and preferably from a school whose philosophy, values, and goals are most congenial to his own.

58. LITHIUM—NEW HOPE FOR MANIC-DEPRESSION

William and Ellen Hartley

One afternoon some years ago, commuters in Grand Central Station, New York City, were treated to an unusual scene. Halfway between the western stairs and the information booth, a handsome, well-dressed man had accumulated a ring of amused listeners. An open sample case lay at his feet. Standing with legs astraddle, he waved bits of lingerie and chanted a litany of sales talk.

"Step right up, ladies and gentlemen. This little number wholesales at $2.70. I can let you have it for $2.65. How about that, lady? You with the pretty eyes."

A station police officer, accustomed to the best and worst in the world, pushed through the crowd. "What's going on here?" he asked no one in particular. A woman giggled and said, "The man's selling panties. They're very pretty, too."

The officer, highly experienced, grasped the man's arm gently above the elbow. "We have an appointment, sir," he said. He sniffed the man's breath. No alcohol, not even the faint odor of vodka which is known as the salesman's drink. This was no drunk.

In the headquarters office, the duty officer examined the salesman's wallet, then placed a phone call. The salesman, meanwhile, was trying to sell lingerie to some off-duty officers getting ready to leave for home.

The duty officer got the man's boss on the phone and explained the situation—that he had been found peddling in Grand Central perfectly sober. The man's boss then informed the officer that the peddler was his star salesman and, as far as he knew, a quiet family-man with no problems.

"Well, something's wrong with him," said the officer. "We'll put him in a cab and send him along. No, we won't charge him with anything."

Later, when the salesman's company sent him to a psychiatrist, he made vigorous efforts to sell bras to the doctor. The odd experience was reported at the past meeting of the American Medical Association. The super-salesman was a manic-depressive who had gone through his manic or excited stage in Grand Central Station. He was a bit like a well known writer who decided on a pleasant afternoon to strip off his clothing and bathe in the New York World's Fair fountain. Neither of these men were insane by clinical standards, nor were they trying to play funny jokes. They were going through the extreme manic phase of manic-depression.

The depressive phase is equally horrible. Astronaut Buzz Aldrin went through it, although Aldrin did not have manic episodes. But the deep depression that almost ruined his life and his marriage is almost characteristic of the depressive interval. Aldrin considered suicide some months after his famous walk on the moon. The moon had

nothing to do with it. Aldrin was simply horribly depressed.

The famous playwright-director Joshua Logan *(South Pacific, Mr. Roberts)* is outspoken about manic-depression. At the 1973 AMA convention, he talked about suicidal tendencies of the manic-depressive. "Regarding suicide—no, not suicide, only a wish to be dead without having to go through the shaming defeat of suicide—I didn't sleep well, because sleep meant oblivion, and that's what I longed for and couldn't get. I didn't really know what to do. I was very, very lost."

Josh Logan also said that the periods of elation in manic-depression are even more frightening. The sufferer works at such a furious rate that judgment may be distorted. This was the situation with the salesman in Grand Central station. He was not insane; to put it crudely, his motor was running without a governor. The same holds true for our naked friend in the fountain.

Some six million Americans suffer from manic-depressive disorders, mild or serious. Of the 30,000 recorded suicides every year, most are victims of depressive disorders. Clear definitions of manic-depression are difficult even for physicians who sometimes confuse manic episodes or depression periods with schizophrenia. According to a British-American study, 30 percent of schizophrenics are mis-diagnosed. They are either manic-depressives or persons suffering from depression, but are fated to improper treatment as a result of confusion about their ailments.

Just to complicate matters more, there are several kinds of affective disorders, thus named because ideas, actions and feelings are mutually affected. One, called bipolar manic-depressive illness, is the most common. The bipolar type affects up to two percent of the population, or about four

million individuals. This type is characterized by highs and lows of hyperactivity and
depression. Between these periods, the person is normal in the sense of not having
extremes in mood.

A characteristic case would be that of a
29-year-old woman in Florida who is normal for weeks or months at a time. During
these periods, she is delightful. But she has
bouts of depression that may last for several
months. These attacks have nothing to do
with menstrual periods, when women are
often depressed. There is no physiological
pattern; the woman simply hits a psychological down that has almost suicidal aspects. She weeps a great deal, has little
energy, even keeps her phone off the hook
to be certain that no one can attempt to
cheer her up.

During her manic episodes, which may
also last for several months, she is active
almost to a frightening degree. A newspaper woman with a family, she can easily
work 18 hours a day. Her editors let her
interview celebrities from noon until dinner. Then she covers night spots until
around 3:00 A.M. After sleeping for two or
three hours, she writes her stories and starts
over again.

During these periods of highs, she feels
perfectly well. But she also goes on wild
shopping sprees and talks so much, and at
such a furious pace, that her friends try to
avoid her. She also attracts young men who
are fascinated by her energy and bewildered
by her periods of depression. In between the
extremes, she is a devoted mother, a sensitive and concerned friend, and a calm, pol-
ished professional writer.

Another affective disorder is unipolar depression, which is characterized by an absence of manic or hypomanic periods.
(Hypomania is mild elation and overactivity.) The behavior pattern is very much
like that of the astronaut, Col. E. E. Aldrin,
Jr., who went into deep depression after his
moon flight. Buzz Aldrin confesses frankly
in his new book, *Return to Earth* (Random
House, 1973), that his depression nearly
cost him his marriage.

"MANIA TAKES ITS TOLL"

Unipolar depression is almost undistin-
guishable from bipolar during the depressed periods, and it takes a shrewd
psychiatrist to tell the difference. Ronald R.
Fieve, M.D., of the New York Psychiatric
Institute, says in *Practical Psychiatry* (May
1973) that patient history is the only way to
distinguish between the two forms.

One thing is certain—manic-depression
is horrifying and destructive. The extremes,
as Josh Logan has put it, are terrifying. It
is quite possible that the person in the
manic phase so overexerts himself that he
subconsciously goes into the depressed
phase to rest his body. This is speculation,
although some psychologists advance it as
valid theory.

Until a few years ago, most manic-
depression of serious nature was treated by
electroshock, chemical shock, lobotomy, or
tranquilizers. Electroshock therapy, in
which an electric current is passed through
the brain, has always been costly and frightening to the patient. In its early days, it may
often have done more harm than good. For
a considerable period of time, the Veterans
Hospitals used electroshock almost indiscriminately on patients ranging from alcoholics to the severely disturbed. Some of
these individuals were "cured" to the point
of being little more than vegetables. As a
result, electroshock treatment has been
greatly improved and is used more selectively—but it still frightens the patients.

Chemoshock is a bit less dangerous, but
all shock therapy is a bit like shooting a
sparrow with a 40 mm cannon. As for tranquilizers, only a very few are moderately
effective with manic-depressives. Chlor-

promazine (Thorazine) is the one commonly used, but all tranquilizers, including meprobamates (Miltown), can have side effects. Some of the tranquilizers dull the senses so much that the patient becomes a comfortable zombie.

Now, however, there is a drug so effective that it is revolutionizing the treatment of manic-depression. This is lithium carbonate, a silvery white alkaline metal. In 1970, the Food and Drug Administration approved lithium, which seems particularly helpful in bipolar manic-depression. (There is still some question about its use in unipolar depression—the type without manic episodes.)

About 80 percent of manic-depressive patients have used it with good effect. Dr. Fieve, mentioned earlier, calls it "psychiatry's first prophylactic agent for a major mental illness." An estimated 50,000 patients, including Joshua Logan and the Grand Central salesman, are maintained on lithium. It does not work with everyone, for reasons still unknown, but the success record is high, particularly in manic periods.

The great value of lithium, apart from what it does, is that it may be taken orally, does not interfere with mental functions, is not addictive, and may be discontinued without withdrawal symptoms. It does have side effects, however, including tremors in the hands and sometimes nausea and vomiting, but these can be eliminated by reducing the dosage.

The strange thing about lithium is that it is not a new discovery in the treatment of manic-depressives. Dr. Fieve and others trace it back to prescriptions by Caelius Aurelianus in the fifth century.

Lithium was isolated in 1818 by August Arfvedson in Sweden. This led indirectly to the discovery that it was often present in mineral waters of the spas of Europe and the United States. People swarmed to drink these waters and gossip politely on the verandas of the great resort hotels. Dr. Fieve notes that Lithium Springs, Georgia, was named for the substance. There was probably not enough lithium in most waters to do much good, but at least it did no harm.

But the substance is highly dangerous for patients with heart or kidney disease. During the 1940's, lithium chloride was used as a salt substitute in products such as Saltisalt and Foodsal. When four persons with heart or kidney ailments died and others were seriously poisoned, the FDA banned lithium.

LITHIUM—HOPE FOR M-D

This was in 1949. In the same year, an Australian named J. F. J. Cade was looking for a chemical cause of mania. He decided to inject guinea pigs with lithium and found, to his surprise, that instead of scampering around they became lethargic. He then tested lithium on ten humans with mania, and found it surprisingly effective. Other investigators had the same results with a large number of patients.

Dr. Fieve has pointed out a peculiar property of lithium. This is the curious fact that the greater the total mania as part of any psychiatric illness, the greater is the overall response to lithium therapy. Moreover, patients do not feel drugged or in a "chemical strait-jacket," as they do when given other tranquilizers.

But it can poison or cause lithium intoxication, and thus must be administered after careful evaluation of the patient and a number of tests. After being used for acute mania, it is often prescribed for stabilization and maintenance. Joshua Logan has been given preventive lithium therapy for about four years, and has said the drug has given him hope for his future life and work.

In a typical case, a brilliant young New

York business executive shifted from periods of mild mania (hypomania) to acute mania. He paced back and forth while dictating at a furious rate, skipped lunches in order to work, sometimes stayed at his desk until late at night. He almost ran instead of walking, talked incessantly, finally began to thumb through correspondence without really looking at it. His troubled secretary decided to bring the situation to the attention of the head of the firm.

The young man was virtually forced into a hospital where he was first given a tranquilizer. After being checked for heart and kidney disease, he began to receive lithium. Since lithium does not take effect until at least five to ten days have passed, he was given electroshock to control his wild agitation.

Finally, when the lithium had taken hold and he had calmed down from the acute, delirious stage, he went on lithium therapy at maintenance level and has progressed well. The only annoyance is that his blood lithium level must be checked regularly.

Lithium therapy is not entirely desirable, however, for some individuals. These are hypomanics whose emotional swings are reasonably mild. Dr. Fieve has pointed out that among some creative persons the best work is sometimes performed in the course of a hypomanic period. In fact, some creative persons give up maintenance therapy. In a report in the *Journal of the American Medical Association* (Nov. 8, 1971) Drs. Fieve and Phillip Polatin described several cases in which creative patients rejected lithium carbonate therapy because they felt it inhibited creativity.

One 62-year-old man had suffered depressive and hypomanic attacks for some 20 years. When depressed, he could not write; when in a hypomanic period, he wrote well and profitably.

He tried lithium carbonate for two years and no longer suffered from depression. But his hypomanic periods also disappeared and he couldn't write. He finally discontinued lithium, wrote furiously, and produced a best-seller.

There have been other instances of this kind, but the two doctors conclude their report by saying that lithium is of great benefit to a majority of patients suffering from manic-depression. Its greatest contribution is control of the manic phase although it also limits depression.

It is true, however, that some doctors still prefer electroshock for treatment of acute mania. But the duration of control is usually quite limited. The only thing so far that keeps manic-depressives on an even keel is lithium therapy. It is one of the most important medical discoveries of recent years.

59.   WEAPON AGAINST PAIN: HYPNOSIS IS NO MIRAGE

Ernest R. Hilgard

Hypnosis works. Laboratory research to date allows us to say that with confidence, even as the clinical applications of hypnosis proliferate. From the pain-filled rooms of cancer patients to antismoking clinics, from dental surgeries to maternity wards, hypnosis is gaining ever wider acceptance as a weapon against pain. While there are many unanswered questions about how hypnosis works and whom it will work for, enough evidence is in to support it fully as a therapeutic tool.

Hypnosis has come a long way from the parlor magic of Franz Anton Mesmer and his theory of animal magnetism. But in part because of those lurid beginnings and in part because of its association with charlatans, bad movies, and entertainers, hypnosis still is suspect in some quarters. Many psychologists argue that the hypnotic trance is a mirage. It would be unfortunate if this skeptical view were to gain such popularity that the benefits of hypnosis are denied to the numbers of those who could be helped. Consider, for example, the experience of women who give birth while in hypnotic trance. Obstetrician R. V. August delivered babies of 1,000 women from 1957 to 1960. Of the 850 women who gave birth under hypnosis, only 36 required chemical anesthesia in addition. And five of the women who relied solely on hypnoanesthesia delivered their babies by Caesarian section.

PHANTOM-LIMB PAIN

C. H. Harding reported successful treatment of migraine and vascular headaches with hypnotic suggestion. Of 90 patients he treated with four to seven sessions of hypnotic induction, 38 percent reported complete relief for periods of up to eight years. Thirty-two percent rated their relief as substantial. Only 11 of the 90 cases reported no relief from hypnotic treatment.

Hypnosis has also been used in the treatment of phantom-limb pain. About 57 percent of all amputees suffer from this peculiar affliction, which feels different from pain in the stump of the limb and is often extremely difficult to relieve. About 33 percent of these cases respond favorably to hypnotic suggestion. C. Cedercreutz and E. Uusitalo of Finland treated 37 cases of phantom-limb pain with hypnotic suggestion. Twenty patients lost all of their pain and another 10 improved so much that medication was no longer needed. Followup studies conducted from one to eight years after treatment revealed that eight patients were still totally pain-free and 10 others still showed some relief. The researchers concluded that, for phantom-limb pain, hypnosis is far better than other available treatments.

While hypnosis is used successfully in clinical settings, the skeptics argue that there is no true reduction in pain. Theodore Sarbin and his colleagues believe that a person adopts the role that is appropriate to his situation. When hypnotized, he plays the role of a hypnotized person behaving as he believes a hypnotized person should. Similarly, Sarbin believes that reports by patients of pain relief indicate only a desire to please the therapist, to perform as he expects. The patient becomes so absorbed by the role, Sarbin believes, that in extreme cases it can lead to phenomena such as voodoo death.

HAND IMMOBILITY

Martin Orne, a psychologist at the University of Pennsylvania, found some truth in Sarbin's notion. He demonstrated hypnosis before two groups of students. Half of the students saw hypnotized subjects whose dominant hand was immobile: this fact was pointed out to the class as characteristic of the hypnotic state. The remaining students witnessed similar demonstrations except that the subject's hand did not become immobile. After the demonstration, members of each group were hypnotized; the hypnotist, however, did not know which demonstration a given student had witnessed. As expected, the students who had observed the model with hand immobility showed that characteristic while the other students did not.

These results are consistent with other studies that show the power of the experimental situation over the behavior of the subject. The efforts of the subject to please the experimenter, even when his demands are unreasonable, are so strong that Orne refers to the "demand characteristics" of the experimental situation. Critics of hypnosis feel that hypnotized subjects may simply be responding to the implied demands of the hypnotist. Response to demands does not lead Orne to reject hypnosis; his point is that the experimental evidence must be viewed critically. Nobody denies that hypnosis includes responses to suggestions, obvious or implicit.

One way to identify hypnosis as something unique would be to produce physiological evidence for the existence of the hypnotic state. It is difficult to prove whether or not a hypnotized person differs physiologically from one who is awake. Those who have been hypnotized report feeling quite different, and we know that at the deepest levels of hypnosis a person may lose any further responsiveness to hypnotic suggestions. The EEG patterns of hypnotized subjects are no different from those of their normal waking state, but they do differ from the patterns associated with sleep. We know that highly hypnotizable subjects produce more alpha waves in the normal waking state than do poor hypnotic subjects. In our laboratory we found a moderately strong correlation between the amount of alpha activity in a person's waking state and his susceptibility to hypnosis, but this correlation has to do with the potential for hypnotic response and not with the hypnotic state itself.

RIGHT AND LEFT LOOKERS

Other work suggests that a correlation exists between hypnotic suggestibility and hemispheric activity. When asked a question such as, "How many letters are in the word 'Washington'?" a person will typically look to the left or the right. About 75 percent of these eye movements will be to one side. Left-eye movements have been found to suggest that the brain's right hemisphere is dominant while right-eye movements are associated with left-hemisphere dominance. Paul Bakan [see "The Eyes Have It," PT, April 1971] gave a test of hypnotic suggestibility to 46 undergraduate students and had them tested for eye movement. He found that left-lookers produced the highest hypnotic suggestibility scores, while the lowest scores came from right-lookers; his work, originally done in our laboratory, has been confirmed and extended here by Raquel and Ruben Gur.

Psychoactive drugs can also affect hypnotic suggestibility. Bernard Sjoberg found that LSD and mescaline increase suggestibility and that this effect lasts beyond the normal effects of the drug. We also know that hypnotic suggestibility is a regular function of age; it reaches a peak between eight and 11 years and then declines gradually. But none of the evidence concerning the physiological correlates of hypnosis proves conclusively that the hypnotic trance has distinctive physiological signs, such as the brain waves and rapid-eye movements associated with dreaming. A better question is whether or not hypnosis produces consequences that are real. We know, for example, that under hypnotic suggestion some people will do things they would otherwise not do. They will erase imaginary words from a blank blackboard, see and hear things that are not there, and not see and hear things that are there.

FREEZING WATER

To find out how real hypnotic effects are, much of the laboratory research has studied the hypnotic reduction of pain. It is possible to get objective measures of the degree of pain and to compare these with subjective reports of pain intensity. If people under hypnotic suggestion endure greater amounts of pain, and if they say they feel less pain than during the waking state, then hypnosis would seem to be genuine.

One technique for inducing pain in the laboratory is to immerse the volunteer's hand and forearm in freezing water. The subject rates the intensity of the pain he feels when awake, and after the hypnotic suggestion that his hand and arm are insensitive. We then compare the two ratings to determine if hypnotic suggestion reduces pain.

In one of our first experiments, we gave 54 volunteers a test of hypnotic suggestibility and then gave them the hypnotic suggestion that they would not feel pain. The subjects then rated the pain they felt during the ice-water test. Pain reduction was clearly related to hypnotic susceptibility. Of the highly hypnotizable subjects, 67 percent showed a 33 percent reduction in pain, while only 13 percent of the least hypnotizable subjects showed as much relief. At the same time only seven percent of the highly suggestible volunteers showed 10 percent or less reduction in pain, while 56 percent of the subjects low in suggestibility showed this small amount of relief.

Our results were confirmed several years later by Michael Evans and Gordon Paul in another laboratory. They also found that ice-water pain could be reduced by hypnotic suggestion and that the amount of reduction increased with a person's susceptibility to hypnosis.

Evans and Paul conducted their experiment with college women. Each volunteer immersed her hand in the icy water for one minute. Then she rated the pain she had felt on a seven-point scale ranging from pleasant to very painful. Later, each subject received one of four treatment procedures. One fourth of the volunteers were hypnotized and given the suggestion that they would not feel pain. Another group was hypnotized but not given the antipain suggestion. A third group was taught self-relaxation and given the suggestion that they would not feel pain. The last group learned self-relaxation but received no suggestion that their ability to feel pain would diminish. After she received one of the four sets of instructions, each woman again immersed her hand in the frigid water and rated the pain she felt. Evans and Paul compared this second rating with the first. Those who received the analgesic suggestion showed a greater reduction in pain than those who did not, but it made no difference whether the suggestion had been given under hypnosis or during the waking state, under self-relaxation.

Other studies of this sort have produced similar results, leading critics of hypnosis to decide that the results of suggested pain reduction are genuine, but that a prior induction of hypnosis is not necessary, and that therefore the concept of hypnosis is superfluous. However, these studies involve random selections of students, which make conclusions regarding the legitimacy of hypnosis of dubious value.

FOUR-MINUTE MILERS

If we asked a random sample of college students to run a mile for us, we would be unlikely to find even one who could run the mile in four minutes. Yet no one would conclude from this fact that a four-minute mile is impossible. The inability of a random sample of people to perform an act does not demonstrate the impossibility of that act. People vary in their skill at any task, and we know that people differ greatly in susceptibility to hypnosis. To determine if hypnotic suggestion can reduce pain intensity it is necessary to test those who are highly responsive to hypnotic suggestion. If these subjects do not show pain reduction then the legitimacy of hypnotism is indeed called into question. If hypnosis is real then those who are highly hypnotizable should show signs that they experience less pain when hypnotized than when not hypnotized, those without hypnotic talent should show less pain reduction, and hypnotic procedures should have no advantage over nonhypnotic ones for them. Because so many of the nontalented are found in the samples studied by Evans and Paul, it is no wonder that they did not find differences favoring hypnosis.

To clarify this issue, Arlene Morgan and Hugh Macdonald joined me in another test of the strength of hypnotic suggestion. Twenty highly hypnotizable subjects were given the ice-water pain test while awake. Then half of the subjects were hypnotized, given the analgesic suggestion, and tested again. The other half were retested in the waking state. If hypnosis works, then the hypnotized subjects should show greater pain reduction than the equally suggestible, but unhypnotized control group. This is exactly what we found. Hypnosis reduced pain an average of 10.3 points, while waking suggestion reduced pain only 4.4 points. The remaining subjects were eventually tested under hypnotic induction. Of the 20 subjects, only four eliminated pain completely. This means that no more than two or three students out of 100 will be able to reach the greatest degree of hypnotic suggestibility. Just as any study that relies on a random sample of students is unlikely to uncover one who can run a four-minute mile, any study that draws a small random sample of students is unlikely to uncover one who will demonstrate the highest levels of hypnotic responsiveness. Even if one or two "virtuosos" appeared by chance, the average performance of the group would be brought down by the unresponsive majority.

DEACTIVATING THE PLACEBO

Further support for the contribution of hypnosis comes from Thomas McGlashan, Frederick Evans, and Martin Orne. They compared 12 highly suggestible subjects with 12 subjects who showed little suggestibility. They induced pain by placing a tourniquet on the upper arm and having the subject squeeze a rubber ball, an act that produces intense pain after a few minutes. The longer a person squeezes the ball, the greater his tolerance of pain. In the McGlashan study, each subject took the test cold without hypnotic induction, then repeated it under hypnotic analgesia, and a third time during the normal waking state, after taking a pill that was supposed to be very effective in killing pain. The pill was actually a placebo, given so that the effects of hypnotic induction could be distinguished from the placebo effect common in drugs [see "The Power of a Sugar Pill," by Frederick J. Evans, PT, April]. The results show clearly that hypnotic suggestion increased tolerance for pain among the highly hypnotizable subjects, but not among those of low suggestibility. For them, there was no greater benefit from hypnosis than from the placebo. But for the highly suggestible subjects, hypnosis produced considerably more tolerance for pain than the placebo.

We have seen that hypnotic suggestion is effective in increasing tolerance of pain. How hypnosis does this is not clear, but we know that imagination plays an important role. A vivid imagination is, in fact, one of the best indications of hypnotic susceptibility. The best hypnotic subjects are those who can imagine with incredible clarity, even while awake. Josephine Hilgard has shown that as children these subjects often had imaginary playmates, and many of them relied on their imagination to escape from unpleasant situations.

CAREFUL FOCUS

Hypnotic induction seems to facilitate the use of imagination. During hypnosis, one woman pretended she was inside the *Venus de Milo* statue. Since she had no arms, she could feel no pain during the ice-water experiment. Another subject pretended he was somewhere else; since he was not in the experimental situation, he could not be hurt. Others imagine that they have been given an injection of an anesthetic; numbness spreads through their arms as the imaginary anesthetic dissipates.

It is not clear why imagination should be helpful in reducing pain. Hypnosis is often described as a state of heightened awareness in which attention is focused intensely on the suggestions of the hypnotist. Perhaps hypnotized subjects are able to focus attention so carefully on some imagined stimulus, such as those the hypnotist suggests, that competing stimuli are physiologically inhibited. All of us have had the experience of becoming so engrossed in a book, a conversation or some other activity that we did not hear our name being called. It is not just that we deny hearing our name; we actually do not hear it. This may not be so different from the experience of the hypnotic subject.

There is overwhelming evidence that some people get relief from pain by hypnotic suggestion; they are not merely withholding reports of suffering to please the hypnotist. The hundreds of patients who have received relief from pain through hypnotic suggestion do not need convincing. And those who may be helped in the future should not be denied the benefits of hypnosis simply because we do not yet understand precisely what hypnosis is or why it works. For now, it is enough to know that it does.

60. FRICTION AND FANTASY: NO-NONSENSE THERAPY FOR SIX SEXUAL MALFUNCTIONS

Helen Singer Kaplan

Since William H. Masters and Virginia E. Johnson published their research on the physiology of sexual intercourse, and talk about sex has become respectable, a growing number of men and women know they are being cheated. They are seeking help at new sex therapy clinics throughout the nation.

In our clinic at Cornell University Medical School, we see couples who have one or more of the six basic sexual problems:

1. Premature ejaculation: inability to control orgasm.
2. Retarded ejaculation: inability to trigger orgasm.
3. Male impotence: inability to produce or maintain an erection.
4. General female sexual dysfunction: lack of erotic response to sexual stimulation, commonly called frigidity.
5. Female orgasmic dysfunction: difficulty in reaching orgasm.
6. Vaginismus: spasm of the muscles at the entrance of the vagina, preventing penetration.

As sex therapists we deal first and foremost with immediate sexual problems, so that women and men can enjoy sex to its fullest. However, we also attack the conflicts and defenses that are obstacles to sexual functioning. We are, of course, concerned with *why* a man persists in wilting his erection by obsessively monitoring his own behavior, or why he is so worried about performing sexually, or what experiences and fantasies make a woman so insecure that she cannot ask her lover to stimulate her clitoris. But we are primarily interested in teaching individuals to abandon themselves completely to the erotic experience of sexual intercourse.

To do this, we teach patients sexual exercises to remove the immediate anxieties and defenses that create and maintain their antierotic environment. We employ psychotherapy when deep anxieties or underlying pathologies impede our progress. I present a detailed discussion of our philosophy and treatment in *The New Sex Therapy,* published by Brunner/Mazel last spring.

FRICTION AND FANTASY

We begin treatment of all sexual dysfunctions with a psychiatric examination of both partners, a detailed history and assessment of their sexual functioning, and an evaluation of the marital relationship. We give the couple a clear picture of what to expect during treatment, and we make a therapeutic contract with them that clearly establishes their responsibility for treatment.

Sex is composed of friction and fantasy; deficiencies in either can produce problems. A pleasurable sexual response depends both on receiving the proper sexual stimulation and responding freely to it. Most couples with sexual problems practice poor, insensitive and ineffectual sexual techniques.

Some inadequate lovemaking results merely from a couple's misinformation or ignorance about sex. Frequently, for instance, neither spouse knows where the clitoris is or recognizes its potential for eliciting erotic pleasure. They have intercourse as soon as the husband has an erection, and he ejaculates without considering whether his partner is ready. Such couples genuinely wonder why the wife does not reach orgasm. Both partners contribute to this sexual ineffectiveness. She will not ask for the kind of stimulation she wants because she is unaware of her own needs; he doesn't know that he's not a very effective lover. So, in silence, they continue their unsatisfactory sexual habits.

In other couples, feelings of guilt or anxiety about erotic needs prevent one or both partners from enjoying sex. They may actively discourage their partners from stimulating them effectively. Careful questioning often reveals that such persons respond to sexual excitement by immediately stopping the activity which produces it. The man who is excited by an actively seductive woman may literally forbid his wife to be aggressive. The woman who is responsive only to slow tender caresses may push her husband away when he tries to kiss her breasts or to caress her buttocks. Patients who avoid effective sexual expression tend to focus on genital stimulation and on orgasm: and are apt to neglect the sensual potential of the rest of their bodies and of nonorgasmic eroticism.

Some persons have as much difficulty giving pleasure as others do in receiving it. These individuals don't provide their partners with enough sexual stimulation because they lack either the knowledge and sensitivity to know what to do, or they are anxious about doing it. Others are consciously or unconsciously hostile towards their mates and don't really want to please them.

SEXUAL DEFENSES

Therapists have overlooked immediate sources of anxiety until the advent of the new sex therapy. Traditional approaches to sexual dysfunction looked for subtle and profound anxiety sources, such as oedipal conflicts and marital power struggles. We find there are also more obvious reasons for sexual anxiety, such as fear of sexual failure, fear that the partner expects too much, or fear that the partner will reject sexual advances. These fears create various sexual defenses and introduce conscious control into lovemaking, which in turn prevents persons from abandoning themselves to the experience.

We have found that the three male dysfunctions, impotence, retarded ejaculation, and premature ejaculation all seem to be associated with some form of sexual conflict, but there are different symptoms for each dysfunction, and each of them responds to different therapeutic strategies and tactics.

1. Premature Ejaculation

Premature ejaculation is one of the most common and easily relieved male complaints. Men with this malady are unable to control voluntarily their ejaculatory reflex. Once they become sexually aroused, they reach orgasm very quickly. Some ejaculate after several minutes of foreplay, others just prior to or immediately upon entering their partner's vagina, and others after only a few pelvic thrusts. The essential problem, however, is not how quickly the man ejaculates, but his inability to control the reflex. In contrast to a premature ejaculator, an effective lover continues to engage in sex play while he is in a highly aroused state. He is able to forestall climax until his partner, who is slower to respond, can reach orgasm. At the least, prematurity restricts the couple's sexuality; at worse, it destroys it.

Most men who suffer this distress are unhappy about their condition, and often employ a variety of common-sense techniques to relieve the difficulty. They shift their attention to nonsexual thoughts during intercourse, tense their anal muscles, bite their lips or dig their fingernails into their palms. In this manner they can delay the onset of intense erotic arousal, but once aroused, they still can't control ejaculation. They feel sexually inadequate, and guilty that they have not satisfied their partners.

The term "primary prematurity" refers to a man who has never been able to control orgasm. If he is otherwise healthy, there is little reason to suspect his difficulty arises from a physical cause. On the other hand, a physician should conduct thorough urological and neurological exams on the secondary ejaculator, a man who has developed the problem after a history of good control. Diseases of the posterior urethra or pathology along the nerve pathways serving the orgasmic reflex mechanisms may cause secondary prematurity. Sex therapy should begin only after a physician rules out any physical basis for the condition.

SMALL COMFORT

Different therapeutic schools emphasize various psychological explanations for premature ejaculation. Psychoanalysts say it is the result of a neurosis, marriage counselors believe it comes from hostilities between the partners, common-sense theorists blame it on excessive sensitivity to erotic sensation. Masters and Johnson contend that stressful conditions during a young man's initial sex experiences bring on premature ejaculation, while Wardell Pomeroy, co-author of the Kinsey reports, says that anxiety is the culprit. All these speculations may be theoretically interesting, but they are of little comfort to the patient.

In 1956, James Semans, a urologist, demonstrated a simple manipulative technique to help cure premature ejaculation. Semans realized that the distinguishing feature of premature ejaculation was the rapidity of the orgasmic reflex. Consequently, his treatment goal was to prolong the reflex. To do this, he directed the patient's wife to stimulate her husband's erect penis until he felt he was just about to have orgasm, and signaled her to stop. When he could recapture control, the patient would tell her to resume stimulation until he again felt the sensations that signaled ejaculation. Again she would stop. Over a period of several weeks the couple practiced this stop-start method until the patient could tolerate stimulation without ordering a halt. At this point, his prematurity was permanently cured.

Semans reported on eight men who were premature ejaculators, and in every case the symptom disappeared. Other clinicians have used his method with the same success. I believe the technique works because it focuses a man's attention on the sensations preceding orgasm. Apparently he has previously failed to acquire control because he has not received, or let himself receive, the sensory feedback necessary to bring the reflex under control.

In our treatment program at Cornell we teach the patient to clearly identify his intensely erotic preorgasmic sensations and, initially, to avoid being distracted by his wife's needs. We advise the couple that, provided they adhere to the prescribed therapeutic exercises, we can cure the symptom in most cases.

We use a variation of the Semans "stop-start" method in our treatment. The couple carries out their exercise assignments in their home. After three or four of these noncoital sessions, the patient usually feels he has attained some improvement in orgasmic control. We then suggest that the couple attempt intercourse using the same stop-start method. They first have coitus with the woman in the superior position, then while both lie on their sides, and finally with the man on top. Since this is usually the most stimulating position for the male, he has conquered his problem when he can maintain control in this position.

HUSBAND FIRST

This procedure can be quite unexciting and frustrating for the wife. Therefore, we suggest that the couple work out an agreement previous to treatment where the husband stimulates his wife to orgasm before or after the stop-start treatment. If the wife is unable to have an orgasm, we tell her that our first goal is to cure her husband's prematurity, then we can shift treatment to her.

If either partner resists any part of the treatment procedures, we root out the cause and intervene with appropriate psychotherapy. This might involve marriage counseling, psychoanalysis or anxiety-reduction techniques. During therapy we continue to reinforce the couple's progress by reminding them that in a relatively short time, most, if not all, premature ejaculators respond to treatment.

2. Retarded Ejaculation

Whereas the man suffering from prematurity cannot control orgasm, the retarded ejaculator cannot trigger it. Men with a mild form of this disorder can ejaculate by employing fantasy or distracting themselves from their sexual worries, or by additional stimulation. A few others have never experienced orgasm. At one time clinicians thought retarded ejaculation was a relatively rare phenomenon. Now it ap-

pears it may be highly prevalent, at least in its mild forms. At Cornell, we are seeing an increasing number of patients with this difficulty.

THE OLD-TIME RELIGION

In its mildest form, a man's ejaculatory inhibition is confined to specific anxiety-provoking situations, such as when he is with a new partner, or when he feels guilty about the sexual encounter. The patient who seeks help, however, usually is more severely restricted in his sexuality. The man who suffers from primary ejaculatory retardation has had the difficulty since his first attempt at sexual intercourse, has never achieved orgasm during coitus, but may be able to achieve it by masturbation, manipulation or oral stimulation. Secondary retarded ejaculators enjoyed a period of good sexual functioning before the onset of retarded ejaculation; commonly, a specific trauma brought on their difficulty. Like the premature ejaculator, the retarded ejaculator often anticipates failure and frustration, which can eventually impair his ability to sustain an erection.

Few physical illnesses play a role in retarded ejaculation. Clinical evidence suggests that a strict religious upbringing, sexual conflict from an unresolved oedipal complex, strongly suppressed anger, ambivalence toward one's partner, fear of abandonment, or a specific sexual calamity are causes of retarded ejaculation.

Our treatment goal is to overcome the mechanism that inhibits ejaculation and resolve the underlying problems that impede sexual functioning. We use a series of progressive sexual exercises to relieve the patient of his anxieties and fears about the sexual act. We start with the couple performing the sexual practices that can elicit any existing ejaculatory capacity. As the patient is successful in one situation, he moves on to a more threatening or difficult one. Concurrently, the psychotherapy sessions at the clinic foster the patient's insight into any of his irrational fears, traumatic memories or destructive interactions with his partner that inhibit ejaculation.

Masters and Johnson cured 14 out of 17 retarded ejaculators using a similar method. Our preliminary results are similar to theirs. One of our successful cases was Mr. J., who had been in psychoanalysis for some time when he came to our clinic.

NO EJACULATION

We traced Mr. J.'s difficulty to the traumatic termination of a sexual relationship. He had left his wife and four children for another woman, who subsequently left him. He became deeply depressed and sought psychoanalytic treatment. Although his depression subsided during analysis, he continued to have ejaculatory problems.

The patient had remarried, and his new wife agreed to cooperate in our sex therapy program. Before entering treatment, they had worked out a way to have frequent and enjoyable sex, except for the limits imposed by his inability to ejaculate during intercourse. They would engage in imaginative sex play and have intercourse until she reached orgasm. Then she would stimulate him manually or orally until he achieved orgasm.

Treatment in this case was brief and effective. First we instructed the couple to participate in sex play without intercourse or orgasm. Then she stimulated him to orgasm with his penis near the mouth of her vagina. Finally, we told the wife to stimulate her husband almost to orgasm, at which point he was to enter the vagina with strong pelvic thrusting. In order to ejaculate during coitus, Mr. J. initially needed to fantasize that his wife was stimulating him orally, but gradually he could ejaculate without distracting himself from lovemaking with fantasy.

At the same time that Mr. and Mrs. J. practiced the sexual desensitization exercises at home, we conducted psychotherapy with them at the clinic. Their relationship had many immature elements in it. He was infantile, jealous and demanding, and haunted by the fear that his wife would leave him. At times, she acted like a stubborn, irresponsible and provocative child. In the therapeutic sessions we discussed the quality of their relationship from this perspective. Two years after we terminated therapy, we were pleased to learn that the patient had retained his ejaculatory competence, felt well, and seemed more assertive and less anxious.

3. Impotence

A man who suffers from impotence is often almost unbearably anxious, frustrated and humiliated by his inability to produce or maintain an erection. Although he may become aroused in a sexual encounter and want to make love, he can't. He feels his masculinity is on the line. Clinicians and researchers estimate that half the male population has experienced at least transient impotence. Men seek help only when the problem becomes chronic.

Primary impotence is the rarest and most severe form of the disorder; men who suffer from it have never been potent with a woman, although they may be able to attain good erections in other situations. Secondary impotence is less severe, but still debilitating. These patients functioned well for some time prior to their erectile difficulties. The prognosis for treating impotence depends on how long the patient has suffered from it and how severe it is. Here again, the prospective candidate should have a thorough physical checkup before he goes into therapy. Stress, fatigue, undiagnosed diabetes, hepatitis, narcotics use, low androgen levels and other physical factors may cause impotence.

DEPRESSION AND DISCORD

Although some traditional therapists believe impotence is always a sign of a deep underlying pathology, we believe there are often more obvious and immediate causes. Fear of sexual failure, pressures created by an excessively demanding wife, and guilt or conflict may prevent a man from producing or maintaining an erection. Therefore, we feel our brief, symptom-focused form of treatment is preferable to lengthy reconstructive insight therapy that essentially ignores the immediate antecedents of impotence. Masters and Johnson report they cured 70 percent of their secondary impotent patients using treatment very similar to ours.

Because depression or marital discord can accompany or cause impotence, we must often relieve these symptoms before we can treat the man's impotence. Therefore, we always combine sexual tasks at home with therapeutic sessions in the clinic. The following case history demonstrates the variability and flexibility of this combined approach.

A 26-year-old Jewish law student applied for treatment. Although he and his 29-year-old West-Indian wife reported they had enjoyed a good sexual relationship during the year and a half they lived together, he began to have erectile difficulty after they were married, and she admitted that even while they lived together, intercourse was often hurried and more infrequent than she wished. Most recently, the patient had been unable to achieve an erection under any circumstances, and had lost all interest in sex. In the course of our initial evaluation and interview, the patient admitted that he had experienced potency problems with

girls of his own ethnic background before he met his wife. But he emphasized that he had functioned well with her at first.

The wife had no sexual problems. She had orgasm during coitus, but only if intercourse lasted for 10 minutes or more. She could climax through clitoral stimulation, but was reluctant to allow him to engage in this activity.

Although there were many elements in the patient's psychiatric and family history that could indicate underlying psychological reasons for his impotence, we did not raise those issues in therapy. They had no immediate relevance to our belief that the cause of the patient's impotence was his wife's demands for frequent intercourse of long duration, and his progressive fear of failure.

We saw the couple in our office once a week. We also instructed them to gently caress each other during sexual play at home, but not to engage in coitus. We encouraged the wife to accept clitoral stimulation to orgasm if her sexual tension became excessive. These exercises produced intense excitement in both partners. He experienced a spontaneous erection, and, "against our advice," their passion led them to try coitus. The wife did not reach orgasm, but the patient felt sufficiently encouraged by his success to attempt intercourse again the following night. This time, he lost his erection when he became afraid he would be unable to sustain it long enough to bring his wife to orgasm.

EROTIC ABANDON

We talked about their experience in the next therapeutic session. When the wife understood the destructive effect of her sexual demands, she admitted for the first time that her husband was not very skilled at clitoral stimulation. Moreover, she said she felt this form of stimulation was "homosexual." We corrected her misconception and encouraged the couple to communicate more freely with each other about their sexual responses.

This couple developed a good sexual partnership, free of the pressures and demands which had caused his impotence. Without making her husband feel deficient the wife achieved postcoital orgasm by clitoral stimulation when she did not climax during intercourse. He learned to abandon himself to his erotic sensations. We terminated treatment after four therapeutic sessions, conducted over a three-week period, and the couple reported no difficulty in sexual functioning a year later.

This case was relatively simple. Others are more difficult. Impotence can be tenacious, and we often have to employ extensive psychotherapy to relieve the anxieties produced by deep-seated pathology or by marital discord.

In contrast to male dysfunctions, the female sexual dysfunctions are not as clearly understood. For example, the term "frigidity" is confusing on two counts. Because it has traditionally referred to all forms of female sexual inhibition, covering both total lack of erotic feeling and the inability to have orgasm, it fails to convey the fact that these are two separate components of the female sexual response. It also implies that women who suffer from inhibitions are cold and hostile to men, which is both inaccurate and pejorative.

Confusion also centers on the relationship between female orgasm and coitus. Some clinicians believe that if a woman cannot achieve orgasm during coitus, she suffers from sexual dysfunction. Others do not attach any particular importance to how a woman reaches a climax. Our clinical experience supports the second viewpoint. A woman who is otherwise orgasmic, but who does not reach orgasm during coitus, is neither frigid nor sick. This pat-

tern seems to be a normal variant of female sexuality for some women. Our impression is that eight to 10 percent of the female population has never experienced orgasm, and of the 90 percent who have, only about half do so regularly during intercourse.

We also believe no one can yet resolve the debate about whether there are one or two female orgasms. But physiological data do give us an idea of how women experience climax. Apparently, the stimulation of the clitoris or the surrounding area triggers orgasm, but women respond to and perceive the climax primarily in the vagina.

Women are slower than men to become aroused, and their arousal signs are much less obvious than the male's erect penis. Because men cannot easily discern whether or not a woman is ready for intercourse, and because women are culturally conditioned to put their husbands' needs first, couples often proceed to coitus before the woman is sufficiently aroused to reach orgasm during intercourse.

GENTLE SENSITIVITY

A woman's reluctance to express her needs, however, is not always based on cultural paranoia. Women may run a real risk of displeasing their husbands if they become sexually assertive. Such behavior repels some men, who regard women who assume active roles in sex as aggressive, castrating females. Other men feel threatened when their wives express sexual needs. They think their partners are challenging their sexual adequacy. Too often men fail to realize that they can become good lovers if they simply supply their partners with gentle, sensitive stimulation instead of perpetual erection.

The inability of some women to become aroused even though they receive adequate stimulation probably indicates some underlying sexual conflict. A restrictive upbringing; a hostile marital relationship; severe psychopathology; conflicts about the female role in lovemaking; fear of men, of losing control, of rejection and abandonment can cause female sexual dysfunctions.

4. Female Sexual Dysfunctions

General sexual dysfunction, usually referred to as frigidity, is the most severe of the female inhibitions. Women plagued with it derive little, if any, erotic pleasure from sexual stimulation. They are essentially devoid of sexual feelings. Many nonresponsive women consider sex an ordeal. Those who suffer from primary frigidity have never experienced erotic pleasure, and those who have secondary general sexual dysfunctions responded at one time to sexual stimulation, but no longer do so. Typically, these patients were aroused by petting before marriage but lost the ability to respond when intercourse became the exclusive objective of all sexual encounters.

To help these nonresponsive women, we create a relaxed, sensuous ambience to permit the natural unfolding of sexual responses during lovemaking. To help foster such an environment, we encourage the couple to communicate openly about their sexual feelings and wishes, and we prescribe systematic sensuous and erotic experiences for the couple to perform at home.

Masters and Johnson developed a technique called sensate focus which is an ingenious and invaluable tool in treating general female sexual dysfunction. This exercise consists of having the couple forego sexual intercourse and orgasm while the wife caresses her husband's body, after which he stimulates her in like manner. By telling the wife to act first, we help counteract her guilt about receiving something for herself, and her fear that her husband will reject her. When we free women from the pressure to produce orgasm, they often experience erotic and sensuous sensations for the first time.

When the patient reports that she feels sensuous and erotic during the sensate focus exercises, we expand the caressing to include light, teasing genital play. After the husband caresses his wife's body he gently touches her nipples, clitoral area, and vaginal entrance. The woman guides his actions verbally and nonverbally. If, during these sessions, he becomes too sexually aroused, we tell the patient to bring him to orgasm manually or orally after she has had a chance to experience nonpressured, reassuring genital play.

PREMONITORY SENSATIONS

Genital stimulation typically produces a definite increase in the patient's sexual responsiveness. When she reaches a high level of erotic feeling during these exercises, the couple moves on to intercourse. On top of her husband, she initiates coitus with slow and exploratory thrusts at first, while she focuses her attention on the physical sensations emanating from her vagina. If her partner's urge to ejaculate becomes too intense during her thrusting, we tell the couple to separate. The husband manually stimulates his wife until his premonitory orgasmic sensations disappear and they can resume intercourse. They repeat this cycle several times until she feels like driving for orgasm. If she does not want to try to reach climax, the couple proceeds with coitus until the husband reaches orgasm.

Frequently these sexual experiences evoke highly emotional responses and resistances in the patient. We use these feelings to help identify the specific obstacles which impede her eroticism. We deal with these obstacles on both an experiential level and in psychotherapy.

There is a good chance that women who suffer from general sexual dysfunction will improve. To a great extent the outcome of treatment seems to depend on the quality of the patient's relationship with her husband. If he does not reject her and she has no deep-seated psychopathology, the great majority of these women learn to enjoy sex and to reach orgasm.

5. Female Orgasmic Dysfunction

Problems in reaching orgasm are probably the most prevalent sexual complaint of women. A woman suffers from primary orgasmic dysfunction if she has never experienced an orgasm, and from secondary orgasmic dysfunction if the disorder developed after a period of being able to reach orgasm. An inorgasmic woman has an absolute problem if she can't achieve orgasm under any circumstances, and a situational one if she can reach a climax only under specific circumstances. Women who suffer solely from orgasmic problems frequently have strong sex drives. They fall in love, enjoy sex play, lubricate copiously, and love the sensation of phallic penetration. They simply get stuck at or near the plateau phase of the sexual response.

Women who can achieve orgasm only by masturbation when they are alone, or those who must use vibrators for half an hour to reach orgasm obviously have a problem. But when a clinician sees a woman who can climax during masturbation, or when her husband stimulates her either manually or orally, but she cannot reach orgasm during coitus, he often faces a dilemma. It is difficult for a therapist to decide whether she is suffering from a pathological inhibition or whether she merely exhibits a normal variation of female sexuality. If the clinician cannot uncover any sexual anxieties, conflicts or fears during his initial interview with the couple, he should probably reassure them that she functions within the normal sexual range, and encourage them to work out lovemaking patterns that satisfy them both. However, if they still want to achieve coital orgasm, we will accept them, and try to increase her sexual responsiveness. Some of these women learn to climax during coitus, and others do not.

AT HOME, ALONE

The first goal of therapy with a woman who has never experienced orgasm is to eliminate as many inhibiting factors as possible from the sexual environment so she can have her first climax. Because it is the rising tide of clitoral sensations which triggers the female climax, and because women are least threatened when they are alone, we first instruct the inorgasmic woman to masturbate at home alone in an environment free from possible interruption. If several attempts at this fail to produce orgasm, we tell her to use an electric vibrator to stimulate her clitoris. Some sexologists feel the vibrator is the only significant advance in sexual technique since the days of Pompeii. Because the patient may become "hooked" on this device, however, we transfer her to manual stimulation as soon as she has had a few orgasms using the vibrator.

When she can stimulate herself to orgasm regularly, we bring her husband into the treatment program. First we instruct them to make love in the usual way, telling her not to make any special effort to achieve orgasm during coitus. After he has ejaculated, and there is no pressure on her to perform quickly, he uses the vibrator or stimulates her manually to orgasm. We tell her to be utterly "selfish," and to focus on her own sensations. After a few of these sessions some women climax during intercourse without the manual stimulation.

One of our patients was a 28-year-old social worker who had never experienced orgasm. Her husband was a 34-year-old physician. They were very much in love, and were frequent and passionate lovers. During the early years of their marriage, Mrs. E. had simulated orgasm because she was afraid her husband would feel hurt and guilty if he knew she could not climax. A year before they sought treatment, she admitted to Dr. E. that she could not reach orgasm, and since then he had tried to bring her to orgasm by clitoral stimulation.

Mrs. E. arrived for the initial interview alone. She explained she had been reluctant to ask her husband to come because of his busy schedule. This was typical of her overprotectiveness of him. We explained that he would have to participate in treatment, and scheduled the first therapy session for two weeks later. In the meantime we instructed her to try to reach orgasm with an electric vibrator.

MISSED SIGNAL

At our next meeting, Mrs. E. told us she had easily achieved orgasm with a vibrator in solitude. But she was afraid to ask her husband to use the vibrator to stimulate her clitoris. She thought it would repel him and make him feel inadequate. He reassured her that this was not true, and said he was eager to try to bring her to orgasm.

We also learned that Mrs. E. never abandoned herself completely to her sexual feelings, because, like many other women, she was overly concerned with satisfying and pleasing her husband. This meant that the couple's lovemaking was never governed by her needs. This was not Dr. E's fault. Often he aroused her to a high level of sexual tension, but at this point she would think, "That's enough, he must be getting tired." And she would signal him to begin coitus. Not surprisingly, he misinterpreted her signal to mean that she was ready to commence coitus because she too was ready to have an orgasm.

It became clear that the patient's orgasmic inhibition was not associated with severe psychopathology or marital difficulties. It was her great need to please her husband, motivated by her own insecurity.

We treated this couple by enhancing the communication between them, prescribing sexual experiences to sensitize Mrs. E. to her own feelings, and by helping her develop a sense of responsibility for obtaining her husband's adequate stimulation to bring her to orgasm. Both the therapist and her husband reassured her that her sexually assertive behavior would not diminish her husband's sexual enjoyment or jeopardize their relationship.

We encouraged Mrs. E. to develop sexual autonomy during lovemaking, and to assume responsibility for obtaining pleasure, first during foreplay and then during coitus. We instructed her to ask her husband to stimulate her, and tell him where to kiss and caress her. If he ejaculated during intercourse, she was to ask him to stimulate her to orgasm. We also helped her stop monitoring her own progress toward orgasm, which distracted her from her sexual sensations.

Dr. E.'s acceptance of Mrs. E.'s growing sexual maturity and activity helped her progress. After 12 sessions, she easily reached orgasm via clitoral stimulation and was beginning to experience coital orgasm. Both enjoyed sex tremendously, and after therapy Mrs. E. became more assertive and happier in general.

More common than the woman who has never had an orgasm is the patient who is orgastic in low tension situations, but cannot reach a climax under circumstances that make her even slightly anxious. She may be able to climax during solitary masturbation, but not when she is with a partner. We treat these patients by uncovering and resolving the specific conflicts which inhibit the patient.

BRIDGE MANEUVERS

With a woman who cannot have orgasm during intercourse, our goals are to identify and remove any psychic blocks or marital problems that inhibit her during coitus, to have her perform erotic tasks to heighten her sexual arousal, enhance her awareness of and pleasure in her vaginal sensations and to maximize clitoral stimulation. We find that techniques that combine coitus with clitoral stimulation are very helpful. These are called "bridge" maneuvers.

A great majority of women, including those who suffer from absolute primary orgasmic inhibition, are able to achieve orgasm after a relatively brief period of therapy. Indeed, orgasmic inhibition is virtually 100 percent curable if the sole criterion for cure is the ability to reach orgasm. But, as mentioned before, some women never reach orgasm during intercourse, which suggests that the phenomenon is a normal variant of female sexual response.

6. Vaginismus

The third, and relatively rare, female sexual dysfunction is vaginismus. Anatomically, a vaginismic woman is normal, but whenever a man tries to penetrate her vagina, the vaginal muscles literally snap the entrance shut so that intercourse is impossible. Physicians often must conduct vaginal examinations on these women under anesthesia. This disorder is due to an involuntary spasm of the muscles surrounding the vaginal entrance. These patients are usually afraid of vaginal penetration, and intercourse. They often suffer from general sexual dysfunction or orgasmic inhibition. However, many women who seek treatment for vaginismus are sexually responsive and highly orgastic.

Vaginismus results from a woman's asso-ciation of pain or fear with vaginal penetration. The precipitating event may be physical pain or psychological stress. A rigid hymen, inflammatory pelvic diseases and tumors, childbirth pathologies, and hemorrhoids may cause it. Strict religious upbringing, a husband's impotence, or the psychological effects of rape also may bring on vaginismus, or it may result from ignorance and misinformation about sex, or guilt caused by deep sexual conflicts.

TOLERATING MOTION

Our basic strategy for treating vaginismus is simple, provided all physical pain-producing conditions have been corrected. Our first goal is to uncover the basis for the patient's phobic avoidance of vaginal entry. Then, with progressive sexual exercises, we try to decondition the involuntary spasm of the muscles that guard the entrance to the vagina.

First we have both the patient and her husband examine her genitals in the privacy of their well-lit bedroom. We tell them to find and examine the exact location of the vaginal opening. In the first sexual assignment, we tell the woman to gently insert her own or her husband's finger into her vagina. When her usual discomfort disappears we tell her to move her finger back and forth inside her vagina until she can tolerate the motion without discomfort. We always allow the woman to control the situation to reduce her fears and apprehensions. Next, the husband or wife inserts two fingers in the vagina, and then rotates them gently, stretching the walls of the vagina. When she can tolerate this, the couple proceeds to intercourse. First they lie still with the man's penis inserted in his wife, then the husband begins gentle thrusting at his wife's signal and withdraws if she wishes him to. Finally the couple thrusts to orgasm. Concurrently we conduct therapy sessions with the couple to work on the patient's phobia about vaginal penetration.

We have achieved excellent and permanent results with women who suffer from vaginismus. Masters and Johnson report they achieved a 100 percent cure rate. We find that the length of treatment is more variable than that for the other sexual dysfunctions because of the tenacity of the phobia. But we have been able to resolve the phobic avoidance in 10 psychotherapy sessions. Within three to 14 weeks, we can go on to cure the vaginal spasm with four to eight home exercise sessions.

Sex therapy promises, and experience suggests it delivers, rapid and permanent relief of distressing sexual problems for many. But we have not scientifically substantiated its merits in a controlled study.

There can be no doubt, however, in light of the clinical evidence and the compelling conceptual considerations which underlie this approach, that the new methods merit further trial and development. We need to know which kinds of problems we can best treat with sex therapy, and under what conditions. We must learn precisely what components of these complex methods are actually responsible for the observed changes. At the present stage in its development, however, sex therapy appears to have great value. Indeed, it may close the door on sexual boredom and agony in America.

Name Index

Subject Index

BOOK MANUFACTURE

The composition of *The Future Is Now: Readings in Introductory Psychology* was by Datagraphics, Inc., Phoenix, Arizona. Printing and binding was performed by R. R. Donnelley, Inc., Crawfordsville, Indiana. Cover design is by Jane Brown. The text type is Times Roman.